CN 374.9768
AN 76504

 Li

Highlander

D1179661

Northern College
Library

NC03051

-LLED

RN COLLEGE LIBRARY
BARNSLEY S75 3ET

THE UNIVERSITY OF TENNESSEE PRESS / KNOXVILLE

Highlander

No Ordinary School

Second Edition

John M. Glen

Copyright © 1996 by The University of Tennessee Press / Knoxville.
All Rights Reserved. Manufactured in the United States of America.
Second Edition.
First Edition by The University Press of Kentucky.

Frontispiece: Early Staff Members, 1933 or 1934. From left, Myles Horton, Rupert Hampton, James Dombrowski, Zilla Hawes, Dorothy Thompson. *Highlander Research and Education Center.*

The paper in this book meets the minimum requirements of the American National Standard for Permanence of Paper for Printed Library Materials. ∞ The binding materials have been chosen for strength and durability.

 Printed on recycled paper.

Library of Congress Cataloging-in-Publication Data

Glen, John M., 1953–
    Highlander : no ordinary school / John M. Glen. — 2nd ed.
        p.   cm.
    Includes bibliographical references (p.).
    ISBN 0-87049-928-9 (pbk. : alk. paper)
        1. Highlander Folk School (Monteagle, Tenn.)—History. 2. Adult education—Tennessee—History. 3. Working class—Education—Tennessee—History. I. Title.
LC5301.M65G55 1996.
374'.9768—dc20   95-41761
                                                                                       CIP

Contents

Illustrations

Acknowledgments

Exploring Highlander's history has been intensely personal and richly rewarding. In studying the school, I have learned much more about the South, about Appalachia, and about the possibilities and problems of radical reform. I also enjoyed the support of many people who offered advice, information, and encouragement as I wrote this book. Unfortunately, I can only thank a few of them by name here.

My greatest professional debts are to two masterful historians and teachers at Vanderbilt University. Dewey W. Grantham introduced me to Highlander, directed my dissertation with skill and subtlety, and made me the beneficiary of his scholarship and his personal warmth. Paul K. Conkin insisted on precise logic and careful wording and drove me to probe the nuances and ironies of my material. Both helped turn my largely unfocused energies into the craftwork of a polished historian. Their colleagues at Vanderbilt, including Richard A. Couto, now at the Jepson School of Leadership Studies at the University of Richmond, also contributed to the development of my work. Cecilia Stiles Cornell and Charles S. Thomas patiently listened to my early ruminations. Vanderbilt's Graduate School provided two grants to finance my research during the summers of 1979 and 1980.

The Department of History at Southwest Texas State University opened new doors when it hired me as a full-time faculty member in 1982. Everette Swinney guided me into the wonders of word processing, and Philip Scarpino and Kenneth Winkle offered especially insightful criticisms of earlier drafts of the manuscript at young faculty seminars. My colleagues in the Department of History at Ball State University have created a stimulating atmosphere that sustains both teaching and serious scholarship.

Archivists are the lifelines between the researcher and the mounds of material confronted in their collections. My own research was greatly aided by the staff at the State Historical Society of Wisconsin. Karen Baumann, former staff members Sarah Cooper and Dale Treleven, and their colleagues were unfailing in their support as I plowed through the Highlander papers in the society's Social Action Collection. The Visual Materials Archives staff generously made available audio recordings and photographs of the school. Former Southern Conference Educational Fund director Anne Braden graciously lifted the restrictions on the Carl and Anne Braden Papers. Other archival staffs were equally cooperative. It is a pleasure to acknowledge the aid I received at the Tennessee State Library and Archives in Nashville; the Southern Labor Archives at Georgia State University; Duke University's Perkins Library; the Labadie Collection at the University of Michigan; and the Southern Historical Collection at the University of North Carolina, whose staff helped me secure Broadus Mitchell's kind consent to examine the Mitchell Family Papers.

My account of Highlander's legal battle with the state of Tennessee was strengthened through the efforts of several people. Dean Robert W. Dubay at Bainbridge Junior College in Georgia furnished useful information regarding the Samuel Marvin Griffin Papers. Sue Bouldin Parrott and her staff at the Grundy County circuit court clerk's office in Altamont, Tennessee, were particularly helpful in locating court transcripts and other legal documents, as was Tennessee state supreme court clerk Ramsey Leathers.

I owe special thanks to the men and women who have been connected with Highlander itself. Initially a bit wary of an "outsider," staff members gradually came to realize that I wanted to do Highlander's history justice, and they never made any attempt to censor my findings. I am especially grateful to former staff member Sue Thrasher and former librarian Linda Selfridge, whose hospitality, friendliness, and generosity made me feel welcome at Highlander. As so many others found, Myles Horton was a constant source of information, inspiration, and enjoyment; his eagerness to share his reminiscences about the school and his confidence in my efforts were of incalculable value. I am indebted to former staff members Septima

Clark, Michael Clark, and Tom Ludwig for talking to me about Highlander's programs and to Aleine Austin, Alice Cobb, Mary Lawrance Elkuss, Charis Horton, May Justus, Catherine Winston Male, Eva Zhitlowsky Milton, Don West, and Joanna and Emil Willimetz for sharing their perspectives on the school. I would also like to thank John Gaventa, Guy and Candie Carawan, and their colleagues on the current Highlander staff for their continued interest.

An earlier version of chapter 1 appears in *Southern Historian* 7 (Spring 1986). Portions of chapter 10 appear in *Border States*, no. 6 (1987), and in *Fighting Back in Appalachia: Traditions of Resistance and Change* (1993), edited by Stephen L. Fisher. I thank the editors of both journals and Temple University Press for permission to use this material. My appreciation also goes to The University Press of Kentucky for publishing the first edition of this book in 1988 and selling every copy.

Finally, there is a personal debt. My daughters, Amy Michelle Stinton and Lorey Julianne Stinton, may never have quite understood why I spent so much time so late at night working on a subject they have yet to understand completely. But they tolerated my moods, accepted the hours, helped select the illustrations, and showed me that there was more to life than scholarship. Most of all, I want to thank my sharpest critic, my most resolute supporter, my wife, and my friend—Kathy Lea Stinton-Glen. She came late to this book and often had to suffer my obsession with it, but in her own unique way she understood. She put aside her own work to help me complete mine. For that, and for her love, I am profoundly grateful.

In revisiting, revising, and renewing this history of Highlander, I received assistance from a number of people who agreed that it was a story worth retelling. My thanks first go to Meredith Morris-Babb at the University of Tennessee Press and the readers who recommended the publication of a second edition, all of whom believe in the importance of Appalachia's past and support scholarship that challenges earlier premises and highlights the region's complexities. After using and packing up many of Highlander's more recent files in the attic of its old farmhouse, I was able to delve more deeply into them again at the State Historical Society of Wisconsin, where the commitment to collecting and preserving the center's written records, fortunately, remains.

Past and current members of the Highlander staff and board of directors have been tough critics. But they also have been willing to discuss, often at length, the work the center and related organizations have pursued in politically difficult times. I particularly want to thank Mike Clark, Joyce

Dukes, Doug Gamble, Sue Ella Kobak, Helen Lewis, Charles "Buck" Maggard, Joe Szakos, and David Whisnant for their perspectives on Highlander and Appalachian activism since the mid-1960s; Hubert Sapp for helping me connect Highlander's efforts to the Deep South over much the same period; John Gaventa and Guy and Candie Carawan for agreeing to interviews specifically for this edition; and Juanita Householder for locating illustrations, both old and new.

Finally, as was the case with the first edition, whatever shortcomings this effort may possess are my own responsibility. I hope its interpretations will continue to be regarded as part of Highlander's ongoing mission: to explore and develop the relationship between education and social change.

Introduction

The name "Highlander" rarely evokes a neutral response, even among those southerners who have heard of it only vaguely. A number of years ago a friend and I were talking with a college freshman from Sewanee, Tennessee, located about nine miles from Highlander's original site near Monteagle. Too young to remember the time when the folk school operated so close to his home, the student seemed puzzled as I recounted its history until I mentioned that it had come under attack for its interracial activities. Suddenly he brightened. "Oh," he exclaimed, "you mean that Communist training school!"

Other southerners have viewed Highlander much differently. Frank Adams, author of a often-cited book on the idea of Highlander, acknowledges that there is a temptation to cast it "in a heroic mold, badgered by men with small minds and governments with mean ways." Yet Adams concedes that his own account is "biased," for Highlander exemplifies his philosophy that "education should foster individual growth and social change and nourish the fundamental value of complete personal liberty while encouraging thoughtful citizenship in community."[1] Others have been even more sweeping and less restrained in their praise.

This book offers a comprehensive and thorough history of the Highlander Folk School that tries to avoid the easy labels and simplistic generalizations that have often confused or obscured its work. Its second, broader objective is to use Highlander's history to examine the course of the organized labor and civil rights movements in the South, as well as the work of southern radicals since the 1930s. Shaped by the Great Depression and the South's system of segregation and racial discrimination, Highlander was an integral part of larger campaigns against economic, political, and racial oppression and reflected both the achievements and limitations of dissent and reform in the region. During its first thirty years it served as a community folk school, a training center for southern industrial labor and farmers' unions, and a major meeting place for black and white civil rights activists. At the heart of Highlander's programs was a belief in the power of education to change society. Through an education based on their experiences, Highlander hoped to empower the poor of Appalachia and the South to take control of their own lives and solve their own problems.

The school opened in 1932 near the small Cumberland Plateau town of Monteagle, Tennessee, with the announced intention of educating "rural and industrial leaders for a new social order" and enriching "the indigenous cultural values of the mountains."[2] During the early and middle 1930s staff members struggled to define Highlander's role in the emerging southern labor movement as well as in the Monteagle community. They aided striking coal miners, woodcutters, textile mill hands, and government relief workers in the surrounding area. They also held workshops at the school for potential union leaders and operated cooperative, cultural, and recreational programs for Grundy County residents. In 1937 the HFS faculty joined the southern organizing drive of the Committee for Industrial Organization (renamed the Congress of Industrial Organizations one year later). Over the next decade the staff helped organize textile workers in Tennessee, North Carolina, and South Carolina, directed large-scale labor education programs in eleven southern states, and developed a residential program to build a broad-based, racially integrated, and politically active labor movement in the region.

The late 1940s and early 1950s were transition years for Highlander. The declining militancy of the CIO and the maturation of the southern labor movement after World War II eroded the school's relationship with organized labor. For several years staff members worked on behalf of the Farmers' Union in Tennessee, Alabama, and Virginia, but their efforts to create a farmer-labor coalition in the South failed. Meanwhile, Highlander and CIO officials were unable to reconcile their differences over the aims and functions of labor education, and by 1953 the productive relationship between the school and organized labor had dissolved. The frustrations of these and other disappointing experiences led HFS leaders to conclude that racism presented the greatest obstacle to the kind of economic and political order they had envisioned since 1932.

Thus, beginning in 1953, almost a year before the Supreme Court's historic *Brown* v. *Board of Education* ruling, the Highlander staff launched a series of workshops for black and white community leaders and students. These sessions initially centered on public school desegregation and gradually grew to encompass the problems of communitywide integration. A Citizenship School project started on the South Carolina Sea Islands in 1957 taught thousands of black adults to read and write in order to register as voters. In 1960 and 1961, as sit-in protests spread across the South, student activists met at the folk school to explore the possible goals and directions for a new era of black protest. Through these programs Highlander became the educational center of the civil rights movement during the 1950s and early 1960s. But as the school grew more prominent in the struggle for racial equality, southern white segregationists mounted a sustained assault against what they described as a "Communist training school." After a barrage of legislative investigations, propaganda campaigns, and dramatic trials, Tennessee officials revoked Highlander's charter and confiscated its property in 1962.

This did not mean the end of Highlander. In 1961 Highlander officers secured a charter for a new institution to be located in Knoxville and called the Highlander Research and Education Center. During most of the 1960s staff members continued to support the civil rights movement and for a time promoted a multiracial poor people's coalition. At the same time, Highlander increasingly turned its attention to the complex troubles facing the poor and powerless in Appalachia. After moving the center to its present location near New Market, Tennessee, in 1971, the staff helped community and county groups grapple with such problems as strip mining, land and mineral ownership, and occupational and environmental health hazards. Since the 1980s the center has sought to address interrelated economic, environmental, and educational issues that link Appalachian concerns with those faced in communities throughout the South, the nation, and the world.

As its turbulent history suggests, Highlander has been no ordinary school. Its flexible and indefinite educational approach has been difficult to explain, and its programs and personnel have changed many times. Yet there have been certain characteristics common to all of Highlander's major programs that give an overall direction to its work. Staff members have been primarily concerned with developing community leadership, organizing the economically and socially oppressed, and creating broad-based coalitions to push for a more democratic society. To be sure, concepts like democracy, brotherhood, and justice have never been fully spelled out; those who have worked at the school tend to insist that such ideals are expansive and connote more than a precise blueprint of the good society. In general, Highlander has envisioned a system in which people have more control over their lives, achieve a higher standard of living, gain unrestricted access to community services and institutions, associate with whom they choose without penalty, make government responsive to the popular will, and exercise individual creativity that contributes to the common welfare. Similarly, brotherhood—and, in more recent years, sisterhood—has suggested a respect for individuals, love, and human relationships free of prejudices or barriers that prevent the fullest enjoyment of life.[3]

Residential workshops have played a central role in Highlander's efforts to work toward these goals. Lasting anywhere from two days to eight weeks and focusing on specific, concrete subjects, the workshops usually have attracted between fifteen and forty adults of various racial, religious, and educational backgrounds. From the start of the school the purpose has been to help these people solve their community's problems. But the process of analyzing and responding to the problems has been as important as the solutions themselves.

At Highlander there are no grades, credits, examinations, or degrees. The needs of the students largely determine the curriculum of the sessions. Meeting in a relaxed, friendly atmosphere on the Highlander campus, workshop participants define their concerns, discuss what has been done to improve conditions at home, and decide upon the most effective course of action to attain the group's objectives. Staff members refrain from imposing a preconceived set of ideas and use consultants, movies, audio and video recordings, drama, music, and written materials to build on the students' knowledge and introduce new values, options, and perspectives. Participants then evaluate their findings, assess their new understanding of their problems, and develop plans to initiate or sustain activities when they return to their communities. Highlander personnel measure the value of a session by how well the students carry out the decisions they made at the school. Though staff members tend to magnify the results, their work often leads to immediate and genuine gains. The union, organizational, and community leaders who attend Highlander are already in a position to implement what they learn, and a successful workshop often stimulates them into taking more productive action back home.

Indeed, the Highlander faculty regards the residential workshop as only one part of a learning process that has begun before the participants arrived at Highlander and continues long after they have left. Staff members follow the more promising students, help them initiate their own educational projects, and enlist other leaders in support of reform campaigns. Once labor education, literacy training, community leadership, voter education, or economics and environmental education classes have been firmly established, the staff transfers responsibility for the programs to organizations with larger resources. Highlander thus has served as a resource and a catalyst for action, inspiring grassroots leaders to work for greater human dignity and justice.[4]

Like other alternative educational institutions founded in the Appalachian South during the 1920s and 1930s, Highlander's historical roots trace back to the Danish folk schools of the nineteenth century. Bishop Nikolai S. F. Grundtvig (1783–1872) promoted the idea of residential adult education programs to enlighten and enliven the Danish peasantry after centuries of exploitation under a feudalistic system. The first folk schools, established in the 1840s, sought primarily to preserve the language and cultural traditions of Denmark. As the number of schools multiplied over the next fifty years and as their faculties became more committed to advancing the economic and political interests of their students, the folk schools sparked the rejuvenation of the economy, the growth of political sophistication, and the revival of Danish patriotism in the late nineteenth century. By 1900 the folk school idea had spread to Germany, Norway, Sweden, Finland, and England.[5]

There were several American attempts to apply the folk school approach to the South, particularly southern Appalachia, but with limited success. As David Whisnant points out, educational experiments as diverse as the John C. Campbell Folk School and Black Mountain College, both in North Carolina; Commonwealth College, in the Arkansas Ozarks; and the Macedonia Cooperative Community, in northern Georgia, were all "idealistic and admirably motivated; all were directed by energetic and imaginative people; all were in some ways at odds with mainstream values, assumptions, and processes." But all of them failed to bring about "substantial and durable change" because they tried to impose "an essentially alien ideology and social program which ultimately could not be successfully integrated with local ideas, customs, mores, and institutions."[6]

In contrast, Highlander has survived and achieved some meaningful change because it has consistently maintained both a sensitivity to southern culture and a commitment to transforming it. Although the school has worked throughout Appalachia, the South, and elsewhere, its programs are designed to remain rooted in a specific local area. Highlander shapes its curriculum to fit the needs of its students. It focuses not on the symptoms but on the causes of the problems facing black and white southerners, and it both anticipates and responds to larger movements for social change.[7]

This book is therefore more than a chronicle of an extraordinary institution in Tennessee. It is also an analysis of how a particular approach to adult education has been applied to the economic, political, and racial problems of the South and of Appalachia. It is in part a biography of Myles Horton, Highlander's longtime educational director, who devoted his life to challenging entrenched power and privilege. It is a history of modern southern and Appalachian activists, of those who recognized the fundamental importance of race but sought to unite blacks, whites, and other communities of color in behalf of their common class interests. And it is not only a history of the organized labor and civil rights movements in the South since 1932, but also a history of a more complex and difficult campaign for economic and political change in Appalachia and the Deep South since 1964. In sum, it is a history of a school on the cutting edge of social change.

This second, revised edition updates Highlander's history to the early 1990s, making it in the process more Appalachian, more international, and less the personal saga of Myles Horton. That the story can be extended this far reinforces the contention made by Horton, who died in 1990, and others that the school has not been simply the product of one man's vision but a source from which men and women—whites, blacks, and other cultural groups; northerners and southerners; native Appalachians and non-Appalachians—have worked for greater democracy and justice. This edition also makes use of newly available materials and incorporates important contributions made by recent scholarship, especially on the black freedom struggle of the 1950s and 1960s, women's activism, and Appalachia in the 1970s and 1980s.

On the other hand, the distinguishing features of the original study remain intact. Of all the major publications on Highlander—including two books appearing in 1990 that are essentially lengthy interviews with Horton—*No Ordinary School* still stands as the only independent perspective on its history and educational approach. Such a position has been perilous on more than one occasion, reminiscent of the cartoon character who leaps from a burning building toward the safety of the fireman's net below only to be bounced, trampoline-like, into the burning building next door. Yet it helps explain the book's scope and documentation. It also illuminates both the "peak" periods of Highlander's history, when larger movements provided context, clarity, direction, and drama for the staff's work, and the "valley" periods, when the staff explored new issues, cultivated community-based leaders and organizations as vehicles for change, and experimented with new teaching techniques. The result is a more complex story, one that demonstrates that education for social change is hard work, costs money, and is an inspirational as well as laborious human process. No doubt the challenges will continue: as civil rights veteran Julian Bond has observed, if historians find it difficult to be confronted by the subjects of their books, it will remain difficult for those subjects to confront those who endeavor to write their history.

Thus *Highlander: No Ordinary School* stands as a sort of bridge between the school's community, past and present, and a curious yet more skeptical outside public, both of whom might join together in a dialogue that is more often proposed than engaged. Highlander provides the space for such an effort.

1

The Establishment
of Highlander,
1927–1932

In large part, the Highlander Folk
School was the product of a personal and intellectual odyssey by its co-
founder, Myles Falls Horton. During the summer of 1927, while conducting a vacation Bible school in the small Cumberland Plateau town of
Ozone, Tennessee, Horton discovered that bringing local adults together
to discuss their common concerns and to find their own solutions was a far
more effective way to address community problems than a conventional
education program. He spent the next five years trying to translate his discovery in Ozone into an educational approach that would meet the needs
of the people of the southern Appalachian region. The quest took him from
a position as a Young Men's Christian Association student secretary for
Tennessee to the challenging academic atmosphere of Union Theological
Seminary and the University of Chicago and to the folk high schools of
Denmark. He investigated several American labor colleges and alternative
communities and explored the ideas of theologians, educators, sociologists,
socialists, and advocates of Danish folk school education. In the end,
Horton decided that the institutional form of his school and its specific
goals and programs would evolve out of particular situations faced by the
students themselves. Horton's education in effect brought him back to his

informal meetings in Ozone and to a technique based on group discussion and analysis of firsthand experiences. As Horton recalled years later, he and his colleagues had to unlearn much of what they had learned and then begin to learn from the people. The initial work of the Highlander Folk School reflected both this simple lesson and the various influences that led a handful of southern radicals to start a school dedicated to fundamental economic and social change.[1]

One crucial element in this new school was the personality of Myles Horton. Born in Savannah, Tennessee, on July 9, 1905, Horton was a descendant of Joshua Horton, a Scotch-Irish woodsman who evidently had received the first land grant in what is now the northeast corner of Tennessee. Myles's parents, Perry and Elsie Falls Horton, stressed to their four children the Calvinistic values of the Cumberland Presbyterian Church. The Horton family expressed its sense of Christian responsibility by aiding those whites and blacks less fortunate than themselves with food and clothing, exposing young Myles to the concept of social service and to people of different social, economic, and racial backgrounds. Perry and Elsie Horton, both former schoolteachers, also considered education central to an individual's development, and Myles never questioned their insistence that he get an education. At the same time, his father offered an example of personal independence by voting Republican in predominantly Democratic districts and by opposing labor unions for their intrusions on individual freedom.[2]

Myles entered Cumberland University in Lebanon, Tennessee, in the fall of 1924, intending to pursue some form of religious education. Majoring in English literature, he read widely. He especially appreciated Percy Bysshe Shelley's idealism and romantic defiance of authority, and he was impressed by John Stuart Mill's argument that individuals should assume responsibility for their own conduct and act upon their own opinions.[3]

Other lessons came from Horton's experiences outside the classroom. He organized his fellow freshmen against the traditional hazing rites at Cumberland, and he refused to join a fraternity when he heard that students were required to belong to one. While working at a Humboldt box factory in the summer of 1925, Horton astounded other employees by his open support of John T. Scopes, then being tried in Dayton, Tennessee, for violating the state law against teaching evolution in the public schools. As president of the Cumberland YMCA in 1927, Horton attended a conference at the Southern YMCA College in Nashville. There he mingled on an equal basis with people of different races, only to confront the fact that he could not take a Chinese woman into a restaurant or enter a public library with a black man. Resenting such restrictions, the young man began to question racial exclusion and segregation and soon made it "an operating principle that nobody could have their rights interfered with as long as they were tending to their own business."[4] Shortly after the Nashville YMCA conference, John Emmett Edgerton, president of the Southern States Industrial Council and a member of Cumberland's board of trustees, lectured the student body on the mistake wage earners made when they tried to improve their conditions through labor unions. Although he knew little about unions, Horton was outraged by the suggestion that working people had no need to determine their destinies, and he visited Edgerton's textile mill in Lebanon to talk with workers about the necessity of exercising their rights. His activities provoked such a commotion at the university that officials threatened to expel him if he visited the mill again.[5]

The most decisive education Horton received came in the summer of 1927, when he directed a vacation Bible school for the Presbyterian Church, U.S.A., in Ozone, Tennessee. Having spent the two previous summers operating similar schools in the area, Horton had become increasingly dissatisfied with the limited usefulness of his work. In an attempt to make the school more relevant to the interests of the Ozone community, he invited the parents of the Bible school children to attend informal meetings at the church in the evening. To his surprise, he found that the adults were eager to learn more about farming, employment in textile mills, public health, cooperatives, and the general economic conditions of their region. Horton realized that the value of the discussions lay in the group's willingness to share their problems and find some answers to them among the people of the community itself. This experience, Horton said later, "was probably the biggest discovery I ever made."[6] Attendance at the meetings steadily increased, and at the end of the summer Ozone residents urged the young man to forgo his final year of college and remain to start a permanent adult education program. Despite his excitement over the success of his summer experiment, Horton decided that he had not fully assessed the possibilities and problems of a major educational undertaking. He returned to Cumberland in the autumn of 1927, promising his friends in Ozone that he would come back when he had "something to offer."[7]

Following his graduation in the spring of 1928, Horton started to explore the potential for extending his Ozone experience to other communities in Middle and East Tennessee. In the process, Ozone became less a location for a school and more a reference point for Horton's elusive educational ideal. During the summer of 1928 he conducted another children's Bible school in Westel, Tennessee, a small community not far from Ozone, and once again he attracted an increasing number of local adults to informal meetings and talks by experts on education, cooperatives, migration, and labor. Although pleased by the response to the sessions, Horton also recognized that adult education was more effective when it was a permanent part of the community, and in the fall of 1928 he became YMCA student secretary for Tennessee in the hope of finding institutional support for the educational program he had in mind. Traveling to high schools and colleges across the state, he was disappointed to find that none of them appeared to take into account the interests, attitudes, and needs of the people in the southern mountains. He began to realize that he could not work in a "regular" school. He needed an approach, as he said later, "that would allow me to bring people in regardless of anything and talk about anything regardless of anything." That was the way to tap the "vitality of people."[8] Interpreting the YMCA's stated goal of "a worldwide fellowship" of young men literally, Horton held interracial meetings throughout the state, usually without securing the permission of his YMCA superiors. He well knew that such conferences were illegal and dangerous, and he later recalled that his employers were relieved when he resigned his post after a year of service.[9]

By then, Horton was thoroughly perplexed. It was clear that no one would be willing to sponsor the amorphously conceived adult education program of a young man who was unable to convey his ideas clearly. He had not found a way of joining knowledge and action in a concrete plan, and his brief YMCA career had revealed the enormous obstacles to using Christian ethics to change social conditions. He knew that he had to learn more.

Fortunately for Horton, his work for the Presbyterian church and the YMCA during and after his college years had taken him to the home of Abram Nightingale, a Congregationalist minister in Crossville, Tennessee. Under Nightingale's guidance, Horton immersed himself in books about Tennessee and southern history, the culture and problems of southern Appalachia, and the place of morality in a modern capitalistic society. In the summer of 1929 Nightingale bluntly told Horton that he needed more formal education to gain a broader perspective on his concerns and urged him to take courses at Union Theological Seminary in New York City. To overcome Horton's hesitancy, the minister obtained an application for admission to Union and gave the young man a copy of *Our Economic Morality and the Ethic of Jesus* by Harry F. Ward, professor of ethics at the seminary.[10]

Our Economic Morality, Ward's spirited critique of the American scene in the late twenties, helped Horton mesh his own increasingly radical view of contemporary society with his strong religious values. One of the most active reformers among the theologians of the 1920s, Ward insisted that the extremes of luxury and poverty in western societies revealed the material failure of capitalism. He asserted that America's "money-making" economy was fundamentally antagonistic to the Christian ethic of brotherhood, creativity, equality, and "a just and fraternal world." Religion, particularly educated idealists of absolute moral vision, must either redeem modern society and release it from its lust for power or blindly lead "this blind age" into the twilight of decline and destruction. Ward's heavy-handed analysis persuaded Horton that while the faculty at Union might not provide all the answers to his dilemma, it would sharpen his understanding of the social and economic weaknesses of capitalism.[11]

Horton entered Union Theological Seminary in the fall of 1929 with no intention of becoming a minister or obtaining a degree. He attended classes on comparative religion, Biblical history and criticism, ethics, and applied Christianity and read books on socialism, progressive education, and industrial unionism. But his initial hopefulness about his studies gave way to a growing uncertainty about his personal beliefs and plans for a school in the southern mountains. Horton gained a reputation among friendly faculty members and students as a "mystic," though he considered himself an idealist or a "pluralist" without quite knowing what he meant by the terms. He was also ambivalent about his nonconformity, and in January 1930 he feared that he was "in danger of being sidetracked" by religion, by his interest in organized labor, or by some "easier and more popular task." Tempted to leave Union, he nevertheless remained determined to find some effective approach to adult education as well as a "tenable philosophy."[12]

Horton's efforts to educate himself during 1929 and 1930 followed no clear pattern. He worked at a boys' club in the Hell's Kitchen neighborhood of New York City, visited the city's Greenwich House and Henry Street Settlement, served as a volunteer organizer in an International Ladies' Garment Workers' Union (ILGWU) strike in New York, and observed a bitter textile strike in Marion, North Carolina, during the winter of 1929–30. He subsequently visited Brookwood Labor College, a residential labor school near Katonah, New York, dedicated to training potential labor leaders who would usher in a new, nonviolent social order. Brookwood disappointed Horton. The college seemed too formally structured and not readily adaptable either to the rural South or to the educational approach that had seemed so promising in Ozone. In the summer of 1930, while traveling to see what remained of the Oneida colony in upstate New York and the cooperative experiments at Rugby and Ruskin in Tennessee and at New Harmony, Indiana, Horton found little more than

The Establishment of Highlander   13

demonstrations of how a small group of idealists could live apart from society and exert no impact on it. Meanwhile, he continued to search for clues on building an educational program in books on organized labor, the social gospel, socialism, and education, including works by British Fabian Socialist Richard H. Tawney and American educators John Dewey, George S. Counts, Eduard C. Lindeman, and Joseph K. Hart. Dewey's influence was pervasive at the time, but Horton was not convinced that his ideas about learning could be translated into working with non-academic adults. Horton also received an unexpected lesson on the adversity confronting radicals in America when he unwittingly wore a red sweater to a May Day parade in New York and received a clout on the head from a mounted policeman for being a "god damn Red."[13]

The most powerful influence on Horton during his stay at Union during 1929–30 was Reinhold Niebuhr. Leader in the newly organized Fellowship of Socialist Churchmen, member of the pacifist Fellowship of Reconciliation, and prolific author of articles in religious and secular journals, Niebuhr had come to Union from a small parish in Detroit the year before Horton arrived. Enrolling in one of the theologian's seminars on Christian ethics, Horton was overpowered by the passion and complexity of Niebuhr's ideas. He was about to drop the course until other members of the class admitted that they did not fully understand the lectures either. Niebuhr persuaded the young Tennessean to remain in the class, and the two men developed a friendship that was to last the next four decades.[14]

Niebuhr's lectures in the seminar formed the basis for his book *Moral Man and Immoral Society,* published in 1932. The theologian shared Horton's sensitivity to the tension between individual ideals and the cruelties of modern society, as well as his skepticism about the redemptive power of the social gospel. Like Horton, Niebuhr had become convinced by the late twenties that basic changes in the American political and economic system were necessary, even though neither had a clear strategy to bring about such changes. Niebuhr's basic thesis in *Moral Man* was simple: there is a fundamental distinction between the behavior of individuals and of groups, and those individuals seeking to create a better world must adopt coercive methods that they themselves consider ethically "embarrassing." Group conflict is inevitable and unending, and "liberal moralists" invariably involve themselves in unrealistic or confused political reforms because they fail to understand "the power of self-interest and collective egoism in all intergroup relations." Thus the problem reformers face is how to pit power against power in order to obtain an approximation of justice, which Niebuhr defined not as love or as an end to conflict but as a form of equality in a society "in a perpetual state of war." Neither nations nor privileged classes could be expected to transcend their interests to contribute to a new social order, Niebuhr believed. Only the "self-conscious and politically intelligent" proletariat, with its ability to combine "moral cynicism and unqualified equalitarian social idealism," holds the power to make a new order.[15]

But if politics was forever destined to remain an area in which conscience and power met to work out "tentative and uneasy compromises," what chance did the proletariat have of achieving a just social order? Niebuhr ruled out revolutionary socialism, for its "fanaticism" permitted absurdities in religion and cruelties in politics. Evolutionary or parliamentary socialism was not much better, for it was not at all certain that such socialism could force industrial society "in the direction of equality." Nonetheless, if evolutionary socialism could approach an "approximation of a rational social ideal," its nonviolent coercion was preferable to the violence of revolutionary socialism. Perfect justice remained an illusory goal. But the illusion was necessary, Niebuhr concluded, for it generated a "sublime madness" in those who believed in "the possibility of a purer and fairer society than will ever be established." As long as reason and individual ethical impulses sought to minimize the destructiveness of social conflict and to enhance the economic and political power of the "disinherited," Niebuhr was satisfied.[16]

Horton seemed to find new inspiration in Niebuhr's radical yet harshly realistic analysis. He was drawn to Niebuhr's attacks on corporate capitalism and the flaccid idealism of the social gospel, his clear commitment to the interests of the working classes, his call for new forms of education, and his concern with the relationship between spiritual values and material welfare. In an essay written sometime during his year at Union, Horton wrote that the "laws, moral teachings and codes of ethics" traditionally used in confronting problems should be tested for their "validity and utility in the light of the present needs," and those that were obsolete should be replaced with "new thought processes."[17] For his part Niebuhr was sympathetic if uncertain about what Horton intended to do in the southern mountains. Like some northern socialists, Niebuhr hoped that the relative sharpness of class tensions in the South would hasten the emergence of a genuinely radical proletariat. Perhaps Horton's proposed school would help.[18]

Although Horton had not reached any definite conclusions after a year in New York and at Union, his interests had turned from theology to sociology, and in the fall of 1930 he began attending classes at the University of Chicago's prestigious Graduate School of Sociology.[19] Again, Horton did not go to Chicago with the intention of making sociology his profession, and again he approached his studies with optimism. "For the *first time* in my school history," Horton noted to himself at the end of 1930, "I am taking what I want—regardless of credit or degree. My education looks hopeful."[20] From Robert E. Park and other professors he learned that combining "techniques of accurate observation" with personal involvement in a community could enable him to "detect the *real* desires of the people and plan his work in light of this discovery."[21] Park's theory that society was composed of individuals more or less antagonistic to one another, yet united by a set of accommodations that permit them to attain collective aspirations, suggested to Horton that educators should not try to resolve conflicts but seek some way to use them to move people away from the status quo. When people were satisfied that they were "headed in the right direction," Horton noted, there was no reason why they should not "plant" themselves in an environment that was conducive to their "desired type of growth."[22]

Yet Horton continued to question whether his intellectual concerns had any relevance to his plans for a school in Tennessee, and once more he looked for answers outside the classroom. On several occasions during the 1930–31 academic year he visited Hull House and discussed his embryonic ideas with Jane Addams and her colleague Alice Hamilton. Horton agreed with Addams's assessment that his proposed school resembled "a rural settlement house," though he saw his work in terms of an educational program using some of the techniques of settlement houses.[23] He cultivated his interest in socialism as president of a local Socialist club and Midwest representative of the League for Industrial Democracy. Horton's most important discovery in Chicago came in the spring of 1931, when he met a Danish-born Lutheran minister, Aage Møller, who had opened his church to university students for square dancing. One night Møller remarked that he had been a student and teacher at folk schools in his homeland that might provide a model for Horton's own endeavor, and he suggested that the Tennessean visit Denmark and study them. Further encouragement came from Enok Mortensen, pastor of an all-Danish congregation in Chicago, who invited Horton to attend services at his church. Fascinated by the vitality of the small Danish community, Horton spent the rest of the spring of 1931 learning more about the culture, language, and folk schools of Denmark.[24]

The original purpose of the Danish folk schools, as conceived by Bishop Nikolai Grundtvig, was to awaken and develop patriotism and civic responsibility among the nation's long-oppressed rural peasantry. Through what Grundtvig called "the living word," the "people's high schools" were to make students aware of their shared cultural heritage, offer useful technical information, and encourage individual expression as well as a spirit of cooperation that would spread throughout the nation. Grundtvig never realized his own plan for a "Royal School for Life," but Danes had seized upon his idea to restore their country's economic prosperity, social stability, and national pride after suffering a decisive defeat in a war with Prussia and Austria in 1864–65. By the late 1920s the folk schools were widely credited with improvements in agricultural practices and the growth of intellectual activity and political participation among the rural population of Denmark. Their success inspired the formation of similar schools throughout Scandinavia and attracted considerable attention among adult educators in the United States.[25]

Excited by the possibility of adapting the Danish folk school concept to the southern mountains, Horton read everything available on the subject, including John C. Campbell's *The Southern Highlander and His Homeland*. Campbell and his wife, Olive Dame Campbell, who helped her husband collect material for the book and actually wrote most of it herself after his death in 1919, had believed for years that an educational venture patterned after the Danish folk schools might supplant existing mission schools in the mountains, and in 1925 Olive Campbell had established the John C. Campbell Folk School near Brasstown, North Carolina. Horton had learned about the school while he was at Union Theological Seminary, but he had believed it to be little more than a quilt-making cooperative, irrelevant to his own more politically radical interests. He was partly correct. Olive Campbell saw the Danish folk school as an alternative to the urban-oriented curriculum of the traditional rural school system, a way of relieving rural isolation, and a substitute for newer rural schools that stressed individual achievement rather than cooperation. At the same time, she admitted, the folk school approach would have to be readjusted "to conform to generally accepted American ideals."[26] As David Whisnant has pointed out, Olive Campbell maintained "a gradualist, meliorist approach to social change, directing her work at the [John C. Campbell] folk school toward the small-scale economics of family farms and cooperatives, and assuming that individuals could find adequate room for mobility within an essentially unaltered system."[27]

Rejecting Campbell's romantic view of rural life and social reform, Horton nevertheless thought in mid-1931 that he had discovered in the Danish folk school a first-rate model for his own adult education program. Denmark's remarkably rapid improvement certainly seemed to be due to the folk high schools, socialist politics, and cooperative agriculture. But he remained skeptical. How could such schools exert so much impact on the country's development? Møller again urged him to learn the language and investigate the folk schools for himself. By the end of the 1931 spring term, Horton had resolved to go to Denmark. Undeterred by offers of a graduate assistantship from Professor Park and a position as principal of an academy in Tennessee, by his parents' financial needs, even by the pleas of his radical friends to stay and fight for revolutionary changes at home, Horton wanted to fully explore the adaptability of the Danish folk schools to southern Appalachia and to sort through all the ideas and experiences he had accumulated since his undergraduate days. Horton's vision battled with his self-doubt:

> It's hard to go on to Denmark. I'll have to take with me the thoughts of a suffering family and know that I could have prevented, at least some, of the suffering if I had not followed my plans. It's hard to sacrifice one's own family for a mere dream or ideal. But it must be so. In no other way can dreams become realities. If one's own suffering is what's driving one on, how much more is the knowledge of a suffering mother & father and sister. God it's hard. And it can only be justified by relieving the suffering of millions in the future. If I ever weaken may my soul be damned to the deepest hell of suffering. It will take a life intelligently—but not too intelligently—and passionately lived to justify my decision to let my family suffer. Temptations will come. Friends will plead. I'll get hungry for the things I love best. God I must not compromise.

With Reinhold Niebuhr's endorsement, and with the money earned as a research assistant to Dr. T. H. Aimes, a New York psychiatrist whom he had met in Chicago, Horton purchased a first-class ticket to Denmark.[28]

Arriving around September 1931 with little money and only a slight understanding of Danish, Horton spent the next several months traveling, observing, and talking with folk school teachers and students. As his knowledge of Danish improved, he began to give lectures on the United States to civic clubs, labor unions, and folk school groups. Many of his talks, based in part on his reading of Vernon L. Parrington's *Main Currents in American Thought* and Edwin A. Burtt's *Principles and Processes of Right Thinking,* focused on race relations and southern Appalachia, subjects on which he could claim some limited knowledge. In one lecture, Horton depicted racial prejudice in the United States as the product of "a basic economic conflict" between the races, which capitalists manipulated to their advantage, and an individualistic ethic held by both blacks and whites. Dismissing old racial stereotypes, Horton described blacks as a "new racial type created in America and thus more distinctively American" than other "racial or national groups" in the country.[29]

The notes Horton took during his tour, with their references to his symbolic "O school" in Tennessee, show that what he found in the folk schools was intriguing but ultimately disappointing. His rambling, disjointed thoughts suggest deepening frustration and uncertainty. "I never seem to get past the inspirational point," he complained on one occasion. "I don't seem able to clothe any idea in usable dress so that others can see them. At bottom I am damn lazy. There is a curiosity that keeps me working but no clear plan."[30] Never had he felt freer to pursue his educational project. At the same time, he feared that he was faltering, losing faith in his plan, and allowing his ideals to succumb to the temptations of conformity, comfort, and respectability: "Am I pitching my life on a plane to [sic] high? Is the air too thin to hold my weight when I am weary of flying?"[31] The sense of doubt, the feeling that he was drifting from one school to another in Denmark as he had in the United States, plagued him. Horton observed that the strengths of the folk schools lay in their creativity, close student-teacher interaction, highly motivating learning process, and dedication to a spiritually inspired purpose. But he also noted that the original emotionally and morally charged mission that had made the schools successful had been lost or had become hazy. Many of the older, rural schools seemed to be draining "life from a buried past," retaining the form of the earlier folk high schools but not their spirit.[32] Horton responded more positively to the newer, urban folk schools for industrial workers, such as Johann Borup's school in Copenhagen and the Workers' Folk School at Esbjerg. It seemed to him that these schools effectively addressed the specific problems of Danish laborers and farmers while maintaining a commitment to far-reaching social and economic reform.[33]

During the winter of 1931–32 Horton made several tentative decisions about his future work. He would return to the South, "to backward mountain sections at least one hundred years behind the most advanced parts of the country," and begin a loosely structured "workers school" that would avoid "all semblance of a training school."[34] Ideally, his school would be located on a farm, where students and teachers would have time both to reflect and to raise food, but there would be no attempt to glorify rural life. The curriculum would fulfill several functions. Beyond basic subjects such as mathematics and literature, courses would be flexible and oriented toward the students' actual needs, and they would provide the opportunity to introduce new ideas on socialism and labor unionism. Students and teachers would also seek to develop a greater sense of community in the surrounding area by promoting the formation of agricultural cooperatives and by staging social events for local residents. Through this combination of residential and community education, Horton somehow hoped to serve the cause of organized labor and socialism while rooting it in the culture of southern Appalachia. Sowing the seeds of a new social order would take time.[35]

Finally, on Christmas night 1931 Horton decided to end his quest. Unable to sleep, he sat down and wrote out his thoughts. It was time to stop trying to design a curriculum and a teaching approach in advance. He should simply go back to the southern mountains and open a school that would gradually assume its own institutional form and allow the "mountaineers" and factory workers of the region to develop the educational program themselves. The school would be a place where small groups of young southern men and women, black and white, could meet for three to five months at a time to learn "how to take their place intelligently in the changing world." Free of credits and examinations, teachers would help students acquire information relevant to their specific concerns and "broaden" their outlook so that they would be able "to make decisions for themselves and act on the basis of an enlightened judgment." In the years to come, Horton hoped, the school would become "a stopping place for traveling liberals and a meeting place for southern radicals."[36] Horton doubted that the folk school idea would completely solve the problems of Appalachia. By February 1932, however, he was satisfied that his chosen method was "best suited for my personality and for the work I want to do."[37]

Tired and broke, Horton returned to the United States around May of 1932, outlined his plans for a school to Reinhold Niebuhr, and secured his aid in raising financial support for the project. Niebuhr's announcement in late May 1932 of the forthcoming establishment of a "Southern Mountains School" emphasized the larger, more radical goals Horton had developed since his summer in Ozone. The new school, Niebuhr wrote, would train "*radical* labor leaders" in the necessity of both "political and union strategy" in "southern industrial areas." The school was to begin somewhere in the mountains of North Carolina on a budget of three thousand dollars; it would help educationally disadvantaged adults learn how to make decisions about their own lives and bring about "a new social order." Although Niebuhr recognized the risks of starting a new venture in 1932 when so many other radical organizations were suffering financially, he was convinced of the need for a school to develop "an educated radical labor leadership" in the South.[38] Horton persuaded Sherwood Eddy, secretary of the international YMCA, to donate one hundred dollars as the first contribution to the school. With the aid of an advisory board that included Niebuhr, Eddy, Socialist party leader Norman Thomas, and Kirby Page of the Fellowship of Reconciliation, Horton would raise over thirteen hundred dollars by early 1933 and receive the support of such luminaries as John Dewey, Roger Baldwin of the American Civil Liberties Union (ACLU), and Frank P. Graham, president of the University of North Carolina at Chapel Hill.[39]

While fundraising went on, Horton began to assemble a teaching staff. Two of his former classmates at Union, John B. Thompson and James A. Dombrowski, agreed to join him after they completed their graduate studies. Thompson, a native Tennessean and a Phi Beta Kappa graduate of Beloit College, was finishing a bachelor of divinity thesis under Niebuhr on "The Social Consequences of Religious Orthodoxy in the South." Dombrowski was writing a doctoral dissertation on the "Early Days of Christian Socialism in America," in which he attacked the futile dependence of the social gospel on goodwill as a technique for social change and its failure to appreciate the influence of economic power on politics. Thompson would come to Horton's school sometime during the spring of 1933 and stay less than a year; Dombrowski would arrive that fall and remain for nearly a decade.[40]

Horton next began searching for a suitable location for his school. For much of the summer of 1932 he traveled throughout the mountainous regions of Tennessee, Kentucky, and North Carolina, looking for a site that fit the pastoral ideal he had imagined in Denmark. At one point he went to Atlanta seeking advice from Will W. Alexander, executive director of the Commission on Interracial Cooperation. Alexander only vaguely understood Horton's plans, but he knew a young man named Don West who was also interested in establishing a folk school in southern Appalachia, and he suggested that the two young men might work together.[41]

Don West's background, education, and ideological commitments resembled Horton's in several respects. Born in rural north Georgia in 1906, West had worked his way through Lincoln Memorial University in Harrogate, Tennessee, where he had been president of the student YMCA and active in organizing Sunday schools in isolated mountain communities. In 1928 he entered Vanderbilt University and developed a keen interest in folk school education under the guidance of Alva W. Taylor and Joseph K. Hart. After spending a year in Denmark studying folk schools, West returned to Vanderbilt and obtained his bachelor of divinity degree in 1931. In his thesis, a sociological survey of rural Knott County, Kentucky, West passionately argued that the solution to the area's social and economic problems was a Danish system of education that would not only help "mountain people" improve their communities but also move them "to see the advantages of cooperation—Socialism" over "the present inhuman system."[42] Tall, athletic, and given to writing poetry about southern

Appalachia, West assumed the pastorate of a small Congregationalist church near Crossville, Tennessee, while waiting for an opportunity to open his own folk school in the region. He learned that Lilian Johnson of Monteagle, Tennessee, was about to retire and wanted to turn over her farm to someone who would use it for a community project. West visited Johnson in the spring of 1932, impressed her with his plans for a folk school, and prepared to begin work in Monteagle that fall.[43]

Horton, when he met Don West at the Blue Ridge Assembly in North Carolina, found him to be a "mountain socialist" who was "growing more revolutionary every day."[44] After several days of discussion, the two men decided that since each had something to offer—Horton the financial backing for a school and West a physical location for it—they should secure Johnson's property and operate a school as co-directors. By the time they reached Johnson's home in September 1932, the "Southern Mountains School" had become the "Highlander Folk School." The name seemed appropriate. The two men were adopting a label commonly applied to Appalachian culture in the early twentieth century to designate the people they intended to educate in the southern mountains. But first, they had to gain Johnson's approval.[45]

In the early 1930s Lilian W. Johnson aptly described herself as "by nature a promoter and organizer, rather than an educator."[46] Born in 1864 into a wealthy Memphis banking and mercantile family, Johnson had earned a Ph.D. degree at Cornell University in 1902 and gone on to a distinguished career as an educator and advocate of agricultural cooperatives, temperance, women's suffrage, and the establishment of a women's college in the South with a curriculum as broad as that offered at male-dominated universities. In 1915 she moved to Summerfield, a small community near Monteagle, and built a large house as a community and educational center for both children and adults in the area. Over the next seventeen years Johnson promoted numerous local cooperative and educational programs. In 1925 she recruited May Justus and Vera McCampbell to teach reading to children and to offer night classes for adults in Summerfield. Yet most of Johnson's well-meaning efforts failed, largely because her condescending view of the community prevented her from ever understanding why her neighbors would not completely adopt her ideas. By 1932, a weary and elderly Johnson was ready to retire and donate her property to some worthwhile project. Following a series of meetings, she made a simple verbal agreement with Horton and West. The two men could use her property for a school as long as they ran it themselves, developed good relations with the community, and achieved tangible results with their programs. If at the end of one year she was not satisfied, they would have to go.[47]

On November 1, 1932, the Highlander Folk School opened for business. Horton and West—the "two young Galahads," as Alva Taylor dubbed them—had chosen a most appropriate place to begin their work.[48] Located at the southern tip of the Cumberland Plateau, Grundy County was by all accounts a very depressed area. The 9,700 people living in the county in 1930 had known poverty, disease, and illiteracy for many years. The coal and lumber industries on which the county had based its prosperity had collapsed well before the Great Depression, leaving only devastated resources and exhausted cropland that Department of Agriculture officials declared incapable of supporting a farm population. The result was what Horton called a "stranded population," almost entirely dependent upon some form of government relief. For decades younger people had left Grundy County in a futile search for jobs; their return merely worsened its economic problems. The government of Grundy County, according to the Tennessee Taxpayers Association, had "almost ceased to function" because of the inefficiency and indifference of county officials. There was little indication of leadership or sense of community among local residents. There were two county seats, at Tracy City and Altamont, thirty churches, an elementary school, a small resort area, and a number of good farm-to-market roads, but there was no hospital or public library. Most important to Horton and West, there was no adult education program in Grundy County.[49]

The area seemed to offer not only an open field for Horton and West but also a history of economic exploitation and labor protest that suggested at least the possibility of radical reform. The county had been created in 1844 and named after Senator Felix Grundy, a noted criminal lawyer, attorney general under President Martin Van Buren, and a land speculator in the Cumberland Mountains. The discovery of rich coal deposits in the 1850s had begun an almost continual drive for profit in land and coal. Mine operators acquired thousands of acres for as little as twelve and a half cents an acre, and by the 1880s the Tennessee Coal, Iron, and Railroad Company (TCI) had emerged as the largest firm in the county. TCI managers crushed a Tracy City assembly of the Knights of Labor formed around 1884 and bitterly fought a United Mine Workers local organized in 1898. The most dramatic labor conflicts, however, were three coal miners' insurrections in the early 1890s, known in the area as "the wars." County miners reacted to TCI's use of convict labor to reduce their own wages by freeing the prisoners, burning their stockades, and fighting gun battles with company guards. TCI leased its Grundy County property to the Tennessee Consolidated Coal Company in 1905, but the almost annual outbreak of short, violent strikes continued. Nevertheless, by the end of 1926 labor unions in the county had disappeared.[50]

Based on their reading of the problems of Grundy County in 1932, as well as its heritage of union activity, Horton and West believed that the prospects were good for using the Highlander Folk School to improve local conditions and train union leaders. The two men recognized, however, that county residents would be suspicious of a school staffed by college-educated people with unconventional ideas. Thus during the winter of 1932–33 Horton and West worked hard to establish themselves in the community and to explain to curious visitors the nature of their work. At first Horton was discouraged. He and West subsisted on beans and potatoes. Their cash dwindled to about $250, and only a single residence student, the son of an Alabama coal miner, came to Highlander when it opened in November 1932. Gradually, however, the informal meetings the two men held with Summerfield residents in late 1932 evolved into the first regular classes at Highlander. A psychology class was formed after the wife of a neighboring farmer complained about her unruly children. A cultural geography class was started after neighbors looked at snapshots taken by Horton and West in Europe. Discussion of a local coal miners' strike led to a course in economics, and the 1932 presidential campaign was the basis of sessions on political analysis. Throughout the winter an average of twenty people, ranging in age from eighteen to eighty, attended these and other classes, and a handful of residence students held weekly meetings with miners in outlying communities in the county. By early 1933 the three major features of Highlander's adult education program—residential courses, community programs, and extension work—had begun to emerge.[51]

The establishment of the Highlander Folk School ended Myles Horton's five-year search for an adult education program that promised both to benefit the people of southern Appalachia and to transform the social, economic, and political order. During those years he had reached a conclusion that recalled his first summer in Ozone and guided Highlander's work throughout the rest of its history. Numerous elements contributed to Horton's personal and intellectual development: his parents' emphasis on Christian service; his work for the Presbyterian church and the YMCA; his friendship with ministers such as Abram Nightingale and Aage Møller; his classes at Union Theological Seminary and the University of Chicago; his extensive reading in philosophy and education; and especially his relationship with Reinhold Niebuhr and his investigation of the Danish folk schools.

Yet by 1932 Horton had come to the realization, reinforced by his first few months at Highlander, that assembling information on an issue without taking student experiences into account separated education from the actual needs of the people of southern Appalachia. He did not want to re-produce the shortcomings of earlier reform endeavors in the region. For generations missionary and philanthropic groups had raised a great deal of money for schools, institutes, and other enterprises in the southern mountains while leaving the basic problems of the region's poor largely untouched. Instead of relying on missionaries for solutions to their ills, Horton wanted southern Appalachian residents to organize and use their own intellectual and material "resources" to build better communities on "a *sound economic foundation*."[52] Although he knew that encouraging students to make their own decisions about their education would require enormous confidence in the "working people" of southern Appalachia, his school sought to awaken "the best that I believe all possess."[53]

Indeed, Highlander's subsequent contributions to organized labor, civil rights, and Appalachian reform stemmed from the energy and zeal with which Horton pursued his idea of using education as an instrument of social change. It is possible to attribute too much of Highlander's history to a single personality, even to one as commanding as Horton's. Highlander's programs owed much to the thoughts and actions of several strong figures, and Horton himself was deliberately vague about his personal principles, partly because of their shifting emphases over time and partly because his public image overwhelmed and sometimes consumed his private life. Yet he was an extraordinarily independent man, determined to find some way to translate his youthful discontent and experiences into an educational approach that expressed his ideals. Ultimately undeterred by doubts and disappointments, he rarely displayed any resignation or despair, and he was not intimidated by anti-unionists, racists, or the economically and politically powerful. His sense of autonomy prepared him for a life of exhorting others to join him in creating a new social order. He remained informal and spontaneous, and he committed several mistakes, but he never lost sight of his original vision of a more democratic, more moral world.

Yet in 1932 Horton and West were as imprecise about the overall objectives of Highlander as they were about their teaching methods. Both wanted to help "mountain folks" understand and adjust to economic and social developments so that they could "enrich their lives and make life more worthwhile."[54] An avowed socialist in 1932, West announced that Highlander "educates for a socialized nation" in which a social order based on "human justice, cooperation, a livelihood for every man and a fair distribution of wealth" would replace the existing system of "graft, exploitation and private profit."[55] Horton's goals were more restrained and even less definite. He proposed to educate industrial and agricultural laborers to exert greater control over their jobs and to build a new society embodying the ideals of democracy, brotherhood, and justice. The two men expected their appealing goals to attract farmers, miners, and unemployed workers to their two-week leadership training course in January 1933. After years of frustration, Horton believed he had finally found an educational approach that reflected his own commitments to southern Appalachia and to fundamental social change. The procedure might not be clear, he wrote in Denmark in late 1931, but a radical must "champion a cause" and make it "real" to the people of the southern mountains.[56]

2

Early Struggles,
1932–1937

The most striking characteristic of the Highlander Folk School's work between 1932 and 1937 was the contrast between its ambitious objectives and its limited achievements. The school's letterhead summarized its two major goals. First, Highlander sought "to educate rural and industrial leaders for a new social order." No one at HFS ever fully articulated the nature of this new order. But in November 1932 Myles Horton and Don West anticipated that the growth of the coal and textile industries in the South would require the training of local union leaders who would contribute to the rise of a broad-based labor movement committed to fundamental social and economic reform. Equally important was Highlander's second overall aim, "to conserve and enrich the indigenous cultural values of the mountains." From his past experiences Horton knew that he could not impose any educational program on the people he wanted to help and that the success of a southern labor movement would rest largely upon its ability to respect regional customs and traditions.

Yet the Highlander teaching staff encountered a host of difficulties during the early and mid-1930s in trying to give purpose and direction to the school's programs. Staff members provided various services to the Monteagle community, became involved in several violent labor struggles in East

Tennessee, began a food cooperative in Grundy County, and attempted to start another school in Allardt, Tennessee. But their plans often outdistanced what actually occurred. Highlander's role in the southern labor movement was primarily confined to Grundy County and to relatively small communities in the area, and virtually every strike involving HFS staff members was unsuccessful. Organized labor in the South grew more slowly and was less militant than the staff ever liked to admit, and unions remained weak and disorganized. In its eagerness to bring about a new social order, the faculty engaged in radical political activities that did little to further Highlander's programs or to increase their appeal to southern wage earners. Thus HFS teachers were almost continually forced to redefine and reevaluate their policies, curriculum, and commitment to social change, resulting in serious conflicts over the means and ends of the school. Compounding these problems were unrelenting financial troubles. In short, staff members only partially succeeded in developing a coherent program of labor education during Highlander's early years. Nonetheless, by the time the Committee for Industrial Organization initiated its southern organizing campaign in 1937, Highlander had achieved a measure of distinction as a school willing to help transform labor relations in the South.

The earliest classes at Highlander were scarcely adequate to the task of creating anything resembling a new social order. In early 1933 Horton believed that education at HFS should lead to "conscious class action" among southern mine and mill workers and to the development of some type of socialist society. Exposing students to "conflict situations where the real nature of our society is projected in all its ugliness" would keep Highlander's programs from becoming "unrealistic," Horton believed, and actively participating in community affairs would prevent the school from becoming "a detached colony or utopian venture."[1]

Such bold declarations of purpose, however, belied a loosely organized curriculum of relatively traditional courses for a painfully small number of students. A total of eight young men and women enrolled in the first residence term between November 1932 and April 1933. In an effort to increase attendance, Horton and West announced a special two-week leadership training course for area farmers, miners, and unemployed workers that would begin on January 16. One week before that date, however, the federal Reconstruction Finance Corporation offered jobs to most of the prospective students, and only one former hosiery mill worker arrived on the first day of the course. During the five-month residence term the students who eventually came pursued independent studies and attended courses in economics, cultural geography, psychology, history, and literature. They discussed the structure, functions, and benefits of labor unions; wrote spirited essays on such subjects as "Technocracy and Socialism" and "Socialism and Christianity"; and joined local residents in evening meetings on various social and economic problems. But clearly something was missing. By the end of the term in April 1933, the HFS faculty had discontinued all classes except John Thompson's seminar on religion and social change. Teachers, going far beyond the interests of their students, had tended to dwell upon abstractions. In one fabled economics class, held in the school's kitchen, the instructor had propped a blackboard over the sink and used pots and pans to demonstrate how economic theories applied to everyday life. But when students in a psychology class decided to learn "how to think straight," Horton had conducted a "brief survey of the nervous system" in an awkward attempt to supplement the main topic of interest.[2]

Acknowledging the shortcomings of these first residence classes, staff members looked to a coal miners' strike in Wilder, Tennessee, to relate the school's program to the concrete problems facing farm and factory workers in the South. To Horton, the labor conflict offered teachers and students a chance to be involved in a clear-cut class struggle while they gained first-hand knowledge of conditions in the area. Yet the violence between striking miners and coal operators and the isolation of the Wilder community reduced much of its instructive value. There was no powerful labor organization to support the strikers' efforts to secure better wages and company recognition of their local union. And without an effective educational program to offer the miners, Highlander could do little to influence the outcome of the strike.[3]

The Wilder strike began in the summer of 1932. Three companies owned all the coal mines around Twinton and Crawford in Overton County and Wilder and Davidson in Fentress County. The New York–based Brier Hill Collieries owned the mines at Twinton; E. W. and Hubert Patterson operated the mines at Davidson; and W. D. Boyer and L. L. Shivers managed the area's largest mines at Wilder for the Nashville-based Fentress Coal and Coke Company. The Depression forced Brier Hill Collieries to close its mines in the early summer of 1932, and on July 8, 1932, Shivers and the Patterson brothers announced that in order to keep their mines open they would not renew their contract with the United Mine Workers of America (UMWA) local unless its members accepted a 20 percent wage cut. Union miners, who had resented conditions in the mines and mining camps for years, rejected the demand and went on strike, deciding that they would "much rather starve out in the open than starve to death in the mines."[4] The mines remained closed until mid-October 1932, when nonunion miners and a handful of union members resumed work at the Wilder mines under the protection of armed guards. During the next seven months, until June 1933, the violence of the Wilder strike was comparable to the prolonged and bitter conflict between coal miners and operators in "Bloody" Harlan County, Kentucky, during the 1930s. Governor Henry H. Horton dispatched nearly two hundred national guardsmen into the area in November 1932, but the presence of soldiers brought no peace to Wilder.[5]

Myles Horton went to the town in November 1932. If his youthful idealism predisposed him to side with the striking miners, he encountered nothing to alter his sympathies. Horton ate a meager Thanksgiving dinner at the home of Barney Graham, president of the Wilder UMWA local, and was deeply moved by the suffering he observed in the community. He was waiting for a bus the next afternoon when Captain Hubert Crawford arrested him, took him to state police headquarters, seized his notes on the strike, and charged him with "coming here and getting information and going back and teaching it."[6] Released the following morning, Horton immediately began a campaign to build public support for the strike. He charged that newsmen had ignored the coal companies' open contempt for the law, the evidence linking company employees with the demolition of a railroad bridge, the widespread drunkenness among the soldiers, and the threat to kill Barney Graham. But Horton's claims merely provoked angry retorts from national guard officers that radical agitators like him were responsible for the troubles at Wilder. In early December 1932, Fentress coal company officials secured a sweeping injunction against the local union, effectively deciding the fate of the strike. The guardsmen left Wilder shortly before Christmas, but returned again in January 1933 to patrol the area after violence erupted again. Highlander had done nothing to aid the miners, Don West noted, "except stir up a lot of hell."[7]

As an uneasy truce settled over the area in early 1933, HFS staff members and others sympathetic to the union cause turned to the task of providing relief to the families of miners still on strike. Through the Wilder Emergency Relief Committee, Howard A. Kester, southern secretary of the Fellowship of Reconciliation (FOR), supplied desperately needed food and clothing. Although some strikers were concerned that Horton was a "Red," the assistance offered by Horton, West, and their students convinced many of the miners of their good intentions. For the rest of the winter of 1933 small groups from Highlander periodically visited Wilder. They helped with relief work, gathered data on the coal companies and conditions in the community, conducted study sessions on unionism, compiled reports on union and strike activities, appealed for funds to feed the miners' families, and made plans with local union officers to start a cooperative garden project. If the union members could hold out for "a mere living wage," the HFS staff believed, they would not only "save" Wilder but also give inspiration to "southern labor at large."[8]

Nevertheless, as the strike wore on into the spring of 1933 and more and more miners trickled back to work, Kester, Horton, and their associates recognized that the strike would last only as long as Barney Graham was able to hold the union local together. The second withdrawal of troops on February 17, 1933, ignited another wave of dynamite explosions, gun battles, ambushes, holdups, whippings, and fires. To prove their claim that a majority of the men would return to work were it not for Graham and "outside influence," Fentress coal company managers published a letter written by a Highlander student who declared that it was "the historic mission of the working class to destroy the capitalist system."[9] In mid-April 1933 Horton learned of a plan by company guards to kill Barney Graham. State officials failed to heed Horton's warnings that Graham's life was in danger, and on April 30, 1933, the strike leader was dead. Graham's murder "just killed me," Horton later recalled. "If I hadn't already been a radical, that would have made me a radical right then."[10] Nearly three hundred miners, their strike finally broken, returned to work without a union contract and under heavy guard the next day. As further outbreaks of violence occurred, Horton predicted "a war of revenge," and West gravely observed that all was "quiet in Wilder Hollow—the quiet that always comes before the storm breaks."[11]

A Chattanooga *Times* editor noted in June 1933, however, that "Bloody Wilder" was also becoming "ragged Wilder, hungry Wilder, desperate Wilder," whose people could no longer exist without some form of relief.[12] Horton and Alva Taylor of the Church Emergency Relief Committee tried to promote a cooperative project to sustain the miners through the summer, but the strike had devastated the area. The mines at Twinton and Crawford permanently closed in the summer of 1933, and nonunion miners worked for substandard wages under armed guard at the remaining mines at Davidson and Wilder. Banking, telephone, transportation, medical, and educational services all but disappeared. A Tennessee Valley Authority official reported in October 1933 that miners and their families were living in "a condition bordering on starvation."[13] Concluding in the fall of 1933 that there was no hope for the coal industry or for organized labor at Wilder, Kester, Taylor, and other concerned people found jobs and housing for miner families at TVA, Civilian Conservation Corps, and federal resettlement projects in the area. Horton was reluctant to acknowledge the defeat

76504

of the union. At the Socialist party state convention, held at Highlander in June 1933, he and other participants declared that TVA's Cove Creek project would snatch victory away from the striking miners in Wilder and allow coal operators to continue their "ruthless exploitation of the workers."[14]

Indeed, the Wilder strike helped shape Highlander's early labor education program, for it presented the sort of "conflict situation" the HFS staff thought students needed to understand their own pressing problems. The strike taught the handful of teachers and students at the school about the role of newspapers, churches, Socialists, and public officials in labor conflicts; the importance of accumulating and analyzing information from firsthand experience; the potential usefulness of education in advancing the cause of organized labor; and the way in which the South seemed to be "awakening in spots" and providing "real leadership" in communities like Wilder.[15] Highlander's participation in the Wilder strike also brought publicity to the school. Three resident students attending the 1933–34 winter term were members of striking miners' families from Wilder, and the school began to attract the attention of southern labor union officials.[16]

Yet several major institutional problems faced the HFS staff. In 1933–34 Highlander was in deep financial trouble. Horton and West believed that the school's programs should be largely self-sustaining. No salaries were paid during the first fiscal year, and the staff subsisted mostly on turnip greens and beans. The rigid economy kept expenses down to about thirteen hundred dollars that year and enabled the staff to buy books and journals and to extend assistance to places such as Wilder. But the school's meager food supplies dwindled as more people came to Highlander, and funds were needed for car repairs, electricity, postage, insurance, taxes, office equipment, books, traveling expenses, and a new community meeting house. Reinhold Niebuhr worried about the lack of publicity for the school and the apparent nonchalance of staff members toward fundraising, especially at a time when philanthropic aid was scarce. He used his influence to secure money and materials for Highlander and urged Horton to seek foundation grants. During the summer and fall of 1933 staff members launched a fundraising drive that highlighted the community's support of the school, the educational and cooperative projects at Wilder, the services students were providing in "southern labor fields," and the use of Highlander by the Socialist party as a training school.[17] Their campaign produced limited results. Highlander's cash balance was exactly $5.57 on May 1, 1933, and even less on October 1, 1933.[18]

Adding to the strains of developing educational programs under such constricted conditions was Lilian Johnson's concern over the poor treatment of her property and Highlander's controversial involvement in the Wilder strike. While she publicly defended the school in December 1932 against charges of communism, she admonished Horton for his role in the strike and advised him not to teach "divisive" theories and slogans that would alienate those local residents who associated socialism with "the worst kind of trade unionism," "loose living," and other "horrors."[19] Johnson decided in May 1933 to renew the lease on her house and farm for another five years. But Highlander's future remained doubtful, and staff members assumed that they would have to find a new location soon.[20]

Dissatisfied with Highlander's halting steps toward a new social order, Don West left the school on April 1, 1933. He and Horton shared an idealistic commitment to the welfare of the southern labor movement, but from the beginning of their collaboration neither had been entirely comfortable with the temperament and judgment of the other. The result was a series of clashes that created internal chaos at the school. Horton charged that West was too individualistic, too extravagant with school funds, and too inattentive to the day-to-day operations at HFS. West responded that Horton attached too much importance to Highlander as an institution, made unilateral decisions regarding staff hiring and student admissions, and claimed sole responsibility for the school's continued existence. Dissolving the partnership appeared to be the only solution. Afterwards, West first went to Atlanta to head the defense committee for Angelo Herndon, a young black Communist organizer charged with violating an 1869 Georgia insurrection statute. He subsequently made an ill-conceived attempt to foment a student strike at the Berry School near Rome, Georgia, founded the Southern Folk School and Libraries near Kennesaw, Georgia, and supported several Communist causes during the 1930s. In 1967 he and his wife, Constance, established the Appalachian South Folklife Center near Pipestem, West Virginia, dedicated to the teaching and preservation of the region's cultural heritage. He died in September 1992 at the age of eighty-six.[21]

Highlander's internal affairs began to improve with the arrival of Elizabeth Hawes and James Dombrowski in 1933. The Vassar-educated Hawes had spent a year at Brookwood Labor College and a summer at the John C. Campbell Folk School before coming to HFS in the spring of 1933. Free-spirited and devoutly socialist, "Zilla" expected that the Depression would produce a "spontaneous indigenous labor movement" and hoped to stimulate "working people" to begin a revolution "in all its phases."[22] Dombrowski arrived at Highlander in the fall of 1933 after spending most of the year raising funds for the school. Son of a Tampa, Florida, jeweler, Dombrowski had served in France during World War I. After graduating from Emory University in 1923, he organized the Emory Alumni Association and served as its first executive secretary before pursuing graduate work at the University of California at Berkeley, Harvard, Columbia, and Union Theological Seminary. Thoughtful, meticulous, and a committed radical who had been jailed in 1929 for publicly supporting striking mill workers in Elizabethton, Tennessee, Dombrowski was anxious to start working at Horton's "radical labor school," for he saw "some stirring days ahead" in the South.[23]

Meanwhile, the spontaneous strike of local bugwood cutters in July 1933 marked both the beginning of Highlander's acceptance in the community and the first real implementation of the school's educational program. A number of men in the Summerfield area worked for an agent contracted by the Tennessee Products Company of Nashville to provide three hundred cords of cutover timber, known as bugwood, for a distillation process that extracted alcohol and other products from the wood. The woodcutters earned seventy-five cents per cord, half of what they had been paid on previous jobs. After Henry Thomas calculated that he was making between fifty and seventy-five cents for a ten-hour day, he persuaded two dozen of his fellow cutters to go on strike on July 3, 1933. Two days later he and Bill Marlowe, secretary of the Summerfield Socialist party, began to hold meetings at Highlander, where a growing number of cutters and their sympathizers indignantly discussed the low wages, the unfair measuring system, and the exorbitant company store prices. With staff member Dorothy Thompson's help, the strikers formed committees to negotiate with the local agent, investigate whether Tennessee Products could afford pay raises, and gather information on the location of other bugwood cutters in order to bring effective pressure against the firm in Summerfield. The agent offered a five-cent raise and vaguely claimed that the strike violated some new law. In response striking cutters met at Highlander, agreed with Thomas that "it takes sharp tools, a strong back and a weak mind" to cut bugwood at the existing pay scale, and decided to stay together and demand $1.50 a cord and proper measuring procedures.[24]

The bugwood strike was not large, involved no momentous issues, and occurred at a time when Highlander was struggling with its own institutional needs. But the strike gave staff members their first opportunity to respond to a perceived problem within the community and develop a labor organization that could be the basis for broader reforms. Cutting a local Socialist meeting short when strikers arrived at the school "on fire to organize," Dorothy Thompson presided over the formation of the Cumberland Mountain Workers' League on July 10, 1933.[25] Horton helped league leaders draft a constitution for the organization, whose stated purposes were "to prevent wholesale destruction of our forests" and "to better the conditions of the community" by raising the wages of its members.[26] The woodcutters recognized that their goals were contradictory. They did not want to cut down the trees at all, but they also knew that jobs were scarce in the area. Still, it seemed strange to them to be destroying the forests at seventy-five cents a day while the federal government was sponsoring a reforestation camp at the other end of Grundy County. They were determined either to preserve their forests or to be paid a decent wage for their work.[27]

Although the woodcutters won neither higher wages nor recognition of their union, the Highlander staff used the year-long strike and the Cumberland Mountain Workers' League to foster greater confidence among local residents in their ability to run their own affairs. Cutters and sympathetic neighbors picketed the woods to stop all bugwood cutting while they awaited federal intervention in the strike. HFS staff members organized several league committees and turned their meetings into classes where strikers learned the laws and codes governing their industry and the federal agencies responsible for administering them. The cutters wrote letters requesting information, studied the technical reports they received, and made recommendations to their colleagues on the basis of their findings. It was a cumbersome process, and the woodcutters' frustration grew as their grievances were shuttled among various federal agencies. Finally, Horton led a four-man delegation, representing the league as well as two thousand area coal miners and textile mill hands, to Washington in November 1933 to lay their complaints before Secretary of Labor Frances Perkins. The men never saw Perkins, however, and by the time the committee returned from Washington, Tennessee Products officials had announced that they were canceling all contracts for the bugwood.[28]

Only the tenacity of the woodcutters kept the strike alive until mid-1934. The Highlander staff conducted classes during the winter of 1933–34 in support of the cutters' attempts to start a cooperative farm and a small cooperative store and laundry. But by May 1934 the cutters were ready to end the strike and accept the company's offer of one dollar a cord if it would recognize and bargain with their union. The company rejected the proposal, and, after exhausting their appeals to federal mediators and Tennessee Federation of Labor officials, the unemployed cutters formed the Cumberland Mountain Unemployed and Workers' League in July 1934 to seek an increase in relief payments.[29]

Despite its collapse, the bugwood strike was an important step in establishing Highlander as an ally of organized labor and a friendly meeting place for local residents. The strike confirmed Horton's belief that workers were capable of recognizing their most pressing problems and forming unions that could be part of a southwide labor movement. HFS teachers and league members discovered that they could neither depend upon outside agencies to support their interests nor remain unaffiliated with larger and stronger organizations. The bugwood strike opened the way for the development of a community education program at Highlander, and Horton later contended that the staff's experiences during the struggle furnished the basis for its subsequent work with labor, farmer, and civil rights groups.[30]

Highlander's training of local labor leaders, however, did little to improve the school's residence program. There remained a large gap between its vaguely defined goals and the methods used to pursue them. Before each residence term, staff members would announce its purpose, the anticipated size of the student body, the costs of the session, the curriculum they intended to follow, and the results they hoped to achieve. But each session would fall short of their expectations or only partially fulfill their plans, a pattern that was to be repeated well into the 1930s.

The winter residence term of 1933–34 offers a glaring example of the weaknesses in Highlander's early residence program. In late 1933 Horton, Hawes, Dombrowski, Dorothy Thompson, and new staff members Rupert Hampton, a graduate of Union Theological Seminary, and Malcolm Chisholm, an artist and dramatist from Alabama, made plans for a five-month residence session for miners and mill workers on the Cumberland Plateau. Tuition was seventy-five dollars or the equivalent in farm products or labor. Courses would include economics, labor history, psychology, sociology, English, public speaking, dramatics, music, and art. Teachers and students would also participate in strikes, organize local unions, publish a school newspaper, make speeches in a labor chautauqua, and engage in community projects. The session was scheduled to begin on December 1, 1933. But for some unexplained reason, the winter term began in the middle of March 1934 and closed ten weeks later. For at least part of the session Hawes was in Knoxville teaching textile union members; Dombrowski and Chisholm were in Allardt, Tennessee, constructing a new school for HFS; and Horton was in a sanitarium, recovering from mental and physical exhaustion. Thus the responsibility for the term fell largely on the relatively inexperienced Thompson and Hampton. Only four students attended the winter session, and its overwhelmingly academic orientation was painfully evident in the extensive use of textbooks as the basis for class discussions. The staff was consoled only by the claim of one student that she had learned more during her stay at Highlander than she would have by spending a year in high school or college.[31]

Well aware of the shortcomings of the winter term and spurred by a noticeable increase in southern rank-and-file militancy, the Highlander faculty prepared more thoroughly for a six-week summer residence term held during June and July 1934. The format of the term was both more flexible and more sophisticated, with core courses in labor history, labor economics, and sociology, and optional classes in labor journalism, public speaking, dramatics, music, and art. Tuition for the term was thirty dollars, and scholarships were available for those workers on strike or unable to pay. Most of the eighteen full-time students attending the session were from East Tennessee and members of unions like the UMWA, Amalgamated Clothing Workers of America (ACWA), American Federation of Hosiery Workers (AFHW), and United Textile Workers of America (UTWA). All of the students declared themselves united in their concern with "the evils of the present day economic system."[32]

Throughout the term teachers and students made a conscious effort to apply their classroom work to the needs of area labor unions, the Monteagle community, and Highlander. Zilla Hawes covered "the story of the working class from Feudalism up to the present American scene" with the aid of charts, outlines, her own knowledge as an ACWA organizer, and the experiences of students in recent strikes. Myles Horton's psychology class investigated "the prejudices and other psychological handicaps that weakened the Labor Movement," drawing examples from labor situations familiar to the students. James Dombrowski's lectures on Russia prompted an examination of capitalist and Communist economic systems. Students

Early staff members, 1933 or 1934. From left, Myles Horton, Rupert Hampton, James Dombrowski, Zilla Hawes, Dorothy Thompson. *Highlander Research and Education Center.*

also practiced the fundamentals of public speaking and parliamentary law, wrote short plays on the struggles of organized labor, and published a weekly newspaper called the *Fighting Eaglet*. Several special events supplemented the classroom work. "Union Week," held in mid-July for workers unable to stay for the full session, assessed conditions in the southern textile industry and union organizing problems.[33]

Although its importance should not be exaggerated, the decision by faculty and students at the 1934 summer term to study the necessity of cooperation among black and white laborers was an early indication of Highlander's willingness to confront the issue of race relations in the South. Following a talk by Howard Kester of the Conference on Economic and Racial Justice on the close economic link between southern white and black workers, several students asked for "the Negroes' side since the problem was important for the working class."[34] Staff members hesitated. In March 1934 they had reluctantly decided not to invite a group of black students to the school, fearing that "the harm it would do in the community would more than offset any sort of value" from such a visit.[35] Believing that Highlander had since gained enough community support to bring a black speaker to the school, the faculty invited Knoxville College professor J. H. Daves to discuss the need for an interracial alliance of unionized workers. Reaction came swiftly, and guards had to be posted around HFS at night when local opponents threatened to dynamite the school.[36]

Students were generally positive in their appraisal of the summer session, but staff members remained dissatisfied with the organization and conduct of the term. Zilla Hawes reminded her colleagues of the school's "revolutionary purpose" and of the need to bring "the people along with us to revolution and the classless society." Dorothy Thompson was more conscious of the school's need for the tolerance of the Summerfield community and the possibility of losing it by hosting black speakers, drinking alcohol, dressing immodestly, and engaging in loose talk about morality.[37] After several meetings, staff members agreed to screen student applicants more closely, to encourage them to come as representatives of their unions, to set a limit of fifteen students for each session, and to be more observant in their behavior. Each faculty member was to supervise a specific "department." As secretary, Dombrowski was to act as spokesman for the school. As educational director, Horton was to direct the operations of the residence sessions.[38]

The refinements in Highlander's residence program partly reflected its early extension work. As in the bugwood strike, staff members neither initiated nor significantly influenced the results of several strikes in East Tennessee during 1933 and 1934. But their prompt appearance at picket lines and their efforts to promote permanent unified action among strikers enhanced the school's reputation as a friend of labor in the South. Highlander's extension program began when Hawes went to Knoxville as an ACWA organizer, formed the first local of the union in the South in August 1933, and successfully guided workers through a strike for union recognition at the Liebovitz Shirt Factory in Knoxville.[39] After Hawes helped organize a UTWA local at the Brookside Cotton Mill in Knoxville, she and other HFS teachers assisted in an unsuccessful strike against the mill in November 1933. During the winter and spring of 1934, staff members took part in what Dombrowski described as "a losing battle, but a grand struggle" over union recognition at the Harriman Hosiery Mills west of Knoxville.[40] To sustain the strikers' militancy Dombrowski, Hawes, and others from Highlander joined picket lines, organized and addressed union demonstrations, and held meetings with jailed strikers. But in spite of a settlement negotiated by National Recovery Administration officials in July 1934, most of the mill hands doubted that they would ever work at the mills again.[41]

Highlander staff members participated in these and other union activities with an eye toward building an education program to help newly unionized workers understand the procedures, tactics, and purposes of their organizations. Like the residence terms, however, the extension work started slowly. In early 1934 Hawes announced the opening of a branch of the folk school in Knoxville that amounted to a reading room in a local hotel and the city's ACWA headquarters. Once a week she, Horton, and Dombrowski held classes for local union members and sympathizers on such subjects as labor history and the relationship between religion and labor. But the failure to find a suitable location for the branch school severely affected attendance, and by early February 1934 HFS staff members agreed that the entire program needed to be overhauled. The bitter failures of recent strikes also produced recriminations that damaged Highlander's work in Knoxville. In late February 1934 the Knoxville Central Labor Union ousted secretary Frank Torlay for official misconduct, but not before he presented books taken from Highlander's reading room as proof that "communists" and "atheists" were responsible for the loss of the Brookside and Harriman strikes. Thereafter, the HFS staff found it difficult to reorganize their Knoxville center and turned to extension projects elsewhere in East Tennessee.[42]

As some HFS teachers struggled to apply the lessons of their extension work to residence terms, others worked to plant the school's activities more deeply in the Monteagle area. Indeed, the residential, extension, and community programs were about as evenly balanced in the mid-1930s as they would ever be in the folk school's history. And like Highlander's other early educational efforts, the community program made only limited progress. The most ambitious attempt to promote community organizing involved the development of several small cooperative enterprises in 1934. After Dorothy Thompson and Rupert Hampton directed a six-week course on the history and operation of cooperatives, several Summerfield families formed the Cumberland Mountain Co-operative and applied for a $19,600 grant from the Federal Emergency Relief Administration in January 1934. HFS teachers may have seen the proposed farm and canning cooperative as "a demonstration of a society based on the socialist philosophy," but most local supporters of the project were simply "tired of going hungry because of insufficient relief and no jobs."[43] Despite the FERA's apparent enthusiasm for the proposal, Colonel Walter L. Simpson, director of the Tennessee Emergency Relief Administration, vetoed funds for the cooperative because he associated it with Highlander's "communist and anarchist" leadership.[44] Twelve Summerfield women proceeded to organize the Highlander Folk Cooperative on August 1, 1934. By November, eighteen families had canned over eleven hundred jars of vegetables. Cooperative members once again applied for a federal grant in late 1934, and in March 1935 the FERA awarded $7,000 to the Highlander Folk Cooperative, apparently convinced that it had no official connection with the Highlander Folk School.[45]

The cooperative never received the grant. The similarity between its name and that of the folk school led to angry protests that the money would only benefit HFS and "perpetuate the teaching of radical doctrines" in the area.[46] Prominent county citizens and local American Legionnaires complained that the directors of the cooperative were all connected in some way with the folk school, and they generally agreed with Southern States Industrial Council president John Edgerton that Highlander was "a thoroughly Communistic enterprise" whose teachers "devoted themselves to the teaching of anti-American doctrines."[47] Evangelist Billy Sunday added moral indignation to the protest during a revival in Chattanooga in June 1935, when he denounced the grant as a Communist assault upon the American home and the teachings of Jesus Christ. Despite repeated declarations by union leaders, clergymen, and others that the cooperative and the folk school were two separate organizations, TERA officials refused to turn over the grant to the cooperative, and the money reverted to FERA. The collapse of subsequent cooperative efforts, including a tomato patch, a sewing circle, a buying club, and a furniture shop, virtually ended Highlander's attempts to promote cooperatives in the community.[48]

Highlander and its neighbors had learned some hard lessons from the failure of these cooperative experiments. Clearly, Grundy County's resources could not sustain its unemployed population; the cooperatives merely exchanged one form of poverty for another. Moreover, the success of local unions and cooperatives required not only strong popular support but also close affiliation with larger and more powerful organizations. On the other hand, although the Highlander Folk Cooperative hardly constituted a serious threat to the economy of the region, the vehement protests against the FERA grant suggest that Highlander was having an impact well beyond its immediate location. The cooperative also helped the HFS staff gain a critically important community base from which to expand its work throughout East Tennessee. Recognizing the urgency of maintaining this foundation, the faculty made it a policy to remain in contact with Summerfield and the surrounding area, avoiding any paternalistic "social service, ymca attitude" toward local residents.[49] By modifying their programs in response to county problems, staff members would simultaneously enlarge their influence "in an educational way," broaden their "community base of support and protection," and attract a greater number of potential students.[50]

Though Highlander gained some organizational stability during 1934, staff members still faced serious questions about its financial status and permanent location. On October 20, 1934, Horton, Dombrowski, Hawes, Hampton, and Chisholm secured a state charter of incorporation, designating the school as a nonprofit institution for adult workers' education and naming the five teachers as the first board of directors. (The HFS faculty constituted the governing body of the school until 1940.) Funding remained a constant struggle. A decline in individual contributions, poorly planned and managed building projects, and residence term expenses left Highlander "nearly broke" in August 1934.[51] Horton wanted to keep the budget relatively small so staff members would not be forced to spend too much time on financial matters. Nevertheless, he and Hawes were compelled to embark on a fundraising tour of the Midwest and Northeast in the fall of 1934, forming chapters of the Highlander Folk School Cooperators among college "liberal clubs," church groups, and other organizations willing to aid HFS. As before, the campaign brought limited results. Between October 1933 and December 1934, revenue from donations, tuition, guest and conference fees, and honoraria totaled about $8,200; offsetting construction and operating expenses left less than $250 in the school treasury on January 1, 1935. The 1935 budget totaled only $3,427, but Dombrowski estimated that the staff would be hard pressed to raise that amount.[52]

Meanwhile, the continuing uncertainty about what Lilian Johnson would ultimately do with her Monteagle property prompted the HFS staff to begin work on a second Highlander in December 1933. Joe Kelley Stockton, Horton's friend since the late 1920s, had offered the use of several hundred acres for a folk school near Allardt, 145 miles north of Monteagle in Fentress County. Plans for the new residential center were thorough, romantic, and impractical. A volunteer labor force of students, teachers, and local workers was to construct a building large enough to house fifteen students, a furniture-making shop, and a "cottage" for teachers. Staff members hoped to limit the cost of the project to $3,550 by using the wood and sandstone found in abundance on the property for building materials and a nearby waterfall for power. The only remuneration Highlander could provide the work crew, wrote Dombrowski, was "the experience of working in a thoroughly interesting mountain community, good fellowship, and the participation in a significant social adventure."[53]

The hope of transferring Highlander's headquarters to Allardt by the end of 1934 quickly evaporated. In addition to extremely cold weather in February 1934 and the difficulty of assembling a work crew, the cutting of some eighty-five tons of sandstone and hauling it to the building site was an excruciatingly slow and laborious process. Between June and October 1934 a fifteen-man crew of college students and unemployed factory workers from Monteagle struggled daily in the quarry and devoted evenings to reading and informal discussions. The foundation for the first building was not completed until late September. At this rate it would take a decade to finish the project, staff members feared, and in October 1934 they suspended work for the winter because there was no money to support the work crew and maintain the Monteagle school at the same time. Already the work at Allardt had cost over $3,000, and an architect estimated that it would take another $1,300 to complete the main building alone. Despite the HFS staff's resolve to resume construction in the spring of 1935, the Allardt project was doomed. The obstacles facing Highlander, Dombrowski wryly observed in October 1934, seemed to be "in inverse proportion to the size of the school."[54]

Staff members gamely pressed ahead with their residence program for 1935 at the Monteagle school. Enrollment remained low, but Horton showed little concern about the size of the student body. He never would. He and his colleagues wanted to train organizers "with a social vision" and rank-and-file workers to carry on education programs in their own unions and communities.[55]

Among the eight students attending the two-month winter session that began in January 1935 was Zilphia Mae Johnson of Paris, Arkansas. Johnson was a quiet, sensitive, and talented woman of Spanish and Indian blood who had graduated from the College of the Ozarks and become a devoted follower of radical Presbyterian minister Claude Williams. Her father, a coal operator, had forced her to leave home because of "her revolutionary Christian attitudes," Howard Kester explained to Dombrowski, but she remained determined to use her musical and dramatic abilities in "some field of radical activity." Kester arranged for Johnson to go to Highlander with the idea of learning some fundamentals of the labor movement and then going on to "Brookwood or some other more advanced labor school."[56] She never reached Brookwood. Zilphia was "the girl I had been waiting for," Horton told Lilian Johnson, and he married her on March 6, 1935.[57]

The marriage would last until Zilphia's death in 1956, though for some of the school's admirers it never ended. The ardor Myles had for Zilphia was as intense as his commitment to Highlander: "I love you officially and unofficially; morning, noon, and night, asleep or awake; and in every mood or position that I find myself in or can imagine myself to be in," he wrote in the mid-1930s. For Zilphia, the relationship between herself, her husband, and HFS was more complex. It required what she described as a balance between independence and dependence, individualism and collective action, traditional gender expectations and creativity. She sought to establish a measure of personal freedom within "two personalities made richer by the blending of their complements and suppliments [*sic*]," and to extend "the delicate thread" that would enable her to maintain "a home with all the responsibilities involved" and still remain "not only an individual but a more creative individual." Her efforts to achieve that balance was an experience shared by women at Highlander for most of its history.[58]

Dominating the activities of the 1935 residence terms was a strike against the Richmond Hosiery Mills in the Chattanooga area. In February Highlander staff and students lived for a week in the homes of striking hosiery workers, organized educational and recreational activities, visited and spoke at picket lines, and helped stage a demonstration parade of strikers and sympathizers. Staff members hoped that their participation in the strike would attract a larger number of southern American Federation of Labor officials to their 1935 summer session, but the response was disappointing. None of the thirty AFL officials invited to the session's "Build the Union Week" in mid-July attended, and only two of the nine residence students were union members; one of them was Matthew Lynch, an American Federation of Hosiery Workers member from Rossville, Georgia, who later became secretary of the Tennessee Labor Council. Following the six-week summer session, faculty members and students staged a labor chautauqua in August and September 1935. Performing in Atlanta under the auspices of the ILGWU and in Huntsville with the sponsorship of the UTWA, the chautauqua presented plays like *Mopping It Up* (which dealt with the recently enacted National Labor Relations Act), puppet shows, folk dances, and labor songs composed by southern union members.[59]

Highlander's leaders, assessing the promising contacts made during 1935 with unions in Tennessee, Georgia, and Alabama, believed that they now had a clearer understanding of the school's role in the southern labor movement. During the year the staff had officially affiliated with the American Federation of Teachers (AFT), addressed AFL union locals from Elizabethton, Tennessee, to Dalton, Georgia, and won the endorsements of UTWA vice-president Francis Gorman, Southern Tenant Farmers' Union (STFU) secretary H. L. Mitchell, and local labor councils in Chattanooga and Huntsville. The folk school was moving into the southern labor movement "in a big way," Horton wrote in March 1935, and an expanded extension program would not only increase Highlander's standing among unions but also encourage organizers "to fight for us against both capitalists and conservative AF of Lers." Hawes asserted that the school's value to organized labor lay in its willingness to take on the difficult task of developing working-class leadership through an education program combining the study of "fundamental causes" with analyses of the students' experiences as union members. Dombrowski considered HFS part of "the whole labor movement" and a firm supporter of southern workers "at every possible point in their struggles."[60] Thus Highlander's agenda for 1936 was an ambitious schedule of residence terms, extension work, community projects, and labor conferences. Seeing a "desperate need" in the South for trained leaders drawn from the ranks of industrial workers and farmers, Dombrowski, like other staff members, contended that the school was in a strategic position to contribute to "the struggle for social justice."[61]

Yet, with no prospects for moving to Allardt and with an operating deficit of one thousand dollars in May 1935, the Highlander Folk School seemed to be in jeopardy. In September 1935 Lilian Johnson visited Highlander to make a definite decision about her property. Concluding that the school had become an accepted part of the Summerfield community, she deeded the house and forty acres of land to Highlander's directors in October 1935. Johnson never quite understood why Highlander had become involved with labor unions, and she worried about its reputation as a den of immoral square dancing and communism. But she was certain that Horton had never been "communistic" and that much of the criticism of the school had been brought on by Don West, who was not only "too radical" but "not so balanced as he should have been."[62] With the deed Highlander finally gained the institutional stability that led to more students, greater financial support, and an expansion of its efforts to promote industrial unionism throughout the South.[63]

Highlander's 1936 residence sessions reflected the staff's new confidence in their programs and their eagerness to contribute to the advancement of organized labor in the South. Eleven men and women, including five members of southern textile and mine workers' unions, enrolled in the two-month winter residence term that began in January 1936. The eight-course curriculum ranged from labor literature to a class on workers' problems, and a workers' council composed of students, faculty, and community residents governed school activities. Previous attempts to establish such councils had been undermined by the students' tendency to defer decisions to the staff. Beginning with this term, however, students at Highlander were more willing to assume responsibility for all phases of the session, gaining useful experience in parliamentary procedure and union-management relations in the process. The residence group also produced its own weekly bulletin, *Our Verdict,* and staged a reenactment of the 1935 AFL national convention, where John L. Lewis formed what was originally called the Committee for Industrial Organization. Given the faculty's own ideological sentiments and the fact that many of the unions defecting to the CIO were receptive to the school's work, it is not surprising that the students concluded that industrial unions were necessary in the drive for better wages, working conditions, and security. Staff members also attempted to impress students with the need for interracial labor unity through movies, visiting speakers like Howard Kester of the STFU, and a program by a black gospel quartet in February 1936.[64]

After a spring of extension work, publicity tours, and weekend conferences at HFS, staff members began a six-week summer residence term in May 1936. Advertised as a place where men and women could get "in the thick of the campaign to organize the South," Highlander attracted eleven students, most of them southern union members, to the session.[65] Enrollment was beginning to follow a pattern: seasonal employment evidently made it more difficult to recruit students—and male union members in particular—for summer sessions, for with two exceptions all of the students were women. Zilphia Horton's dramatics class was one of the high points of the term. After her marriage Zilphia had studied workers' theater at the New Theatre School in New York. When she returned to HFS she was ready not only to continue the chautauqua style of the dramatics program but also to teach students the rationale behind workers' theater.

The dramatics class prepared a play about a strike, held a mock AFL convention, worked on mass recitations and songs, and presented a program to union audiences in Chattanooga, Knoxville, and Atlanta and to TVA workers at Norris in June 1936. Under Zilphia's direction, the emphasis of the dramatics program shifted away from educating those who observed the plays to educating those who participated in them. Field trips and weekend conferences at HFS for the Tri-State Council of Hosiery Workers and for seventy trade unionists from Georgia and Tennessee rounded out the residence session.[66]

After several years of often sobering experiences, Highlander faculty members believed that they were finally in a position to help transform the unrest among southern factory workers in the mid-1930s into a powerful labor union movement. Persistent fiscal problems hindered any rapid expansion of HFS programs, and the financial status of the school remained heavily dependent on supporters outside the South. Nevertheless, Highlander's total revenue increased from $6,200 in 1935 to almost $9,700 in 1936, and its budget rose from $4,500 in 1935 to $8,905 in 1937. In November 1936, workers began construction of a new wing to double the school's capacity, refurbished the attic of the main building for a dormitory, and built two cabins for staff members. In the staff's opinion southern industrial workers were ripe for revolt, and the obvious need for trained union organizers foretold an even greater role for Highlander in the southern labor movement.[67]

The HFS faculty was equally concerned, however, that its expanded operations should not distance the school from its neighbors. Local attitudes toward Highlander were still mixed in 1935. Complaints of rough outdoor play, too much "freedom," and rowdy Saturday night square dances mingled with sentiments that the school was the center of the community. To improve the institution's image, staff members invited local citizens to hear brief speeches during residence terms, to attend James Dombrowski's Sunday night sermons on religion and social problems, and to participate in the well-established recreational affairs. Hilda Hulbert, who had joined the HFS staff in the fall of 1934, expanded the collection of books in the school library, securing donations from people such as renowned Fisk sociologist Charles S. Johnson.[68]

But it was Zilphia Horton and Ralph Tefferteller who integrated Highlander's cultural program with the curriculum and made the school truly attractive to the community and workers in the region. Music and folk dancing were forms of entertainment as well as education at HFS. They instilled a sense of solidarity among students, fostered a feeling of cultural pride, offered inspiration and hope, and contributed to the development of leadership, if only for group singing. By all accounts both Tefferteller and Horton were very capable and popular teachers. Tefferteller officially joined the staff in the summer of 1935. A native of Blount County, Tennessee, and an alumnus of Maryville College and Union Theological Seminary, "Teffie" was instrumental in the revival of square dancing in the area. Music became a vital part of Highlander's program almost as soon as Zilphia Horton arrived as a student in 1935. She encouraged students to share songs out of their own experiences, using a piano or accordion to help them write music or song lyrics and to lead groups in singing them. The cultural program gained national and even international notice when the British Broadcasting Corporation presented a performance from HFS in March 1937. As the Knoxville News-Sentinel reported, the ballads and spirituals sung by Horton, Tefferteller, Lee Hays (later a member of the famous Almanac Singers), and others were "the genuine article in Southern Highland music."[69]

Meanwhile, Highlander staff members took part in several strikes in the mid-1930s. None of the strikes was successful. But the faculty agreed with ACWA organizer Franz Daniel that "no strike is ever lost" and that every conflict offered a chance to use education in support of southern laborers. In February 1935 HFS teachers and students visited Rossville, Georgia, one of the scenes of a strike against the Richmond Hosiery Mills, and offered to help coordinate strike activities there and at the company's branch mills in Soddy and Daisy, Tennessee. In addition to holding labor history classes and discussions of strike tactics, making speeches, and singing on picket lines, the Highlander group helped plan a Washington's Birthday parade to the Daisy mill. On February 22, 1935, about four hundred strikers and sympathizers staged a noisy demonstration at the mill for several hours until about fifty strikers burst through the front gate and rushed into the yard. They were met by a volley of gunfire from inside the mill which wounded four workers and Highlander librarian Hilda Hulbert; fistfights then broke out between strikers and nonunion workers attempting to leave the plant. Neither Highlander nor the strikers were able to overcome the company's refusal to recognize a union, however, and the hosiery workers went back to work on March 1, 1935.[70]

Highlander's involvement in union and strike activities grew in 1936, but again with few tangible results. On April 6, 1936, some two hundred workers, angry over a ten-hour increase in the work week with no increase in wages, spontaneously walked out of a hosiery mill in Rockwood, Tennessee. The strike was doomed from the start. Former HFS student Matt

Lynch went to Rockwood to organize an AFHW local and asked for Highlander's assistance. The staff scoured the area for surplus food to feed the strikers and their families, set up classes on union organization and strike tactics, and tried to boost the strikers' morale at mass meetings. But as Zilla Hawes bitterly wrote, the strike became a repetition of "the old southern pattern, with violence all on one side, and every authority in the county lined up behind the company with not even an outside chance for redress of any kind."[71] Deputized mill guards used blackjacks and brass knuckles on Lynch and three successive union organizers and terrorized the striking mill hands. In early May, after a local "citizens committee" disrupted a union rally, Horton asked for the person who had been making public statements accusing Highlander of being communistic. When Captain Robert H. Thompson, head of the committee, replied that he had been responsible, Horton snapped, "Any man who says our school is communistic lies," sparking a fight between the two men and nearly a brawl between the two groups.[72] The company finally crushed the strike in June 1936; once more, striking workers had been powerless before the overwhelming onslaught of anti-union forces.[73]

Highlander's participation in a strike by five hundred hosiery workers at the Holston Manufacturing Company in Knoxville in September 1936 further enhanced its reputation among labor leaders, though the walkout itself was apparently unnecessary. Staff members, joined by teachers from the University of Tennessee and TVA employees, held classes on the picket lines as early as 4:00 or 5:00 A.M. on parliamentary law, contracts, labor history, and current events. This arrangement allowed the instructors to run classes for workers on both the night and morning shifts. Despite Highlander's support of the strike, Zilphia Horton suspected that no real issue was at stake, and the strikers voted to go back to work in mid-October 1936.[74]

The largest and most successful extension program undertaken by Highlander in the mid-1930s—and one that gave the staff a solid foothold in the community—was a union organizing and education campaign among Works Progress Administration workers in Grundy County. In 1935 WPA relief workers earned $19.20 a month, the lowest possible WPA wage rate in the Southeast. With 60 percent of the county's population on some form of government relief in June 1935, most of the workers resigned themselves to accepting the poor wages in return for steady jobs on road- and school-building projects. Myles Horton and some local residents believed that county WPA supervisors and foremen were political appointees generally "out of sympathy with the New Deal" who "ran things to suit themselves."[75] Yet the workers hesitated to form unions, vaguely feeling that it was not right to organize against the government. Realizing that the workers needed more information on the WPA, the HFS staff began offering informal classes in late 1935 on the agency's administrative orders. Among other things, the workers discovered that though the orders clearly divided jobs into skilled, intermediate, and unskilled categories, every relief worker in the county was working for unskilled wages. When they also found that there were no rules against unions, Tracy City relief workers established Local 848 of the International Hod Carriers, Building and Common Laborers' Union (CLU), AFL, in January 1936. Over the next several months the Highlander staff started several more locals in the county, as well as a Grundy County Women's Auxiliary for female WPA workers.[76]

With this organizational base, Highlander staff members attempted to carry out an education program throughout Grundy County. During the spring and summer of 1936 they attended two to four union meetings each week and helped Common Laborers' Union locals form committees to resolve the most immediate problems on the WPA projects. HFS teachers and union officers devised an inexpensive dues system, held mass meetings and weekend institutes at the folk school, circulated assurances from WPA officials that relief workers had the right to organize, and carefully trained local leaders in WPA grievance procedures. The primary task, however, was to raise the wage scale on WPA projects. By classifying Grundy County as an agricultural area, southern state WPA administrators had placed it in the lowest possible wage category. After amassing data with Highlander's assistance showing that the county should be reclassified as industrial, union committees wrote letters to President Franklin D. Roosevelt, national WPA administrator Harry L. Hopkins, and state WPA administrator Colonel Harry S. Berry, protesting both the inadequate wage rates for common laborers and a cut in the number of people on the county relief rolls.[77]

Meanwhile, the union's unsettled grievances accumulated. Project supervisors reportedly gave nonunion men preferential treatment, and one foreman declared that he was "getting damn tired of fooling with these union men."[78] In frustration, CLU relief workers halted nine of the fifteen WPA projects in Grundy County in March 1937, demanding union recognition, county reclassification, and the replacement of the county WPA administrator with someone "more honest and more human."[79] State administrator Berry held Highlander responsible for the strike, angrily charging that a "communistic organization has for months been feeding muscovite hops to relief clients in Grundy County" and suggesting that workers go elsewhere if they could do better.[80] By the end of the month CLU members had returned to work with assurances from WPA officials that their demands for union recognition and proper grievance procedures would be met, but there was no resolution of the county reclassification issue. As HFS teachers and relief workers drew up further protests, Berry and the CLU clashed again during the summer and fall of 1937 over the wages paid on WPA malaria control and road projects on Tennessee Consolidated Coal Company property. Officers of the international union finally prodded federal WPA administrators into settling the dispute, and in December 1937 local WPA officials agreed to comply with the agency's wage rate categories.[81]

Highlander's efforts in Grundy County and elsewhere during the 1930s made it part of a small, fragile network of individuals and groups committed to helping the region's poor and powerless, black and white, through education, union organizing, and community activism. Between 1933 and 1937 the faculty attended or hosted numerous conferences on race relations, workers' education, the TVA, and the relationship between church and labor. In 1934 Dombrowski organized the first meeting of the Conference of Younger Churchmen of the South to provide fellowship for those attempting to apply Christian principles against "the irrationalities and brutalities of the present economic order."[82] Renamed the Fellowship of Southern Churchmen in 1936, the group remained the voice of prophetic religion in the South for the rest of the thirties.[83]

Highlander had few institutional ties with other southern schools oriented toward workers' education. Basic differences in philosophy and program blocked any connection with the John C. Campbell Folk School; Commonwealth College in Mena, Arkansas, was too doctrinaire in its teaching approach; and North Carolina's Southern Summer School for Women Workers lacked the kind of community contacts the HFS staff worked so diligently to maintain. On the other hand, Highlander was unable to develop a productive relationship with the Southern Tenant Farmers' Union, a small but well-known example of interracial unionism in the 1930s. STFU's campaign to organize black and white sharecroppers in the face of arrests, evictions, and violence attracted considerable publicity. The HFS staff invited the union to send members to its residence terms, and in 1936 Horton taught at two STFU training institutes in Mississippi and Arkansas. But a heated dispute with Commonwealth College had made STFU leaders suspicious of all labor schools, and a desperate lack of funds made it virtually impossible for the union to send students to HFS. Collectively these associations established another theme in Highlander's history: although it sympathized and often worked with other reform groups in the South, it remained committed to its own agenda for radical change.[84]

At the same time, Highlander's promotion of a southern labor movement and its stated objective of a new social order meant that almost from the day it opened the school confronted charges that it was a breeding ground for "radical social agitators whose baneful influence is felt throughout this section."[85] Industrialists, news reporters, members of the American Legion, and others branded staff members as disruptive or meddlesome elements in the community and, more commonly, as Communists. As Highlander's reputation grew, the attacks intensified. Southern employers firmly believed that labor unionism meant the loss of profits, prestige, and prerogatives. Unions menaced what they saw as the region's greatest economic attraction—a docile labor force, willing to work for very little pay. Any group supporting the labor movement thus could expect to encounter the same resistance union members faced: "citizens committees" that attributed organizing campaigns to outside or radical agitators, "back-to-work" movements, and threatened or actual violence. The attacks upon Highlander during the early and middle thirties often occupied an inordinate amount of the staff's time and occasionally affected its work. Yet HFS teachers never hesitated to proclaim their socialist sympathies, their intention to train southern workers to unionize, and their willingness to challenge the power and interests of employers.

The accusations against Highlander erupted shortly after the school began operations. In December 1932 the Grundy County Board of Education barred the use of any county school building by Horton and West because they taught "political matters" that were "'Red' or communist in appearance."[86] Two years later John Edgerton, founder of the Southern States Industrial Council and president of the Tennessee Manufacturers Association, declined Horton's invitation to present his organizations' views at Highlander, proclaiming that "this enterprise of destruction" was "about the boldest and most insulting thing to the Anglo-Saxon South that has yet been done."[87] In 1935 the Knoxville *Journal* and the Chattanooga *Times* reported that documents found in STFU organizer Ward H. Rodgers's possession following his arrest on charges of fomenting anarchy proved that Horton, Dombrowski, and Hawes were part of a group of radical agitators promoting unionization, racial equality, and a united front of Communists and Socialists in the South. Dombrowski called the allegations that HFS was a Communist school "absurd" and pointed out that it was the school's policy to remain "non-factional in fact and spirit." Noting that no one who had criticized Highlander publicly had ever visited the school, Dombrowski reiterated the staff's position that it welcomed any properly conducted investigation at any time.[88]

These were relatively minor and scattered incidents. A more serious attack on Highlander occurred in May 1935, when Horton, Dombrowski, Howard Kester, and representatives of other progressive groups convened the All-Southern Conference for Civil and Trade-Union Rights. Participants at the interracial meeting in Chattanooga were to discuss a proposed platform calling for the repeal of all sedition and antilabor laws, the recognition of "bona fide" labor unions, the abolition of lynching and the poll tax, the "disbanding of all armed fascist bands" such as the Ku Klux Klan, and the freeing of all "victims of capitalist persecution." The conference was not being run by Communists, Dombrowski asserted; the aim was to make it "broadly representative," and Socialist party members had been "actively concerned in it right along."[89]

But the Americanism committee of the Chattanooga American Legion saw the All-Southern Conference as nothing more than a meeting of "reds." Declaring that the Legion's campaign against radicalism in America was "more important than the World War," committee chairman Raleigh Crumbliss pressured the Chattanooga Odd Fellows to cancel the rental of their hall to the conference on May 1.[90] Dombrowski blasted the legionnaires' display of "unofficial Hitlerism" and proceeded to rent a hall from the Knights of Pythias, a black fraternal group.[91] But after the Legion committee "advised" the Pythians, the conference was again homeless. Dombrowski finally secured a room over the Villa DeLuxe, a black beer garden. On May 26, about half an hour before the conference was to begin, approximately thirty-five legionnaires joined twenty-five police officers outside the building and compelled the proprietor to order the delegates out of the hall. The legionnaires then sped off in pursuit of the reputed "reds," determined that the conference would not meet in Hamilton County. Informed that some delegates had been seen near Cleveland, Tennessee, the men raced to the scene and found only the graduation exercises of Bob Jones College. Meanwhile, the fifty-nine delegates who had survived the location changes met at Highlander, where they made speeches denouncing the American Legion, passed resolutions adopting the general platform of the conference, and formed a committee to build a broader and more permanent organization.[92]

The All-Southern Conference debacle fueled the American Legion crusade against HFS. When Legion officers announced that a statewide rally would be held at Monteagle on July 12, 1935, observers generally understood that the purpose of the demonstration was to intimidate Highlander. During the night before the rally, a large, bronze American eagle perched on a concrete and rock base in front of the Monteagle motel was mysteriously dynamited, immediately arousing suspicions against the folk school. On the following day, with most of the HFS staff on a field trip to Alabama, several hundred legionnaires gathered to paint stars and stripes on the eagle's pedestal and hear speakers rail against the Communist menace to America. Monteagle citizens were largely indifferent to the Legion's presence, and some stood guard at the school in an unexpected bit of good fortune that Dombrowski attributed to Highlander's community program. Correspondents from the Chattanooga *News* ridiculed the Legion rally and printed pictures of school residents standing in Highlander's garden "fomenting political unrest amid bean bug life."[93]

Ironically, it was the *News* that sparked another major controversy over Highlander in 1937. On February 6 the paper published an article in which Lyle C. Stovall, chairman of the Chattanooga American Legion Americanism committee, revealed that a state highway patrolman posing as a newspaper reporter had investigated the school and found it to be "an immoral and dangerous institution." According to Stovall, the probe disclosed that immorality, drunkenness, and the singing of the Communist "Internationale" occurred at HFS, which was not a school but "an instrument of fomenting class consciousness and teaching strike techniques." The Chattanooga *Free Press* joined the attack the next day, repeating most of the allegations in spite of Stovall's complaint that his comments had been distorted.[94]

As soon as the two news stories appeared, Horton, Dombrowski, and their colleagues decided to rally "all the labor and liberal support" they could gather, make Chattanooga *News* editor George Fort Milton "pretty damn sick" of the controversy, and "stop these attacks once and for all."[95] Throughout the rest of February 1937, Norman Thomas, Reinhold Niebuhr, clergymen, TVA employees, labor organizations, and other friends of Highlander bombarded Milton with letters. Most significant to HFS staff members was the petition signed by over four hundred county residents expressing their appreciation of the faculty's work on their behalf. Thrown off guard by the protest, Milton initially refused to publish the letters of complaint. He defended the *News* report as an attempt to prevent "an unfriendly illiberal competitor," presumably the *Free Press*, from running "a great sensational expose of an allegedly Communist School."[96] But as the number of complaints grew, Milton printed the letters and beseeched Horton to call off the campaign. Horton and Dombrowski contemplated taking legal action, but concluded that the support the school received from organized labor, the community, and friends was "a significant vindication of our technique" and sufficient proof of Highlander's value to the area.[97]

While HFS staff members managed to forestall the potential damage of the *News* attack, they spent so much time combating it that they failed to respond quickly to a call for aid during a textile strike in Cleveland, Tennessee, in February 1937. Embittered by the loss of the strike, Zilla Hawes and her husband, Franz Daniel, accused the faculty of trying to develop a workers' education program apart from the labor movement. A "responsible" labor school, Hawes declared, "must be ready to serve at all times in spite of apparent sacrifice," and the most convincing answer to the redbaiting of the press would have been an immediate response to the strike in Cleveland.[98] Hawes saw in the preoccupation with defending the school a greater concern with Highlander as an institution than with its role in the labor movement. Dombrowski accepted responsibility for the error in judgment, pointing out that he and his colleagues were "still young, and ready to learn, and still feeling our way."[99] But he thought that Daniel and Hawes were overreacting to the staff's first major mistake in the past five years, and he resented the idea that Highlander's allies had joined the American Legion and a hostile press in openly criticizing the school.[100]

Dombrowski's irritation reflected a larger problem the Highlander staff faced in reconciling its commitments to the interests of the southern working class, to organized labor and radical reform groups, and to the residents of Grundy County. The conflicts were particularly sharp in the 1930s, but they would trouble the folk school for most of its history. In the early 1930s most staff members described themselves as Socialists, and in early newspaper interviews Myles Horton predicted that some new economic system would replace capitalism. Though he stressed that Highlander had "no special plan for improving social conditions" and that its staff was willing "to support any party or any plan which will secure the needed changes in our social structure," he personally believed that socialism was the best answer to America's economic and political problems.[101] Throughout the early and mid-1930s staff members served as organizers for the Socialist party, conducted schools for Socialist organizers, spoke at Socialist meetings, and attended party conferences. But Horton and Dombrowski considered such activities as a means of building interest in Highlander; they did not see the school as a vehicle to spread the party's gospel. Like many Americans in the 1930s, HFS teachers found socialism appealing because it expressed their sense of injustice and gave some coherence to their radical idealism.[102]

The rise of the Popular Front in the mid-1930s reaffirmed both Highlander's willingness to work with any organization for the advancement of the southern working class and its determination to maintain institutional independence. To varying degrees Dombrowski, Horton, and Hawes envisioned the rise of a radical coalition in support of an aggressive, interracial movement of industrial workers and farmers in the South. One expression of this ideal was a conference at Highlander in December 1934, where southern Socialist and Communist party representatives drafted a six-point agenda for building a united front in the South; another was the All-Southern Conference for Civil and Trade-Union Rights. The Popular Front, however, blurred ideological distinctions and left non-Communists open to criticism, especially from Socialists who suspected that groups like the HFS staff were too inclined to work with Communists. Yet neither Horton nor any other faculty member ever took the final step and joined the Communist party. Highlander's leaders found it impossible to agree among themselves on a specific political program anyway, and Horton confessed in 1935 that he had been so absorbed in the school's programs that he had little time to think about the larger issues of American radicalism. Thus the Highlander staff's radicalism reflected its willingness to experiment with new and unorthodox ideas, techniques, and leaders to combat the problems southern workers faced. Its primary allegiance was to the southern labor movement and to the work of the school.[103]

By 1937 the people at Highlander had developed an educational program that included summer and winter residence courses, year-round extension work, and a community program of cooperatives and cultural events. About 160 students had attended residence terms, over 1,650 had been reached through extension classes, and at least another 1,000 had been present during special institutes.[104] Such numbers hardly indicate that Highlander had become a sweeping success after five years of operation. Its early years were marked by small and awkwardly run residence terms; geographically limited, often ineffective, and almost always controversial involvement in labor conflicts; virtually no improvement of economic conditions in Grundy County; and several confrontations with powerful anti-union and antiradical forces. At best the southern labor movement seemed to be slowly awakening.

Yet between 1932 and 1937 Highlander gained a reputation among labor unions, educators, and political leftists as one of the few schools in the South clearly committed to the cause of organized labor and economic justice. Despite numerous setbacks, staff members energetically pursued their original objectives and established policies and teaching techniques that would guide Highlander's programs for the rest of its history. Horton, Dombrowski, and Hawes believed that potential labor leaders could be educated to help their fellow workers if they had a chance to discuss their problems, discover new ideas, and act upon what they learned. "Workers' education," Horton pointed out in 1936, "must furnish heat as well as light."[105] In the process of working with labor organizers and union officials directly responsible to the rank and file, HFS teachers became more knowledgeable about the development of union leadership and the pace at which they could bring about the reforms they desired.

As a result, Highlander's educational approach in the early and middle 1930s laid the basis for larger, more influential programs. Residence students became organizers for mine and textile workers' unions, served as local and area union officers, held their own classes for union members, and returned to HFS as advisers and teachers. The community program helped maintain the culture of the southern mountain region and led to a greater acceptance of the school in the Monteagle area. Although Highlander's extension program reached only a small part of the southern work force, staff members used it to build union contacts in Grundy and neighboring counties, train union organizers and local leaders, keep in touch with events and trends in the southern labor movement, and help students in the field after they left the school.[106]

Highlander's efforts did not go unnoticed by union officials. UTWA vice-president Francis J. Gorman observed in 1935 that HFS promised to be "of inestimable value to the trade union movement of the South" because it provided organized workers with "an excellent opportunity to prepare themselves for the battle just ahead."[107] Indeed, Highlander's programs achieved a level of proficiency just as New Deal legislation and the formation of the Committee for Industrial Organization were stimulating the growth of labor unions in the South. In 1937 CIO leaders asked HFS to take part in their drive to organize the entire region, for they knew that the staff was ready to provide a workers' education program based on several years of hard-earned experience. With the CIO drive, the school became a vital part of the southern labor movement; Horton hoped that its contribution would enable southern workers "to envision their role in society and in so doing, make the labor movement the basis for a fundamental social change."[108]

3

Building
and Defending
a Program,
1937–1941

As Highlander's 1937 winter residence term opened on January 6, staff members stepped up their efforts to establish a sound workers' education program before an anticipated CIO organizing campaign in the South got underway. The eleven students enrolled in the six-week session took classes on labor economics, labor history, public speaking and parliamentary procedure, union tactics, and dramatics. They produced a play and a student newspaper, attended conferences and union meetings, and assisted strikers in Laager, Sherwood, and Cleveland, Tennessee. Meanwhile, HFS leaders sought to double the school's financial support for 1937 by joining Commonwealth College in a "Southern Resident Labor Colleges" campaign to raise about thirty-five thousand dollars by the end of April. As with previous HFS fundraising drives, the results were disappointing. In May 1937, however, the United States Treasury Department decided to grant tax exemption on donations to the folk school, providing an important stabilizing influence on the institution's financial status. James Dombrowski expected that the ruling would lead to a long-term increase in contributions and would allow the staff to expand its work just as Highlander was "assuming more and more importance in the developing of a strong labor movement in the area."[1]

Dombrowski was right, for between 1937 and 1941 Highlander became a significant part of the southern labor movement. In the mid-1930s the school had gained a favorable reputation among local union officials, union organizers, and area mine and mill workers that impressed several national labor leaders. Thus when the CIO announced its campaign to organize textile workers in March 1937, the directors of the drive enlisted Highlander's help in recruiting and educating thousands of new union members throughout the South. As staff members pursued several major extension projects in the late 1930s and early 1940s, they continued to hold semi-annual residence terms, experiment with new educational programs, and solidify their base of support among their neighbors. Highlander's success in conducting larger and more effective residence sessions and in organizing area workers into a relatively powerful economic and political force brought reprisals and efforts to expel the school from Grundy County. But by the end of 1941, the faculty had developed a program that contributed substantially to the growth of southern industrial unions.

After spending the summer of 1937 working for the CIO's Textile Workers Organizing Committee (TWOC) in Tennessee, North Carolina, and South Carolina, HFS staff members returned to Monteagle to conduct one of the most productive residence terms in the school's short history. Eager to build on the gains of the TWOC, they approached their work with a new seriousness: in December 1937 they banned alcoholic beverages from the school during residence terms, and during the 1938 winter session they stressed the practical issues involved in building a strong local union. Fifteen of the eighteen students attending the residence term were CIO members; several served as union officials or organizers in their hometowns. Myles Horton's union problems class covered organizing methods, strike tactics, race relations, and how to operate a union hall. Ralph Tefferteller used the ACWA *Rules of Order* instead of *Robert's Rules of Order* to teach parliamentary procedure. New HFS staff member William Buttrick, a North Carolina native and Duke University graduate who had taught at Commonwealth College, at the Southern Summer School for Women Workers, and in WPA education programs, attempted to relate student experiences to a Marxian analysis of the American economic system. Union business agents outlined the duties of their position, and a TWOC attorney discussed National Labor Relations Board procedures. Eighteen regional and area union representatives spoke on the history of their organizations and the impediments to union growth in the South. In every respect, staff members declared, the six-week session had met the needs of new CIO unions in the South.[2]

Shortly after the 1938 winter session the Highlander staff turned once again to the struggles of unionized WPA workers in Grundy County. Despite the apparent resolution of the dispute over wage rates in late 1937, the battle between relief workers who had joined the CLU and state and county WPA officials had continued into 1938. Some WPA union leaders were reaching the conclusion that political action was necessary to secure adequate relief measures and end discrimination against union members on WPA projects. Seizing the opportunity to build a coalition of all local labor unions and to extend Highlander's influence, Horton visited every organization in Grundy County and in neighboring Marion County to drum up interest in a nonpartisan political conference patterned after the powerful Labor's Political Conference of Chattanooga and Hamilton County. He then helped organize a mass meeting in Whitwell, Tennessee, on April 24, 1938, where more than 250 people representing some twenty UMWA, CLU, Workers Alliance, and American Federation of Teachers locals in Marion and Grundy Counties formed political conferences for each county. By midsummer 1938 ten of the eleven unions in Grundy County had affiliated with the conference. With the assistance of HFS teachers, conference officers drafted a constitution and selected a slate of candidates to back in the June Democratic primary and the August general election.[3]

Ralph Tefferteller, extreme right, with Common Laborers' Union and Workers Alliance members, ca. 1937–38. *State Historical Society of Wisconsin.*

Highlander staff members, union officials, and conference leaders faced formidable odds as they campaigned on behalf of what were commonly called "labor's candidates." The incumbent candidates had the support of not only the county Democratic committee but also the Tennessee Consolidated Coal Company, which union forces believed had indirectly controlled local politics for years. The most immediate task was to weld county workers into a strong political force; even that required the creation of a delicate balance among AFL, CIO, and independent labor organizations. To help coordinate union activities, longtime local resident Dolph Vaughn became Highlander's field representative as well as business agent for all county WPA unions. HFS personnel and union members produced a mimeographed paper called the *WPA Worker* to promote labor's candidates. Near the end of the campaign, county officials denied the use of the courthouse to all unions; a local mine owner and other employers accused the labor candidates of being under "the Communistic influence of the Highlander Folk School and of the Workers Alliance"; and conference leaders suspected that their opponents had amassed a large campaign fund to buy poll tax receipts and bribe voters with whiskey.[4]

The campaign nevertheless resulted in a series of narrow victories for the candidates endorsed by Labor's Political Conference of Grundy County. In the August 1938 general election, union forces elected a sheriff, a school superintendent, and three road commissioners, perhaps the most important officials of all in a county where 85 percent of the population was on relief and dependent on WPA road projects. The conference candidate for governor, Prentice Cooper, carried the county handily, and in the congressional race, union members helped re-elect Sam D. McReynolds by a large margin. Conference supporters believed that their electoral success would further increase membership in WPA unions and provide greater security for workers on WPA projects. Following the election, Dolph Vaughn began several National Youth Administration projects in the county. Representatives of eight UMWA, CLU, and Workers Alliance locals in Grundy, Marion, and Franklin Counties formed a tricounty conference to serve as a permanent clearinghouse for members in the area. Highlander staff members held a weekend training institute in October 1938 for CLU and Workers Alliance officers, and in November HFS teachers began weekly classes on the WPA's structure and operations.[5]

Alarmed at the prospect of losing control of the county, opponents of Labor's Political Conference launched a drive in the fall of 1938 to undermine the power of the sheriff and the road commissioners and to discredit Highlander. According to Horton, the defeated county "political machine" cut Sheriff Roy Thomas's salary in half, eliminated his mileage allowance, cut off the electricity in the county building, and warned the former union miner to resign or be "starved out."[6] For two months after the election, the road commissioners received no salary, and it took just as long to secure a contract with the WPA giving them authority over appointments of foremen and timekeepers. By the end of the year, there was little doubt among union members in Grundy County that WPA officials were "sabotaging" the work of the commissioners and usurping "in every way possible" their power over personnel and work projects.[7]

The controversy escalated in January 1939, when the county road commissioners threatened to terminate a major farm-to-market road project if the WPA did not comply with the terms of its contract with them. State WPA administrator Harry Berry, already known for his opposition to WPA unions, swiftly responded that the commissioners were attempting "to build roads by the hammer and sickle rather than with the pick and shovel." He blamed Myles Horton for the controversy and announced that he would withdraw WPA funds unless the commissioners resigned.[8] When the three men retorted that they were duly elected county officials and had no intention of resigning, Berry ordered the farm-to-market project closed on January 18, throwing about 700 men in Grundy County out of work and drying up the sole source of income for an estimated 2,500 people. The road commissioners offered to compromise with the WPA, and nearly 1,000 people held a mass meeting and parade in Tracy City to demonstrate their support for the commissioners and to demand the resumption of the road projects. But Berry refused to negotiate.[9]

The showdown between Grundy County unions and the WPA came in February 1939. New WPA projects re-employed 326 men to work on state highways in the county, thus circumventing the commissioners' authority and leaving most union members without jobs. Angry workers retaliated by following a plan devised by union leaders and the HFS staff. On the morning of February 10 a small group of unemployed men reported for work at the Tracy City relief office. They left when the county relief administrator refused to issue work cards to them. But a few minutes later they returned with their wives and announced that they intended to remain in the office until they received jobs. By the end of the day some 150 men and women had moved into the building. On February 11 Dolph Vaughn led a parade of an estimated 500 WPA workers into Tracy City and held a protest rally in front of the relief office to call for a resolution of the WPA crisis. Tracy City had been stood "on its ears," Dombrowski wrote, and if the demonstration succeeded unions and Highlander would be "riding high in the county."[10]

There had been precedents for what was called the stay-in, most notably the sit-down strikes in a number of industries in 1937. But the week-long demonstration at the Grundy County relief office was different in that it involved entire families and came to resemble a short Highlander residence session. The WPA office, Horton remarked, "turned into a combination union club room, relief kitchen, and sleeping quarters."[11] HFS teachers and union families operated a soup kitchen, read labor papers and pamphlets, held discussions on the goals of the protest, organized press, relief, and negotiating committees, heard speeches of encouragement from regional union leaders, produced a mimeographed paper entitled *We the People* to bolster morale and to publicize the strikers' demands, and appealed to HFS contributors for financial help. As news of the demonstration spread across the state, WPA labor relations director Nels Anderson arrived from Washington on February 16 to settle the dispute. Anderson instructed county WPA foremen to stop discriminating against union members and to make more relief jobs available. But he also warned that he would take the WPA entirely out of Grundy County unless the demonstrators moved out of the relief office. That afternoon all but one critically undernourished woman vacated the building.[12]

The WPA stay-in produced no more than a temporary victory for the unions. The men rehired by the WPA worked on state projects, once again bypassing the road commissioners; local union members seemed "aimless" and "discouraged" to HFS office secretary Rosanne Walker.[13] Encouraged by reports that Berry was willing to negotiate, about three hundred Grundy County citizens met on February 26, 1939, and elected an eighteen-member committee, chaired by druggist E. W. Cheek, to work with various government agencies on county improvement programs. The Highlander staff's hope that the unions were now in a position to consolidate their power was short-lived. Berry rejected a contract acceptable to local WPA officials and the road commissioners. Cheek promptly dissolved the committee, and at a second mass meeting on March 12 he and a Consolidated Coal Company official named Swan attempted to form a new county rehabilitation committee composed entirely of nonunion men. As tempers flared over this obvious subterfuge, county welfare director Lude Goodman declared that the crux of the dispute was the Highlander Folk School. Since most citizens in Grundy County would have nothing to do with the school, he asserted, no one on the committee should be affiliated with it. Horton retorted that a majority of county citizens had not hesitated to cooperate with organized labor in the recent elections or to elect HFS and union representatives to the first committee. Attacking the school, he argued, amounted to attacking the county unions. The contending factions finally agreed to form two committees to elect delegates to a coordinating committee. The compromise proved futile.[14]

By the summer of 1939 union forces had clearly lost the battle for economic and political control of Grundy County. Berry still refused to work with the road commissioners, and appointees of the defeated county politicians retained their foreman and timekeeper jobs on WPA projects. Membership and morale in the WPA unions declined as Congress sharply cut WPA relief appropriations. Reductions in the WPA rolls and a decrease in Highlander's income left Dolph Vaughn without a job and ended the school's fieldwork program. In an attempt to retain some political power, members of Labor's Political Conference of Grundy County disbanded and in August 1939 joined other unions in a county unit of Labor's Non-Partisan League (LNPL). Unions had not lost all influence. In a special election held in September 1939 to replace Congressman Sam McReynolds, who had died in office, the LNPL-backed candidate, Estes Kefauver, carried Grundy County by a four-to-one margin. Local union members also asked the HFS staff to conduct classes in the fall of 1939 on politics and unionism.[15]

In the end, however, a countywide coalition of labor groups was not enough to prevent the collapse of unions and the WPA in Grundy County. Highlander staff members had attempted to carry out an effective and practical political education program. They had helped organize unions among relief workers and developed local leadership to solve some of the county's most immediate problems. Labor's Political Conference had scored an unprecedented victory for organized labor in the area, and the dramatic stay-in had gained local support as well as the attention of state and federal officials. In subsequent years, the HFS staff used the experience of the WPA struggle to fashion education programs for CIO unions, farmers' groups, civil rights organizations, and community activists in southern Appalachia and the Deep South.

Nevertheless, Highlander played a peripheral role in Grundy County after 1939, serving largely as a social and recreational center and as the sponsor of several cooperative projects. Beyond the greater attraction of participating in the southern labor movement, HFS staff members were no longer sure that their community program could ever reach enough local residents to improve economic conditions in the area. While the school continued to host Saturday-night square dances, no one on the staff could devote much time to helping the community.

Some residents were embittered by the withdrawal of Highlander from the community; others reportedly would have nothing to do with the folk school after the demise of the WPA unions; and still others regarded its dances as the source of drinking and loose morality. In contrast, a number of local families appreciated the nursery school it operated during the late 1930s and early 1940s. Opened in June 1938, the nursery was a substitute for the older brothers and sisters who usually took care of local children while their mothers worked in the summer resorts at Monteagle. Claudia Lewis, who had taught at the Bank Street Cooperative Schools in New York City, joined the HFS staff in the summer of 1938 as director of the school. Lewis tried to incorporate Highlander's educational approach in the nursery school and teach the children not only cooperation but also "habits of questioning and curiosity about the things that concern them."[16] After she left Highlander in 1941, the nursery was directed first by Joan Payne of Sarah Lawrence College and then by Eva Zhitlowsky of Black Mountain College. Although the project was popular among the children and their parents, it was never well funded, and the nursery closed in 1943. Postwar efforts to revive the program died for lack of financial support.[17]

As Highlander's relationship with Grundy County gradually declined, staff members turned to the needs of union locals across the South for trained leadership. While a majority of the students attending Highlander's 1939 residence terms were CIO members, others registered for the sessions as well, including AFL unionists, college students, and Workers Alliance relief workers. Expenses for each student amounted to about one hundred dollars for each six-week term, but students or their sponsoring locals paid only forty-two dollars, with the difference apparently covered by scholarships donated to HFS. The growing size of the student body reflected Highlander's expanding contacts with unions across the South. Forty-four men and women from ten southern states and representing ten national and international unions enrolled in the winter and summer terms. At least a dozen were either presidents of their local unions or union officers. Several students came from Carolina mill towns where Horton had recently worked as a TWOC organizer. Despite the increase in enrollment, the HFS staff acquiesced to southern union and community sentiments and did not admit southern black workers as students. But staff members continued to welcome black guests and lecturers to the school, and their hopes for a chance to change their racial policy rose after Telesfora Oviedo and Juanita Munos, the Mexican-born president and treasurer of a Pecan Workers Union in San Antonio, Texas, attended the winter session without incident.[18]

The 1939 residence terms offered the same basic courses as in previous years—labor history, union problems, public speaking, parliamentary law, economics, and labor journalism—but the focus shifted from the problem of organizing southern workers to the maintenance and expansion of union operations. For example, in the union problems course Myles Horton and visiting teachers led discussions on the immediate concerns of local union leaders, such as contract negotiations, grievance procedures, improving attendance at union meetings, and the legal restrictions on organized labor. In an experimental "Work Shop" course taught by Mary Lawrance, who had joined the HFS staff in September 1938, students learned how to use visual aids in workers' education by producing posters, handbills, charts, and other mimeographed material pertinent to the specific issues facing their unions. Residence students also had extensive contact with union activities in the region. Winter term students operated a soup kitchen, raised funds, and made speeches in support of the stay-in of Grundy County WPA workers, and students at both sessions sang and performed mass chants and plays written in HFS dramatics classes before union and workers' education conferences in Dalton, Georgia, and Chattanooga, Laager, and Nashville, Tennessee.[19]

The most noteworthy feature of the 1939 residence terms, however, was the large number of union officials, government spokesmen, and prominent southern reformers who participated in Highlander classes. These visitors included representatives of textile, hosiery, rubber, mine, and steel workers' unions; federal agencies like the TVA, NLRB, and Social Security Board; and such reform groups as the Southern Conference for Human Welfare. Their presence attracted "carloads" of interested union members from Tennessee, Alabama, and Georgia.[20] Beyond reporting on the current work of their organizations, speakers often addressed broader subjects, such as the "philosophy of labor," workers' education, labor legislation, foreign affairs, and racism among southern laborers. UMWA international representative James H. Terry bluntly told the white student body at Highlander's winter term, "if we raise the negro, we raise ourselves," and Arthur Raper of the Commission on Interracial Cooperation assisted staff members in breaking down prejudices among several students during the summer term.[21] The HFS staff reported that the fifty-seven men and women who spoke during the two sessions, representing nearly every labor and progressive organization in the South, helped make the 1939 residence program "by far the most successful in the history of Highlander."[22]

Short-term institutes and conferences became regular features of the HFS residence program in the late 1930s. Union educational directors used the weekend institutes to tell new members about the history and current operations of their organizations and to discover and develop effective local leaders without having to pay employers for the union members' lost time. In 1938, for example, AFHW educational director Larry Rogin, one of the few union officials who, in Horton's opinion, truly understood the value of workers' education, began to conduct annual summer conferences at HFS for union members from Tennessee, Georgia, and Alabama. Between 1938 and 1941 Highlander staged its own series of conferences for southern union, YMCA, LNPL, and cooperative officers. Staff members included weekend institutes on organizing methods, union political action programs, and other topics during residence terms, and they participated in several conferences on the role of workers' education in establishing more permanent unions in the South. Through such institutes the HFS staff made further headway in relating its educational efforts to the political, cultural, and economic needs of southern labor unions.[23]

Meanwhile, Highlander's music and drama programs not only gave strength and vitality to residence sessions but also contributed to the school's reputation among southern workers. After Ralph Tefferteller left HFS in 1938 to work for the ACWA, Zilphia Horton assumed responsibility for the cultural program and developed a highly effective and popular approach to teaching and disseminating songs. By skillfully changing a few lines to familiar tunes, she turned hymns, traditional ballads, and popular songs into forceful expressions of protest. "Old MacDonald Had a Farm," for instance, became "John L. Lewis Had a Plan" with the resounding refrain "CICIO." A Pentecostal hymn called "I Shall Not Be Moved" became the celebrated labor song "We Shall Not Be Moved." Horton and HFS students transformed "Rock a Bye Baby" into "Workers' Lullabye," and they rewrote "Dixie" as "Look Ahead, Working Men." Under her direction, students sang at union meetings, workers' education conferences, rallies, and strikes throughout the region. During her years at HFS, Zilphia collected hundreds of songs, published at least ten songbooks, and mimeographed thousands of song sheets for residence sessions and picket lines. The "real musical merit" of folk songs, she wrote in 1939, was not their form but the way they expressed the struggles of working people.[24]

Through Highlander's dramatics program Zilphia Horton and other staff members showed students how drama could be used to educate union members, reinforcing in the process the school's emphasis on learning from experience. Ideally, the HFS staff believed, plays written and performed by workers for workers should entertain as well as address important labor questions, clarify the union point of view, stimulate attendance at union meetings, and develop individual poise and self-expression. At the outset of each dramatics course students identified certain problems affecting their unions and acted them out in a spontaneous improvisation. After Horton gradually introduced various dramatic techniques, students selected a topic and a cast for an improvisation before his or her local organization. Criticism followed each performance, and if necessary the cast performed once again. There were some drawbacks to this method. Although Horton encouraged spontaneity, students often felt compelled to memorize lines if a script was available, and the denouement of their plays was sometimes little more than simple declarations of "Solidarity Forever." Yet by the end of a residence term students had often gained enough critical and creative ability to present an improvisation with coherent dialogue and to repeat it when it was particularly effective.[25]

As local unions, other workers' education centers, and Highlander groups performed the plays developed at the school in the late 1930s and early 1940s, staff members printed scripts of the more popular improvisations. The most frequently requested plays in the Highlander repertoire were *Gumbo* and *Labor Spy*. Written by students in 1937, *Gumbo* was a story about the attempts of sharecroppers to organize a union in the Mississippi Delta. Unlike later HFS productions, *Gumbo* was full of poetic dialogue, black spirituals, and strident speeches. Its intent was praiseworthy, but all-white audiences found it difficult to accept the necessity for interracial cooperation among southern workers when the play was not relevant to their actual experiences and when whites wore blackface to play black characters. Subsequent plays, such as *Labor Spy*, written in 1938, contained more straightforward dialogue and pursued themes that were more understandable to both performers and audiences. Students based *Labor Spy* on Leo Huberman's *The Labor Spy Racket*, an analysis of the espionage tactics used by anti-union industrialists. The play opens with the owner of a mythical southern textile corporation hiring a detective to keep a CIO union out of his factory. The detective tricks a hardworking union man into becoming an informant, but in the final scene the worker reveals his treachery when he opposes a strike call and is forced to resign from the union. By paying close attention to setting, characters, and dialogue, students produced a play that vividly illustrated a problem confronting southern labor unions.[26]

The HFS dramatics program gained tremendous impetus following the 1938 premiere of *People of the Cumberland*, a documentary written by Elia Kazan and directed by Robert Stebbins and Eugene Hill. The movie portrayed conditions in the Cumberland Mountain region, the struggle for union organization, and Highlander's activities among southern workers. The opening sequences depicted "a bad land" of abandoned mines, destroyed forests, decaying mills, eroded soil, and "lonely and forgotten people." But with the help of Highlander, unions, and the New Deal, men and women had begun to organize, "determined that there be no more waste, no more disease, the families no more burned out and lost"; scenes of a Fourth of July celebration in La Follette, Tennessee, suggested a healthy, prosperous future for union families.[27] Shown at Highlander fundraising events, at union meetings, and at the White House for Eleanor Roosevelt, *People of the Cumberland* received mixed reviews. But because the film appeared to have achieved results with nonprofessional actors, Zilphia Horton, visiting dramatist Chouteau Dyer, and an unusually able dramatics class wrote and performed several plays in 1939. Their productions included *Lolly-Pop Poppa,* a musical farce satirizing employer paternalism; *North-South,* a sketch on how industrialists perpetuated sectional antagonisms among workers to serve their own ends; and *Stretch-Out,* a commentary upon the institution of a 12 percent wage cut and an increased production pace. After the outbreak of World War II, HFS students wrote plays on such subjects as the poll tax and the role of organized labor in the war.[28]

Just as the music and dramatics programs tried to improve organized labor's public image in the South, so Highlander's writers' workshops sought to train those who would publicize union activities. The writers' project, however, never lived up to its promise. The first Summer Workshop for Student Writers began in August 1939 under the joint auspices of Highlander and the Communist-led League of American Writers, an arrangement that James Dombrowski insisted did not violate the staff's policy of keeping the school free of party labels. During the two-week session visiting essayists, poets, and editors taught courses on short story and poetry techniques, script writing, and labor journalism to fourteen aspiring writers. Among the guest lecturers at the workshop were author Sherwood Anderson and Vanderbilt University professor Herman C. Nixon. Conscious of the need to tie the project more closely to the interests of southern labor groups, Highlander and the league sponsored a second workshop in July 1940 for eighteen students, many of them members of southern mine, rubber, office, and newspaper workers' unions. Although several curricular and financial problems hampered the 1940 session, the HFS faculty considered the program important enough to hold two more workshops in 1941 and 1942 under the direction of staff member Harry Leon Wilson, Jr., whose father wrote the popular novel *Ruggles of Red Gap.* Staff members scheduled a fifth workshop for July 1943, but a poor response forced them to discontinue the sessions and incorporate labor journalism courses into the regular residence program.[29]

Work camps combining manual labor and educational experiences were another part of Highlander's expanding education program in the late

1930s and early 1940s. During the summer of 1938, instead of holding the usual residence term, the HFS staff turned the school over to the American Friends Service Committee for a two-month work camp. About two dozen university students worked on various improvements around the school, built a recreation field for Summerfield, and participated in a community canning project. To acquaint these primarily northern college students with current labor issues in the South, camp directors, HFS staff members, and local union, NLRB, and TVA representatives led nightly discussions on such topics as the coal and cotton industry, the TVA, and the migration of rural southerners to industrial centers. Pleased with the accomplishments and potential value of the work camp, the Highlander faculty directed two more camps in 1940 and 1941 in cooperation with Work Camps for America. Students at the 1941 work camp largely ran the one-month program themselves. They compiled reports on economic and social conditions in Grundy County, heard lectures from visiting speakers, started a daily wall newspaper, and produced a short movie and a mimeographed book describing the Highlander camp. One camper, William Elkuss, an Austrian refugee who had been a student activist at the University of Paris before he came to America to complete his education at Columbia University, became a member of the HFS staff. Plans for another work camp in the summer of 1942 never materialized, and the faculty suspended the entire program for the duration of World War II.[30]

Still another Highlander endeavor begun in the late thirties was a series of junior union camps designed to teach the children of union members the principles of unionism and thereby lay the foundation for a strong labor movement in the future. Former HFS students Horace and Margaret Bryan organized and directed the first camp, held in June 1940 for thirteen children of Nashville ACWA members and Summerfield union people. Each morning opened with a general business session, in which the staff and the young campers planned the day's activities and discussed union issues, the problems facing youth, and the experiences and goals of the children. The staff encouraged the children to participate in the running of the camp by having them elect officers and form committees to oversee various projects. It was a rudimentary program, but the HFS staff found the initial effort successful enough to conduct more junior union camps over the next four years for youngsters from union families in Tennessee, Georgia, Kentucky, and Arkansas. Zilphia Horton and other camp directors thought that their success in promoting the physical and personal development of the campers would enhance the school's public relations once the children told their parents about its work. But after 1944 the costs of operating the camps, the declining number of junior unions, and especially the increasing amount of time devoted to residence terms for adult workers brought an end to the program.[31]

As they broadened the scope of the residence program, Highlander's leaders continued to join forces with other reform groups in the South. The most prominent southern alliance in the late 1930s and 1940s was the Southern Conference for Human Welfare (SCHW). Like other southern white progressives, HFS staff members regarded SCHW partly as a response to the findings of the National Emergency Council, whose 1938 report on the South led President Roosevelt to label it "the Nation's No. 1 economic problem," and partly as a potentially powerful interracial coalition seeking fundamental political, economic, and racial change. Myles and Zilphia Horton and Bill Buttrick were among the twelve hundred to fifteen hundred delegates attending the first SCHW convention in Birmingham in November 1938. Other participants included Eleanor Roosevelt, Supreme Court Justice Hugo Black, Aubrey Williams of the NYA, prominent southern politicians and newspapermen, black college presidents, a sizable group of black and white CIO officials, a smaller contingent from the AFL and railroad brotherhoods, two dozen Socialists, and a handful of Communist party members.[32]

Myles Horton was initially optimistic about SCHW. Although apprehensive about its top-heavy organizational structure, he thought that the conference could attract union and white middle-class support while maintaining its forthright stand against segregation. But for most of its existence SCHW's militant reputation and allegations of Communist influence hindered its efforts to provide an organized platform for southern reformers. In 1939 HFS staff members assisted the SCHW Committee on Civil Rights in the lawsuit of Tracy City resident Henry Pirtle against the Tennessee poll tax, and in 1940 Eleanor Roosevelt met with a group from Highlander at the SCHW convention in Chattanooga and later donated the first of several one-hundred-dollar scholarships to the school. Although the controversy over Communist infiltration subsided after James Dombrowski became executive secretary of the conference in 1942, SCHW remained in serious financial and organizational trouble and formally dissolved in 1948. Its educational arm, the Southern Conference Educational Fund, survived and became one of the most strident opponents of segregation in the South.[33]

By the end of the 1930s Highlander and its alumni were exerting a noticeable impact on the southern labor movement. Although financing the school's programs was still difficult, Highlander took in more than fourteen thousand dollars in 1939, and the staff estimated that during the year it had served about two thousand people in twenty-one CIO, AFL, and independent unions through its extension work, special institutes, and residence terms. Six former students had been elected presidents of their union locals, twenty-two others had become union organizers, many had assisted in or directed local union membership drives and strikes, and several alumni had become involved in various phases of workers' education in Tennessee, South Carolina, Arkansas, and Kentucky. In all, nearly four hundred students, 93 percent of them union members and 87 percent from the South, had enrolled in Highlander residence terms between 1932 and 1939. During that period, at least eighteen hundred people attended special institutes at the school, and over forty-six hundred workers took part in HFS extension classes. In November 1939 staff members and former students organized an alumni association to coordinate union education projects, plan financial campaigns, recruit students, and keep abreast of problems besetting southern labor unions.[34]

At the same time, Highlander's opponents viewed its accomplishments as part of a growing radical assault upon the established political and economic order of the South, and beginning in the fall of 1939 a new series of attacks attempted to discredit the school and banish it from the state. The opening salvo came in October 1939, when Nashville *Tennessean* publisher Silliman Evans assigned one of the paper's top reporters, John McDougal Burns, to investigate Highlander. At HFS Burns introduced himself as John McDougal, an instructor on leave from Texas Christian University interested in the school's operations. During his two-day stay, staff members treated Burns with the same cordiality accorded the many people who visited Highlander each year. Yet they became suspicious when Burns began to inquire about the school's affiliation with labor unions and other groups and about the extent of Communist sentiment in the area. Their doubts increased after Burns left suddenly and two *Tennessean* photographers arrived to take pictures, ostensibly for a Sunday feature story on the school. Discovering the reporter's true identity and anticipating his purpose, HFS staff secretary William Buttrick asked the managing editor of the *Tennessean* for an opportunity to correct any piece written by Burns on Highlander. Other staff members sought legal advice about obtaining an injunction against the newspaper, and some friendly *Tennessean* newsmen tried to forestall publication of Burns's report. It was too late.[35]

In six front-page stories beginning on Sunday, October 15, 1939, Burns told how Highlander was "a center, if not the center, for the spreading of Communist doctrine in 13 Southeastern states." Burns never defined what he meant by communism. Nonetheless, in his first report he charged that HFS leaders had consorted with people accused of being Communists; that the faculty had sent students into southern labor unions to teach the "red doctrine" and had held conferences to expound "communist theories"; that the staff had organized units of the Workers Alliance, described before a congressional committee as having Communist origins, and had kept in close contact with Commonwealth College, notorious for its Communist orientation; that the school's teachers entertained "many leftists of national reputation," maintained a library "well stocked with communist literature and history," and used every opportunity "to spread the leftist doctrine"; and that local resident Dillard King was proud that his fellow citizens had "already begun to overthrow the government" in Grundy County with Highlander's help. Burns elaborated on these themes in subsequent installments. In the issue of October 16, he asserted that Myles Horton had told him that "Everyone realizes that capitalism is a failure and that we should examine Communism" as a solution to the nation's problems, even though Horton was in California on a fundraising tour during Burns's visit. While Highlander's influence was negligible in Monteagle, Burns concluded, the citizens of Grundy County had become amazingly knowledgeable about the economic issues affecting them and were presumably ready to initiate the revolutionary program taught at the school.[36]

Reaction to the *Tennessean* series was immediate and tumultuous. Highlander's adversaries applauded the attack: Chattanooga *Free Press* editors nominated the *Tennessean* for the Pulitzer Prize. HFS office secretaries received harassing telephone calls, and after the final article appeared a carload of men drove up to the school's front gate, shouted curses, and threatened to return and "bomb this place."[37] That night Highlander personnel trained floodlights on the main building, armed themselves, and stood guard with friends from Summerfield around the school. Buttrick and his colleagues considered suing the *Tennessean* for libel, but they agreed that a lawsuit would be expensive and probably only bring "all the 2 × 4 politicians and red-baiters down upon our heads."[38] Instead, they concentrated on winning public opinion to their side. On October 18, 1939, a small newspaper called the Nashville *Times* published a statement by Buttrick categorically denying that the HFS staff had connections with any political party. The *Tennessean* printed a second statement on October 22, in which Buttrick outlined Highlander's purpose and program and charged that Burns's articles contained "such a network of errors and misrepresentations" that intelligent readers should "simply brand the whole series as one grand falsehood." Buttrick then suggested that the *Tennessean* probe was not only "the opening gun" in a drive to secure southern Democratic votes for Vice-President John Nance Garner in the 1940 presidential campaign by discrediting unions opposed to him, but also part of "a nationwide witch-hunt," fueled by wartime hysteria, to smear all labor and progressive organizations.[39]

During the month following the Burns exposé, *Tennessean* editors were besieged with copies of affidavits, petitions, and at least forty letters denouncing the attack. Faculty and students at Commonwealth College assailed the series, but the newspaper presented their letters as evidence in the case against Highlander. More valuable to the HFS staff were the protests sent to the *Tennessean* by university professors, ministers, labor union officials and members, former students, staff members, and work camp participants. Only a few of these letters were published, however, and Horton and Dombrowski suspected that the newspaper's executives destroyed the rest. Meanwhile, *Tennessean* editors stoutly maintained that Highlander's "ideological partiality for the cause of Communism" was the issue, not Silliman Evans's friendship with Garner, and that in "lifting the veil" that obscured the school's operations they had performed a public service.[40]

HFS leaders realized that some bold stroke was necessary to refute the attack and clarify once more the misconceptions about Highlander. Under considerable public pressure the *Tennessean* printed James Dombrowski's defense of the school on November 19, 1939, along with a list of those who had written to criticize the articles. Denying that the HFS staff had ever knowingly hired a Communist or received support from any political group, Dombrowski described Highlander as "a school for democratic living" and cited both the prestigious backgrounds of the school's supporters and the improvements it had helped bring to the lives of thousands of southern workers. Dombrowski pointed out that staff members emphasized "the free play of an unfettered mind coming to independent judgments" at HFS, and he invited the public to visit the school and judge it on the same basis.[41] Dombrowski and Claudia Lewis pursued the same themes at two well-attended meetings in Nashville on the nights of November 19 and 20. Highlander's leaders, Dombrowski explained, were motivated by a desire "to relate religious idealism to the social problems of today, particularly to relate the social aspirations of religion and the labor movement." Accordingly, the school trained leaders for southern labor unions, used cooperative procedures to solve basic community problems, and helped labor groups develop their own cultural and educational programs.[42]

Highlander had resolved very little in its dispute with the *Tennessean*. Dombrowski was elated by the largely sympathetic public response he encountered in Nashville and at later meetings in Knoxville and Chattanooga, and staff members derived grim satisfaction when the *Tennessean* endorsed Garner's presidential candidacy in December 1939. Yet the controversy took its toll on the school's treasury. By the end of 1939 income was about sixteen hundred dollars below operating expenses, and with the economic future uncertain after the outbreak of war in Europe, HFS leaders settled for a 1940 budget that did no more than maintain existing programs.[43]

Nor did Highlander's enemies abate their criticism. The *Tennessean* groused that it was still mystifying why any institution based on Christian principles should be tolerant of Communist ideas. Rumors arose in Nashville that Highlander was a free-love commune with a library full of Communist literature and that Dombrowski was not only a Communist but a convicted criminal as well. In the spring of 1940 House Committee on Un-American Activities chairman Martin Dies of Texas announced that his committee had received a large amount of material on Highlander in connection with its probe of alleged radical activities in the South. Horton welcomed any legitimate investigation of the school. But since a Federal Bureau of Investigation agent who visited Highlander in the summer of 1939 had found no evidence of subversive activity, Horton thought that HUAC would simply issue "occasional smearing releases which are always gobbled up and featured by the southern press." His more immediate concern was the possibility that one of the "local defense committees" springing up throughout the state might pay the school "a vigilante visit." Staff members had repelled such attacks in the past and would do so again if necessary. They were also working hard to re-elect the union-backed sheriff in the August 1940 county election, for his defeat would be a "disastrous" loss of legal protection for Highlander.[44]

The election, however, completely reversed the political gains made by HFS and local unions in the previous two years and unleashed an unprecedented barrage of attacks on the school. Tennessee Consolidated Coal Company officials and members of the old county political ring campaigned aggressively and decisively defeated the union-backed candidates for sheriff, school superintendent, and road commission chairman. The storm over Highlander broke even before the polls closed on August 1. During the primary Horton and Grundy County LNPL members had secured the approval of Representative Estes Kefauver's field manager to campaign in the congressman's behalf. As the LNPL handed out leaflets supporting his record, Kefauver began receiving complaints that he was being advertised as Highlander's candidate in Grundy County. Resenting the idea of being identified with any group without his knowledge, the congressman wired county residents that he protested the unauthorized advertisement. Citizens calling themselves "100 percent Americans" immediately circulated a leaflet quoting Kefauver's telegram as proof that the congressman "is in no way, shape or form connected with, influenced by, and neither does he endorse the Highlander Folk School."[45] On August 11 the Chattanooga *News-Free Press* reproduced a copy of Eleanor Roosevelt's one-hundred-dollar check to HFS to bolster its allegation that the First Lady financed subversive activities. Alvin Henderson, cashier of the First National Bank in Tracy City, whose president was secretary of the Tennessee Consolidated Coal Company, told HFS staff members Leon Wilson and James Dombrowski that he had done nothing unethical in publicizing Highlander's bank records, for the school was "against the government" and an institution whose affairs were a matter of public interest.[46] The bombardment continued in September when a reporter from the staunchly Republican Nashville *Banner* claimed that local residents were anxious to get rid of Highlander, for it had given Grundy County an undesirable reputation as it spread its "un-American influence."[47]

The most thorough defamation of Highlander came in November 1940 with the appearance of Joseph P. Kamp's pamphlet *The Fifth Column in the South*. Kamp headed the Constitutional Educational League, well known for its pro-Fascist, anti-Semitic, anti-labor, and anti–New Deal propaganda. Reprinting Eleanor Roosevelt's check on the inside front cover of his pamphlet, quoting liberally from the Nashville *Tennessean* series on Highlander, and distorting the meaning of HFS publications, he branded the school "a training center for Communist agitators" and "a fountain head of propaganda for revolution."[48] Although it cost twenty-five cents, many copies of the pamphlet were available for free throughout Grundy County. HFS staff members had no doubt that Consolidated Coal had financed this latest blast at the folk school after one Tracy City resident received a copy of the tract from the owner of the company.[49]

The attacks galvanized both Highlander and its local opponents. On November 8, 1940, Alvin Henderson asked to visit the school with some friends. Staff members had no illusions about Henderson's intentions, but they invited him and one or two companions for dinner on November 12. On the night of November 8, the staff received startling news: C. H. Kilby, Tennessee Consolidated Coal Company secretary, counselor-chairman of the Tracy City Junior Order of United American Mechanics, and a man who had become, according to a Knoxville-based FBI agent, almost obsessed with ridding Grundy County of HFS, had announced that he and other local organizations were going to march on the school to protest its presence in Tennessee and its "disintegrating effect upon our community in general."[50]

Discovering that most of the groups Kilby claimed to represent were not taking part in the mass march, Dombrowski addressed an open letter to Kilby in which he expressed his fear of the almost certain violence that would occur when an uncontrollable crowd of two or three hundred people confronted the school's indignant friends and neighbors. Instead of a "spectacular demonstration," the HFS chairman called for a "genuine conference" to assess Highlander's standing in the community.[51] Although Kilby scoffed at the possibility of a riot, staff members appealed to CIO officials, state officers of the Junior Order of United American Mechanics, and Governor Prentice Cooper to head off the march. On the afternoon of November 12, barely four hours before the announced time of the march, Kilby called Highlander and said that his citizens' committee agreed to meet with HFS leaders at a neutral site. Kilby wanted to hold the conference at a Monteagle roadhouse, but he reluctantly accepted Saint Luke's Common Room at the University of the South.[52]

Each side marshaled its forces before the conference. About one hundred people convened at the Tracy City high school auditorium, where Henderson explained that confusion and the threat of legal action had forced a cancellation of the march. He then proposed the formation of the Grundy County Crusaders, whose slogan would be "no ism but Americanism" and whose purpose would be to carry on "a crusade against all un-American activities and subversive influence that may exist in our County, Community, State and Government." Henderson and Kilby orchestrated the election of a permanent committee of the Crusaders and oversaw the unanimous approval of a resolution asking Highlander to leave Grundy County. Meanwhile, a smaller group of Summerfield citizens met at the folk school to express their resentment against the attacks and to begin circulating a petition pledging their continued support of HFS programs.[53]

The confrontation between Highlander and Grundy County Crusaders representatives began at 9:00 P.M. on November 12 and lasted some five hours. Kilby and Henderson opened the meeting with charges calculated to produce fireworks, accusing Highlander of communistic teachings and subversive activities. They did not press their charges once Dombrowski and Horton presented evidence describing the school's programs, its independent status, and the support it received from the community. Instead, the Crusaders peppered the staff with questions about its involvement in local strikes, the performance of plays and songs criticizing the nation's "commercial system," and the portrayal of conditions in Grundy County in *People of the Cumberland*. A Chattanooga *Times* reporter observed that Kilby "rose to oratorical heights with some of his questions," but staff members answered each accusation frankly and at length. When the Crusaders objected to Dombrowski's publicized statement that HFS had helped overthrow "the power of a large coal company" in the 1938 elections, Dombrowski responded that the staff had aided union members in electing their own candidates and thereby break the political power of the coal company. At that point, the *Times* reported, Kilby stepped out of his Crusader role to announce that as an employee of the Tennessee Consolidated Coal Company for fifteen years he had "never known its management to make any attempt to influence the votes of its employees."[54] Crusader spokesmen derided favorable appraisals of HFS, while Highlander representatives ridiculed allegations that the folk school had cost county residents jobs and forced Kilby to admit that none of the organizations he claimed to speak for were officially affiliated with the Crusaders. As a Chattanooga *News-Free Press* writer noted, "there was no love-fest at the completion of the lengthy, tension-packed meeting."[55]

The conference temporarily stymied the Crusaders' efforts to oust Highlander from the county. While a *News-Free Press* editor grumbled that the institution remained intact because "some intelligentsia" had out-talked the "plain country folk" of Grundy County, a Chattanooga *Times* editor more perceptively observed that Highlander's leaders could now win over their opponents by welcoming any visitor interested in learning precisely what they were trying to do.[56] Staff members did not let that opportunity pass. Following the conference, Dombrowski and his colleagues outlined Highlander's work to Governor Cooper and at public meetings in Sewanee and Nashville. The faculty scored a major public relations victory on November 22 when the third national convention of the CIO unanimously approved a resolution endorsing the school and condemning efforts to "discredit and defame" Highlander as "an attack on the progressive labor movement of the South."[57] The folk school had already received the unanimous endorsement of the Tennessee State Industrial Union Council in May 1940, and CIO president John L. Lewis had commended Highlander's work in October 1940. But the national CIO endorsement was an especially timely and powerful symbol of support by labor leaders representing four million workers. Staff members intensified their publicity campaign, stressing that the Crusaders were not only attacking a bona fide institution promoting the interests of organized labor but also fomenting bitterness against the school at a time "when all groups should be working together to create a real national unity."[58]

If the HFS staff had won what William Buttrick called "the first round" in its battle with the Crusaders, no one doubted that C. H. Kilby and Alvin

Henderson would renew their efforts to force Highlander out of Grundy County.[59] As rumors reached the school that the Crusaders were preparing a pamphlet describing how Highlander was building a Soviet America, Kilby announced a second mass meeting at which the Crusaders would adopt further resolutions against the school. Between 60 and 150 people, including Myles Horton, Leon Wilson, and Claudia Lewis, met in the county high school gymnasium on the night of December 3, 1940. Embarrassed by the presence of the Highlander trio, Alvin Henderson read a long, rambling indictment of the school's activities. Next C. H. Kilby disclosed that he had affidavits supporting his contention that HFS staff members taught communism (the affidavits, the FBI later reported, were probably dictated by Kilby and signed by "irresponsible" persons). Students sang a song about the "Russian Red Flag" at the end of each class, he asserted, and then they lined up and gave "the Russian Red Salute." To the deadly serious audience, and to the amazed Highlander observers, Kilby demonstrated the salute several times, moving his arms in exactly the same motion a song leader uses at the beginning and end of songs. The group rapidly passed resolutions declaring that the Crusaders were 100 percent behind organized labor, that its leaders should confer with HUAC chairman Martin Dies, and that high-ranking federal officials should be asked not to sponsor a forthcoming benefit for Highlander in Washington, D.C., because they did not know the true purpose of the institution.[60]

Despite the Crusaders' warning, the Highlander benefit concert in Washington went on as scheduled on December 6, 1940. It was not only a smashing financial and public relations success, but it also brought a decisive shift in Highlander's struggle with the Crusaders. As one historian of the school has remarked, the sponsors of the affair "read like a Who's Who of the New Deal and organized labor," including Supreme Court Justice Hugo Black, cabinet members, congressmen, administrators of major federal agencies, and other prominent persons.[61] An audience of around five hundred people heard a poetry reading by Archibald MacLeish, then Librarian of Congress; a ballad performed by the Washington Choral Society and the Howard University Glee Club; and a collection of folk, blues, and workers' ballads sung by Zilphia Horton and famed black blues singer Huddie "Leadbelly" Ledbetter. The national attention given to the Washington concert improved the public perception of Highlander as a legitimate institution. Its success boosted the morale of the HFS staff, and the Crusaders never seemed as intimidating thereafter.[62]

Yet the Crusaders had not exhausted every means of combating the school. In January 1941, state representatives Beverly O. Briley and Joe R.

Taylor introduced a criminal syndicalism bill into the Tennessee legislature. Proclaimed by Briley as "Tennessee's answer to Nazi Bunds, Fascist groups, and Communistic organizations," the bill made it a felony to advocate, suggest, or teach criminal syndicalism, sabotage, or the use of violence to achieve change, foment revolution, or gain profit.[63] As union and HFS leaders saw it, the term *criminal syndicalism* was defined vaguely so that it could be used against labor organizing and as a license to prosecute Highlander. Myles and Zilphia Horton joined Tennessee CIO state secretary Paul Christopher, CIO public relations representative Lucy Randolph Mason, and others in lobbying against the measure in Nashville. Under such pressure, Briley and Taylor withdrew the bill. Meanwhile, the Grundy County Court passed a resolution read to them by C. H. Kilby on February 3, 1941, which asked state authorities to direct the district attorney to indict Highlander as "the largest center of communistic teaching in the South."[64] Dombrowski noted with astonishment that the county court heard no testimony before adopting a resolution "so badly worded and so devoid of all legal fact" that it was both amusing and grounds for a lawsuit against the county. Others in the county were reaching similar conclusions about Kilby's antics: area miners had begun calling the Crusaders the "Crucifiers."[65]

By the spring of 1941 support for the folk school was as strong as it had ever been. UMWA locals in Whitwell and Tracy City, along with the Tennessee Conference for Democracy, a group representing AFL, CIO, and Railroad Brotherhood organizations in the state, passed resolutions condemning the Crusaders' campaign against Highlander and organized labor. Governor Cooper informed Horton that he would lend his assistance if any trouble arose again. The district attorney announced that he was unable to find enough evidence to bring charges against the institution. On February 1, 1941, Eleanor Roosevelt delighted the HFS staff by renewing her contribution to Highlander. She had concluded that the school's enemies opposed it not "because of any communist activities, but because they are opposed to labor organization and, therefore, labor education," which in her opinion was "a most unwise and short-sighted attitude."[66] By the end of March 1941 the Crusaders faced almost total defeat. Highlander's leaders launched a new publicity and fundraising campaign, removed the school's funds from the First National Bank of Tracy City, and explored the possibility of legal action against Alvin Henderson for publishing Roosevelt's check. By the time the Tennessee State Industrial Union Council reaffirmed its support for Highlander in June 1941, Horton was fairly certain that the attacks on the school had finally subsided.[67]

Nevertheless, the controversies of the past two years left a bitterness that was not easily dissolved. Highlander's battle with the Crusaders had taken so much time and money that the staff felt compelled to curtail its residence program during the spring of 1941 in order to devote itself to the fundraising drive. In May delegates at a meeting of the Murfreesboro district of the Methodist church refused to restore James Dombrowski's ministerial license and resolved that the church should in no way support HFS. Two weeks later the state council of the Junior Order of United American Mechanics adopted a resolution submitted by C. H. Kilby branding Highlander as communistic, un-American, and subversive. In October 1941 an FBI agent conducted an investigation of Highlander. Using Kilby's office as his headquarters, the agent neither visited the school nor talked with local residents who worked closely with it; he also spurned repeated invitations to visit HFS, as well as a homemade applesauce cake. In response to the school's protests, another agent arrived in early 1942. Staff members gave him unlimited access to their records. As they expected, he found nothing but further instances of anti-unionists using the terms "labor organizer" and "Communist" interchangeably. Indeed, after finding Kilby's methods repeatedly suspect, the *Tennessean* articles politically motivated, and Highlander hardly deviating from its efforts to aid labor unions, the FBI concluded that there was "very little indication of Communistic influence while there is abundant indications [sic] that the school is liberal and radical and, therefore, opposed by Conservatives." Bureau director J. Edgar Hoover ordered an end to any further active investigation of HFS in October 1942.[68]

Highlander staff members could withstand attacks from opponents like the Crusaders; more troubling was the criticism leveled at them from people they considered allies in the southern labor movement. Throughout Highlander's history, and particularly in the turbulent period before World War II, conservatives and radicals alike could not accept the school's refusal to commit itself to a specific political position. In mid-1941 the faculty learned that Frank McCallister of the Workers' Defense League, Franz Daniel of the ACWA, and others were making it known that Highlander's policies were consistently helpful to the Communist party in the South. McCallister denied making such statements, claiming that he had never been able to determine what ideological line the school followed. He knew only that Horton and Dombrowski were "socialists with a little 's'" who bitterly resisted Socialist party attempts to hinder their educational program.[69] Such an ambiguous position enraged Franz Daniel. A long-time friend of Horton and Dombrowski, Daniel had become disenchanted with workers' education in the late thirties and began denouncing Highlander as "communistic." He admitted that his accusations were not true. But because staff members were not *anti*-Communist, Daniel announced in May 1941 that he and his wife, Zilla Hawes, were severing all ties with the "Communist stooges" at Highlander.[70] For her part Hawes insisted that the school could not stand apart from the bitter power struggle within the CIO between John L. Lewis and Sidney Hillman or from the domestic repercussions of the German invasion of the Soviet Union in June 1941; it could not remain "all things to all groups in the liberal movement at one and the same time."[71] HFS leaders would not compromise their position. ACWA officials issued a statement in April 1942 indicating that Daniel's attitude did not reflect the union's sentiments. But like Highlander's other opponents, Daniel did not change his opinion of the school.[72]

Throughout the controversies of 1939–41, Highlander's residence program remained largely intact. Revising the residence schedule to leave the summer free for short-term conferences and other projects, the faculty held two six-week residence terms in the spring and fall of 1940, a two-week session in May 1941, and a six-week term beginning in August 1941. Even with these adjustments, recruiting students became more difficult as work in defense industries increased. Enrollment remained generally stable, however, averaging around twenty-two students each term. Highlander's core curriculum of union problems, labor history and economics, public speaking and parliamentary law, dramatics, and labor journalism courses continued to provide practical training in conducting the affairs of local unions. One noticeable trend during the residence terms was the greater coordination among classes in addressing the central problems of union organization. Students in a union problems class, for example, spent several periods discussing contract negotiation and enforcement. They then used the parliamentary procedure class to introduce motions for a new contract and to appoint a committee to represent them in contract talks, just as they would in regular union meetings. Later, in the dramatics course, students improvised a short play depicting the union representatives' negotiations with a factory owner.[73]

A second, more significant trend during the 1940–41 residence terms was the involvement of major southern labor union figures in classes, panel discussions, and weekend institutes. Their participation, along with the creation in December 1940 of an HFS executive council composed largely of AFL and CIO officials, confirmed Highlander's growing prominence in the southern labor movement. During the fall term of 1940, for instance, ACWA southern director Bernard Borah held a class on contracts; Paul

Christopher, vice-president of the Textile Workers Union of America, led discussions on grievance procedures and shop committees; and LNPL southern director Alton Lawrence talked about the potential political activities of local unions. A total of 181 workers from twenty-three unions affiliated with the AFL, CIO, Railroad Brotherhoods, and Farmers' Union attended two weekend institutes at HFS in the fall of 1940 and the spring of 1941. Highlighting the 1941 summer term were five weekend conferences for over 150 union members led by New Orleans regional CIO director Fred Pieper, Richard Deverall of the United Auto Workers, Allen McNeil of the Mine, Mill, and Smelter Workers, and other regional labor leaders. These special programs were in addition to the almost steady stream of university professors, political activists, TVA employees, federal government officials, and labor leaders from virtually every union in the South who came to Highlander during the residence terms.[74]

The HFS staff also pressed forward in its efforts to persuade southern white union members that racially integrated labor unions were as practical as they were morally desirable. Staff members used what Myles Horton called a "method of natural exposure" to overcome racial prejudices. Residence classes studying the connection between race relations and labor organization inevitably concluded that there must be equal opportunities for blacks and whites if both races were to improve their living conditions. When blacks such as Fisk University sociologist Charles S. Johnson came to HFS either as speakers or as casual visitors, the faculty showed them as much consideration and courtesy as any other guest and maintained normal eating and sleeping arrangements. Not all students altered their racial attitudes. Yet Horton asserted that white students generally had no objections when blacks simply fit into the daily routine of the school, and some students subsequently became "instrumental" in bringing blacks into their unions.[75]

Between 1937 and 1941 the Highlander Folk School emerged as a vital center of labor education in the South. Indeed, the controversies besetting the school in the late 1930s and early 1940s occurred largely because of the faculty's success in educating local leadership for unions throughout the region. To be sure, staff members suffered several setbacks during the period. Their efforts to promote a political coalition among union members in Grundy County produced only a temporary victory. Most of Highlander's experimental projects, such as the writers' workshops and junior union camps, did not attract enough support to last very long. While HFS leaders took pride in maintaining a financially and ideologically independent institution, their position entailed risks that they may not have fully appreciated. By 1941 total income had grown to nearly

$16,500, but the school also finished the year with a $1,300 deficit, and the number of individual contributors declined while remaining decidedly nonsouthern.[76] The insistence on making no ideological commitments beyond the southern labor movement left the staff vulnerable to charges of communism from people of wildly disparate political backgrounds. Out of an exaggerated fear of Highlander's influence, conservatives raised the specter of "communism" to undermine the school's challenge to southern labor, political, and racial customs. Other attacks on HFS stemmed from factional feuds among labor leaders or between Socialists and Communists. Yet the heart of the dispute, which persisted for decades, lay in the difficulty of classifying Highlander. Horton, Dombrowski, and their colleagues contended that they operated a school based upon democratic principles and the everyday problems of southern workers and their families. Many people simply did not believe them.

Yet judged by the amount of cooperation shown by southern labor leaders, by the people who contributed to HFS, and by the activities of its alumni, Highlander had undeniably earned a solid reputation as a southern labor school. Dozens of union officials took part in the residence terms, and over nine hundred people from thirty-six states made contributions to the school in 1940. Staff members measured the true worth of their work, however, by the fact that over 50 percent of the folk school's alumni had held official positions in their unions by 1940. Former students organized and presided over the only United Rubber Workers of America local in the South, directed an ILGWU educational program in Atlanta, edited a union newsletter and served on an industrial union council committee in Louisville, negotiated a new contract for textile workers in Lumberton, North Carolina, and served as vice-president of the Tennessee State CIO. HFS leaders were naturally pleased that each student left the school, as one wrote, "more able to go out in the world as a working man and stand up for my constitutional rights."[77] But they also recognized that keeping Highlander's work relevant to the needs of southern laborers required actual organizing experience and education programs supplementing union campaigns. In the decade after 1937 the staff conducted extension programs that made Highlander even more clearly a school for workers in the South.

4

Extension Work, 1937–1947

When CIO leaders announced the formation of the Textile Workers Organizing Committee in March 1937, Highlander staff members leaped at the chance to become part of what James Dombrowski called the "most important event in southern labor history."[1] The potential effects of the TWOC drive to organize the southern textile industry were indeed enormous. A million people worked in the industry in 1937, about 450,000 in the South alone; a successful campaign by the CIO would create the largest union in America. It was also commonly accepted that the organization of the textile industry, the largest employer of southern wage earners, held the key not only to the success of industrial unionism but also to any shift in economic and political power in the South. Dombrowski considered it imperative that Highlander become fully involved in the TWOC campaign if it was to fulfill its promise as a southern labor school. Other HFS leaders agreed. To Myles Horton the TWOC campaign seemed to signal the beginning of a true "labor movement," a "democratic, radical, social movement" determined to secure economic benefits for all southern laborers and to use political action and education to improve their lives.[2]

For a decade after the start of the 1937 TWOC campaign the Highlander staff conducted extension programs for unions across the South. HFS teachers served as union organizers and managed the educational side of union drives, helping local officers maintain and enlarge their activities and teaching workers how to bargain collectively and live successfully under union contracts. Through their fieldwork, staff members hoped to learn firsthand about the problems of southern laborers and union organizing, to improve Highlander's curriculum and teaching approach, to educate a larger number of workers than would be possible in residence sessions, and to strengthen the overall effectiveness of the school in promoting the southern labor movement. Highlander had become a fairly well-known center for workers' education by the late 1930s, and its extension programs between 1937 and 1947 enhanced that reputation. Although the CIO was only moderately successful in organizing southern industries by the end of World War II, the gains its leaders could claim were in part the product of the efforts of Myles Horton, Mary Lawrance, and other staff members to further the development of organized labor in the South.

TWOC chairman Sidney Hillman of the ACWA and his colleagues wanted to avoid the mistakes made in previous union organizing campaigns in the South. Textile workers had exhibited a strong desire for unionization in the massive strike of 1934, but organizing was difficult because the industry was so fragmented. Each branch—cotton, woolen and worsted, rayon, silk, hosiery, and others—had its own distinctive market, technology, and labor force. Half the industry produced cotton goods, and almost four-fifths of the mills in this subindustry were in the South. But the mills were scattered in dozens of small towns throughout the southern Piedmont. Intense competition and an abundant labor supply resulted in long hours, low wages, and poor working conditions. Well aware that their profits depended on cheap labor, mill owners fiercely resisted any attempt to organize textile workers, often with the aggressive support of the local community. Owners commonly crushed union drives by replacing unskilled and semiskilled union members with readily available nonunion workers; by playing on the distrust of rural laborers toward outsiders, particularly northerners; by hiring large numbers of women who generally worked for lower wages than men; and by threatening to replace white union members with black nonunion workers.[3]

Hillman and his lieutenants sought to overcome these and other barriers to textile unions through a carefully planned, well-financed strategy sensitive to the peculiar problems of southern cotton textile workers. The first phase of a local TWOC campaign would be educational. Organizers would publicize the TWOC's affiliation with the CIO to disassociate it from the past failures of the United Textile Workers. They would emphasize the respectability of the new union, its benefits to workers and the community, and its ability to withstand employer retaliation after the initial outburst of organizing excitement. Next, they would seek a National Labor Relations Board representation election, and, once elected, they would demand the negotiation of contracts with employers, using political pressure and resorting to strikes only where necessary. Throughout this process, organizers would attempt to persuade white workers that they could include black workers in their unions and thus increase their economic clout without necessarily altering existing southern race relations. They would also appeal to the poorest and most reluctant workers through a pledge card campaign, in which mill hands signed cards designating the TWOC as their collective bargaining representative and paid no dues until the union secured a contract and established a new local. Finally, to blunt charges that the drive was an invasion of Yankees, Jews, and Communists, TWOC leaders hired A. Steve Nance, a popular leader who had been president of the Georgia Federation of Labor, to direct the critical Deep South campaign, and employed 160 southerners as organizers, including Lucy Randolph Mason, Franz Daniel, and Myles Horton.[4]

The Highlander staff eagerly responded to Nance's invitation to participate in the first major CIO organizing drive in the South. On April 1, 1937, the entire faculty attended a conference in Atlanta marking the start of the TWOC cotton campaign. Horton quickly volunteered Highlander's services, and his colleagues agreed to suspend the residence program and devote themselves entirely to the southern drive until the end of 1937. Staff member Beckie Barton became an assistant to Zilla Hawes, who headed the TWOC district office in Greenville, South Carolina, one of the largest and most anti-union textile centers in the nation. Zilphia Horton went to La Follette, Tennessee, to help ACWA organizer Charles Handy, an HFS alumnus, set up the office of a new thousand-member shirtworkers local. James Dombrowski edited a special issue on religion and labor for the *TWOC Parade* to counter the influence of anti-union evangelists who were condemning the union and the CIO.[5]

Meanwhile, Nance hired Myles Horton as a full-time TWOC organizer and immediately sent him to Bennettsville, South Carolina, to avert a strike and to sign up members for the union. The Duncan K. McColl Company employed eleven hundred workers in five Marlboro cotton mills, one in Bennettsville and the other four in nearby McColl, South Carolina. The mill hands had little union experience, but sentiment at the Bennettsville plant was strongly in favor of an immediate strike. It would be more effective, Horton believed, to shift the emphasis from striking to organizing and to use Highlander's educational techniques to help the workers assume responsibility for a campaign that would produce strong interracial unions at all five mills. He first persuaded the Bennettsville mill hands to delay striking until they and the workers in McColl had been organized, and then he coordinated a membership drive that by mid-April had signed up 90 percent of the Marlboro workers, both black and white, for the TWOC. While waiting for TWOC officials to negotiate a contract, Horton and volunteers from the two mill towns carried on an organizing campaign in Laurinburg, North Carolina, signing up 80 percent of the eight hundred employees at the local mills and winning a 10 percent wage increase. When Marlboro mill executives refused to sign a contract acceptable to union members, employees went on strike on May 7, 1937. After eight days mill owners agreed to a 12 percent raise, a checkoff for union dues, and a preferential union shop. Horton recalled that Marlboro mills president Duncan McColl had a "heart attack" when he learned that black workers would earn the same wages and considerations as white workers under the contract.[6] Horton had done a remarkable job. Through his appealing personality and broad-based organizing approach he had recruited over eleven hundred workers for the TWOC, and he had helped bring about one of the first TWOC contracts in the South and the only one obtained by the union in South Carolina during the drive.[7]

As soon as the Marlboro mill workers returned to work in May 1937, Horton went to Lumberton, North Carolina, in response to reports of threats and wholesale discrimination against textile union members. The Mansfield and Jennings mills on the eastern and northern edges of town had a history of tough resistance to union organizers. But by 1937 management dominance of community life—the East Lumberton council met in the Mansfield mill office and the company paid policemen's salaries—had become distasteful to many workers. Wages were not the primary reason for organizing, one worker later said; more important was the mill hands' desire "to have something to say about their working conditions, their jobs."[8] Arriving in Lumberton in mid-May, Horton and TWOC organizer Richard F. Strickland met with a delegation of union members who had talked to Horton in McColl. As the men discussed the growing interest among mill workers in the TWOC, the mayor of Lumberton, company overseers, and their followers gathered in the street below Horton's hotel room and demanded that the "outsiders and trouble makers" leave town.[9] That night anti-unionists fired shots and threw rocks at the homes of three workers who had attended the meeting and smashed the windows of Strickland's car. The next morning Horton called Steve Nance and asked to stay and organize the mills, since it was the only answer to such treatment.[10]

Throughout the organizing campaign Horton tried to instill in the Lumberton textile workers a sense of their independence and power. The reputation he had won in McColl was enough to bring a few dozen Lumberton workers into the TWOC. To increase membership Horton held small meetings where he encouraged workers to discuss their problems and explained the implications of those difficulties and the necessity of unions. From these meetings he recruited about ten people who actually ran the organizing drive. Within a week after his arrival, the organizers had signed more than one hundred new union members and, with the help of more than one hundred union people from McColl and Bennettsville, staged the first union meeting held in public in Lumberton. By the end of May, 65 percent of the 650 Mansfield mill employees and 95 percent of the 350 Jennings mill employees had signed TWOC membership cards.[11]

Horton did not want the new union members to strike before the NLRB held hearings on their complaints against the Lumberton mills. But on June 7, 1937, a few days before the start of the hearings, employees at the Jennings mill walked out in protest of a 50 percent increase in their work load with no change in their hourly wage. Horton was certain that the company's managers had provoked the strike in order to close the plant for remodeling without paying the workers, to cut labor costs during a slack production period, to block the NLRB hearings as long as possible, and to discredit the union and his work. Since the larger Mansfield mill was the key to the success of the strike, Horton hastily called a mass meeting in East Lumberton and persuaded a majority of the machinists in the weaving room to strike on June 10 in support of the Jennings mill workers, bringing Mansfield mill operations to a halt. On June 11 Mansfield mill officials called for help from the county sheriff and city police to guard against possible disorder and asked for a postponement of the NLRB hearings because of the "violence" of the strike. But the hearings proceeded as scheduled, and the vast majority of the striking mill hands, many of them women, refused to go back to work. Frustrated, H. B. Jennings, president of the two Lumberton mills, ordered the dismissal of union members, the eviction of workers from company houses, and the cutoff of credit at the company store.[12]

The three-month Lumberton strike, as one labor newspaper reporter wrote, became "the story of [the] textile employers' war to check unionization of workers by T.W.O.C. Organizer Myles Horton."[13] During the summer of 1937, as arrangements for a NLRB election slowly developed, local

TWOC leaders carefully followed what Horton called "a policy of peaceful action."[14] On June 12, Governor Clyde R. Hoey sent a detachment of highway patrolmen from Raleigh to Lumberton to preserve order. The union planned to have a large picket line that day, but Horton went to the Mansfield mill and sent all but a handful of pickets home. When the patrolmen roared up to the plant, they found only two union banners in front of the mill and a group of young men and women playing guitars and banjos instead of the expected four to five hundred angry strikers. The next day Horton organized a large picket line, and for about a week every time the state patrolmen began the two-hour journey to Lumberton, newsmen from the Raleigh *News and Observer* called Horton and warned him to thin out the picket line before the patrolmen arrived. To maintain interest and enthusiasm among the strikers, Horton held informal classes on the picket lines and, along with several union leaders, conducted mass meetings five nights a week. For decades after the strike he enjoyed telling the story of five men who came by his hotel room one evening brandishing pistols and announcing that they were going to take him out of Lumberton permanently. Horton got a .45 army pistol from his dresser and offered his services as an organizer to help the men decide who was going to be killed in their mission. After some sober reflection, the men got back in their automobile and drove away.[15]

Despite Horton's efforts to maintain peace, neither the striking union members nor the mill managers and police officials would give ground. On June 17, 1937, the police arrested six strikers for allegedly assaulting a nonunion employee during a union meeting and charged Horton with inciting the attack. A local judge rejected all testimony denying the charges and sentenced Horton and two other men to thirty days in jail, but upon appeal prosecutors dropped the case. On June 25, former mill policeman Alto B. Stephens, already under bond for assaulting a picketing mill hand, struck Horton as he was talking to a reporter. The treasurer of Mansfield mills posted bond for Stephens, who paid a ten-dollar fine after being convicted of the attack. When Horton tried to obtain an injunction barring highway patrolmen from forming lines through which nonstriking workers could enter the mills, company officials, the mayor of Lumberton, and highway patrol officers asked for an injunction against picketing by Horton and TWOC members. The judge denied all injunctions, declaring that local authorities could preserve order. In July, however, a highway patrol lieutenant threatened to rearrest Horton if violence occurred anywhere near the picket lines, regardless of whether he was on the scene or not, and the sheriff declined to provide Horton with protection after nonstriking workers threatened to kill him if he ever returned to the mills. Clearly, peaceful picketing was all but impossible. Since the stretchout had ended, and since an increasing number of strikebreakers were filling the mills, the strikers decided to go back to work while retaining their TWOC membership.[16]

Having exhausted their delaying tactics, Mansfield officials consented to hold NLRB elections to determine the collective bargaining agent of the workers, and on September 22, 1937, the TWOC won handily, receiving over 60 percent of the vote in the two mills. When mill managers still refused to negotiate with the union, the TWOC filed further charges with the NLRB. The prospect of another labor board hearing and another strike persuaded the mills' president to sign a contract on January 29, 1938, providing for union recognition, a seniority system, arbitration procedures, and union dues checkoff, but no wage increase. In the end, Horton observed, "organization won over violence and hysteria," and the primary aims of the eight-month TWOC campaign in Lumberton had been secured by the contract.[17]

While Horton worked for the TWOC in the Carolinas, other staff members began an educational program for a newly organized local of the Amalgamated Clothing Workers of America in La Follette, Tennessee, about forty miles north of Knoxville. Two shirt-making factories in La Follette, owned by a New York company, normally employed about one thousand women who earned between six and seven dollars for a fifty- to sixty-hour work week. When the shirtworkers went on strike in January 1937, former Highlander student Charles Handy and other organizers quickly established an ACWA local. By mid-March, with the support of hundreds of area UMWA members, the ACWA won contracts at both plants providing for a closed shop, wage increases, shorter hours, and other provisions. Yet company executives maintained that the shirtworkers really did not want the union, and during the spring of 1937 they tried to induce the women to desert the ACWA. Handy asked the HFS faculty to teach the new union members the fundamentals of labor organization, and, at the end of May 1937, James Dombrowski, Ralph Tefferteller, and HFS librarian Margaret Musselman joined Zilphia Horton in La Follette to begin a carefully designed Workers Education Rally. The Highlander teachers planned to experiment with new educational techniques that could be applied on a larger scale throughout the South. They would first concentrate on educating a small group of the ablest union members and cultivating their leadership abilities. They would then work through a social and recreational program to build among local union members "a greater emotional loyalty to the union" and a better understanding of the entire labor movement.[18]

Highlander's six-week program in La Follette proved more of a recreational than an educational success. After staging an opening rally on May 29 for between 125 and 150 clothing, mine, and lumber worker families, HFS staff members conducted two group discussions each week during June 1937. Following brief singing sessions and presentations on parliamentary procedure, Dombrowski, Zilphia Horton, and Tefferteller used charts and booklets called union primers to take the shirtworkers step-by-step through the structure, functions, and benefits of the ACWA and CIO. Attendance gradually increased, and by the end of the rally around one hundred union members were participating in the classes. The HFS faculty had to be content with teaching elementary ideas, for most of the students knew very little about their union. Some miners attending the classes did not know what the letters CIO meant, and when Dombrowski asked who was the head of the CIO one miner replied, "Theodore Roosevelt."[19]

Shirtworkers, miners, and their families responded far more enthusiastically to the more informal features of the Workers Education Rally. Staff members brought books and pamphlets from Highlander and established a small library in the local ACWA hall, helped produce a weekly shop paper called *Shirt-Tale,* and organized recreational activities that would popularize the union among shirtworkers. In late June the local union's education committee organized a Union Label Fair featuring exhibits and raffles of union-made goods, two union fortune tellers, and a union label tobacco-spitting contest. The rally ended with an Independence Day Labor Celebration attended by over four thousand people and acclaimed by the HFS staff as "one of the finest demonstrations of labor solidarity ever seen in this part of the country."[20]

While Highlander's teachers believed that some elements of the La Follette experiment could be used in other union education programs in the South, they also recognized its shortcomings. Their plans had been too ambitious and had not encouraged the shirtworkers to assume responsibility for the project. A majority of union members in the area never attended the lectures and discussions, and too many of those who came to the classes had difficulty understanding the teaching materials. Nonetheless, shirtworkers were enthusiastic about continuing all of the rally's activities after the Highlander group left La Follette. Thus the staff took satisfaction in noting that the educational rally had given the ACWA local "greater prestige in the eyes of the union membership and a firmer position in the community."[21]

By the end of 1937 the TWOC campaign had made substantial progress in North but little headway in the southern textile industry. The drive had enjoyed some immediate success. By September 1937 the

TWOC had negotiated sixteen agreements covering 17,500 southern mill hands, and more than 100,000 southern workers had reportedly signed pledge cards. But the cards hardly ensured contracts, and the campaign never recovered its momentum after an economic recession in the fall of 1937. Employer resistance to textile unions hardened. Union contributions declined. Competent organizers struggled with exhaustive work loads. In the spring of 1939 the United Textile Workers reorganized as an AFL affiliate and began competing with the TWOC for the allegiance of textile workers. By the time the TWOC became the Textile Workers Union of America (TWUA) in May 1939, union contracts covered only 7 percent of the South's 350,000 mill workers, and the contracts themselves were on precarious ground. For example, new owners of the Marlboro mills in Bennettsville and McColl had refused to renew the union agreements when they expired in December 1937; they had closed the mills in April 1938 and then reopened them one month later with a totally nonunion labor force. In September 1939 workers at the Jennings mill in Lumberton went on strike and secured a new contract, but the agreement expired in 1940, and workers remained unorganized for several years. Thrown on the defensive, TWUA leaders turned to protecting and consolidating their existing strength. Like its predecessors, TWUA became "a northern organization which constantly looked southward for its salvation."[22]

Meanwhile, Highlander staff members were beginning to reevaluate their extension work. In August 1937, Myles Horton went to Charlotte as a field representative for the CIO in North Carolina, where he helped plan a general union drive and organized various groups of workers. Although he had intended to remain with the CIO until the end of the year, he resigned his post and returned to Highlander in October 1937. Horton had concluded that union officials were more interested in controlling members than in developing a spirit of independence and initiative among them. He had also learned that organizing was not necessarily educating. While he enjoyed battling mill owners and their allies, he preferred to teach workers to establish and manage their local unions themselves. His HFS colleagues were reaching similar conclusions about the limitations of their fieldwork. They had come to recognize that any extension program on the magnitude of the La Follette project precluded their involvement in any other effort. What Highlander needed was an extension program that supplemented residence sessions rather than replaced them. The most effective approach, they decided, was to bring students to HFS from places where a staff member was carrying on an extension program and send them back, as Horton wrote, "with additional enthusiasm and equipment."[23]

Implementing this revised strategy would be twenty-three-year-old Mary Lawrance, who became Highlander's full-time fieldworker in 1939. The Pennsylvania-born daughter of southern parents had first become interested in organized labor during her college days at Duke University, where she had worked with local tobacco and hosiery workers and chaired a statewide YWCA student-industrial committee. Lawrance quickly grasped Highlander's central premise that an effective educational program had to be "simple, clear, dynamic and practical" and based upon personal knowledge of the problems and experiences of the people involved. These lessons were underscored in early 1940, when Lawrance went to Louisville to hold classes for local Teamsters and textile workers' unions and found herself "convincing a few staunch union members to be stauncher union members." Her mistakes taught her to organize classes that addressed issues related to the union's growth, to make sure that there was a prior demand for them, and to include the entire membership of the union in an educational program.[24]

Lawrance's first chance to test her ideas about labor education came in June 1940, when a union committee in Alcoa, Tennessee, asked Highlander to help it revive interest in the Aluminum Workers of America (AWA) local. The AWA had a nationwide contract with the Aluminum Company of America, and the five-thousand-member Alcoa local was the largest in the nation. Yet its strength was deceptive. Most workers lived on farms well outside the town and rarely came to union meetings. Jealousy between workers in the fabrication and reduction plants, tedious union meetings, a lack of publicity, and a domineering president had also bred apathy among AWA members. The local's executive board and officers doubted that Lawrance could do anything to stimulate interest, and only a handful of the twenty-two workers attending the first union meeting after her arrival had the faintest idea of why she was in Alcoa.[25]

Confronted with such major problems, Lawrance directed all her efforts to the basic goal of building interest in the union. The local's Saturday night meetings were usually lifeless affairs, but Lawrance's announcement that the next regular meeting would feature a speaker and an entertainment program attracted about seventy-five people to the union hall. Lawrance led the group through a few labor songs, passed out sample copies of the *AWA News* to arouse interest in a shop newspaper, and circulated short questionnaires on possible classes for union members. She then reorganized the ladies' auxiliary to help plan entertainment for future union meetings and set up a Worthy Worker Club for the wives of black workers who might involve their husbands in the union. After about a month of work, Lawrance persuaded the executive board to form a planning committee that would set the agenda of each general meeting, equip the union hall for recreational and social activities, and coordinate the affairs of the women's clubs. As attendance at the meetings grew and more people participated in her program, Lawrance recruited three men to help her produce more editions of the *AWA News* and persuaded the executive board to underwrite the distribution of the paper at the plants so workers could see what the local was accomplishing.[26]

Lawrance could go no farther with her program in Alcoa. When she announced the beginning of classes on labor history and union publicity, the response was negligible. Frustrated by the inability of executive board members to progress beyond the idea that all they needed was a leader, Lawrance decided to demonstrate that the union already had a strong group of capable members by holding an all-day conference to plan an education program addressing the union's organizational problems. But factions within the union used the gathering to ask the entire executive board to resign, and the ensuing uproar overwhelmed the last week of her work. Lawrance left Alcoa in August 1940 doubting that the program could continue without the involvement of the local's leaders. Indeed, the union soon reverted to its earlier lethargy. Lawrance had been able to develop new leadership and to produce some enthusiasm and activity among union members; she had also shown that no education program could be sustained unless the local union assumed responsibility for it. Her experiences in Alcoa became the basis for stronger and more successful Highlander extension programs in the 1940s.[27]

The coming of World War II enabled southern labor unions to take advantage of the dramatic rise in employment and favorable federal policies to increase membership, raise wages, and improve their public image. By November 1941, Lucy Randolph Mason proclaimed, the CIO had organized "hundreds of thousands" of workers in the South. CIO membership in the New Orleans area had grown from 675 in 1939 to about 15,000 in 1941. New locals in Atlanta were "springing up in every direction." It had been "too dangerous for CIO men to stay in Memphis" in the late 1930s, but now thousands of workers had joined CIO unions and won contracts in a number of industries. There were already several CIO locals in Chattanooga, and unions had begun aggressive campaigns in the Knoxville area.[28]

But this rapid expansion also meant that the leadership of thousands of unionists was largely inexperienced in conducting union activities and that new members often knew little about union operations. The Highlander staff therefore began in 1941 to work closely with industrial union councils to coordinate labor education programs for union officers and the rank and file. Usually HFS would contribute the services of Mary Lawrance or another staff member while a local council or some other organization paid for the costs of the program. Lawrance and her colleagues sought to make union members realize that the fate of organized labor was at stake in the war. Their goal was to turn "union card-carriers" into "union crusaders" who would make their unions a powerful force in civic affairs and defend them against the attacks "launched by the anti-labor crowd under the smokescreen of patriotism."[29] As it became more difficult to recruit students for residence sessions, Highlander's leaders affirmed in August 1942 that extension projects should be "the main consideration" in their overall educational program during the war.[30]

Highlander's commitment to large-scale extension work began with a successful program for CIO unions in the New Orleans area in 1941 and 1942. The CIO had grown so rapidly in the area between 1939 and 1941 that union officials had not been able to educate new members in the mechanics of building and maintaining union strength. Thus when the HFS faculty offered to conduct a year-long education program for New Orleans unions in January 1941, Louisiana CIO regional director Fred Pieper and the New Orleans Industrial Union Council quickly accepted the proposal. Mary Lawrance arrived in the Crescent City in April 1941 and found that establishing the program would be a formidable challenge. CIO unions stretched from the New Orleans waterfront to towns fifty miles away. Fortunately for her, most union members lived in the city of New Orleans, on the south bank of the Mississippi River, or around area sugar plantations. After spending a week gathering information on the unions, Lawrance held a meeting with about 120 local officials to launch an officers' training school. Using charts, a "Labor Information Please" question-and-answer exercise, and a short improvisational skit, Lawrance skillfully demonstrated the usefulness of classes in labor history, union problems, parliamentary law, union publicity, and labor dramatics. By the end of the meeting the officers were eagerly signing up for the subjects they wanted to study.[31]

During the initial four-week training school, Lawrance kept the classes informal and focused on the practical needs of the unions. Officers worked on speeches they later delivered at union meetings, practiced parliamentary procedure, analyzed the grievances they planned to discuss with plant managers, and made posters for picket lines. Lawrance consolidated the labor history and union publicity classes into a general union education class and added special classes for local officers of the Inland Boatmen Division of the National Maritime Union and the Transport Workers Union. In addition to these scheduled sessions, Lawrance corrected mistakes in parliamentary procedure at hosiery workers meetings, discussed the duties of shop stewards with female sugar workers, and assisted members of a striking furniture workers' union. By the time she left New Orleans in May 1941 to participate in Highlander's spring residence term, Pieper and the industrial union council had become enthusiastic supporters of her work. Four local officials attended the HFS residence session to learn how they could assist Lawrance when she went back to New Orleans to start a second training course, and Pieper proposed that twenty active locals contribute five dollars a month to sustain the education program.[32]

When Lawrance returned to New Orleans in June 1941, local union leaders were still struggling to carry out their functions efficiently. She thus placed special emphasis during the second phase of the extension program on the training of officers, shop stewards, and committee members. During the next three months she showed the officers how to handle grievances, collect dues, schedule department meetings, organize committees, and conduct wage surveys. To encourage them to use these practices, Lawrance wrote an officers' handbook entitled *How To Build Your Union* and conducted short programs on grievance procedure, parliamentary law, and other simple union problems at furniture, construction, sugar, transport, inland boatmen, and hosiery workers' union meetings. She reached still other union members by speaking at meetings, publicizing union activities, writing articles for a local newspaper, establishing a labor library, devising model report blanks for use in collecting dues, and helping to organize the first Labor Day parade in New Orleans in many years. To mobilize the workers against pending anti-union legislation, Lawrance set up union legislative committees and printed weekly bulletins on the latest political developments. By the end of the second period of the extension program in August 1941, attendance at union meetings, membership, and dues collections had increased; a shop paper had been started; and morale had risen noticeably. The educational program had been "successful far beyond our expectations," Pieper happily told Lucy Mason, and he planned to make it a permanent part of the New Orleans CIO program.[33]

Lawrance began the third session of the New Orleans training program in October 1941, intending to develop new union leaders to replace the officers being drafted into the armed forces. With the entry of the United States into the war, however, she altered the program to reach as many CIO members as possible and to place further stress on building a sound steward system. In January 1942 she discontinued virtually every class in favor of informal discussions at department, steward, executive board, and general membership meetings. Lawrance usually began with a summary of the world crisis and the potential threats to the labor movement and then outlined some practical ways to make members more active in union affairs. To help stewards appreciate their added obligations because of the war, Lawrance held banquets and conferences for them, organized councils, and mimeographed a "Pointers for Stewards" bulletin. In October 1942 Highlander staff members Myles and Zilphia Horton and Maria Stenzel joined Lawrance at a three-day institute to recapitulate the lessons of the New Orleans program. The HFS teachers, CIO directors, and officials from the War Production Board, Office of Price Administration, and United States Employment Service used a radio dramatization, government war films, and panel discussions to impress upon workers their responsibilities to their unions and the importance of organized labor's role during and after the war. Leaders of a United Sugar Workers local responded to the institute by establishing a labor-management committee, placing union representatives on rationing boards, and checking retail prices in their community, hoping to make their union "bigger and stronger and more vital to the war effort."[34]

Highlander's New Orleans program made a solid contribution to the organization and education of CIO members in the area and set a pattern for later HFS extension projects. As Lawrance pointed out, too much of the New Orleans program depended upon her individual efforts, and attendance in the classes was never as high as she would have liked. Union militancy did not increase, and officers and members did not become more proficient in running their locals simply because they participated in the course. Nevertheless, Lawrance had created a sound program that taught officers as well as the rank and file not only the techniques of building union strength but also the relationship of their efforts to the larger labor movement. Some union members who attended Highlander residence terms became full-time organizers; others began educational activities that ensured the continuation of the program after Lawrance's departure. Most important, as word of Highlander's work in New Orleans spread, other union leaders in the South invited the HFS staff to carry out similar extension programs in their area. For example, in October 1942 staff members directed two institutes at Goose Creek and Ingleside, Texas, that helped the Oil Workers Organizing Campaign win a labor board election at the Humble Oil Company by a three-to-one margin.[35]

Having tested and refined their educational techniques, Mary Lawrance and her Highlander colleagues conducted major extension projects in Atlanta, Knoxville, and Memphis for thousands of union members over the next three years. When the six-month Atlanta program began in November 1942, Lawrance's objective was to teach members of local steel, textile, rubber, furniture, and other CIO unions about the responsibilities the war had thrust upon them. Wartime conditions prevented Lawrance from scheduling formal classes, and the racism among white union members inhibited her attempts to build a strong labor movement in Atlanta. Despite these constraints, Lawrance was able to educate several hundred men and women each week through fifteen-to-thirty-minute programs that became a regular part of nearly a dozen local union meetings. Using charts, outlines, and other materials prepared by Highlander's new research department, Lawrance led discussions on grievance procedure, the duties of stewards and committee members, contract enforcement, parliamentary law, and other basic union problems. Lawrance and a new CIO victory committee also began monthly forums to help Atlanta unionists understand the operations of wartime government agencies affecting labor.[36]

During 1943 Lawrance and the CIO victory committee broadened the scope of the Atlanta extension project to involve local unions more directly in legislative affairs and in community activities vital to the war effort. Lawrance and union officials developed a legislative committee system that responded quickly when the Georgia legislature began consideration of an antistrike measure in the spring of 1943 and successfully blocked passage of the bill. Local unions donated blood and money to the Red Cross, set up servicemen's committees to contact members in the armed forces, organized an informal banquet for soldiers stationed in and around Atlanta, and took turns sponsoring a "CIO night" once a month for servicemen. A black servicemen's committee scheduled entertainment programs for black soldiers. A consumer council examined price controls, grade labeling, and point rationing, devising a system to report price ceiling violations. Lawrance and the victory committee also prodded unions in war plants into forming production and transportation committees and helped organize union demolition crews to aid in the state scrap program. To publicize the unions' support of the war effort, Lawrance supervised the production of a "Victory Action" newsletter and hung a large "Victory Action" chart, which measured the unions' progress in various local projects, in the Atlanta Industrial Union Council hall. By the end of the extension program in May 1943, Lawrance believed that most local unions had become better organized, that the servicemen's projects had gained momentum, and that the legislative committees, monthly forums, and public relations work had been well established.[37]

In May 1943 Lawrance accepted a salaried position as educational director for the Tennessee State Industrial Union Council while remaining on the HFS staff. Her first assignment in her new post was a six-month extension project for CIO unions in Knoxville. Since most area locals were fairly well organized and active, Lawrance's major concern was to build unity among the unions so that they could wield greater political and consumer influence and expand their participation in the war effort. Between May and December 1943 Lawrance conducted some of the same basic grievance, contract, and union problems courses she had held in Atlanta and New Orleans, but the results of her work were disappointing. Although she continually urged local unions to set up their own legislative committees, the constant turnover of members due to service inductions and the reluctance of most committees to proceed without her help handicapped union political activity. Some locals formed cost-of-living committees and circulated ten thousand cards pledging union members not to pay more than the current legal prices, but the anti-inflation campaign was complicated by the resistance to price controls among CIO unionists living on farms. Union members also showed little interest in rolling bandages, became frustrated when Red Cross officials did not schedule convenient hours for blood bank donations, and refused to open a labor servicemen's center after the dormant Knoxville United Service Organization suddenly announced the opening of its own canteen in the fall of 1943.[38]

Yet as Lawrance had hoped, the proximity of Knoxville to Highlander permitted a closer coordination of the residence and extension programs. In September 1943, Myles Horton went to the Rohm and Haas Plexiglas plant in Knoxville, where managers had aggravated racial tensions among fifteen hundred white and black workers to hamper an organizing campaign. Horton managed to relieve the tense situation, improve race relations in the plant, and form interracial organizing committees, all of which contributed significantly to the CIO victory in the NLRB election later that fall. Lawrance then directed a three-day institute in November 1943 to train the new union's officers on grievance procedure, and Zilphia Horton helped enliven the discussion by leading the singing of labor songs. Attendance at union meetings following the institute rose dramatically, and in January 1944 local officers signed the first contract ever made by the Glass, Ceramic, and Silica Sand Workers in Tennessee.[39]

Memphis had long presented a special challenge to both the CIO and Highlander. Overcoming the opposition of Shelby County political boss Edward H. Crump, the city administration, AFL unions, and even to an uncertain extent the southern racial caste system, CIO unions had grown steadily in the late 1930s and early 1940s. Yet the inexperienced leaders of these new interracial locals badly needed training in the mechanics of unionism, and in October 1941 the Highlander staff had held a three-day conference for the United Auto Workers in Memphis to kick off an extension program for all CIO members in the city. By mid-November HFS staff member Harry Lasker, who had done volunteer work among textile unions while a student at the University of North Carolina, had started several classes on basic union problems, promoted the formation of legislative and education committees, and provided other educational services to eight local unions. But Lasker's conscientious efforts produced wretched results. From the beginning, race presented such a formidable barrier that Lasker felt compelled to teach separate classes. The program was poorly financed, local unions failed to work with one another, and union members remained largely unorganized and indifferent, even to the more entertaining portions of the program. The enmity of the Crump machine was always a potential threat, and the city police warned Lasker and local organizers against preaching social equality. Lasker was bravely optimistic about the future of the extension program, and after he volunteered for the Army Air Corps Myles Horton went to Memphis in early 1942 to revive the program, but to no avail.[40]

Nearly two years later Highlander and the state CIO began another educational program for Memphis union members, and this time conditions on the home front and the HFS staff's greater experience in extension work generated a better response among the workers. In November 1943 Mary Lawrance initiated a year-long program that eventually reached more than twelve hundred union members in Memphis every two weeks. In addition to running classes on administrative procedures at local union meetings, Lawrance aided steward councils in their educational efforts, organized a forum on the War Labor Board, conducted citywide officers' training institutes, and worked particularly hard to strengthen large locals at the Firestone, Ford, and Fisher Body plants through shift meetings, conferences with women auto workers, and shop newspapers. As the Memphis education program progressed, Lawrance tried with mixed success to promote union education and political action programs and to consolidate the various wartime projects of union members. Although she was never completely satisfied with the coordination of the educational and political activities, virtually every CIO local in the city became involved in the war effort through the creation of the first CIO Servicemen's Canteen in the South in March 1944. Servicemen responded magnificently to the canteen, Lawrance reported, and as they met CIO men from all over the country Memphis workers developed a stronger faith in unionism and a greater pride in being CIO members. Local union members also scheduled special nights at the canteen for black servicemen and held ward parties at local hospitals for disabled veterans. To check any attempt by employers to pit veterans against workers over jobs, Lawrance established veterans' committees to inform returning servicemen of their rights under the GI Bill and to urge them to join the CIO in the fight for full employment.[41]

The end of World War II changed the style more than the content of the Highlander extension program. HFS leaders wanted to resume the school's traditional emphasis on residential education, and the expansion of the civilian labor force, the termination of most overtime work, and Mary Lawrance's accomplishments made student recruitment easier. Lawrance launched an education program for sixteen unions in Chattanooga in August 1945 that continued intermittently until the fall of 1947, but shorter extension projects became more common. Between August 1945 and July 1947, Lawrance, Bill Elkuss, Catherine Winston, and their Highlander colleagues carried out extension programs for white, black, and Mexican-American members of textile, furniture, mine, agricultural, and rubber workers' unions in Tennessee, Georgia, Alabama, North Carolina, Texas, and the tri-state district of Oklahoma, Missouri, and Kansas. Despite assorted shortcomings, these projects aroused greater interest among union members in further labor education programs, attracted students to Highlander residence sessions, and laid the groundwork for union-sponsored institutes and special terms at the folk school.[42]

Zilphia Horton leading singing on a picket line in Chattanooga, 1940s. HFS staff members Bill Elkuss, seated third from right, and Mary Lawrance Elkuss, seated fourth from right. *State Historical Society of Wisconsin.*

In the decade after Highlander began full-time extension work in 1937, the staff held education programs for CIO unions in virtually every southern state. The school's extension activities reached over 10,000 local labor leaders between 1937 and 1945; during that same period the CIO organized some 400,000 members in the South, and AFL officials claimed 1.8 million southern members by 1946. The Highlander staff liked to think that each extension program was unique, for the particular demands of local unions varied at each location and changed over time. Yet the general purposes of each program were to build strong, efficient, well-run unions; to encourage and coordinate various union activities in the community; to make union members more aware of the importance of legislative and political action; and to develop among them a sense of the potential power of the southern labor movement. Several HFS staff members became skilled organizers and educational directors in great demand by unions across the South; some of their more promising students became union educators themselves. Mary Lawrance became a particularly effective field organizer, capitalizing upon favorable local circumstances, drawing upon her considerable administrative skills, working well with both male and female unionists, and searching for ways to bring black workers into the ranks of organized labor.[43]

The central problem for any extension program, as Lawrance and her Highlander colleagues clearly recognized, was to persuade local unions to implement these principles themselves. Staff members could start union education programs and meet some short-term goals. But the success of the programs rested on the willingness of union leaders to continue the classes, meetings, and other projects after Highlander had begun them. This did not happen in many cases. As late as 1944, the school's executive council expressed concern that unions were not doing enough to finance the educational programs, even though interest in workers' education had increased significantly.[44]

A more general problem for Highlander's extension program in the late 1940s involved changes in the American labor movement itself. Many of the shortcomings of the extension program stemmed from the staff's attempt to take unions beyond their concern with basic wage and hour issues. Yet folk school leaders believed that unions too often judged their success solely on bread-and-butter issues and not on their ability to influence elections or promote new labor legislation. As they feared, union leaders failed to capitalize upon the advantages gained during the war, grew defensive, and narrowed their vision. Highlander's optimistic belief that it would be able to respond to the shifting needs of workers and that unions would remain receptive to its work was well founded in the early postwar years. But the growing conservatism of union officials and the gradual restriction of union activities clashed with Highlander's broad, grassroots approach to labor education and its efforts to build a militant and progressive labor movement in the South. Highlander's residence terms for the CIO during most of the 1940s were among the most successful in the school's history. Nevertheless, the growing disparity between the goals of organized labor and those of Highlander almost completely ruptured relations between them by the end of the decade.

5

The CIO Years, 1942–1947

Between 1942 and 1947 the American labor movement grew steadily in size and influence. Wartime labor shortages, legal support for the right to organize, and the energetic, if not always successful, prosecution of cases before the War Labor Board swelled union membership from approximately 10.5 million in 1941 to about 15.4 million at the end of 1947. Accompanying this picture of progress, however, were signs that the labor movement was headed toward troubled times. Less than one-fourth of the AFL's membership and well under 10 percent of the CIO's membership lived in the South in 1947. Some state legislatures sought to undermine the legal position of unions during and after the war, and employers who cooperated with unions during the war did so almost solely out of patriotic necessity, quickly moving to reassert their authority once the crisis had passed. Meanwhile, union members became convinced that they had suffered long enough under wartime government controls while business profits soared, and they prepared to improve their living standards once they regained the freedom to negotiate and strike. The result of the bitter postwar struggle over wages and the allocation of power between organized labor and management, as David Brody has observed, brought employers and union officials into an "unacknowledged collaboration against shop-floor militancy."[1]

The early and mid-1940s also marked the culmination of the Highlander Folk School's participation in the southern labor movement. In 1942 staff members proudly noted the school's vital role in the development of labor unions in the South. Around 90 percent of Highlander's alumni were serving as national, regional, or local union officials and organizers, and numerous AFL and CIO unions and officers had endorsed the school's work. Yet the faculty also recognized the need for a broader educational program. Anti-union forces were seeking to reverse earlier gains, government agencies were determining the rights of laborers, and unions were sacrificing "their most effective weapon," the right to strike, in order to facilitate war production. Highlander had to commit its resources to the defeat of fascism wherever it existed and to the new wartime issues facing southern workers. Union members needed to fight for a greater voice in the war effort, Myles Horton argued in early 1942, for the influence of organized labor after the war depended on what it secured during the war.[2]

In January 1942 the HFS executive council drew up a revised statement of purpose that reflected such concerns. Highlander intended "to assist in the defense and expansion of political and economic democracy," council members declared, and to strengthen unions through education. The council also reaffirmed earlier policies: the needs of labor unions would determine the nature of Highlander's educational programs; the school would function as a "rural settlement house" in the community; and the teaching staff would own and manage HFS cooperatively, remain unaffiliated with any organization, and receive financial support from unions and their allies throughout the country.[3]

Guided by these objectives, the Highlander faculty developed some of the most effective residence programs in the institution's history between 1942 and 1947. During these years staff members sought to build a broad-based, racially integrated, and politically active southern labor movement and to foster a greater appreciation for the contributions workers' education could make to it. For a time it seemed quite possible that they would achieve their goals. Between 1944 and 1947 Highlander hosted annual Southern CIO Schools for potential local union leaders from across the region. Staff members promoted the activities of the CIO's Political Action Committee, a coalition formed in 1943 to influence state and national elections and to secure favorable legislation. HFS leaders also urged white union officers and members to participate in interracial workshops at the school, believing that the sessions would help improve the fortunes not only of the CIO but of all southern laborers. Once the United Auto Workers (UAW) held an integrated workshop in 1944, reportedly the first time black and white students attended the same classes at a southern labor school, the faculty made some headway in persuading other unions to accept the school's nondiscriminatory policy.

Yet if Highlander and the southern labor movement appeared to be pursuing common objectives by the end of World War II, there were indications that unity was tenuous. While Highlander was still able to meet the needs of southern labor unions after the departure of several strong personalities, including James Dombrowski in 1942, the school's policies and programs became largely dependent upon Myles Horton. More ominous signs of stress were evident in Highlander's very minor role in the 1946 CIO organizing drive and the decreasing involvement of union officials in the school's CIO terms. These and other problems pointed to a fundamental disagreement over the role of unions in postwar America: as the HFS staff gave greater attention to civil rights, political action, and the potential of a farmer-labor coalition, CIO leaders cast off much of their earlier militancy and concentrated upon securing wage increases and fringe benefits. The resulting tensions between Highlander and the CIO were not easily resolved.

Soon after the United States entered World War II, Highlander leaders attempted to make the school part of the national defense effort while continuing to serve the interests of southern unions. In January 1942 the executive council proposed that the Office of Civilian Defense use the school as a defense training center for union leaders in the South. Under this plan OCD and union representatives were to hold special sessions at HFS on how workers could protect their plants from sabotage and air raids, solve production problems, and sustain employee morale. Despite several CIO endorsements, the OCD hesitated to accept the offer because of Highlander's relatively isolated location, the difficulty of getting workers to leave defense industry jobs, the radical reputation of the school, and a reluctance to work with organized labor. Highlander therefore established a research department in October 1942 under the direction of Bill Elkuss to carry on the folk school's defense program. Elkuss produced interpretive pamphlets and outlines on wartime labor legislation and government agencies and issued weekly bulletins on the latest legislative developments. In September 1944 staff members began publishing *INFO,* a biweekly newsletter for servicemen containing items of interest to labor union members. These projects did not transform Highlander into the defense training center envisioned in 1942. But they did encourage the exchange of information among unions, helped educate union members on the labor issues created by the war, and boosted the prestige of the school.[4]

Executive council and faculty members also hoped to improve Highlander's work during the war by strengthening its financial status, a perennial problem that had become especially acute by 1942. Income was greater than ever before, but so was the budget. Expenditures in 1941 totaled nearly $14,000, while revenues amounted to $12,700. Merely to duplicate the existing program in 1942 would cost nearly $18,000, and the burdens the war had placed upon many of Highlander's most faithful contributors made fundraising extremely difficult. Confronted with a "pitifully low" number of donors and a lack of financial support from labor unions, HFS leaders initiated a major financial drive to coincide with the institution's tenth anniversary.[5] A benefit concert in Washington, D.C., in May 1942, featuring renowned black baritone Paul Robeson, as well as the formation of a National Sponsoring Committee that included Eleanor Roosevelt and other prominent individuals, sparked a gradual rise in contributions to the school during 1942. The fundraising drive climaxed in October 1942 with a day-long celebration of Highlander's ten years of work in the South. Noting that the school had grown from a single house in 1932 to seven separate buildings on two hundred acres of land a decade later, Myles Horton announced that the staff was more confident in its teaching methods than ever before and certain that union demands for its services would continue to increase.[6]

The tenth anniversary campaign may have been a public relations success, but it did not relieve Highlander's financial woes. At the end of 1942, income totaled just under $11,700. Despite efforts to cut expenses to a minimum, the inadequate financial response of CIO unions forced the cancellation of a year-end publicity and fundraising project, compelled several staff members to resign, and made it difficult to find replacements for them. Although the executive council continued to press labor leaders for more financial support, unions gave less than half the amount donated by individual contributors in 1943, and the school's total income was only $13,334. Increased revenues from unions nearly doubled Highlander's income over the next two years, but the $23,316 the school received in 1945 fell far short of its projected operating budget of $31,585. HFS leaders nevertheless remained optimistic. They anticipated that the return of peace would release enough funds to allow the start of a building program, the expansion of Highlander's labor education programs, and the beginning of new projects among southern farmers.[7]

In addition to the persistent fundraising problem, Highlander struggled during the war years to replace staff members who had been an integral part of the school for much of its history. Ralph Tefferteller, Zilla Hawes Daniel, and Claudia Lewis had left HFS by the end of 1940, and their positions had been filled by a series of competent, though less experienced, men and women.[8] The departure of James Dombrowski in January 1942 was a far more serious matter, however. For almost nine years Dombrowski had managed the school's affairs with a steady hand, coordinating staff activities, handling administrative duties, raising funds, organizing workshops, and acting as official spokesman of the school. He complemented the improvisational teaching style, gregarious personality, dramatic flair, and undaunted optimism of Myles Horton with a self-effacing, cautious personality and a more meticulous and reflective teaching approach that lent clarity and purpose to the efforts of Horton and other staff members. Indeed, the two men were largely responsible for the effectiveness of Highlander's labor program.

But in mid-1941 Dombrowski found himself laboring under several burdens that intensified his desire to find a position where he could devote more time to the issues that concerned him. Certainly the school's administrative affairs had ceased to challenge him, and his attempts to gain more freedom to teach or to participate in organizing campaigns had been repeatedly frustrated. Equally troubling to Dombrowski was the inordinate amount of time and energy he spent explaining and justifying Highlander's operations to an often skeptical public. Horton and Dombrowski never wavered in their insistence that the institution was open to people of all creeds and colors. But Dombrowski acknowledged that this policy had led to misunderstandings and conflicts with both allies and opponents, and while his HFS colleagues agreed that racial prejudice presented an enormous barrier to their goals, few were willing to join him in confronting the issue. The strained relationship between Dombrowski's fiancée, Ellen Krida, and Myles and Zilphia Horton was still another source of discontent. Krida refused to live at HFS, and Dombrowski found the long separations trying. Finally, tensions developed between Dombrowski and Horton, occasionally over financial matters but primarily over differences in personality. Together, these problems produced severe strains within an intensely private man, and on January 22, 1942, Dombrowski resigned as chairman of the HFS staff to become executive secretary of the Southern Conference for Human Welfare.[9]

Dombrowski's resignation created one major personnel problem for Highlander in the early 1940s; the war created others. The induction of Harry Lasker and Bill Elkuss into the army, the death of Bill Buttrick after a long illness, and the departure of four other staff members during 1942 substantially reduced the size of the staff. By early 1943, Leon Wilson and Myles Horton were the only male staff members, and there was no assurance that they would remain much longer. In the fall of 1942 Wilson had applied for conscientious objector status on the basis of his long-standing humanitarian opposition to war and military service. When the Marion County, Tennessee, draft board held that conscientious objection must be based on religious scruples and classified him as 1-A, Wilson resigned from the staff in order to prevent "another wave of malicious slander" against the school.[10] Highlander's opponents were elated when Wilson was charged with draft evasion in March 1943, calling his arrest a vindication of their fight against a disloyal institution. But the precautions Wilson had taken to disassociate himself from Highlander and the staff's public endorsement of the American war effort checked further criticism.[11]

The turmoil on the staff continued when Myles Horton faced induction in April 1943. Although he was thirty-seven years old, and although he and Zilphia had recently become the parents of a baby boy, Horton and the Highlander executive council agreed that he would not ask the Selective Service for an exemption, since it was likely that married men with children would be inducted that year. Instead, Horton persuaded the local draft board to grant him a sixty-day deferment to allow him to reorganize the school's affairs and convert Highlander's forty-acre farm to the production of crops needed for the war effort. Horton intended to cite these and other wartime projects as evidence that Highlander was essential to the national defense. He then could apply for a release from duty after he became thirty-eight years old, the age limit for active servicemen, and return to HFS. The remaining staff members maintained a grim determination to carry on the education program in his absence. They were relieved, however, when Horton reported for induction on June 30, 1943, and returned home the same day. According to Zilphia, army doctors decided that Myles's age, "his looking like an intellectual and not applying for a commission," and his status as head of an "unestranged family" disqualified him from military duty.[12] In May 1943 the HFS staff had reaffirmed its belief that the school as a whole was more important than any one person. But it also seemed clear, with Dombrowski gone and Mary Lawrance in the field conducting extension programs, that Highlander's fortunes would hinge upon the ideas and actions of Myles Horton for at least the next several years.[13]

Beset with financial and personnel problems, as well as with the difficulty of operating the school during wartime, the HFS staff conducted a relatively modest program of union training in 1942 and 1943. Following a labor problems seminar for a handful of college students in July 1942, twenty-seven regular and five part-time students from CIO and AFL unions began a six-week residence term focusing on "Labor's Part in Winning the War" in August. Staff members incorporated new courses on the operations of government agencies affecting labor, and speakers included southern CIO officials Paul Christopher and Lucy Randolph Mason, United Rubber Workers of America (URWA) publicity director Robert Cruden, and Virginia Durr of the National Committee to Abolish the Poll Tax. By most reports the term succeeded in educating local union leaders about their wartime responsibilities, but HFS teachers privately expressed dissatisfaction with virtually every course. The majority of the problems, the faculty concluded, stemmed from the presence of college students who lacked practical work experience yet dominated class discussions. Staff members therefore decided that in any future labor session, college students would be educated from the workers' perspective.[14]

Another problem affecting the 1942 residence program was Highlander's attempt to steer clear of disputes within the labor movement. Shortly after the war began, CIO president Philip Murray attacked United Mine Workers president John L. Lewis's proposal to resume unity negotiations with the AFL. Lewis led his union out of the CIO and announced that the UMWA would seek to extend its jurisdiction over all unorganized workers through its catchall District 50. In this context, Highlander's indefinite postponement of a two-week term for District 50 workers in the spring of 1942 led to rumors that HFS had abandoned its nonfactional policy to oppose District 50. Claiming that other rumors labeled Highlander a District 50 school, Horton reaffirmed the school's policy of staying out of jurisdictional fights. Several southern CIO officials, including a few HFS executive council members, objected to this neutrality. "If the school teaches only parliamentary law and avoids the major issues," southern Gas, Coke, and Chemical Workers director Bernard Borah warned Horton, "it will find itself on the road to uselessness" in the labor movement.[15]

Nevertheless, Highlander stayed out of the fight, and as the American labor movement entered a period of relative harmony with the re-admission of the UMWA to the AFL in October 1943, the HFS staff stabilized the school's internal affairs and carried out an informal residence program. Since the war was making it difficult to recruit either workers or students for residence terms, Horton and his colleagues were compelled to concentrate on their extension program, delay the start of a three-month labor education seminar for college students until June, and replace the summer term with a two-week War Workers' Vacation Camp. Mindful of the problems they had encountered in 1942, staff members carefully limited the contacts between union members and the eight college women attending the seminar until late August, when Highlander held its first camp for vacationing war workers. Two dozen trade unionists, soldiers, schoolteachers, YWCA secretaries, and students held informal discussions on the labor movement, politics, and current events. Staff members then devoted the rest of 1943 to field work in Tennessee, searching for opportunities to maximize Highlander's contribution to organized labor during the war.[16]

One exciting opportunity came with the CIO executive board's decision in July 1943 to create the Political Action Committee (PAC). Chaired by ACWA president Sidney Hillman, the PAC was designed to mobilize union support for President Franklin Roosevelt and Democratic congressional candidates sympathetic to organized labor. Highlander's faculty had long advocated political action by labor unions as part of a broad working-class coalition that would transform the South into the most progressive region in the country. But just as unions were the "medium" through which they conducted their education program, staff members had to foster political activism among southern workers through unions, moving "as far in a progressive direction as we can go and still carry the unions with us."[17] CIO-PAC therefore represented a significant development in the labor movement's commitment to political as well as economic change.[18]

The PAC never lived up to its promise, but in 1944 it projected an image of immense political power. In August, sixty Tennessee CIO officials representing twenty-four national unions and over seventy thousand workers met at Highlander and formed the Tennessee Citizens Political Action Committee (TCPAC) along with a system of local and area political action committees. Opponents of HFS and the CIO rushed to denounce the entire campaign. Nashville *Banner* editors noted that Highlander, notorious for its aggressive radicalism and Communist teachings, had now become "the vehicle for Sidney Hillman's 'education' of Tennessee—his faculty of shock troops in these parts."[19] To counter such charges the PAC launched a massive publicity campaign, printing and distributing more than fifteen million pieces of literature in the South, including an HFS-produced leaflet on Tennessee voting requirements. PAC leaders claimed that their organization's efforts contributed substantially to Roosevelt's victory as well as to the election of six governors, seventeen senators, and 109 congressmen in 1944. Despite continuing criticism from James G. Stahlman of the *Banner,* who bluntly equated TCPAC with the Highlander "Communists," TCPAC delegates would meet at the folk school again in February 1945 to plan future activities, and HFS staff members would continue to work against anti-union legislation in Congress and in the Tennessee legislature.[20]

Another part of the CIO's wartime agenda directly involving Highlander was the education of union leaders who could take on the responsibilities of those officers serving in the armed forces. At the 1943 national CIO convention, several southern regional directors proposed a month-long training program at HFS in the spring of 1944. The directors agreed to sponsor the residence session, serve as speakers or teachers, and recruit thirty-five industrial union council or local union leaders from ten southern states for the term. National CIO director of research and education J. Raymond Walsh, Tennessee CIO director Paul Christopher, and Myles Horton assumed joint direction of the "Southern CIO School," and the tentative curriculum of the term reflected their particular interests. The primary emphasis was to be on the union's organizational and political action programs, but there would also be such familiar Highlander courses as labor economics, labor history, public speaking and parliamentary law, and union publicity. Staff members regarded the session as "a significant development in the field of Workers' Education," for it marked the first time regional labor officials ever "requested, worked out details, and offered to finance such a program."[21]

Although the first Southern CIO School, held during a period of stringent labor shortages, failed to attract many students, it served as a prototype for later CIO terms. The session began on May 1, 1944, with only eight local union leaders in attendance. While forced to scale down its original plans, the HFS faculty, with the aid of some thirty speakers and visiting teachers, carried out the classes scheduled for the term. A new community relations course examined the steps unions might take to establish a good working relationship with various civic groups, to start a program for servicemen, and to combat racial discrimination. Two members of the Training Within Industry division of the War Manpower Commission taught a week-long course on labor-management problems, the first of its kind for union members in the South. Supplementing the course work were an all-day conference on political action and postwar employment sponsored by the Chattanooga Industrial Union Council and a weekend conference on farmer-labor unity held with the Summerfield Farmers' Union. The term ended with a banquet and celebration that included group singing led by Pete Seeger, a former Almanac Singer then stationed at Camp Sibert.[22]

Students, southern CIO officials, and HFS staff members alike considered the 1944 Southern CIO School a success in spite of the small number of students. One North Carolina student claimed to have learned more about CIO policy, racial discrimination, and political action at Highlander than he had in four years as an officer of his local. A student from Texas reported that he and his fellow students left the school "much more devoted to the Labor Cause than we had been theretofore," and Lucy Mason asserted that the staff had accomplished some "miracles" during the term.[23] Faculty members measured their effectiveness partly by the fact that four of the students became union organizers after they returned to their locals; more important was the unanimous vote of the CIO southern regional directors to hold another month-long session at Highlander in 1945.[24]

CIO leaders generally recognized that wartime labor education programs should not only train new local union officers but also bolster attempts to organize black workers. Despite an official policy of nondiscrimination, prompted at least in part by the key position of blacks in some of the industries on which CIO strength was based, racial discrimination persisted in many locals, particularly in the South. Nevertheless, southern CIO leaders at least rhetorically supported interracial unionism, and some made determined efforts to battle racial prejudice among white union members. A few CIO unions in the South took advantage of wartime labor shortages to secure concessions for black workers, to encourage the racial integration of union locals, and to argue that racial equality was a necessary war measure, if not a moral imperative.[25]

The Highlander staff also prodded southern CIO unions to admit black workers, not only because of its commitment to racial equality but also because of the need to square the school's racial practices with its principles. Highlander had always encouraged black visitors, invited black speakers, participated in interracial conferences, and helped existing biracial unions. During the 1937 TWOC drive, staff members had organized interracial locals, and later they had conducted extension programs for blacks in Tennessee, Louisiana, and elsewhere. In January 1942, Lewis Jones, a Fisk University sociologist, had become the first black member of the HFS executive council. But the school was not really racially integrated. Most residence students came from union locals that had no black members at all, and HFS policy was to accept only those students sent by their unions. Staff members tried to overturn the prejudices of white workers by exposing them to the problems of black workers, but they hesitated to have black students enrolled in the same residence terms. In August 1942, however, Highlander's leaders announced that residence terms would henceforth be interracial and that students should be informed in advance that there would be no discrimination at the school. As a kind of test of this new policy, the HFS faculty held a low-key interracial conference in May 1943 featuring Max Yergan, director of the Council on African Affairs.

Later that year Myles Horton offered his services to unions faced with racial troubles, and in September 1943 he helped ease tensions at the Rohm and Haas Plexiglas factory in Knoxville through "personal work" with black and white leaders in the plant.[26]

The campaign to integrate Highlander residence sessions finally paid off in 1944, when United Auto Workers regional director Thomas J. Starling accepted the staff's invitation to hold a week-long summer term for local union officers in southern war plants. Unlike many CIO unions in the South, the UAW's greatest strength lay outside the region; thus union leaders were able to move against racial discrimination in their southern locals without jeopardizing the UAW's fortunes. When Starling asked whether he could send a black committeeman from Memphis to the session, Horton replied that any black union member could come provided that white students selected by the UAW knew in advance about Highlander's nondiscriminatory policy. That apparently was enough for Starling, and the first Southern UAW Summer School began on June 5, 1944, with fifty-six people in attendance, including two black committeemen from Memphis and a black steward from Atlanta. The HFS faculty assisted members of the UAW education and consumer division staff conduct classes on such topics as the economics of the auto and aircraft industry, collective bargaining, political action, UAW history, and postwar planning. Students also wrote a wall newspaper, formed a council to plan group activities, and operated a cooperative store.[27]

The 1944 UAW Summer School was not only the first interracial school held by any union in the South but also the largest group ever to attend a single session at Highlander, and it all proceeded, in Horton's words, "without a hitch."[28] White students had simply accepted black students as fellow union members. Horton attributed the success of the session partly to Highlander's mountain location, for it had allowed the union members to work, play, and discuss their common problems relatively isolated from outside pressures. The folk school's ability to hold such terms was not lost on state CIO leaders. In June 1944 the Tennessee State Industrial Union Council recommended the expansion of Highlander to accommodate larger numbers of students and urged other CIO unions to follow the precedent established by the interracial UAW school.[29]

Highlander's busiest summer in its history, and certainly the most successful since the beginning of the war, ended with a flurry of activity. After holding a junior union camp in July 1944, four staff members conducted a series of institutes for sixteen CIO locals in Virginia and the Carolinas. A general workers' residence term followed in mid-August. Although Horton recognized that some whites might not attend the planned interracial session and that recent friction with some of the school's neighbors might make it more difficult to have blacks at Highlander, he and his associates agreed that closing the term to black union members would set back their efforts to integrate the school. Much of the work of the one-week term—attended by eight white and two black local officers of the Mine, Mill, and Smelter Workers (MMSW), the United Furniture Workers of America (UFWA), and the Glass, Ceramic, and Silica Sand Workers—centered on the contributions local unions could make to the 1944 CIO political action campaign. Students drew up several recommendations that were adopted by state CIO representatives who convened at HFS at the end of August to form the Tennessee Citizens Political Action Committee. After the general workers' term, Carl Haessler of the Federated Press directed a one-week labor journalism course at the school for sixteen students from five AFL and CIO unions.[30]

By the end of 1944 Highlander had become perhaps the most important labor education center in the South. That year, over 100 local labor leaders had enrolled in residence sessions; almost 1,300 students had participated in extension classes; and over 1,000 union members had been to twenty-one HFS-directed conferences and institutes throughout the South. Staff members had produced more than 2,500 songbooks and song sheets, several thousand leaflets on political action, and hundreds of pamphlets on parliamentary law and other subjects. Union contributions and payments to Highlander had increased from $3,364 in 1943 to $8,429 in 1944. The goals and strategies of the CIO and the school had become virtually identical. Southern CIO-PAC director George S. Mitchell issued a glowing endorsement, and Tennessee CIO subregional director W. A. Copeland, who had initially been skeptical about HFS and its independence from "outside influences," was now impressed by the abilities of the school's staff and convinced of its commitment to the CIO.[31] To meet the growing demand for the school's services, the HFS executive council approved a budget of $31,585 for 1945 and a campaign to raise $65,000 for the construction of a dormitory and a library as a memorial to former staff member Harry Lasker, who had died in 1944 from injuries received in a plane crash. Highlander's leaders also indicated their willingness to maintain the current direction of their program by electing several southern CIO directors to the council and United Steel Workers regional director William Crawford to the chairmanship.[32]

Workshop participants gathered in front of Highlander's main building in the 1940s.
State Historical Society of Wisconsin.

Highlander staff members capitalized on their previous gains during 1945, but their accomplishments did not come easily. Southern CIO directors took a strong role in planning the Second Southern CIO School, held between May 7 and June 3, 1945. Thus while the HFS staff managed to schedule classes on the broader issues confronting unions in the postwar South, the emphasis of the curriculum reflected the regional directors' interest in CIO policy and the principles of industrial union councils. The directors also agreed to raise the $5,000 needed to cover the expenses of the month-long term from CIO unions and the national office. But many individual unions were reluctant to help defray the costs of the term, and CIO vice-president Allan S. Haywood did not think that the national organization could afford any substantial amount for the term. As a result, Highlander was compelled to advance more money for tuition, publicity, and recruiting than it ever received.[33]

A more complex issue was whether to send black union members to the Southern CIO School. All of Highlander's publicity since the summer of 1944 had stressed its interracial terms. Staff members were committed to continuing this policy, and they believed that tensions among students

116 *The CIO Years*

could be reduced by notifying whites in advance of Highlander's racial policy, by limiting the number of black students, and by restricting extra-curricular activities. If past experience was any indication, white CIO local leaders who attended the school would move to a more liberal position on race. Yet there remained the possibility that a month-long biracial CIO school could aggravate racial prejudice in Grundy County, and, as a poll taken by Paul Christopher revealed, southern CIO directors, slower to change than the rank and file, were unwilling to risk it. Although Maryland regional director Frank J. Bender fully supported the idea of a racially mixed group at a single CIO school, Alabama regional director Carey Haigler flatly asserted that the prejudice prevalent in the Monteagle community necessitated separate sessions for black and white workers. The views of other regional officers fell between these two. Most insisted that they personally favored having black union members at Highlander but were worried about community reaction to the CIO school and doubted whether many white union members from their areas would attend integrated classes. Acting Kentucky regional director Joseph D. Cannon warned that the CIO school should not go "an inch farther than is absolutely safe," for a single mistake "would set the school back for years and give the C.I.O. a black eye in the entire south." The purpose of the CIO, Cannon pointed out, was to organize workers into a powerful industrial union. All other issues, including the race question, were secondary to that goal.[34]

On the basis of the regional directors' response, Christopher and Horton decided not to have black students at the CIO school. Horton took some consolation from the fact that the directors had faced the issue squarely. Perhaps it was expecting too much of the directors "to go the whole way on the Negro question at once," he admitted.[35] But the decision disappointed several CIO locals that had planned to send white and black students to the CIO school, and the Alabama state CIO executive board voted to make the next session at Highlander interracial or seek another location for the school. Protests also came from the national CIO office, especially from the Committee to Abolish Racial Discrimination, and for a time it seemed that the entire term might be canceled. National and southern officials finally decided to go through with the CIO school at HFS, and two black union officers attended the session. But the controversy made any future CIO commitment tentative.[36]

For all the trouble in planning the term, the twenty-six local union leaders who attended the second CIO School not only learned a variety of organizational skills but also gained a better understanding of the broader goals the CIO hoped to pursue after World War II. The course work, reflecting the concern of organized labor over the number of jobs that would be available when the war ended, focused on the theme of sixty million jobs and how the CIO could help bring them about. Each week a visiting regional director—Paul Christopher of Tennessee, William Henderson of Arkansas, Ernest B. Pugh of Virginia, and Charles Gillman of Georgia—taught classes on CIO policies and postwar strategies, and at the end of the term Allan Haywood outlined the tasks that lay ahead for the CIO in the South. Complementing familiar Highlander courses on union problems, union-community relations, parliamentary law, public speaking, union publicity, and current events were short courses conducted by James Dombrowski of SCHW, George Weaver of the CIO Committee to Abolish Racial Discrimination, George Mitchell of the CIO-PAC, and several representatives of CIO committees, reform groups, and government labor agencies. Students gained some idea of the importance of farmer-labor unity when they attended a meeting of the local Farmers' Union at Highlander, and they followed HFS custom by forming a governing council and operating their own cooperative store. While they left questions of racial discrimination in their unions unresolved, the students unanimously elected Henry White, president of a Memphis transport workers union and one of the two black students at the term, president of the student council.[37]

Reactions to the 1945 Southern CIO School were decidedly mixed. Although generally satisfied with the results of the term, HFS staff members were sharply critical of the lack of teaching experience among visiting CIO officials, the omission of courses on labor history and economics, and the narrowness and lack of coordination of class discussions. Other problems concerned the students themselves. One drank too much alcohol, and Zilphia Horton noted the bitterness expressed by male students against women in industry. Racism created still more dissension. Although one student who came to the term possessing "the usual racial prejudice" went back home "unprejudiced," two other white students from Alabama left at the end of two weeks because the session was integrated.[38] Moreover, Highlander received only $2,353 for the CIO school, well short of the $5,000 the CIO had promised to pay. On the other hand, virtually all of the students assumed new offices within their unions after the term, and an Oil Workers local in Arkansas and the executive board of the Arkansas-Oklahoma Industrial Union Councils adopted resolutions endorsing the school. It had not been the easiest residence term for staff members. But the CIO school gained important official sanction when the Tennessee State Industrial Union Council recommended a third CIO term at Highlander.[39]

Following the Southern CIO School, Highlander hosted a succession of residence sessions that solidified its status as the CIO's southern training center for union leaders. In June 1945 the UAW held its second annual summer school at HFS, where staff members, George Mitchell, and several UAW officials covered the economics of the auto industry, leadership training, consumer problems, and union operations. There was no apparent trouble among the five black and sixteen white southern auto workers attending the term. The AFHW sponsored two weekend institutes at Highlander in June and September 1945 under the direction of national education and research director William L. Rafsky for forty-six branch members in the Chattanooga area. Carl Haessler taught his third labor journalism course at Highlander in August 1945. The one-week workshop attracted eighteen students—including the black vice-president of a Georgia UAW local—from CIO, AFL, and Farmers' Union locals as well as from the American Veterans Committee. The lone exception to the school's interracial policy during 1945 was a two-week term in July restricted to twenty-five white URWA members from Alabama, Tennessee, and North Carolina. These short sessions were not particularly notable. Yet the popularity of the HFS summer courses among CIO unions had become great enough that a proposed institute for the United Packinghouse Workers of America was canceled because the facilities could not accommodate enough students. For the moment, Highlander's relationship with the CIO seemed secure.[40]

With the end of World War II and the rapid dismantling of government controls, labor-management relations quickly shifted from War Labor Board hearings to collective bargaining conferences and picket lines. President Harry S. Truman appealed to union and business leaders to reach new agreements during the reconversion period; both sides chose instead to square off in tests of economic strength. In a wave of strikes that swept the country in 1945 and 1946, unions sought wage increases sufficient to match the effects of inflation, but rapidly rising prices frustrated the goal of a higher living standard. At the same time, many Americans came to believe that the responsibility for rising prices and most other economic problems lay with organized labor. Public reaction against unions grew steadily, and after the disastrous defeat of union-backed candidates in the 1946 elections, Congress and over thirty state legislatures enacted the largest number of anti-union laws since the late nineteenth century, culminating in the Taft-Hartley Act of June 1947. In short, the return to a relatively uncontrolled economy and the perceived intransigence of organized labor put unions on the defensive, leading to a greater emphasis on securing wage increases and on maintaining control over the rank and file.[41]

Highlander's residence program after the war remained responsive to the needs of the southern labor movement, even as CIO support for the school was slipping away. Although southern regional directors were willing to sponsor a third CIO School at HFS in May 1946, strikes and preparations for an organizing drive forced them to spend far less time in planning the term than in previous years, and the slow union response to fundraising appeals once again placed Highlander's financial status and recruiting efforts on precarious ground. The nineteen students attending the CIO school represented seven unions with a combined membership of 16,714 workers in the South, but only one CIO southern regional director took part in the one-month term. To be sure, several officials from the national CIO, CIO-PAC, and member unions were guest speakers or teachers in courses on union problems, publicity, and organizing tactics. But without the usual complement of union and government officials, HFS staff members taught virtually all the classes on their own. The curriculum included shop steward training, labor legislation, parliamentary law and public speaking, and labor history and economics. Tom Ludwig, who had joined the HFS staff in early 1946 to develop a Farmers' Union program in Tennessee, taught classes on farmer-labor cooperation, and near the end of the term, students participated in a Farm-Labor Unity Conference.[42]

Student reports about the 1946 CIO School generally contained high praise for staff members and their ability to help students solve the most difficult union problems, but they concealed the tensions that seemed to prevail for most of the term. The costs of carrying out the session left a one-thousand-dollar deficit that Highlander could ill afford. Faculty members acknowledged that the course work should have been better coordinated and more pertinent to the students' specific problems.[43]

It was the interracial policy that proved the most troublesome issue during the 1946 CIO School, however. Five white students arrived for the term unprepared for the full implications of an integrated term at HFS, and they soon threatened to leave if blacks were not segregated at meals. Confronted with a serious setback to their efforts to improve race relations among southern union members, staff members pointed out that there was enough room for white students to eat at separate tables. In the meantime, they stressed the CIO's nondiscriminatory policy in the classroom, made sure that all student committees were interracial, and invited black and white speakers to the school. The denouement of the controversy came when the leader of the antiblack faction, a Ku Klux Klan supporter, discredited himself by refusing to sign a student letter protesting President Truman's treatment of striking railroad workers. During the remainder of the term and most subsequent HFS residence sessions, white and black students interacted freely. Staff members became more adamant in expecting students to adapt to their interracial program, but they also considered several steps to accommodate white objections to integrated housing, bathing, and eating facilities. Despite claims that Highlander's experiences proved that southern white and black workers were willing to work together, it was clear that the problems of interracial education were still not completely resolved.[44]

Highlander staff members could understand that southern CIO officials would choose to prepare for the "Operation Dixie" organizing campaign rather than participate in the 1946 CIO School, but they were undoubtedly dismayed by their exclusion from the drive. In the spring of 1946, both the CIO and the AFL launched campaigns to unionize the large number of unorganized workers in the South, and by the end of 1947 the AFL claimed about five hundred thousand new members and the CIO four hundred thousand. But increasingly burdensome costs, difficulties in enlisting in-plant advocates, racial antagonism, anticommunism, and the intransigent opposition of employers—all familiar barriers to unionism in the South—hindered further organizing efforts. Sensitive to the AFL's widely publicized charge that its rival was led by Communists, CIO campaign director Van Bittner recruited 85 percent of his staff from the South and rejected offers of help from outside groups, including the Southern Conference for Human Welfare "and any other organization living off the CIO."[45]

Bittner's comment reflected a shift in thinking among CIO leaders about the goals of their union in postwar America and its relationship with organizations like SCHW and Highlander. CIO officers at all levels seldom forgot that their unions existed primarily to protect the economic interests of their members, and the end of the war brought a renewed stress on organizing as many workers as possible and improving union benefits. Political action, labor education, and racial change became less pressing concerns, and the growing internal crisis over communism led CIO officials to distance themselves from groups that did not directly serve their organizational needs or adhere to the national union's policy. Highlander thus received mixed signals from the CIO, for its effective work for the union went hand in hand with its broader concern for basic economic, political, and racial reform in the South. The staff's offer to conduct education programs during the CIO organizing campaign met with a curt refusal from public relations director Alan Swim, who declared in July 1946 that "all programs should be requested by the State Director of the CIO Drive."[46] Yet in January 1947 the school was still on the list of groups approved by the CIO executive board. While staff members remained optimistic about their future role in the southern labor movement, the differences between Highlander and the CIO were becoming more evident.[47]

Another indication of the rift developing between the folk school and the CIO appeared during Highlander's postwar fundraising drive. In April 1946 the HFS executive council approved a campaign to raise $100,000 for an expanded program and a new building to house the library, classrooms, and a community meeting hall. Council members decided that southern CIO unions should begin to repay Highlander for years of selfless aid by donating $50,000. But because of the CIO's commitment to its southern organizing drive and its wariness toward the school, the expected union contributions never materialized. Facing the prospect of insufficient funds for current operating expenses, the HFS staff turned to nonunion sources to meet its financial needs. During 1946 and 1947 Highlander committees conducted fundraising campaigns in Boston, New York, Chicago, Washington, Atlanta, and Nashville. In July 1946 Highlander was one of ten organizations in the country to receive $6,000 from the proceeds of a Frank Sinatra film, *The House I Live In,* in recognition of the school's efforts to promote racial harmony, and in December 1946 the Julius Rosenwald Fund awarded a $15,000 grant to develop an education program for potential community leaders in the rural South. Yet total contributions to the residence program amounted to only $20,567 in 1946, and the building fund was less than $5,000. Accepting Horton's argument that contributors would respond to a "concrete symbol of achievement" like a new school building, HFS leaders earmarked all but $45,000 of the school's 1947 budget of $239,000 for the building fund.[48] Once again, however, Highlander's expectations far exceeded the amount of money actually raised during the year. While revenues rose to $43,000 in 1947, expenses increased as well, compelling the executive council in January 1948 to reconsider the school's construction plans.[49]

The coolness of the CIO and financial constraints led to a more circumspect and self-supporting program during 1946. The AFHW sponsored three training institutes at Highlander for over fifty union shop committee members and potential leaders from local branches in Tennessee and Georgia. Seventeen black and white tobacco, food-processing, and cottonseed oil compress workers from seven southern states attended the first Food, Tobacco, and Agricultural Workers (FTA) leadership training school at HFS in April 1946. In the wake of recent racial disturbances in nearby Columbia, staff member Catherine Winston and FTA education director Cornelia M. Anderson carefully confined the term's activities to the folk school, and the one-week term took place without incident. Meanwhile, Bill Elkuss helped union veterans in Chattanooga establish a new interracial American Legion post and held informal classes for about fifty black veterans, teachers, and members of the local National Association for the Advancement of Colored People (NAACP). Despite their uneasiness about the overall decline in union support, HFS teachers hoped that working with groups outside organized labor would give additional strength to the southern labor movement.[50]

When several other terms for individual unions failed to materialize, the HFS staff held a two-week general workers' term in September 1946 for fifteen white and three black students from seven different southern CIO unions. After almost fourteen years of practice and experimentation, the faculty had fashioned a fairly well-ordered curriculum divided between what it called tool courses, which covered the mechanics of union building, and background courses, which sought to stimulate student thinking about labor history, economics, and current events. An even more important development was the complete integration of the black students into the activities of the term. Five white students had not been informed in advance of Highlander's interracial policy, and though the staff's strategy of creating a friendly atmosphere and providing "optional" sleeping quarters and bathrooms checked any open protest, several white students initially resented the presence of black students. After two white Memphians held informal sessions to discuss race relations, however, the white objections ended. Staff members contributed to this effort by gradually introducing the topic of racial discrimination during the classes and evening programs and by making no attempt to force integration. By the end of the term the students had cultivated a group spirit absent from any previous HFS interracial session.[51]

Highlander's 1947 residence program was not significantly different from that of the previous year; once again it was marked by special terms for particular unions and by the limited participation of CIO leaders. Throughout the year the AFHW, FTA, UAW, URWA, MMSW, and Farmers' Union sponsored short interracial sessions for local officers, covering not only the mechanics of union building but also broader subjects like political action and farmer-labor cooperation. The highlight of the residence program was the fourth annual Southern CIO School, held during June and July. In addition to reducing student fees from the customary one hundred dollars to seventy-five dollars and buying extra tents and beds to accommodate the fifty students promised by the CIO, the staff acceded to Paul Christopher's demand that HFS dismiss the school's housekeeper because she was an admitted Communist party member and openly hostile to certain southern CIO officials. Since the Communists disliked the school anyway and had long tried "to impair Highlander's effectiveness," Christopher pointed out, the faculty could not risk antagonizing labor leaders whose support it could hardly afford to lose.[52] Staff members were irritated by the failure of CIO officers to fulfill their pledge of fifty students and by the planning and scheduling of the term, but they found the twenty-two black and white workers who came to the CIO school from ten unions in seven southern states an unusually able group. Because most of the national CIO officials who came to the session stayed for only one week, the term became as flexible as any Highlander residence term. One student wrote a song on securing world peace, brotherhood within the labor movement, and farmer-labor unity, while a white student, living for the first time with black workers, concluded that people of all races and religions should unite to solve their common problems.[53]

Despite the overall success of these residence sessions, there were ominous signs of a change in Highlander's relationship to the labor movement. As union officials assumed greater control over their organizations' educa-

Staff member Estelle Thompson leading a class at a Highlander CIO School, ca. 1947. *State Historical Society of Wisconsin.*

tion programs, they became more interested in using the folk school for training sessions on union policy than in allowing the HFS faculty to hold classes on a broad array of economic, political, and social issues. The increasing value placed on union discipline by CIO leaders also clashed with Highlander's emphasis on developing local union initiative, and the conflict revived old suspicions about the political loyalties of the HFS staff. In early 1947 the faculty agreed that Highlander should remain officially neutral regarding "Socialist-Communist issues" and the battle between the Progressive Citizens of America (PCA) and the Americans for Democratic Action (ADA). Personal opinions were "another matter," however, and most staff members evidently shared Myles Horton's opinion that former vice president and PCA standard-bearer Henry A. Wallace represented "the only strong voice speaking out against steps that will lead to war."[54] This sort of neutrality was unacceptable to the URWA, one of the first industrial unions to endorse the school. Disturbed by the large number of unannounced visitors and by the staff's unorthodox teaching methods during the union's two-week term in August 1947, URWA officials and students came to believe that Highlander was communistic and that every visitor "was either a spy for the rubber industry or a communist from New York." To the URWA there were too many people at HFS who did not understand the problems of union members or the South. Highlander, of course, was partly responsible for this growing independence of southern labor unions. But the consequences were nonetheless disconcerting.[55]

Highlander's program in the 1940s depended to a large extent on the willingness of southern CIO unions to use the school's services. World War II strengthened the bonds between Highlander and the CIO; the return of peace weakened them. Despite the uneven results of the residence terms and extension work, the halting steps toward integration, and the inconsistent support of the CIO, Highlander had been instrumental in the growth of southern labor unions. Between 1932 and 1947 more than 6,800 students had enrolled in HFS residence sessions and institutes, and over 12,000 union members had participated in extension classes. Most students found that their stay at Highlander gave them a broader understanding of the labor movement as well as a sense of confidence in their own abilities. Many of them subsequently became local union officers and thus were able to pass on the lessons they had learned at Highlander to union members throughout the South. In certain southern communities, such as Gadsden, Alabama, HFS alumni significantly contributed to the development of local union strength through organizing campaigns, political action programs, and community welfare projects. Student progress in improving community race relations was slower. However much they might agree on the need to end racial discrimination and prejudice, few workers of either race believed that the integration found at Highlander could be extended to the rest of the South.[56]

Meanwhile, a fundamental reordering of priorities in the American labor movement after 1945 signaled a retreat from the broad concerns of the previous decade. There were over two million organized workers in the South at the end of World War II, but the CIO southern organizing drive stalled in the face of strong employer resistance and a postwar reaction against large-scale union operations. A growing body of legislation, capped by the passage of the Taft-Hartley Act, sharply curtailed the power of organized labor. The demands of labor leaders for improved security clauses, coupled with employer demands for stronger clauses defining the rights of management, resulted in postwar contracts that committed both sides to the containment of independent activity by union members. Complicating matters for the CIO was the growing internal crisis over communism. Convinced that the Republican victory in the 1946 congressional elections made further association with Communist and other "leftist" groups politically costly, CIO leaders pledged themselves to a Democratic triumph in 1948 and condemned those who supported Henry Wallace and the Progressive party. In effect, the CIO adopted a position that tested the loyalty of its nonlabor allies. As HFS and other organizations eventually discovered, to advocate independent political action or to argue for an expansion of union militancy rather than a return to basic trade union issues meant expulsion from the CIO.[57]

Highlander's leaders could hardly agree to any narrowing of the concerns of the southern labor movement. But in identifying the school's policies and programs with those of the CIO, the HFS staff was vulnerable to pressures from union leaders. Some of them believed that staff members interfered too much in the internal politics of the CIO. Paul Christopher assured CIO secretary-treasurer James Carey that Highlander was not communistic and that it had consistently conformed to CIO policies since 1938. Even so, Christopher thought he detected "some kind of campaign against Highlander" that was having "more effect than I've observed in a long time."[58] The TWUA maintained its official distance from the school, and at a meeting with HFS representatives in January 1947 members of the Tennessee State CIO Council raised questions about the alleged Communist sympathies of several staff members. The council members admitted that much of the criticism of Highlander came from state CIO leaders and not the rank and file. Nonetheless, they wanted to know whether the school would alter its policies to conform more closely to changes in CIO policy, including the ban on activities with organizations not approved by the union. Highlander would not. Horton and his colleagues insisted that they could not shape their policies to satisfy the "whims of any particular person or group" without impairing the school's overall effectiveness.[59]

By the end of 1947, Highlander's leaders and teachers realized that they needed to find new ways to reach an even greater number of workers in the South. If the CIO had substituted organizational activity for the rank-and-file militancy of the 1930s, Highlander had not abandoned its hopes for a fundamental transformation of southern economic, political, and racial practices. In January 1948 the HFS executive council affirmed the decision to broaden the school's program. Noting with approval that a growing number of CIO unions had begun their own education programs, council members decided that the HFS staff should concentrate on strengthening unions with "less well developed educational programs." The staff should still work with southern labor unions. But Highlander should also devise "some broad principles" of cooperation with the National Farmers' Union so that it could become the union's southern education center. The "greatest contribution" the school could make to the "overall movement" for progressive change in the South, council members concluded, was to bring together "all branches of organized labor, farmers and sympathetic non-labor groups" to work on their common problems. By organizing southern farmers and developing a farmer-labor coalition, Highlander could help build a vehicle for reform more powerful than the CIO itself.[60]

The executive council meeting of 1948 marked the beginning of a momentous shift in the educational program of an institution that had been known as a "CIO School" for the past decade. It had not been an easy step to take, and it was not done without regret. "We had a movement at one time in the CIO," Myles Horton recalled in 1975. The CIO had represented not simply a drive for better wages and working conditions but also "people organizing to do things in their community, taking political action, learning about the world, carrying on educational programs to start cooperatives, to do a lot of things." Education had been "the spark that kept those things ignited," while the CIO had been the "cement" that held the movement together. If the southern labor movement had remained in the hands of the rank and file, Horton added, then the unions could have stayed "strong and fresh" as they had been in the 1930s.[61] But that freshness rapidly disappeared after World War II, creating a growing division between Highlander and the CIO and redirecting the school's efforts toward the development of a farmer-labor coalition that would speak out courageously for the rights of southern blacks.

6

Transition Years,
1944–1953

The late 1940s and early 1950s were
years of transition for the Highlander Folk School. As southerners began
to adjust to the far-reaching economic and racial changes produced by
World War II, Highlander's leaders struggled to give overall purpose and
direction to an expanded education program. The executive council's decision in January 1948 to broaden contacts with labor, farmer, and nonlabor
groups was both a reflection of the deteriorating relationship with the CIO
and a reaffirmation of goals the teaching staff had pursued since 1932,
when Myles Horton and Don West announced their intention to educate
both rural and industrial leaders for a new social order. For years staff members had done little to organize southern farmers or to include them in
their programs, and they had remained vague about how they intended to
bridge the different interests of farmers and laborers and forge a coalition
powerful enough to transform the South.

But by 1947 Horton thought he saw "signs of unity" that could be "made
to grow up to something big." He was confident that Highlander could
secure the backing of southern labor unions for a farmer-labor coalition; he
knew that the school's supporters had long been attracted to the idea of a
broad grassroots reform movement in the South; and he believed that south-

ern farmers and factory workers shared certain economic and political interests. Rural and urban workers together could lay the basis for what Horton called a "real democracy." If not, they would leave "the reigns [sic] of government in the hands of a mercenary minority."[1] By 1953, however, HFS leaders would conclude that working with existing labor and farmer organizations left unresolved the most important and most complex problem in the South—race. Thus, as much of the region tried to withstand assaults on its racial traditions, Highlander confronted the issue head-on, laying the foundation for a direct challenge to the South's most basic beliefs and practices.

The Farmers' Educational and Cooperative Union of America, commonly called the Farmers' Union, was the smallest, the second-oldest, and historically the most militant major farm organization in the country. Founded in Texas in 1902 by a former Populist and Farmers' Alliance organizer, the union spread rapidly throughout the South and into some border and western states and numbered about 117,000 members nationwide by 1910. Membership declined steadily over the next three decades, and the Upper Mississippi Valley replaced the South as the core of Farmers' Union support. But after James Patton became national president in 1940, the union grew at a rate comparable to that of the American Farm Bureau Federation and renewed its strength in the South. Many Tennessee farmers who joined the Farmers' Union in the 1940s had either been members themselves or had fathers who had belonged to it during its heyday before World War I.[2]

Highlander was not so much interested in the numerical strength of the Farmers' Union as in its ideology and potential role in a farmer-labor coalition in the South. Although the union worked primarily in behalf of middle-income farmers, HFS staff members believed that its concern with the plight of low-income farmers enhanced its chances for growth in Tennessee, where as late as 1949 around 40 percent of the state's commercial farmers sold an average of seven hundred dollars' worth of products annually. Highlander also was attracted to the union's emphasis on cooperatives as a means of curbing the exploitation of small farmers, building unity among union members, and reasserting some control over the individual farmer's livelihood. Even the position of the Farmers' Union on nonfarm issues attracted Highlander. In 1934 the union approved the admission of black farmers to its ranks, and during the 1940s it consistently backed fair employment practices legislation and other civil rights proposals. Union leaders generally agreed with the goals of organized labor, sought to overcome farmer antipathy toward labor unions, and encouraged alliances with organized workers to win legislative battles. Finally, the Farmers' Union was committed to using adult education to help farmers take intelligent action to solve their grievances.[3]

In the spring of 1943 Myles Horton decided that if Highlander was to remain "in the forefront in the fight for a progressive South," it had to begin the "pioneering job" of organizing the Farmers' Union in Tennessee.[4] Staff members would recruit an "interested nucleus" of farmers for the union, develop a program that would help them do "something real politically," and establish the basis for farmer-labor political action. After some hesitation over the scope of Horton's proposal, the HFS executive council decided in January 1944 that "farmers would be a big asset" to organized labor and authorized the staff to offer its services to the Farmers' Union.[5] Two months later state legislative representatives of the AFL, CIO, and Railroad Brotherhoods formed a committee to promote the unionization of Tennessee farmers and agreed to pay for several thousand subscriptions to the National Farmers' Union newspaper to publicize the organizing drive. Eager to take advantage of this show of support, Highlander assumed almost complete responsibility for getting the campaign under way. Aubrey Williams, former head of the National Youth Administration and southern organizing director for the Farmers' Union, made Horton the official representative of the union in Tennessee. Staff members quickly devised an education program, helped conduct meetings for potential members in various parts of Tennessee, and assigned Zilphia Horton's sister, Ermon Faye Johnson, to work full-time on the project. By the end of 1944 the National Farmers' Union had designated Highlander as its education center for the southern states.[6]

Recognizing the need to organize Tennessee farmers as the first step in training rural leaders, Highlander staff members made a symbolic beginning by forming a Farmers' Union local in Summerfield in the spring of 1944. The HFS community program had already won the support of area farm families, and Summerfield was close enough to the school to keep expenses low and allow the staff to introduce labor union members attending residence sessions to the problems of the small farmer. In March 1944 the Summerfield Cooperative voted to affiliate with the Farmers' Union, and by early May, forty-five families had paid their membership dues, elected officers, sponsored several community projects and events, formed education and political action committees, and received a charter as the first Farmers' Union local in Tennessee. Yet the Summerfield group was never a full-fledged farmers' organization. Not all of its members were full-time farmers, and the local was too small to sustain any large-scale cooperative project or to operate independently of Highlander. After 1944, union members carried on various educational and recreational activities, formed a sewing co-op, built a cooperative cannery, and contributed to the election of a pro-union slate of county, state, and national candidates in

1946. Nevertheless, by 1947 larger Farmers' Union locals in other counties overshadowed the Summerfield union, and local members gathered primarily to express their grievances and discuss current events.[7]

The HFS staff believed that Greenhaw, Tennessee, would provide a better test of the potential growth of the Farmers' Union, for the people living in and around the small Franklin County community had no previous exposure to the school's work. Beginning in November 1944, Horton met with local farm families and found considerable dissatisfaction with the Farm Bureau and with low market prices, as well as an interest in soil conservation and producers' cooperatives. Horton proceeded to establish a Farmers' Union local in the spring of 1945 and, more important, recruited a farmer who could provide leadership for the new union. Homer Crabtree, the son of an old Farmers' Alliance member and operator of a fairly large family farm, quickly assumed a prominent role in the Greenhaw local. As secretary-treasurer of the organizing committee he showed that he knew what to expect from opponents of any farmers' union. When James Stahlman of the Nashville *Banner* warned Tennessee farmers in March 1945 against being fooled by the "Communists" who sent representatives from Highlander's "hot-bed of radicalism" to recruit for the Farmers' Union, Crabtree shot back that the state's farmers did not need editors and publishers of "corrupt sheets of yellow journalism" to do their thinking for them.[8]

By mid-1945 the Greenhaw Farmers' Union was a thriving local. With about seventy paying and seventy nonpaying farm families in the union, members set up a cooperative, signed a contract to sell their crops at a price above the existing rate at the county market, and began buying fertilizer at a significant discount. Horton reported that some of the largest farmers in the county joined the Farmers' Union to take advantage of the contract, and he contended that each move made by Farm Bureau officials against the Greenhaw local increased interest in the union. After participating in a week-long leadership training institute sponsored by Highlander in July 1945, union members staged "family nights" to try to keep young people away from less productive diversions, and the education committee launched a campaign to turn the local grade school into a community recreation center. Such activities helped publicize the Farmers' Union in other parts of Tennessee. One leaflet pointed out that the Greenhaw local showed how farmers could organize and contribute to the development of "a People's movement by the Farmers of Tennessee."[9]

Highlander staff members hoped that the Greenhaw Farmers' Union would spark the expansion of the union into other areas of the state, but during 1945 and 1946 their efforts brought more verbal than financial support.

Tennessee labor unions were slow to help finance a proposed organizing campaign, and National Farmers' Union president Patton offered only words of encouragement. Determined nevertheless to cultivate the growing interest among Tennessee farmers in the union, Horton borrowed $500 from the Highlander treasury and began working full-time for the Farmers' Union in July 1945 with the aid of seventeen volunteer fieldworkers. In October the organizing drive received an important boost when the Brotherhood of Railroad Trainmen donated $3,750 to pay the expenses of Horton and another organizer. With that contribution the Farmers' Union campaign gained momentum. World War I hero Sergeant Alvin York agreed to speak on behalf of the union. In the spring of 1946 the Reverend Eugene Smathers of Big Lick, Tennessee, drafted a statement endorsing the Farmers' Union and signed by more than twenty rural ministers. That May, Horton, Smathers, Crabtree, and other farm leaders formed the Tennessee Organizing Committee of the National Farmers' Union and called for the development of farmer-owned, farmer-controlled cooperatives as part of a broad "program of economic reform."[10] The committee elected A. C. Lange of Carroll County chairman, Crabtree secretary-treasurer, Horton director of organization, Ermon Faye Johnson state education director, and Tom Ludwig state field representative.[11]

Leaders of Highlander's Farmers' Union program, ca. 1949. From left, Aubrey Williams, A. C. Lange, Tom Ludwig of the HFS staff, J. A. Knight, H. N. Hatley, national Farmers' Union president James Patton, and Myles Horton. *State Historical Society of Wisconsin.*

Ludwig had joined the HFS staff in early 1946. Born in Arkansas in 1919, Ludwig had organized a student workers' association and worked as a machinist, longshoreman, and CIO organizer while attending the University of California at Berkeley. During World War II he taught vocational counseling at Fort Oglethorpe in Georgia, encouraging black soldiers or those with union backgrounds to lead discussions on the difficulties facing returning veterans. Ludwig heard about Highlander while stationed at Oglethorpe and often took soldiers to Mary Lawrance's labor education classes in Chattanooga. When he received his discharge he decided to forgo graduate study in Europe in favor of working through the folk school to organize farmers, establish cooperatives, and secure credit for Farmers' Union members.[12]

Meanwhile, Highlander's campaign to build a strong farmers' organization in Tennessee reached its height in Greene County, a relatively prosperous area in the eastern part of the state. Local dairy farmers were generally satisfied with the prices set by the Pet Milk Company, which had a virtual monopoly of milk sales in the county. Yet they also believed that the company's procedures for weighing, testing, and handling their product were inadequate, and they chafed at their dependence on Pet Milk's purchasing and payment plans. Persuaded by Horton that the Farmers' Union was "a fighting organization," over one hundred farmers formed the first local in Greene County in August 1945 and set up a dairy cooperative to help farmers negotiate with Pet Milk.[13] Within a month the cooperative had over three hundred members, and Horton expected that there would soon be a thousand Farmers' Union members in the county. While Emmon Faye Johnson prepared an education program for the new union locals, Horton worked to counteract attempts by Farm Bureau spokesmen, local agricultural agents, and area newsmen to halt the organizing drive, and by the end of 1945 he had helped establish the East Tennessee Dairy Cooperative Association. Since farmers throughout Tennessee sold milk to condenseries, creameries, and cheese factories, the growth of the Farmers' Union in Greene County had statewide implications, Horton asserted in early 1946. Indeed, dairy farmers in adjoining counties were already asking for assistance in setting up union locals and cooperatives.[14]

For a few years the Greene County Farmers' Union was perhaps the strongest farmer organization in East Tennessee. Waging intensive publicity and organizing campaigns and working closely with members of the United Gas, Coke, and Chemical Workers inside the Pet Milk plant, Ludwig and union negotiators won agreements from the company in 1946 and 1947 providing for faster processing procedures, a licensed milk inspector at the condensery, and a Farmers' Union dues checkoff. These contracts and other projects increased interest in the union and the cooperative, and by the end of 1947 the county Farmers' Union had over five hundred members. Highlander staff members and union leaders agreed that the farmers' gains were at least partly due to the assistance of CIO members at Pet Milk, and at the staff's urging Farmers' Union and CIO officers explained the contracts to their members and established an informal farmer-labor committee. Farmers' Union members also supported several strikes during 1947 in Greeneville and in Winston-Salem, North Carolina.[15]

The growing power of the Greene County Farmers' Union stimulated HFS staff members and local leaders into expanding their efforts throughout East Tennessee. When Pet Milk officials reduced the rates they paid dairymen in the summer of 1947, cooperative officers launched a drive to organize every milk producer who sold to the company between Abingdon, Virginia, and Knoxville in order to halt further decreases. Horton and other union representatives waged a brisk organizing and educational campaign, and by the end of 1947 nearly three hundred Virginia farmers selling to Pet condenseries in Abingdon and Bristol, Tennessee, had formed five Farmers' Union locals. They established a cooperative patterned after the one in East Tennessee, placed a milk checker inside Pet's Abingdon plant, and pursued the same program that had proven so effective in Tennessee.[16]

Despite such signs of progress, there were limits to the influence of the Greene County Farmers' Union. Horton annually contended that the county union could potentially include two thousand members. But union rolls evidently never listed many more than five hundred farmers, and even a two-thousand-member local would still leave a majority of the county's six thousand farmers unorganized. Moreover, the first dues checkoff in August 1948 caused resentment among some union farmers who protested that they had not authorized anyone to deduct money from their milk checks. The union suffered a major setback in 1949 when it tried in vain to force the Greeneville Power and Light Company, a TVA distributor, to extend electric service throughout the county and then failed to secure a federal loan for an electric cooperative. The stalemate over rural electrification aggravated several other problems for the Farmers' Union and the East Tennessee Dairy Cooperative, and membership began to decline. Handicapped by the hospitalization of HFS staff member and union organizer Louis Krainock, Highlander was unable to stop the slide. By 1950 the staff's role in East Tennessee was largely confined to teaching classes at a cooperative insurance training institute, attending Virginia Farmers' Union meetings, and holding conferences at the folk school and in various communities in the area.[17]

Highlander's efforts to build the Farmers' Union in Carroll County, a section in West Tennessee somewhat poorer than Greene County, were also no more than a partial and temporary success. After meeting with Horton and Ludwig in December 1945, some fifty county farmers formed a new union and elected A. C. Lange chairman. Almost immediately the group encountered difficulties. Many potential members became skeptical when Alvin York failed to appear at a union rally; farmers refused to pay dues until the union showed signs of strength; and the county Farm Bureau gave members stock in a new cooperative to retain their allegiance. Lange, who shouldered nearly the entire burden of the organizing work himself, was reluctant to challenge local racial attitudes by admitting black farmers into the union. With the help of Horton, Ludwig, and Homer Crabtree, Lange established five Farmers' Union locals in Carroll County with between four and five hundred members by July 1946, and that fall union farmers opened a cooperative feed mill. The formation of a union local for the county's black farmers in 1947, the first such organization in the state, raised Horton's hopes that other black farmers in Tennessee would join the union, and over the next two years he and Zilphia held education conferences and rallies for both black and white union members. But after mid-1949 the Farmers' Union in Carroll County declined as rapidly as it had grown. A campaign to expand the cooperative foundered, and co-op directors failed to secure favorable freight rates. Local leaders showed no initiative and left union affairs almost completely in Lange's hands. Above all, as had been the case in Greene County, only a fraction of Carroll County's thirty-three hundred farmers joined the union.[18]

Indeed, reviving the Farmers' Union in Tennessee was proving to be more challenging than expected. Highlander's organization of union locals in a few counties, as well as its involvement in the creation of a Tri-State Farmers' Union Cooperative in Chattanooga in August 1946, had not significantly advanced the fortunes of the union in the state. Nevertheless, the National Farmers' Union board of directors considered the Tennessee organization strong enough to grant it territorial status at the end of 1946, giving it official representation at national conventions and other privileges under the union's constitution. President Patton strongly endorsed the school's successful application for a fifteen-thousand-dollar grant from the Julius Rosenwald Fund, declaring that the HFS staff was making "more fundamental progress toward building rural leadership and the development of cooperatives than any single group has in the South."[19] The Tennessee Farmers' Union had grown from two to seventeen locals during 1946, and under Ludwig's editorial direction the *Tennessee Union Farmer* developed into an eight-page monthly publication distributed throughout the state. By January 1948, Patton was ready to establish an "official connection" with the school and confirm its status as the center for the union's education program in the South.[20] Even the chances for a farmer-labor coalition seemed promising. County farmer-labor committees, the use of the Farmers' Union market in Chattanooga by striking CIO workers, and other activities suggested growing cooperation between Tennessee's organized farmers and laborers.[21]

In an attempt to build on these signs of progress, HFS staff members conducted a series of residence terms for regional, state, and local farm leaders. At its first Farmers' Union school in February 1947, the Highlander faculty held classes for twenty-six black and white Tennessee farmers on leadership training, rural health and education, farm legislation, and union-community relations, while national officials covered the history, policies, and operations of the union. The success of the one-week session suggested to Horton that union leaders could "push ahead much more rapidly" in developing "a real organization" in Tennessee.[22] Thus in July 1947 he, Aubrey Williams, and *National Union Farmer* editor Benton Stong organized a more ambitious Southwide Leadership Training School for over fifty Farmers' Union members and their allies from six southern states. HFS teachers, along with James Patton and other union officials, led discussions on parliamentary law, farmer-labor relations, agricultural and community problems, and the benefits of cooperatives. Once again students and faculty members were enthusiastic about the term, and Horton proclaimed at the last session that there were enough students "right here in this room to set the whole South on fire."[23] Highlander hosted two more Farmers' Union schools in 1948 and 1949 for members from Alabama, Tennessee, and Virginia, focusing on the types of cooperatives best suited for a given area, union and cooperative operations, and organizing techniques.[24]

But HFS staff members learned that their residence program, like their extension work, could do little for the Farmers' Union and even less for the farmer-labor coalition ideal. They took the "fairly advanced step" of offering a Farmer-Labor School in September 1947, hoping that it might lead to closer ties between organized farmers and laborers.[25] Such hopes proved far too optimistic. Both the National Farmers' Union and the CIO were unwilling to cover the expenses of the term. Staff members seemed uncertain about the kinds of courses that would attract industrial workers to the Farmer-Labor School, and their publicity reflected their ambivalence. Most disheartening was the low attendance: only sixteen Farmers' Union, labor union, and cooperative members registered for the two-week session.

Students and teachers spent much of the first week analyzing the economic problems facing working-class people in the South, forming a Farmer-Labor Cooperative Association, and opening a co-op store. During the second week the group considered farmer-labor political action with the assistance of CIO-PAC and several labor union representatives. In the end, several students promoted closer farmer-labor relations in their home towns, but the term produced no real effect at all.[26]

In December 1947 National Farmers' Union officers, Alabama union president Aubrey Williams, and Myles Horton decided to try another organizing strategy to broaden the union's appeal in the South. While they agreed that the trade union activity and politics of the "Mountain-Piedmont area" made it the "logical place" to begin a regional campaign, they also believed that such sections as southern Alabama and the Abingdon, Virginia, area offered good opportunities for smaller, more localized union development.[27] In early 1948 the *Tennessee Union Farmer* became the *Union Farmer*, with special sections for Alabama, Virginia, and Tennessee members as well as stories of union affairs throughout the South. Later that year national directors expanded Horton's jurisdiction to include Virginia, and between 1948 and 1950 HFS staff members and Farmers' Union representatives tried to sustain the organizing drive by holding a series of short education conferences in Tennessee, Alabama, and Virginia and attending various state conventions, county union board meetings, and cooperative insurance training institutes.[28]

Highlander's major project for the Farmers' Union in the late 1940s was the development of a fertilizer cooperative in south Alabama. During the spring and summer of 1947, Alabama, Tennessee, and Georgia farmers formed the Farmers' Union Fertilizer Cooperative to produce inexpensive, high-grade, and easily available fertilizer that would reduce the dominance of private companies over the market. In October 1947 the cooperative board of directors selected the area around Andalusia, Alabama, to begin operations. Tom Ludwig and local farmers J. D. Mott and Paul Bennett recruited some twelve hundred farmers for twenty Farmers' Union locals in Covington, Conecuh, and Butler Counties, sold shares in the fertilizer cooperative to area farmers, and enlisted both white and black union members to work at the plant. Ludwig then directed the construction of a large building and railroad dock in 1948, and almost immediately co-op members began saving thousands of dollars by ordering fertilizer in carload lots. By the spring of 1949 there were 850 members in the cooperative, and in November Bennett bought the first ton of fertilizer produced at the plant. Beyond the considerable reduction it brought in fertilizer costs, the cooperative seemed to demonstrate that a regional fertilizer service could be used to stimulate the growth of the Farmers' Union in the South.[29]

Indeed, neither the Farmers' Union nor Highlander showed signs of slackening their efforts at the end of the 1940s. In March 1949 national union representative Lee Fryer recommended the creation of a chain of cooperatives extending from south Alabama to western Virginia as the basis for "a fully rounded" and permanent Farmers' Union program in the South.[30] The regional cooperative campaign developed rapidly under Ludwig's direction. By mid-1949 over twenty stores in south Alabama were handling Farmers' Union label feed; carloads of insecticides were coming into south Alabama; distribution centers extended into north Alabama; and negotiations were under way to provide milling services for union members in Tennessee and Virginia. To finance the system, Aubrey Williams and Myles Horton formed Farmers' Union insurance companies in Alabama, Virginia, and Tennessee. In 1950 and 1951 HFS staff members conducted educational projects designed to promote union programs. For example, following a leadership training institute in Altoona, Alabama, in 1950, local farmers completed construction of a feed cooperative, established a cooperative cotton gin and store, and furnished food to striking miners in the area.[31]

Although these activities seemed to portend a bright future for the Farmers' Union in the South, national officers abruptly decided to withdraw from the region in 1951 and concentrate their resources in the Midwest, where the union already had substantial strength. The reasons for the shift in policy were never made clear. Union leaders had never been significantly committed to the South; Fryer had proposed the regional cooperative system in part because he believed that more cooperatives should be organized before other projects received funding. But as Horton remarked in 1949, the cooperative federation moved "about as fast as sorghum molasses does in the wintertime," and the poverty of many southern farmers, aggravated by sharp declines in net farm income in 1949 and 1950, made it difficult to accumulate much capital for the Farmers' Union.[32]

Organizing strategies and a relatively small southern membership may have hastened the departure of the National Farmers' Union. The Farm Bureau made greater headway than the union in the South after World War II because it adjusted more effectively to changing patterns in southern agriculture, including the migration of small farmers to urban areas and the declining number and increased acreage of individual farms. The Farmers' Union advocacy of racial integration and cooperation with organized labor may have appealed to the Highlander staff, but it often hindered organizing campaigns among southern white farmers. Farm Bureau membership in the South rose 53 percent between 1945 and 1950, from 311,899 to 477,290. Farmers' Union family memberships in the region, though they increased 121 percent between 1938 and 1953, still totaled only 59,389 in 1953. James Patton's centralization of power at the national level also clashed with Highlander's faith in the capabilities of grassroots leadership and, in Horton's opinion, neglected the specific needs of union members in the South.[33]

Finally, the Farmers' Union retreat from the South may have stemmed from the effects of the Cold War on organized labor and allies like Highlander. In 1949 a Greene County union leader was accused of associating with "a known Communist, Myles Horton," and a journalist covering the 1949 Alabama Farmers' Union convention for *Alabama,* a magazine representing large farming interests in the state, belittled the union, Zilphia Horton, and "her notoriously radical husband."[34] Highlander had long experience in dealing with such charges, but the attacks carried weight with the Farmers' Union. Although its national convention decided not to take an explicitly anti-Communist stand in 1948, delegates yielded on the issue in 1952. Meanwhile, the increasingly cautious CIO intensified the pressure. In 1948 the Tennessee State CIO Council questioned whether its contribution to the *Union Farmer* was warranted, given the newspaper's alleged endorsement of presidential candidate Henry Wallace. Myles Horton pointed out that the Tennessee Farmers' Union received little support from the CIO other than a few favorable resolutions, but CIO officials remained skeptical. The CIO was acting "like a spoiled baby," Ludwig angrily wrote in 1952, demanding that the Farmers' Union "hold its hand but not hold hands with anybody else" even as the labor organization befriended the Farm Bureau.[35]

Political and financial considerations may indeed have lain behind the Farmers' Union decision to pull out of the South. Yet Horton offered the most telling insight into the short-lived attempt to revive the union when he concluded years later that Highlander, which had conducted labor education programs in response to the rise of the southern labor movement, had reversed the process and tried to develop an education program for a farmers' movement that did not exist. The Farmers' Union program was never a major part of the school's overall work, and only a very small number of union farmers attended residence terms at HFS. Yet the effort added another dimension to Highlander's reputation as a place where black and white farmers and industrial workers could discuss their common concerns. Tom Ludwig later asserted that the program was a "brilliant failure," for if the staff had not found a solution to the fundamental problems facing southern farmers, it had helped a few thousand farmers in Tennessee, Alabama, and Virginia learn how to address those problems and regain some control over their lives.[36]

During the years Myles and Zilphia Horton and Tom Ludwig spent working with the Farmers' Union, Bill and Mary Lawrance Elkuss supervised education programs for southern industrial unions. Generally the work proceeded smoothly, and Highlander continued to reach a large number of union members across the South. But the excitement and sense of purpose that had infused the programs in the past had faded in the late 1940s. In 1948 nearly 140 students representing local textile, rubber, and mine workers' unions in ten southern states attended residence sessions, and the extension program served several hundred union members in Tennessee, South Carolina, Georgia, and Alabama. At the small but effective Fifth Annual Southern CIO School in September 1948, members of the national CIO education department and several regional and state officials helped the HFS staff teach subjects covered during earlier CIO schools. As in most of the other residence terms that year, there was good rapport between black and white students. Highlander's work with labor unions declined when Bill and Mary Elkuss left the staff in 1949. Nevertheless, extension courses and residence sessions that year reached 1,001 students.[37]

A new feature of Highlander's program in the late 1940s and early 1950s was a Film Center. Emil Willimetz, a former student who had been working as a photographer at the school, proposed in 1948 that he and two filmmakers produce and distribute low-cost documentary films and other visual aids and train local union leaders in their use. Operating as a self-sustaining group, the Film Center staff gave demonstrations on the use of filmstrips and other graphic materials at residence sessions; showed films and led discussions at education conferences; trained union organizers in photography; established movie circuits for southern labor and farmers' union locals; and recorded various events for Highlander publicity and fundraising campaigns. The center steadily expanded as the demand from unions and other organizations increased. However, many of these groups were unable to pay for its services, creating a drain on Highlander's resources. The common perception that the center was an integral part of the school compelled the faculty to ensure its survival—and at considerable cost—until persistent financial difficulties finally closed the center in 1954.[38]

The Highlander faculty also revived its community program in the late 1940s in an effort to strengthen local acceptance of the school and its interracial activities. Staff members showed movies and taught folk songs at the local grammar school, sponsored a sewing co-op, held square dances and other recreational events, began a farm demonstration project, and guided production of the *Summerfield News*. Zilphia Horton was president of a community club between 1950 and 1952. New facilities also made Highlander more attractive to local residents. A community building opened in 1947. Unitarian work campers helped complete construction of the Harry Lasker Memorial Library in 1948, and other Unitarian work groups landscaped the grounds around Highlander Lake, a three-acre artificial lake that was ready for use in 1953. Meanwhile, Joanna Creighton joined the staff in 1948 to work full-time in the Summerfield community. Creighton, who received her professional training under former staff member Claudia Lewis at the Bank Street School for Teachers in New York, reopened the HFS nursery school and made it the core of a coordinated community program by early 1949. These efforts seemed to improve relations between Highlander and Summerfield residents by the early 1950s, leading HFS leaders to hope that enough community support existed to allow them to push for even greater change in the South.[39]

Yet operating such a wide array of programs and projects placed serious strains on Highlander's financial resources in the late 1940s and the early 1950s. The HFS treasury hit "rock-bottom" in early 1948, and the faculty devoted a good deal of time over the next several years to organizing fundraising committees and contacting potential donors, particularly in major cities outside the South.[40] Publicity about the folk school stressed its work with well over 20,000 farmer and labor leaders between 1932 and 1948, its promotion of greater farmer-labor unity, and the implications of its interracial policy. The half-hearted response of organized labor deeply troubled HFS leaders. Contributions from individuals rose from $7,898 in 1946 to $20,064 in 1947, and over the next four years averaged $17,311 annually. Foundation grants reached a postwar high of $14,303 in 1948 before dropping sharply in 1949, 1950, and 1951. In contrast, union contributions and payments to the school totaled over $6,600 in 1946 but fell to $930 in 1948; in 1950 and 1951 labor groups donated less than $800. This decline was partly the result of the unions' growing investment in their own education departments, a trend Horton regarded as "inevitable and advisable." Yet C. W. Danenburg of the United Chemical Workers reached the crux of the issue when he stated in 1949 that CIO unions might contribute more money if Highlander took "a public position on the question of the fight between left and right wing forces in the CIO."[41]

As Danenburg's comment suggests, the growing crisis over communism within the American labor movement was altering not only the structure and functions of labor unions but also the relationship between organized labor and institutions like Highlander. The problem presented little difficulty for the AFL, with its long history of anti-Communism. But it was a far more serious matter for the CIO. Communists had been prominent figures in the CIO from its beginning, accepted for their organizing skills and their commitment to industrial unionism. After World War II, however, the Communist issue sparked bitter factional battles within some CIO affiliates and divided union leaders over whether to channel the CIO's political power through the Democratic party or through an independent third party. Soviet-American conflicts, Republican victories in the 1946 congressional elections, the subsequent passage of the Taft-Hartley Act, and President Harry Truman's restored standing among labor unions because of his opposition to the measure intensified the pressure. The Communists' decision to commit themselves in the 1948 election to the Progressive party and its presidential candidate, Henry Wallace, coupled with Truman's unexpected victory, provided the final impetus for the expulsion of Communist-led unions. Delegates at the 1949 CIO convention, charging that left-wing unions put the interests of the Communist party before something called "CIO policy," voted to expel the United Electrical, Radio, and Machine Workers and the Farm Equipment Workers, and by mid-1950 unions claiming to represent over one million members had been driven out of the CIO.[42]

The Communist expulsions ended all serious political debate within the CIO and signaled that its crusading days were over. Much less time, money, and attention would be given to those outside organized labor. Instead, the CIO would concentrate on gaining concessions for a more disciplined rank and file. Those still attached to the idea of a popular front searched for some way to distinguish between what they called totalitarianism and democracy or tried in vain to defend the rights of Communists while remaining independent of them. Neither position could prevent the demise of the Southern Conference for Human Welfare in 1948 or the Communist-front charges lodged against the Southern Conference Educational Fund in 1950. Other institutions, such as the Southern School for Workers and the Georgia Workers Education School, closed in 1950 for lack of union support.[43]

The Communist controversy within the CIO also took its toll on Highlander and decisively affected its educational program. The troubles began during the CIO's postwar southern organizing drive, when director Van Bittner not only excluded staff members from the campaign but also became incensed when one of his more proficient organizers, Louis Krainock, joined the HFS faculty in early 1948. Nearly a year later Myles Horton was concerned that a "very unhealthy situation" still existed between the CIO and HFS.[44] Indeed, Horton's alleged attacks on union leaders for straying from the "liberal movement," his supposed endorsement of Henry Wallace, his opposition to loyalty tests and to the outlawing of the Communist party, and his willingness to have a Progressive party conference at the school did nothing to calm union officers.[45] For his part, Horton was worried that CIO leaders intended to follow "no consistent principle" unless it served the union's needs "at a given moment." Their criticism of Highlander's residence terms for the leftist-led FTA and MMSW because they were "unofficially on the CIO's blacklist" seemed to mean that the HFS staff was to "ignore at times the expressed policy of the organization as a whole and line up with the controlling faction." (It was perhaps no coincidence that both the MMSW and FTA were more racially integrated and more vigorous supporters of civil rights than other southern CIO unions; FTA also counted a notable number of black women as officials and organizers.)[46]

The increasing pressure to conform to national CIO policy divided the executive council at its January 1949 meeting. C. W. Danenburg declared that the only question was whether Highlander "should try to satisfy those groups which demand a public statement." To do so, Horton asserted, would require changing the school's policy of pursuing "a positive, not a negative, program," and he doubted that any statement would halt rumors "circulated by people who know they are not true anyway." After considerable debate, the council appointed a committee composed of Horton, Aubrey Williams, and Paul Christopher to draw up a revised statement of purpose. When the committee could not agree on a suitable revision, the council postponed any decision until it had drafted a statement satisfactory to the CIO and the school.[47]

It soon became clear that it would be difficult for Highlander to meet the demands of the CIO. In March 1949 Horton met with CIO education director Stanley Ruttenberg and associate director George Guernsey in Washington. He found them "extremely friendly" and willing to accept a simple statement from Highlander affirming its "program for democracy." He received a much different message from CIO general counsel Arthur J. Goldberg. Declaring that the day had passed when someone "could carry water on both shoulders," Goldberg maintained that the HFS staff had little choice but to follow CIO policy if it wanted to work with the union in the South, even though the faculty also worked with organizations other than the CIO. Although convinced that "any effort to compromise would be futile," Horton agreed with Ruttenberg to "let things drift along" unless the issue upset plans for a scheduled CIO-Rubber Workers session at

Highlander.[48] In June, Guernsey suddenly notified Horton that the CIO had decided to cancel the term. Ruttenberg explained that it had become virtually impossible to recruit enough students to go to Highlander because two or three southern directors believed there was "some left wing 'Communist' influence" at the school. Ruttenberg did not share this opinion, but he noted that the HFS council had not approved an amended statement of purpose condemning "all kinds of totalitarianism including communism, fascism and nazism" which would allow the CIO to send students to HFS.[49] When Horton demanded to know the names of the southern directors making such charges and asked about Highlander's freedom to work with other groups, Ruttenberg curtly replied that Horton was raising "false issues" and that he would recommend the removal of the school from the CIO's list of approved organizations.[50]

Horton responded by upholding Highlander's traditional determination to remain an independent institution. "I am at sea as to the meaning of democracy if the right to face ones' [sic] accusers has become a false issue," Horton protested. He saw nothing wrong in questioning the implications of the CIO's proposed amendments. He argued that a school serving a variety of groups should not take "a public position" on matters affecting those organizations, and any statement adopted by the HFS council should oppose all forms of totalitarianism. Horton also had reservations about the influence of the anti-Communist Association of Catholic Trade Unionists on Catholic labor leaders, but in raising the issue he had been branded as a religious bigot and an "anti-Catholic Southerner."[51] Horton's objection needlessly created further controversy. Nevertheless, he did not intend to allow the CIO to call Highlander Communist when to him the real issue was the role of the Catholic church in the labor movement. Since 1934 HFS leaders had consistently stated that the school was unaffiliated with any political party. If Highlander now permitted one group to determine its policies, there was little chance that it would survive, for the history of American labor schools showed that no "partisan school" ever lasted very long. Highlander therefore would go its own way and pursue its growing interest in interracial problems until the crisis had passed.[52]

Horton's stand revealed another side of the Highlander "tradition"—the nagging doubts in some people's minds that Horton fully appreciated the CIO's fear that communism could destroy the labor movement. Several union and nonunion supporters backed the school's determination to remain independent. But they also worried that Horton was clouding the issue and making it impossible for CIO affiliates to come to Highlander's aid. Paul Christopher assured Ruttenberg that Horton had always been "a strong Socialist" who possessed "an amazing tolerance of the viewpoints of others, including Communists," and a tenacious belief in the right to support certain ideas and organizations without condemning ideas and organizations opposed to them. Even though the end of the cordial relationship between the CIO and Highlander could have "embarrassing repercussions" for both sides, Christopher acknowledged that if HFS leaders refused to take a forthright stand against the Communists the union had no choice but to sever its ties with the school.[53] Roger Baldwin of the ACLU also believed that Horton was hedging on "a clear moral issue." Since the CIO wanted only a declaration that Highlander was a "pro-democratic institution," not that it accepted all CIO policies, the council should announce its rejection of all "anti-democratic influences" before the dispute became uncontrollable.[54]

Highlander's leaders tried to meet the CIO halfway without compromising the school's independence. Shortly before the November 1949 council meeting, Horton, Aubrey Williams, George Guernsey, CIO Southern Organizing Drive director George Baldanzi, and CIO southern public relations director Lucy Randolph Mason drafted a revised statement of principles. The key section read: "With a democratic goal, we are in a position to fight anything that gets in the way, whether it be totalitarian communism or fascism or monopoly-dominated capitalism." Stanley Ruttenberg then asked that part of the clause be changed to read: "whether it be [the] totalitarianism of communism or fascism, or the monopoly-domination of capitalism." Such quibbling made it "meaningless" to discuss the original statement, Horton declared to council members. Fearing that the CIO might well demand more concessions, the council decided to remove the entire clause from the Highlander policy statement.[55]

With the onus of the controversy on them, CIO officials sought to come to terms with Highlander. In December 1949 Guernsey requested a revision of the HFS council meeting minutes to make the CIO's position seem less harsh and leave room for further negotiations. In the revised version, Mason indicated that the CIO wanted an "acceptable" statement on communism from Highlander, "voluntary concessions" regarding its services to CIO rivals, and possibly some determination of council membership.[56] Horton objected to this obvious attempt to control Highlander's policies and programs. Guernsey then suggested in early 1950 that if the executive council adopted the original policy statement the CIO would resume relations with Highlander. Horton was skeptical about the proposal. He had discovered that the Communist charges against Highlander came primarily from three CIO officers—Roy R. Lawrence of North Carolina, W. A.

Copeland of Tennessee, and Carey Haigler of Alabama—who equated interracial practices with communism because they countenanced racial discrimination in their unions. But once Ruttenberg gave assurances that the CIO desired only a statement similar to the one initially adopted, the HFS council unanimously voted in April 1950 to insert the original amendment into the school's statement of purpose.[57] (See Appendix 1 for approved statement of purpose.)

Horton regarded this resolution as a victory for Highlander; evidently the CIO had accepted the staff's intention to pursue an independent, flexible, and positive program. In his view the whole dispute had been an "embarrassing and uncalled for episode" arising from the CIO's preoccupation with its "internal problems," and the HFS faculty should "never again" allow such a crisis to inhibit its teaching effectiveness.[58] He regretted that he had injected the question of Catholic trade union activities into the conflict. But George Baldanzi's announcement in mid-1950 that "it was part of CIO policy to support" Highlander meant that the way was now clear for the development of some badly needed education programs for CIO members in the South.[59]

Yet the folk school was hardly free of the suspicions generated by the volatile combination of interracial education and Cold War politics. In the fall of 1950 Horton learned that two FBI agents had been asking Summerfield residents about black students at HFS and reportedly implying that its nondiscriminatory policy "would be considered communistic by a majority of Southern people."[60] Horton wondered why the agents chose "to harass neighbors with questions linking Negroes with communism" when "they could catch us red handed practicing racial democracy by a visit to the school."[61] The effect of the investigation was nonetheless clear: previously tolerant neighbors were once again having doubts about Highlander's racially integrated classes. In the spring of 1951, as he worked to allay the misgivings of Summerfield citizens, Horton pressed the FBI to consent to the HFS council's demand for written interviews. Having ordered the bureau's active file on Highlander closed nearly a decade earlier, FBI director J. Edgar Hoover was furious that his agents had discussed the school with anyone, tried to explain away their refusal to respond to Horton's protest by dismissing him as a "trouble maker," and investigated HFS "in a crude and inept manner."[62] The public position of the bureau, however, was that no official investigation of the school had taken place, and when neither the Department of Justice nor the ACLU offered help, Horton reluctantly concluded in June 1951 that the matter should be dropped. Highlander remained off the attorney general's list of subversive organizations. But the staff was only beginning to appreciate the extent to which some people in postwar America believed that the school was communistic because it was racially integrated.[63]

Though Highlander had weathered the storms of the past few years, the turmoil had had a chilling effect on the creativity and vitality of its education program in the early 1950s. The school became more a place where unions sponsored conferences or training sessions on specific topics than a center where southern farmer and labor leaders learned to organize and work on their common problems. To be sure, the residence and extension programs remained fairly active. CIO education and research department officials sponsored one-week interracial terms at HFS in 1951, 1952, and 1953 as part of their attempt to keep the Southern Organizing Campaign alive. Several individual unions held sessions at Highlander between 1950 and 1953, and the HFS faculty carried out extension projects for labor, farmer, and cooperative groups in virtually every southern state. A series of conferences, seminars, and workshops conducted in the early 1950s for representatives of rural community centers, ministers, union leaders, and college students, as well as the participation of staff members in numerous meetings on education, labor, religion, and racial discrimination, added to Highlander's regional and national reputation. Yet Highlander's efforts seemed to lack the spark evident in previous years, and they reflected the growing distance between the school and organized labor.[64]

Myles Horton made one more attempt to shore up Highlander's battered relationship with the labor movement when he agreed in 1951 to direct an education program for the United Packinghouse Workers of America (UPWA). Highlander's involvement was to be limited, but the project seemed worthwhile to Horton, staff members, and the executive council for several reasons. UPWA officers wanted Highlander's help in implementing their plans for an extensive education program in the South, and a contemporary survey showed that a large majority of union members were willing to attend union-sponsored classes. UPWA members could also appreciate the merits of a farmer-labor alliance, for many of them worked in plants that processed farm products. In Horton's opinion the UPWA had the best record among unions in the South in addressing racial issues: the number of African-American members had been growing since World War II, and blacks occupied local leadership positions throughout the nation. Finally, the absence of an anti-Communist amendment in the UPWA constitution led Horton to believe that he could conduct an educational program that was in line with Highlander's own policies. He admitted to the HFS council that the undertaking might not advance the school's long-term interests. But he pointed out that his job with the union provided funds for other projects and offered a chance to test labor education techniques both inside and outside the South. Highlander and the UPWA, he added, would work together as long as they agreed on the purposes of the program and the union's education staff did a satisfactory job.[65]

Horton planned to organize an education staff that would start an instructor-training program and extend it to every UPWA local. Like previous HFS extension projects, the UPWA program would be based on what Horton now called the "percolator" system, in which ideas came "from the workers up," instead of the "drip" system, in which union officials transmitted policy from the international to the local.[66] Once the education staff had begun shop steward-training courses in union districts across the country, Horton hoped to turn the classes over to local discussion leaders or instructors, thereby freeing the staff and field representatives for a more general program covering race relations, farmer-labor relations, political action, and other issues. In time, Horton contended, the entire program could become self-sufficient as UPWA locals learned how to manage their own affairs. UPWA district directors therefore should not expect "conventional or immediate results"; it took time to make union members realize that "education had to do with recognized problems and that the solution is in their hands."[67]

The first task was to develop a new UPWA education staff. In early 1952 Horton, HFS staff members, and union officials conducted a month-long training session at Highlander and at Camden, New Jersey, for five educational representatives selected from more than one hundred candidates. The three-man, two-woman staff studied the union's goals and activities, practiced teaching techniques, and wrote two instructor's manuals for shop steward classes. The group then began working in five districts—Des Moines, Kansas City, Fort Wayne, New York City, and Atlanta—where UPWA organizing drives were in progress. Some UPWA teachers proved more effective than others, and some union officials hesitated to accept the instructor-training program and the strengthening of shop steward functions. Nevertheless, Horton was able to report some encouraging results at the UPWA constitutional convention in May 1952. A number of UPWA locals had begun to hold their own steward-training sessions; new leadership had emerged in several locals; and officers had noted a marked improvement in the handling of grievances, increased attendance at union meetings, and "a more energetic dealing with management in general."[68]

Following the UPWA convention, Horton's staff devoted the rest of 1952 to the second step in the education program—the training of local union instructors. By the end of the year forty instructors had begun to achieve results similar to those attained by the education staff and on a much larger scale. Through their shop steward classes and discussions at local union meetings, the instructors stimulated the formation of organizing committees, strengthened the UPWA steward and committee systems, and initiated a variety of projects ranging from flood relief to political action. Meanwhile, the education staff continued to hold district and local leadership schools, steward-training sessions, and conferences with UPWA executive boards, steward councils, and union committees. The leadership schools led to the breakup of formerly all-white departments and to an increase in the number of black, Mexican-American, and women stewards. While Horton acknowledged that a few UPWA officials still resisted the program's unconventional teaching approach, he remained confident that it would eventually demonstrate that UPWA members were "capable of handling their own affairs, including union education."[69]

Yet organizational, political, and racial problems hounded Horton and his UPWA staff almost from the beginning of their work. Despite Horton's pleas for time and cooperation, union officers grew impatient with the inexperience of the staff and the progress, direction, and costs of the program. In April 1952 Lewis Corey, an ex-Communist who had been an enemy of Highlander for years and who had become education director of the UPWA's AFL rival, the Amalgamated Meat Cutters and Butcher Workmen, charged that Communists were controlling the UPWA. As proof he cited the appointment of Horton as UPWA education director, a man who had been "under attack for at least fifteen years as a communist" and whose folk school was "known as a communist front."[70] Horton quickly ended the controversy by publicizing the Amalgamated's past support of Highlander. But it was not so easy to combat opposition within the UPWA to the union's nondiscrimination policy. One staff member reported that prejudice and indifference at an Indiana plant had stymied efforts to desegregate several all-white departments and that there was little backing anywhere in his district for the union's antidiscrimination drive.[71]

Above all, the education program provoked increasing resistance from UPWA officials who sensed a challenge to their authority. Vice-President A. T. Stephens led the opposition. In August 1952 he began to voice his displeasure with the expenditures of the education department, its departure from the original idea of educating UPWA members on specific union concerns, its declining number of classes, and its inability to promote the antidiscrimination campaign. Schools in certain areas had been ineffective, Stephens contended, because they had not been run by the union's regular forty-member staff. He therefore had no intention of scheduling further schools until "some basic policy matters" had been "straightened out" and the education program showed "a heck of a lot more direction."[72] In reply, Horton blamed the lack of cooperation shown by UPWA field representatives for at least some of the problems, and he remained firm in his commitment to the training of local union instructors. By the end of 1952 the dispute was clearly defined. Stephens wanted a "drip" system of education emphasizing topics selected by the union hierarchy, an approach exactly opposite from Horton's "percolator" system that stressed the development of leadership from the rank and file.[73]

The HFS executive council had its own misgivings about the value of the UPWA program to Highlander. In December 1952 several members questioned whether the school was gaining any advantage from its association with the union, since Horton's involvement in the project had forced the faculty to make potentially costly adjustments at HFS. Pointing to the overall similarities in the goals of Highlander and the UPWA, Horton insisted that opposition to the education program would cease once union officials realized how much it freed field representatives for other endeavors. The program's basic principles were sound; it was completely financed by the union; it could be duplicated; and it offered an unprecedented opportunity for Highlander to influence the entire American labor movement. Persuaded by Horton's arguments, the council approved the Highlander-UPWA arrangement for the next fiscal year.[74]

Within six months of the council meeting, Horton's faith that the HFS-UPWA relationship could survive and prosper had been demolished. In January 1953 Stephens proposed that the education staff be replaced by district program coordinators under the direction of Vice-President Russell Lasley and himself. Instead of building local union leadership, the coordinators would promote those parts of the UPWA program that met the specific needs of each district at a given time. Stephens brushed aside Horton's suggestions that the education and coordinator programs be combined and that union members should discuss rather than be told what to do in their locals. Any possibility of compromise disappeared when Stephens and the coordinators held a UPWA staff school at Highlander in March 1953. Excluded from the term's planning sessions, Horton found the classes so arbitrarily conducted and so divorced from the intent of the education program that he resigned from the UPWA the day the school ended. He later reported to the HFS council that none of the ideas or personnel developed by the education staff had been carried over into the coordinator program. The education program had been dropped largely because it had not enhanced "the political strength of some of the more ambitious International officials."[75] Yet it had proven that UPWA members were capable of educating themselves and that Highlander's teaching approach could be adopted by unions throughout the country.[76]

Another, perhaps ironic, result of Horton's resignation was the dissolution of Highlander's official relationship with the CIO. In August 1953 Paul Christopher informed Horton that HFS had been removed from the CIO list of approved schools. No one at the national CIO office offered an explanation for the decision. Horton later learned that CIO officials had mistakenly identified Highlander with the allegedly Communist UPWA staff school held at HFS earlier that year. The UPWA had been cleared of those charges, and CIO leaders reportedly "had a big laugh" when they discovered that HFS had severed its connections with the UPWA because of the school, but no one took Highlander off the CIO blacklist.[77] Another source told Horton that a union official criticized by the HFS faculty for his Jim Crow policies and use of Ku Klux Klan sympathizers as organizers had initiated the CIO action against the school. Once more the staff found itself victimized by the loose association of racial integration with communism. Weary of the CIO's somersaults over the past several years, Horton reaffirmed Highlander's willingness to serve the southern labor movement and anyone else who wanted its help.[78]

Highlander faced yet another crisis in February 1952 when a tornado ripped through the school grounds, but in this case the tenacity of the HFS community and the generosity of supporters brought positive results. The tornado demolished part of the Horton family home; twisted the roofs off the main building, library, and nursery-community building; damaged several smaller structures; and uprooted hundreds of trees. No one was injured, but Highlander had practically no insurance to cover the more than fifteen-thousand-dollar damage done to the buildings. It was thus an indication of the school's value to the Summerfield community that neighbors arrived to help twenty minutes after the storm had passed and then attended a community meeting at HFS the next night to plan tree-clearing operations. It was also a measure of the staff's dedication to its work that field trips and residence sessions proceeded on schedule, and the Film Center, library, and nursery school reopened within two weeks of the tornado. Highlander committees throughout the country launched emergency fundraising efforts, and many individuals renewed and raised their annual donations. By the end of September 1952 the school's total income had risen to over $66,500, its highest level in several years. Highlander was clearly in a position to be of greater service to unions in the South.[79]

Myles Horton.
State Historical
Society of Wisconsin.

Zilphia Horton.
State Historical
Society of Wisconsin.

By the end of 1952, however, Highlander's leaders were ready to explore new approaches to new issues. As Myles Horton drolly observed, the tornado had somewhat forcefully reminded him that "institutions should be destroyed every twenty years and obliged to start over."[80] Thousands of men and women had been educated at Highlander and across the South after World War II, but the campaign for a farmer-labor coalition had not succeeded, and the school's relations with organized labor never completely recovered from the controversies with the CIO. Zilphia Horton lamented in 1952 that unions had "become so reactionary and . . . so complacent" that they had "lost their ideals, and I don't care anything about singing for people like that."[81] These and other experiences had taught staff members that an enormous obstacle had to be overcome before they could attain the kind of political and economic order they had envisioned since 1932. Whenever they had tried to build unions, coalitions, or virtually anything else, they had eventually confronted the barrier of racism. The past two decades had established Highlander's reputation among labor, farmer, interracial, religious, and progressive organizations, and the advances made by these groups had demonstrated the value of its teaching techniques. What was now needed was a program to unite black and white people in a struggle for common goals.

The best way to restore Highlander's sense of purpose and direction, Myles Horton concluded, was through a revitalized education program. In December 1952 he pointed out to the executive council that in recent CIO residence terms there had been "too much top down stuff" that did not meet the needs of union members. Highlander should be "moving out," he asserted, setting an educational agenda that "cut across all lines," attracted people without regard to affiliation, and promoted the school's overall policies. Council chairman George Mitchell of the Southern Regional Council agreed that staff members should work on the broadest and most significant problems facing all southerners, thereby giving the school "a new vitality" and creating "something new for the people of the South, a movement of the people."[82] With this vague declaration of independence and an enthusiasm recalling the early days of its involvement in the southern labor movement, the HFS staff began a program that soon centered on the issue of public school desegregation. During the ensuing decade Highlander would become the education center of a movement that profoundly challenged and reshaped not only southern society but the entire nation.

7

From School Desegregation to Student Sit-Ins, 1953–1961

"We are at our best at Highlander when we are pioneering," Myles Horton declared in 1953, and until 1961 the Tennessee school was in the forefront of the drive to end racial segregation in the South.[1] Highlander's programs during the 1950s reflected the growing struggle for legal, political, and social equality by black Americans. Indeed, to a great extent the focus and direction of the staff's work came to depend upon the civil rights movement. It furnished HFS teachers with powerful allies who could join them in confronting the racial prejudice that had frustrated their efforts to organize industrial workers and small farmers. It gave the folk school the clear-cut purpose it had largely lacked since the end of World War II. Its gains demonstrated the effectiveness of Highlander's educational approach and helped spread those techniques throughout the South. And its goals and rhetoric expressed the faculty's own vaguely defined vision of a more democratic and humane political and economic system.

Highlander had been ready for the civil rights movement for a long time. From the beginning of the school in 1932, Myles Horton and his colleagues had been committed to interracial education. During the 1930s and 1940s, however, most southern labor union leaders did not share that commitment, and, despite extension projects involving black and white laborers and the decision in 1942 to integrate HFS classes, only white students attended residence terms until 1944. In the late 1940s and early 1950s, staff members turned their attention to strengthening the education programs of unions that frequently included a large percentage of black members. They organized both black and white farmers for the Farmers' Union and encouraged them to participate in residence workshops and cooperative enterprises together. Under Horton's direction, the UPWA education program had trained local officers to recognize and end racial discrimination in their locals. By 1953 Highlander's teachers had made local and regional leaders of numerous organizations aware that there was a school in the South where blacks and whites could meet to explore their common interests, and they had gained the respect of those pushing for racial equality. Black journalist Carl T. Rowan asserted in 1952 that only a few white southerners like Horton were willing to "go further" than "the Southern liberals, the 'freedom-for-you-sometime-soon' gradualists" and to say that racial segregation was the "root and perpetrator of all the evils" facing the modern South.[2]

Highlander was thus prepared to both anticipate and respond to important developments in race relations during the 1950s. In April 1953, as the Supreme Court was considering the case of *Brown v. Board of Education of Topeka, Kansas,* the HFS executive council met to determine "the most pressing problem for the people of the South" that the school could take on. Asserting that the greatest challenge was "not the problem of conquering poverty, but conquering meanness, prejudice and tradition," George Mitchell submitted that Highlander's "new emphasis" should be on the desegregation of public schools. This program, he believed, would have an immediate relevance to "the coming upheaval in the South" following the Supreme Court's ruling either to outlaw school segregation or to enforce complete equality in educational facilities.

Mitchell's proposal represented a gamble for Highlander. There was no indication that the *Brown* decision would be far-reaching, nor any certainty that the HFS staff could bring black and white southerners together on so sensitive an issue as school desegregation. But the council finally decided that the time had come for Highlander "to extend its activities into wider fields of full democratization." The staff should hold two experimental workshops during the summer of 1953 that would prepare representatives of labor, church, interracial, and civic groups to provide leadership during the transition from a segregated to an integrated public school system in the South. Characteristically, HFS leaders acknowledged that the desegregation program was "a tremendous undertaking" but predicted that with the cooperation of many individuals and organizations "the job can be done."[3]

Highlander's 1953 workshops on "The Supreme Court Decisions and the Public Schools" were carefully designed to lay the groundwork for school desegregation drives in the South. Irene Osborne of the American Friends Service Committee, who had worked with civic groups to desegregate schools in Washington, D.C., helped plan and conduct the two sessions. To provide a black perspective on the issue, Paul Bennett, a graduate student at Howard University and a former Farmers' Union leader in Alabama, served as director of the workshops. The seventy-one northerners and southerners who attended the sessions generally assumed that the Supreme Court would deliver some sort of antisegregation ruling, and they regarded the pending decision as an unprecedented opportunity to develop useful approaches to the integration of public schools in the South. Workshop members agreed that desegregation had to be a "grass-roots affair," with citizens working through community groups to push school and other public officials into action. Anna Kelly of Charleston, South Carolina, cited as an example the meetings called by her local YWCA and other interested organizations to "prepare a favorable climate" in the city for the anticipated Supreme Court ruling.[4]

Following further discussions, participants produced materials designed to help them proceed with local school desegregation efforts. A guide and checklist based on Osborne's mimeographed "Working Toward Integrated Public Schools in Your Own Community" outlined how a campaign could grow from a small interracial core of influential people to a coordinated effort involving various organizations committed to school integration. A committee led by Dean B. R. Brazeal of Morehouse College drew up a report calling for the integration of public school faculties as part of any desegregation plan. Workshop members also helped create a filmstrip, *The High Cost of Segregation,* depicting the ill effects of segregation on housing and health as well as schools, and compiled a list of films and filmstrips on similar topics. With these workshops Highlander had confronted what its staff called "The South's Number One Problem" almost a year before the Supreme Court handed down its decision in *Brown v. Board of Education.*[5]

Clearly, Horton wrote in late 1953, Highlander was "on the right track" in its approach to public school integration.[6] It was also obvious that a larger staff would be needed to refine the plans devised at the initial workshops and help students implement those plans in communities throughout the South. The closing of the financially troubled Film Center in February 1954 meant the loss of Emil and Joanna Creighton Willimetz as well as Mort and Ann Isaacs, who had been on the staff since November

1952. The burden of carrying on Highlander's program now fell on Myles and Zilphia Horton and three new staff members, Henry and Betty Shipherd of Swarthmore, Pennsylvania, and Monteagle resident Julie Mabee. Before coming to the school in June 1954, Henry Shipherd had worked in the Philadelphia area with labor, veterans, cooperative, and civic organizations. He had also taught at a previous HFS residence session. Betty Shipherd had engaged in various neighborhood projects in suburban Philadelphia. Myles Horton had enough confidence in their abilities to commit a substantial proportion of the school's funds to building a house for the Shipherd family. Mabee joined the staff in August 1953 to work on Highlander's community leadership training program. With these staff additions and the help of outside consultants, Horton hoped to make the school responsive to any opportunities opened by the desegregation of public schools in the South.[7]

Highlander's program acquired new significance when the Supreme Court rendered its decision in *Brown v. Board of Education* on May 17, 1954. The Court, reversing *Plessy v. Ferguson* (1896), unanimously concluded that "in the field of public education the doctrine of 'separate but equal' has no place. Separate educational facilities are inherently unequal." The victorious team of NAACP lawyers, headed by Thurgood Marshall, pointed out that the Court had struck down racial segregation only in tax-supported educational institutions. Nevertheless, black Americans generally greeted the ruling as the beginning of the end for all state-enforced segregation. Myles Horton was overjoyed. He was on a fundraising tour and happened to be in the Supreme Court building when the justices announced their decision. After quieting him down, Marshall joked that it was "more than an accident" that Horton was present on such a momentous occasion. The Highlander staff was "more in the swing of things" now that the Court had ruled against public school segregation, Horton told former HFS teacher Ralph Tefferteller. "It all goes to prove that the law will finally catch up to you if you live long enough." Technically, Highlander was still in violation of a Tennessee law prohibiting integrated private schools, but Horton was confident that "no one will dare raise the issue."[8]

About a month after the *Brown* decision the HFS staff hosted its second summer workshop on public school desegregation, convinced that acceptance of the Supreme Court's ruling would come "more quickly and with less violence than the majority of people believe possible."[9] Most of the twenty-four black and white participants were teachers from the South; some of them came from the same Alabama, Georgia, South Carolina, and Tennessee communities as those who had attended the 1953 workshops.

As in the previous sessions, participants described their personal encounters with school segregation and examined recent integration efforts in the South. Most of the discussions went no further, however, and while the students developed guidelines to enlist civic groups in the cause of better schools for all southern children, at least one was disappointed that the group did not try to translate individual experiences into some useful general knowledge. The most important product of the school integration workshop was inspiration. Black southerners were especially elated by their stay at HFS and left with the conviction that complete public school integration was possible. No one doubted that there would be stiff resistance from white school officials. But one workshop member, a black schoolteacher from Columbia, South Carolina, persuaded the state NAACP president to launch a school desegregation campaign and told local audiences that "I always knew what I wanted to get done, but now I feel like I know *how* I'm going to get it done."[10]

Another inspired participant who would soon play a major role in the school's civil rights efforts was Septima Poinsette Clark. Born in Charleston, South Carolina, in 1898, Clark earned a bachelor's degree from Benedict College and a master's degree from Hampton Institute through summer school, extension, and night classes between 1929 and 1946. She had begun her teaching career in 1916 on Johns Island, located six miles outside Charleston, and spent most of the next forty years teaching in the Charleston and Columbia school systems. Clark was active in many civic, education, health, and religious organizations and a board member in several of them. At the suggestion of former Highlander student Anna Kelly, she attended the 1954 workshop at HFS. There she found southern whites willing to treat her and other southern blacks as equals and to eat and sleep in the same room with them, and when she returned to Charleston she urged local interracial organizations to make use of Highlander's resources. Her experience, Clark later wrote, made her "more vociferous," "more democratic," and more conscious of the need for "reliable facts" in pressing for integration.[11]

In August 1954 Clark and some forty farmers, trade unionists, educators, college students, and civic leaders attended Highlander's workshop on "World Problems, the United Nations, and You." The stated purpose of the session was to relate the economic problems of the South to the rest of the world and to the work of the UN. But its underlying intent was to promote a greater understanding among black and white southerners of race relations in their home communities through discussions of the effects of discriminatory practices around the world. When the week-long workshop began, most of the participants had only a hazy notion of what the United Nations was and how it could possibly be related to their own experiences. But with the help of the HFS staff and several outside consultants, they were able to establish some vague links between public school desegregation, the development of community leaders, and support for the United Nations. They generally agreed with Horton's suggestion that a local campaign on behalf of the UN, emphasizing that the world was composed of many different religions, races, and ideologies, could be used to "help raise the sights and understanding" of many of the same community leaders who would be making decisions concerning the integration of schools, hospitals, and other institutions.[12] But for Esau Jenkins, a black community leader from Johns Island who had come to the workshop with Septima Clark, the most immediate problem was to help his neighbors learn how to read and write so they could register to vote. The Highlander staff's promise to set up night classes marked the start of a long and productive relationship between the school and the people of the South Carolina Sea Islands. Whatever steps workshop participants took to create a world based on the "equality and dignity of man," Horton asserted, would add up "to a real march toward the future."[13]

After the two major summer workshops of 1954, the Highlander faculty began to press for the rapid desegregation of public schools, for in Horton's view "the place for gradualism is after, not before integration of schools."[14] Taking heart from the progress HFS graduates and others were making in local desegregation drives in Tennessee, South Carolina, Alabama, and Georgia, staff members resolved to expand their program in 1955 in order to accelerate the trends begun in these communities. Expansion, however, meant raising additional funds. Total income for the 1953 fiscal year had decreased slightly from the previous year to around $59,000, reflecting the decline in labor union support and the fears of some contributors about the new direction Highlander was taking. During 1954 the school's income increased to almost $67,000, but HFS teachers wanted to double the size of their program, especially after the Supreme Court made its decision on the implementation of the *Brown* ruling. By the end of the 1955 fiscal year Highlander's income would total nearly $74,000, with an overwhelming percentage of donations coming from individuals and foundations.[15]

An expanded program at Highlander also meant stimulating local southern black leaders into taking positive steps to achieve integration. HFS residence terms had already begun to attract more black interest. Until 1954 only 10 to 15 percent of the students at the school were black, but during that summer about 50 percent of the workshop participants were black. The next, more difficult task was to translate the inspiration whites and blacks received at Highlander into action. As Horton pointed out in March 1955, black leaders should realize that most southern whites were not going to desegregate anything unless blacks built up the necessary "steam." Sympathetic whites could increase the pressure by pushing for integration in a "reasonable" length of time. This white support in turn would persuade blacks that school desegregation could be done "in a peaceable and orderly fashion." Horton did not think that the process would be free of "trouble." But by continuing to bring the races together as equals to work toward a common goal, the Highlander staff could try to minimize racial conflict, to "keep down trouble not by keeping the lid on but by taking the lid off."[16]

During the summer of 1955 HFS staff members sought to generate more steam for integration through labor unions and the subject of the United Nations. In May the faculty held a one-week workshop for thirty-five blacks and whites from sixteen southern locals of the United Furniture Workers of America. Horton had not modified his earlier criticism of organized labor. Yet he thought that southern unions should face up to the problem of desegregation, for it would improve their chances for organizing black workers and make them "a progressive force in the community."[17] Thus while the UFWA members covered familiar union-related topics, they also considered the importance of labor participation in the drive for school desegregation. The sixteen participants at the July 1955 workshop on the United Nations, like those at the 1954 session, tried to connect local economic problems with those concerning the UN in the rest of the world. Sometimes they succeeded. For example, they agreed that just as the UN facilitated the exchange of information so that nations did not have to go through the same struggles faced by other nations before them, so they could add information about other people's experiences to their own to achieve their goal. In both workshops Highlander teachers tried to show how the school's strategies and techniques could be applied to virtually any significant community issue, including school integration. But for black students like Bernice Robinson, a Charleston beautician attending the UN session, the mere fact of living with whites at Highlander was far more valuable than the workshops themselves, and she immediately began to help her cousin Septima Clark involve more people in community activities on Johns Island.[18]

The highlight of the 1955 residence program was the two-week summer workshop on public school desegregation. Almost fifty teachers, union members, college students, and civic leaders came to the session well aware that the Supreme Court, in its May 1955 implementation decision on the *Brown* ruling, had made local school officials responsible for drawing up plans for desegregation, requiring only that the process go forward "with all deliberate speed." The HFS faculty believed this decision made it all the more imperative that workshop members design a flexible, effective approach to local school integration. The picture presented by the participants at the beginning of the session indicated how difficult that task would be. The Little Rock, Arkansas, board of education had already devised a gradual desegregation plan, but union and citizens' committees in Knoxville, Charleston County, South Carolina, and Bessemer and Tuskegee, Alabama, had not been able to move far on school desegregation or voter registration. Rosa Parks of Montgomery, Alabama, doubted that the city's blacks would unite behind any major challenge to segregation. Despite their pessimism, these reports allowed participants to consider common problems, and for the first time black workshop members talked candidly about their concerns. Septima Clark later suggested that prior to this session most black students had hesitated to speak before whites, fearing that news about what they said at Highlander would at the least cost them their jobs back home. They remained cautious. But perhaps because of the size of the student body, the large percentage of black participants, a more experienced HFS staff, and the context in which they met at the school, black students showed a greater willingness to speak openly to the rest of the workshop group.[19]

Once the participants identified their problems, they went to work on planning strategies for public school desegregation in their communities. Consultants Irene Osborne and Herman Long, director of Fisk University's Race Relations Department, provided examples of successful desegregation programs in the District of Columbia, Arkansas, Texas, and states in the Upper South. Equipped with such information, one group of students prepared an organizing pamphlet, *A Guide to Community Action for Public School Integration,* and a mimeographed series of recommendations that citizens' groups could use to lobby for integration. A second group studied the mechanics of school desegregation by selecting two communities, one where blacks and whites lived in the same areas and another where they were segregated, drawing maps designating neighborhood boundaries and the location of school buildings, and then preparing suitable desegregation plans. The workshop ended with participants once again praising their interracial experiences at Highlander and pledging to use their guides when they met with local school boards.[20]

After two years of workshops, however, Highlander staff members still were not certain they were doing all that could be done in behalf of public school integration. During 1955 they had worked with over two hundred potential leaders, the majority of them black, and they had distributed thousands of copies of the *Guide to Action* throughout the nation. Foundations were awarding grants for further desegregation workshops. While news from former students in the Deep South indicated that blacks were retreating before growing white opposition, other alumni reported that they had intensified their drives for public school desegregation. Affirming that the staff was headed in the right direction, HFS leaders voted in October 1955 to expand the residence program again in 1956. John Hope II of Fisk University pointed out that Highlander had been most effective in its work with organized labor when something had aroused factory workers to act. Staff members therefore would have more opportunities to press for school integration "as the situation gets worse" in the South and as demands for compliance with the *Brown* decision increased. "The problem is that the stakes are much higher now," Hope declared, and though education was the issue now, there would be even greater changes before long.[21]

Hope's prediction was largely fulfilled when Rosa Parks was arrested on December 1, 1955, in Montgomery, Alabama, for refusing to yield her bus seat to a white passenger. There has been much speculation about why Parks did not obey the driver's instructions. Spokesmen for white Montgomery then charged that her protest was part of an NAACP plot to destroy the city's transportation system; historians and journalists later romanticized it as the act of a woman who refused to stand simply because her feet hurt. Actually, Martin Luther King, Jr.'s comment that Parks "had been tracked down by the *Zeitgeist*—the spirit of the time" may be closer to the mark, for Parks had been preparing for that moment on the bus all her adult life.[22]

Parks, a seamstress in a Montgomery department store in 1955, was one of the few black high school graduates in the city. She had joined the local chapter of the NAACP during World War II and had served as its secretary and adviser to its youth auxiliary. On the recommendation of longtime HFS supporter Virginia Durr, Parks attended the school's 1955 desegregation workshop. As she said years later, "That was the first time in my life I had lived in an atmosphere of complete equality with the members of the other race." In early 1956 Virginia Durr also noted the impact of Highlander on Parks: "When she came back she was so happy and felt so liberated and then as time went on she said the discrimination got worse and worse to bear AFTER having, for the first time in her life, been free of it at Highlander. I am sure that had a lot to do with her daring to risk arrest as she is naturally a very quiet and retiring person although she has a fierce sense of pride and is in my opinion a really noble woman."[23] The workshop itself had not brought on Parks's defiance. It was one of many accumulated experiences that made her sensitive to racial discrimination and to the possibility of living in a fully integrated society.[24]

Although Highlander had no direct role in the bus boycott that followed Parks's arrest, the protest in some ways resembled the integration strategies designed at its workshops. E. D. Nixon, president of the Alabama NAACP and a veteran of the Brotherhood of Sleeping Car Porters, and Jo Ann Robinson, president of the Women's Political Council in Montgomery, regarded the arrest of the dignified and respected Parks as a long-sought opportunity to organize the city's blacks to protest their mistreatment by whites. While Robinson mimeographed leaflets calling for a boycott of city buses on December 5, Nixon persuaded some forty black leaders, mostly ministers, to meet at the Dexter Avenue Baptist Church, where they agreed to support the boycott. In response to the overwhelming success of the boycott's first day and the conviction of Parks for violating the state law enforcing racially segregated seating on city buses, black leaders formed the Montgomery Improvement Association (MIA) and unanimously elected Martin Luther King, Jr., president. Under the leadership of King and other MIA officers, blacks stayed off city buses for 381 days. At first the MIA sought only to reform the practice of segregation, demanding more courtesy from bus drivers, the hiring of black drivers for predominantly black routes, and passenger seating on a first-come, first-serve basis, with blacks sitting in the back of the bus and whites in the front. But city and bus company officials refused to compromise, and as the months went by Montgomery blacks escalated their demands to attack the entire system of segregation. Finally, the Supreme Court in November 1956 upheld a lower court ruling invalidating Alabama's bus segregation laws, and on December 21 unsegregated buses rolled through Montgomery. The bus boycott, the first major triumph of the civil rights movement, marked the beginning of a new direct action campaign against segregation led by young black southerners, as well as King's emergence as the foremost black spokesman in America.[25]

During the boycott, the Highlander staff's immediate concern was to find a source of financial support for Rosa Parks. The price of her protest had been high. By mid-February 1956 she had lost her job; her husband, a barber, had lost customers; both her husband and her mother had fallen ill; her rent had been raised; demands for pictures and interviews as well as boycott meetings had made it very hard for her to earn any income—and the contributions pouring into Montgomery went to the boycott itself. The HFS faculty gave moral and some financial support to Parks and offered her a job as a speaker and recruiter. Parks took part in a few Highlander activities and attended other HFS workshops, but her family soon moved to Detroit, where she eventually joined the staff of Michigan Congressman John Conyers, Jr.[26]

A further effect of the Montgomery bus boycott was to move Highlander's program beyond the issue of public school desegregation to the entire range of problems involved in attaining a racially integrated society. In March 1956 HFS leaders decided that the three one-week workshops scheduled for that summer should concentrate on working toward integration in specific areas. The staff should pay special attention to East Tennessee in the first workshop, to the relation between union members and integration in the second, and to the Deep and Coastal South in the third. More important, while the focus of the workshops ought to remain on school desegregation, students should also consider such topics as passive resistance, registration and voting, and the integration of transportation, housing, and parks.[27]

Suddenly, tragedy struck. On April 11, 1956, Zilphia Horton died. Her shocking death aroused intense emotions, when it was discussed at all, among those who knew her. At the time a single letter written by Myles offered the only explanation. While working at the school one day, he wrote, Zilphia accidentally "picked up a glass which she thought was water" and drank a small amount of carbon tetrachloride, used to clean office typewriters. She immediately recognized her mistake, forced herself to

Septima Clark, left, and Rosa Parks at Highlander in the late 1950s. *Highlander Research and Education Center.*

vomit, called her doctor, and learned that the situation was not serious. For the next couple of days she maintained her routine without mentioning the incident to anyone, reassuring her daughter Charis that her continued vomiting was due to an upset stomach. Finally, on the way to the hospital in Sewanee, Zilphia told Myles what had happened. A few days later doctors advised her to go to the Vanderbilt University Hospital in Nashville. She died of uremic poisoning shortly thereafter.[28] Her passing produced an outpouring of grief from Highlander's neighbors and friends around the world. Myles was distraught. His children, Thorsten and Charis, went to live with his sister Elsie Pearl in Murfreesboro, close enough to allow occasional visits. It was indicative of Horton's commitment to Highlander and the emerging civil rights movement, and of the man himself, that he forced himself to carry on the school's work. Years later he observed that "you solve personal problems not by maximizing them and dissecting them and concentrating on them and brooding over them; you solve them by getting interested in something bigger than yourself. Then your problems are unimportant to you."[29]

For three decades the circumstances surrounding this incident remained shrouded in a kind of protective silence. Years of correspondence, staff meeting minutes, and other documents, as well as oral interviews, yielded little more than cryptic clues or vaguely stated rumors. With so little evidence available, even cautious suggestions about the impact of Zilphia's disenchantment with labor unions and apparently diminished role at Highlander, or Myles's perplexing account of how a strong-smelling office chemical could be mistaken for water, produced indignant protests.

In the late 1980s, however, family and former staff members provided a more complete story. Zilphia's disillusionment with organized labor was shared by the rest of the faculty, but she had continued to sing for labor and farm groups as well as at black churches and gatherings; she also helped initiate Highlander's new project on the South Carolina Sea Islands. More important, staff member Anne Lockwood was with Zilphia when she picked up that lethal glass and agreed with her that the doctor's comforting diagnosis over the telephone made it unnecessary to broadcast what had occurred. Some contemporaries strongly insist that Zilphia was taking a swallow of moonshine for medicinal purposes, a common practice in Appalachia and her native Ozarks. What seems most clear is that the liquid, whether it was carbon tetrachloride or white lightning, aggravated a pre-existing kidney ailment that was not discovered until Zilphia entered Vanderbilt Hospital. Thus the life of a buoyant, dynamic, and charismatic woman ended because of a fatal mistake. The impact of her death on the school was immediately apparent.[30]

Despite his resolve to continue his work, the trauma of Zilphia's death contributed to Myles's decision to force the resignation of Henry and Betty Shipherd. The Shipherds had not adjusted well to Highlander. Before joining the faculty, Henry Shipherd had hobnobbed with several wealthy Philadelphians, and in his fundraising efforts for the school he appealed to their paternalism, suggesting at one point that staff members could use "some top down help from the men who own and operate the factories and mills."[31] Horton simply could not countenance such an idea. The Shipherds also may not have fully appreciated the consequences of mingling with blacks in the South. In light of these and other problems, Horton announced on April 16, 1956, that either he or the Shipherds must resign within one week. Zilphia had given Highlander a "quality" that "a number of us believe is worth preserving and building upon," he said. But some people "who would like to recreate Highlander in their own image" failed to recognize that quality and were destroying the very essence of the school. He and the Shipherds simply could not run the school together.[32]

The Shipherds wanted to postpone the decision, but Horton refused to wait. On April 21 prominent members of the executive council met with Horton and Henry Shipherd in Atlanta. Horton explained that while his dispute with the Shipherds stemmed mainly from honest disagreements over control of the school's funds, there were philosophical differences and personal misunderstandings as well. Shipherd responded that it was too soon after Zilphia's death to take any action, that he and his wife had obligations to those who had donated funds to the school through them, and that they had incurred a debt of about ten thousand dollars in behalf of Highlander. The council members reached a predictable verdict. Horton was to settle all debts with the Shipherds, carry on the school's programs, and draft new amendments to the HFS charter and bylaws that would clearly establish administrative responsibility. Council members refused to blame the Shipherds for the problem, and they did not condone Horton's ultimatum. But the Shipherds had to leave Highlander because their concern with "regularity" clashed with the "dream" the Hortons had been pursuing for more than twenty years.[33] After negotiating a financial settlement, the Shipherds resigned on April 30 from a school that they maintained was "bigger than any one person—or persons." "The price was steep," Horton conceded, "but worth it."[34]

Horton quickly turned to the task of rebuilding the HFS staff for the upcoming summer program, and in May 1956 he hired Septima Clark to direct the three workshops on integration. As she recruited students for the sessions, the Charleston school superintendent notified her in June that her contract would not be renewed for the coming school year. Clark never received an explanation for her dismissal. She suspected that her NAACP membership was the determining factor, for the South Carolina legislature had decreed in 1956 that city and state employees who belonged to the NAACP would be fired from their jobs. She also believed that her interracial activities in Charleston, her friendship with retired federal district judge J. Waties Waring (whose 1947 ruling had outlawed the state Democratic party's white primary), and her association with Highlander played a part. Horton immediately persuaded her to become Highlander's full-time workshop director. Despite their differences in background and personality, Horton soon appreciated Clark's organizing abilities and her quiet yet determined approach to integration. Several temporary staff members and more than the usual number of consultants would help carry out the residence sessions.[35]

Considering the turmoil of the past spring, the 1956 workshops on integration were remarkably successful in helping local leaders who wanted to do more than desegregate public schools. Most of the more than 110 students and 60 visitors who came to the sessions in July and August were from the South, and over half the students were black. Each morning workshop members assessed the problems they faced in ending segregation in their hometowns. Rosa Parks and the Reverend Robert Graetz gave inspiring accounts of the Montgomery bus boycott. L. A. Blackman of Elloree, South Carolina, impressed the students even more with his description of a black counterboycott in Orangeburg County and how he had stood before an open meeting of the Ku Klux Klan after a Klan leader called upon members to run him out of town and announced, "I've been here seventeen years, and I have no idea of leaving."[36] After these discussions, participants formed committees to study four major phases of the battle over integration. Committees on passive resistance concluded that it would be better to describe the steps being taken to attain racial justice in the South as nonviolent resistance, which connoted active opposition to segregation through economic, legal, political, and spiritual means. Committees on voting and registration examined ways to thwart voting restrictions and stimulate black voter registration. Participants investigating the actions of citizens' groups stressed the importance of organization and cooperative action. The fourth set of student committees urged further legal challenges to southern segregation laws and greater support for local school desegregation plans.[37]

In addition to these residence sessions, Highlander staff members became quietly involved in a bitter school desegregation battle in Clinton, Tennessee. Shortly after twelve black students began attending the white

Clinton High School in the fall of 1956, segregationist crusaders descended upon Clinton and whipped up the fears and racial prejudices of many white townspeople. Rioting soon followed. State troopers and national guardsmen moved in to restore order, but for months the black students entered the high school to a torrent of abuse. As the turmoil subsided, Septima Clark went to Clinton and arranged a weekend retreat at Highlander in December 1956 for the eight remaining black students. Staff members also sponsored a tutorial program for the students. Only six of the black youngsters stayed at Clinton High School for the rest of the school year. But Bobby Cain graduated with the rest of his class in 1957, becoming the first black graduate of an integrated public high school in Tennessee.[38]

HFS leaders eagerly planned an expanded agenda for 1957. After three years of workshops, increased black enrollment had raised overall enrollment considerably, but there had been no comparable increase in the number of southern white students. Staff members recognized that they needed to work harder to bring whites together with blacks and to maintain contact with them after they left the school. The residence program also needed to focus more sharply on specific community issues rather than broad topics. With these goals in mind, the executive council approved a twelve-month schedule of workshops for 1957, highlighted by a twenty-fifth anniversary celebration in the fall. The budget for the twelve workshops, extension work, interracial children's camps, and other projects amounted to nearly $109,000, almost $40,000 more than Highlander's total income for the 1956 fiscal year. The council did not consider this sum unobtainable. Horton pointed out that the next two or three years were critical in the integration struggle, and that Septima Clark's abilities and the activities of former HFS students would bring additional contributions. But then, Horton confessed, "I am a good dreamer."[39]

Indeed, Highlander's leadership badly misjudged the amount of momentum behind the movement to desegregate public schools. Over the next three years the drive to secure black rights would proceed very slowly. State legislatures throughout the South solidly opposed compliance with the *Brown* decision. Citizens' Councils and allied organizations sprang up in every southern state and reached the peak of their size and influence by the end of 1956. This white resistance severely inhibited recruiting and fundraising efforts. Highlander's bank account was exhausted by the middle of February 1957, and then foundation contributions abruptly stopped on February 20, when the Internal Revenue Service revoked the school's tax-exempt status. Income during the 1957 fiscal year was only forty thousand dollars; the operating deficit was nine thousand dollars, and only an eighteen-thousand-dollar balance built up during the previous fiscal year kept the debt from being much higher. HFS leaders nevertheless urged staff members to press forward with their integration workshops, for they had "a head start" over other organizations in gaining the confidence of both blacks and whites. As Horton and John Hope asserted, Highlander had to tackle the tough job of finding "the hundreds of silent, quiet, troubled whites" who were willing to discuss integration and convincing blacks that "there are some white people who are worth trusting as allies."[40]

For most of 1957, staff members struggled to carry out the residence program. Because of the shortage of funds, they held only eight workshops instead of the scheduled twelve. At least two of these sessions barely passed as workshops on integration. Enrollment was erratic and often lower than Horton and Clark desired. An average of twenty to thirty people took part in each workshop. Most of the sessions centered on current efforts to achieve integration in various southern communities. In the January workshop, Cortez Puryear, president of the Winston-Salem, North Carolina, NAACP chapter, recounted his organization's partial success in desegregating the city's public facilities. At the June workshop E. D. Nixon detailed his earlier efforts to encourage blacks to become registered voters in Alabama and outlined his plans to enlarge the campaign. Participants in the July workshop considered the strategic role of ministers and black technicians in breaking down prejudice and stereotypes. Over two hundred local leaders attended these and other residence sessions, including a larger number of whites than the previous year. Through the workshops the participants learned more about the importance of organized protest, interracial cooperation, and black registration and voting.[41]

The centerpiece of the 1957 residence program occurred on Labor Day weekend, when about 180 people, mostly southerners, gathered at Highlander to celebrate the school's twenty-five years of service in the South and to consider future action in the drive for integration. Former staff member John B. Thompson, now dean of the Rockefeller Memorial Chapel at the University of Chicago, served as director of the seminar. Anniversary planners designed the event as an expanded version of a Highlander workshop, where participants would gain an understanding of the "underlying human aspects" of the civil rights movement and thus handle more effectively the problems that would "inevitably accompany the forward movement toward integration in the South."[42] The celebration included reports on the "integration beachheads" being established in the South, panel discussions of the overall impact of integration on the region, and an overview of Highlander's history. Workshop groups examined the implications of integration for religious groups, educators, trade unions, civic organizations, and youth. The anniversary weekend was a time of joy as well: Ralph Tefferteller brought back memories of Highlander's early days as he called square dances, and Pete Seeger led the participants in group singing.[43]

The celebration culminated in speeches by Aubrey Williams and Martin Luther King, Jr., which John Thompson aptly described as "the Old Testament" and "the New Testament" on integration in the South.[44] Williams, editor of *Southern Farm and Home,* attacked the policy of massive resistance pursued by public officials in the South, warning that these men were "playing with fire." Nearly a hundred years ago the South had suffered enormously "in a similar stand against the morals of mankind," Williams said, and apparently the rigid defenders of segregation were willing to pay that fearful price again. Citizens had the right to criticize laws or court decisions, but when publicly elected officials openly refused to comply with the Supreme Court decision on school desegregation, they were "advocating defiance and rebellion against the government." Williams concluded that these men had not considered the consequences of their resistance, for they were "gambling with the future well-being of every home, every family, every child, every church, school, business in the South."[45]

In contrast to Williams, with his dark vision of the future, King believed that the South was on the threshold of a new era in race relations. In spite of the Ku Klux Klan and Citizens' Council, he asserted, hundreds of white southerners were moving to implement the Supreme Court rulings and "make the ideal of brotherhood a reality." The Highlander staff had worked toward this ideal for twenty-five years, he added, giving the South "some of its most responsible leaders" during its transition from a segregated to an integrated society. Though the fight for integration would be long and difficult, the determination of blacks to gain freedom and equality through nonviolence would eventually overcome the oppression of segregation. King called upon his listeners to remain "maladjusted" to the racial discrimination, economic exploitation, and "physical violence" found in America and to work for the day when freedom and justice would extend to all races and classes.[46]

The anniversary seminar was a memorable occasion for both supporters and opponents of Highlander. The Nashville *Banner* announced that the anniversary had brought together many of the instigators of the South's current racial strife; one story bore the misleading headline "'Stuff of Rebellion Planted,' Williams Says at Highlander."[47] An even more sensational attack was the publication in October 1957 of *Highlander Folk School: Communist Training School, Monteagle, Tenn.,* by the Georgia Commission on Education.

The report began with the assertion that "During Labor Day weekend, 1957, there assembled at Highlander the leaders of every major race incident in the South." This broadside marked the start of a concerted attack by southern white supremacists that would ultimately close the folk school.[48]

Against a background of almost incessant criticism and litigation, Highlander staff members pushed ahead with their integration program in 1958 and 1959. Horton believed that Highlander now had its best teaching and office staff in years, and under Septima Clark's direction the workshops had grown in number, scope, and quality. Old friends and new allies had rallied to the school's defense. After the IRS restored Highlander's tax-exempt status in December 1957, foundation support in both 1958 and 1959 rose spectacularly, and annual income during these years amounted to over $110,000. Highlander's role in the civil rights movement was important enough, the executive council declared in January 1958, that the staff "positively has the right and the responsibility to carry on a vigorous campaign to educate people to their rights as citizens."[49]

Meanwhile, several new staff members joined Horton and Clark in 1959. Esau Jenkins and Bernice Robinson, already important figures in the folk school's extension work on Johns Island, became part-time members to expand the Citizenship School project. Alice Cobb, a soft-spoken white woman with a master's degree from Union Theological Seminary, took a two-year leave of absence from her position as director of rural fieldwork at Scarritt College in Nashville to supervise Highlander's special projects and publicity. A white folk singer with a master's degree in sociology named Guy Carawan, who had been inspired by a visit to HFS during the summer of 1953, returned six years later and volunteered to revive the music program.[50]

Strengthened by the increases in financial support and personnel, the HFS staff held a series of workshops in 1958 and 1959 based on the theme of "Citizenship and Integration." One pair of workshops encouraged professional social workers and members of health, welfare, and human relations groups in the South to take a more active part in integrating their communities. The thirty to fifty participants at each "Community Services and Segregation" session generally agreed that inexperience and segregated agency staffs, clientele, and services had hindered their attempts to help needy people regardless of race. Welfare workers could therefore assist integration campaigns by pursuing projects related to law and order, voter education, housing, and similar topics; by reinforcing each other's efforts; and by enlisting the support of church leaders to make their services more widely available.[51]

A second set of Citizenship and Integration workshops focused on registration and voting, reflecting the staff's view that securing and exercising the right to vote was essential to achieving full integration. Sixty black and white southerners at the 1958 workshop decided that they could stimulate voter registration through an educational campaign that counteracted the distortion of issues by the local press and made the registration and voting process more attractive and convenient. This session received more publicity than usual when Eleanor Roosevelt visited the folk school and spoke before a crowd of about three hundred on the need for the South to guarantee equal voting rights for all citizens. The editor of the Chattanooga *News-Free Press* sniffed that Roosevelt's address would not damage either her reputation or Highlander's "since both already have sunk so low."[52] But her remarks delighted HFS staff members. Roosevelt had reaffirmed their contention that the need for voter education was critical, especially when most of the 2.5 million functional illiterates the U.S. Census found in eight southern states in 1950 were still subject to literacy tests for voting. The twenty-four participants at the 1959 session, representing states that required literacy tests, learned how to organize local education programs to help adults pass the tests and complete ballots.[53]

The HFS faculty completed its Citizenship and Integration series with sessions on "Community Development" in July 1958 and "Community Leadership and Integrated Housing" in July 1959. Most of the approximately forty participants in each workshop were from Charleston, the Sea Islands, and eastern Tennessee, areas where there had been Highlander-sponsored programs for several years. While some students came from white communities and others from black, they shared a common concern about the problems involved in building local support for integrated and adequate community services. Students at the 1959 workshop learned a valuable, unexpected lesson about the sort of resistance they could expect in their hometowns when local and state police officers raided the school and arrested four staff members, charging them with possession of alcohol, drunkenness, and resisting arrest. During the raid participants sang what was still known as "We Will Overcome" to bolster their courage; the HFS staff considered this "a vivid example under fire [of] the kind of leadership they had all come to learn about."[54]

Several other residence sessions at Highlander during the late 1950s followed up some of the topics addressed during the Citizenship and Integration series. In September 1958 an experimental workshop on migration struggled to devise an educational program that could smooth over the tensions arising from the movement of blacks and whites from the rural South to urban areas across the region. In September 1959, despite pending litigation against the school, staff members held on schedule a workshop to review Highlander's Citizenship School program and to plan an expansion of the schools to other southern communities. Three interracial workshops in late 1959 and early 1960 on "Social Needs and Social Resources" attracted an average of twenty-three ministers and lay church workers interested in extending public and private welfare services to the entire community. By the end of the 1950s, well over one thousand southerners, black and white, had participated in the residence program on integration.[55]

Highlander's prominence in the southern struggle for black rights stemmed from its ability to anticipate and respond to shifts in the focus of civil rights activity. Staff members maintained that flexibility in 1960 and 1961, when college and high school students began sit-in demonstrations against segregated public facilities in the South. Highlander quickly became a place where student leaders could come to discuss the ideology, goals, and tactics of their protest. At the same time, as Myles Horton recognized, the students gave the school "a new lease on life" by creating "a crisis situation" around which the staff could develop a new education program.[56]

On February 1, 1960, four black students from North Carolina Agricultural and Technical College ignited a decade of protest when they remained seated at the segregated F. W. Woolworth lunch counter in downtown Greensboro after they were refused service. Although similar demonstrations had occurred before, the drama of the Greensboro sit-ins galvanized young people in other cities into action. By the end of February, sit-ins had taken place in other North Carolina towns and in more than thirty cities in seven states, including Nashville, Atlanta, and Montgomery. By mid-April the demonstrations had reached more than one hundred communities throughout the South, involving at least fifty thousand black and white participants. Despite thousands of arrests and other setbacks, the sit-ins led to the desegregation of lunch counters in scores of cities in fourteen states. More significant, the sit-ins set in motion a wave of events that transformed the civil rights movement. The demonstrations marked a shift in tactics from a largely legalistic approach to direct action based upon the power of the black community. The student protesters challenged the leadership of existing civil rights organizations and pushed the movement beyond the issue of constitutional rights to the economic concerns of black Americans. They also managed to convert, at least temporarily, a disparate collection of local protests into a coordinated campaign that accelerated the entire process of change in race relations.[57]

For six years prior to the sit-ins, the HFS staff had held workshops for black and white college students that had generally failed to stimulate them into moving against racial segregation either on or off campus. Staff members were therefore initially surprised by the sit-ins, but they endorsed the protests almost instinctively. In March 1960 Horton attended a mass meeting in Nashville and found the student demonstrators, some of whom had taken part in HFS college workshops, willing to work not only with adult black leaders but with whites as well. Horton hoped this would mean greater biracial participation in the sit-ins, for in his view black student leaders could use the assistance of whites who could "join them without dragging their feet."[58] He also learned that while the students were determined to desegregate Nashville's lunch counters, they disagreed over what their protests had accomplished and over their next move. Highlander's role now seemed clear to Horton. Through a series of workshops he and his colleagues would try to help black students control the pace and direction of their protests while encouraging both black and white adults to support and defend them. Horton realized that it would be a delicate task, for black students were impatient with their elders' campaigns against segregation, including Highlander's own efforts. Changes had to come fast enough to prevent violence, and the students' civil disobedience must be reconciled with the older concept of orderly progress.[59]

On April 1, 1960, the HFS staff opened its seventh annual college workshop, to its knowledge the first fairly large gathering of representative sit-in leaders since the demonstrations had started. The planning committee of adult consultants and former college workshop members, including Marion Barry of Fisk University, had originally scheduled several broad topics on race relations and college life. But as Barry and other students became leading figures in the sit-ins, the planning group decided that the focus of the session should be on the demonstrations and their impact on college students and the civil rights movement. Eighty-two persons, over half of them black, came to "The New Generation Fights for Equality," a much larger group than any previous college workshop had attracted. More than seventy students from seventeen colleges in seven states enrolled; most of them, black and white, were sit-in veterans.[60]

The "New Generation" workshop charted a new course for Highlander's residence program and revealed some of the elements that would characterize the civil rights movement during the 1960s. Many of the discussions concerned the role of white students and adults of both races in a protest begun by black students, led by them, and with few exceptions involving only them. There was little agreement among student demonstrators on the merits of cooperating with adults. Students from Nashville appreciated the support they had received from several interracial church and community organizations. But others doubted the wisdom of working directly with such agencies, and some argued that the protests should be restricted to college students. White students then wondered about their own part in the campaign, for they were not certain that southern black students wanted their assistance. Herman Long of Fisk University raised more pointed questions about the protest. Observing that the sit-ins represented the kind of direct action against racial discrimination that adults would not likely undertake themselves, Long nevertheless urged the students to establish closer ties with "the larger community" and to define their philosophy and goals more clearly. The students especially needed to explain their use of nonviolence and to resolve "the whole dilemma of law and morality" if their movement was to have "permanent relevance." Horton took a different approach. Assuming the roles of an "average liberal white person" and an "average Negro businessman," sympathetic with the protests but seeking assurances that the students were acting "entirely within the law," he prodded workshop participants to define and defend their ideas.[61]

The students' response to the problems posed by Long and Horton was diverse and ambiguous, yet also indicative of their militance, idealism, independence, and concern with action rather than philosophy. Three leaders of the Nashville sit-ins argued that litigation against segregation took second place to nonviolent civil disobedience. Bernard Lafayette declared that the student protestors were "on the side of moral right" in opposing laws imposed on blacks without their consent. For John Lewis and James Bevel, the "moral principle" of nonviolence ultimately meant being willing to go to jail and to refuse bail in order to end the racist system that imprisoned them.[62] Not all of the students were as firmly committed to mass demonstrations against the law as the Nashville activists, however, and they formed committees to consider the next steps in their cause. The communications committee proposed the formation of a regional coalition to promote, coordinate, and finance the southern student movement. A second committee produced a brief, simplistic "philosophy" of the movement: "We believe in democracy. We are Americans seeking our rights. We want to do something. We are using nonviolence as a method, but not necessarily as a total way of life. We believe it is practical." Another committee called for "further and better planned" sit-in demonstrations and for picketing and economic boycotts where they would be "practical" and "effective." Finally, a community relations committee reaffirmed the general sentiment of the workshop that the demonstrators should work more closely with sympathetic white and interracial agencies without permitting them to take control of the students' desegregation drive. White students could join the campaign, Ezery Kinder of Claflin College added, for "in a democratic movement, all are welcome and useful."[63]

The students left Highlander not only with a set of guidelines for future protests but also with a collection of adapted spirituals and modern melodies that would become known as "freedom songs." During the weekend, Guy Carawan learned some of the songs the demonstrators had sung in jail—an assortment of popular tunes, religious hymns, rock and roll music, and calypso songs. Candie Anderson, a white exchange student attending Fisk University who would marry Carawan about a year later, had developed a new version of "They Go Wild over Me," first sung by the Industrial Workers of the World. Carawan introduced the students to songs he and Zilphia Horton had collected from union members and South Carolina Sea Islanders, including "We Shall Not Be Moved," "Keep Your Eyes on the Prize," "This Little Light of Mine," and "We Shall Overcome." The Carawans later recalled that the students were immediately attracted to these older songs.[64]

Indeed, before long "We Shall Overcome" would become the anthem of the civil rights movement, although most of those who sang it were unaware of Highlander's role in its evolution. Originally a religious folk

A student workshop at Highlander, April 1960. John Lewis, first row left; Bernard Lafayette, second row center; Anne Lockwood Romasco, first row right. *Highlander Research and Education Center.*

song that evolved into a formal Baptist hymn, members of a CIO food and tobacco workers' union in Charleston, South Carolina, changed its lyrics during a strike in 1945 and sang "We Will Overcome" to maintain morale on the picket line. The following year two women from the union local attended a workshop at Highlander and taught the song to other students. Recognizing its emotional appeal, Zilphia Horton slowed the tempo, added new verses, and began singing and teaching it to HFS students and at various gatherings in the South. Pete Seeger learned the song from Zilphia in 1947 and revised it further, altering "we will overcome" to "we shall overcome" and including more verses during his concerts around the country. The song's popularity did not spread far beyond the school and a few folk singers during the 1940s and 1950s. Guy Carawan was introduced to the song by a West Coast folk singer named Frank Hamilton. Carawan helped give the song its contemporary format and taught it and other freedom songs at HFS workshops and civil rights gatherings throughout the South during the early 1960s.[65]

Two weeks after the close of Highlander's 1960 college workshop, sit-in leaders met to form the Student Nonviolent Coordinating Committee (SNCC). The initiative for the founding conference, held in mid-April 1960 in Raleigh, North Carolina, came from Ella Baker, executive director of the Southern Christian Leadership Conference (SCLC). Recognizing that few black students were prepared to lead a sustained drive against segregation, Baker sought to bring student leaders together in an organization that would keep their protest active, nonviolent, and free of adult control. The Raleigh conference attracted more than 120 black college and high school students from twelve southern states and the District of Columbia, as well as a dozen southern white students, delegates from northern and border state colleges, and representatives of thirteen other groups, including Guy Carawan. The delegates voted to establish a temporary Student Nonviolent Coordinating Committee that would have no official ties but would cooperate with all other civil rights groups. A permanent structure for the organization would be created in October 1960. SNCC's leadership included several members of Highlander's "New Generation" workshop, foreshadowing a relationship that would persist well into the 1960s. Marion Barry, later elected mayor of Washington, D.C., became SNCC's first chairman in 1960; John Lewis would rise to national prominence as chairman of SNCC between 1963 and 1966 and became a Georgia congressman in 1986; Bernard Lafayette served as a SNCC field secretary until 1963; and James Bevel worked closely with SNCC while remaining a militant member of the SCLC staff.[66]

As in the past, Highlander's leaders responded to this new protest movement against southern segregation by reshaping the policies and programs of the school. The executive council ended the exclusion of college students from the rest of the residence program, for the student demonstrators had assumed the kind of "direct community responsibility" found among adults who came to HFS.[67] The council also decided that the school's earlier relationship with labor unions should apply to civil rights organizations: the staff would work with all major interracial and black protest groups, and workshop participants must be recognized leaders of their organizations. The school should seek to broaden the interests of sit-in leaders and encourage the development of black political power, but the residence program should also examine the role of southern whites in a struggle initiated and led by southern blacks. Horton and his colleagues recognized that the black students' determination to chart their own "course of action" had "shocked the good white people who think of themselves as friends of the Negro."[68] But achieving racial justice now required more than improved communication between the races. Citing the late black sociologist Charles S. Johnson, Horton asserted that "communication depends upon the agenda, and will be restored when Southerners accept the new agenda. This is what Highlander offers to the white Southerner—a New Agenda."[69]

Accordingly, Highlander's next workshop, held in May 1960, outlined "The Place of the White Southerner in the Current Struggle for Justice." Horton sparked considerable discussion among the thirty-six whites and twenty-eight blacks attending the session when he pointed out that with blacks assuming leadership of the fight against segregation, the pivotal question now was what whites could do to help them in the battle. Plenty, black adults and college students replied. Black activists like Ella Baker and the Reverend Fred S. Shuttlesworth, president of the SCLC-affiliated Alabama Christian Movement for Human Rights, stressed the need for whites themselves to break down racial barriers. Workshop groups explored how whites and blacks, individually and collectively, could pressure businessmen and politicians to end segregation and black disfranchisement, foster constructive relations between the races, and mobilize support for desegregation drives. As Anne Braden of the Southern Conference Educational Fund (SCEF) reported, workshop members found that southern blacks certainly wanted whites to join the struggle, but not if they were going to be a "drag" on the movement or if they sought "the old pattern that has often prevailed even in liberal interracial organizations—that of white domination."[70]

Now convinced that southern whites had an important role to play in the civil rights movement, the HFS staff held two more workshops designed to examine the part white college students could take in the protest. In November 1960 "The Place of the White College Student in the Changing South" attracted thirteen black and forty-seven white college students from sixteen southern and northern schools, as well as about fifty observers from the University of the South in nearby Sewanee. All of the black students and a few of the white students had participated in sit-ins. Along with Anne Braden of SCEF, James Wood of SCLC, and Lewis Jones of Tuskegee Institute, they served as teachers for the rest of the curious, sympathetic, but as yet uncommitted white group. The students acknowledged that they needed to develop a coherent ideology and long-range goals. Yet white students were particularly concerned with the question of whether they could gain the trust of black activists, even if they were not prepared to engage in acts of civil disobedience. Black participants responded that while whites should not expect to become the policymakers of the student protest movement, blacks welcomed anyone willing to bear its responsibilities and sacrifices equally.[71]

At the "New Frontiers for College Students" workshop in April 1961, eighty-seven persons, mainly students, met to assess the impact of the student protests on the South and to consider the future direction of the movement. Participants included Ella Baker, Dorothy Cotton, Bernard Lee, Wyatt Tee Walker, and C. T. Vivian of SCLC; black student leaders Lonnie King, John Lewis, and Ruby Doris Smith of SNCC and Timothy Jenkins of the National Student Association; Robert Zellner, who was to become SNCC's first white field secretary that summer; and the Reverend Andrew Young of the National Council of Churches, who would soon return to the South to administer the Citizenship School program for SCLC. (One month later Lewis, Lee, Walker, Vivian, and six other black and white students at the workshop would be among those who began "freedom rides" to desegregate bus station waiting rooms in the South.) As in previous HFS workshops on the student movement, participants only started to find answers to the issues raised by the protests. Beyond vaguely agreeing that the goal of the struggle was to secure racial justice and enhance human freedom, they shared no single set of organizing beliefs, differed on their commitment to nonviolence and direct action, and only tentatively defined the role of whites in the movement. But what seemed to matter most to the participants, what gave the workshop value, was the full and candid exchange of views between young blacks and whites and between college students and older adults. Highlander's college workshops in 1960 and early 1961 at least furthered the idea of an interracial movement for integration led by independent young southern blacks.[72]

While staff members adjusted the residence program in response to the emerging southern student movement, three other workshops reflected their earlier concern with black voter registration and public school desegregation. At a one-week session on voting and registration in June 1960, thirty-nine civic leaders and prospective black voters concluded that a carefully planned voter education program would overcome two major impediments to the growth of black voting in the South: the lack of black political participation and the difficulty of getting blacks to register and go to the polls. The forty-two blacks and seven whites attending a political leadership and community development workshop in July 1960 studied the provisions of the Civil Rights Act of 1960, drew up a simple list of instructions for blacks intimidated or prevented from voting, and proposed various adult education projects to encourage voter registration, broaden local leadership, and integrate public schools. Once the doors to segregated schools were opened, black and white parents must send their children through them; so in August 1960 HFS teachers held a workshop for parents who would be enrolling their children in integrated schools that fall. Assisted by ministers and officials from recently desegregated schools, the mostly black workshop group discussed the problems facing black and white children, adults, administrators, and the local community as school integration went into effect.[73]

Another outgrowth of the staff's interest in public school desegregation was a Youth Project conducted during the summers of 1960 and 1961. The project was to provide six weeks of interracial living in which young people could pursue creative projects requiring cooperation with members of other racial, ethnic, and cultural groups, learning how to smooth over the troubles southern students might have in newly integrated classrooms. Young northerners would learn more about the South and benefit from associating with blacks their own age who were engaged in the struggle for integration. Confident that the project would have great educational value, the HFS faculty predicted that it might suggest a new approach to preparing southerners for a racially integrated society.[74]

The Youth Project fostered more intercultural and interracial communication than even the optimistic HFS staff anticipated. In 1960 staff members initially planned to bring about twenty-five to thirty black and white youths to Highlander, covering most of their expenses with a ten-thousand-dollar pledge made by entertainer Harry Belafonte. Although Belafonte did not completely fulfill his pledge, his fundraising efforts, along with individual contributions and foundation grants, enabled over forty black, white, Native-American, and Mexican-American high school students from nine southern and four nonsouthern states to participate in the project. This diverse group shared their interests in the arts, took field trips, held panel discussions, attended workshops for adults, and worked and played together. Most important, as the HFS staff saw it, the youths formed friendships across color and cultural lines and gained a greater appreciation of the need to break through racial barriers once they returned home. The most sensational result of the project was the arrest and conviction of three children of the Reverend Fred Shuttlesworth for refusing to sit in the back of a Greyhound bus en route to their home in Birmingham. Their appeal, and their nine-million-dollar damage suit against Southeastern Greyhound Lines for its segregationist practices, sparked a Justice Department probe of the incident. Highlander executive council members were so impressed by the Youth Project that they voted to hold a second one in the summer of 1961. The interracial experience had less dramatic impact than the year before, but once again the thirty-five black and white high school students attending the camp learned how to live together in harmony.[75]

The 1961 residence program closed with three workshops projecting a civil rights movement with a broader leadership base, a greater degree of unity, and more concerted action by black and white southerners. At the "New Leadership Responsibilities" workshop in January, fifty-two black beauticians from Tennessee and Alabama explored the ways in which they and other women whose jobs left them relatively free of white economic pressure could build upon their extensive contacts in black communities to promote the cause of racial equality. In February the HFS staff sought to promote more cooperation within the civil rights movement by bringing together thirty-one representatives of organizations formed in the wake of the student sit-ins to consider "New Alliances in the South." After studying how economic boycotts and other integration campaigns had grown out of sit-ins in places such as Atlanta and Nashville, the workshop participants concluded that maintaining the momentum of their movement would require stronger organizations, clearer channels of communication, more adult allies in the South, and the establishment of long-term goals. As the Reverend Fred Shuttlesworth put it, "It takes massive organization to overcome massive resistance."[76]

Drawing upon the findings of these two sessions, staff members held their last workshop at the Highlander Folk School in May 1961 to draw up "The New Agenda for the Southerner." Nashville student leader Diane Nash, James Wood of SCLC, and the eighteen other participants discussed at length the responsibilities of southern black and white civil rights activists at the individual, institutional, and community levels. They also analyzed the challenges posed by the Black Muslims, the nationalistic sect that served as a reminder of the considerable antiwhite sentiment among blacks. The growth of the Black Muslims suggested to workshop members that civil rights groups had not yet reached the vast majority of black Americans and that they must work to secure equal economic opportunities as well as the right to vote.[77]

The summer that followed the "New Agenda" workshop was a difficult time for Highlander. In April 1961 the Tennessee Supreme Court had upheld a lower court ruling revoking the HFS charter and closing the school. As their lawyers prepared an appeal to the United States Supreme Court, staff members continued to operate, but now on the periphery of the civil rights movement.

Meanwhile, the first "freedom riders" sponsored by the Congress of Racial Equality (CORE) set out in two buses from Washington, D.C., in May 1961 to dramatize the persistence of racial segregation in interstate travel terminals in the South. The riders endured beatings and arrests at the beginning of their journey, and the violence escalated when they reached Alabama. In Anniston a white mob bombed and burned one bus and beat riders on both buses. When the CORE contingent decided to end their freedom ride after being assaulted again in Birmingham, Diane Nash of SNCC quickly assembled an interracial group in Nashville to continue the protest. After further setbacks in Birmingham, the freedom riders proceeded to Montgomery, where a thousand angry whites attacked them as they stepped off the bus. The injured included former HFS students John Lewis and James Zwerg, a white exchange student attending Fisk University. The bruised and bandaged riders went on to Jackson, Mississippi, where police arrested them when they tried to enter the bus station's white waiting room. During the following months, over three hundred black and white freedom riders from across the country were arrested in Jackson and sent to Parchman state prison and other Mississippi jails when they refused to pay their fines. Guy Carawan led the singing at mass meetings in Jackson that summer supporting the riders and their "jail-no bail" strategy. As the campaign spread to bus, railroad, and airport terminals in other states, the Interstate Commerce Commission ordered the desegregation of all interstate transportation facilities, but there was only partial compliance in the South.[78]

The freedom rides infused southern student activists with a new, more militant spirit. The question was whether that militancy should be directed toward registering black voters. For its part, the John F. Kennedy administration wanted civil rights organizations to become more involved in voter registration work, arguing that the vote was the key to racial change in the South and that registration drives would be more productive than further demonstrations. SCLC leaders were already convinced of the value of voter education, but SNCC leaders were not so certain, and they met at Highlander in August 1961 to resolve the issue. Marion Barry, Diane Nash, and some SNCC members insisted that nonviolent direct action should remain their primary policy, charging that white liberals and federal officials were attempting to divert the student movement into slower, safer channels. Charles Jones and other SNCC leaders asserted that a voter registration drive would help transform the protests against segregation into a massive campaign for black advancement. Ella Baker finally proposed the establishment of two SNCC divisions: Nash would be in charge of direct action and Jones would direct voter registration projects. The compromise left no one entirely satisfied, but SNCC now had an organizational framework that ensured its survival. Two weeks later the Highlander Research and Education Center opened in Knoxville, and in October 1961 the Supreme Court refused to review the Tennessee court order revoking the HFS charter. After twenty-nine years of struggle, the Highlander Folk School closed its doors.[79]

The Highlander residence program between 1953 and 1961 both anticipated and reacted to the dynamics of the civil rights movement during the period. Frustrated by the racism that had hindered their work with southern labor and farmers' unions, staff members sensed that the Supreme Court's decision on school desegregation might offer an opportunity to confront that barrier and bring about an end to the entire system of southern segregation. Beginning in 1953, therefore, Highlander workshops focused on the issue of public school desegregation, sometimes directly, sometimes through subjects like the United Nations. Staff members did not foresee the impact Rosa Parks's protest and the Montgomery bus boycott would have on the scope and strategy of the civil rights movement. But they quickly grasped the implications of the boycott, and their workshops soon addressed the problems of integrating public facilities throughout southern society. They attempted to involve more blacks and whites from a wider range of occupations and backgrounds and to pay more attention to the potential power of black voters. And when student sit-ins erupted across the South in 1960, HFS teachers again readjusted their residence program to help student leaders evaluate the impact of their demonstrations, examine the role of whites in the movement, form new alliances, and develop new strategies of protest.

There was continuity in Highlander's workshops as well. Over and over again, almost regardless of the subject, black and white workshop participants were most impressed by the experience of living and working together on the basis of complete equality. Indeed, perhaps the most important accomplishment of the residence program during the 1950s and early 1960s was that it made the school an important "movement halfway house," a visible and successful demonstration of an integrated society.[80] Blacks learned that they could and should take the lead in insisting on the full rights of citizenship, and whites found that integration in many ways enhanced their own economic and political interests. Yet like the civil rights movement as a whole, the residence program came under increasing fire from white segregationists. By 1961, the drive for black equality, and Highlander's role in it, had made some headway. But the gains had been limited, and much remained to be done.

8

The Citizenship
Schools,
1953–1961

The same process of anticipation and re-
action that marked Highlander's residence program also characterized its
extension program between 1953 and 1961. Between 1953 and 1956, staff
members experimented with a project designed to train grassroots leadership for communitywide reform efforts. Conceptually vague from the start,
the program foundered in most cases. But the idea took hold on Johns Island, South Carolina, primarily because residents of the island were not so
much concerned with something called community development as with a
single essential problem: illiteracy as a barrier to voter registration. In response, Highlander began sponsoring Citizenship Schools on the island in
1957. Over the next several years the program spread throughout the Sea
Islands and the rest of the South. It moved from voter registration into a
broad range of political party and electoral activities, including campaigns
for representation on the boards of local organizations. Ultimately it led to
the operation of a Southwide citizenship education program by the Southern Christian Leadership Conference. The Citizenship Schools were
Highlander's most significant contribution to the civil rights movement
and perhaps the most important single program the folk school staff ever
developed.[1]

Originally, Highlander's Community Leadership Training Program was an attempt to demonstrate that the staff could build community leadership in much the same way as it had educated union leaders. In the wake of his disappointing experiences with labor unions, Myles Horton decided that HFS teachers should work less with organizations and more with individuals concerned about some community problem. In late 1952 he began conferring with Carl Tjerandsen of the Emil Schwarzhaupt Foundation about securing funds to test some community organizing techniques that Horton had rejected in the past but now thought might have some merit. Horton proposed to develop leaders among poor farmers in southern Appalachia and among southern blacks who would stimulate community interest in "the nature of a democratic society and the individual's role as a citizen," broaden participation in local, state, and national affairs, and spark efforts to "change attitudes which limit democracy." The primary aim of the program would be to train these leaders in the use of educational methods that would not only promote "rural citizenship" but also establish a "continuous relationship" between Highlander and these leaders. In April 1953 the Schwarzhaupt Foundation awarded $44,100 for a three-year program that Horton believed would result in "some effective and lasting local leadership."[2]

Initially, however, the leadership training program produced very little, at least partly because the project's staff members had trouble grasping its purpose and their own function in it. After defining a "true community" as "a number of people having common ties or interests and living in the same locality," Ann Isaacs, Emil Willimetz, and Julie Mabee started work in the fall of 1953.[3] From the start, the trio confused their efforts to organize community projects with the idea of training local leaders to initiate such projects themselves. When Mabee formed a group in Monteagle to improve the local public school and then move on to other projects, residents advised her that any issue beyond school improvement would bewilder townspeople, and Horton told her that involving the HFS staff in the organization would defeat the intent of the training program. Meanwhile, Isaacs and Willimetz tried to arouse interest in the program in Whitwell, Tennessee, and Altoona, Alabama, by introducing themselves as representatives of the Alliance of Southern Communities, a group concerned with developing local leadership. They never liked using the name, and they could not resolve the dilemma of remaining in the background while motivating others to address community problems. Willimetz wondered how he and his colleagues could explain "what we mean by a democratic way of functioning in a community" when virtually no one in Altoona showed any interest in the program.[4] Clearly the staff was not taking into account whether community members wanted to do anything at all or trust outside organizers.[5]

By mid-1954, Horton realized that the leadership training program was not working. Staff members could not "cook up" a project for a community. The training program would succeed only when there was a "crisis situation" or when a local leader decided that something needed to be done to solve a pressing problem.[6]

The program showed more promise in Kodak, Tennessee, because a local leader there wanted to organize a community group and turned to Highlander for help. Yet once again the project was no more than a partial success, for other Kodak residents did not share the HFS staff's perception of their problems. For some time people living in and around Kodak, a community of about two thousand people located twenty miles east of Knoxville, had been complaining to an insurance agent named Max Cate about the poor quality of their schools, roads, mail and milk routes, and other services. A number of them wanted to do something about their grievances, but no one seemed to know how to begin. Cate thought that a Farmers' Union local might stimulate the community into action, and through Tom Ludwig, state manager of the union's insurance company, he asked Horton for assistance. After a tour of Kodak in July 1954, Horton suggested that Cate build interest in a community organization through a series of monthly meetings. Several dozen people began attending the meetings, and by the end of 1954 the group had elected a slate of officers and voted to affiliate with the National Farmers' Union.[7]

The Farmers' Union local provided the springboard for further community action in Kodak. When members raised the possibility of establishing a milk cooperative in early 1955, Horton and William Jones, a rural sociologist at the University of Tennessee, helped organize a committee to survey local dairymen and assess the feasibility of a cooperative in the Kodak area. Horton urged the committee members to get the information themselves, believing that the milk issue was a good way to bring more people into the union and to find and develop new local leaders. After spending the rest of 1955 studying various details of the proposal, union members decided not to begin a cooperative. There were not enough milk producers in the Kodak area, and the cost of a cooperative would be prohibitive if it processed only local milk. Yet the conduct of the survey itself was important. It had involved a significant number of Kodak citizens, identified several potential leaders, and encouraged residents to undertake projects ranging from the opening of a new community center to a letter-writing campaign supporting an exemption of animal feed from a state sales tax. In an attempt to connect the Kodak program with Highlander's residence workshops, Horton and Ludwig conducted weekend conferences on the impact of desegregation on the Sevier County school system. Horton asserted that the improved "quality of life" in Kodak and the widespread interest in community affairs marked "a great change from the general apathy of the past."[8]

Although Horton thought that the Kodak project involved "Universalities" applicable to much of the South, it never managed to fulfill his vision of an ongoing program of community reform.[9] There was still no clear definition of the program's purpose and Highlander's role in it. No new organizations arose to complement the work of the local Farmers' Union, and members made no attempt to broaden the scope of its concerns. For example, the union took no action on school desegregation because there were no black members and the issue evidently did not directly affect Kodak. The program lost much of its direction when Cate and the local union president moved away and Ludwig left the Farmers' Union. Most important, as Horton observed later, most Kodak citizens lacked the incentive to solve their community problems themselves. They had long been accustomed to having outside experts assess their problems and then telling them what to do. They could not or would not accept the idea of acting on their own to improve their community, and few were willing to attend a leadership training workshop at Highlander. In the end, the vitality of the Kodak project lasted only as long as the HFS staff was involved in it.[10]

In contrast, the Sea Islands provided a fertile setting for substantial and permanent results. The Sea Islands lie in a chain along the coast of South Carolina and Georgia. Johns Island, about six miles south of Charleston, is the largest of the group. Extending south from it are Wadmalaw, Edisto, and Daufuskie Islands. Slightly over four thousand people lived on Johns Island in 1954; the other islands had smaller populations. Nearly 67 percent of Johns Island's population was black, and on the other islands the proportion ranged as high as 85 to 90 percent. Until the WPA built causeways and bridges in the 1930s, Sea Islanders could reach Charleston only by boat. Most blacks on Johns Island earned meager incomes operating their own small farms or working for others on large truck farms or in Charleston homes, factories, and shipyards. Illiteracy was widespread. Septima Clark had first gone to Johns Island in 1916 to teach in a crude two-room school; four decades later, she lamented that the islanders had made little progress in their battle against ignorance, poverty, disease, and superstition. Only one out of ten black adults on the island was literate, about the same percentage as the number of registered voters. The islanders were isolated culturally as well. They spoke Gullah, a dialect bearing distinctly African traits that had evolved among their slave ancestors. They had divorced themselves from the mainland, and they remained deeply suspicious of outsiders, especially whites, who came to the islands. In short, conditions on Johns Island and the other Sea Islands were such that virtually any change would be dramatic.[11]

When Esau Jenkins came to Highlander's 1954 workshop on the United Nations, staff members met a leader who would make their communitywide education program a success. Jenkins was a remarkably active man and clearly a major figure on Johns Island. He had supplemented his fourth-grade education by taking night classes on the island and in Charleston, and after converting his small cotton farm into a truck farm he had learned the rudiments of Greek in order to do more business with Greek vegetable merchants in Charleston. Later, as islanders began to work in Charleston, Jenkins operated a small bus line to transport them to the city and back. He was president of the island's PTA, a church school superintendent, assistant pastor of his church, and a member of the Charleston NAACP executive board. He was also the perennial president of the Johns Island Citizens' Club, a two-hundred-member organization interested in school and community improvement, and chairman of the Progressive Club, a fifteen-member group he had organized in the late 1940s to provide legal aid to blacks.[12]

Esau Jenkins, right, instrumental in starting the Citizenship School program on the South Carolina Sea Islands, ca. 1954. *Highlander Research and Education Center.*

Jenkins was convinced that the right to vote was the key to Johns Island's problems. One morning Alice Wine, one of his bus passengers, asked him to help her learn to read and write so she could pass South Carolina's literacy test for voter registration. Jenkins secured and circulated copies of the state constitution and voting laws among all his nonvoting passengers. During the forty-five-minute drive to Charleston he talked about the definitions of words in that part of the constitution that made up South Carolina's literacy test and about registration and voting procedures. After arriving in the city and while waiting for passengers for the return trip to Johns Island, he discussed further the meaning of the passages with the islanders. Wine eventually received her registration card by memorizing the pertinent section of the state constitution. But she still wanted to learn to read, and Jenkins knew that he was not equipped to teach that skill to others.[13]

At Highlander, Jenkins was emphatic about what he wanted to do about voter registration on Johns Island. He explained that the most pressing need on the island was adult education, for only a few black residents were able to read and write well enough to meet voting requirements. Encouraged by the HFS staff's offer to help finance a night school for adults if he could find a place and a teacher for it, Jenkins decided to run for school board trustee on Johns Island. He never expected to win. But he wanted to prove that a black person could seek political office without being killed and to use his campaign to arouse interest in voter education. Jenkins's candidacy spurred a small increase in black voter registration, and in the election against three white candidates he polled 192 out of 200 black votes and finished third, high enough to prompt the chairman of the county council to change the office of school trustee from an elective to an appointive position. More important, Jenkins formed a committee to maintain the momentum of the registration campaign, in effect starting the kind of community organization that Highlander had tried to develop elsewhere.[14]

Impressed by Jenkins's initiative and by Zilphia Horton's report of her visit to Johns Island in November 1954, HFS staff members made a series of trips during 1954 and 1955 to explore the possibility of starting a leadership training program on the island. They encountered a mixed picture. There was some cautious interest in the connection between education, political action, and integration; a potential set of leaders among Citizens' Club members; and a general understanding of the need to decentralize the responsibility for voter registration and other projects. Myles Horton had a difficult time, however, in convincing Jenkins and his neighbors that

Highlander's program would help them make even greater progress. Jenkins could "think in terms of getting people active," Horton confessed, but the whole idea of leadership training was "meaningless" to him.[15] Even so, Horton thought that the Sea Islands could provide a successful model of the leadership training program. First, there was a clear desire to increase the number of registered black voters. Between 1944 and 1954 only about two hundred black islanders had registered to vote, but in 1955, prodded by Jenkins's insistence that the ballot was essential to gaining recognition from white society, over one hundred had registered. Second, the geography of the area would allow HFS teachers to approach each island as a separate, manageable project, and to use their experiences on Johns Island to improve the program on Edisto, Wadmalaw, and other islands. The economic status of the black population also promised success for the leadership training program. Although most black islanders barely lived above the subsistence level, many owned their own farms or operated small businesses. Horton believed that this made them less vulnerable to economic pressure from whites yet still hungry for some way out of their poverty.[16]

What most convinced Horton that Highlander could help on the Sea Islands was the ability of Jenkins and Septima Clark to carry out the leadership training program. Horton knew that the project would work only if the HFS staff remained in the background. He also recognized that the black islanders must have black leaders. Indeed, Clark and other Johns Island teachers asked Horton to keep whites away from the island during the initial stages of the program in order to allay the residents' suspicion of outsiders and their fear of white reprisals. But since someone had to keep Highlander informed, Horton hired Clark in February 1955 to file reports that would help the staff analyze the development of community leaders, prepare a leadership training manual, and secure funds for the project. As she worked with Jenkins on the voter registration drive, Clark was careful not to give the impression that she was interfering with his efforts. At the same time, she tried to persuade Jenkins that cultivating new leaders would supplement rather than detract from his campaign. She encouraged him to put registered voters to work, no matter how indirectly their tasks affected the voter registration program. Gradually Jenkins gained confidence in Clark's knowledge of Johns Island and began to understand the value of spreading the responsibilities of leadership. He now realized the importance of giving others tasks that helped produce "better citizens in a community," he wrote Horton in April 1955. "My old ways of doing were slow."[17]

Once Jenkins had grasped the objectives of the Highlander program, the next step was to recruit other Johns Islanders for residence sessions on leadership training. Workshops on the island proved nearly as effective as workshops at HFS. During the summer of 1955 Clark brought three carloads of islanders to the folk school. Among them was George Bellinger, Jenkins's bus-line competitor and possibly the wealthiest black man on Johns Island; his cooperation was crucial to the success of the entire program. Bellinger eventually agreed to support not only the voter registration campaign but also the effort to establish a credit union and a low-cost housing project on the island. By September 1955 he and other residents who had attended Highlander workshops had emerged as a core group of leaders on Johns Island. Horton thought the program could continue without further residence sessions. But Jenkins and other islanders wanted more training, and in February 1956 they attended a series of one-day workshops on Johns Island that revealed the strengths and shortcomings of the leadership training program. One workshop group studied cooperatives with Bernice Robinson, who had been working with the islanders since returning from an HFS workshop. Other participants learned that loans could be secured for homes costing far more than most of the existing dwellings on Johns Island. Yet the time it took a third group to read the section of the South Carolina constitution required for voter registration re-emphasized the problem of illiteracy on Johns Island.[18]

Despite signs of progress, Horton's prediction in March 1955 that it would take about two years to register all the potential black voters on the Sea Islands was proving far too optimistic. Horton wanted to direct the program toward public school desegregation and use that issue to stimulate black political activity on Johns Island and in the Charleston area. But Jenkins continued to concentrate solely on voter registration, convinced that the election of black public officials would be enough to solve the island's problems. At the same time, Horton's vague description of the leadership training program and his initial difficulty with the Gullah dialect hindered communication between himself and Jenkins. Many Johns Islanders responded cautiously to the program. A number of black residents stayed away from meetings attended by Highlander staff members. One man apparently kept his truck engine idling during such meetings in case he needed to make a quick escape. Some black islanders criticized Jenkins for going too far. Whites who learned about his activities almost certainly agreed. Every day it seemed that one or two blacks would withdraw their names from a petition or send "a smart back-tracking letter" to the editors of Charleston's newspapers, Clark complained.[19]

More than anything else, Highlander's leadership training program was not addressing the problem of adult illiteracy. The three hundred blacks who were registered voters in 1956 may have been virtually all of the blacks on Johns Island who could meet South Carolina literacy requirements; the vast majority simply could not read well enough to gain the franchise. Horton had assumed that the islanders would have to participate in other community activities before they would become involved in a literacy program for voter registration. Two years of limited success, however, suggested that taking the opposite approach might produce more results. After all, Johns Island blacks remained convinced that literacy would solve their most basic problems. They were unwilling to enroll in the adult education program offered by the Charleston County public school system not because they were uninterested, as officials claimed, but because they did not want to go to a public school, stuff themselves uncomfortably behind children's desks, and use the same reading materials ordinarily used by first graders. Johns Island needed a different kind of school, Horton decided. It should be physically comfortable and staffed by nonprofessional teachers who were familiar to the adults and able to show them that literacy could be achieved quickly and open up new opportunities for voting as well as a variety of community projects. Horton had no particular teaching method in mind. But Clark had taught illiterate adults before, and if her approach was a bit too traditional for Horton, she might still keep the literacy program going.[20]

In the fall of 1956 Horton, Clark, and Jenkins moved to set up an adult school on Johns Island that residents would soon call the Citizenship School. The Progressive Club tried unsuccessfully to secure the use of the local high school and the island's Methodist center, and a white man outbid the club for the purchase of an old schoolhouse from the county school board. But when the man offered to sell the property, Jenkins asked Horton if Highlander could lend the money to buy the place for the adult school. HFS had received a grant of $56,150 from the Schwarzhaupt Foundation in July 1956 to continue the leadership training program for another three years; Horton was therefore able to help the Progressive Club acquire the building for $1,500. By January 1957, Johns Island residents had remodeled the old school so that it could fill several functions. There was room in the front for a cooperative grocery store, and there was enough room in the back for recreational events, Progressive Club meetings, and, most important, adult literacy classes. Through contributions, club dues, proceeds from the cooperative, and rental fees from other groups, the club eventually repaid its debt to Highlander.[21]

Horton and Clark then persuaded Bernice Robinson to teach the first class at the adult school. Horton reminded Robinson that after she had attended a HFS workshop she had told him that she would be willing to do anything to help the school. But she was a beautician and a dressmaker, Robinson protested; she had no experience as a teacher and no college education. That made no difference to Horton and Clark. Robinson had finished high school, and she would be teaching only the most elementary subjects. They needed a teacher who would not follow standard teaching practices, who would have a fresh perspective on education, and who was familiar with the Highlander program. Most important, they needed a black woman whom the islanders would trust and who could communicate with them. Highlander would provide the funds for the project, and staff members would supervise its overall operations. Robinson finally agreed to try teaching and began recruiting students for the school.[22]

On January 7, 1957, Robinson stood nervously before her first class on Johns Island. She had brought with her some elementary school teaching materials, but she very quickly realized that they were too juvenile for the group. Reassuring the ten women and four men in the room that she did not consider herself a teacher and that they were all going to learn together, Robinson then asked them what they wanted to learn. It was an inspired question, for the subsequent success of Highlander's Citizenship School program stemmed from its ability to respond to the expressed needs of its students. The islanders told Robinson that they first wanted to be able to write their names. Next, they wanted to learn to read well enough to understand a newspaper, the Bible, and that part of the state constitution required under South Carolina voter registration laws. They also wanted to know how to fill out mail-order catalogue forms and money orders to pay for their purchases. Finally, the men who worked on the wharves in Charleston wanted to be able to do some arithmetic in order to keep track of their hours and the amount of cargo they moved. The group decided to meet two hours a night, two nights a week, for the next two or three months. Robinson also agreed to teach a group of high school girls how to sew. To symbolize the goals of the class, she tacked up a copy of the United Nations Declaration of Human Rights and announced that she wanted each student to read and understand it by the end of the school term.[23]

Robinson's teaching approach was simple and direct. At Clark's suggestion, she had the students learn to write their names through the kinesthetic method, tracing their signatures over and over again on a sturdy piece of cardboard until they could reproduce it on a blank sheet of paper. This process was hardly dull. One adult insisted that he had signed his name with an X all his life and did not intend to change; another liked to put capital E's in the middle of a word because he thought they looked pretty there. Teaching the class to read was a more complex task. After familiarizing the students with the alphabet and with words describing such things as their occupations, Robinson wrote stories about their daily activities and had those with some ability read these accounts and newspaper articles aloud to the group. Words that gave the readers trouble became the basis for spelling lessons. When the adults had acquired a small vocabulary, Robinson introduced them to the voter registration section of the South Carolina constitution and drilled them in the spelling, pronunciation, and definition of the more difficult words. To assist the students, Jenkins secured a voter registration application. The Highlander staff mimeographed it in larger type, and Robinson posted a chart-sized copy of the application on the classroom wall. Clark produced a workbook on voting, social security, taxes, and the functions of the county school board. Once the students learned basic arithmetic by studying items like grocery store advertisements, Robinson provided copies of mail-order forms and money orders and instructed them to read the directions, fill in the blanks, and compute the amount of money they owed.[24]

Robinson found that the patience she needed to work with the islanders was more than compensated for by the progress of the class. "I have never before in my life seen such anxious people," she reported. "They really want to learn and are so proud of the little gain they have made so far." Horton visited the school in early 1957 and marveled at "the expression on the faces of the people learning to read and write and spell, especially the older people."[25] Enrollment rose to thirty-seven adults, and other islanders would stay in the cooperative store and listen to the activities in the next room. By the end of the term in February 1957, sixty-five-year-old Annie Vastine, who had never been able to read or write before, was able to recognize her name. Alice Wine took great pleasure in reading during her leisure time, writing to her brother, and serving as a clerk in the cooperative grocery. The ultimate test of the program, however, was whether the adults became registered voters. Since South Carolina voting laws stipulated that residents had to re-register every ten years, the islanders decided to wait until 1958, the next re-registration year, before attempting to qualify as voters. In the meantime, Robinson conducted a second session that began in December 1957. In February 1958, all of the voting-age adults who had attended the five months of classes read the required paragraph, signed their names, received their registration certificates, and returned to the island shouting with joy.[26]

Bernice Robinson at the first Citizenship School on Johns Island, 1957. *State Historical Society of Wisconsin.*

Highlander's literacy education program helped accelerate the voter registration drive on Johns Island and in Charleston County during 1958 and 1959. Each step forward met white resistance. As local registrars realized that an increasing number of blacks were passing the literacy test, they began to scrutinize registration forms, required black applicants to read other sections of the state constitution, and refused to register those who had failed the test before. In March 1959 the Charleston *News and Courier* joined the opposition, editorializing that anyone who taught black voters to become "bloc conscious" did the race an "injustice."[27] In response, Jenkins and other local black leaders organized voter registration rallies, and Robinson held informal classes to rehearse registration and voting procedures. Robinson also launched an intensive campaign to register eligible black voters in Charleston County before the 1959 local elections. Equipped with a dozen copies of the South Carolina statutes secured with the help of a sympathetic lawyer in Virginia, Robinson coordinated a staff of local HFS alumni who reviewed the state's voting regulations with black adults, formed car pools to take them to the registrar's office, and took turns standing outside the office to give last-minute reviews and moral support. Largely as a result of such efforts, nearly seven hundred black residents in Charleston County passed the literacy test during the ten-day registration period before the election.[28]

Bolstered by the success of the Johns Island adult school and the voter registration drive, as well as by the growing demands of local blacks for political recognition, Highlander's Citizenship School program spread to other Sea Islands and into the city of Charleston. The literacy classes still involved only a small portion of the black population. But as the number of schools grew, a pattern emerged that essentially repeated the process followed on Johns Island. The first step had to be taken by local leaders, for Horton and the HFS faculty now knew that there was "no faster or more effective way to bring about integration than to assist Negroes in a program of their own making."[29] During 1958 two residents of Wadmalaw Island, a social worker on Edisto Island, and a beautician in North Charleston asked for Highlander's help in starting Citizenship Schools. Black citizens living on St. Helena and Daufuskie Islands and in a section of Johns Island called Promised Land made similar requests in 1959. Each area faced certain problems that their leaders thought could be solved after the number of black voters increased. The North Charleston beautician wanted city officials to do something about the unpaved streets and dilapidated rooming houses in her neighborhood. For those who lived on Daufuskie Island the primary goal was communication with the mainland, specifically the construction of a road that would end the 112-mile trip by car and launch between Charleston and the island.[30]

The second step in expanding the program involved the development of local support for Citizenship Schools. Clark made frequent visits throughout the islands to promote the program. Jenkins had once assumed full responsibility for starting a new project; now he passed on the methods used on Johns Island to other islanders and urged them to take action on their own. Mass meetings also built enthusiasm for the schools. Once enough interest had been established, Clark or Robinson brought prospective teachers to one of Highlander's residence sessions. Since few of these people had professional teaching experience, the workshops not only taught them how to organize and run literacy classes but also gave them confidence in the sincerity of the HFS staff. Finding places to hold the Citizenship Schools was not usually a problem. On both Wadmalaw and Edisto Islands Presbyterian preachers opened church facilities to the schools. Robinson used the shop of the North Charleston beautician for one of her classes.[31]

Following the approach adopted by Robinson on Johns Island, Citizenship School teachers helped an increasing number of black adults become registered voters between 1958 and 1961. During the winter of 1958–59, schools in North Charleston and on Johns, Wadmalaw, and Edisto Islands trained 106 students, some as young as fifteen and others as old as seventy-six, but most between the ages of forty and fifty. Sixty-one of them had previously registered to vote, and the rest passed the literacy test by April 1959. Because of the interest in the upcoming 1960 presidential election, over 150 black residents of Wadmalaw, Edisto, and Johns Islands, Promised Land, and North Charleston enrolled in Citizenship Schools during the winter of 1959–60. About one hundred adults attended classes regularly, and sixty-five became registered voters. By March 1960 there were about two hundred voters on Edisto Island, five times as many as there had been in 1958, and the number of blacks on Johns Island who had registered since 1956 had increased an estimated 300 percent by the fall of 1960. These trends continued during the winter of 1960–61, as 105 out of 111 black students in four Citizenship Schools in North Charleston and on Edisto and Wadmalaw Islands qualified to vote.[32]

Meanwhile, Highlander staff members worked to broaden the scope of the program. They held a series of workshops on James Island during the winter of 1958–59, where participants covered such topics as cooperatives, driver's education, and health care. In 1959 Clark and Robinson collected materials from earlier literacy schools into a twenty-page booklet that could be used throughout South Carolina. It contained information on Highlander, maps of the United States and South Carolina, pertinent sections of the state's voting requirements, short chapters on political parties, taxes, social security, and other subjects, and sample copies of voter registration, mail-order, and money-order forms. Later Clark and Robinson produced similar booklets for schools in Tennessee and Georgia. During the Citizenship School sessions of 1959–60 and 1960–61 Guy Carawan conducted "singing schools," music training courses held about once a week after the regular literacy classes. Carawan learned some of the old island spirituals and folk songs from the students and introduced them to new songs from other parts of the country, using the lyrics not only to help teach reading and writing but also to foster a greater appreciation for the traditional music of the Sea Islands. Alice Cobb incorporated a consumer education project into the program in 1960, and area residents built an experimental concrete-block house to demonstrate how local families could plan, finance, and construct low-cost housing themselves.[33]

By the end of the 1950s, Highlander's Citizenship School program had helped produce an active, relatively sophisticated group of black voters on the Sea Islands. Robinson became a part-time member of the HFS staff to coordinate the operations of area schools, and the islanders started work on other projects. Those on Edisto Island launched an "each-man-get-a-man" campaign, pledging every student at the literacy school to recruit another person to qualify and register to vote. Students also held monthly meetings to study voter registration laws and to review candidates and issues before an approaching election. In 1961 Jenkins formed "second step" political education classes to encourage newly registered voters to go to the polls for more reasons than because someone told them to do so. With some help from Robinson, Jenkins conducted classes on Johns, Wadmalaw, and Edisto Islands and in Charleston and nearby Awendaw once a month, leading discussions about Charleston County representatives in the state legislature, the South Carolina congressional delegation, and the availability of federal funds for local housing, health, and cooperative projects.[34]

Above all, the Citizenship Schools contributed to the growth of black political power in Charleston County. It is difficult to ascertain the number of adults who attended the schools. Between 1954 and 1961, Highlander sponsored thirty-seven education programs in South Carolina, most of them literacy schools, involving nearly thirteen hundred participants. Most Citizenship School graduates became registered voters, and many of them may well have stimulated other eligible blacks to secure the franchise. It is also difficult to gauge the effect of the Civil Rights Acts of 1957 and 1960 on black voting in the Charleston area, since county officials did not keep separate black and white voter registration rolls. Nevertheless, in 1956 there were only two hundred blacks registered on Johns Island, and few of them voted. Four years later there were some seven hundred blacks registered on the island, and voter turnout was usually almost 100 percent. Jenkins estimated that there were about five thousand blacks registered in Charleston County in 1954; a decade later there were nearly fourteen thousand. The new black electorate soon had an impact on area politics. In 1960 Johns Island's black voters turned out in record numbers, blacks outvoted whites for the first time in the history of Edisto Island, and blacks came within six votes of outvoting whites for the first time in Wadmalaw Island's history. A black candidate for the county board of directors outpolled his two white opponents to capture the St. Helena township seat, and Esau Jenkins had become a recognized political leader in the Charleston area. Many local black leaders attributed these changes to Highlander's Citizenship School program. "Everybody is jubilant for the Highlander Folk School," Jenkins later declared, for it had "helped them see the light."[35]

Horton and his colleagues were naturally pleased by this success, but by the middle of 1959 they had come to believe that Highlander should gradually decrease its role in the program. They were already receiving more requests for new schools than they could handle, and the potential size and scope of the program was far greater than they were ready or able to administer. Horton envisioned a program for thousands of people involving hundreds of thousands of dollars, putting "some real money in the South in terms of integration."[36] But such a budget would be too large for Highlander, Horton asserted, and the school's overall goals would suffer if the faculty was tied to a single project. Moreover, the announcement of a joint SCLC-NAACP campaign to add over a million African Americans to the voting lists by the November 1960 election was a clear indication that a massive black voter registration drive was about to begin, despite rabid white opposition across the South. Thus in July 1960 the HFS executive council approved the staff's plan to aid the registration campaign by helping local black leaders establish and operate their own Citizenship Schools. Over the next year, staff members developed the program to the point where it could be adopted by both local and regional civil rights groups.[37]

During the winter of 1960–61, Highlander's teachers found out how well the Citizenship School program could foster the growth of black voter registration by organizing eight schools in Huntsville, Alabama, and Savannah, Georgia. Although conditions in Huntsville and Savannah were similar to those on the Sea Islands, Bernice Robinson and Septima Clark were unfamiliar with the two cities and thus had to work harder than they had on the islands to build local support for the Citizenship Schools. Yet once they had determined each community's needs and trained leaders at HFS workshops, the new schools adopted goals and teaching methods like those on the Sea Islands, and they achieved similar results. In Huntsville, 115 students enrolled in five Citizenship Schools sponsored by the Madison County Voters' League; eighty-six had registered to vote by the end of March 1961. In Savannah, a black chemist named Hosea L. Williams, head of the Chatham County Voters' Crusade, asked for Highlander's help in strengthening local black leadership and the group's voter registration drive. Four teachers attended HFS training sessions, established three Citizenship Schools in December 1960, and successfully trained seventy-four out of ninety-two students to qualify as voters.[38]

Reassured by the progress in Huntsville and Savannah, the Highlander staff accelerated its efforts to transfer the responsibility for the program to other southern civil rights organizations. In December 1960 Horton announced that Highlander's resources were available to any group wanting to establish citizenship education classes. These groups were to select potential teachers and supervisors, finance their training at HFS workshops, and bear the costs of operating the schools. Staff members would train the teachers, standard-ize and publish procedures for running the classes, and work on improving teaching materials and methods to make the Citizenship Schools more eco-nomical and efficient. Not every staff member and local leader liked Highlander's new role, and some especially objected to the shift in the financial burden of the program. But with the legal status of the folk school in jeopardy and with the expanding number of Citizenship Schools, Horton insisted that the staff had little choice if the program was to continue.[39]

Accordingly, Highlander staff members held a series of one-week teacher-training workshops throughout 1961, as well as a set of three-day "refresher" sessions designed to help Citizenship School teachers adjust their work to fit the particular needs of their communities. At two experi-mental workshops in November 1960 and January 1961, seventy-five par-ticipants, including Esau Jenkins, experienced teachers from the Sea Is-lands, and new teachers from Huntsville and Savannah, developed a curriculum for the training program. They analyzed the instructional methods and materials that had proven effective on the Sea Islands, re-viewed the operations of Citizenship Schools, and discussed how to evalu-ate the effect of the classes on students. The HFS staff used their findings to conduct three training workshops in February, March, and April 1961 for nearly sixty teacher trainees sent by SCLC, the Montgomery Improve-ment Association, the Southeastern Georgia Crusade for Voters, and sev-eral county voting rights leagues. Any adult who lived in the community where a school was to be located and who had at least some high school education, an ability to read well aloud and write clearly on the black-board, and some familiarity with state voting and election systems and community services could become a teacher. As a result, the trainees, rang-ing in age from sixteen to seventy, included farmers, retired teachers, col-lege students, ministers, and unemployed laborers. Some were college graduates; others had only an elementary school education. All the train-ees sent by the Southeastern Georgia Crusade for Voters were knowledge-able about politics in their region; in contrast, the trainees sent by the Fayette County [Tennessee] Civic and Welfare League had seen a voting ballot for the first time in November 1960.[40]

Despite their diverse backgrounds, workshop participants found that their Citizenship Schools brought rapid results. The eighty-eight teachers trained at the January, February, March, and April workshops returned to more than forty communities in the South and enrolled between fourteen hun-dred and fifteen hundred adults in citizenship classes. By the end of Sep-tember 1961, over seven hundred of these students were registered voters.[41]

For as long as they could during 1961, the Highlander faculty followed up the training workshops by working with teachers on new citizenship education projects in Alabama, Tennessee, and Georgia. Nine Citizenship Schools held in Montgomery, Alabama, during the spring and summer of 1961 enrolled 435 students, and 243 became registered voters. Another Citizenship School project begun in the spring of 1961 was part of an intense struggle by blacks in West Tennessee for the right to vote. Although blacks made up two-thirds of the population in Fayette County, located on the Mississippi border, and in neighboring Haywood County, no blacks in Haywood County and only 420 of the nearly 10,000 eligible blacks in Fayette County were registered to vote. When local blacks began a registration drive in 1959, whites retaliated with delaying tactics and wholesale economic discrimination. Following the November 1960 election, white landowners evicted seven hundred black tenant farm families from the land; in virtually every case some member of the family had registered and voted. In response, the Original Fayette County Civic and Welfare League organized a "tent city" to house the evicted families during the winter of 1960–61. Their plight attracted national attention and eventually led to the intervention of the Justice Department. Fifteen men and women from Fayette County and twelve students from Lane College attended teacher-training workshops at HFS, and with funds provided by the staff set up twelve Citizenship Schools. Ninety-five of the 141 adults who enrolled in the schools became registered voters by July 1961.[42]

Meanwhile, the Citizenship School program was flourishing in southeastern Georgia. In January 1961 Hosea Williams and over forty local black leaders formed the Southeastern Georgia Crusade for Voters to coordinate an education project that would enhance an areawide voter registration drive. According to a Crusade for Voters survey, 77,400 blacks were eligible to vote in nine southeastern Georgia counties, but only 21 percent, or 16,350, were registered voters, and only about 60 percent of them voted. In comparison, there were about 80,000 whites registered to vote in the same counties, and an average of 70 percent voted. The result was a familiar one in the rural South: though blacks made up at least 45 percent of the population and a majority in two counties, there were no elected black officials in the area. Once the Crusade for Voters had been organized the Highlander staff moved rapidly, holding training workshops for twenty-nine prospective teachers, advancing over $2,000 to support their work when they returned home, and securing an $11,500 grant from the Schwarzhaupt Foundation to finance additional teacher training. By the middle of May there were twenty-one Citizenship Schools operating in thirteen counties in southeastern Georgia. Over 600 black adults enrolled in the classes, and at the end of the session in August, 110 registered to vote.[43]

Highlander's legal troubles with the state of Tennessee ended its involvement in the project, but the education and voter registration campaign continued. The Southeastern Georgia Crusade for Voters affiliated with SCLC in September 1961 and stepped up its efforts to increase black political power. The results were dramatic. Between 1959 and 1962 over 220 Citizenship School teachers received training, and through their classes and other campaigns 42,100 blacks registered to vote. By 1963 numerous public facilities in Chatham County had been desegregated, and the number of blacks in Savannah's municipal government and police force had increased significantly. As Horton had envisioned, the Citizenship Schools had not only stimulated black voter registration but had brought other benefits as well.[44]

By the summer of 1961, however, the program was in the hands of the Southern Christian Leadership Conference. For two years Septima Clark had been urging Martin Luther King, Jr., to adopt the Citizenship School project. King was initially reluctant, but Clark eventually convinced him that the schools had achieved more tangible results than SCLC's voter registration efforts, that they could be established across the South, and that they offered an effective alternative to the appeal of the Black Muslims among southern blacks. In late 1960 King announced that SCLC would take control of the program and named Dorothy Cotton of the SCLC staff coordinator of Citizenship School operations. In February 1961, with the aid of the HFS staff, SCLC officers applied for a $31,787 grant from the Field Foundation to carry on the program. Since SCLC did not have tax-exempt status, Highlander would administer the funds on behalf of the conference. Clark was to join the SCLC staff to train Citizenship School teachers and would receive her salary from the grant. SCLC leaders planned to send 240 potential teachers to twenty-one Highlander training workshops during 1961; these teachers in turn would open Citizenship Schools for over 20,000 blacks in the South that year.[45]

Opponents of Highlander and SCLC were quick to criticize the new alliance. The Nashville *Banner* and the Chattanooga *Times* reprinted an article from the *New York Times* that reported that "some observers" believed the affiliation "raised serious questions of prestige" for SCLC, for "the delicacy of the racial problem and Highlander's controversial status" would make it difficult for "Southern whites of liberal or moderate persuasion to deal with the conference." The Chattanooga *News-Free Press* condemned both groups and their plan "to train Negro leaders to agitate for all kinds of forced racial integration." Even the black Pittsburgh *Courier* worried that it was "a dubious alliance" that would do little to help SCLC.[46]

The Field Foundation complicated the transfer far more than any critics when it made an award of $26,500 to SCLC on the condition that the funds not be administered by the HFS staff or used at the folk school pending a final court decision on its future. Highlander's precarious legal position made the foundation's directors wary of jeopardizing their own tax-exempt status by giving more money to the school. Following a series of negotiations between Horton, James Wood of SCLC, Maxwell Hahn of the Field Foundation, and Wesley Hotchkiss of the American Missionary Association of the Congregational church, the AMA agreed to receive and administer the grant on behalf of SCLC. The AMA had a tradition of funding adult education and community service programs, and the Congregational church had several residence centers in the South that could be used for training workshops, including Dorchester Community Center in McIntosh, Georgia. Under the new arrangement the AMA would put Highlander staff members on its payroll and finance training workshops away from the school.[47]

Meanwhile, Horton and Wood formed the Citizenship School Committee in June 1961 to ensure the survival of the program regardless of what happened to Highlander. The committee included Horton, Wood, Herman Long of the AMA Race Relations Department, and a young black minister named Andrew Young. Inspired by a recent HFS workshop, Young had accepted Horton's invitation to join the staff in the spring of 1961. Young thought the civil rights movement needed someone who was "somewhat secure in an integrated society and is able to appreciate the Negro's possible contributions." He also wanted to provide "a little theological perspective" for civil rights activists, for he believed that "what they hunger for most is some form of ideology that can hold them together as a movement." Young did not know whether he could fulfill these functions, but he believed he could help "by bringing together many people who can, and Highlander seems to be the place to do it; perhaps the only place."[48] Because of Highlander's uncertain future, however, Young bypassed the school to become the AMA's administrator of the SCLC grant, in effect acting as a bridge between the groups involved in the transfer of the Citizenship School program.[49]

Septima Clark and Bernice Robinson objected to the slow and complex maneuvering of the Citizenship School program, revealing the tensions that beset the Highlander staff during its fight to keep the school in operation. In November 1960 Clark sensed considerable strain among HFS staff members over the fate of the program, but trusted that they would "never scorn" the people they served and "cater only to men in gray Flannel Suits."[50] But as delays in starting the SCLC program continued, and as Highlander's financial troubles grew, both Clark and Robinson came to believe that the situation would never clear up. Clark also suspected that there was little interest in her or the teacher-training program. The two women therefore took the Peace Corps examination at the end of May 1961. They explained to a shocked Horton that when the decision to separate Highlander's and SCLC's Citizenship School activities had changed the entire operation of the program, they had decided to work together regardless of who paid them. They refused "to be swapped around like horses."[51] Since Horton had told Clark that HFS could not assume responsibility for her job with SCLC, and since SCLC had not made any commitment to her at all, Clark felt abandoned by the conference and was ready to take her services elsewhere.[52]

Already under pressure to maintain Highlander's residence program while battling for the school's existence, Horton managed to ensure the continuation of the Citizenship School program and to persuade Clark and Robinson to remain with it. Clark accepted Horton's reassurances that HFS and SCLC were committed to the project, and as the Field Foundation began funding the program she left Highlander to work with SCLC while serving as a consultant to the school. Robinson decided to stay on the HFS staff and provide her services to SCLC upon request. Clark had been justified in complaining about the uncertainty of her position, but the dispute evidently created some ill feeling between Clark and her former colleagues, and she never seemed truly satisfied with her relatively limited role in the SCLC education program.[53]

By August 1961, HFS staff members had met all their existing commitments to Citizenship School projects in Georgia, South Carolina, and West Tennessee, and had turned over administrative responsibility for the teacher-training program to the Citizenship School Committee. Since 1953 the HFS staff had directed 129 extension programs reaching an estimated 4,500 black and white southerners. The Citizenship School program had grown rapidly after 1958 and promised to expand further through SCLC's Citizenship Education Project. At Dorchester Center, Andrew Young, Septima Clark, and Dorothy Cotton trained local black leaders to operate schools patterned closely after Highlander's earlier efforts. In later years Cotton and Young agreed that the Citizenship Schools represented a vital part of the civil rights movement in the South. Young, who later became a United States congressman from Georgia, ambassador to the United Nations, and mayor of Atlanta, noted in 1981 that the South was "full" of black political leaders "who had their first involvement in civil rights in that Citizenship Training Program."[54]

While the emergence of the civil rights movement in the 1950s gave Highlander more influence in the South than it had ever had before or would ever have later, the movement gained added value and momentum from Highlander's efforts. Staff members had tried for years to break through the barriers separating southern blacks and whites. Thus when the Supreme Court issued its *Brown* decision in 1954, the HFS staff quickly proceeded to develop education programs that would promote interracial understanding and a commitment to achieving racial justice. As in the 1930s, the effectiveness of those programs, particularly their flexibility in responding to the changing emphases of the civil rights movement, was the result of the ability and leadership shown by such people as Septima Clark, Bernice Robinson, and Myles Horton, working in a sort of creative tension with one another. They and the rest of Highlander's teachers conducted almost ninety workshops on public school desegregation, integration, voter registration, leadership development, and the issues raised by college student demonstrators for nearly forty-four hundred black and white adults and youths from across the South and the nation. Citizenship Schools spread from the South Carolina Sea Islands to Georgia, Alabama, and Tennessee, helping thousands of blacks gain the literacy skills needed to vote, as well as the confidence to become active participants in their communities.[55]

Yet the impact of Highlander's efforts should not be measured by enrollment figures alone. Participants came to residence workshops motivated not simply to learn more about the nature of the problems they faced, but also to use that knowledge to involve others in campaigns to improve the lives of southern blacks. Similarly, once Clark and Robinson had shown how black adults on Johns Island could become registered voters, the Citizenship School program spread rapidly and eventually brought HFS and SCLC leaders together to train teachers to organize their own schools for even greater numbers of potential voters. Yet what Highlander taught above all else was the possibility for blacks and whites to live and work together on an equal basis, something few places in the South could or would permit in the 1950s and early 1960s. Pleased that black Americans at long last were taking control of their own destinies, Horton believed that they needed "white allies in the process of integration, so as to avoid antagonism when the goal is achieved." Highlander therefore was "important as a symbol—the Negro must know that there is such a place in the South where he can discuss his problems with members of the white race."[56]

9

Highlander under Attack, 1953–1962

As the role of the Highlander Folk School in the civil rights movement expanded, the school became the target of a series of attacks spearheaded by southern segregationists. Fearful of the Communist threat to the United States, and furious over the Supreme Court's *Brown* decision, opponents once again began to denounce the school as a Communist training center bent on fomenting racial strife and disrupting established values and institutions in the South. From 1954 until the closing of the folk school in 1961, staff members had virtually no rest from investigations, explosive publicity, and threats against them and their allies. A Senate internal security subcommittee made Highlander part of an official probe in 1954, the Internal Revenue Service temporarily revoked the institution's tax-exempt status in 1957, the Georgia Commission on Education mounted a propaganda campaign against HFS in the same year, and the Arkansas attorney general joined the hunt for subversives at the school in 1958. The drive to shut down Highlander climaxed at the end of the decade with an investigation by Tennessee state legislators, a raid on the school directed by a Tennessee district attorney, and two dramatic trials that resulted in the repeal of the HFS charter and the confiscation of folk school property in 1962. But by then Myles Horton had secured a charter for a new institution to be called the Highlander Research and Education Center. "Highlander is an idea," Horton liked to say, and though its enemies could close the school they could not stop its teachers from pursuing political, economic, and racial justice.

The offensive against Highlander generally followed a predictable pattern. Adversaries based each new set of accusations upon earlier charges, some dating as far back as the 1930s. Their assaults included the construction of conspiracies, allegations emphasizing guilt by association, and testimony furnished by former Communists of dubious integrity. The criticism intensified in proportion to the geographic scope of Highlander's operations. In some cases southern white politicians attempted to exploit voter concern over integration and communism to their own advantage by attacking HFS. Then, after years of trying to rid the South of Highlander, the school's foes finally succeeded when they took a new approach and focused on apparent violations of the HFS charter rather than on larger ideological controversies.

The defense of Highlander also had a familiar ring. Staff members remained as steadfast to the ideals guiding their work during the 1950s as they had been in earlier crises, even though it meant the loss of Highlander as an institution. Their battle with southern segregationists consistently won them admiration and sympathy outside the South. But at the same time, HFS leaders never achieved more than a standoff against their opponents in Grundy County, Tennessee, and the South. The school's defenders, therefore, could not prevent Highlander from becoming a casualty of the region's massive resistance to desegregation during the 1950s. Finally, Horton and his colleagues characteristically were more concerned with developing effective education programs than with adhering to financial and administrative procedures permitted under the HFS charter. Yet it was this tendency that proved the downfall of the folk school.[1]

Highlander's past associations with labor, farmer, and civil rights organizations ensured that it would be swept up in the "Great Fear," when millions of Americans after World War II suspected that the growing power of the Soviet Union, American foreign policy reversals, and the accelerating pace of domestic change were somehow due to radical activities at home. This fear, fanned into hysteria by Wisconsin Senator Joseph R. McCarthy, became an irresistible issue for politicians of both major parties and for "self-confessed" former Communists seeking notoriety and profit. A professional informer named Paul Crouch fired the opening salvo at Highlander in September 1953. Crouch told a Chattanooga reporter that during his reign as the "open head" of the Communist party in Tennessee between 1939 and 1941 there had been "about 25 members" in Monteagle, most of them connected with the folk school run by Myles Horton and James Dombrowski. Horton responded that Crouch was repeating the old mistake of confusing Highlander's "democratic policy," which included extending equal rights to blacks and whites, with communism.[2] Offering to match Crouch's unnamed followers with a list of twenty-five "outstanding Americans" who had backed the school in the past, Horton declared, "If independence and the right to be different is un-American, the recent converts to democracy should say so."[3]

Two months later, Tennessee Congressman Pat Sutton sought to make Highlander an issue in his campaign to defeat Senator Estes Kefauver in the 1954 Democratic senatorial primary. During a speech in November 1953 Sutton reportedly labeled HFS, Dombrowski, and Horton as Communist. Horton challenged Sutton to put his claim in writing, and the congressman replied with a six-page diatribe released to such newspapers as the Chattanooga News-Free Press, a persistent critic of the school. Sutton wrote that in his speech he had urged Tennesseans to join "in the fight against those that do not believe in America and our Constitution" and to check the record of Highlander, Dombrowski, and Horton to "see if it's the type school or the type men you want to teach your boys and girls." Sutton based his statement on information taken from the "House of Representatives files," which included the testimony of Paul Crouch and others before the House Committee on Un-American Activities. Horton curtly thanked Sutton for proving "beyond a doubt that the Highlander Folk School has been working with labor unions and opposing racial prejudice." Noting that opponents had been trying to "smear" the school since its founding in 1932, Horton told the congressman to look for some other way to get votes: "The mud won't stick." For his part Kefauver carefully avoided the Highlander issue in his race against Sutton. That was all he needed to do. Sutton, described as a "two-bit McCarthy" by the Chattanooga Times, lost the primary to Kefauver by more than a two-to-one margin.[4]

By the spring of 1954, however, Mississippi Senator James O. Eastland was linking past criticism of Highlander and similar organizations in the South with fresh invective against their advocacy of racial integration. A wealthy planter from Sunflower County, Eastland entered the Senate in 1941 and quickly became one of its most virulent defenders of white supremacy. Later he became an ardent follower of Joseph McCarthy and the ranking Democrat on the Senate Subcommittee on Internal Security. Convinced that the movement to end segregation was the work of a Communist conspiracy, Eastland thought that if he could expose those who promoted racial equality as subversives he could demolish whatever influence they had in the South and block the desegregation of public schools. A well-publicized anti-Communist campaign could also serve him well in the tough fight he faced in the 1954 election. Accordingly, Eastland announced in March 1954 that he would investigate the Southern Conference Educational Fund as part of a general probe into alleged Communist-front activity in the South. SCEF president Aubrey Williams, executive director James Dombrowski, board member Myles Horton, and former board member Virginia Durr were among those who received subpoenas to testify before the Internal Security Subcommittee in New Orleans that month.[5]

If Eastland wanted to discredit as many prominent southern white integrationists as possible, SCEF was a good place to begin. In 1946 the board of directors of the Southern Conference for Human Welfare formed SCEF to separate the educational from the political activities of the organization. Dombrowski, who had left Highlander in 1942 to serve as executive secretary of SCHW, became SCEF director in 1947. By 1954 he and Williams had turned SCEF into a small but highly vocal critic of southern segregation. While Eastland could not easily dismiss the distinguished black and white southerners who sat on the SCEF board of directors as "outside agitators," there were other avenues of assault available. He could use HUAC's earlier charges that SCHW was a Communist front to imply that SCEF was a vehicle for carrying on the same programs as its parent organization. He could stress Williams's reputation in the 1930s as a radical and outspoken New Dealer whom the Senate had refused to confirm as Rural Electrification Administrator in 1945, in part because of his racial attitudes. He could intimate that Virginia Durr, sister-in-law of Supreme Court Justice Hugo Black, wife of former Federal Communications Commission director Clifford Durr, Progressive party candidate for the Senate in 1948, and anti-poll tax activist, had introduced Communists into the highest levels of government. And he could complete the web of conspiracy by connecting SCEF with the already controversial Highlander Folk School.

When the hearings opened on March 18, 1954, the senator and subcommittee special counsel Richard Arens quickly indicated the direction the SCEF probe would take.[6] For three days Eastland and SCEF officers battled not over the functions of the fund but over the alleged Communist activities of Dombrowski, Durr, Horton, and Williams. While the bulk of the testimony did not directly concern Highlander, Eastland and Arens included the school as part of their general offensive against SCEF. After Dombrowski took the stand and identified officers and directors of the fund, Eastland and Arens grilled him for several hours on the influence of Communists in SCHW, his associations with alleged Communists and

Communist-front groups, and his endorsements of peace plans and amnesty petitions. Paul Crouch and John Butler, another Communist-turned-government-informer, then named Dombrowski as a high-ranking party member. Crouch also asserted that he had conferred with Dombrowski at SCHW meetings and at Highlander, an institution that cooperated closely with the Communist party. No one had ever introduced him as a Communist, Dombrowski replied, and he would have immediately corrected anyone who had done so. He had never seen or heard of Butler, and while it was conceivable that he had encountered Crouch among the hundreds of people he had met at Highlander it was never as a Communist party member. When Crouch insisted that he had heard Dombrowski discuss at Highlander "the actual hideout" of top Communist figures, Dombrowski shot back, "That is a lie, sir." Eastland finally dismissed Dombrowski without permitting him to describe even briefly the activities of SCEF, supposedly the purpose of the hearings.[7]

Eastland and Arens handled Durr and Williams more cautiously because of their Washington connections, but they too faced rough treatment for their past activities and associations. Durr was defiant when she appeared before Eastland. The senator denied her request to read a statement expressing her "total and utter contempt of this Committee," and when the questioning began Durr only identified herself, acknowledged that she was Clifford Durr's wife, and denied that she was a Communist or under party discipline.[8] To every other question she either refused to answer or replied simply, "I stand mute." After Butler and Crouch linked her to various allegedly Communist causes in the 1930s and 1940s, Eastland excused Durr, who coolly proceeded to powder her nose before she left the stand to the delight of press photographers covering the hearings. During his testimony, Williams freely discussed SCEF programs and the fund's ties to SCHW but denied any Communist influence. Williams also insisted that he had never met Crouch, never belonged to the Communist party, and never knowingly consorted with Communists. When Butler claimed to have met "Comrade Williams" in 1942 and attended a Communist meeting with him, Williams became furious, threatening to sue Butler the minute he repeated such statements outside the hearing room. (Butler declined to risk a slander suit.) After Crouch also claimed that Williams was a secret member of the party, Eastland allowed Clifford Durr, who was serving as counsel for Williams and Horton, to cross-examine Crouch, a right denied previous witnesses.[9]

Durr immediately began to draw from Crouch the story of his career as a Communist, repeatedly showing that the government informer's recollection of past events was vague and inconsistent and suggesting that he had been "trained in deception." Crouch alleged that most of the Communist party was composed of "secret, concealed members in all walks of life" who coordinated their efforts with "the few known Communists." That was how "left Socialists" like Dombrowski and Horton, "having nothing fundamentally different" from Communists, worked with the party. Crouch cited a meeting at Highlander in 1940 where he had supposedly stated that Communist officials were "anxious to get the maximum results" from the school without letting it become public knowledge. Among other things, he testified, Dombrowski and Horton had agreed to allow Tennessee's Communist chieftains to send an emissary named Mildred White to HFS to recruit for the party and spread "the Communist Party line among the student body there." Crouch also claimed that Horton had turned down his invitation to become a Communist with the remark that he was "doing you just as much good now" as he would as a party member. As Durr pressed Crouch for more specific information, Arens interrupted to ask the witness whether Durr was a Communist. When Crouch assured Arens that Durr had been a party member at one time, Durr became a witness and flatly denied the allegation. He demanded that either he or Crouch be indicted for perjury and left no one in doubt as to who he thought had lied.[10]

Perhaps sensing that the probe was not going well for them, Eastland and Arens called Horton into a closed session. Horton asked to testify publicly, announcing that he would answer any questions about himself without invoking the Fifth Amendment but did not intend to talk about those who were not at the hearings to defend themselves. He made clear his opposition to this and similar congressional investigating committees for the "undemocratic methods" they used under "the guise of fighting communism." Although some legislators might equate the fight for racial equality with communism, Horton maintained that public school integration would "spectacularly refresh the democratic thesis everywhere," reaching into the farthest corners not only of Asia and Africa but of Mississippi as well. Failing to budge Horton from his position, Eastland reluctantly allowed him to testify in open session.[11]

Horton's public appearance at the hearings was brief and tumultuous. Almost immediately he and Eastland began to quarrel over whether the alleged Communist organizer Mildred White had been a student at Highlander. Horton could not recall her specifically, but he asserted that if she had come to HFS it was as a union member, not as a Communist party member. Before he could outline the school's admission policy, Eastland slammed his fist on the table and barked that if Horton could not remember White he could not explain the basis of her attendance at Highlander. At that point Arens inquired about Dombrowski's affiliation with Highlander. Horton remained silent while Clifford Durr objected that Dombrowski had already testified about himself. Impatiently Eastland burst out, "Is that any reason why this witness should not answer?" Insisting that he be given a chance to state his reasons for not answering, Horton exclaimed, "Mr. Chairman, you listened to Communists and ex-Communists talk here—won't you listen to an American citizen talk?"[12] As Eastland pounded his gavel for order, Horton began to read in a rising voice a statement on civil rights by President Dwight D. Eisenhower until the senator ordered Horton out of the hearing room. Two United States marshals grabbed Horton and propelled him toward the door. "They're treating me like a criminal," he shouted, turning to yell at Eastland, "You are just putting on a show here, that's all!"[13] The struggle continued out in the corridor as the marshals attempted to throw Horton to the floor, one of them snapping that they had been warned he was a dangerous troublemaker. Shaking with fury, Horton concluded that Eastland had deliberately planned to evict him from the hearings because of his stormy executive session with the senator.[14]

The hearings reached a dramatic climax when Crouch returned to attest to the alleged Communist sympathies of SCEF leaders. Crouch identified five men, four of them former SCHW officers, who he said had operated a Communist espionage ring inside the White House before World War II. Neither President and Mrs. Roosevelt nor Justice Hugo Black suspected that these men were Red agents, Crouch asserted, but Virginia Durr "had full knowledge" of the conspiracy.[15] When Crouch finished and stepped down from the witness chair, Clifford Durr suddenly lunged at him and roared, "You son of a bitch! I'll kill you for lying about my wife!" In the ensuing bedlam, attorneys and marshals restrained Durr while the informer stood to one side grinning. Friends led the white-faced and trembling Durr out into the corridor, where he suffered what doctors later diagnosed as a mild heart attack. After he was taken to a local hospital, someone rushed up to ask if help had arrived. Horton bitterly commented, "What difference does it make—they'll assassinate you one way or the other."[16] Shaken by Durr's outburst, Eastland told reporters at the end of the hearings that he might issue contempt citations against witnesses who had refused to testify, but he did not think the Durrs or Williams were Communists.[17]

If Eastland turned to McCarthyism to convince the public that white southerners who sought integration were isolated Reds, then the SCEF hearings produced disappointing results. In a widely reported poll taken by the Montgomery *Advertiser* of the nine journalists who covered the hearings as to who represented "the greatest threat to American ideals," Eastland received four votes, Crouch two, and Arens, Dombrowski, and a subpoenaed witness named Max Shlafrock one each.[18] Newspaper editorials in the South as well as outside the region generally echoed Montgomery columnist Allen Rankin's characterization of the hearings as "incredible" and a "tragi-farce" and often tied Eastland's probe to his re-election campaign.[19] Eleanor Roosevelt, Reinhold Niebuhr, Roger Baldwin of the ACLU, Ralph J. Bunche of the United Nations, ministers, educators, and two labor union presidents were among those who commended Horton for his position in New Orleans. But some Tennessee newspapers were noticeably critical. The editor of the Chattanooga *News-Free Press* sneered that Horton "added no honor to the reputation of his unrespected Highlander Folk School" by creating such "disorder" at the hearings that he was ejected. The editor of the Grundy County *Herald* remarked that Horton's statement in New Orleans—"Where I come from Mountain Men don't scare easily"—applied to himself as well, for he was "a lowlander and an outsider and a thousand years at Summerfield would not change that fact."[20]

For the moment, however, Horton seemed to have succeeded in defending Highlander's policies and his own principles. At a public meeting at HFS in late March 1954, Horton gave his version of the SCEF hearings, declared once again that the staff had never knowingly accepted funds or students from the Communist party, and asserted that the best answer to communism was to develop "a program of individual rights" that would "win out over Communism."[21] Senator Eastland never again conducted hearings on communism in the South, and Paul Crouch died in disgrace and virtually unnoticed in November 1955. Two months earlier the Senate Internal Security Subcommittee had published its report on SCEF. Not surprisingly, it completely accepted the testimony of Crouch and John Butler regarding SCHW, SCEF, and Highlander. Neither the United States attorney general nor the Subversive Activities Control Board acted on the subcommittee's recommendation that they investigate SCEF, but the damage had been done. Although SCEF continued to work on many fronts in the civil rights movement during the 1950s and 1960s, the Communist stigma haunted the organization and contributed to its gradual decline in importance. Highlander had weathered the storm better than SCEF, perhaps because their programs and public relations approaches differed, because of the greater regional and national prominence of SCEF leaders, and because the public generally did not identify the school with either SCHW or SCEF.[22]

In May 1954, shortly after the SCEF hearings, the Supreme Court issued its momentous ruling against public school segregation, touching off a prolonged and bitter racial battle in the South. As the Highlander staff conducted residence workshops on integration and began to develop its Citizenship School program, whites in the states of the old Confederacy rallied to the defense of racial segregation. While a few southern political leaders such as Estes Kefauver cautiously counseled acceptance of the *Brown* decision, far more voiced the sentiments of James Eastland, who condemned the Supreme Court for being "indoctrinated and brainwashed by Left-wing pressure groups." Marvin Griffin won the 1954 Democratic gubernatorial primary in Georgia with a campaign pledge that, "come hell or high water," he would prevent the "meddlers, demagogues, race baiters and Communists" from destroying the right of states to maintain segregated schools.[23]

Southern white resistance to desegregation took several forms. Public school officials and state legislators adopted measures to obstruct or restrict school desegregation, ranging from pupil placement plans to legislation providing for the closing of public school systems. Some ninety different private groups organized to defy the *Brown* decision and to mobilize whites against the supposedly conspiratorial attempt to desecrate racial orthodoxy and undermine southern society. After its establishment in 1954, the Citizens' Council quickly became the most vocal and powerful segregationist force in the South, and at its peak in 1956 the council and associated groups claimed as many as 250,000 to 300,000 members. The more prominence Highlander achieved as an education center for civil rights activists, the more likely it would become the object of segregationist attacks. Indeed, the staff's promotion of racial integration and black voter registration posed an immediate, tangible challenge to the very traditions southern segregationists were determined to uphold.[24]

But the next blow against Highlander came from an unexpected source. In February 1957, H. T. Swartz, director of the Tax Rulings Division of the Internal Revenue Service, informed the HFS staff that the institution no longer qualified for the tax-exempt status granted it in 1937. Charging that Highlander's classes were principally concerned with the organization of labor unions and with building pressure for or against pending legislation and political candidates, Swartz objected to the faculty's announced intention of "deliberately" using education "for the realization of certain social and cultural values." Swartz conceded that some HFS activities were "educational in character." But in his view the staff did not operate the school "exclusively" for educational purposes or for any purpose by which HFS could legally qualify as a tax-exempt corporation.[25]

Surprised by the IRS ruling, staff members immediately began a drive to restore the tax exemption. Horton suspected that the trouble really stemmed from the school's integration program. Nevertheless, it was essential to reverse the decision quickly, for the HFS treasury was unusually low after several residence sessions during the winter of 1956–57. School attorneys began working to have Highlander reclassified as a tax-exempt institution, while staff members tried to maintain their 1957 workshop schedule by slashing expenditures and salaries. Horton resigned from the SCEF board of directors and all other organizations that required travel. Urgent requests went out to supporters for special, taxable contributions. In response, almost twice as many individuals sent donations to HFS in 1957 as in 1956, though the total was barely enough to cover the costs of the summer projects. Meanwhile, Marvin Griffin and James Eastland cited the tax revocation as further evidence of Highlander's illegal operations, and a petition circulated in Monteagle attacked the "integrationists" at HFS for teaching ideas "contrary to our southern way of life and Americanism."[26]

Highlander's financial crisis ended with the restoration of tax exemption in December 1957. At the suggestion of an IRS official, the HFS board of directors, composed of Horton, Tracy City author May Justus, and retired University of the South professor Eugene Kayden, amended the school's charter to conform to the agency's 1954 code on tax-exempt institutions. The IRS was then satisfied. H. T. Swartz wrote that contributions to the school were again exempt from federal income taxes under the agency's 1937 ruling. Clearly, the reinstatement of Highlander's tax exemption was crucial to its education program. In 1957 only $4,000 of its total income of $39,000 had come from foundations; in comparison, by the end of the 1958 fiscal year the school's income had shot up to nearly $114,300, with foundations granting over $73,000. Horton and Septima Clark were still not certain why the IRS had moved against HFS, but they could expect their foes to try again to stop their fight against segregation.[27]

An interracial children's camp brought more trouble to Highlander. In 1954 the Georgia legislature had created the Georgia Commission on Education to develop legislative strategies for the preservation of public school segregation. Three years later Governor Marvin Griffin had appointed a new executive secretary to the commission, an ambitious young Atlanta lawyer named Truman V. Williams, Jr. Under Williams's direction the commission mounted an aggressive propaganda campaign and worked with the Georgia Bureau of Investigation on undercover investigations of civil rights groups. One of the commission's targets, the interracial Koinonia Farm near Americus, Georgia, led it to Highlander. Koinonia's leaders took part in an attempt to desegregate Georgia State College in 1956, prompting a GBI probe into Koinonia's operations and its plans for an integrated children's camp. When legal obstacles and violence made it impossible to hold the camp in Georgia, Highlander and Koinonia jointly sponsored camps at the Tennessee school in 1956 and 1957, where GBI agents apparently continued their surveillance. Meanwhile, the Commission on Education learned in 1957 about the twenty-fifth anniversary celebration to be held at Highlander during Labor Day weekend. Calculating that the affair, and especially the presence of Martin Luther King, Jr., might provide material for the charge that racial integration was a Communist plot, commission officials dispatched a photographer named Edwin Friend to infiltrate the meeting.[28]

Friend registered at the anniversary seminar as an employee of the Georgia water pollution department and a free-lance photographer on vacation with his wife. Also registering were a black woman who had been an HFS student and her husband, Abner Berry, who said he was a free-lance reporter who might write an article on Highlander. Berry did not tell Horton that he was a correspondent for the Communist party's *Daily Worker*. But Horton accepted Berry's and Friend's stories at face value and paid little attention to the two strangers during the anniversary. At one point he saw Friend and Berry together, but when he approached they stopped their conversation and denied knowing each other. During the festivities Friend took numerous pictures of blacks and whites discussing the implications of integration for the South, listening to speeches and folk singing, and eating, swimming, and square dancing together. Almost every one of Friend's shots included Berry. When Horton requested a photograph of Martin Luther King, Jr., Aubrey Williams, Rosa Parks, and himself sitting in a row before they addressed the celebrants, Friend waited until Berry squatted in front of the group before taking the picture. Horton complained that he did not want to buy that print, but he still had no inkling of the motive behind Friend's actions.[29]

The results of Friend's work became painfully clear shortly after the anniversary weekend. In early October 1957, T. V. Williams and Friend presented to the Georgia Commission on Education photographs and other evidence purporting to show that the leaders of every recent major racial conflict had gathered at Highlander to discuss "methods and tactics for precipitating racial strife and disturbances." Williams also released a list of anniversary participants, which included Abner Berry of the *Daily Worker*. In Governor Griffin's opinion the report furnished "irrefutable" facts about "where some of the South's racial trouble originates."[30] Horton dashed off a public statement of protest and then tried to unravel the mystery of Abner Berry. The journalist had published a favorable summary of the seminar in a September 1957 issue of the *Daily Worker* and later apologized to Horton for the trouble he had brought to the school. Horton still was surprised and angry that Berry had not revealed his true identity to him, for "any informed person knows that such an article can do untold harm to every pro-integration group in the South."[31]

In October the Georgia Commission on Education published a four-page, glossy, newspaper-sized work bearing the sensational title *Highlander Folk School: Communist Training School, Monteagle, Tenn.* The report hammered on the theme that the participants at the anniversary weekend were un-American, immoral, Communist conspirators responsible for every major civil rights controversy since the *Brown* decision. Articles quoted the testimony of Paul Crouch and John Butler before the Eastland committee in 1954, listed the "Communist Affiliations" of those attending the Labor Day conference, and summarized HUAC citations of a number of organizations and journals. Filling the inside pages of the report were pictures of racially mixed groups taken by Friend at HFS. Detailed captions characterized Martin Luther King, Jr., as a representative of "the ultimate in 'civil disobedience,'" Pete Seeger as a typical entertainer who supported the "Communist apparatus," and Aubrey Williams as perhaps the greatest ally of the Communist party "in its conspiracy against peace between the races" in the South. Friend's shot of Berry crouching in front of Horton, King, and Williams depicted the "'four horsemen' of racial agitation." Only one photograph, the largest, had no caption. It showed a black man and a white woman in a square dance requiring the partners to clap their hands behind each other's head; in the commission's view, this was interracial mixing of the worst kind.[32]

The exposé touched off a bitter public debate over Highlander. The Commission on Education circulated some 250,000 copies of the paper across the nation, and estimates of the number of reprints distributed by Citizens' Council and Ku Klux Klan groups by the end of 1959 ran to over one million. Several southern newspapers launched their own attacks on the basis of the commission's findings. The editor of the Maryville-Alcoa *Times* observed that if HFS was actually in league with the Communist party, "the sooner it is gotten rid of the better." The Atlanta *Constitution* opened a seven-part series on the folk school by quoting Horton as saying that Highlander was not Communist but "in the same field." Later installments reproduced portions of Crouch's New Orleans testimony, suggested that most Grundy Countians had "scorned" Highlander for years, and hinted at secret workshops, suspicious supporters, and interracial intimacies.[33]

The "'four horsemen' of racial agitation," Labor Day weekend, 1957. Crouched in foreground, Abner W. Berry; first row, Martin Luther King, Jr., second from right; Aubrey Williams, third from right; Myles Horton, fourth from right. Also seated: Rosa Parks, sixth from right. First published by the Georgia Commission on Education, this photograph appeared on billboards in the 1960s with the caption "Martin Luther King at Communist Training School."

In time the Georgia commission's report became a staple of segregationist propaganda. The commission itself reiterated the accusations in its 1958 pamphlet *Communism and the NAACP* and its 1961 publication *CORE and Its Communist Connections.* Mississippi Governor Ross Barnett displayed the "four horsemen" photograph as proof of the civil rights movement's Communist leadership while testifying against a major civil rights bill before a Senate committee in 1963. *American Opinion,* the official organ of the John Birch Society, printed the picture as a postcard. The same scene also appeared on billboards across the South during the mid-1960s with the headline "Martin Luther King at Communist Training School."[34]

As in the past, Highlander's defense came largely from outside the South. To be sure, there were some black and white southerners who expressed support for the school. Elsewhere, however, the reaction was almost entirely favorable to Highlander. The editor of the Littleton, Colorado, *Arapahoe Herald* exaggerated when he commented that Governor Griffin "believes that anyone who favors integration must be a Communist. That makes about 125 million Communists in the United States."[35] But Highlander's staff did its best to encourage such sentiments in a nation-wide public relations campaign emphasizing its commitment to racial integration in the face of southern resistance to federal law. In December 1957 Horton released a statement signed by Eleanor Roosevelt, Reinhold Niebuhr, Monsignor John O'Grady of the National Conference of Catholic Charities, and former University of Wisconsin law school dean Lloyd K. Garrison. The four charged Griffin with "irresponsible demagoguery" and urged Americans to join them in subscribing to Highlander's "policies of equal opportunity."[36] Horton also considered filing suit against Griffin for his "slanderous attack," and challenged the governor to state "personally, and without immunity" that he was a Communist. Griffin declined, saying only, "You lie down with dogs and you're going to get fleas."[37] The HFS executive council eventually decided not to take legal action against Griffin, for it saw "little likelihood of receiving a fair trial in a Georgia court." Instead, the council adhered to its conviction that Highlander's "best defense" was to continue its present course and remain open to all who came in good faith to participate in its educational activities.[38]

The impact of the Georgia Commission on Education's tract was not immediately apparent. The FBI dismissed the "Communist Training School" claim during its initial probe into Martin Luther King's activities in 1961, and a HUAC spokesman later reported that no federal agency had cited Highlander as subversive. The commission itself declined in importance after T. V. Williams resigned amid accusations of using the agency to interfere in Georgia's 1958 gubernatorial primary; his replacement disavowed the report on Highlander. Abner Berry remained an enigma. When Horton later encountered him at the United Nations, Berry claimed that he had never known Edwin Friend or realized that the photographer was manipulating him. Insisting that he had never meant to harm either HFS or the civil rights movement, Berry said he had concealed his identity because he thought it might embarrass the school. The tragedy, he ruefully added, was that he had left the Communist party shortly after writing his *Daily Worker* article. Horton charitably accepted his explanation. But what had begun as a rejuvenating anniversary celebration had become part of a smear campaign that frightened Highlander's supporters and placed the school in an increasingly vulnerable position.[39]

The segregationist offensive against Highlander escalated during 1958, fueled by the school desegregation crisis in Little Rock, Arkansas. In September 1957 President Eisenhower had ordered federalized National

Guardsmen and one thousand army paratroopers to enforce the court-ordered admission of nine black students to previously all-white Central High School. By the time Arkansas Governor Orval Faubus ordered the closing of the city's high schools for the 1958–59 school year, Little Rock had become a symbol of southern resistance to racial desegregation. When Highlander lost its fire insurance policy in September 1957 and again in April 1958, Horton suspected that the Citizens' Council and its "Kluxer associates" were supplementing their threatening letters and anonymous telephone calls to Highlander with economic pressure against the school.[40] Staff members obtained the equivalent of insurance by securing over twenty-seven thousand dollars in pledges to pay for any possible damage to HFS property, as well as a seventy-five-thousand-dollar extended coverage policy from Lloyd's of London. In 1959 the Grundy County school board yielded to the Tracy City American Legion's demand that it dismiss local grade school teacher Vera McCampbell because of her association with Highlander. The barrage of propaganda also continued, with one gazette labeling Highlander "Little Moscow of U.S.A." and another linking the Little Rock school crisis to the "Communist Training School."[41]

Meanwhile, legislative committees in Louisiana, Florida, Mississippi, and Arkansas held hearings between 1957 and 1959 on the causes of racial unrest in the region, seeking not so much information as confirmation that the civil rights movement was subversive. Two professional witnesses imported to testify before these committees were Manning Johnson, a black ex-Communist, and J. B. Matthews, a former HUAC investigator. Both placed the Communist label on the NAACP, the Southern Regional Council and its human relations council affiliates, SCEF, and Highlander. Ardent segregationist Attorney General Bruce Bennett paraded Johnson, Matthews, and similar witnesses before the special education committee of the Arkansas Legislative Council in December 1958. As expected, the committee concluded that an interlocking network of integrationists had schemed to make the Little Rock desegregation crisis "a world-wide incident," that the NAACP was sympathetic toward Communist causes, that Highlander had been "used for communist and communist front purposes for the past 25 years," and that these and other groups had aided the international Communist conspiracy.[42]

These findings reinforced Attorney General Bennett's crusade against the NAACP and prompted him to carry the campaign into Tennessee and against Highlander. His battery of lawsuits against the NAACP and his "Southern Plan for Peace" were part of an unsuccessful attempt to wrest the 1960 Democratic gubernatorial nomination from Governor Faubus.

Yet Bennett also believed that eliminating the NAACP would preserve segregation in Arkansas and that to rid the state of the association he must root out allied organizations and institutions like Highlander. In January 1959 he told reporters from the staunchly anti-HFS Nashville *Banner* and Chattanooga *News-Free Press* that the school was "a gathering place for Communists and fellow travelers." Suggesting that Highlander be closed on the grounds that it constituted a "nuisance," Bennett offered his services and information from the Arkansas investigation if Tennessee officials decided to take action.[43]

The Tennessee legislature heeded Bennett's advice and initiated the final, decisive drive against the folk school. On January 26, 1959, state representatives Shelby Rhinehart and Harry Lee Senter introduced a resolution authorizing Governor Buford Ellington to appoint a committee to investigate Highlander and its involvement "in activities subversive to and contrary to the form of good government."[44] Rhinehart, a first-year representative whose district included Grundy County, simply wanted to discover whether the accusations against HFS were true. But Senter, a champion of segregationist causes from Sullivan County, declared that the investigation would "show the world that we are Americans, and not dedicated to one-world or one-race." To build support for the resolution, a lobbyist for the segregationist Tennessee Federation for Constitutional Government distributed copies of the Georgia Commission on Education tract on Highlander. After adding two minor amendments, the house easily approved the resolution. Barton Dement, a veteran legislator and "Un-reconstructed Rebel" from Rutherford County whose trademarks were a long, thin tie and ten-gallon white hat, then guided the measure through the state senate, arguing that Highlander was "a finishing school for Communists" who advocated "the intermingling of the races." The senate passed the resolution on a voice vote and sent it to Governor Ellington for his signature.[45]

Growing opposition to the original resolution slowed final approval of the investigation. Horton arrived in Nashville to insist that the legislature settle the question of subversion at Highlander once and for all. Asserting that the real issue was Highlander's interracial policies, he invited the legislators to visit the school, examine any and all of its records, and either prove Attorney General Bennett's charges and close HFS or put an end to the rumors. Apparently fearing that the probe might prove more expensive than productive, Governor Ellington returned the bill to the general assembly, protesting that it allowed the committee to hire a legal staff without any specific appropriation for it and that the legislators should take the responsibility for naming committee members. Senter and Rhinehart immediately introduced another resolution that was milder in form, broader in authority, and amended to meet Ellington's objections. The new measure briefly noted the charge of subversion, authorized the speakers of each house to appoint the five-member committee, and limited the total expense of the investigation to five thousand dollars. When two representatives branded the appropriation a waste of money, Senter retorted that Horton had "tantalized" legislators with an invitation to Highlander and then "challenged" them "to put up or shut up." How long were his colleagues "going to stand by and allow the Communists and do-gooders and one-worlders to take over?" Senter cried. "Our purpose is to root out that which is evil." On February 4 the house approved the revised resolution seventy-four to four.[46]

Six days later the senate adopted House Joint Resolution 30. Dement rested his case for the measure by inviting Carl H. Kilby to deliver his personal report on Highlander to the senate. Described as "a minister, gospel singer, and businessman," Kilby was also secretary of the Tennessee Consolidated Coal Company and the ringleader of the Grundy County Crusaders' campaign against Highlander in 1939. Kilby spoke rapidly and passionately as he recounted the school's "nefarious" activities. Instead of an investigation, he shouted, the legislature should enact a bill "with teeth in it" and revoke Highlander's charter. Dement then called for approval of the resolution, asserting that no one should be "scared" of trying to rid the state of "this cancerous growth." Despite the complaint of one senator that sponsors were "waving the flag of Communism" before he and others had even received copies of the proposal, the senate voted for the investigation twenty-two to nine. Opponents remained convinced that the probe would simply squander five thousand dollars, and as Ellington signed the resolution on February 12 he wondered whether the inquiry would accomplish anything.[47]

Reaction to the planned investigation was sharply divided. The Nashville *Tennessean* condemned the legislative "witch hunt" as a mere "smoke screen" created "to harass and intimidate the institution because of its candid advocacy of integration." The Chattanooga *Times* and Knoxville *News-Sentinel* agreed with the *Tennessean* that the probe would only promote Bruce Bennett's political ambitions, violate the "democratic concept" of free speech, upset efforts to maintain peaceful race relations in the state, find old information at taxpayer expense, and give Tennessee "the distinction of reviving McCarthyism." Outside the South, the St. Louis *Post-Dispatch* and other newspapers chastised both Bennett and the Tennessee legislature for their "ugly and uninformed bit of persecution" against Highlander. Conversely, the Nashville *Banner,* Charleston *News and Courier,* and Hamilton County

(Tennessee) *Herald* shared the sentiments of the Chattanooga *News-Free Press,* which depicted the probe as an effort to alert citizens "to the sordid story of this festering sore atop the mountains in the heart of Tennessee."[48] Newspapers and Governor Ellington received letters from across the state and from the Alabama House of Representatives favoring the investigation, while southern and northern HFS supporters echoed Reinhold Niebuhr's contention that Highlander was facing "political blackmail" because of its stand on integration.[49]

Under pressure to produce results before the legislature adjourned in mid-March 1959, the Highlander investigating committee convened on February 20. Chaired by Senator Dement, the all-Democratic committee included Senator Lawrence T. Hughes of Shelby County and Representatives Senter, J. Alan Hanover of Shelby County, and Cartter Patten of Hamilton County. J. H. McCartt, district attorney for the Nineteenth Judicial Circuit, served as special counsel. Armed with affidavits, copies of Highlander's 1934 charter, and information from the 1954 Eastland hearings and the Georgia Commission on Education, the committee met in secret session to hear Bruce Bennett present his evidence against HFS. Bennett also showed what was probably Edwin Friend's film of the 1957 Labor Day seminar at Highlander, identifying several persons in it as "known Communists." Horton may have hoped that the probe would help educate Tennesseans about HFS, but the committee clearly intended to search for any possible way to indict and close the school.[50]

On February 21, 1959, the legislative committee began its probe with a closed hearing in Tracy City, the seat of Grundy County, to determine Highlander's reputation in the area. It was all bad, according to the five men testifying during the five-hour session. County judge Malcolm Fults, county school superintendent E. J. Cunningham, and Grundy County *Herald* editor Herman Baggenstoss estimated that at least 95 percent of the county's residents disapproved of the school, believed that its staff was connected with some sort of communistic activity, and would be happy to see HFS located somewhere else. These three witnesses listed several reasons for the tainted image, most of them having to do with the staff's union organizing efforts during the 1930s. Fults and Baggenstoss denied that Highlander's involvement in the civil rights movement concerned the community, arguing that because there were no black residents in Grundy County there could be no "integration problem." Furthermore, even though they had no firsthand knowledge of HFS programs and had turned down invitations to attend events there, the three men did not regard Highlander as an educational institution at all. It had no normal faculty, awarded no diplomas, never had its courses approved by state officials, and never fulfilled its announced purpose of training rural and industrial leaders. In short, they insisted, Highlander had contributed nothing to the county.[51]

Two other witnesses at the Tracy City closed hearing provided more sensational testimony. Carl Kilby had never set foot on HFS premises and had had nothing to do with the school since his days with the Grundy County Crusaders, and the only contact a "retired" soldier named Carrington M. Scruggs had with Highlander occurred during his teenage years in Summerfield twenty years before. Each man nonetheless announced that he had extensive information about Highlander that he would divulge only to the committee, Kilby claiming that the FBI had taken his files and Scruggs alleging that his "classified" testimony had to be cleared by military intelligence.[52] Kilby railed away at Highlander and its supposedly immoral, Communist practices. He swore that HFS teachers constantly sought to insinuate "their nefarious communistic ideas into the heart" of various organizations and that Horton—who was "as mean as the devil"—discouraged children from going to church, told one young woman there was no God, and did not call on ministers at the school to say grace. During his youth, Scruggs testified, he had seen Zilphia Horton dressed like a Russian peasant woman, the "red book," the *Daily Worker,* and "Russian speaking students" singing "The Red Flag" at HFS, and he believed the Horton children had "Russian names." In time Scruggs had come to realize that Highlander was "operated out of Moscow" and was working for the violent overthrow of the United States government. Yet both Kilby and Scruggs admitted that they had never observed any immoral or subversive activity at Highlander.[53]

Indeed, among all the rumors and recollections offered during the session the only damaging evidence concerned the Highlander charter of incorporation. In 1933–34 HFS staff members, uncertain whether Lilian Johnson would give her Monteagle property to them, had secured a charter and begun building a folk school at Allardt in Fentress County. After Johnson had signed over the deed to her property in 1935, the staff had ended the Allardt project but neglected to refile the charter in Grundy County as required by Tennessee law. It was a minor point at this stage of the investigation, but it provided the legislators with an opening through which to move against the school.

Following a brief visit to Highlander, the legislative committee continued its investigation with a public hearing in Tracy City on February 26. Although Chairman Dement and Special Counsel McCartt announced that the committee intended to be fair and impartial, those who defended HFS quickly became embroiled in disputes with the legislators over integration and communism. Two professors at the University of the South described Highlander as "an inspiring example of democracy at work" and found not the "slightest trace" of subversion at the school. Both admitted that in supporting public school desegregation they and HFS teachers had not taken a popular position, and committee members readily agreed. Senter interpreted the two professors' remarks to mean that they advocated the "amalgamation of races." In contrast, the thirteen Grundy County residents who expressed disapproval of the folk school went virtually unchallenged. Emmett Thomas of Tracy City had never witnessed any "free love" at Highlander, but he and Summerfield laborer Henry Dyer had seen blacks and whites swimming together in the school's pond. Three local public officials concurred that Highlander could not really be a school for union organizers when Horton did not belong to any union. Other witnesses critical of Highlander confounded the committee with contradictory testimony. McCartt introduced affidavits signed in 1940 and 1941 by Summerfield residents Roy Layne and Ford Cox in which they accused the HFS staff of such offenses as displaying the "Russian flag," praising the "Russian form of Government," and carrying Young Communist League membership cards. Cox repudiated his affidavit before the committee, however, and Layne confessed that he did not recall seeing any red flags or YCL cards, or hearing staff members recruit for any organization, Communist or otherwise.[54]

The most significant disclosure during the hearing was by county register of deeds Violet B. Crutchfield. She confirmed that the Highlander charter had not been recorded in Grundy County, and also reported that part of the folk school property had been conveyed to Myles Horton in August 1957. To the committee this suggested that Horton was running Highlander for profit and violating its tax-exempt charter. The transfer of property had been made with the best of intentions but appeared legally suspect. In 1956 the HFS executive council, concerned about the financial security of the Horton family, moved that the board of directors draft a plan for deeding an appropriate amount of property to Horton. Based upon Septima Clark's report that Myles and Zilphia Horton had worked without salaries until 1954 and that Zilphia had used her eleven-thousand-dollar inheritance to renovate their home, board members recommended that the house and the land surrounding it be transferred to Myles and his heirs in appreciation of a quarter-century of service to Highlander. After consulting with attorneys, school treasurer May Justus signed over the home and some seventy acres of land to Horton in August 1957. No exchange of money was involved, and Horton and the HFS community continued to regard his home as part of the school.[55]

The questions raised by the warranty deed to Horton enabled the legislative committee to discredit Justus's spirited defense of Highlander. For an hour and a half the author and retired teacher matched wits with the legislators, often drawing applause from the two hundred spectators at the hearing. Contending that the school had contributed a great deal to the community, Justus saw "nothing immoral" in the Georgia Commission on Education picture of a black man and white woman square dancing together. When McCartt pointed out that Tennessee law prohibited interracial marriages, Justus snapped that she did not regard a square dance as part of a marriage ceremony. Noting that one of Highlander's stated purposes was to train rural and industrial leaders, McCartt asked when the staff had ever given a diploma to a student "to go out and be an industrial leader?" "I didn't know diplomas were required for training industrial leaders," Justus replied. The standoff continued until committee members zeroed in on Justus's ignorance of Highlander's financial affairs. Even though she was secretary-treasurer, Justus admitted that she did not solicit, disburse, or record the school's funds, nor did she fully understand the legal procedure involved in transferring HFS assets to Horton. But she did know that it had been Lilian Johnson's "dying wish" that the land around Horton's home be given to him, and Justus was confident that the property would remain part of the school's facilities. The legislators were incredulous. Hanover challenged Justus to name any other educational institution that gave its real estate away to faculty members, and Senter declared that the Highlander Folk School no longer existed, for Justus had "given it all to Myles Horton." The committee had at last found an issue with which to close Highlander.[56]

The final round of legislative hearings took place in Nashville on March 4 and 5. The principal witness at these sessions was Myles Horton, counseled by Nashville attorney and HFS executive council member Jordan Stokes III. During much of Horton's nearly six hours on the stand Bruce Bennett whispered suggestions to the investigating team as it delved into the school's allegedly subversive and immoral policies while accumulating further evidence of apparent charter violations. The tenor of the committee's examination of Horton was set almost immediately. Handed a copy of the HFS charter, Horton acknowledged that he had not recorded it in Grundy County. Stokes advised Horton to keep the document so the admitted defect could be corrected. But Dement declared that the committee had already subpoenaed the charter and instructed the husky sergeant-at-arms to take it away from Horton. Stokes leaped to his feet and demanded that the record show that the charter was "physically bodily removed from the witness's hands." Senter sarcastically remarked that Stokes had "made a nice picture" for news photographers, and Dement ordered the record to show that Horton "volunteered" to give the document to the sergeant-at-arms.[57]

Following this exchange, committee members interrogated Horton extensively about past accusations against him and Highlander. Again and again Horton firmly denied any connection between the school and so-called Communist and subversive organizations. He dismissed Paul Crouch as a "professional liar" who had never been to HFS. Furthermore, the picture from the Georgia Commission on Education report on Highlander that McCartt construed as an embrace between a black man and white woman was actually a square dance step, and to the delight of the audience Horton demonstrated the step with McCartt as his would-be partner. Horton assured Senter that he was a religious man, but he did not start meetings with an invocation because Highlander was not "a religious school," and he would not go to local churches because they excluded blacks. On the other hand, Highlander had long been integrated, prompting Senter to ask if it had operated in violation of Tennessee law "before the 1954 'Black Monday' decision of the Supreme Court." "Yes, sir," Horton shot back; the only segregation at HFS was between men and women, which he thought was "a reasonable sort of a necessary arrangement." Horton ended his first appearance before the committee by emphatically stating that neither he nor any Highlander student, teacher, or official was a Communist, subscribed to Communist publications, or solicited contributions from Communist groups. All he wanted was "to be left alone to teach," Horton declared, though that now seemed to be "the hardest thing to manage."[58]

Horton faltered only when questioned about the transfer of HFS property to him in 1957. In light of May Justus's testimony in Tracy City, however, it was a glaring shortcoming. Horton maintained that the board of directors had deeded him a piece of land in lieu of "back salary." Under Hanover's probing, Horton admitted that he did not know the exact amount of back pay owed him or his current salary. He knew he had no legal claim to any back salary and that if he had wanted the land he could have had it long ago. But he insisted that he had made no demands on the school and had every intention of leaving the property with Highlander and letting it serve as security for his two children. Hanover did not believe him. "That guy is running a racket at that place," he told newsmen later, and at the committee's request Horton turned over all of the school's financial statements since 1932, together with a card file of contributors.[59]

After their close examination of Horton, the legislators allowed their star witnesses, Edwin Friend and Bruce Bennett, to testify with complete impunity. Friend showed a film he had made at Highlander's twenty-fifth anniversary depicting blacks and whites in front of the HFS library and swimming together in the school's lake, where Friend asserted bathing suits were optional. A school that permitted such scenes, he said, was subversive of "the way that I have been taught to live in America" as well as of "Southern tradition," which had taught him "to keep the races separate." Bennett's testimony was largely a recitation of evidence from past congressional investigations. As he summarized the activities of Pete Seeger, James Dombrowski, Aubrey Williams, and others, Bennett diagrammed on a blackboard his version of the Communist-directed southern conspiracy, placing Highlander in the center and connecting it to the people he named as well as to SCHW, SCEF, and the Little Rock school crisis. According to this analysis, Highlander was "flying in formation with a lot of people who have as their goal the destruction of these United States as we know them, and putting the Communist Party into power in the United States." Was HFS therefore a "Communist-dominated institution?" Senter asked. After a moment's hesitation, Bennett replied that it was. When he had finished, Bennett shook hands with each committee member and said, "Run 'em out, boys, run 'em out. That's the main thing."[60]

Arkansas attorney general Bruce Bennett explaining Highlander's role as the center for "subversion" in the South to Tennessee legislative investigating committee, 1959. *State Historical Society of Wisconsin.*

Not content with the image they had already created of Highlander, the legislators heard more witnesses and filed more affidavits implicating the HFS staff in various subversive offenses before calling Horton to the stand once more to answer questions about the school's financial affairs. Squirming restlessly in his chair as Hanover questioned him closely, Horton listed Highlander's bank accounts and its funds for general operating expenses, insurance, and special projects like the Citizenship School program. Exasperated by his testimony, Hanover submitted that Horton had shuffled HFS funds so that no one could "find out what you really had." Staff members had to make their records very clear to the IRS and to their contributors, Horton replied hotly, and foundations would not award grants to the school if they were not satisfied. "That's no proof," Hanover interrupted.[61] Stokes jumped up to object that the representative was arguing with the witness. Hanover retorted that he intended to repeat his questions as long as Horton evaded them. "I am not trying to talk around anything," Horton protested, "I am trying to explain the program to you." Senter then complained about the sources of Highlander's financial support and began plucking cards naming HFS donors from the filing case Horton had turned over to the committee. "Some of these are not even from Tennessee," Senter shouted as he drew the first card. "Who is Mrs. Ora E. Johnson, Severe Street, Clarksville, Arkansas?" "That is my mother-in-law," Horton answered. As a more relaxed Horton identified nearly two dozen contributors, Hanover caustically remarked on how well he remembered names but not HFS finances, while Senter's parting shot was to charge Horton with promoting any program that spent "good old American dollars." The committee then adjourned, convinced that they had unearthed enough evidence for court action against the folk school.[62]

In its report the legislative committee recommended the revocation of Highlander's charter for legal and financial transgressions. Throughout their report the legislators placed the word "School" in quotation marks to emphasize their view that HFS was not an educational institution "in the normal sense of the word." For all its efforts to uncover subversive activities at Highlander, the committee devoted only a small portion of its report to the issue. "A great deal of circumstantial evidence," it declared, indicated that HFS was "a meeting place for known Communists or fellow-travelers." The legislators directed their harshest attacks at the school's financial affairs, condemning Horton's "rather strange attitude" in describing "funds and bank accounts of undetermined amount and purpose" as well as the confusing testimony he and May Justus had given to explain the transfer of HFS property to him in 1957. The committee concluded that the Highlander charter should be revoked for two reasons. First, its officers had not filed the document in Grundy County in conformity with state laws respecting nonprofit institutions. Second, its board of directors had sold property to Horton, violating not only the Tennessee code governing general welfare corporations but also the school's own charter. On the basis of the committee's report, both houses of the Tennessee legislature adopted Senate Joint Resolution 47 on March 3, 1959, directing Albert F. "Ab" Sloan, district attorney of the Eighteenth Judicial Circuit, to bring suit for the forfeiture of the charter.[63]

As committee members congratulated themselves and Tennessee newspapers vehemently debated their actual accomplishments, Horton vowed to continue the school regardless of the fate of the charter. Legal observers doubted that a case could be made against HFS for the merely technical misfiling of the charter. As one journalist wrote, the investigation simply proved "beyond a doubt that the school is interracial."[64] The probe had produced considerable rancor on both sides. Following the hearings Horton invited committee members to attend workshops at Highlander so they could see for themselves how the school operated. "Hell, no, I'm not going," responded Senator Lawrence Hughes. None of the other legislators accepted the invitation either.[65] Horton denounced the investigation as an example of segregationist and antilabor demagoguery and ridiculed the concern of "ardent states' righters from Arkansas and Georgia" about a school in Tennessee.[66] He appreciated the letters of support from human relations councils and individual citizens, as well as the increase in contributions from Tennessee residents in the wake of the investigation. At the same time, he uneasily noted, the staff suffered "the psychological strain of expecting court action every day."[67]

Suddenly, on July 31, 1959, the last night of a community leadership workshop, county and state law officers led by District Attorney Sloan raided Highlander, intent on finding evidence with which to close the school. About forty blacks and whites were gathered in the HFS dining room to watch a documentary film, *The Face of the South*. Bernice Robinson and a few other adults sat cooling themselves on the front lawn. Around 9:00 P.M. Robinson noticed several automobiles driving onto school grounds. A man in street clothes appeared and began herding those on the lawn toward the main building. A woman screamed, and the group inside froze. By the time Robinson entered the dining room there were nearly twenty armed uniformed and plainclothes men in the room. Apparently aware that Horton was attending an adult education conference in Germany, Sloan called for Septima Clark and told her he had a warrant to search the building for liquor. "Well, go right ahead," Clark replied, "You won't find any whisky in this house." A short time later an officer arrested Clark, a teetotaler, for "possessing whisky." When Brent Barksdale, a young white HFS office worker and nondrinker, inquired about Clark's legal rights, a trooper snarled, "We know how to take care of little men like you," grabbed him by the belt, and marched him out the door after Clark. Perry MacKay Sturges, another white office worker, asked if Clark could call an attorney, and he too was arrested and pushed outside. Guy Carawan followed the crowd to the door, where he was arrested as well. The charges against the three men were public drunkenness, interfering with officers, and resisting arrest.

Meanwhile, the rest of the workshop group remained seated, watching the movie nervously. A patrolman yanked the projector cord from its socket, plunging the room into darkness for the next hour and a half. Solomon S. Seay, a black minister from Montgomery, heard someone begin to whistle "We Will Overcome" softly. A black teenager started singing the tune, and soon all of the students joined her, adding a verse that would become a permanent part of the song: "We are not afraid, We are not afraid tonight." The singing continued until a policeman turned on the lights, recorded the names of those who would identify themselves, and allowed the group to leave.

The raiding party was becoming uneasy, for after ransacking the main building it still had found no liquor. The officers moved to other school buildings and eventually to Horton's home at the edge of the Highlander campus. There they discovered opened bottles of rum and gin and a wooden keg containing a small amount of liquid that Sloan assumed was moonshine whiskey. After searching all the cars parked at the school, the patrolmen left with the arrested four and arrived at the county jail at Altamont at 1:00 A.M. As they took Clark's fingerprints, Sloan jokingly asked her if she had "a good taste of that liquor." Clark irritably volunteered to undergo a blood test for alcohol, but no one accepted her offer. Vera McCampbell secured her release at 2:30 A.M. by posting a $500 bond. McCampbell also tried to pay the bail of $250 for each of the three men, but Sloan held them in jail overnight "to sober up" before releasing them the next morning.[68]

Sloan now believed he had sufficient grounds to stop Highlander. The legislative investigating committee had given him "information mostly on integration and communism," Sloan told reporters, but he was not "satisfied" that he could use it in court. The raid, based on an informant's tip, was therefore his "best shot and I think now I'll be successful" in securing the revocation of the HFS charter. As Representative Harry Lee Senter praised Sloan for the raid, the Highlander community joined Jordan Stokes in branding it "a Gestapo-type act with trumped-up charges" staged solely for the purpose of closing the school. Students at the fateful workshop agreed that they had not seen or smelled any alcoholic beverages during their stay. Highlander's defenders pointed out that the authorities had not seized liquor at the school itself but in Horton's private home. While technically correct, this argument conflicted with testimony before the legislative committee that the home served as part of the school. In effect, Sloan had forced Highlander into at least one legally untenable position.[69]

At a wild three-hour preliminary hearing on August 6, 1959, two Grundy County justices of the peace ruled that Septima Clark should be bound over to the county grand jury on the charge of illegal possession of whiskey. Representing Clark was Cecil Branstetter, a Nashville attorney who had assisted Stokes during the legislative investigation. From the outset Branstetter challenged the validity of the search warrant, demanding in vain that Sloan produce the informant who provided the pretext for the raid and stressing that the liquor reportedly found in Horton's home was not on Highlander property and not within the boundaries described in the warrant. When the court overruled him, Branstetter called Clark as his only defense witness. The liquor had never been in her possession, Clark declared, and the Horton residence was not HFS property. Sloan shook his finger at Clark and warned that she was liable under perjury statutes if she "falsifies the records." Branstetter objected that the district attorney was intimidating the witness. Make "this bird" sit down, Sloan cried to the court. "I object to being called a bird," Branstetter shouted. In his summation Branstetter exclaimed that he had "never before seen a witness so abused" as Clark had been by the district attorney, apparently because she was black. During his closing argument Sloan roared that "any attorney who could bring color or race into a case is not worthy of hanging his license on the wall in this state" and insisted that Clark was arrested because officers discovered whiskey at Highlander and she was the only school official present.[70] The court agreed and ordered that Clark be held under the same $500 bond already posted.[71]

Because of the length of Clark's hearing, the arraignment of Barksdale, Sturges, and Carawan took place on August 12. Their hearing was a virtual duplicate of the first, but it lasted only thirty-five minutes and lacked the fireworks that marked the earlier session. Three officers who had participated in the raid testified that the defendants had been drunk, had tried to prevent Clark's arrest, and then had resisted when officers took them into custody. Branstetter once more contested the legality of the search warrant, but presented no testimony in his clients' defense. The two magistrates bound each man to the grand jury with bonds of $250, which May Justus promptly paid. The grand jury later indicted all four HFS staff members, but in 1960 it dismissed Clark's case and directed that the charges against the three men be dropped upon payment of "officers' costs."[72]

Indeed, Sloan was after Highlander itself, not some of its staff. Immediately following the second arraignment, he filed a petition with Circuit Court Judge Chester C. Chattin seeking not only the padlocking of the school as a public nuisance but also an order dissolving the corporation and canceling its tax-exempt charter. Some of Sloan's charges concerned the alleged misuse of the charter: Horton ran Highlander "for his own financial benefit"; he "dictated" school policy and carried out its programs "as though it were his own"; and the institution's "haphazard" operations depended on the day-to-day "fantasies and vagaries" of its leaders. Other, more sensational accusations involved immorality: the folk school was a place where "the sale, furnishing, storing and consumption of intoxicating beverages" occurred, and where "a boisterous, noisy, rowdy, and drunken crowd makes a habit of gathering and becoming drunk." Witnesses had seen "men and women, unmarried to each other," going into cabins at the school together "and remaining there for long periods of time," or walking in nearby woods "locked in each others arms and engaging in many other practices of lewd and lascivious character." In light of such disreputable practices, Sloan asked Chattin for a temporary injunction against further activities at HFS until the circuit court convened in November 1959 to determine whether the injunction should be made permanent.[73]

The Highlander case was becoming a drama rivaling that heard in the same judicial circuit a quarter century earlier, a Chattanooga *Times* writer suggested, when John T. Scopes went on trial for violating Tennessee laws against the teaching of evolution in public schools. The raid and ensuing legal action gained regional, national, and international attention, as did the contention by Highlander's leaders that the school's interracial policies and civil liberties were at stake in the forthcoming trial. Letters to HFS, the press, and Governor Ellington deplored the attack on the institution and attested to the staff's sober and orderly behavior. Returning from Europe in late August 1959, Horton stamped the raid as a "very, very underhanded" move and announced that the effort to "discourage" Highlander's integrated program would fail.[74] Sloan's charges were "preposterous," Clark asserted. "The real complaint," she said, was that Highlander "has always been an integrated school."[75] HFS programs went on as scheduled, and Horton and Clark invited newspaper reporters and friends to attend the trial in the interest of "fair play" and justice.[76]

The hearing on the petition to padlock Highlander's buildings began on September 14, 1959, in what one newsman described as a "near-carnival atmosphere" in the Grundy County courthouse at Altamont.[77] The prosecution team consisted of Sloan, his assistant C. P. Swafford, and attorneys Sam Polk Raulston and A. A. Kelly, a well-known trial lawyer in Middle Tennessee who generally kept the tempestuous Sloan under control during the trial. Assisting Cecil Branstetter with the Highlander defense was Nashville attorney George Barrett. The packed courtroom was about evenly divided between local citizens anticipating a dramatic legal battle and black and white friends of the school from several southeastern states. Myles Horton relaxed at the defense table, often with one arm draped over the back of his chair. Sloan and Branstetter clashed frequently during the three-day proceedings, but Judge Chattin remained firmly in command, warning both attorneys several times that he "didn't come up here to referee an argument between you all."[78]

The state's strategy was to depict Highlander as a place that illegally stored and sold alcoholic beverages, winked at interracial liaisons, and had a bad image among area residents. A series of witnesses told lurid tales of drunkenness and blatant promiscuity at the school, but Branstetter easily showed that most of them had police records, tarnished reputations, or personal vendettas against Horton. Hazel Mae Thomas swore that during her visits to HFS she had noticed racially mixed couples nude inside cabins having sexual intercourse, drunks of "all ages and all sexes and all colors," and a mountain of empty beer cans and whiskey bottles at the garbage dump used by the institution. Under Branstetter's cross-examination Thomas admitted that she had been arrested for larceny, but hotly denied that Horton had ordered her to stay away from HFS because she had stolen money and property repeatedly from staff members and students. "If Myles Horton told you that, he told you a damned lie," Thomas stormed. Other local residents claimed to have seen at Highlander such things as beer being sold, blacks and whites drinking, and four couples having sexual intercourse on a lawn fifteen feet from a county road. Two of the witnesses had gone to reform school, one had served a prison term, and one had been jailed more than thirty times for drunkenness. Tired of hearing the same list of charges, Branstetter at one point protested that these witnesses had been told what to say. Sloan jumped to his feet, had Lawrence Petty deny that the prosecution had prompted him, and with his finger pointed at Branstetter roared, "Tell that nitwit over there."[79]

The prosecution made a better argument for the consumption of beer at Highlander than for immorality. Establishing that the HFS staff had no license to sell beer, Sloan called to the stand two beer truck drivers who reported delivering several dozen cases of beer to the school in 1955 and 1956. Beer trucks had come onto the grounds often when he worked at Highlander during the 1940s, Ike Church testified, and he had bought beer and seen students and teachers "in a drunken condition" there. After Church remarked that the folk school's reputation was generally bad, Branstetter asked him, as he had other state witnesses, if the real reason for its unpopularity was because blacks attended its classes. "Well, people don't like it," Church bluntly replied, "don't allow them on this mountain." To emphasize the presence of alcohol at Highlander, Sloan called on Sheriff Elston Clay for his account of the July 31 raid. The prosecution suffered a major setback, however, when Chattin accepted Branstetter's contention that the search warrant used in the raid was illegal. Chattin's unexpected ruling not only cut short Clay's testimony but also effectively quashed the indictments against the four staff members arrested during the raid.[80]

To complete the state's case, four men who had testified before the Tennessee legislative investigating committee on Highlander's subversive activities took the stand to elaborate on their charges. Edwin Friend once again told the story of his trip to the twenty-fifth anniversary to "find out whether or not that malignancy of the NAACP and communism was leaking over into Georgia" and recalled purchasing beer and observing participants drinking during the celebration. HFS supporters burst out laughing when he declared that his greatest concern in going to the affair was whether Martin Luther King, Jr., "would advocate the murder of the white people" to force federal intervention in public school desegregation in the South. Tracy City grocer Carl Geary and county judge Malcolm Fults, who had accompanied Sloan to the school's dump to inspect "the largest collection of beer cans and whiskey bottles in the State of Tennessee," stated that the refuse confirmed Highlander's reputation as an "integrated whore-house," a "hot-bed" of subversion, and "a cess pool of vice and crime." Fults and Herman Baggenstoss of the Grundy County *Herald* maintained that integration was not the cause of Highlander's notoriety, for it had lost whatever local backing it had long ago. Twenty witnesses had appeared for the prosecution over a two-day period, but Judge Chattin indicated that "the only issue" was whether or not the Highlander faculty had been selling beer.[81]

Highlander's defense, as one newsman reported, opened with "a parade of some of the most articulate representatives of this culture," including college professors, ministers, and community leaders.[82] Each defense witness emphatically denied that the HFS staff sold intoxicating beverages or oversaw drunken, boisterous, or immoral conduct. All of them had been involved in various Highlander activities, but Sloan argued that the HFS curriculum was not on trial and prevented any testimony about it. The most impressive testimony came from seven professors from the University of the South. While four had drunk beer during social gatherings at the school, most doubted whether proof of actual beer sales at HFS would change anyone's opinion of the institution. Highlander's reputation was "mixed" in the Sewanee area because some residents "radically disapproved of integration of any sort," Wilford Cross pointed out, and these "social and political" considerations made the folk school controversial. The prosecution belittled the professors' knowledge of HFS by stressing that none of them had stayed there overnight or had discussed the school's reputation with citizens living near it.[83]

To demonstrate that there was local support for Highlander, four Summerfield residents who had extensive, direct contact with the school took the stand in its behalf. John Clark had made regular rounds of the campus as a night watchman and had never discovered any whiskey or moral misconduct. Highlander's relations with the community were poor because people "don't like the colored folks," Clark drawled. "That is the main burning issue." During a decade of living and working on the HFS grounds, James Hargis had seen beer trucks and beer in a cooler but never intoxicating beverages for sale, drinking by employees, or bootlegging operations. "You get paid to keep your ears and eyes shut, don't you?" Sloan demanded on cross-examination. "I get paid to do a job," Hargis shot back, "I don't hear all this stuff that other people have heard." In all the years they had known the institution, May Justus and Vera McCampbell averred, they had found nothing wrong and recalled seeing beer served only on one special occasion. The prosecution challenged both women's testimony, contending that neither of them had ever spent the night at Highlander and that McCampbell's dismissal by the Grundy County school board reflected the school's bad reputation in the area. Like Justus, McCampbell responded that "reputation is what people say we are but character is what we are." The same axiom held true for Highlander, for "a lot of people have the idea that when any two races get together that there is going to be immorality," no matter what.[84]

With the sale of beer at Highlander becoming the key issue in the trial, Myles Horton and Septima Clark provided honest but critically damaging testimony. Both categorically denied all charges, but Horton assumed full responsibility for having beer on HFS property. When workshop participants wanted beer, he explained, he arranged to have it available at the school since no nearby establishment would serve racially mixed groups. Students and guests either paid an extra fee to defray the cost of the beer or operated a "rotating fund" by voluntarily putting money in a cigar box to replace what they drank. Although Horton insisted that this system did not constitute selling beer, he admitted that he had devised the rotation plan against the advice of colleagues and friends, and during her testimony Clark expressed her own disapproval of the policy. The prosecution closely cross-examined both school leaders in an effort to cast doubt on their credibility. At one point Sloan asked Horton if he stored liquor in his house, quickly adding "You don't have to answer. You can holler the Fifth Amendment." Banging his gavel sharply, Chattin halted the district attorney before Branstetter could object to the remark. "I'm notifying the witness—" Sloan began to protest. "If there is any notifying to be done here, I'll do it," Chattin growled, "You settle down and treat this man with some respect whether you like him or not." Yet Sloan's antics did not obscure the legal question of whether there was a distinction between the rotating fund for beer at Highlander and the sale of beer in violation of Tennessee law.[85]

After impassioned closing arguments by each side, Judge Chattin announced his decision. The state had completely failed to support its charge of immorality, he said, and there was "no proof at all whatever" of fighting, drunkenness, and boisterous crowds. Yet there was a "great preponderance" of evidence showing that beer was for sale at Highlander. Horton himself admitted it, despite his explanation of a rotating fund, and many witnesses had seen beer trucks and purchased beer at HFS. Even Clark had opposed the way the staff handled the beverage. Since it was a nuisance to sell beer without a license and illegal to possess beer for resale, Chattin issued a temporary padlock order on the school's main building pending a hearing on a permanent injunction in early November 1959. He made it clear that he was not prohibiting legitimate activities elsewhere on the campus, and he gave Highlander officials ten days to move staff members and equipment out of the building before his order went into effect.[86]

Grimly encouraged by a ruling that amounted to a temporary compromise, Highlander leaders set out to win the battle for public opinion. As Sheriff Clay and his deputies placed locks on the doors to the main building on September 26, Horton told reporters "You don't need buildings to run a school"; state authorities could not "padlock an idea" like Highlander.[87] While staff members held workshops in other school buildings, editorials in southern, northern, and black newspapers defended the school's right to exist, identified racial integration as the true source of the controversy, and sharply criticized the severity of the punishment for the sale of beer, normally a misdemeanor under Tennessee law. Protests flowed into Governor Ellington's office from across the nation and from overseas. The Montgomery Improvement Association, Southern Christian Leadership Conference, Council of the Southern Mountains, and Fellowship of Reconciliation condemned the attack as a threat to every individual and group working for integration in the South. Nearly one hundred prominent citizens, most from outside the South, signed a statement calling on Tennessee officials to allow the HFS staff to pursue its programs without harassment. In addition to such faithful supporters as Eleanor Roosevelt, Martin Luther King, Jr., and Reinhold Niebuhr, the list eventually included former TVA director Gordon Clapp, Southern Regional Council vice-president Marion Wright, Roger Baldwin of the ACLU, A. J. Muste of the FOR, Brotherhood of Sleeping Car Porters president A. Philip Randolph, and former baseball player Jackie Robinson. Through meetings and special fundraising appeals, Horton and Clark raised money for a defense fund to cover the anticipated legal expenses.[88]

A few days before the November 1959 hearing, racial integration finally became an explicit issue in the Highlander case. Sloan filed an amended petition adding to his original public nuisance charges the sale of beer and other commodities, the sale of property to Horton, and the exploitation of the school by Horton and other HFS officers for their personal profit. He further complained that Highlander's interracial classes were in violation of a 1901 Tennessee law that made it "unlawful for white and colored persons to attend the same school." Each of these actions in Sloan's view constituted grounds for the revocation of the HFS charter and the confiscation and sale of all its assets. Up to this point Sloan had given repeated assurances that integration had nothing to do with his efforts to close the folk school. But the Supreme Court had not ruled out segregation in private schools such as Highlander, he now argued, and a 1956 Tennessee Supreme Court decision overturning the state segregation act applied only to public institutions.[89]

Branstetter rejected the supposed legal loophole as well as Sloan's other charges, maintaining that the segregation law was "unconstitutional," "null and void," and inapplicable because the courts had pronounced it "no longer in effect."[90] The sole purpose of the amended petition, Branstetter submitted, was to "harass, annoy, and seek to deprive" Highlander of its "civil liberties and constitutional rights" because it was a racially integrated school. Furthermore, if Tennessee's fifty-eight-year-old segregation statute still applied to HFS, then the charters granted to all of the state's private colleges and universities should be annulled.[91] Sloan nevertheless predicted victory in what he called "the final hearing" on Highlander. Horton agreed that the forthcoming trial would be a "last-ditch fight" which would determine whether it was "possible to carry out the mandate of the Supreme Court of the United States and to push back the prejudices and dogmas of the die-hard reactionaries."[92]

The chances for a successful defense of Highlander virtually disappeared soon after the four-day charter-revocation trial began on November 3, 1959. A. A. Kelly moved to dismiss the state's request for a permanent injunction against HFS and to proceed solely on its petition to revoke the charter. State law prohibited this procedure, Branstetter protested; the prosecution could not drop the nuisance part of its petition and at the same time indict Highlander for charter violations. Rejecting Branstetter's complaint that the state was using a "shotgun approach in an effort to try to find something" against the school, Judge Chattin permitted the deletion of all references in the petition to HFS as a public nuisance. The defense gained two partial victories when Chattin ordered the padlocks removed from Highlander's main building and quashed a state subpoena commanding Horton and May Justus to bring school records into court. But Sloan's amended petition also asked for a jury to try the issues of the case, and over Branstetter's objection Chattin directed that one be impaneled. Although the eleven-man, one-woman, all-white jury selected over the next day and a half claimed to have no prejudice against HFS, most of the jurors were opposed to interracial classes. Once the jury was seated, Chattin ruled out all but two of the nine charges brought against the school. He instructed the jurors to determine only whether Highlander was operated for the personal gain of Horton or any other official, and whether the staff had purchased and sold beer, whiskey, and other merchandise, reserving for himself the question of whether the school was violating Tennessee's segregation law.[93]

To Branstetter and Highlander's supporters the jury's decision was inevitable. Gone were the charges of integration, communism, immorality, and drunkenness. The trial now would proceed on relatively complicated questions concerning the school's financial and administrative procedures and the transfer of HFS property to Horton.

Given Chattin's ruling in the September hearing on the question of beer sales, the prosecution's strategy was to stress that questionable financial practices extended throughout Highlander's operations. Two merchants testified that they had sold candy, chewing gum, gasoline, and kerosene to the school; Dosia Church and others asserted that the staff resold these items for profit; and Grundy County court clerk William R. Hargis reported that the institution had no license to retail any product. Chattin rebuffed the prosecution's attempt to introduce evidence obtained in the July raid on the folk school. But over Branstetter's vigorous objections, he allowed the state's attorneys to read passages from the September trial concerning the alleged sale of beer at HFS and the experiences of Edwin Friend during Highlander's anniversary in 1957, showing his pictures of the event to the jury as they read his statements.[94]

To clinch the state's case, A. A. Kelly sought to show that the property transferred to Horton in 1957 was proof the HFS president had personally profited from his position. Under subpoena, accountant H. V. Herrell produced his audits of the school's accounts since 1957. The net worth of Highlander's assets had increased from almost $125,000 in 1957 to about $175,000 in 1959, but a $32,000 debt incurred in 1957 left a net increase in assets of only $18,000 for the three-year period, not a large sum for a school. Herrell also noted that the percentage of income allocated for staff salaries was lower than at similar institutions. Two real estate brokers then estimated that the total market value of the land and buildings deeded to Horton was well over $30,000. Under cross-examination both men acknowledged they had made their appraisals from a distance and had not actually gone onto the grounds to inspect the property. Nevertheless, the state's attorneys continued to contend that Horton had not only received valuable assets from Highlander but also permitted the use of school funds to make improvements on them. Finally, Kenneth R. Herrell of the Tennessee Department of Revenue corroborated the prosecution's charge that the property transfer and the sale of goods for profit were illegal under Highlander's tax-exempt charter. Kelly and his colleagues then rested their case, satisfied that they had revealed definite charter offenses.[95]

Judge Chattin indicated that Highlander was indeed in trouble. Before presenting his case, Branstetter moved for a directed verdict in favor of the defense. He argued that Horton had not personally benefited from the school, that its financial records clearly showed staff salaries lower than at other institutions, and that there were less drastic remedies to halt commercial activity than the revocation of the HFS charter. Chattin denied the motion. The judge considered it "a serious thing" when an officer of a corporation could obtain land and buildings "under the guise" of back salary. He noted that he could enjoin the HFS staff from selling commodities and invalidate the deed for the property given to Horton, and Branstetter suggested that Chattin could also enjoin the faculty from conducting integrated classes. But Highlander was a private school incorporated under state law,

Chattin responded, and if the *Brown* decision applied only to public schools, then Highlander had violated Tennessee law on that count as well.[96]

Tensions mounted in the packed courtroom as Myles Horton took the stand to contest the charges against him and Highlander. Repeatedly denying that staff members had sold anything for profit, Horton told how he and Zilphia had worked without pay until 1954, when the school's financial condition had become sound enough to allow the executive council to begin paying salaries to the staff. Horton received twelve hundred dollars that year, and by 1959 his salary had increased to nine thousand dollars, though he pointed out that he had been offered many jobs paying much more. The council's decision in 1957 to deed Horton his home and seventy-six acres of land, he added, was in recognition of the years he had served without salary. Sloan challenged every point of Horton's testimony. When Horton explained that he could not document his salary because several school records had been lost or not returned after the legislative investigation in early 1959, Sloan accused him of making "that same alibi" during the probe. In truth, Sloan cried, "you took this deed to the property of Highlander Folk School, you didn't give them anything in exchange for it, did you?" "I gave them a pretty good part of my life and my wife's life," Horton answered heatedly. But there was nothing to prevent him from taking a high-paying job, selling the property, and "walking out," Sloan persisted. "I couldn't do it," Horton countered, "I'm not that kind of person." Later Sloan tried once more to pin the personal profit charge on Horton and received a lecture on how the controversy over Highlander really represented an effort by state officials "to harass a school that was integrated." "Are you through, Mr. Horton?" Sloan said in disgust. "You asked for it," Horton replied.[97]

As in the September hearing, an imposing list of witnesses appeared for the defense. But their testimony was anticlimactic, and the jury appeared unmoved by statements on the merits of Highlander from people who did not live in Grundy County. Morris R. Mitchell, president of the Putney Graduate School of Teacher Education in Vermont, expressed the sentiments of other educators who appeared during the trial when he stated that HFS was "one of the most valuable schools in America" for pioneering "new forms and ideals" in education and that Horton could easily command a much higher salary elsewhere. Sewanee contractor Riley Finney, who had repaired the Horton home and been paid by Zilphia personally, admitted that he was no appraiser but estimated the present value of the property at fifteen to twenty thousand dollars, well below the assessments of the state's witnesses.[98]

Once testimony ended, few doubted the outcome of the trial. Kelly maintained in his closing argument that Horton had lived on tax-free property for more than twenty years and then "cut the melon" and took his slice, a tract of land and a home worth more than thirty thousand dollars. It was "smart, shrewd thinking, but it is not legal thinking," Kelly contended, and there was no record to substantiate the claim that the property was transferred to Horton in compensation for back salary. Branstetter emphasized the evidence refuting the notion that Horton was motivated by personal profit, and he passionately urged the jury not to let "fundamental prejudices" close a school "trying to help the community and the world." In his emotionally charged summation Sloan mocked Highlander's contributions. Horton ran the school according to his own "whiffs and whims" and deeded property to himself "for nothing." "We can do without that type of business in Grundy County," the district attorney roared.[99]

In his summary of the case, Chattin withdrew the charge of commercial sales at Highlander, since in his view there was no disagreement about it, and instructed the jury to consider only whether the school had been operated for Horton's personal gain. At Branstetter's insistence, the judge explained that the transfer of property in lieu of back salary did not constitute "personal gain." But after deliberating forty-five minutes, the jury returned a unanimous verdict that Horton was guilty of profiting from Highlander. Chattin allowed HFS programs to continue and gave the prosecution and defense time to file briefs on the legal points of the case before deciding the school's fate.[100]

On February 16, 1960, Chattin held that Highlander should forfeit its charter for permitting Horton to operate the school for his own benefit, selling beer and other commodities without a license, and practicing racial integration in its classrooms. On the first charge the judge fully agreed with the jury's verdict. Under state law a corporation could not convey property to one of its officers, and Horton's personal gain was "a misuse and abuse" of Highlander's charter and a perversion of its purposes. Chattin next determined that the unlicensed sale of beer at HFS was a direct violation of its charter as well as state criminal and public nuisance laws. Finally, the judge found Highlander guilty of violating the 1901 Tennessee segregation statute, which he upheld. Although Highlander insisted that *Brown v. Board of Education* and the Fourteenth Amendment guaranteed its right to conduct integrated classes, Chattin believed that the state's segregation laws "as applied to private schools are constitutional and valid." Each offense was enough to justify charter revocation. Chattin therefore ruled that he would appoint a receiver to "wind up" Highlander's affairs and liquidate its holdings. One week later the judge declared the deed transferring land to Horton void, revoked the institution's charter, instructed HFS officials to prepare a complete inventory of property, and enjoined them from disposing of any assets. Chattin modified his order on March 7 to allow normal school operations pending the final outcome of its appeals.[101]

The ongoing newspaper debate over the Highlander case intensified after the charter revocation decision. The Chattanooga *News-Free Press* led the southern press offensive against the school. "From its Red-tinged beginnings," its editor jeered, HFS had been "a notorious, disgraceful, leftwing, integrationist institution of highly questionable purposes." It had "gone along imperturbably, angeled by a band of nationally-known leftwing quacks." But now these supporters found themselves standing by a place convicted of bootlegging activities and operating for its director's private profit. In contrast, northern, labor, black, and religious journals expressed indignation that Highlander should be persecuted because of its interracial policy. The Chattanooga *Times* sadly viewed the trial as "a monumental case of persecution and political self-glorification that does Tennessee damage in the eyes of a freedom-loving nation."[102]

Highlander's response to the ruling was to carry on its education programs while exhausting every possible legal appeal. Branstetter immediately announced that he would file a motion for a new trial. Both he and Horton expected Chattin to reject the request and thereby clear the way for an appeal to the state supreme court, where an adverse ruling presumably would allow Branstetter to take Highlander's case to the United States Supreme Court. Publicity and fundraising tours by Horton and Septima Clark during the winter of 1959–60 raised more money for the legal defense. Executive council chairman B. R. Brazeal, dean of Morehouse College, formed a Legal Education Committee in February 1960 to direct appeal efforts. Meanwhile, scores of favorable statements flowed into HFS from across the country and around the world. Especially encouraging to the staff was the increased support for Highlander in Tennessee and the South. Relations with local residents also improved, though Horton wryly commented that such cordiality might only represent "respect for the dead."[103]

Indeed, there was a growing realization among Highlander leaders that the folk school was doomed. As soon as the November 1959 trial had ended, they had begun conferring with wealthy contributors about buying back the Monteagle property at auction, and after Chattin's February 1960 decree Horton announced that offers of land for a new school had come from Arkansas, Kentucky, North Carolina, and an unidentified neighbor. The executive council decided that a more satisfactory alternative was to establish a trust agreement creating an institution legally separate from HFS, so that if the Monteagle campus closed the staff could move the entire program to the new location. By April 1960 longtime benefactor Ethel Clyde had purchased a seventy-five-acre tract of land in Jefferson County about twenty miles from Knoxville. On June 17, 1960, the day before Branstetter presented his motion for a new trial to Judge Chattin, the trustees of the Highlander Research and Training Center signed the trust agreement and elected Horton president, May Justus secretary-treasurer, and the HFS executive council as policymaking board. Highlander was now ready to operate in either Grundy or Jefferson County, and even if the folk school remained open the staff planned to use the center for extension work in East Tennessee. In the meantime school officials kept the trust agreement confidential and waited for a decision on Branstetter's appeal.[104]

The Highlander legal battle and education program hardly missed a step when Chattin overruled Branstetter's motion for a new trial on June 24, 1960. The HFS attorney cited thirty-two errors and violations of law and judicial procedure in the November trial, but Chattin found that none of them warranted a rehearing of the case. Horton promptly announced that Highlander would appeal the charter revocation decree to the Tennessee Supreme Court. As Branstetter prepared his argument, HFS staff members maintained their residence and extension program schedule. In July 1960 the executive council revealed the school's plans to expand into East Tennessee, emphasizing that this move represented a further development of projects begun in 1956. Lewis Sinclair, a TVA economist, vice-chairman of the Knoxville Area Human Relations Council, and the first black man to receive a graduate degree from the University of Tennessee, joined the council to assist in the expansion.[105]

Highlander leaders were not surprised when, on April 5, 1961, the state supreme court upheld Chattin's charter revocation ruling, but they had not anticipated that the judges would frustrate any further appeal by circumventing the issue of segregation in private schools. In their opinion, the five judges concurred with the circuit court's findings that the operation of Highlander for Horton's private gain distorted the stated purposes of the school and was "injurious to the public." The record was also "replete" with evidence that Horton sold beer and whiskey in direct violation of the HFS charter and state law. These two propositions alone were sufficient to annul the charter, the judges concluded. It was therefore "unnecessary for us to pass upon the constitutional question as to the mixing of white and colored, male and female, in the same school." As a prerequisite to filing a writ of certiorari to the United States Supreme Court, Branstetter petitioned the state supreme court to rehear the case. In May 1961 the judges rejected Branstetter's request and granted a stay of execution of the lower court's order closing HFS pending the final outcome of its appeal. Yet the Tennessee court had effectively confined the issues at stake to the state level, thus removing any federal question for the Supreme Court.[106]

Highlander was now in "real trouble," Horton admitted.[107] As Senator James Eastland wished for a United States Supreme Court of "the same caliber" as the Tennessee Supreme Court and sympathizers denounced the "injustice" of the decision, HFS forces fought desperately to save the institution.[108] In April 1961 Horton married Aimee Isgrig, a native of Wisconsin and executive director of the Illinois Commission on Human Relations, in a quiet ceremony at Highlander. The new couple immediately set out on a fundraising tour, for mounting legal fees, the loss of tax-exempt foundation grants, and growing demands for the school's services had severely depleted its treasury. Supporters in New York, Boston, California, and elsewhere sponsored concerts, meetings, and other fundraising affairs. Horton and the rest of the staff negotiated the transfer of the Citizenship School program to SCLC, minimized expenses, and in some cases worked without salary. Yet Highlander's debt was over seventy-five hundred dollars for the 1961 fiscal year, and the constant struggle to meet financial commitments, along with the uncertainty over the school's future, virtually immobilized HFS operations.[109]

While the chances that their appeal would be heard by the Supreme Court were slim in the absence of any clear-cut constitutional issue, Branstetter and George Barrett based their petition to the high court on the violation of Highlander's Fourteenth Amendment rights because of its interracial character. The two attorneys argued that the Highlander case was the first in Tennessee history in which a corporation's charter had been revoked through court proceedings. It presented "an unmistakable picture" of officials manipulating state law to deny the school its rights. A prejudiced jury had found personal gain in the conveyance of property to Horton for two decades of subsistence living, and the state supreme court had "simply ignored" its own earlier rulings in determining that the rotating fund for beer at HFS constituted commercial activity. Furthermore, these findings were "merely make-weights" designed to protect the state's action from further review. The judgments against Highlander stood "as a warning to any who would challenge the segregationist traditions of Tennessee that they will be subjected to harassment by the full power of the state, and will be treated as a class apart in the application to them of state law."[110]

The ACLU agreed with Highlander's petition, and NAACP lawyer Thurgood Marshall offered to advise the defense, but Branstetter and Horton knew that a supporting brief from the Department of Justice would be critical to the success of the appeal. Horton invited supporters to emphasize to the department the importance of HFS in the struggle for civil rights in the South, and by August 1961 over seventy individuals had written Attorney General Robert F. Kennedy, Solicitor General Archibald Cox, and Burke Marshall, head of the Civil Rights Division, urging them to intervene on the school's behalf. The list, reflecting much of Highlander's twenty-nine-year history, included Reinhold Niebuhr, professors from Columbia University and the University of Chicago, Farmers' Union president James G. Patton, United Nations undersecretary Ralph J. Bunche, Esau Jenkins, and Eleanor Roosevelt. The initial response of the Justice Department was sympathetic but cautious. Cox wrote to one HFS backer that "everything I have seen indicates that this is a case of unjust oppression."[111] Yet after further study Marshall regretfully informed Branstetter that the department would not file an *amicus* brief because there was no substantial federal question involved and no general question affecting other legal issues of interest to the United States. The Highlander defense searched for some other way to bolster its appeal, but without the Justice Department's help the possibility of a Supreme Court review evaporated.[112]

Deciding that the time had come to implement the plan for preserving the Highlander idea, Myles Horton and four colleagues secured a charter for the Highlander Research and Education Center on August 28, 1961. While carefully worded to meet state requirements, the charter specifically stated that the new corporation would be racially integrated. It was no secret that the center would incorporate the folk school's programs as much as possible. But issuing the new charter was a purely administrative act, and Tennessee officials could not block it as long as the center met certain legal criteria. The five incorporators quickly adopted a constitution and bylaws for the center, designated the HFS executive council as its advisory council, and elected Horton, Justus, Eugene Kayden, Lewis Sinclair, and University of the South professor Scott Bates as its first board of directors. Highlander Center's temporary headquarters was to be an aging, two-story mansion located in a racially mixed neighborhood in Knoxville. Leased from former staff member Tom Ludwig, the Riverside Drive building was large enough to accommodate small workshops and several staff apartments until more permanent facilities could be built on Highlander's property in Jefferson County.[113]

The prospect of a new Highlander in Tennessee operating no differently from the old, regardless of what the Supreme Court did, predictably outraged opponents and even puzzled some supporters. A state charter was mandatory for the center even if its purpose was the same as that of the folk school, Horton explained, and Burke Marshall had promised that the Justice Department would intervene if there was further harassment from Tennessee officials. Horton also expected less opposition in Knoxville, though as a precautionary measure the staff would lease facilities and rent equipment. There was never any question in his mind that Highlander should remain in the South. "I am weary of being an amateur lawyer," Horton wrote in October 1961, "and would like to try my hand again at adult education."[114]

On October 9, 1961, the U.S. Supreme Court refused to review the Tennessee Supreme Court's decision upholding the charter revocation order, bringing the legal existence of the Highlander Folk School to an end. HFS leaders agreed that continued litigation would be fruitless. Asked by reporters what might happen to the school, Branstetter suggested that it be turned over to the Citizens' Council. Horton once again pointed out that though the state courts could circumvent justice to close Highlander, no one could "confiscate the ideas" the staff would take with it to Knoxville.[115] On November 7, the Grundy County circuit court appointed attorney F. Nat Brown receiver of the institution's physical assets, valued at about $136,000. The battle between the folk school and the state of Tennessee was over.[116]

The sale of the Highlander property, Scott Bates observed at one point, resembled "a picnic, a circus" and "the dissection of a corpse." In mid-December 1961 over one thousand people braved a biting wind, hard rain, and muddy roads to attend the auction of furnishings and equipment. Officials conceded that the campus had been looted and burglarized' after a court order had padlocked it several weeks earlier. Eager buyers nevertheless jammed their way into the various buildings on the grounds to bid on linen, farm supplies, furniture, and similar items, while Monteagle women's groups operated concession booths. Although Bates and other local HFS supporters were prepared to pay at least $3,000 for the school's 5,000-volume library, the unsympathetic auctioneer rescheduled the bidding to allow a secondhand book dealer to purchase it for $425. Brown reported that the auction brought in more than $10,000. But with $25,000 in claims against the school, including $20,000 in legal fees, the land and buildings also would have to be put up for sale.[117]

There were some last-ditch efforts to save the Monteagle estate when the announcement of the second auction appeared in June 1962. Howard Frazier, who had known Horton since their high school days, initiated a plan to buy the school on a cooperative basis for the center, and Horton explored the possibility that SCLC or a few wealthy supporters might acquire the property. But board members, contributors, and Horton himself eventually agreed that despite their emotional ties to the old campus, Highlander should be based in Knoxville. No one from Highlander was present, therefore, when over one hundred persons bid on the last remnants of the folk school on July 7, 1962. The 175 acres, fourteen buildings, and nine residences netted $43,700 for the state treasury. In light of Chester Chattin's recent appointment to the state court of appeals and A. F. Sloan's promotion to the Grundy County circuit court bench, Horton considered it fitting that Sam Polk Raulston, a member of the team that prosecuted HFS, was the high bidder on the library building. As state newspapers proclaimed the death of the most controversial school in modern Tennessee history, the Highlander Center faculty pressed forward with a voter education project in Mississippi. In a new form, the Highlander idea continued.[118]

The Highlander Folk School was closed because of the difficulty of staying at the forefront of social change in the South while maintaining an administratively sound institution. Highlander's greatest strength was its fatal weakness. Certainly the staff's forthright advocacy of racial integration and its role in the civil rights movement during the 1950s was at the root of every criticism leveled against the school. Judge Chattin had simply made the issue explicit. Yet even if opponents concealed the real motivation for their assaults and even if HFS officers had valid reasons for their decisions, students and visitors had drunk beer on Highlander grounds, Myles Horton had received Highlander property, and Highlander's financial affairs were often disorderly. Thus Mississippi Senator James Eastland, Governor Marvin Griffin's Georgia Commission on Education, Arkansas Attorney General Bruce Bennett, and members of the Tennessee legislative investigating committee were largely frustrated because they attacked Highlander's ideology, giving Horton and others an opportunity to defend the school eloquently and often persuasively. On the other hand, the probing questions of state representative Alan Hanover and attorney A. A. Kelly and the maneuvering of the Tennessee Supreme Court did far more damage because they exposed Highlander's loose institutional practices and held it strictly accountable to its charter and to state laws governing general welfare corporations.

It would have been unrealistic to expect Highlander personnel to be absolutely meticulous in running the school. Other nonprofit groups in Grundy County and across Tennessee provided beer for their members, and an overriding concern with administrative and bookkeeping tasks would have sapped the dynamism of HFS educational projects. Yet in the late 1950s Highlander was bound to come under scrutiny because of the intense opposition to racial integration among a massive number of white southerners. Flexibility and informality might have been tolerated during the 1930s but not in the superheated atmosphere two decades later. Indeed, a 1963 survey showed that HFS had enjoyed strong support among Summerfield residents until blacks began attending workshops and integration became the central focus of its program. Horton and his colleagues were slow to understand that in a legal system designed to control radical dissent opponents would use that system, even resort to legal technicalities, to accomplish what no other form of attack was able to do.[119]

Horton learned quickly, however, and in the long run Highlander perhaps benefited from the crisis. Reiterating that Highlander was above all an idea, he too used the law to establish a new school that virtually duplicated the original but could not be touched as long as it met state requirements. Moreover, unlike many whites, Horton knew that the civil rights movement would continue regardless of what happened to a white-led educational institution, and the emergence of a new generation of black activists in the early 1960s suggested that Highlander's emphasis on school desegregation had reached its limits. The closing of the folk school thus contributed to the revitalization of Highlander as an idea and as an institution. The challenge for its staff, as it had always been, was to anticipate and respond to shifts in the struggle for racial equality and human justice, and to find new ways of educating white and black southerners to take more control of their own lives.

10

Highlander Center: New Directions, New Struggles

As it continued to work with the poor and powerless in the years after 1961, the central challenge facing the Highlander Research and Education Center was to sustain the focus and clarity that characterized the Highlander Folk School's programs. Through a series of strategic shifts, experimental projects, and new methodological approaches, the center sought to contribute as much to education and progressive change in the "valley" period of the late twentieth century—a time without a unifying movement for social change—as it had during "peak" periods defined by the southern labor and civil rights movements. Even as its longevity was celebrated, Highlander's history became at once a burden and a standard of effectiveness.

Highlander also endeavored to forge alliances among diverse groups with common interests and to link local and regional concerns to global developments. The center remained an important part of the civil rights movement during most of the 1960s; inspired by their participation in the Poor People's Campaign of 1968, Highlander teachers promoted the formation of a multiracial coalition that broke apart in the early 1970s. By then the staff had returned to Highlander's roots to focus once again on the problems confronting the people of southern Appalachia. There it worked with a complex network of groups, leaders, followers, and tendencies—a movement of movements that never achieved cohesion. Yet its persistence, and its revelation of the interregional and international implications of local crises, led Highlander in the 1980s and 1990s to address economic, health, and environmental issues that transcended race and culture in Appalachia, the Deep South, India, Central America, and southern Africa. Highlander currently believes its role no longer involves a single issue or constituency; it must bring together people and build common ground, nurture voices and spaces of resistance, and help educate for a multi-issue, multicultural, multiregional movement. The cumulative effect of these changes on the center has been at least as great as its contributions to the varied struggle for grassroots democracy, economic empowerment, and environmental justice.

The Highlander Center's earliest programs in Knoxville were largely a carryover from the folk school. Leasing the old mansion on Riverside Drive in 1961 seemed prudent to Myles Horton. Local labor unions and black community groups with which the staff had worked in the past could provide some protection against further repercussions from the legal battle over the Monteagle school. The house served as the center's headquarters and accommodated small residence workshops, and in early 1962 the faculty rented the manse of nearby Shiloh Presbyterian Church for larger meetings, a community center, and student housing. Staff members then began to conduct workshops, seminars, and evening classes to familiarize Knoxville citizens with the kind of education provided at Highlander. Such activities included a lecture-discussion series called "Problems of a Free Society," weekly meetings with local college students, and a voter education program. In addition to directing Citizenship School classes in Knoxville, Bernice Robinson and other staff members attended teacher-training sessions at Dorchester Center in Georgia and conferred with Esau Jenkins and other local leaders on the future of the Citizenship Schools on the South Carolina Sea Islands.[1]

Even with this promising start, Highlander Center was not free of the controversies that had surrounded the folk school. In November 1961 the Knoxville City Council passed an emergency zoning ordinance, clearly aimed at Highlander, requiring council approval of new school parking plans. Mayor John Duncan assured Horton in early 1962 that city officials would take no action against the center. But local American Legion and John Birch Society members objected to Highlander's very existence, and a new Citizens' Council chapter was formed to prevent the center's "communist-related" staff from spreading "racial strife throughout the South." The Knoxville *Journal* carried articles charging the school's teachers with

Civil rights meeting in the early 1960s. Standing, extreme left, Andrew Young; fourth from left, Septima Clark; fifth from left, Aimee I. Horton; fifth from right, Candie Carawan; fourth from right, Bernice Robinson; extreme right, Guy Carawan. *State Historical Society of Wisconsin.*

training black agitators and associating with "admitted Communists, known Communists, and fellow travelers."[2] Highlander's tax status was another troublesome matter. When attorneys for the center applied for a tax exemption in August 1961, IRS officials balked at considering the request until Highlander had been in operation for one year; they then pressed for more detailed information on its charter, programs, and financial affairs before finally granting tax-exempt status in March 1963.[3]

The IRS ruling seemed to dispel any lingering uncertainty among staff members and supporters over Highlander's immediate future in Knoxville. Financial support grew rapidly. Both the number of workshops and student enrollment increased steadily. C. Conrad Browne left Koinonia Farm to become associate director at Highlander in July 1963. And Knoxville residents generally came to tolerate the school's presence in the city.[4]

Yet by mid-1963, Highlander's leaders had already decided to curtail activities in the Knoxville area and to commit the center's resources to voter education and other extension work in the Deep South. As with the Citizenship School program of the 1950s, Highlander's goal was to develop independent education centers that would continue to function after staff members had initiated them. In part this shift came in response to

SNCC's transition in 1962 from student protests to a broader campaign for black voting rights. Following a Highlander workshop for SNCC staff members and other volunteers on voter education techniques in June 1962, Robert Moses, head of SNCC's Mississippi Voter Education Project, asked Bernice Robinson to conduct further sessions in Mississippi. During the summer of 1962 and the spring and summer of 1963, Robinson directed a series of workshops in support of voter registration drives in Jackson, Edwards, Ruleville, Greenwood, and other towns with the help of SNCC fieldworkers and local leaders.

Holding workshops in the Mississippi Delta was difficult and dangerous. White segregationists harassed, intimidated, and assaulted teachers and students. Several prospective students in one town were afraid to attend a workshop because of the possibility of white reprisals, Robinson reported. "This fear is real, not imaginary."[5] Yet SNCC executive secretary James Forman attributed at least some of the gains made during the voter registration drive to Highlander's education projects. The center's 1963 workshops eventually included over fifteen hundred participants; SNCC workers, along with other former Highlander students, gradually assumed greater responsibility for the sessions; and the number of black voters grew. The "freedom vote" campaign in the fall of 1963, climaxed by a symbolic election in which over eighty thousand blacks chose their own candidates, dramatized the desire of black Mississippians to vote.[6]

The result was the 1964 Mississippi Freedom Summer Project. Shortly after the "freedom vote" election, Moses, Horton, and Mississippi CORE director David Dennis supervised a workshop for the Council of Federated Organizations (COFO), where SNCC, SCLC, and CORE representatives began to hammer out plans to bring northern white students to Mississippi to accelerate the voter registration drive. Many black activists opposed the use of white volunteers. But eventually they agreed that the project would focus national attention on the state, force federal intervention on behalf of the campaign, and help publicize the efforts of the Mississippi Freedom Democratic Party (MFDP) to challenge the credentials of the all-white regular state party at the 1964 Democratic National Convention in Atlantic City.

Highlander's role in Freedom Summer was largely limited to the planning stages of the campaign. A higher profile would make COFO vulnerable to the red-baiting charges still being leveled against the school; the presence of white civil rights workers in Mississippi was risky both for themselves and for local blacks; and experience had taught staff members that they were most effective in laying the groundwork for larger campaigns. Highlander therefore confined itself during Freedom Summer to running a small, experimental White Community Project for COFO. After two weeks of orientation in Oxford, Ohio, and at Highlander Center, eighteen white students moved into Biloxi intending to establish support for COFO among middle-class white moderates. While most of the students were southerners, none had previous organizing experience in white communities, and at a midsummer workshop under the direction of Myles and Aimee Horton they reported few tangible results. Sharp disputes over tactics subsequently contributed to the abrupt demise of the project.[7]

The fate of the White Community Project reflected the larger failure of the Freedom Summer Project to achieve the breakthrough in civil rights sought by SNCC and other groups. Despite the bravery of the project workers, only sixteen hundred Mississippi blacks actually registered to vote. Racial tensions between black activists and white volunteers were a constant problem. There was no massive federal intervention in the state, and the Democratic National Convention turned back the Freedom Democratic party's attempts to unseat the regular Mississippi delegation. Although Horton urged SNCC leaders to develop their own education program, using Highlander teachers only as advisers, clashes over proposals to expand and improve the organization's programs increased. SNCC was losing faith in the power of nonviolent, interracial reform.[8]

Highlander's second major civil rights program during the 1960s was the Southwide Voter Education Internship Project, designed to cultivate greater political sophistication among new black voters in the Deep South. In the staff's view Charleston County, South Carolina, had become a model for other southern black communities since the start of the first Citizenship School on Johns Island in 1957. An ongoing voter registration campaign had helped over ten thousand black citizens gain the franchise by mid-1963, black candidates had run for city and county offices, and schools and other public facilities had been desegregated. In the summer of 1963 Highlander staff members and Esau Jenkins agreed to make such accomplishments part of a demonstration program combining residence workshops and internship training for black leaders across the South. Between July and October nearly nine hundred black adults in the Charleston area, along with over fifty interns from six southern states, participated in seventeen Citizenship and Political Education Schools. The interns examined case studies of local civil rights efforts and lived with area black leaders to learn how to set up adult education programs and other civic activities in their hometowns. Guy and Candie Carawan, who had moved to Johns Island in June 1963, led singing during the workshops and staged a folk music festival.[9]

Over the next four years the internship project spread throughout Charleston County and into neighboring Berkeley and Dorchester Counties. Several thousand blacks and whites attended Citizenship and Political Education Schools. Although the results of the internship program were less clear, the Highlander faculty could cite several inspiring examples. After recovering from a beating she and other civil rights activists received on their way home from a Johns Island workshop, Fannie Lou Hamer enrolled in another Highlander workshop in Mississippi. She became a leading figure in the Mississippi Freedom Democratic Party and was a congressional candidate in 1964. In the same year, the Reverend Franklin D. Rowe became the first black candidate for public office in Ben Hill County, Georgia, since Reconstruction, and along with another intern he directed a voter registration campaign in Fitzgerald, Georgia, in 1965.[10]

In response to the growing number of southern blacks running for public office, Highlander offered a series of workshops for city, county, and state candidates between 1966 and 1968. During one-week sessions at the center and in Mississippi and Georgia, Highlander board member Lucy Montgomery, black Georgia state representative Julian Bond, MFDP strategist Lawrence Guyot, and other consultants covered such topics as the techniques of political campaigns, the relative merits of working through existing parties and forming independent black organizations, and the duties of candidates once they won election. The Mississippi candidate-training workshops jointly run by Highlander, MFDP, and the Delta Ministry in 1967 proved especially useful—eighteen of the twenty-two victorious black candidates in the state's off-year elections had participated in the sessions. When these victors encountered white harassment following the elections, the workshops addressed the problems of assuming office and developing more black political candidates.[11]

Highlander Center thus attained nearly as much prominence in the civil rights movement of the 1960s as the folk school had gained during the previous decade. Yet the billboards bearing the caption "Martin Luther King at Communist Training School" that appeared across the South in 1965 were reminders that this renewed importance also meant a resurgence of attacks against the institution. In June 1963 the sheriff of Blount County, Tennessee, a local stronghold of the Ku Klux Klan, led a 3:00 A.M. raid on a Highlander-sponsored North-South work camp, where about two dozen black and white students were building a campsite on privately owned land. Armed with guns but no search warrant, the posse herded the group to the county jail in Maryville and charged them the next day with disorderly conduct, lewdness, possession of alcohol, and contributing to the delinquency of minors. Eventually the work campers won appeals reversing their lower court convictions. But after area newspapers linked the work camp with communism and interracial sex, the camp site mysteriously burned to the ground. Several windows at Highlander Center were smashed, the staff received threatening telephone calls, and a Maryville cafe owner beat Horton and defense attorney Edward D. Lynch as they tried to eat breakfast in the diner.[12]

The assault on Highlander reached its peak between 1965 and 1968. Staff members endured a storm of adverse publicity in the Knoxville *Journal*, a KKK parade past the center, repeated vandalism, firebombs, burglaries, gunshots, and taped telephone messages branding Highlander as a "malignant organization" whose "red spiders" taught "hate, violence and riots."[13] In the fall of 1966, Knoxville grocer and city councilman Cas Walker, the school's most outspoken opponent in the city, asked for a council resolution requesting the state attorney general to revoke Highlander's charter. Council members took no action, but in January 1967 Walker's nephew, state representative Odell Cas Lane of Knoxville, introduced two resolutions into the Tennessee legislature calling for a committee to investigate Highlander's "subversive" activities and for city, county, and state law enforcement officials "to use all legal means to cut this cancerous growth from our state."[14] In contrast to its aggressive prosecution of Highlander in 1959, the general assembly only reluctantly approved the formation of a committee in May 1967, and the inquiry itself never materialized. Governor Buford Ellington signed the resolution, apparently knowing that its sponsors had inadvertently failed to appropriate funds for the probe. Highlander directors and ACLU lawyers then secured two restraining orders from United States District Court Judge William E. Miller blocking the proposed investigation, and in January 1968 Miller enjoined the legislature from proceeding further until it had found a constitutionally adequate definition of "subversion." Despite Lane's vow to continue his campaign, state officials did not appeal Miller's decision, reconciling themselves to the idea that Highlander would remain in Tennessee.[15]

Even before the attacks on Highlander subsided, the staff was moving beyond its work in the civil rights movement to the more formidable task of organizing the poor in southern Appalachia as part of a new multiracial poor people's coalition in America. In 1964 Horton and his colleagues recognized that the school needed to consider a new direction. As a matter of policy Highlander withdrew from social movements once they were underway in order to encourage independent action, and despite the steady demands for their services staff members maintained that the black struggle for freedom should have black leadership. The growing number of black organizations and leaders confirmed Highlander's earlier conclusion that it was no longer a necessary element in the civil rights movement. So too did the militancy of young black activists: conservative journalists inaccurately reported that Horton had taught Stokely Carmichael the idea of Black Power, but the Highlander staff agreed with the black leader's contention that whites could best aid their cause by organizing poor whites, the only group blacks could accept as allies. The center's approach also emphasized working with people in potential social movements. Horton noted that while black protest had sparked organized activities among Chicanos, Puerto Ricans, and Native Americans, he doubted whether these groups could become a powerful force for change without white allies. Organizing poor, predominately white Appalachians would therefore help create a genuinely multicolored coalition capable of affecting national policy.[16]

Appalachia itself seemed ripe for change. President Lyndon B. Johnson had declared his War on Poverty in 1964, and the early wave of media attention on the mountain poor was accompanied by the infusion of millions of dollars in federal aid, dozens of Community Action Programs, and hundreds of antipoverty warriors. The Highlander staff suspected that the campaign would ultimately disappoint large numbers of people in Appalachia. But there were signs, such as the roving picket movement of unemployed coal miners in Perry County, Kentucky, that these same people could be aroused to challenge the external forces that exploited the region's economy, an effort which by necessity would link up with other poor and working-class groups across the country.[17]

Context, crises, and opportunity thus dovetailed nicely in Highlander's analysis. There was one additional benefit for the center. An Appalachian program would allow Highlander to come back to its home region, to address problems that had been subordinated to the larger southwide labor and civil rights campaign, and perhaps to achieve a true balance between its original goals of developing a new social order and preserving the indigenous cultural values of the mountains.

Highlander's first steps in building an Appalachian movement were tentative but nonetheless promising. In March 1964, thirteen volunteers recruited by the white student project of the Student Nonviolent Coordinating Committee attended a three-day workshop to examine Appalachia's problems and plan a project that would contribute to the War on Poverty. The group quickly learned the dimensions of the challenge facing the poor and unemployed in areas like eastern Kentucky: a deteriorating coal industry, increasing mine mechanization, a quiescent United Mine Workers of America, a history of dissent and agitation undermined by self-serving outside crusaders, racial prejudice coexisting with a tradition of interracial union activism and common economic concerns, an unresponsive public welfare system, and a handful of protest groups. Workshop participants concluded that change in Appalachia would begin when its people became aware of the tremendous gap between the announced intent of federal antipoverty programs and what they actually delivered. Student volunteers must "make the transition from thought to responsible action," Sam Shirah of SNCC declared. They should help indigenous leaders understand government procedures and how they and their neighbors could make them serve their needs, setting the stage not only for increased assistance but for further community organization as well. The emphasis had to be on education, Horton observed, if the young activists hoped to strengthen the independence rather than the dependence of the Appalachian people.[18]

Over the next three years, while most of Highlander's energies went to the development of black political leadership in the Deep South, Horton and a few other staff members tried to assess the mood in Appalachia as they experimented with several education programs. They worked with established organizations like the Council of the Southern Mountains and the Glenmary Sisters, a Catholic order in Virginia, as well as with a larger number of newer groups, such as the Southern Student Organizing Committee, the Appalachian Economic and Political Action Conference, Federation of Communities in Service, the Marrowbone Folk School, and the Congress for Appalachian Development. During the summer of 1965, four young men, including Myles Horton's son Thorsten, attempted to replicate the beginnings of the Citizenship Schools through an exploratory project in the once flourishing coal mining town of Habersham, Tennessee. There they maintained a low profile, quietly encouraging local people to take the initiative in public affairs and see how their grievances were part of larger economic and political issues. Their experiences formed the basis of a series of workshops at Highlander for community leaders and Appalachian Volunteers (AVs), a federally funded group radicalized by their involvement in the War on Poverty. As the workshops grew in size and scope, participants thought they saw the beginnings of an Appalachian-wide movement; some started their own educational programs in places like Wise County, Virginia, and Harlan County, Kentucky. Highlander staff members Guy and Candie Carawan showed workshop groups how music and singing could become tools for organizing and staged Appalachian music projects and festivals at the center and in eastern Kentucky.[19]

A general strategy for Highlander's Appalachian program began to emerge out of this "action research," as Horton called it.[20] Staff members learned that the region's poor must first be activated to form their own organizations before there could be any serious steps toward a widespread social movement. Short-term projects, like the one in Habersham, could not arouse any sense of urgency among the poor to organize. The college student and summer volunteers who came to the mountains had neither the experience nor the patience to wait until the poor themselves were ready to act. The War on Poverty's Community Action Programs, even when not compromised by the interests of local elites, usually pursued limited goals. Organizing in Appalachia therefore should not become too broad, too sweeping, too hasty. Instead, Highlander should concentrate on the nurturing of indigenous leadership and, along with other activist groups in the region, continue to experiment with organizing models that were responsive to the diversity of Appalachian communities. Eventually a social movement would grow out of these grassroots efforts, and then a formal alliance could be created to reinforce and give breadth to the local actions.[21]

Highlander had chosen a familiar path, guided by the presumption that its historic "bottom-up" approach to community organizing would work in Appalachia. The situation may be less structured than the labor movement of the 1930s, staff members admitted, but there were appealing parallels between Appalachia in the 1960s and the early days of the civil rights movement. The region contained a cadre of young but experienced organizers. Several issues, most notably strip mining, were generating unrest in coal mining areas. Appalachians were increasingly disillusioned with top-down, Washington-controlled solutions to poverty. And the similarities between the plight of the Appalachian poor and that of southern blacks remained tantalizingly close. Enough was "stirring" in Appalachia to indicate the emergence of a regional movement that could become part of a national coalition of the poor, Horton reassured board members in 1967; it was "just a matter of figuring out how much we're going to put into it."[22]

Events in 1968 seemed to confirm Highlander's analysis of the effort it would take to build a multiracial poor people's movement that respected its component parts. Shortly before his death in April 1968 Martin Luther King, Jr., announced a poor people's march on Washington, D.C., that he hoped would unite the dispossessed of all races, appeal to the nation's conscience, and compel the federal government to provide jobs and income to all who needed them. Such an agenda thrilled Horton. Following a meeting in Atlanta where more than fifty nonblack organizations endorsed the campaign, he exulted to Andrew Young that he had seen "a glimpse of the future . . . the making of a bottom up coalition."[23]

But government officials were unmoved by the sight of several thousand poor people living near the Lincoln Memorial, and the Poor People's Campaign was soon mired in mud, violence, chaotic administration, ineffective demonstrations, and disputes among black, Latino, and Native-American leaders. A contingent from Highlander stayed in Resurrection City and conducted music and cultural workshops until police closed the shantytown in June 1968. Horton and Mike Clark, a former Appalachian Volunteer who had recently joined the Highlander staff, left Washington disappointed that the domineering black management of the campaign had made it impossible to mount a broad-based program for radical change. Yet the virtual absence of organizations representing Appalachians and poor whites generally underscored how Highlander could substantially contribute to the multiracial coalition, and the well-run alternate community created at Hawthorne School in Washington during the campaign by five distinct ethnic groups testified to the ability of poor people to work together as equals for a common cause.[24]

Other developments signaled the beginning of the end for the War on Poverty in Appalachia. Federal appropriations steadily declined, state officials closely monitored funding proposals and reports, Community Action Programs operated under tightening budgetary and administrative constraints, community centers closed, the number of antipoverty warriors decreased, and the once-hopeful signs of progress disappeared. The Appalachian Volunteers became a particular target of state and local officials wary of any grassroots ferment. In 1968 the governors of West Virginia and Virginia refused to approve an extension of federal antipoverty grants to the Appalachian Volunteers in their states, and the Kentucky Committee on Un-American Activities held hearings on alleged subversion in Pike County, effectively killing the possibility of further grants to the AVs in that state. This shift in government attitudes was significant. An Appalachian movement would now have to proceed largely without the direct aid of federal legislation, agencies, revenue, and intervention, support that had helped the labor and civil rights movements make important gains.[25]

Highlander thus entered a complex transition period through which the staff discovered that hopes for a multiracial poor people's alliance were premature, that the center's resources should go toward the mobilization of Appalachian protest, and that even this step would take time. At Resurrection City, Reies Tijerina, leader of the *Alianza* campaign in New Mexico to regain the land members believed had been stolen from their ancestors, had urged Horton to establish an education center in the Southwest to help

Mexican-American and Native-American groups gain greater economic and political power. By mid-1969 Horton had organized Highlander West, directed by white activist and bilingual newspaper editor Craig Vincent, Native-American anthropologist Shirley Witt, and Chicano journalist and labor organizer Gilberto Ballejos. A succession of workshops in 1969 and 1970 spurred a number of protests and projects by Mexican-American women in Albuquerque, workers at the University of New Mexico, *Alianza* activists, and members of seven Native-American tribes. Yet Highlander West's activities were spread too thinly. The distance between New Mexico and Tennessee also made it very hard for the Highlander Center staff to coordinate a program for a complicated and constantly shifting Chicano movement.

The Chicago project was equally frustrating. In 1969 Horton found considerable potential for using Highlander's services to support the fledgling educational activities of Appalachian and Puerto Rican youth groups in the city. But there was little response to Horton's proposals, and in mid-1970 the staff ended the project. Staff members made a dramatic attempt to link together all of the racial groups involved in Highlander programs by holding workshops in Knoxville in 1970 and 1971, where black, Mexican-American, Native-American, Filipino, Puerto Rican, and Appalachian participants laid the groundwork for a future multiracial alliance.[26]

Yet it was clear by the early 1970s that the possibility of a multicolored poor people's movement in America was rapidly disappearing. Activists splintered into rival factions and reluctantly acknowledged that the poor did not constitute a unified class of economically oppressed people. Even if such unity existed, the poor represented only a small fraction of the nation's population, and in a time of growing conservatism it would be increasingly difficult to achieve any significant reform.

Change in Appalachia was also becoming more problematic. In 1969 Myles Horton recalled that five years earlier he had projected the development of a program to the point where it could be passed on to others, much as the Citizenship School program had been transferred to Southern Christian Leadership Conference. But it had been "very difficult to get the poor to assert their independence in the face of a horde of missionaries, primarily from the government, who are always master-minding them." Activists in Appalachia were suffering from a "poverty of ideas," pursuing dead-end strategies and repeating previous mistakes.[27] Highlander had not sufficiently tested its own ideas. The center's workshops, however, pointed to the need for an education program, run by poor people themselves, which would establish a regional identity for an Appalachian movement. Since no areawide organization or structure existed to provide a base for such an effort, this education program had to be flexible and inclusive, addressing a wide variety of local issues while highlighting the common experiences of people from different sections of the region.[28]

The Appalachian Self-Education Program (ASEP) was Highlander's attempt to meet those needs. Once again the Citizenship Schools provided the model, tempered by the experiences of several former Appalachian Volunteers and native-born activists who joined the staff in the late 1960s. Instead of offering the poor the illusion of power, as many Community Action Agencies had done, the ASEP sought to insure their empowerment. There was to be no formally recognized leader or group, no pre-established guidelines, no organizing around a particular issue, no organizer-centered or agency-generated change. The ASEP would consist of community workshops whose agenda and content would be entirely determined by poor people. Community leaders would learn to be educators rather than organizers. The workshops would build contacts within and between communities, inspire confidence among participants, acquire information as well as the tools for using it, and foster a collective identity. Cultural components would celebrate the value of local and traditional art and music. Research and other special services would furnish materials and new technology, such as videotape recorders, to accelerate the spread of knowledge. Highlander's Appalachian staff would be "field coordinators" for the ASEP. They would travel extensively throughout West Virginia, eastern Kentucky, and eastern Tennessee; identify potential workshop leaders; help them set up their own sessions at the center and elsewhere; supply information and consultants when requested; and serve as liaisons between local groups.[29]

As Mike Clark recognized at the start of the program, the decentralized, nondirective intent of the ASEP made it different from anything Highlander had tried before. There were few organizations in Appalachia through which to channel the program's educational activities; there was no one primary need in the region but a number of localized problems varying considerably from one community to the next; and beyond giving power to the powerless, the ultimate goals of the program were vague and distant. Progress would therefore come slowly. Ending old habits of dependency on outside reformers and local elites would be hard. Community groups struggled with an enormous range of problems, and all of them had to overcome a legacy of powerlessness. The workshops themselves would require months of patient fieldwork by the Highlander staff, searching for sparks of response to the self-education idea. Yet if small, democratically run, autonomous groups could begin to formulate programs and policies at the local level and then work together to pressure local agencies and institutions to deliver according to the wishes of the community, mountain society would be "turned inside out": poor people would gain a new image of themselves, look to one another for ideas and support, and secure political justice and economic independence.[30]

It was this vision of Appalachia finally breaking free from the forces oppressing it that would motivate a new generation of Highlander staff members. Animated by a variety of influences—the anti–Vietnam War movement, the War on Poverty, community struggles against strip mining, the effort to establish Appalachian Studies programs at colleges in the region—the staff pursued the ideal of democratizing economic and political power in Appalachia with a passion not easily expressed in reports to the center's board of directors, grant proposals, and public presentations. There was constant experimentation, considerable creativity, and a determination to identify those institutions, laws, and practices that perpetuated the region's problems. There were also debates over the relative merits of specific issues; questions about the constituencies to be served by Highlander; disputes over theory, analysis, and pedagogy; and internal tensions over long-term strategy. The Appalachian program placed Highlander in a new context, without the frame of reference offered by an active, developed social movement. Over time the vision would become more complex—and more elusive.

The primary challenge of the ASEP was to build a movement without organization. It was true, as Highlander and War on Poverty veterans could testify, that organizations often set in motion forces that defeated the insurgency that gave rise to a social movement. The question was whether an Appalachian movement based on local initiative would benefit from a deliberately unstructured education program.

In the tumultuous years of the late 1960s and early 1970s, keeping the issues specific seemed to be the key. Highlander responded to a request by the Council of the Southern Mountains for assistance in establishing closer ties with the poor by holding workshops on both the Council and the ASEP for people from West Virginia, southeastern Ohio, eastern Kentucky, southwest Virginia, and eastern Tennessee. The staff went one step further at the Council's 1969 conference at Fontana Lake, North Carolina, and supported the efforts of a coalition led by blacks, poor people, and students mobilized by Sue Ella Easterling of the Council's Youth Commission to force a major reorganization of the group. Highlander staff member Almetor King, a founding member of the new Council Commission on Black Appalachians and Commission on Poor People's Self-Help, won election to a reconstituted board of directors whose majority represented the poor.[31]

Following the Council "revolution," Highlander explored the possibilities of starting new poor people's organizations through workshops attended by disabled miners, welfare recipients, housewives, subsistence farmers, and individuals wanting to form tenants' rights groups and credit unions. Staff members found very specific problems blocking collective action by the poor: pride, fear, dependency on outside help, inadequate government programs, and racial, legal, and financial barriers. In response, the staff intensified its fieldwork, seeking to fashion an indigenous model of democratic problem solving. Assistance to groups like Pickett United for Self-Help and LBJ & C Development Corporation in eastern Tennessee and in various "hot spots" of discontent in eastern Kentucky coal counties resulted in marketing and purchasing cooperatives, job training projects, community centers, fights against strip-mining abuses, and demands for school and road improvements. Additional workshops at Highlander studied ways to establish welfare and tenants' rights organizations, to use music to promote regional pride and social awareness, to assess how lawyers could advise poor people's groups without controlling them, and to use newspapers and other media techniques as organizing tools.[32]

Highlander's Appalachian program seemed to be gaining momentum. A regional network of activists who had first met at the center was growing, as were the number of requests for help from poor people's groups. Just as it had done during earlier social movements, Highlander was once again serving as both a meeting place and a vital source of information. At the same time, the focus of the program was shifting. Having seen too many groups falter or dissolve after reaching a certain goal, too many leaders quit because of physical exhaustion or political pressure, and too many artificially created leaders divorcing themselves from the people they were presumably helping, staff members announced in 1971 that they would concentrate on educational methods that involved groups rather than individuals from groups. The staff would continue to avoid any paternalistic or "power-broker" relationships with community organizations. But it would seek workshop participants more motivated to work on local problems and more willing to make connections with other organizations. Even more critical was Highlander's decision to hold workshops on specific issues rather than generalized subjects like community organizing. Staff members were taking a calculated risk in adopting this strategy, reckoning that while there were few signs of unity among the dozens of organizations struggling in the mountains, Appalachia faced issues of such crisis proportions that its people, for all their diversity, would have to forge a regional movement for their own survival.[33]

If issue organizing held out the promise of broader, more durable, even bolder citizens' associations, which issues had sufficient galvanizing power, and how could Highlander turn them into a "true peoples movement" in the mountains?[34] The center's staff chose to address the question on three general fronts. First, residential workshops examined local issues that would sustain grassroots organizations. For a time staff members thought that the regionwide controversy over Area Development Districts—multicounty planning units that wielded virtually complete control over federal expenditures within their boundaries—could lead to a program involving thousands of people in a fight against "the most important change in local government since the Revolutionary War." Although that campaign never materialized, other workshops sought to build upon community struggles over strip mining, welfare rights, school reform, and other issues.[35]

A second front, research and advocacy, was headed by James Branscome, a former Appalachian Regional Commission staff member who had challenged Kentucky coal operators through the anti-strip-mining group Save Our Kentucky. Branscome forcefully asserted that institutions in Appalachia professing to serve the region's people were actually working for their "extinction." With a critical eye that spared no institution (including Highlander), he wrote hard-hitting articles on the ARC, Appalachia's public school systems, federal and state regulatory agencies, and especially the Tennessee Valley Authority, attacking the agency's coal policies and opening its decision-making structure to public scrutiny for the first time in its history.[36]

Long-term leadership development programs constituted the third part of Highlander's strategy. Former miner Charles "Buck" Maggard, the staff's connection to the coal fields and subsistence farms of southeastern Kentucky, asserted that the cutoff of federal antipoverty funds would leave Appalachian people hungry, aware, and ready to develop their own independent leadership. He and Branscome spent weeks at a time traveling up mountain hollows in North Carolina, Virginia, eastern Kentucky, and southeastern Ohio, looking for and listening to people with a good sense of leadership, passing on their ideas to leaders elsewhere—allowing the process, as Maggard put it, "to spread like molasses."[37]

This reorientation was one of several signs in the early 1970s that Highlander was making a decisive break from an analysis dating from the civil rights movement to one rooted in Appalachia. The shift was also expressed physically. Facing the prospect of an urban renewal project that would either raze the Riverside Drive headquarters or leave no room for expansion, the faculty moved in 1972 to a 104-acre farm near New Market, Tennessee, twenty-five miles east of Knoxville and about a mile from the Jefferson County tract turned over to the school in 1960. Even Highlander's administrative leadership reflected the transition after Myles Horton's retirement in 1970, passing from Conrad Browne to Frank Adams and then in 1972 to Mike Clark. For board members and supporters who understood the school in terms of earlier social movements, the implications of these changes were unclear. A nationwide capital fund drive eventually raised over $250,000, but in the process provoked sharp disputes between campaign directors Herman and Betty Liveright, who argued that donors responded most readily to appeals emphasizing Myles Horton and the civil rights movement, and staff members who resisted the idea of using either the past or a single personality to promote the center. At the same time, the staff was generally unclear about its educational roles. These concerns perhaps reflected a vague uneasiness over whether a broad-based movement was indeed emerging in Appalachia.[38]

Thus in the mid-1970s the Highlander staff took another hard look at the relationship of its education program to Appalachia. Many of the community organizations that had emerged during the War on Poverty or in

Nimrod Workman, center, retired West Virginia coal miner, performing at "Mountain Movement Music" workshop, Highlander Center, 1972. *Doug Yarrow/Highlander Research and Education Center.*

response to issues like strip mining had become inactive. The energy crisis of 1973–74 brought rapid economic expansion to some parts of the region as coal, oil, and gas prices boomed, while other areas suffered severe declines as small factories closed and small farmers lost their land. In Highlander's view the one constant in this changing picture was the growing power of corporations and government agencies in the mountains and their increasing lack of accountability to the public. Clark believed that an Appalachian movement was still very much alive, but it was not the poor people's coalition Highlander had anticipated in the mid-1960s. The movement was taking "a new direction." Older activists and groups were "weeding themselves out." Union members and middle-class professionals were asking critical questions about the future of the region. Single issues were becoming part of larger, multifaceted issues. Local problems had connections to national and international developments. Highlander's uncertainty in this situation, Clark asserted, stemmed from an educational base that had become "extremely nebulous," with a great deal of time, money, and effort being spent in Appalachia and little to show for it. Staff members agreed that the center needed to leave behind what Clark called "the myth of Highlander." They had to gain a new sense of purpose, to widen their constituency to include people in Appalachia and elsewhere who shared common concerns, to expand their activities to areas outside the region's coal fields, and to develop programs around a nucleus of issues that had broad, long-term significance.[39]

A new, intensive wave of institution-building programs followed. Dozens of workshops during the late 1970s and early 1980s brought several thousand Appalachian people together on an extensive range of issues: strip mining, land ownership, coal taxation, tax reform, toxic wastes, industrial health and safety, housing, welfare rights, public school reform, child development, elderly rights, and more. A request from coalfield clinics established by the UMWA for help in extending primary health care to rural communities led to the formation of the Appalachian Health Leadership Exchange Project (AHELP), coordinated by Helen Lewis, Ron Short, Craig Robinson, and Robin Gregg. To support community control of the clinics, AHELP recruited physicians, educated clinic board members and staffs on health care finance and delivery issues, organized health forums in three states, and promoted a network of assistance among the clinics that proved vital when the 1978 UMWA contract sharply cut back benefits from its Welfare and Retirement Funds.[40]

Highlander also renewed its ties with organized labor when staff members June Rostan and Bingham Graves set up a high school equivalency degree program for Knoxville area members of the Amalgamated Clothing and Textile Workers Union (ACTWU). The program spread to ACTWU locals elsewhere in Appalachia. Meanwhile, training in labor education began at Highlander for union officers from across the South. These and other workshops, such as sessions on the debilitating lung diseases suffered by textile mill workers and coal miners, reflected a renewed emphasis by Highlander on the links between Appalachia's problems and those found in the rest of the rural South.[41]

Research at Highlander moved away from the individualistic approach favored by James Branscome to become a more formal part of the center. Operating on the principle that information is power and that it can be effectively used to change society, a Resource Center, directed by Rhodes Scholar John Gaventa and Juliet Merrifield, not only provided research assistance and data but also trained citizens to do their own research and thus participate effectively in public policy decisions. Research projects documented the economic and environmental record of coal companies, occupational health and safety issues and legislation, and the interlocking relationships between corporations and public officials. In the late 1970s and early 1980s, Merrifield, Helen Lewis, and other staff members worked with Bumpass Cove, Tennessee, residents to block the dumping of toxic wastes in a nearby landfill, and, along with a citizens' group in Kingsport, Tennessee, they called attention to the possibility that chemicals at the Tennessee Eastman Company were hazardous to both employees and city residents. Although the Bumpass Cove Citizens Group became publicly divided after one of its officers turned against Highlander, and although the Kingsport Study Group may have been little more than a nuisance to local industrialists, the latter's persistence compelled Tennessee Eastman to make further efforts to comply with environmental regulations. Moreover, the links forged by the Kingsport group with conservationists throughout the region indicated that any emerging Appalachian movement would likely have an environmental component.

Highlander also participated in a major collaborative study of land ownership in Appalachia. Funded in part by a grant from the Appalachian Regional Commission, about one hundred activists and academics associated with the Appalachian Alliance pored over tax rolls and deed books in eighty selected counties in six Appalachian states—West Virginia, Virginia, Tennessee, North Carolina, Alabama, and Kentucky—to determine the owners of some twenty million acres of land and mineral rights. Despite some methodological complaints, the eighteen-hundred-page survey, completed in 1981, confirmed what Appalachian natives had known for decades: corporate and absentee ownership of huge amounts of land and minerals was responsible for inadequate tax revenues, public services, housing, and schools; shrinking farm lands; and environmental abuses.[42]

The Bumpass Cove, Kingsport, and land study projects reflect the attentiveness staff members gave to grassroots activities that might coalesce into some larger effort. Their experience with emerging indigenous leaders who needed technical assistance, organizing support, and sometimes a shot of self-confidence led to the creation of the Southern Appalachian Leadership Training (SALT) program. Selected local leaders engaged in a period of intensive, individualized study on a particular community problem, such as the construction of an unwanted dam or the lack of flood relief. In the process SALT trainees honed their leadership skills; learned to take maximum advantage of what government and other outside agencies had to offer; shared ideas with other community leaders, organizations, and responsive professionals; and deepened their commitment to their home communities. The center's cultural program continued to encourage the sharing of folk traditions among mountain and Deep South communities through Guy and Candie Carawan's workshops and performances before black and white audiences in Tennessee, Kentucky, West Virginia, and Georgia. A coalition formed in 1977 that for a time possessed considerable potential as a vehicle for reform was the Appalachian Alliance, composed of over thirty community groups seeking to speak with a more unified voice on regional problems and public policies. Bill Horton, who coordinated the land ownership study with John Gaventa, became coordinator of the Alliance in 1981, and at various Highlander workshops Alliance representatives considered strategies addressing health, energy, education, economic, and gender issues.[43]

Highlander's leadership was comparatively slow to appreciate the growing prominence of gender as an analytical, organizing, and unifying concept. Women at the center had become increasingly conscious of the irony of working at an institution whose commitment to change had been historically carried out to a significant degree by women; whose workshops had inspired and empowered women for decades; whose efforts in Appalachia had brought it into contact with leaders like Eula Hall and Edith Easterling; yet whose policy decisions, administrative duties, and workshop agendas were determined by men. During the 1970s Betty Liveright, Joyce Dukes, and other staff women had organized workshops specifically designed for women, and the center's leadership passed resolutions supporting the incorporation of women's perspectives in its programs. Yet it was the question of providing child care during workshops that enabled Highlander women to confront the "old boy network" and "blue jean machismo" of the male staff. For many years the center had adhered to a "no kids or dogs" rule. Most staff men did not regard child care as important; after all, they asserted, Highlander was an adult education center. Finally, after several years of lobbying by board member Sue Ella Kobak (née Easterling), staff members Helen Lewis and Candie Carawan, and other women; after the number of staff members with children grew; and after the center became involved in such efforts as the Coal Employment Project, which was aimed at pointing out the health hazards facing women mining coal underground, Highlander established what proved to be an exemplary child-care program in 1982. Thereafter the number of workshops devoted to women's issues increased rapidly, encouraging the formation of groups like the Southeast Women's Employment Coalition to support local efforts to achieve job equity and economic opportunities for women.[44]

In the course of all this activity, the lexicon of Highlander staff members and activists generally underwent a subtle yet significant change. Talk of an Appalachian *movement* that would tie into a larger poor and working people's movement virtually disappeared. In its place came more carefully chosen words about technical assistance, support systems, and, most commonly, *networks*. Despite promoting a positive image of Appalachia, sponsoring nearly two hundred residential workshops and countless meetings elsewhere, linking hundreds of community leaders with one another, coordinating groundbreaking research projects that challenged corporate wealth and power, and establishing a thriving campus with a broad financial base, the Highlander staff concluded that an analysis that had made sense in the 1960s was no longer viable.[45] Perhaps earlier efforts to create a social movement in Appalachia had been naive or raised expectations too quickly. Perhaps the idea of a regionwide struggle drew too readily on the examples of the labor and civil rights movements when there were not enough points of cohesion among the many localized struggles in the mountains. Perhaps Highlander's focus on regional and local issues overlooked the possibilities of achieving change at the state level. Perhaps the revelation of complex, interlocking sets of problems made the task of defining and sustaining an organized movement too difficult, too costly, or unnecessary. Or perhaps groups like Highlander had not adequately communicated their purposes, activities, and accomplishments. Whatever the reason, the new reality was that developing progressive leadership, supporting grassroots organizing, and fashioning a campaign on the people's terms that was simultaneously tailored to varying community needs—and in a time of economic contraction and political conservatism—would be, for the foreseeable future, a long, laborious process.

Yet the Highlander community was troubled by the way this changing context was blurring the definition of Highlander's work. In 1979 Clark observed that the most serious problem facing the center was its lack of educational structure and the consequent inability of those who came there to identify with its ideas, or even understand them. Some members of the staff, as well as an increasingly assertive executive committee and board of directors, saw Highlander as "perilously close to being all over the map" in the late 1970s and early 1980s, with program priorities that were vague, too crisis oriented, or reflecting personal commitments rather than the long-term interests of Highlander. Still others asked questions about the relationship between program technique and content, the center's diverse constituencies, staff responsibilities for raising funds and organizing programs, the growing academic orientation of the staff, and the possibility that Highlander's major goal should not be coalition building but the sowing of seeds for a coalition to be built by others. Hubert Sapp, a former assistant to Martin Luther King, Jr., who succeeded Clark as director in 1982, thought the essential issue was one Highlander had confronted throughout its history: "What balance do we strike between foresight and foreknowledge of [a] new movement, and the ability or the potential to respond to things as they emerge?"[46]

With the celebration of Highlander's fiftieth anniversary in 1982 came the third major refocusing of its educational program since Myles Horton and his colleagues had turned their attention to Appalachia in the mid-1960s. This new strategy emerged at a time when Highlander's history was receiving both praise and criticism—and demonstrating how far that past reached into the present. In 1983 Representative Ronald Dellums of California and Mayor Andrew Young of Atlanta nominated Highlander for the Nobel Peace Prize, emphasizing its efforts on behalf of the civil rights movement. That same year North Carolina Senator Jesse Helms raised objections on the floor of the Senate to the passage of a bill honoring Martin Luther King, Jr., with a federal holiday in his name, citing evidence linking the late civil rights leader to the Highlander Folk School, "a Communist, or at least a pro-Communist, training school." James J. Kilpatrick and other conservative columnists also revived the old canard, but an aggressive response from the center, and pressure from a significant number of newspapers, forced Kilpatrick to print a retraction in 1984.[47]

Highlander's recent programmatic approach acknowledges its historic role in bringing together grassroots groups across issues, races, and cultures. At the same time, the center has recognized the need to address issues common to Appalachia, the Deep South, and other areas of the world in the specific context of the 1980s and 1990s. The decision to continue working in Appalachia while moving to a wider issue orientation made analytical sense and held considerable appeal for staff members. The center's environmental health, land ownership, labor education, and other projects had revealed important connections between struggles in Appalachia and the Deep South. A broader geographical scope would therefore enable Highlander to act on requests for help not only from mostly white communities in Appalachia, but also from communities about the same distance away in the Deep South's Black Belt. That new focus in turn resolved a dilemma created by the impression that Highlander's Appalachian program restricted the center's efforts to build respect for racial and cultural diversity. With the actual or threatened dismantling of antipoverty, affirmative action, and labor programs by the Ronald Reagan administration, it also seemed imperative to focus not on specific strategies but on the overall task of reversing what Highlander viewed as a growing trend toward militarism, corporatism, and attacks on the disadvantaged. Finally, given the globalization of environmental, economic, and information issues, Highlander believed it needed to respond in kind.[48]

Aware that this analysis posed enormous organizational challenges, Hubert Sapp and his colleagues concentrated on five general, interrelated priorities. The first and foremost, as staff members liked to say, was "to keep your feet on the ground within the region." This self-admonition took on a variety of forms. Residential workshops on mineral leasing, racism and economic justice, occupational and environmental health, women's health and safety, unemployment, and other issues reflected the attempts of a variety of local groups and constituencies in Appalachia and the South to contend with the erosion of protective legislation and services. A Community Empowerment project encouraged, with limited success, Appalachian and Deep South community groups to share their respective experiences of anti-strip-mining campaigns and especially voter registration campaigns and see them as part of a long-term struggle for community survival and development. Helen Lewis assisted Maxine Waller and the Ivanhoe Civic League in their efforts to revitalize that small southwest Virginia town through industrial development, home renovation, civic improvement, and community history projects. Despite tight financial constraints, Jane Sapp, Linda Paris-Bailey, and Guy and Candie Carawan worked to tie the cultural program into the community empowerment concept. They created the space for folk singers and other "culture bearers" to reclaim community traditions; built networks among both artists and cultural workers; conducted field research and workshops in Alabama,

South Carolina, Kentucky, and elsewhere; and, in the Highlander tradition, made music, singing, storytelling, and other cultural expressions part of other programs.[49]

Meanwhile, the center addressed a series of issues that possessed environmental, economic, and political ramifications and thus the potential for unifying an otherwise diverse array of community groups. Toxics replaced rural health clinics as a particularly prominent Highlander concern during the 1980s. The long-running battle between the Yellow Creek Concerned Citizens (YCCC) of Bell County, Kentucky, and a sewage treatment plant pumping chemicals into Yellow Creek sparked efforts to promote ties among similar anti-pollution fights through campaigns to secure information on toxic dumpsites, Stop The Poisoning (STP) workshops, conferences on health and safety hazards, and a Community Environmental Health Program, coordinated by YCCC leader Larry Wilson. Staff members could point to success stories annually. They found it equally important that the drive for environmental quality challenged divisive "jobs versus environment" claims and threats that industries would be forced to "run away" to other communities, states, regions, and nations with less stringent regulations.[50]

Yet as the restructuring of the international economy continued throughout the 1980s, bringing fundamental dislocations to Appalachia and the South and expanded poverty to many communities, Highlander could only try to demystify the change and introduce alternative development strategies. A three-year Highlander Economic Education Project, headed by Bill Horton, Helen Lewis, and Sue Thrasher, developed curricular materials on economic development with local leaders from Virginia, Tennessee, West Virginia, and Alabama, and then used them in classes, workshops, and conferences at Highlander and at community centers and colleges in southwestern Virginia. John Gaventa and other researchers documented the impact of plant closings on workers throughout the South, and in 1989 the center joined with the ACTWU and the Commission on Religion in Appalachia to launch the Tennessee Industrial Renewal Project, a coalition that might help broaden Highlander's educational effort. Labor education itself fell into a holding pattern at Highlander in the mid-1980s, a reflection of the besieged state of organized labor. But when Virginia coal miners went on strike against Pittston Coal Company in 1989, staff members joined the dispute with gusto, walking the picket lines, leading singing at rallies, coordinating support activities, and doing what they could to help the miners gain the victories won in the strike.[51]

Highlander's other three priority areas sought to develop the tools and resources for social change. First, the enormous scope of the issues the center proposed to address, as well as cutbacks in sympathetic federal agencies and nonprofit groups, prompted a renewed emphasis on leadership development among both adults and youths. After a period of independence, a renamed and scaled-down Southern and Appalachian Leadership Training program returned to its original Highlander home in 1986–87. Following workshops at the center and in their home communities, SALT Fellows helped form day-care and community improvement centers, establish literacy education programs, improve occupational health and safety safeguards, and mount rallies against school consolidation, domestic violence, federal dam projects, strip-mine abuses, and inadequate public school instruction. Highlander's Summer Youth Workshops also reappeared in the mid-1980s after a hiatus of nearly twenty-five years. The intent of the program was to bring together a select group of older black, white, and Native-American teenagers from southern and Appalachian communities engaged in local struggles and cultivate their potential as citizen activists, assisting in the process the long-term needs of community groups for a new generation of volunteers, staff members, and leaders. Thus in addition to recreational activities, youth workshop participants explored a wide assortment of issues and creative activities through which they might not only express themselves but also place their communities' concerns in a larger context. The workshops continued into the 1990s and acquired a more urgent agenda as the crises facing America's youth became more prominent.[52]

Second, Highlander worked to build national and international networks of like-minded organizers, educators, and researchers. Staff members annually hosted meetings and workshops of regional and national alliances, coalitions, and associations concerned with justice, education, and leadership, and welcomed union and community leaders from dozens of countries in Europe, Africa, Asia, and Latin America. In the wake of the 1984 industrial disaster in Bhopal, India, Highlander mounted an intensive research, publication, and publicity campaign in cooperation with a delegation of Indian labor activists, who toured communities facing similar chemical dangers in Kentucky, West Virginia, and North Carolina. Highlander also became part of a global adult education network represented by such organizations as the International Council on Adult Education and the Latin American Council on Adult Education. In addition to co-sponsoring a North/South conference in Managua, Nicaragua, in 1983, as well as exchange programs for adult educators in that country and Appalachia during the mid- and late 1980s, Highlander staff members traveled extensively to share ideas about community-based education and the control of scientific knowledge.[53]

Highlander staff and friends meet with labor activists from India, 1985. Standing, left to right: Linda Selfridge, D. Thankappen, Sue Ella Kobak, Jane Sapp, Myles Horton, Peggy Kiggins, Lucy Phenix, Larry Bostian, Cinday Allen, Sue Thrasher, Hubert Sapp and son Edward, Helen Lewis, Nina Reining, Guy Carawan, Ganesh Pandey, Candie Carawan. Seated: Sylvie Key, Rajesh Tandon, Robert Sapp, Jacob Gaventa, Juliet Merrifield, Jonathan and John Gaventa, Vijay Kanhere. *Highlander Research and Education Center.*

Third, as Highlander continued to publish studies that challenged dominant perspectives on education, economics, and the environment, staff members engaged in what John Gaventa called "sharing the tools" of participatory research, and the "vision" it implies, with a growing number of grassroots groups and professionals. In 1981, in addition to its work on the land ownership study, Highlander published *We're Tired of Being Guinea Pigs,* a handbook on how citizens could confront local environmental health hazards. Two years later Tom Schlesinger completed *Our Own Worst Enemy,* a book-length report on the impact of military production on the upper South, along with *How To Research Your Local Military Contractor* for citizen researchers. Some publications were products of Highlander workshops, such as *Picking Up the Pieces,* on women and work, and *Water: You Have to Drink It with a Fork,* on industrial waste in water supplies. Other workshops offered participatory research training and helped develop media and computer technology skills. Still other Highlander-based research investigated such issues as land and coal taxation, rural poverty and natural resources, the impact of plant closings, and current economic problems in Appalachia and the South, a project that in 1990 resulted in *Communities in Economic Crisis.*[54]

Each component part of Highlander's work was timely, informative, and in many cases effective; the problem for staff members was to communicate its coherence and overall purpose to board members, supporters, and sometimes to one another. Public statements stressed the center's responsiveness to the need for community empowerment, accessible information, and global links to local struggles. Privately, staff and board members were concerned that the programs collectively lacked definition, coordination, or vision. The staff's fieldwork did not seem to weave back into an integrated residential curriculum. Several board members questioned not the idea of international linkages, but the role of Highlander in them. Foundation grant proposals appeared to have the effect of compartmentalizing programs, leaving some more financially secure than others. At the same time, prospective funders had difficulty understanding Highlander's educational process. Though Highlander's budget soared past the half-million-dollar mark in the mid-1980s, and a Fiftieth Anniversary fundraising campaign successfully met its million-dollar goal by 1985, an unanticipated, serious deficit in 1986 required a revision of the center's financial management system. Defining the center's constituency had become very difficult. Some feared that Highlander was becoming less a center for education than a center for conferences. Hubert Sapp's consensus-building administrative style and the staff's desire for a greater voice in decision making was disconcerting to those who viewed Highlander in terms of an older, director-centered structure.

In short, if Highlander was not living up to the distinctive educational pedagogy of Myles Horton, it was burdened with the image of Horton as the patriarch of a tradition-bound institution. Horton himself suggested in 1986 a fresh evaluation of the history of the school and the South as a way to re-energize the "Highlander spirit" and adapt it to contemporary conditions. The drafting of a new Statement of Mission in 1987 represented an effort to clarify and stabilize the center's vision in a context far different from the time when the folk school drew up a Statement of Purpose in 1950 (see Appendix 2).[55]

This reassessment was a difficult but necessary task, for Highlander's history is in many ways the history of dissent and reform in Appalachia and the American South since the onset of the Great Depression. Highlander was only one part of the struggles to organize labor unions during the 1930s and 1940s, achieve racial justice during the 1950s and 1960s, and challenge corporate power in Appalachia and the South during the 1970s and 1980s. Yet it played a crucial role in these movements because it did one thing better than any other institution in the region: educate industrial workers, farmers, blacks, and the poor to understand the nature of their grievances and nurture the seeds of their discontent. To be sure, in the long run the overall progress made by the labor and civil rights movements was not determined by the Highlander staff's work. Southern industry has remained basically nonunionized and anti-union, and despite important, tangible gains, the full promise of the black freedom struggle has yet to be realized. Indeed, the problems afflicting Appalachia and the Deep South are more intractable than ever before. Nevertheless, Highlander's education programs have made citizen activism in the region different and stronger than it might otherwise have been.

From the start, Highlander has sought to seize the moment when communities in the South and Appalachia have struggled against traditional structures of power and control. Devoted in their early years to aiding mine, lumber, and textile workers in Tennessee, staff members anticipated the formation of the Congress of Industrial Organizations and its attempts to form industrial unions in the region, and by the mid-1940s Highlander had become a major education training center for the CIO in the South. The school then served as a bridge between the labor and civil rights movements as the staff began an assault on racial discrimination in the late 1940s and early 1950s, and it achieved even greater prominence between 1953 and 1961 as a principal gathering place for the leaders of the drive for racial equality. It attracted Rosa Parks, Martin Luther King, Jr., Andrew Young, and dozens of other black activists, initiated a massive literacy campaign among southern blacks, started voter education projects, inspired blacks to become political candidates, vote, and participate in civic affairs, and forged productive alliances with SCLC, SNCC, and other civil rights groups.

The influence of the folk school often went unnoticed because of the staff's basic educational strategy of developing leadership among the rank and file of unions or community groups, emphasizing issues defined by them, and responding to their needs. Still, another measure of Highlander's significance was reflected by both its friends and its enemies. The list of supporters was consistently impressive, including prominent citizens like King, Eleanor Roosevelt, and Reinhold Niebuhr, educators, ministers, musicians, government officials, journalists, and officers of labor, farm, religious, philanthropic, and reform organizations. Highlander's opponents were equally powerful. Staff members endured threats, beatings, gunshots, arson, attacks from the American Legion, the Grundy County Crusaders, and the KKK, and a more or less constant barrage of denunciations from southern industrialists, politicians, and newsmen. There was also official harassment in the form of investigations by congressional committees, the

Internal Revenue Service, and the Tennessee state legislature, surveillance by the Federal Bureau of Investigation, well-publicized diatribes by the governor of Georgia and the attorney general of Arkansas, and ultimately the revocation of the folk school's charter and the confiscation of its property by Tennessee state officials. Highlander Center had to face similar assaults for most of the 1960s and is still viewed with skepticism by those who know only vaguely about its controversial past. Whether Highlander is perceived as a source of inspiration or as a dangerous revolutionary threat has depended very much on one's response to the changes that have taken place in southern and Appalachian society since the 1930s.

While each phase of the school's history has had its own issues, programs, and consequent successes and failures, and while its name, location, and personnel have changed over the years, Highlander's principles and purposes have remained constant. Its leaders have dedicated themselves to the idea that education could be used to push for fundamental social, economic, and political change leading to what they saw as a more democratic and humane society. They therefore sought to make Highlander a school where people could build on the knowledge they had gained from experience so that they could take charge of their own lives. The poor and the powerless, whatever their racial, ethnic, or geographical backgrounds, had similar characteristics as well as similar problems, the staff believed, and in informal group discussions they could identify their common goals and find ways of working collectively toward attaining them. This interaction in itself was important. It also provided motivation—the feeling, for example, that interracial cooperation was possible because it was being practiced at Highlander.

The Highlander faculty held classes throughout the South and Appalachia, on picket lines and shop floors, in union halls and community centers, in individual homes, and outdoors. Yet it was through Highlander's residence program that labor, farmer, civil rights, environmental, and other activists came to appreciate the staff's commitment to helping them solve their problems. For students, staff members, and visitors alike, the campuses of both the folk school and the center, with their acres of woods and meadow, panoramic views, spacious main buildings, libraries, cabins, and other attractive features, offered an emotionally uplifting experience that reflected the school's ideals. People lived, worked, played, and learned together in a setting most had never known before; they came into contact with new ideas and new people and returned home ready to spread the lessons Highlander had taught them.

This nondirective, open-ended educational approach was easy to explain but difficult to carry out, and it did not always work. Students, especially in the early years of the school, were often frustrated by the lack of coherence in residence workshops. Critics were to some extent correct when they pointed out that the staff's methods did not always produce lasting results or that its programs were too incremental and fragmented to create the broad-based coalitions it continually promoted. The folk school's loose structure extended to its administrative and financial affairs as well, and it cost the staff dearly in 1961 when HFS was closed. But such weaknesses were also the source of Highlander's strength and longevity. By not becoming attached to a single issue, organization, or movement, Highlander avoided the danger of rising or falling with one victory or defeat. By emphasizing decentralization and diversity, it could respond to the energies and interests of those who came to its workshops. The limitations, contradictions, and failures of numerous reforms since the 1930s gave substance to the staff's insistence that unless people at the bottom educated themselves to take their destinies into their own hands there could be no meaningful change in Appalachian, southern, or American society.

Highlander's achievements and longevity also have been due, to a considerable degree, to Myles Horton. The overall success of the institution has not depended solely on his efforts. Indeed, the school was strongest when educators like James Dombrowski, Zilphia Horton, Mary Lawrance, Septima Clark, Bernice Robinson, Mike Clark, Helen Lewis, John Gaventa, and many other committed men and women served on the staff. Yet Horton seemed to have a genius for anticipating the emergence of major reform movements in the region and for using Highlander's educational methods to contribute effectively to them. Horton's faith in the abilities and influence of Highlander students was often overstated; his hopes for a transformation of southern economic, political, and racial practices were repeatedly disappointed; and his vision of a new social order was never sufficiently clear. Nevertheless, Horton worked through Highlander to help the poor and oppressed critically examine the conditions affecting their lives and discover their capacity to change them. He urged students to realize that they had not only a right to a higher standard of living and decent treatment but also the potential to resist the attempts of the rich and powerful to exploit them.

Horton also tried to educate by the example of his own life. For both his friends and his enemies, Horton symbolized a challenge to the South's traditional beliefs and practices. He shared his own enthusiasm and ability to learn from others in helping people learn how to learn. He gave people the willingness to wage the long fight as well as the sensitivity to find solutions without creating new problems in their place. Most of all, Horton imparted a belief that a time would come when there would be greater human dignity and justice. Until then, he and his colleagues would keep pushing toward their objectives, continually setting their sights on higher goals. He never saw himself as being satisfied, nor did he see any reason to be satisfied. Southern and Appalachian citizens may not have understood or agreed with him, but they knew he was on the side of the dispossessed. That reputation sustained both Horton and Highlander.

The dilemmas that have recently confronted Highlander stem from problems in Appalachia and the South that are all too familiar to activists in the region. By the end of the 1980s there were few of the unifying elements that had undergirded the labor and civil rights movements, an unnerving diversity of community organizations, and a great deal of diffused dissent. New difficulties loomed ahead. The economies of Appalachia and the South, as the center has documented, were actually declining. Single-issue groups were discovering that their approach circumscribed their ability to inspire or achieve change and that the problem they confronted had many dimensions. Meanwhile, grassroots organizations were receiving diminishing support. A new generation of activist leadership had not yet fully emerged. Highlander's quandary was therefore the product of a generation-long adjustment by the staff, board, and supporters to the realization that, in the late twentieth century, the character, methods, and problems of social change could not be the same as they once were.

Highlander's work in the 1990s thus reflects its ongoing efforts to reorient its mission so that the center remains a vital part of broader regional, national, and international movements. It continues to address economic and environmental crises, encourage community revitalization from the grassroots up, locate unity within diversity, promote participatory research, build leadership, and strengthen popular culture. Yet it operates in a dramatically changed context. Shortly after completing an autobiography and a book about adult education and social justice with Brazilian educator Paulo Freire, Myles Horton died of brain cancer in January 1990 at the age of eighty-four; more than a thousand people gathered at the center that May to pay tribute to him. John Gaventa, who served as director between 1989 and 1993, ensured Highlander's stability through the post-Horton era and left a healthy institution for current director Jim Sessions, former head of the Commission on Religion in Appalachia. In recent years about half of the center's governing board has been composed of people of color, and about half have been women. Its workshops, annual budgets, and endowments have grown substantially. It has hooked into various computerized information networks.[56]

New Directions, New Struggles 281

Most significant, Highlander has a greater sense of responsibility for maintaining a gathering place, an educational center, a safe haven, and a space where strategies for progressive change can be developed. For activists working in a difficult political climate buffeted by social and economic dislocations and post–Cold War uncertainties, the center stands as a symbol of tenacity and hope. The labor and civil rights movements that shaped so much of the school's past stand as singular instances in American history of major social movements that made dramatic advances in a relatively short time. Each sought to secure basic rights and enjoyed success as long as their efforts centered on those rights. Each had a centralizing organization and at least one charismatic national leader—John L. Lewis and Martin Luther King, Jr. And each demanded and eventually received a governmental commitment to their causes. The mobilization of a grassroots coalition to resist exploitation and empower the people will remain arduous. The critical question for Highlander is not whether it will go on, but how it will choose to move ahead.

1 APPENDIX

Highlander's 1950
Statement of Purpose

Highlander Folk School:
Statement of Purpose,
Program, and Policy

We reaffirm our faith in democracy as a goal that will bring dignity and freedom to all; in democracy as an expanding concept encompassing human relations from the smallest community organization to international structure; and permeating all economic, social, and political activities.

Democracy to us means that membership in the human family entitles all to freedom of thought and religion, to equal rights to a livelihood, education and health, to equal opportunity to participate in the cultural life of the community and to equal access to public services.

We hold that democracy is inactive unless workers are given a full voice in industry through unions; or farmers are given a voice in the market place through cooperatives; or where freedom of thought and discussion is limited; that democracy is outlawed by legally entrenched discrimination and segregation; that there must be diversity of approach but each step must be in conformity with the goal, which is dishonored by each undemocratic act.

With a democratic goal, we are in a position to fight anything that gets in the way, whether it be totalitarian communism, or fascism or monopoly-dominated capitalism.

The purpose of the Highlander Folk School is to assist in creating leadership for democracy. Our services are available to labor, farm, community, religious and civic organizations working toward a democratic goal.

The nature of a specific educational program will be determined by the needs of the students.

Use of the services of the School by individual organizations will be in accordance with their own policies so long as these policies do not conflict with the purposes of the School. A staff member will assist in planning and coordinating all programs.

The Highlander Folk School is a chartered institution, cooperatively owned by the teaching staff. It has no affiliations. The policies and program of the School are wholly determined by an Executive Council composed of the staff and recognized Southern leaders.

Highlander Folk School is supported by contributions from individuals, organizations served by the School, foundations and tuition.

The times call for an affirmative program, based on a positive goal. An army of democracy deeply rooted in the lives, struggles and traditions of the American people must be created. By broadening the scope of democracy to include everyone, and deepening the concept to include every relationship, the army of democracy would be so vast and so determined that nothing undemocratic could stand in its path.

Approved by the Executive Council, April 3, 1950

2 APPENDIX

Highlander's 1987
Mission Statement

Statement of Highlander's Mission
November 1987

The Highlander Center works with people struggling against oppression, supporting their effort to take collective action to shape their own destiny. It seeks to create educational experiences that empower people to take democratic leadership towards fundamental change.

Highlander works with community groups primarily in Appalachia and the deep South. Because we are located in the poorest region of the world's richest and most powerful nation, we work with people who benefit least from our society as it is now structured. We also maintain exchanges and linkages with national and international groups, because we recognize the global dimension of economic and political injustice.

We bring people together to learn from each other. By sharing experience, we realize that we are not alone. We face common problems caused by injustice. Together we develop the resources for collective action. By connecting communities and groups regionally, we are working to change unjust structures and to build a genuine political and economic democracy.

We accomplish our purposes in a variety of ways. Residential workshops and educational training sessions at our New Market, Tennessee farm and center bring together representatives of communities facing specific struggles throughout the region. Our library and audiovisual resource center are available to individuals and groups wanting information about Highlander's history or about current social issues and strategies. Through our participatory research and cultural program we seek to affirm and document the knowledge, concerns, and struggles of the people with whom we work. Highlander staff persons also develop and conduct workshops across the region, link communities grappling with common issues and provide other education assistance in the field. Finally, through its youth, internship and other programs, Highlander strives to develop leadership within communities so that those who participate go on to share with others and to multiply what they have learned.

If real democracy is to be achieved, it will start with grassroots action. As diverse people respond to local circumstances, they must build broader movements which confront and change the policies and structures which dominate our lives. The power of the Highlander experience is the strength that grows within the souls of people, working together, as they analyze and confirm their own experiences and draw upon their understanding to contribute to fundamental change.

Approved by Highlander Staff and Board of Directors, November 1987

Notes

Introduction

1. Frank Adams, *Unearthing Seeds of Fire: The Idea of Highlander* (Winston-Salem, N.C.: John F. Blair, 1975), xv, 190.

2. These goals are expressed in numerous Highlander documents in the early 1930s.

3. For more on Highlander's definitions of democracy and brotherhood, see Myles Horton, "The Community Folk School," in *The Community School,* ed. Samuel Everett (New York: D. Appleton-Century, 1938), 265–67, 271–72; Horton, "Education at Highlander," MS for *New South Student,* ca. 1968, Highlander Research and Education Center Papers, Box 110, State Historical Society of Wisconsin, Madison (hereinafter cited as HC Papers); *The New Agenda for the White Southerner in His New South,* Highlander Folk School Occasional Papers, no. 1 (Monteagle, Tenn.: Highlander Folk School, 1960), Highlander Folk School Manuscript Collection, Box 12, Tennessee State Library and Archives, Nashville (hereinafter cited as HFS Coll.); Horton, conversations with Alice Cobb, Spring 1970, transcripts, Myles Horton Papers, Box 3, Highlander Research and Education Center, New Market, Tenn.; Michael Clark, "Meeting the Needs of the Adult Learner: Using Nonformal Education for Social Action," *Convergence* 11 (1978): 45; transcript, "The Adventures of a Radical Hillbilly," *Bill Moyers' Journal,* program no. 725, June 5, 1981, 2, 3, 6.

4. Highlander's general educational approach, and its consistency over time, is summarized by Horton in "The Community Folk School," 273–85; Gary J. Conti and Robert A. Fellenz, "Myles Horton: Ideas that Have Withstood the Test of Time," *Adult Literacy and Basic Education* 10 (1986): 1–18; Mike Clark, memorandum to All Health Workshop staff, May 2, 1978, Highlander Research and Education Center Papers, 1990 additions, Box 35, State Historical Society of Wisconsin, Madison (hereinafter cited as HCadd). Highlander's most recent files, organized into Administrative, Current, Director's, Financial (and other) Reports, General Correspondence, and Research categories, were transferred in 1990 to the State Historical Society of Wisconsin and added to the existing Highlander Papers. The specific box location of these partially processed documents will be cited where possible. See the bibliographical essay for other discussions of Highlander's educational approach.

5. David Whisnant, *All That Is Native and Fine: The Politics of Culture in an American Region* (Chapel Hill: Univ. of North Carolina Press, 1983), 128–29; Royce S. Pitkin, *The Residential School in American Adult Education* (Chicago: Center for the Study of Liberal Education for Adults, 1956), iii–iv, 5–7; Horton, "Decision-Making Processes," in *Educational Reconstruction: Promise and Challenge,* ed. Nabuo Shimahara (Columbus, Ohio: Charles E. Merrill, 1973), 327.

6. Whisnant, *All That Is Native and Fine,* 174–75, 177.

7. Horton, "Some Thoughts on Residential Adult Education," 1959; Horton, "Folk School in U.S.A.," paper published in the 1966 *Year Book of the Folk Schools of Scandinavia,* both HC Papers, Box 83; Horton, "Highlander's Citizenship School Idea," ca. 1961, HFS Coll., Box 2; Whisnant, *All That Is Native and Fine,* 125–39, 169–70, 172–79. See also Richard J. Altenbaugh, *Education for Struggle: The American Labor Colleges of the 1920s and 1930s* (Philadelphia: Temple Univ. Press, 1990); Joyce L. Kornbluh and Mary Frederickson, ed., *Sisterhood and Solidarity: Workers' Education and Women, 1914–1984* (Philadelphia: Temple Univ. Press, 1984).

1. The Establishment of Highlander, 1927–1932

1. Horton, interview with Dana Ford Thomas, Mar. 9, 1959, Knoxville, Tenn., 4; "Statements on the Origin of Highlander by Myles Horton and Questions by Aimee Horton," Nov. 1966, 1, 4, 11–12, both HC Papers, Box 54; Horton, interviews with author, Highlander Research and Education Center, Aug. 9, 1978, June 3, 1980; "Adventures of a Radical Hillbilly," 2–3. The Thomas interview is quoted at length in Thomas Bledsoe, *Or We'll All Hang Separately: The Highlander Idea* (Boston: Beacon Press, 1969), 23–50.

2. Horton, "Autobiographical Notes," ca. 1942, Box 2; Neil J. O'Connell, "The Religious Origins and Support of the Highlander Folk School," paper presented at the Southern Labor History Conference, Georgia State Univ., Atlanta, May 5, 1978, 2–5, Box 5, both Horton Papers; "Statements on the Origin of Highlander," 24–25; Horton, Thomas interview, 4–5; Aimee I. Horton, "The Highlander Folk School: A History of Its Major Programs Related to Social Movements in the South, 1932–1961"

(Ph.D. diss., Univ. of Chicago, 1971), 12–14. Aimee Horton's work was subsequently published as *The Highlander Folk School: A History of Its Major Programs, 1932–1961* (Brooklyn, N.Y.: Carlson, 1989); citations in this study refer to her dissertation.

3. Horton, personal notes on John Stuart Mill, *On Liberty and Other Essays* (New York: Macmillan, 1926), 34–35, 90–91, Horton Papers, Box 1; Horton, "Early Reading and 'Think Notes,'" HC Papers, Box 54; O'Connell, "Religious Origins and Support," 5–6; "Statements on the Origin of Highlander," 25; Horton, interview with author, June 3, 1980; "Adventures of a Radical Hillbilly," 4.

4. Horton, Thomas interview, 13.

5. Ibid., 11–13; O'Connell, "Religious Origins and Support," 6–7; Horton, interview with author, June 3, 1980.

6. Horton, Thomas interview, 2.

7. Horton to Mrs. J. Malcolm Forbes, May 25, 1932, quoted in A. I. Horton, "Highlander, 1932–61," 16–18; Horton, Thomas interview, 1–3; O'Connell, "Religious Origins and Support," 7–8; Hulan Glyn Thomas, "A History of the Highlander Folk School, 1932–1941" (M.A. thesis, Vanderbilt Univ., 1964), 10–12; Horton, "Autobiographical Notes."

8. Horton, Thomas interview, 6.

9. Horton, untitled talk at Rockwood, Tennessee, Presbyterian Church, 1928; Horton, untitled sermon at Crossville, Tennessee, Congregational Church, ca. 1928, Myles Horton Papers, State Historical Society of Wisconsin, Madison (hereinafter cited as MHP); O'Connell, "Religious Origins and Support," 8; Horton, Thomas interview, 6–7, 13–14; A. I. Horton, "Highlander, 1932–61," 21; H. G. Thomas, "Highlander, 1932–41," 12–14; Horton, interview with author, June 3, 1980.

10. Horton to P. J. Andreasen, Oct. 13, 1934, HC Papers, Box 5; Horton, Thomas interview, 7; O'Connell, "Religious Origins and Support," 9; "Statements on the Origin of Highlander," 16–17; H. G. Thomas, "Highlander, 1932–41," 14–15; Horton, interview with author, June 3, 1980.

11. Harry F. Ward, *Our Economic Morality and the Ethic of Jesus* (New York: Macmillan, 1929), 20, 323, and elsewhere. See also "Statements on the Origin of Highlander," 18; Donald B. Meyer, *The Protestant Search for Political Realism, 1919–1941* (Berkeley: Univ. of California Press, 1961), 145–53.

12. Horton, notes on southern mountains school, Union Theological Seminary, 1929, Horton Papers, Box 2; Horton, personal notes, Union Theological Seminary, Jan.–May 1930, HC Papers, Box 54. See also Horton, schedule of classes at Union Theological Seminary, Jan. 1930, HC Papers, Box 54; Horton, Thomas interview, 6, 7, 10; O'Connell, "Religious Origins and Support," 10.

13. "Statements on the Origin of Highlander," 4–8, 13–16, 18, 26. See also Horton to Arthur Swift, Nov. 6, 1965, Box 27; Horton, notes on Marion and Gastonia, N.C., textile strikes, ca. 1929, Box 64, both HC Papers; Horton, personal notes, ca. 1930, on Richard H. Tawney, *The Acquisitive Society* (New York: Harcourt, Brace and Howe, 1920), Box 1; Horton, "Tennessee Mountains: Rugby," ca. 1930, Box 5, both Horton Papers; Fannia M. Cohn, International Ladies' Garment Workers' Union, to Horton, Mar. 15, 1930, MHP, Box 6; A. I. Horton, "Highlander, 1932–61," 22–27; Horton, Thomas interview, 10; O'Connell, "Religious Origins and Support," 10;

H. G. Thomas, "Highlander, 1932–41," 16–17; Horton, interview with author, June 3, 1980. Horton later asserted that John Dewey's influence on his own educational approach had been overemphasized; when he once told the educator that he did not claim to be one of his disciples, Dewey "remarked that he was delighted because most of his misinterpreters claimed to be his disciples." Horton, "Some Rough Notes," Dec. 2, 1974, MHP, Box 10. On Brookwood Labor College, see Altenbaugh, *Education for Struggle,* and Charles F. Howlett, *Brookwood Labor College and the Struggle for Peace and Social Justice in America* (Lewiston, N.Y.: Edwin Mellen Press, 1993).

14. "Statements on the Origin of Highlander," 16; O'Connell, "Religious Origins and Support," 11; Meyer, *Protestant Search for Political Realism,* 218; Horton, interview with author, June 3, 1980; "Adventures of a Radical Hillbilly," 6–7; Richard Wightman Fox, *Reinhold Niebuhr: A Biography* (New York: Pantheon, 1985), 111–13.

15. Reinhold Niebuhr, *Moral Man and Immoral Society: A Study in Ethics and Politics* (New York: Charles Scribner's Sons, 1932), xi, xx, 19, 144, and elsewhere.

16. Ibid., 4, 199, 209, 219–22, 237, 277. See also Meyer, *Protestant Search for Political Realism,* 223, 229–30, 252, 268; Fox, *Niebuhr,* 136–41; Richard H. Pells, *Radical Visions and American Dreams: Culture and Social Thought in the Depression Years* (New York: Harper and Row, 1973), 141–47.

17. Horton, "The Bible as a Psycho-Social Agent," Union Theological Seminary, ca. 1929–30, HC Papers, Box 54.

18. Horton, personal notes, Union Theological Seminary, 1929, Horton Papers, Box 2; Horton, Thomas interview, 8; O'Connell, "Religious Origins and Support," 14. Niebuhr's enthusiasm for the South as a seedbed of radical Protestantism, as Donald Meyer and Richard Fox suggest, was particularly evident in the mid-1930s. *Protestant Search for Political Realism,* 343–44; *Niebuhr,* 157.

19. Horton's undergraduate degree in literature and year of seminary study did not meet the admission standards of the University of Chicago, so he enrolled at Chicago Theological Seminary and cross-registered for the sociology courses he wanted.

20. Horton, personal notes, Univ. of Chicago, Dec. 10, 1930, HC Papers, Box 54.

21. Horton, personal notes, Univ. of Chicago, Mar. 9, 1931, Horton Papers, Box 2.

22. Horton, personal notes, Univ. of Chicago, Nov. 27, 1930, HC Papers, Box 41. See also Ralph H. Turner, ed., *Robert E. Park on Social Control and Collective Behavior: Selected Papers* (Chicago: Univ. of Chicago Press, 1967), ix–xlvi.

23. "Statements on the Origin of Highlander," 18; Horton to Alice Hamilton, Mar. 5, 1969, HC Papers, Box 96.

24. Horton, personal notes, Univ. of Chicago, Oct. 1930, HC Papers, Box 54; Horton, Thomas interview, 8; "Statements on the Origin of Highlander," 2, 15, 18, 31; H. G. Thomas, "Highlander, 1932–41," 20–21; A. I. Horton, "Highlander, 1932–61," 28–30; O'Connell, "Religious Origins and Support," 15.

25. [Horton?], "Folk School Must Meet Folk's Need," ca. 1936, HFS Coll., Box 6; O'Connell, "Religious Origins and Support," 15–17; H. G. Thomas, "Highlander, 1932–41," 18–19. See also Horton, "Grundtvig and Danish Folk Schools," *Mountain Life and Work* 20 (Winter 1944): 23–25; Joseph K. Hart, *Light from the North: The Danish Folk Highschools: Their Meanings for America* (New York: Henry Holt, 1927); Holger Begtrup, Hans Lund, and Peter Manniche, *The Folk High Schools of Denmark*

and the Development of a Farming Community (London: Oxford Univ. Press, 1926); Whisnant, *All That Is Native and Fine*, 128–36.

26. John C. Campbell, *The Southern Highlander and His Homeland* (New York: Russell Sage Foundation, 1921), 297.

27. Whisnant, *All That Is Native and Fine*, 105–79, quotation 174. See also Horton, personal notes on books about Danish folk schools, 1931, HC Papers, Box 41; Horton, interview with author, June 3, 1980; Horton, Thomas interview, 8–9; O'Connell, "Religious Origins and Support," 17–18; Campbell, *Southern Highlander and His Homeland*, 190, 257–58, 289–98, 316; Henry D. Shapiro, *Appalachia On Our Mind: The Southern Mountains and Mountaineers in the American Consciousness, 1870–1920* (Chapel Hill: Univ. of North Carolina Press, 1978), 195, 237–39.

28. Quotation from Horton, notes written on 900 Park Avenue, New York City, stationary, June 18, 1931, MHP, Box 13. See also Zilla (Elizabeth) Hawes to Horton, Apr. 16, 1931, Box 15; Aage Møller to Horton, July 18, 1931; [Horton?], translations of excerpts from Fred. Norgaard, *Denmark fra 1864* (Copenhagen: H. Aschehang, 1920), both Box 41, all HC Papers; A. I. Horton, "Highlander, 1932–61," 31–32; H. G. Thomas, "Highlander, 1932–41," 21–22; Horton, Thomas interview, 9–10, 14–15; "Statements on the Origin of Highlander," 27; O'Connell, "Religious Origins and Support," 18; Horton, interview with author, June 3, 1980.

29. Horton, "Negroes in the U.S.," notes for Danish lecture, Esjberg F.H.S., ca. 1931–32, HC Papers, Box 41. See also Horton, Thomas interview, 16; "Statements on the Origin of Highlander," 17; H. G. Thomas, "Highlander, 1932–41," 23–24; Horton, interview with author, June 3, 1980.

30. Horton, personal notes, Denmark, ca. 1931–32, HC Papers, Box 54.

31. Horton, personal notes, Denmark, Feb. 11, 1932, Highlander Papers, unprocessed files, Highlander Research and Education Center (hereinafter cited as Highlander Papers).

32. Horton, personal notes, Denmark, Nov. 1931, Horton Papers, Box 2.

33. Horton to P. J. Andreasen, Oct. 13, 1934, Box 5; Horton, personal notes, Denmark, ca. 1931–32; Horton to Paul Hansen, Apr. 2, [1932?], both Box 41; "Pre-Highlander Notes by Myles Horton," ca. 1931–32; Horton, "Discussion with Fjerland," Feb. 3, 1932; Horton, personal notes, Denmark, ca. Nov.–Dec. 1931, Mar. 14, Apr. 21, 1932, all Box 54, all HC Papers; Horton, personal notes, Denmark, Feb. 11, 1931, Highlander Papers, unprocessed files; Horton, personal notes, Denmark, ca. 1931–32, Horton Papers, Box 2; Horton, "Influences on Highlander Research and Education Center, New Market, Tennessee, USA," paper presented at "Grundtvig's Ideas in North America" conference, Holte, Denmark, June 16–19, 1983, MHP, Box 3; Horton, Thomas interview, 17–18; "Statements on the Origin of Highlander," 9; A. I. Horton, "Highlander, 1932–61," 35–36; Horton, interview with author, June 3, 1980.

34. Horton, personal notes, Denmark, ca. Nov. 1931, HC Papers, Box 54; Horton, personal notes, Denmark, Dec. 2, 1931, Horton Papers, Box 2; A. I. Horton, "Highlander, 1931–61," 33.

35. Horton, personal notes, Denmark, ca. Nov.–Dec. 1931, Horton Papers, Box 2; Horton, personal notes, Johann Borups High School, Feb. 1932, Box 41; personal notes, Denmark, Nov.–Dec. 1931, Jan. 19, 1932, Box 54, all HC Papers; "Pre–Highlander

Notes by Myles Horton," 1931; "Statements on the Origin of Highlander," 23; A. I. Horton, "Highlander, 1932–61," 32, 33, 36–37.

36. Horton, "Christmas Night, 1931, Copenhagen, Denmark," HC Papers, Box 2.

37. Horton, personal notes, Johann Borups High School, Feb. 1932, ibid., Box 41. See also Horton, conversations with Cobb; Horton, Thomas interview, 18–19; "Statements on the Origin of Highlander," 19–21; A. I. Horton, "Highlander, 1932–61," 37–38; Horton, interview with author, June 3, 1980.

38. Reinhold Niebuhr to potential contributors to the "Southern Mountains School," May 27, 1932, HC Papers, Box 22.

39. Summary of Cash Receipts, June 1932–Feb. 28, 1933, Box 3; Roger Baldwin to Horton, June 6, 1933, Box 6; John Dewey, statement on Highlander, Sept. 27, 1933, Box 10; Sherwood Eddy to Horton, May 12, Aug. 30, 1932, Box 11; Elizabeth Gilman to Reinhold Niebuhr, May 31, Dec. 9, 1932; Niebuhr to Gilman, Dec. 13, 1932; Frank P. Graham to Horton, May 25, 1933, all Box 13; Niebuhr to Horton, Aug. 18, [1932]; Kirby Page to Horton, Aug. 16, 1933, both Box 22; John Thompson to Myles and Aimee Horton, Apr. 11, 1962, Box 28; Horton, personal notes, Paris, Apr. 1932, Box 54, all HC Papers; "Statements on the Origin of Highlander," 12; Horton, Thomas interview, 20–21; H. G. Thomas, "Highlander, 1932–41," 24–26; Meyer, *Protestant Search for Political Realism,* 343.

40. Dombrowski's dissertation was eventually published as *The Early Days of Christian Socialism in America* (New York: Columbia Univ. Press, 1936). See also John Thompson, vita, ca. 1941, HC Papers, Box 3; H. G. Thomas, "Highlander, 1932–41," 27; O'Connell, "Religious Origins and Support," 19.

41. Accounts differ as to where and when Horton visited Alexander. Will W. Alexander to Sherwood Eddy, May 26, 1933, HC Papers, Box 5; H. G. Thomas, "Highlander, 1932–41," 28–29; O'Connell, "Religious Origins and Support," 19; Stanley Lincoln Harbison, "The Social Gospel Career of Alva Wilmot Taylor" (Ph.D. diss., Vanderbilt Univ., 1975), 372.

42. Donald West, "Knott County, Kentucky: A Study" (B.D. thesis, Vanderbilt Univ., 1931), 88.

43. "Georgia Poet Points to Plight of Downtrodden," St. Louis *Post-Dispatch,* Apr. 14, [1946?], HC Papers, Box 76; Jesse Stuart, "Portrait of a Mountain Boy," *Cumberland Empire,* ca. 1932, 35–38; West, "Knott County"; West, "Hogism: A Parable of the Barnyard," *Epworth Highroad* (Nov. 1933): 30; H. G. Thomas, "Highlander, 1932–41," 28–29; Harbison, "Alva Wilmot Taylor," 372, 410–12; O'Connell, "Religious Origins and Support," 19–20; May Justus, interview with Alice Cobb, Nov. 10, 1977, Appalachian Oral History Program, Mars Hill College, Mars Hill, N.C.; Anthony P. Dunbar, *Against the Grain: Southern Radicals and Prophets, 1929–1959* (Charlottesville: Univ. Press of Virginia, 1981), 29–31; West to author, Nov. 10, 1980.

44. Horton to Paul H. Ritterskamp, Oct. 31, 1932, Socialist Party of America Papers, Box 116, Manuscript Dept., Perkins Library, Duke Univ., Durham, N.C.

45. Discrepancies abound in previous accounts of the meeting between Horton and West, the decision to adopt the name Highlander Folk School, and the relative contribution of each man. West appears to have been responsible for the name change. He had used "highlander" in his thesis to describe the people of Knott County, and he

later said that his wife, Constance, made the suggestion to call the new school Highlander. Horton to Reinhold Niebuhr, July 6, 1966, Box 22; Horton and Don West to Lilian Johnson, Sept. 17, 1932, Box 61, both HC Papers; H. G. Thomas, "Highlander, 1932–41," 29–31; Horton, Thomas interview, 21; O'Connell, "Religious Origins and Support," 19; Horton, interview with author, June 3, 1980; West to author, Nov. 10, 1980; Shapiro, *Appalachia On Our Mind,* 110–12.

46. Alanna J. Mozzer, "Lilian W. Johnson—Wellesley Class of 1885," unidentified magazine clipping, ca. 1932, Horton Papers, Box 3.

47. Lilian Johnson to "My Dear Friends," Jan. 20, 1917; Johnson to members of Cumberland Mountain KinCo, Apr. 1921; Lilian W. Johnson, *Who's Who in America,* [1947?], all HC Papers, Box 16; "A Pertinent Suggestion. From the Memphis Commercial Appeal of Nov. 19, '01," MHP, Box 13; Mozzer, "Lilian W. Johnson"; Horton, Thomas interview, 21–22; Justus, Cobb interview; Septima Poinsette Clark, with LeGette Blythe, *Echo in My Soul* (New York: E. P. Dutton, 1962), 122–29; Horton, interview with author, June 3, 1980.

48. Alva W. Taylor, "Building Gains Over the South," *Christian Century* 49 (Sept. 21, 1932): 1148.

49. Horton, "Report on Grundy County, Tennessee," Mar. 21, 1939, HC Papers, Box 53; *A Report of the Survey of the Finances and Management of the Government of Grundy County, Tennessee* (Nashville: Tennessee Taxpayers Association, 1934); Horton, "Community Folk School," 269–71; A. I. Horton, "Highlander, 1932–61," 40–44; H. G. Thomas, "Highlander, 1932–41," 4–6.

50. James Dombrowski, "Early History of Grundy County," ca. 1940; Horton, notes on Grundy County, ca. 1939, both HC Papers, Box 52; A. I. Horton, "Highlander, 1932–61," 44–46; Fran Ansley and Brenda Bell, ed., "Miners Insurrection/Convict Labor," *Southern Exposure* 1 (Winter 1974): 144–47; James B. Jones, Jr., "Strikes and Labor Organization in Tennessee During the Depression of 1893–1897," *Tennessee Historical Quarterly* 52 (Winter 1993): 256–64.

51. Horton and West, "Christmas Greetings from Highlander Folk School," Dec. 1932, Horton Papers, Box 2; Horton to Elizabeth Gilman, Dec. 22, 1932, Box 13; Horton to Elizabeth Hawes, Nov. 30, 1932, Box 61; Horton and West, "The Highlander Folk School," ca. 1933, Box 73, all HC Papers; Horton, "Educational Theory: Mutual Education," 1933, Horton Papers, Box 2; Horton, "The Highlander Folk School," *Social Frontier* 2 (Jan. 1936): 117; Horton, "Community Folk School," 272–73; Justus, Cobb interview; Leon Wilson, "Highlander Folk School: An Informal History," *Mountain Life and Work* 16 (Fall 1940): 16; A. I. Horton, "Highlander, 1932–61," 50–52; Horton, interview with author, June 3, 1980; Horton, untitled statement on Highlander as community school, June 3, 1980, in author's possession.

52. Horton, untitled introduction to talk on Denmark, 1932, HC Papers, Box 66; Horton, "Autobiographical Notes."

53. Horton, personal notes, ca. 1931–32, HC Papers, Box 41, and Horton and West, "Highlander Folk School," ca. 1933. See also Horton and West, "The Highlander Folk School, Monteagle, Tennessee," ca. spring 1933, Box 1; Horton, untitled notes, n.d., Box 2; Horton, "An Idea on Learning," ca. 1931–32, Box 41, all HC Papers; Horton, "Autobiographical Notes"; Horton, "Highlander Folk School," *Progressive Education*

(Apr.–May 1934): 302–3; Horton, interview with author, Aug. 9, 1978; "Adventures of a Radical Hillbilly," 9–10; Horton, "Decision-Making Processes," 327, 334, 338–39.

54. Horton and West, "Highlander Folk School," ca. 1933.

55. West, "Highlander Folk School," ca. 1932, Socialist Party Papers, Box 625.

56. Horton, personal notes, Denmark, Nov. 1931, HC Papers, Box 41. See also Horton, "Educational Theory"; Horton and West, "Highlander Folk School, Monteagle"; Horton, "Highlander Folk School Idea," ca. 1933, Box 54; Horton and West to editor, *Cumberland Outlook,* ca. Jan. 1933, Box 61, all HC Papers; West to Ethel M. Davis, Nov. 10, 1932, Socialist Party Papers, Box 117; "Statements on the Origin of Highlander," 3, 11, 12, 22, 29–30; Horton, Thomas interview, 19–20; Horton, "Highlander Folk School," *Mountain Life and Work* 17 (Spring 1941): 16.

2. Early Struggles, 1932–1937

1. Horton, "The Highlander Folk School Idea," ca. July 1933, HC Papers, Box 2. See also Horton and West, "Highlander Folk School, Monteagle."

2. Horton, "Experimental Education," ca. 1933, quoted in A. I. Horton, "Highlander, 1932–61," 52–53. See also John B. Thompson to Arthur L. Swift, Feb. 6, 1933, Box 28; Horton to Elizabeth Hawes, Nov. 30, 1932; Horton and West to editor, *Cumberland Outlook,* ca. Jan. 1933, both Box 61, all HC Papers; Horton and West, "Christmas Greetings," Dec. 1932; Horton, "Educational Theory"; table of residence term attendance, 1946, HFS Coll., Box 11; "The Highlander Folk School," *Rural America* 11 (May 1933): 12, 16; Horton, "Highlander Folk School," *Social Frontier,* 117.

3. Horton, "Educational Theory," Horton Papers, Box 2. The following account of the Wilder strike is based in part on Vernon F. Perry, "The Labor Struggle at Wilder, Tennessee" (B.D. thesis, Vanderbilt Univ., 1934); Fount F. Crabtree, "The Wilder Coal Strike of 1932–33" (M.A. thesis, George Peabody College for Teachers, 1937); Mikii Marlowe, "Wilder," MS, n.d., HC Papers, Box 83; Howard Kester, "Early Life of Howard Kester, about 1937," 9–10, Southern Tenant Farmers' Union Papers, Microfilm 4602, reel 60, Southern Historical Collection, Univ. of North Carolina at Chapel Hill (hereinafter cited as SHC); Fran Ansley and Brenda Bell, "Strikes in the Coal Camps: Davidson-Wilder, 1932," *Southern Exposure* 1 (Winter 1974): 113–33; Dunbar, *Against the Grain,* 1–15; H. G. Thomas, "Highlander, 1932–41," 68–72; Robert F. Martin, *Howard Kester and the Struggle for Social Justice in the South, 1904–77* (Charlottesville: Univ. Press of Virginia, 1991), 46–53.

4. James Crownover and C. D. Ferguson, statement on UMWA activity in Wilder area, ca. 1932, quoted in Perry, "Labor Struggle at Wilder," 26.

5. Compilation of newspaper articles about the Wilder strike, 1932; *Cumberland Outlook,* Dec. 2, 1932; Horton, "Strike of the Wilder Miners," 1933; Horton, "Comments on the Wilder Case," Sept. 1933, all HC Papers, Box 76. See also John Hevener, *Which Side Are You On? The Harlan County Coal Miners, 1931–1939* (Urbana: Univ. of Illinois Press, 1978); Philip Taft, "Violence in American Labor Disputes," *Annals of the American Academy of Political and Social Science* 364 (Mar. 1966): 127–40.

6. Horton to Tennessee newspapers, Nov. 28, 1932, HC Papers, Box 76.

7. Don West to Howard Kester, Feb. 15, 1933, Howard A. Kester Papers, Box 1, SHC. For accounts of Horton's arrest, see Chattanooga *Times,* Nov. 30, 1932; *Cumberland Outlook,* Dec. 2, 1932, both HC Papers, Box 76; Ansley and Bell, "Strikes in the Coal Camps," 122–23. See also Horton to Elizabeth Hawes, Nov. 30, 1932, Box 61, and various reports and clippings in Box 76, all HC Papers.

8. "The Wilder Miners' Battle Against Starvation," ca. 1932–33, HC Papers, Box 76. See also John B. Thompson to Norman Thomas, Feb. 23, 1933, Box 27; Walker Martin, HFS student, reports on Wilder strike, Jan. 11, ca. Jan. 15, 1933; Horton, "The Wilder Strike," ca. Mar. 1933, all Box 76; all HC Papers; Kester to Horton, Feb. 22, ca. Feb. 22, Mar. 22, 1933, all Box 3, all Horton Papers; Kester, "Trouble in the Tennessee Coal Fields," Dec. 4, 1932; Kester, report on Wilder, Tennessee, Jan. 1933; Kester to Don West, Feb. 21, 1933, all Kester Papers, Box 1; Harbison, "Alva Wilmot Taylor," 236, 380; Robert F. Martin, "A Prophet's Pilgrimage: The Religious Radicalism of Howard Anderson Kester, 1921–1941," *Journal of Southern History* 48 (Nov. 1982): 520; Kester, interview with Jacquelyn Hall and William Finger, July 22, 1974; Kester, interview with Mary Frederickson, Aug. 25, 1974, both Southern Oral History Program, SHC.

9. Walker Martin to Arkley L. Bilbrey, Jan. 31, 1933, reproduced in Crabtree, "Wilder Coal Strike," 16–17.

10. Horton, quoted in Ansley and Bell, "Strikes in the Coal Camps," 129. Miners and coal company officials vehemently disagreed over the circumstances of Barney Graham's death. Evidently two mine guards employed by Fentress Coal, Jack "Shorty" Green and John W. "Doc" Thompson, confronted Graham on the main street of Wilder. Shots rang out, and by the time miners reached the scene Graham lay dead, his body riddled with at least ten bullets and severely beaten. Armed mine guards held union members at bay for three hours before finally turning their leader's corpse over to them. Green was later indicted for the murder of Graham but was never convicted.

11. Horton to Reinhold Niebuhr, May 2, 1933, Box 22; Don West, Federated Press news release, May 8, 1933, Box 76, both HC Papers. See also clippings and notes in HC Papers, Box 76; Howard Kester to Horton, May 29, 1933, Horton Papers, Box 3.

12. Chattanooga *Times,* June 1, 1933, quoted in H. G. Thomas, "Highlander, 1932–41," 71.

13. Memorandum, C. C. Killen to F. W. Reeves, Nov. 3, 1933, HC Papers, Box 76.

14. News release, Socialist Party of Tennessee, state convention, Monteagle, June 11, 1933, Socialist Party Papers, Box 625. See also clippings and notes, Box 76; unidentified newspaper clipping, 1934, Microfilm 795, all HC Papers; Harbison, "Alva Wilmot Taylor," 239–40.

15. John B. Thompson to Lilian Johnson, May 29, 1933, HC Papers, Box 76.

16. Thompson to Kester, May 25, 1933; Kester to Thompson, May 29, 1933; Horton to Wilder strikers, Nov. 30, 1933, all HC Papers, Box 76; Horton, "Educational Theory"; Horton, "Highlander Folk School," *Social Frontier,* 117.

17. Form letter to prospective donors, May 1, 1933, HC Papers, Box 44.

18. Summary of cash receipts, June 1932–Feb. 28, 1933, Box 3; Horton to Alfred Baker Lewis, June 30, 1933, Box 18; Niebuhr to Horton, Feb. 27, July 24,

1933; Niebuhr to James Dombrowski, Nov. 8, 1933, Jan. 22, 1934, all Box 22; Thompson to Swift, Feb. 6, 1933, Box 28; Thompson to "Archie," Apr. 17, 1933, Box 44; list of contributors, 1933, Box 48; Horton to the editors of the *Christian Century, Nation, New Republic, World Tomorrow, New Leader,* and *Christian,* May 3, 1933, Box 53; Dombrowski to "Br. Beauchamp," Apr. 13, 1933, Box 76, all HC Papers; *Highlander Fling* 1 (Dec. 1933). Copies of most issues of the *Highlander Fling* can be found in HC Papers, Box 84, and HFS Coll., Box 12. "The Highlander Folk School," *World Tomorrow* 16 (Apr. 12, 1933): 343.

19. Lilian Johnson to editor, Chattanooga *Times,* Dec. 8, 1932; Johnson to Horton, Dec. 8, 1932, both HC Papers, Box 16.

20. Johnson to Horton, Dec. 8, 12, 1932, Box 16; Horton to Niebuhr, May 2, 1933, Box 22; news release, May 3, 1933, Box 41, all HC Papers; H. G. Thomas, "Highlander, 1932–41," 38–41; Horton, interview with author, June 3, 1980.

21. [Walker Martin?], "Criticism of Highlander Folk School," May 11, 1933, Box 2; West to Horton, Apr. 3, Dec. 16, 1933; announcements, Southern Folk School and Libraries, Kennesaw, Georgia, ca. Apr., Dec. 1933, all Box 29, all HC Papers; Alva W. Taylor to Horton, Oct. 17, Nov. 11, 1933; Sherwood Eddy to Horton, Oct. 17, 1933; West to Horton, ca. Oct. 1933; Horton to Bruce Bliven, Nov. 1, 1933, all Horton Papers, Box 7; West to Horton, May 12, 1933, MHP, Box 15; *New Republic* 76 (Oct. 4, 25, 1933): 216, 292; "The Highlander Folk School," *Rural America,* 16; Horton, interview with author, June 3, 1980; West to author, Nov. 10, 1980; Dunbar, *Against the Grain,* 52–59; Charles H. Martin, *The Angelo Herndon Case and Southern Justice* (Baton Rouge: Louisiana State Univ. Press, 1976), 111–13; Hannah Bynum, "For One We Lost: Poet Don West," *Southern Exposure* 20 (Winter 1992): 6–7; Bob Henry Baber, "Remembering Don West (1906–1992)," *Appalachian Heritage* 22 (Spring 1994): 27–30.

22. Elizabeth Hawes to Horton, Feb. 4, 1932, HC Papers, Box 15.

23. Dombrowski to Horton, June 15, 1933, HC Papers, Box 15. See also Horton to Dombrowski, ca. July 25, 1933, Box 2; Hawes to Horton, Feb. 4, 1932; Dombrowski to Horton, July 24, 25, 26, 1933, all Box 15; Dombrowski to Samuel Marcus, Oct. 16, 1933, Box 20, all HC Papers; Horton, interview with Mary Frederickson, July 24, 1975, Southern Oral History Program, SHC; Dombrowski, vita, ca. 1940s, Carl and Anne Braden Papers, Box 17, State Historical Society of Wisconsin; Dombrowski, "From a Mill-Town Jail," *New Republic* 60 (Oct. 2, 1929): 171–72; Morton Sosna, *In Search of the Silent South: Southern Liberals and the Race Issue* (New York: Columbia Univ. Press, 1977), 142–43; Thomas A. Krueger, *And Promises to Keep: The Southern Conference for Human Welfare, 1938–1948* (Nashville: Vanderbilt Univ. Press, 1968), 104–5; Frank T. Adams, *James A. Dombrowski: An American Heretic, 1897–1983* (Knoxville: Univ. of Tennessee Press, 1992), 5–63; John Egerton, *Speak Now Against the Day: The Generation Before the Civil Rights Movement in the South* (New York: Alfred A. Knopf, 1994), 160, 162.

24. Thomas quoted in Dorothy Thompson, notes on bugwood strike, July 5–29, Aug. 3, 1933, HC Papers, Box 52. See also Aimee Horton, "Crisis Education at Highlander," 3–6, Box 16; Thompson to Alva W. Taylor, July 6, 1933, Box 52; Horton, "Fog on the Mountain," 1940, 3, Box 83, all HC Papers; Michele Fowlkes

Marlowe, "Participation of the Poor: The Southern White in Social Movements" (M.S. thesis, Univ. of Tennessee, 1967), 33–34, 42–44; Horton, interview with author, June 3, 1980. For another account of Highlander's efforts in Grundy County during the 1930s, see Michael E. Price, "The New Deal in Tennessee: The Highlander Folk School and Worker Response in Grundy County," *Tennessee Historical Quarterly* 43 (Summer 1984): 99–120.

25. Dorothy Thompson, notes on bugwood strike, July 10, 1933.

26. Constitution of the Cumberland Mountain Workers' League, July 20, 1933, HC Papers, Box 52.

27. A. Horton, "Crisis Education at Highlander," 6; Dorothy Thompson to Alva Taylor, July 15, 1933, Box 27; Horton to Tennessee Products Company, July 29, 1933; Thompson to Frances Perkins, July 29, 1933; Thompson, notes on bugwood strike, July 5–29, Aug. 3, 1933; "Oath to be taken by Members of the Cumberland Mountain Workers' League," July 27, 1933; Will L. Brown to Franklin D. Roosevelt, May 3, 1934, all Box 52, all HC Papers; Marlowe, "Participation of the Poor," 44, 48–49; Horton, "Fog on the Mountain," 4.

28. Horton, "Fog on the Mountain," 4. See also news releases, clippings, letters, and statements in HC Papers, Box 52 and Microfilm 795; *Highlander Fling* 1 (Dec. 1933); A. I. Horton, "Highlander, 1932–61," 64–65; Marlowe, "Participation of the Poor," 45–46; Horton, "Community Folk School," 274–75.

29. A. Horton, "Crisis Education at Highlander," 2; correspondence, clippings, notes, and news releases, HC Papers, Boxes 52, 66; *Highlander Fling* 1 (Dec. 1933); Horton, "Community Folk School," 275–76; Marlowe, "Participation of the Poor," 46–47, 49–51.

30. A. Horton, "Crisis Education at Highlander," 2; A. I. Horton, "Highlander, 1932–61," 67, 74–76, 109.

31. Summer School Report and Summary of Reports of Other Educational Activities, Sept. 1933–1934, Box 1; announcement, "Highlander Folk School, Monteagle, Tennessee, 1933–1934," Nov. 1933, Box 61, both HC Papers; report on winter session of ten weeks, Mar. 19–May 25, 1934, HFS Coll., Box 14; [Dombrowski?] to Ruth Baldwin, Dec. 6, 1933, William H. Baldwin Papers, Box 1, State Historical Society of Wisconsin; *Highlander Fling* 1 (Dec. 1933, May 1934).

32. *Fighting Eaglet* (HFS student publication), no. 1 (June 1934), HC Papers, Box 61. See also Summer School Report and Summary of Reports; Horton to Dombrowski, ca. summer 1934, Box 15; announcement, Six Weeks' Summer School [June 18–July 28], 1934; report on summer school—June 18 to July 29, 1934; list of 1934 summer term students, all Box 61; *Cumberland Outlook,* May 3, 1934; *Hosiery Worker,* July 1934, both Microfilm 795, all HC Papers; *Highlander Fling* 1 (May, Sept. 1934); Horton, "Tennessee Highlander Folk School," *Concerning Workers' Education* 1 (Aug.–Sept. 1934): 17.

33. Summer School Report and Summary of Reports, 1–5. See also Horton to Dombrowski, ca. June 1934, Box 15; Horton to prospective students of Labor Union Week, July 3, 1934; *Fighting Eaglet,* nos. 1, 2, 5 (June, July 1934), all Box 61; course outline, History of the American Working People, ca. 1934, Box 62, all HC Papers; *Highlander Fling* 1 (Sept. 1934); Horton, "Tennessee Highlander Folk School," 17.

34. Staff members, "To Our Friends of Summerfield and Neighboring Communities," 1934, HC Papers, Box 1.

35. Staff meeting minutes, Mar. 18, 25, 1934, HC Papers, Box 2.

36. Summer School Report and Summary of Reports; Dombrowski to "Bryant," Aug. 6, 1934, Box 8; Dombrowski to Francis Henson, July 23, 1934, Box 13; [Dombrowski?] to Al Keedy, Aug. 6, 1934, Box 31; *Fighting Eaglet,* nos. 3, 4 (July 1934), Box 61, all HC Papers; R. F. Martin, "A Prophet's Pilgrimage," 521–22.

37. Zilla Hawes, "Recommendations," Sept. 1934; Dorothy A. Thompson, "Criticism of Highlander Folk School," Sept. 1934, both HC Papers, Box 2.

38. "Myles Horton's Criticism," Sept. 1934; Rupert Hampton, "Criticisms," Sept. 1934; staff meeting minutes, July 29–31, 1934, all Box 2; *Fighting Eaglet,* no. 5 (July 1934), Box 61, all HC Papers.

39. Summer School Report and Summary of Reports; *Bread and Roses: The Story of the Rise of the Shirtworkers, 1933–1934* (New York: Amalgamated Clothing Workers of America, n.d.), 21, cited in A. I. Horton, "Highlander, 1932–61," 113–14.

40. Dombrowski to Niebuhr, Feb. 27, 1934, HC Papers, Box 44.

41. Summer School Report and Summary of Reports; Dombrowski to Oscar B. Hawes, Feb. 6, 1934, Box 14; Dombrowski to Rupert Hampton, Jan. 27, 1934, Box 15; Dombrowski to Harry F. Ward, Mar. 4, 1934, Box 29; New York *Sun,* June 30, 1934, Box 53; Zilla Hawes, "The Amalgamated Comes South," ca. Sept. 1933, Box 63; Dombrowski, "Aims and Methods of the Highlander Folk School," Chattanooga *Federation News,* Mar. 1934, Microfilm 795, all HC Papers; *Highlander Fling* 1 (Dec. 1933, Jan., Spring 1934). See also John Dean Minton, *The New Deal in Tennessee, 1932–1938* (New York: Garland Publishing, 1979).

42. Summer School Report and Summary of Reports; announcement, Highlander Folk School for Workers in Knoxville, 1933, Box 1; plans for extension work and union contacts, Sept. 1934–Sept. 1935, Box 2; Hawes to Horton, ca. Feb. 1933, Feb. 18, 1934, Box 15; staff meeting minutes, Allardt, Feb. 4, Apr. 2, 1934, Box 31; notes on educational program, Jan. 13, 20, 1934, Box 52; announcement, Highlander Folk School for Workers in Knoxville, ca. 1933, Box 63; Knoxville *Journal,* ca. Feb. 26, 1934; Knoxville *News-Sentinel,* Mar. 20, 1934, both Microfilm 795, all HC Papers; *Highlander Fling* 1 (Jan. 1934).

43. Summary of activities, 1933–34, Box 37; Will L. Brown to Franklin D. Roosevelt, May 3, 1934, Box 73, both HC Papers.

44. Simpson quoted in John W. Edelman to Hawes, July 27, 1934, Box 11; Dombrowski to Ted Schultz, TVA, Sept. 22, 1934, Box 73, both HC Papers.

45. Summer School Report and Summary of Reports; recent activities, 1934, Box 1; Dombrowski to Elizabeth Gilman, Dec. 5, 1933, Box 13; Dombrowski to Lilian Johnson, Nov. 6, 23, 1934, Box 16; summary of activities, 1933–34, Box 37; Cumberland Mountain Cooperative, application to FERA, Jan. 5, 1934; report on the Highlander Folk Cooperative, Sept. 1934; Dombrowski to Lilian Harris, Oct. 31, 1934; Mrs. E. E. Eldridge to Judge Barton Brown, TERA, ca. Feb. 1935; Highlander Folk Cooperative to whom it may concern, Mar. 28, 1935, all Box 73, all HC Papers; *Highlander Fling* 1 (Nov. 1934, May 1935); Horton, "Fog on the Mountain," 5; A. I. Horton, "Highlander, 1932–61," 69–71.

46. Chattanooga *Times,* Apr. 4, 1935, HC Papers, Microfilm 795.

47. Knoxville *Journal,* Mar. 28, 1935, HC Papers, Microfilm 795.

48. Recent activities, ca. 1934, Box 1; Dombrowski to Ruth Catlin, Apr. 13, 1935, Box 8; Dombrowski to Sherwood Eddy, Apr. 26, 1935, Box 11; Dombrowski to George N. Mayhew, Apr. 8, 1935; Dombrowski to Udo Rall, Apr. 26, 1935; [Leona Graham?], FERA, to Jane Tabrisky, July 12, 1935, all Box 73; Chattanooga *Times,* Mar. 25, Apr. 4, 11, June 4, 1935; Chattanooga *News,* Apr. 9, 10, 11, 12, 20, 1935, Microfilm 795, all HC Papers; Horton, "Fog on the Mountain," 6–7.

49. Staff meeting minutes, Dec. 19, 1934, HC Papers, Box 31.

50. "County Program," ca. 1934, HC Papers, Box 2.

51. Hampton to Dombrowski, ca. Aug. 1934, HC Papers, Box 15.

52. Charter of Incorporation, State of Tennessee, notarized July 31, 1934, approved Oct. 20, 1934, Box 1; Rupert Hampton, "Criticisms," Sept. 1934; Hawes, "Recommendations," Sept. 1934; "Myles Horton's Criticism," Sept. 1934, all Box 2; annual statement, Oct. 1, 1933–Jan. 1, 1935, Box 3; Dombrowski to Kay Day, Aug. 6, 1934, Box 10; Dombrowski to Lilian Johnson, Oct. 23, 1934, Box 16; Dombrowski to Joe Kelley Stockton, Dec. 16, 1934, Box 27, all HC Papers; *Highlander Fling* 1 (Spring, Sept. 1934); Ruth Baldwin to Dombrowski, Feb. 18, 1934, Baldwin Papers, Box 1; A. I. Horton, "Highlander, 1932–61," 57; Horton, interview with author, June 3, 1980.

53. Dombrowksi to Norman Thomas, Mar. 7, 1934, HC Papers, Box 27. See also "Present Activities and Plans of the Highlander Folk School," ca. 1933, Box 1; Dombrowski to A. E. O. Munsell, Jan. 23, 1934, Box 21; Dombrowski to Al and Dot Keedy, Mar. 18, 1934; "Table of Costs for a Building to be Erected at the Highlander Folk School, Allardt, Tennessee," 1933, both Box 31, all HC Papers; *Highlander Fling* 1 (Dec. 1933); "Books and Kitchen Gadgets," *Nation* 138 (Jan. 3, 1934): 21.

54. Dombrowski to Ruth Baldwin, Oct. 5, 1934, and see Feb. 27, Aug. 6, 1934, Baldwin Papers, Box 1. See also Summer School Report and Summary of Reports; staff meeting minutes, July 29–31, Oct. 14, 1934, Box 2; summary of expenses—Monteagle and Allardt, Dec. 1934, Box 3; Horton to Dombrowski, ca. June 1934; Frances Thompson to Horton, Sept. 16, 1934, both Box 15; Dombrowski to Stanley Reese, Oct. 5, 1934, Box 23; Dombrowski to Stockton, Dec. 16, 1934, Box 27; Dombrowski to Al Keedy, Aug. 6, 1934; daily report, Allardt, Sept. 20, 1934, both Box 31; summary of activities, 1933–34 (to supplement Educational Report), Box 37, all HC Papers; *Highlander Fling* 1 (Jan., Spring, Sept. 1934); Horton, interview with author, June 3, 1980.

55. Horton to W. R. Amberson, Dec. 12, 1934, HC Papers, Box 5.

56. Howard Kester to Dombrowski, Jan. 23, 1935; Kester to Zilphia Mae Johnson, Jan. 24, 1935, both Kester Papers, Box 1.

57. Horton to Lilian Johnson, May 5, 1935, HC Papers, Box 16. See also Hilda Hulbert to Dorothy Thompson, Mar. 7, 1935, HC Papers, Box 15; Zilphia Horton to Myles Horton, July 17, 1936, Zilphia Horton Papers, Box 15, State Historical Society of Wisconsin (hereinafter cited as ZHP).

58. Quotations from Myles Horton to Zilphia Horton, Jan. 12, ca. 1936, MHP, Box 3; Zilphia to Myles, "Thursday eve," ca. 1936; notes "from Zi's class on community

singing at Lequemac," ca. 1935–36, ZHP, Box 15. See also Myles to Zilphia, Jan. 19, "Sunday," "Monday," "Monday Morning," "Tuesday morning," "Wed. Night," ca. 1936, MHP, Box 3; "I ask myself why I love you," ca. 1935–36, ZHP, Box 15.

59. Report for 1935; report on extension activity, Feb. 14–Apr. 12, 1935; report of activities for 1935 and winter term of 1936, all Box 1; Hawes to Joseph Scholssberg, ACWA, June 5, 1935, Box 5; Hilda Hulbert to Roger Baldwin, Feb. 19, 1935; Hawes to "Cousin Lou," Feb. 20, 1935, both Box 6; report on Richmond Hosiery Mills strike, ca. Feb. 22, 1935, Box 41; report on summer activities, summer session, June–Aug. 1935; *The Snag* (HFS student publication), nos. 2, 3 (July 2, 10, 1935), all Box 61; *Cumberland Outlook,* Feb. 14, 1935, Box 67; unidentified newspaper clipping, ca. Mar. 6, 1935; *Southern Voice,* May 1, 1935; unidentified Huntsville, Ala., newspaper, Aug. 1935, all Microfilm 795, all HC Papers; *Highlander Fling* 1 (May, Aug. 1935); A. I. Horton, "Highlander, 1932–61," 84–85; Anne W. Petty, "Dramatic Activities and Workers' Education at Highlander Folk School, 1932–1942" (Ph.D. diss., Bowling Green State Univ., 1979), 82–92.

60. Horton to Dombrowski, Mar. 4, 1935, Box 15; Hawes to Coy Fulton, Feb. 11, 1935, Box 12; Dombrowski to William Jeanes, May 11, 1935, Box 11, all HC Papers.

61. Dombrowski to Mary E. Ketchell, Jan. 31, 1935, HC Papers, Box 51. See also report for 1935; Horton, untitled essay on folk education, Oct. 16, 1935, both Box 1; Hawes to Brody Boyd, Mar. 28, 1935, Box 5; Dombrowski to Roger Baldwin, Mar. 4, 1935, Box 6; Henry T. Parmley to William Green, AFL, Dec. 24, 1935, Box 33; [C. R. Cuthbert?] to Green, Oct. 20, 1935, Box 56; Nashville *Labor Advocate,* ca. Nov. 28, 1935; Chattanooga *Times,* Dec. 12, 1935, both Microfilm 795, all HC Papers; announcement, *The Highlander Folk School. Fourth Year. Winter Term—January 6–February 29, Summer Term—May 18–June 27, 1936,* HFS Coll., Box 11.

62. Lilian Johnson to Mal Nisbet, Nov. 6, 1935, HC Papers, Box 16.

63. Staff meeting minutes, May 31, 1935, Box 2; Horton to Hilda Hulbert, Oct. 17, 1935; Dombrowski to Franz Daniel and Hawes, Aug. 31, 1935; Dombrowski to Hawes, Sept. 30, 1935, all Box 15, all HC Papers; Justus, Cobb interview; Horton, interview with author, June 3, 1980.

64. Report of activities for 1935 and winter term of 1936; report for the year 1936, both Box 1; staff meeting minutes, Dec. 9, 11, 1935, Jan. 3, 14, Feb. 11, Mar. 4, 1936, all Box 2; summary of students, winter 1936, Box 32; winter term announcement, Jan. 11–Mar. 6, 1936; "Educational Procedure, Winter Term—1936"; untitled notes on workers' councils, 1936; *Our Verdict,* nos. 1–5 (Jan. 21, 28, Feb. 8, 13, 20, 1936), all Box 61, all HC Papers; Petty, "Dramatic Activities at Highlander," 94–95.

65. Announcement, summer school for workers, May 18–June 27, 1936, HC Papers, Box 61.

66. Report for the year 1936; Hawes to Odean Enesvedt, June 16, 1936, Box 11; Hawes to Charles Prouty, June 2, 1936, Box 23; summary of students, summer 1936, Box 32; *The Lookout,* no. 1 (June 7, 1936), Box 61, all HC Papers; untitled report, HFS, June 10, 1936, HFS Coll., Box 14; Petty, "Dramatic Activities at Highlander," 99–101.

67. Report for the year 1936; staff meeting minutes, Oct. 1936, Box 2; financial report, 1935; treasurer's report for 1936; budget for 1937, all Box 3; list of "Early

Contributors," 1936, Box 48; Dombrowski to William B. Benton, June 5, 1936, Box 51, all HC Papers; untitled report, HFS, June 10, 1936, HFS Coll., Box 14.

68. Report of activities for 1935 and winter term of 1936, Box 1; staff meeting minutes, Jan. 16, Feb. 13, 1935, Box 2; Hilda Hulbert, summary of activities, ca. 1935, Box 3; Charles S. Johnson to Hulbert, Jan. 10, 1935, Box 16; Dombrowski to Robert Marshall, Dec. 26, 1936, Box 20; Dombrowski to W. Burnett Easton, Jr., Jan. 7, 1935, Box 51; Hulbert to Tommie D. Barker, Jan. 24, 1935, Box 53; Hulbert to Mrs. L. A. Mead, Jan. 30, 1935, Box 61; *Cumberland Outlook,* ca. fall 1934–winter 1935, Microfilm 795, all HC Papers; Horton, "Community Folk School," 278–79.

69. Knoxville *News-Sentinel,* Mar. 14, 1937, HC Papers, Box 66. See also report for the year 1936; Tefferteller, summary of activities, ca. 1934–38, Box 3; Tefferteller to Felix Greene, BBC, Feb. 24, 1937; news release to editors of county newspapers, Mar. 10, 1937; "Highlander Folk School short wave broadcast from Monteagle to England, 3/13/37," all Box 66; Knoxville *Labor News,* Mar. 18, 20, 1937, Microfilm 795, all HC Papers; untitled report, HFS, June 10, 1936, HFS Coll., Box 14; *Highlander Fling* 1 (May 1935, Sept. 1936), 2 (Spring 1937).

70. Report for the year 1935; report on extension activity, Feb. 14–Apr. 12, 1935, both Box 1; Horton to Alice and James Dombrowski, Feb. 5, 1935, Box 5; Hulbert to Roger Baldwin, Feb. 19, 1935, Box 6; Hulbert, "Excerpts from Diary Kept during Strike," Feb. 1935; notes on Richmond Hosiery Mills strike, ca. Feb. 22, 1935; Horton and A. L. DeJarnette, news release, Feb. 24, 1935, all Box 41; William Marlowe to Dombrowski, Feb. 22, 1935, Box 61; *Cumberland Outlook,* Feb. 14, 1935, Box 67; Dombrowski, "A Civil Liberties Tour in the Tennessee Valley," 1939, 21–24, Box 82; Chattanooga *Times,* Feb. 23, 1935; Chattanooga *News,* Feb. 25, 1935, Microfilm 795, all HC Papers; *Highlander Fling* 1 (May 1935); Horton, "Highlander Folk School," *Social Frontier,* 118; H. G. Thomas, "Highlander, 1932–41," 72–75.

71. Hawes to Charles Handy, Apr. 29, 1936, HC Papers, Box 14.

72. Chattanooga *Times,* May 8, 1936, cited in H. G. Thomas, "Highlander, 1932–41," 78.

73. Staff meeting minutes, May 15, 1936, Box 2; Hawes to Charles Prouty, May 2, 1936, Box 23; Dombrowski to William B. Benton, June 5, 1936, Box 51, all HC Papers; Dombrowski, "A Civil Liberties Tour," 12–13; H. G. Thomas, "Highlander, 1932–41," 75–80; Max York, "Labor's Tall Man on the Hill: The Matt Lynch Story," Nashville *Tennessean Magazine,* July 1, 1962, 8–9.

74. Report for the year 1936; Zilphia Horton to Myles Horton, July 23, 1936, Box 15; "Field Work Programs—1933–1942," Box 58; "A Unique Labor School," *American Teacher* (Nov.–Dec. 1936), Box 82; Nashville *Labor Advocate,* Nov. 12, 1936, Microfilm 795, all HC Papers; Zilphia Horton to Myles Horton, Sept. 23, 1936, ZHP, Box 15; *Highlander Fling* 1 (Sept. 1936); H. G. Thomas, "Highlander, 1932–41," 80–81; Horton, Frederickson interview.

75. Horton, "Fog on the Mountain," 8.

76. Report of activities for 1935 and winter term of 1936; report for the year 1936; unidentified notes, Jan. 11, 1936; Horton to E. E. McDaniel, Feb. 17, 20, 1936, both Box 52; Charles E. Allred et al., *Grundy County, Tennessee: Relief in a Coal Mining*

Community, Tennessee Agricultural Experiment Station, Report 11, Univ. of Tennessee, Knoxville, Box 53, all HC Papers; Myles Horton to Zilphia Horton, Nov. 30, 1935, "Tuesday morning" [1935], Feb. 20 [1936], Box 3, MHP; Horton, "Fog on the Mountain," 8–9; A. I. Horton, "Highlander, 1932–61," 77–78.

77. M. R. Etter to Rep. Samuel D. McReynolds, Feb. 7, 1936; N. R. Patterson to Horton, Mar. 3, 1936; "Interview with District WPA Administrator," July 9, 1936, all HC Papers, Box 52; Officers of Common Laborers' Union Local 848 to Franklin D. Roosevelt, Harry L. Hopkins, and H. S. Berry, July [18?], 1936, HFS Coll., Box 10; Myles Horton to Zilphia Horton, "Sunday" [1936], MHP, Box 3; *Highlander Fling* 1 (Sept. 1936); Horton, "Fog on the Mountain," 9–10; A. I. Horton, "Highlander, 1932–61," 78–82; Berthe Daniel, "Tennessee's Mountaineers," *Letters* 3 (Sept. 28, 1936).

78. Quoted in Horton, "Fog on the Mountain," 11.

79. Telegram, E. W. Birdwell to Franklin D. Roosevelt, Mar. 11, 1937, Box 52; Chattanooga *Times,* Mar. 12, 1937, Box 53, both HC Papers.

80. Knoxville *News-Sentinel,* Mar. 13, 1937, HC Papers, Microfilm 795.

81. Tefferteller, "Report on Field Trip," Aug. 20, 1937, Box 44; chairman and secretary of CLU Local 930 to Harry L. Hopkins, Mar. 19, 1937; "A petition to Mr. Harry L. Hopkins, WPA Administrator," Mar. 25, 1937; E. E. McDaniel to Hopkins, Mar. 31, 1937; "A Record of Events Leading up to the Strike of Local Union 930," Sept. 1937; Charles Adams to Hopkins, Oct. 13, 1937; Adams, complaint to NLRB, Oct. 1937; "Demands of Local 930 of International Hod Carriers," Oct. 1937, all Box 52, all HC Papers; Horton, "Fog on the Mountain," 11–15.

82. Dombrowski, "Radical Religion in the South," 1939, 9, HC Papers, Box 44.

83. Report for the year 1936; announcement, "Fellowship and Conference," Paris, Ark., Aug. 13, 1934, Box 29; Conference of Younger Churchmen of the South, "Findings," May 27–29, 1934; Thomas B. Cowan, "History of the Fellowship of Southern Churchmen," ca. 1937, both Box 44; report, Southern Workers' Education Conference, July 26–29, 1934, Box 77, all HC Papers; report on Conference on Workers' Education, Jan. 16–17, 1937, HFS Coll., Box 5. See also David Burgess, "The Fellowship of Southern Churchmen: Its History and Promise," *Prophetic Religion* 13 (Spring 1953): 3–11; Martin, *Howard Kester,* 114–18, 121–22, 124–25; Dunbar, *Against the Grain,* 59–61, 74–75, 256–57.

84. Report for the year 1936; Olive D. Campbell to Horton, Feb. 5, 1934, Box 8; Horton to Dombrowski, Apr. 7, 1936, Box 15; H. L. Mitchell to Dombrowski, Oct. 21, 1935, Box 21; Horton to Dombrowski, ca. Dec. 1936, Box 25; Horton, field report on Commonwealth College, Aug. 28, 1934, Box 39, all HC Papers; Horton to Mitchell, Apr. 24, 1936, reel 2; Horton to Mitchell, Oct. 13, 1936; leadership training course for the STFU, Dec. 13–22, 1936, both reel 3, all STFU Papers; Horton, Frederickson interview. See also Dunbar, *Against the Grain,* 68–70, 101–4, 130–35; Martin, *Howard Kester,* 82, 86–100, 104–7; Mary Frederickson, "A Place to Speak Our Minds: The Southern School for Women Workers" (Ph.D. diss., Univ. of North Carolina at Chapel Hill, 1981); Frederickson, "Recognizing Regional Differences: The Southern Summer School for Women Workers," in *Sisterhood and Solidarity,* 148–86; Donald H. Grubbs, *Cry From the Cotton: The Southern Tenant Farmers' Union and the New Deal* (Chapel Hill: Univ. of North Carolina Press, 1971); Altenbaugh, *Education for Struggle.*

85. *Grundy County Herald,* ca. fall 1936, HC Papers, Microfilm 795.

86. *Cumberland Outlook,* Dec. 15, 1932, in "Opposition to Highlander and Criticism of Its Activities as Gathered from Newspaper Clippings, 1932–1941," HC Papers, Box 33.

87. John E. Edgerton, Tennessee Manufacturers Association news release, June 28, 1934, HC Papers, Box 33.

88. Dombrowski to Raymond F. Lowry, June 29, 1935, HC Papers, Box 5. See also "Opposition as Gathered from Clippings, 1932–1941"; John E. Edgerton to Horton, June 19, 1934, Box 11; *Cumberland Outlook,* ca. Dec. 18, 1932; Chattanooga *News,* ca. Feb. 3, 1933; Chattanooga *Times,* Jan. 28, 1935; Knoxville *Journal,* Mar. 31, 1935, all Microfilm 795, all HC Papers; George Brown Tindall, *The Emergence of the New South, 1913–1945* (Baton Rouge: Louisiana State Univ. Press, 1967), 444–45.

89. *Call for the All-Southern Conference for Civil and Trade-Union Rights,* ca. May 26, 1935, HFS Coll., Box 6; Dombrowski to Mary W. Hillyer, Apr. 25, 1935, Kester Papers, Box 1.

90. Chattanooga *News,* May 5, 1935, HC Papers, Microfilm 795.

91. Chattanooga *Times,* May 3, 1935; Chattanooga *News,* May 6, 1935, HC Papers, Microfilm 795.

92. General Platform of All-Southern Conference for Civil and Trade-Union Rights, May 26, 1935, Box 31; Chattanooga *Times,* May 3, 5, 7, 27, 1935; Chattanooga *News,* May 5, 6, 27, 1935, all Microfilm 795, all HC Papers; "The All-Southern Conference for Civil and Trade-Union Rights," ca. May 27, 1935, HFS Coll., Box 5; Dombrowski to H. L. Mitchell, May 11, 1935, STFU Papers, reel 59; H. G. Thomas, "Highlander, 1932–41," 114–16; untitled editorial, *Nation* 140 (June 12, 1935): 671.

93. Chattanooga *News,* July 13, 1935, HC Papers, Microfilm 795. See also "Opposition as Gathered from Clippings, 1932–1941"; Dombrowski to William H. Baldwin, Aug. 7, 1935, Box 6; Dombrowski to Jennie M. Flexner, Sept. 26, 1935, Box 12; Chattanooga *Times,* May 7, June 13, July 11, 12, 1935; Chattanooga *News,* July 11, 12, 1935, all Microfilm 795, all HC Papers; *Highlander Fling* 1 (Aug. 1935).

94. Chattanooga *News,* Feb. 6, 1937; Chattanooga *Free Press,* Feb. 7, 1937, both Microfilm 795; Lyle Stovall to Horton, Feb. 7, 1937, Box 33, all HC Papers.

95. Horton to Roger Baldwin, Feb. 8, 1937; Dombrowski to Albert E. Barnett, Feb. 10, 1937, both HC Papers, Box 33.

96. George Fort Milton to Barnett, Feb. 10, 1937, Box 6; Milton to Niebuhr, Feb. 17, 1937, Box 33, both HC Papers.

97. Horton to Roger Baldwin, Feb. 13, 1937, HC Papers, Box 33. See also Dombrowski to Barnett, Feb. 8, 1937, Box 6; various individuals and unions protesting *News* article to George Fort Milton, Feb. 7–12, 1937; petition, "We the Citizens and Neighbors of Highlander Folk School" to Milton, Feb. 16, 1937; Milton to Norman Thomas, Feb. 22, 1937, all Box 33; Chattanooga *News,* Feb. 9, 11, 13, 16, 18, 23, 1937; Chattanooga *Labor World,* Feb. 12, 1937, all Microfilm 795, all HC Papers; *Highlander Fling* 1 (Spring 1937).

98. Hawes to staff, Feb. 15, 1937; Hawes to Dombrowski and staff, Feb. 28, 1937, both HC Papers, Box 14.

99. Dombrowski to Hawes, Mar. 3, 1937, HC Papers, Box 14.

100. Hawes to Ruth Catlin, Mar. 2, 1937; Hawes to Dombrowski, Mar. 9, 1937; Dombrowski to Hawes, Mar. 24, 1937, all Box 14; Chattanooga *Times,* Feb. 16, 1937, Box 39; Chattanooga *News,* Feb. 16, 1937, Microfilm 795, all HC Papers; *Highlander Fling* 1 (Spring 1937).

101. Knoxville *News-Sentinel,* Jan. 21, 1933; Chattanooga *News,* Feb. 1, 1933; Chattanooga *Times,* Aug. 27, 1933, all HC Papers, Microfilm 795.

102. Present activities and plans, 1933, Box 1; Hawes to Horton, Mar. 15, [1933?]; Horton to Dombrowski, ca. spring 1933, both Box 15; Nancy Lea Smith to Dombrowski, Mar. 15, 1934, Box 26; Chattanooga *News,* ca. summer 1933, Box 41; minutes, Tennessee State Socialist Conference, Feb. 19, 1933, Box 68; Federated Press news release, June 1933, Microfilm 795, all HC Papers; Horton to *America For All* (Socialist Party newspaper), Nov. 1, 1932, Box 116; Ethel M. Davis to Don West, Nov. 4, 1932, Box 117; Horton to Clarence Senior, Dec. 19, 1932; Senior to Horton, Dec. 29, 1932, both Box 120, all Socialist Party Papers; Senior to Kester, Feb. 14, 1933; Kester to Senior, Feb. 21, 1933; minutes, Southern Conference, Socialist Party, Jan. 2–3, 1937, all Kester Papers, Box 1. See also Pells, *Radical Visions and American Dreams,* 61–86; Tindall, *Emergence of the New South,* 607–8, 618; Bernard Karsh and Phillips L. Garman, "The Impact of the Political Left," in *Labor and the New Deal,* ed. Milton Derber and Edwin Young (Madison: Univ. of Wisconsin Press, 1957), 83–88.

103. Horton to P. J. Andreasen, Oct. 13, 1934; Dombrowski to J. E. Carnes, Dec. 16, 1934, both Box 8; Hawes to Horton, Sept. 10, 1935, Box 15; Dombrowski to Kester, Oct. 16, 1934, Box 17; Horton to Griscom Morgan, June 9, 1935, Box 21; Dombrowski to Stan and Nancy Smith, Dec. 28, 1934, Box 26; *Daily Worker,* Jan. 5, 1935, Microfilm 795, all HC Papers; C. A. Hathaway to Horton, Aug. 9, 1934, Horton Papers, Box 1; Horton, Hawes, and Dombrowski to Joe Kelley Stockton, Jan. 3, 1935; "Notes on Southern Tour of Paul Porter and Clarence Senior," May 1935, both Kester Papers, Box 1; Kester, Hall and Finger interview; Martin, *Howard Kester,* 119–20.

104. Table of attendance at residence terms, residence institutes, and extension classes, 1932–45, HFS Coll., Box 11.

105. Horton, "Highlander Folk School," *Social Frontier,* 118.

106. "Union Contacts in Grundy and Marion Counties," [1936?], HC Papers, Box 52; *Highlander Fling* 1 (Sept. 1936); Horton, "Highlander Folk School," *Social Frontier,* 118.

107. Francis J. Gorman to Horton, Oct. 22, 1935, Box 28; Nashville *Labor Advocate,* Nov. 18, 1935, Microfilm 795, both HC Papers. See also Egerton, *Speak Now Against the Day,* 158–62; Egerton, "Highlander in the Thirties: An Appalachian Seedbed for Social Change," *Appalachian Heritage* 22 (Winter 1994): 5–9.

108. Horton, "Highlander Folk School," *Social Frontier,* 118.

3. Building and Defending a Program, 1937–1941

1. Dombrowski to Anna Bogue, William C. Whitney Foundation, May 8, 1937, HC Papers, Box 51. See also budget for 1937, Box 3; Henry Sherwood, U.S. Treasury Dept., to HFS, May 6, 1937, Box 34; Bogue to Dombrowski, Jan. 14, 1937;

Dombrowski to Bogue, Jan. 18, Feb. 8, May 18, 1937, all Box 51; report of fifth winter term, Jan. 6–Feb. 10, 1937; *The Foghorn,* nos. 1, 3 (Jan. 23, Feb. 6, 1937), all Box 61; pamphlet, *Southern Resident Labor Colleges,* ca. Jan. 1937, Box 85, all HC Papers.

2. Summary of activities, Jan.–Oct. 1938, Box 1; staff meeting minutes, Dec. 26, 1937, Box 2; *Let Southern Labor Speak* (Monteagle: Highlander Folk School, 1938), Box 62; news release, Dec. 23, 1937, Box 66; Chattanooga *Times,* Dec. 23, 1937, Jan. 15, 1938, Microfilm 795, all HC Papers; announcement, *Highlander Folk School, Monteagle, Tennessee. Fifth Year, Fall and Winter Terms,* Sept. 1–Oct. 30, 1937, Jan. 10–Feb. 20, 1938, Box 11; *Highlander Folk School Review, Winter Term 1938,* Box 12, both HFS Coll.; Horton to Paul Christopher, Dec. 12, 1937, AFL-CIO Region VIII Records, 1930s–1970s, Box 44, Southern Labor Archives, Georgia State Univ., Atlanta (hereinafter cited as Christopher Papers); *Highlander Fling* 1 (Dec. 1937, Jan. 24, Feb. 7, 18, 1938); Joseph Yates Garrison, "Paul Revere Christopher: Southern Labor Leader, 1910–1974" (Ph.D. diss., Georgia State Univ., 1976), 189–90.

3. "Community Forums," Apr. 17, 1938, Box 13; Horton to Jimmie Cox, May 23, 1938, Box 41; Constitution and By-Laws, Labor's Political Conference of Grundy County, Apr. 24, 1938; Chattanooga *Times,* Apr. 25, 1938; Horton to E. L. Oliver, Labor's Non-Partisan League, May 18, 1938, all Box 52, all HC Papers; Horton, "Fog on the Mountain," 16–18.

4. Horton to John L. Lewis, Sept. 3, 1938, HC Papers, Box 53. See also summary of activities, Jan.–Oct. 1938, Box 1; Horton to Floyd Reeves, July 8, 1938, Box 23; Horton to Dolph Vaughn, Jan. 4, 1941, Box 33; Horton to J. C. Cox, May 20, 1938; "Labor's Political Conference—Grundy County, 1938–1939," unsigned MS, Oct. 8, 1939, both Box 52; "Instructions of WPA Locals in Grundy County," ca. July 1938; *WPA Worker* 1 (Aug. 2, 1938); Horton, "Saga in the Tennessee Mountains," ca. July 1944, all Box 53, all HC Papers; Horton, "Fog on the Mountain," 18, 20–21; Bee Rich, "Democracy's Drama in the Hills," *Social Work Today* 8 (Jan. 1941): 14; H. G. Thomas, "Highlander, 1932–41," 118–21.

5. Summary of activities, Jan.–Oct. 1938; Horton, "Report on Grundy County"; Horton to Nels Anderson, Aug. 30, Nov. 4, 1938; Horton, announcement of WPA weekend training institute, Oct. 1, 1938, all Box 53; Nashville *Labor Advocate,* Aug. 18, 1938; Chattanooga *Times,* Oct. 10, 1938, both Microfilm 795, all HC Papers; *Highlander Fling* 1 (June 1938).

6. Horton, "Fog on the Mountain," 22.

7. Chronology of events, WPA controversy, Feb. 15, 1939, HC Papers, Box 53. See also "Labor's Political Conference"; chronology of events, WPA controversy, ca. Feb. 13, 1939, HC Papers, Box 52; Horton, "Saga in the Tennessee Mountains"; Horton, "Fog on the Mountain," 22–24.

8. Nashville *Tennessean,* Jan. 17, 1939, HC Papers, Microfilm 795.

9. Dombrowski to Elia Kazan, Jan. 31, 1939, Box 17; chronology of events, ca. Feb. 13, 1939, Box 52; "Grievances of Road Commissioners to WPA," 1938; "List of Complaints by County Highway Department Against W.P.A.," Jan. 1, 1939; statement by HFS regarding WPA controversy, Jan. 19, 1939; D. F. Steinbaugh, WPA state director, to Harry S. Berry, Jan. 25, 1939; Dillard King to David Lasser, Workers Alliance of America, Jan. 30, 1939; proposal of Grundy County road commissioners

to WPA, ca. Feb. 1939; Dolph Vaughn to Francis Harrington, WPA, Feb. 5, 1939; chronology of events, Feb. 15, 1939, all Box 53; Grundy County *Herald,* Jan. 19, 1939; Chattanooga *Times,* Jan. 29, 1939; Chattanooga *Free Press,* Feb. 3, 1939, all Microfilm 795, all HC Papers; Horton, "Fog on the Mountain," 22–25.

10. Dombrowski to Hawes, Feb. 13, 1939, HC Papers, Box 14. See also Horton to Nels Anderson, Dec. 21, 1940, Box 33; William Buttrick to David Lasser, Feb. 18, 1939; Dillard King to Mary K. Gorman, editor, *Work,* Mar. 1, 1939, both Box 53; Chattanooga *Times,* Feb. 10, 11, 1939, Microfilm 795, all HC Papers; chronology of events, ca. Feb. 13, Feb. 15, 1939; Horton, "Saga in the Tennessee Mountains"; Horton, "Fog on the Mountain," 25–27.

11. Horton, "Fog on the Mountain," 27.

12. Rosanne Walker to Dombrowski, Feb. 17, 1939, Box 16; *We The People,* nos. 1, 2, 3 (Feb. 10, 12, 15, 1939); Dombrowski to contributors, Feb. 10, 1939; Horton to David Lasser, Feb. 12, 1939; Dombrowski to Ethel Clyde, Feb. 13, 1939; Buttrick to Lasser, Feb. 18, 1939; Dillard King to Mary K. Gorman, Mar. 1, 1939, all Box 53, all HC Papers; chronology of events, Feb. 15, 1939; Horton, "Fog on the Mountain," 27–29.

13. Walker to Dombrowski, Feb. 17, 1939, HC Papers, Box 16.

14. Walker to Dombrowski, Feb. 25, 1939; Horton to Dombrowski, Feb. 27, 1939, both Box 16; Walker to Tefferteller, Feb. 18, 1939, Box 27; news release to the Chattanooga *Times,* Feb. 24, 1939; Walker to Charles Stinnith, Feb. 25, 1939; Dillard King to Mary K. Gorman, Mar. 1, 1939; Grundy County citizens meeting, Mar. 12, 1939, all Box 53; Mary Lawrance Elkuss, interview with Aimee Horton, Nov. 7, 1963, Box 64, all HC Papers; Horton, "Fog on the Mountain," 29–35.

15. "Labor's Political Conference"; Horton, "Saga in the Tennessee Mountains"; Horton, "Fog on the Mountain," 35–40; *Highlander Fling* 2 (Sept. 1939); Horton, interview with author, Aug. 9, 1978.

16. *Highlander Fling* 2 (Jan. 1939).

17. Mary Lawrance, report on community program (Sept. 1938–Aug. 1939); achievements in 1939; report on activities, Jan. 1–July 1, 1941, all Box 1; staff meeting minutes, July 25, Aug. 3, 11, 1938, Box 2; "The Great Axel, Secretary," to Mrs. James Booboo [sample form letter?], Sept. 27, 1939, Box 51; pamphlet, *Give This Child the Chance for a Normal Life,* ca. 1940, Box 65, all HC Papers; *Highlander Fling* 2, 3, 5 (Jan., June 1939, May 1940, Feb., July 1941, Feb. 1943); Claudia Lewis, "The Summerfield Nursery School," *Bank Street Alumni News,* bulletin no. 1 (May 1, 1939). Lewis reported on her nursery school experiences in "Equipped with an Oak Tree," *Childhood Education* 16 (Jan. 1940): 208–10; "It Takes Courage and Dignity," *Progressive Education* 17 (Oct. 1940): 387–92; "Cocoa Beans at Five," *Progressive Education* 18 (Dec. 1941): 414–18; and *Children of the Cumberland* (New York: Columbia Univ. Press, 1946).

18. Achievements in 1939, Box 1; Martha Biehle to Dombrowski, Feb. 1, 1939; Dombrowski to Biehle, Feb. 7, 1939; Dombrowski to Roger Baldwin, Mar. 29, 1939, all Box 6; Dombrowski to Elia Kazan, Jan. 31, 1939, Box 17; Horton to A. Philip Randolph, Nov. 30, 1938, Box 22; data on residence terms, 1932–1945, Box 32; list of students, winter term 1939; Horton to secretaries of local unions, and to secretaries of Textile Workers Union of America locals, June 3, 1939; list of summer term students, July 3, 1939, all Box 62; Chattanooga *Times,* Oct. 31, 1938; *Industrial Leader,*

Feb. 24, 1939, both Microfilm 795, all HC Papers; announcements of residence terms, 1939–40, HFS Coll., Box 11; *Highlander Fling* 2 (Jan. 1939).

19. Achievements in 1939; Dombrowski to Israel Ben Scheiber, July 28, 1939, Box 51; schedule of classes, Jan. 1939; *Daily Worker,* Feb. 17, 1939; *Students Union Problems Note Book,* winter term 1939, all Box 62; William Buttrick, news release, Feb. 19, 1939, Box 66; *Industrial Leader,* Feb. 17, 24, Aug. 18, 1939; *Work,* Sept. 14, 1939, all Microfilm 795, all HC Papers; *We the Students,* winter term 1939, 8–11, 13, 16, 20–21; *Highlander Fling* 2 (Sept. 1939).

20. *Highlander Fling* 2 (Sept. 1939).

21. Dombrowski to Albert Barnett, July 11, 1939, Box 6; Horton to J. B. S. Hardman, July 8, 1939, Box 13; *H.F.S. Voice* 1 (Jan. 23, 1939), Box 62, all HC Papers.

22. Achievements in 1939. See also "Speakers at HFS (Summer 1939)," HC Papers, Box 62; *Students Union Problems Note Book*; *We the Students,* 6–7; *Highlander Fling* 2 (Jan., June, Sept. 1939).

23. Staff meeting minutes, Oct. 3, 1938, Box 2; Horton to Tefferteller, Nov. 29, 1938, Box 61; report, Carolina Conference on Workers' Education, Charlotte, N.C., Mar. 25–26, 1939, Box 77; Chattanooga *Times,* June 5, Aug. 28, Oct. 10, 1938; *Hosiery Worker,* Sept. 8, 1938, July 14, 1939, all Microfilm 795, all HC Papers; report of findings, Third Chattanooga Workers' Education Conference, May 18–19, 1940, HFS Coll., Box 6; *Highlander Fling* 2, 3 (Jan., June, Sept. 1939, Feb., July 1941); A. I. Horton, "Highlander, 1932–61," 159–61; A. A. Liveright, *Union Leadership Training: A Handbook of Tools and Techniques* (New York: Harper and Brothers, 1951), 205; Larry Rogin, interview with Bill Finger, Nov. 2, 1975, Southern Oral History Program, SHC; Horton, Frederickson interview.

24. Zilphia Horton quoted in *Highlander Folk School Review, Winter Term 1938,* 23, HFS Coll., Box 12. See also "Random Notes by Myles Horton on Singing and Music at Highlander," n.d., Box 13; Zilphia Horton, "How to Present a New Song," ca. 1930s, Box 66; labor songbooks, Box 84; *Industrial Leader,* June 16, 1939, Microfilm 795, all HC Papers; *Highlander Fling* 2 (Jan., Sept. 1939). For an analysis of Zilphia Horton's "musical surgery," see Glyn Thomas, "Hear the Music Ringing," *New South* 23 (Summer 1968): 38–39.

25. Zilphia Horton, "Dramatics," 1939, HC Papers, Box 58; Chouteau Dyer, drama workshop report, summer 1939, 3, 5–9; preface to *Five Plays About Labor* (Monteagle: Highlander Folk School, Aug. 1939); "An Experiment in Drama at the Highlander Folk School," fall term 1940, all HFS Coll., Box 9.

26. Lee Hays to Zilphia Horton, ca. 1937, HC Papers, Box 58; *Gumbo,* 1937; *Labor Spy,* 1938, both HFS Coll., Box 9; *Highlander Folk School Review, Winter Term 1938,* 17–18; *Highlander Fling* 1 (Spring 1937); Petty, "Dramatic Activities at Highlander," 103–9; Leo Huberman, *The Labor Spy Racket* (New York: Modern Age, 1937), 50–51.

27. *People of the Cumberland,* soundtrack transcript, HC Papers, Box 65.

28. Summary of activities, Jan.–Oct. 1938; *The Year 1941. Ninth Annual Report of the Highlander Folk School,* 4, both HC Papers, Box 1; Dyer, drama workshop report, 3, 7–8, 13; *Five Plays About Labor*; "An Experiment in Drama," 4–7; *Highlander Fling* 1 (June 1938); Petty, "Dramatic Activities at Highlander," 110–12, 125–28, 130–31. Contemporary reviews of *People of the Cumberland* include *Daily Worker,* July 8, 1938;

CIO News, May 28, 1938; *Fight,* June 1938; New York *Post,* ca. May 2, 1938, all Box 65; *Vassar Miscellany,* May 1938; Grundy County *Herald,* Aug. 25, 1938, both Microfilm 795, all HC Papers; *Nation* 146 (May 21, 1938): 595–96. Leslie Fishbein, *"People of the Cumberland* (1938): A Dialectic in Perplexity," *Labor History* 25 (Fall 1984): 565–76, is one of several recent evaluations of the film.

29. Ninth Annual Report, 1941, 5–6; report on activities, July–Sept. 1941, Box 1; Dwight Macdonald to Dombrowski, Aug. 4, 1939; Dombrowski to Macdonald, Aug. 10, 1939, both Box 19; announcements and reports of writers' workshops, 1939–43, Box 63; news releases, June 5, July 28, 1941, Box 66; Chattanooga *Times,* Aug. 21, 1939, Microfilm 795, all HC Papers; *Highlander Fling* 2, 3, 5 (June, Sept. 1939, May, Aug. 1940, July, Nov. 1941, Feb., June, Sept. 1943); Lillian Barnard Gilkes, "Experiment at Highlander," *Direction* 2 (Nov. 1939): 10–11.

30. Ninth Annual Report, 1941, 6; reports on activities, July–Sept. 1941, 1942, both Box 1; Horton to Charles E. Handy, July 26, 1938, Box 14; work camp announcements and publications, 1938, 1940; Robert E. Lane, Work Camps for America, to Horton, May 24, 1941; Horton to Lane, June 9, 1941; Dombrowski to Lane, July 2, 1941, all Box 77; Chattanooga *Times,* June 25, 1938, Microfilm 795, all HC Papers; "Study Program of the Work Camp," July 1941, HFS Coll., Box 15; *Highlander Fling* 2, 3 (May, Aug. 1940, July 1941), Lane, "Work Camps Come of Age," *Threshold* 1 (Oct. 1941): 27–28.

31. Annual Report, 1944, 3, Box 1; Margaret Bryan to Griselda Kuhlman, May 28, 1940, Box 55; announcement, 1942 Junior Union Camp, June 1–7, 1942; analysis of assembly activities, 2d Junior Union Camp, ca. July 5, 1942; special staff meeting on the Junior Union Camp, July 12, 1942; news releases, May 27, 1941, July 16, 1942, all Box 56; news releases, June 28, 29, 1942, May 22, 1943, Box 66; Summerfield *News* 4 (July 15, 1944): 2, Box 85; *Advance,* Aug. 1940; Chattanooga *Times,* June 23, 1941, both Microfilm 795, all HC Papers; *Highlander Fling* 2, 3, 4, 5 (May, Aug. 1940, Feb., July 1941, June 1942, Feb., June, Sept. 1943). See also John P. Beck, "Highlander Folk School's Junior Union Camps, 1940–1944," *Labor's Heritage* 5 (Spring 1993): 28–41.

32. Staff meeting minutes, July 12, Nov. 8, 1938, Box 2; Southern Conference for Human Welfare, plans and purposes, enclosed in Louise O. Charlton and Luther Patrick to Horton, Aug. 13, 1938, Box 70, all HC Papers. For accounts of SCHW's origins, see Krueger, *And Promises to Keep,* 3–39; Linda Reed, *Simple Decency & Common Sense: The Southern Conference Movement, 1938–1963* (Bloomington: Indiana Univ. Press, 1991), 1–22; Dunbar, *Against the Grain,* 187–91; Sosna, *In Search of the Silent South,* 88–97; Egerton, *Speak Now Against the Day,* 177–97; John A. Salmond, *Miss Lucy of the CIO: The Life and Times of Lucy Randolph Mason, 1882–1959* (Athens: Univ. of Georgia Press, 1988), 152–55; Harvard Sitkoff, *A New Deal for Blacks: The Emergence of Civil Rights as a National Issue,* vol. 1: *The Depression Decade* (New York: Oxford Univ. Press, 1978), 128–31, 261; Adams, *James A. Dombrowski,* 133–35; Tindall, *Emergence of the New South,* 636–37.

33. Horton to Dombrowski, Sept. 20, 1938, Box 15; Horton to Tefferteller, Nov. 29, 1938, Box 61; Horton, news release, July 26, 1940, Box 62; Chattanooga *News-Free Press,* Apr. 16, 1940, Microfilm 795, all HC Papers; Horton to Charles H. Martin, May 16, 1978, Horton Papers; *Highlander Fling* 2, 4 (Mar., May 1940, June 1942); Krueger, *And Promises to Keep,* 44–47, 60–67, 80–84, 88–89, 96–103, 139–91; Reed,

Simple Decency & Common Sense, 22–128; Adams, *James A. Dombrowski*, 135–221; Egerton, *Speak Now Against the Day*, 296–301, 439–46, 530; Sosna, *In Search of the Silent South*, 97–100, 142–49; Dunbar, *Against the Grain*, 191–95, 213–19; Tindall, *Emergence of the New South*, 638–41; R. F. Martin, "A Prophet's Pilgrimage," 527–29; Salmond, *Miss Lucy of the CIO*, 155–66.

34. Annual statement for 1939, Box 3; Dombrowski to Ethel Clyde, July 27, 1939, Box 9; minutes of Alumni Association meeting, Nov. 26, 1939; "Statistics on Students at Highlander, 1932–1939," both Box 32, all HC Papers; *Highlander Fling* 2 (Jan., June, Sept. 1939); *We the Students*, 33; statistics on residence and extension classes, 1932–1945, HFS Coll., Box 11.

35. Zilphia Horton to Horton, ca. Oct. 15, 1939, Box 15; Daniel Duke to Rosanne Walker, Oct. 10, 1939; William Buttrick to A. V. Goodpastor, Nashville *Tennessean*, Oct. 10, 1939; Buttrick to Dombrowski, Oct. 15, 1939; Zilphia Horton to Horton and Dombrowski, Oct. 15, 1939, all Box 33, all HC Papers.

36. Nashville *Tennessean*, Oct. 15, 16, 17–20, 1939, Microfilm 795; Buttrick to Maxton Champion, Oct. 30, 1939, Box 33, all HC Papers.

37. Nashville *Tennessean*, Oct. 22, 1939, HC Papers, Microfilm 795; Claudia Lewis, "Reminiscences of Highlander, 1938–1941," 4–5, HFS Coll., Box 16.

38. Buttrick to Dombrowski, Oct. 27, 1939, HC Papers, Box 16.

39. Nashville *Times*, Oct. 18, 1939; Nashville *Tennessean*, Oct. 22, 1939, both HC Papers, Microfilm 795. See also Daniel Duke to Buttrick, Oct. 25, 1939; Buttrick to Duke, Oct. 26, 1939, both Box 10; Dombrowski to Buttrick, Oct. 19, 23, 1939; Buttrick to Dombrowski, Oct. 20, 23, 28, 30, Nov. 1, 1939, all Box 16; Buttrick, "Statement on the Article about Highlander Folk School," Oct. 16, 1939; Lawson, "Telephone call at 6:05 p.m., October 17, 1939," both Box 33; Chattanooga *Free Press*, Oct. 17, 30, ca. Nov. 1939, Microfilm 795, all HC Papers.

40. Nashville *Tennessean*, Oct. 22, 1939, Microfilm 795, and Oct. 24, 1939, Box 33, both HC Papers. See also Buttrick to Dombrowski, Oct. 23, 25, 1939, both Box 16; Dombrowski to George N. Mayhew, Nov. 16, 1939, Box 20; letters to the editor of the Nashville *Tennessean* in defense of HFS, Oct. 16–Nov. 15, 1939; affidavits signed by Claudia Lewis, Dillard King, and Roy B. Thomas, Oct. 21, 1939; Buttrick to friends of Highlander, Oct. 24, 1939; Buttrick to Stanton Smith, Oct. 25, 1939; Buttrick to Champion, Oct. 30, 1939; Horton, "The Nashville *Tennessean*'s Red-Scare," Oct. 1939, all Box 33; Nashville *Tennessean*, Oct. 20, 22, 29, 31, Nov. 5, 1939, Microfilm 795, all HC Papers. For Commonwealth College's response, see Morris Engel to Buttrick, Oct. 17, 24, 1939; Buttrick to Engel, Oct. 23, 27, 1939, all HC Papers, Box 39.

41. Nashville *Tennessean*, Nov. 19, 1939, HC Papers, Microfilm 795.

42. "The Philosophy and Program of the Highlander Folk School: A Summary of a Discussion by James Dombrowski, Chairman, Highlander Folk School, at the Hillsboro Presbyterian Church, November 19th, and in the Chapel, Doctor's Building, Nashville, Tennessee, November 20th, 1939," HC Papers, Box 82. See also Albert E. Barnett, form letter announcing meeting at the Methodist Board of Missions chapel, Nov. 15, 1939, Box 6; Dombrowski to Mrs. Walter Gellhorn, Nov. 22, 1939, Box 13; Dombrowski to Evelyn Preston, Nov. 28, 1939, Box 22; Dombrowski to Stanton Smith, Nov. 22, 1939, Box 26, all HC Papers.

43. "Plans for 1940: Special Needs," ca. 1939, Box 1; Dombrowski to Jacob S. Potofsky, Dec. 6, 1939; Dombrowski to J. S. Bixler, Dec. 6, 1939, both Box 5; Dombrowski to Barnett, Nov. 16, 1939, Box 6; Dombrowski to Hawes, Dec. 1, 12, 1939, Box 14; Dombrowski to Niebuhr, Nov. 22, 1939; Dombrowski to Evelyn Preston, Nov. 28, 1939, both Box 22; Dombrowski to Anna Bogue, Oct. 15, 1939, Box 51, all HC Papers; Horton, "The *Tennessean*'s Red-Scare."

44. Horton to Beatrice Griffiths, June 7, 1940, HC Papers, Box 13. See also notes concerning Dies Committee investigation, ca. Oct. 16, 1939, Box 6; Horton to Griffiths, Mar. 13, 1940, Box 13; Horton to Lilian Johnson, July 24, 1940, Box 16; Horton to Estes Kefauver, Apr. 24, 1940; Kefauver to Horton, Apr. 30, 1940, both Box 17; George N. Mayhew to Dombrowski, Dec. 4, 20, 1939, Box 20; Nashville *Tennessean,* Oct. 16, Nov. 22, 1939; Chattanooga *News-Free Press,* Apr. 16, 1940, all Microfilm 795, all HC Papers; Adams, *James A. Dombrowski,* 115–16. According to a 1940 FBI memorandum, the bureau's files "failed to reveal" that an investigation had been made. In light of subsequent investigations, the agent's visit to HFS may not have been official—or he may not have been an agent at all. S. J. Tracy, "Memorandum for the Director" [J. Edgar Hoover], Dec. 6, 1940, *FBI File on the Highlander Folk School* (Wilmington, Del.: Scholarly Resources, 1990), microfilm, reel 1 (of 1).

45. Leaflet, "Vote for Estes Kefauver for Congress, Third Congressional District. Is 100 Per Cent American," ca. Aug. 1, 1940, HC Papers, Box 52.

46. Leon Wilson, "Summary of Conversation with Mr. Alton [*sic*] Henderson, Tracy City First National Bank," Aug. 15, 1940, HC Papers, Box 33; Chattanooga *News-Free Press,* Aug. 11, 1940, in "Opposition as Gathered from Clippings, 1932–1941."

47. Nashville *Banner,* Sept. 24, 1940, HC Papers, Microfilm 795. See also Dombrowski to Horton, Aug. 3, 1940, Box 16; "Reconstruction from memory of telegram fastened on wall of voting place, Monteagle, Tennessee, August 1, 1940"; Horton to Estes Kefauver, Aug. 23, 1940, both Box 17; Dombrowski, "Answer to 1940 Attack (Grundy County Crusaders)," 1940; "The Attack of the Grundy County Crusaders on the Highlander Folk School," Dec. 18, 1940, 3–4, both Box 33; flier, "Look at the Record of this Man: Estes Kefauver," July 1940; Chattanooga *News-Free Press,* Aug. 4, 1940; Kefauver to Horton, Aug. 30, 1940; Horton, "Letter to Estes Kefauver," ca. Nov. 1940, all Box 52, all HC Papers; Horton, "Fog on the Mountain," 41; Adams, *James A. Dombrowski,* 122–23.

48. Joseph P. Kamp, *The Fifth Column in the South* (New York: Constitutional Educational League, 1940; reprint, Knoxville: Conservative Citizens Committee, 1967), 20, and see 18–25, Highlander Papers, Ser. 2, Box 1. Eleanor Roosevelt's support of Highlander, as interpreted by Kamp, was also featured in the Nov. 1940 issue of *The Fiery Cross,* the official organ of the Ku Klux Klan.

49. Barnett to A. D. Clement, Law Enforcement Commission of Tennessee, Jan. 6, 1941; Barnett to Gerald Foley, Jan. 16, 1941, both Box 6; Constitutional Educational League, advertisement for Kamp, *Fifth Column in the South* and *The Fifth Column in Washington,* Nov. 1940; Leon Wilson, "Crusaders of the Cumberland," ca. Nov. 30, 1940, both Box 33, all HC Papers; "Attack of the Grundy County Crusaders," 3; Horton, "Letter to Estes Kefauver"; *Highlander Fling* 2 (Nov. 1940).

50. C. H. Kilby quoted in Nashville *Tennessean,* Nov. 9, 1940, and Nashville *Banner,* Nov. 9, 1940, both HC Papers, Microfilm 795.

51. Dombrowski, open letter to C. H. Kilby, Nov. 10, 1940, Box 33; Nashville *Tennessean,* Nov. 11, 1940; Chattanooga *News-Free Press,* Nov. 12, 1940, both Microfilm 795, all HC Papers.

52. Barnett to A. D. Clement, Jan. 6, 1941, Box 6; Dombrowski to Lilian Johnson, Nov. 10, 1940, Box 16; Malcolm Ross to Gov. Prentice Cooper, Nov. 28, 1940, Box 24; A. L. Henderson to Dombrowski, Nov. 7, 1940; Dombrowski to Henderson, Nov. 8, 1940; Buttrick and Wilson, notes on interview with C. H. Kilby, Nov. 9, 1940; Kilby to Dombrowski, Nov. 9, 11, 1940; HFS to Jimmie Zirkle and Henry Carruthers, JOUAM, Nov. 10, 1940; Barnett to Clarence E. Floyd, JOUAM, Nov. 12, 1940; Paul Christopher to Kilby, Nov. 12, 1940; Christopher to Zirkle, Nov. 12, 1940; Christopher to Horton, Nov. 12, 1940, all Box 33; Horton, news release, Nov. 15, 1940, Box 66; Chattanooga *News-Free Press,* Nov. 12, 1940, Microfilm 795, all HC Papers; Wilson, "Crusaders of the Cumberland"; "Attack of the Grundy County Crusaders," 4–10; Adams, *James A. Dombrowski,* 123–24; Federal Bureau of Investigation, Knoxville Office, report on Highlander Folk School—Internal Security, Apr. 10, 1941, *FBI File on HFS.*

53. Bee Rich, "Free Transcription Proceedings, Mass Meeting, Tracy City High School Auditorium, November 12, 1940," HC Papers, Box 33. See also news release, ca. Nov. 12, 1940; Dombrowski, fundraising letter, Nov. 21, 1940; petitions circulated and signed by Summerfield area residents, Nov. 1940, all HC Papers, Box 33; "Attack of the Grundy County Crusaders," 9–12; Wilson, "Crusaders of the Cumberland." Besides Kilby and Henderson, the Crusaders' committee included seven men who were well known in Grundy County for their ties to the Tennessee Consolidated Coal Company and their antipathy toward Highlander. Further investigation, HFS staff members argued, would probably reveal an even greater connection between the Crusaders and the coal company.

54. "Summary of Meeting between the Staff of the Highlander Folk School and the Committee from the Grundy County Crusaders, St. Luke's Chapel, Sewanee, Nov. 12, 1940," Box 33; Chattanooga *Times,* Nov. 14, 1940, Microfilm 795, both HC Papers.

55. Chattanooga *News-Free Press,* Nov. 13, 1940, HC Papers, Microfilm 795. See also Summary of Meeting between HFS and the Committee; Wilson, "Crusaders of the Cumberland"; "Attack of the Grundy County Crusaders," 12–13; Nashville *Tennessean,* Nov. 13, 1940; Nashville *Banner,* Nov. 13, 1940; unidentified Sewanee student publication, Nov. 14, 1940, all HC Papers, Microfilm 795; Adams, *James A. Dombrowski,* 124–25.

56. Chattanooga *News-Free Press,* Nov. 13, 1940; Chattanooga *Times,* Nov. 18, 1940, both HC Papers, Microfilm 795.

57. Copy of CIO resolution, Nov. 22, 1940, HC Papers, Box 33.

58. Leaflet, "The Best National Defense Is a Healthy Intelligent People," ca. 1940, HC Papers, Box 62. See also Barnett, open letter, "When News Is Not News," Nov. 19, 1940, Box 6; Barnett, invitation to Highlander meeting in Nashville, Nov. 14, 1940; Barnett to Silliman Evans, Nov. 14, 1940; news releases, 1940; leaflets,

"Come and See for Yourself!" and "Who Are the Real Americans?" ca. 1940, all Box 33; news releases, Nov. 22, 29, 1940, Box 66; Chattanooga *News-Free Press,* Oct. 28, Nov. 14, 24, 1940; Chattanooga *Times,* Nov. 14, 23, 1940; Nashville *Tennessean,* Nov. 4, 23, 24, 1940; Grundy County *Herald,* Nov. 21, 1940; Sewanee student publication, Nov. 21, 1940, all Microfilm 795, all HC Papers; Wilson, "Crusaders of the Cumberland"; *Highlander Fling* 3 (Feb. 1941).

59. Buttrick to Tefferteller, Nov. 28, 1940, HC Papers, Box 27.

60. Buttrick to Dombrowski, Dec. 3, 1940, Box 16; staff notes on second Grundy County Crusaders meeting, Dec. 3, 1940, Box 33; Claudia Lewis to Barbara Payne, Dec. 8, 1940, Box 65; Chattanooga *News-Free Press,* Nov. 19, 29, Dec. 2, 3, 4, 1940, Microfilm 795, all HC Papers; "Attack of the Grundy County Crusaders," 14–16; Knoxville FBI Office, report on Highlander Folk School—Internal Security, Sept. 12, 1941, *FBI File on HFS.*

61. H. G. Thomas, "Highlander, 1932–41," 142–43.

62. A theater benefit held in New York City in January 1941 also enhanced Highlander's image. "Come and See For Yourself!"; Washington Committee for the Highlander Folk School, announcement of benefit, ca. Dec. 6, 1940, HC Papers, Box 45; *Highlander Fling* 3 (Feb. 1941); *New York Times,* Dec. 7, 1940; "A Good School Under Fire," *New Republic* 103 (Dec. 9, 1940): 776; G. Thomas, "Hear the Music Ringing," 40.

63. Nashville *Banner,* Jan. 23, 1941, quoted in Highlander publicity release, "Hitler Would Like This," Jan. 28, 1941, HC Papers, Box 33.

64. Copy of "Resolution on Highlander Folk School Passed by Grundy County Court," Feb. 3, 1941, HC Papers, Box 33.

65. Dombrowski to Barnett, Feb. 17, 1941, Box 6; Dombrowski to Franz Daniel, Feb. 13, 1941, Box 10; Horton to Malcolm Ross, Jan. 13, 1941; [Dombrowski?] to Ross, Feb. 19, 1941, both Box 15; Louise Dichman to Jane Lawson, Jan. 25, 1941, Box 18; Horton to Bee Rich, Apr. 21, 1941, Box 24; Dombrowski to Edgar S. Brightman, Dec. 18, 1940, Box 33, all HC Papers; Lucy R. Mason to Eleanor Roosevelt, Jan. 29, 1941; Mason to Allan S. Haywood, Feb. 24, 1941, both Lucy Randolph Mason Papers, Manuscript Dept., Perkins Library, Duke Univ.

66. Eleanor Roosevelt to Dombrowski, Feb. 1, 1941, HC Papers, Box 24.

67. Executive council meeting minutes, Mar. 23, 1941, Box 1; Horton to Barnett, Jan. 13, 1941; Dombrowski to Barnett, Feb. 13, Mar. 29, 1941, all Box 6; Horton to Kefauver, Feb. 27, 1941; Horton to N. R. Patterson, June 19, 1941, both Box 17; Dombrowski to Eleanor Roosevelt, Jan. 24, Feb. 6, 14, 1941, Box 24; copy of resolution passed by UMWA Local 7708, Tracy City, Tenn., Dec. 21, 1940; "Resolution Unanimously Passed, February 23, [1941], by the Tennessee Conference for Democracy Called by Representatives of the Rail Road Brotherhoods, A.F. of L. and C.I.O."; Dombrowski to Alvin Henderson, Apr. 3, 1941; news release, "Highlander Endorsed by Tennessee State Industrial Union Council," June 1, 1941, all Box 33; Jane Lawson, HFS daily record—begun Jan. 1, 1941, Box 41; Horton, news release, Mar. 24, 1941, Box 66, all HC Papers; *Highlander Fling* 3 (Feb. 1941).

68. Quotation from Knoxville FBI Office, report on Highlander Folk School—Internal Security, Sept. 12, 1941, *FBI File on HFS.* See also Dombrowski to Eleanor Roosevelt, Feb. 6, 1941; Lucy R. Mason to Roosevelt, Jan. 13, 1942, both Box 24;

Wilson, untitled memorandum on FBI investigation, Oct. 11, 1941, Box 33, all HC Papers; Myles Horton to Zilphia Horton, Feb. 1942, Box 3; *Unionist* (ACWA Local 362 newspaper), May 5, 1940, Box 9, both MHP; "Opposition as Gathered from Clippings, 1932–1941"; Knoxville FBI Office, reports on Highlander Folk School—Internal Security, Apr. 10, Dec. 30, 1941, Apr. 1, 1942; Knoxville FBI Special Agent file: Highlander Folk School, June 1, 1941; W. A. Murphy, Special Agent in Charge, Knoxville FBI Office, to Director [J. Edgar Hoover], Oct. 12, 1941; memorandum, Hoover to SAC, Knoxville, Oct. 23, 1942, *FBI File on HFS.*

69. Frank McCallister to Paul Christopher, Dec. 24, 1941, Christopher Papers, Box 52A.

70. Daniel quoted in Dombrowski to Virginia Durr, July 3, 1941, HC Papers, Box 11. See also Dombrowski to Franz Daniel, June 9, 1941, Box 10; Durr to Dombrowski, ca. July 3, 1941, Box 11, both HC Papers.

71. Zilia Hawes Daniel to Dombrowski, Nov. 4, 1941, HC Papers, Box 14.

72. Executive council meeting minutes, Jan. 11, 1942, Box 1; Franz Daniel to Rose Bush, ACWA, Aug. 4, 1941, Box 10; Dombrowski to Virginia Durr, July 3, 1941, Box 11; Lucy R. Mason to Eleanor Roosevelt, Jan. 13, 1942; Dombrowski to Malcolm Ross, Jan. 14, 1942, both Box 24, all HC Papers; HFS executive council to Jacob S. Potofsky, Feb. 11, 1942; Potofsky to executive council, Apr. 27, 1942; Christopher to Horton, May 12, 1942; HFS executive council meeting minutes, Aug. 29, 1942, all CIO Organizing Commitee, Knoxville, Knox Co., Tenn., Papers, Box 146, Manuscript Dept., Perkins Library, Duke Univ.; Egerton, *Speak Now Against the Day,* 162.

73. Ninth Annual Report, 1941, 2–4; Horton to Louise Dichman, June 5, 1941, Box 10; Dombrowski to [Franz Daniel?] Sept. 30, 1940, Box 16; Horton, news releases, ca. Sept. 1940, Aug. 27, 1941; *Highlander Folk School Students Speak,* Sept. 1940; leaflet, "Highlander Folk School, Monteagle, Tennessee: A Southern Workers School. Two Weeks Term, May 12–24," [1941]; data on spring session, May 12–24, 1941; Zilphia Horton to Mary Lawrance, Aug. 1, 1941; leaflet, "Special 2 Weeks Term, September 14–27," [1941]; report: summer term—1941, all Box 62; *Grundy Grouch* 1 (Sept. 13, 1941), Box 84, all HC Papers; *Highlander Fling* 2, 3, 4 (Mar., May, Nov. 1940, July 1941, Mar. 1942).

74. Ninth Annual Report, 1941, 2–5; Horton, news release, Sept. 1, 1940; highlights of the year 1940; list of speakers during the spring term, Apr. 1941; report: summer term—1941, all Box 62; Horton, news releases, May 26, Sept. 26, 1941; Bettye Goldstein, news release, Sept. 14, 1941; news release to the Chattanooga *Times* and other newspapers, Sept. 22, 1941, all Box 66; *Grundy Grouch* 1 (Sept. 13, 1941), Box 84; Chattanooga *Times,* Sept. 11, 1940; Chattanooga *News-Free Press,* Oct. 28, 1940, both Microfilm 795, all HC Papers; *Highlander Fling* 2, 3 (May, Nov. 1940, Feb., July, Nov. 1941).

75. Horton to Arthur Raper, May 21, 1940, HC Papers, Box 39.

76. Ninth Annual Report, 1941, 25–26; list of renewals and new contributions by state, 1941, HC Papers, Box 3.

77. Alumni advertisement, ca. fall term 1941, CIO Org. Comm. Papers, Box 147. See also Horton to Walter Wanger, Jan. 15, 1940, Box 28; Dombrowski, "Answer to 1940 Attack," Box 33, both HC Papers; *Highlander Fling* 2, 3 (Mar. 1940, Apr. 1941).

4. Extension Work, 1937–1947

1. Dombrowski, "Outstanding Achievements in 1937" (William C. Whitney Foundation Report), HC Papers, Box 51.

2. Horton, interview with William R. Finger, Dec. 6, 1974, Southern Oral History Program, SHC. See also Dombrowski, confidential memorandum for the staff, May 8, 1937, HC Papers, Box 2; Edward Levinson, *Labor on the March* (New York: Harper and Brothers, 1938), 240.

3. Irving Bernstein, *Turbulent Years: A History of the American Worker, 1933–1941* (Boston: Houghton Mifflin, 1971), 616–18; Walter Galenson, *The CIO Challenge to the AFL: A History of the American Labor Movement, 1935–1941* (Cambridge: Harvard Univ. Press, 1960), 594; Paul David Richards, "The History of the Textile Workers Union of America, CIO, in the South, 1937 to 1945" (Ph.D. diss., Univ. of Wisconsin, 1978), 2–7, 20, 25, 39; John Wesley Kennedy, "A History of the Textile Workers Union of America, C.I.O." (Ph.D. diss., Univ. of North Carolina, 1950), 52–55, 118; Egerton, *Speak Now Against the Day*, 162–66. See also James A. Hodges, *New Deal Labor Policy and the Southern Cotton Textile Industry, 1933–1941* (Knoxville: Univ. of Tennessee Press, 1986); Robert H. Zieger, "Textile Workers and Historians," in *Organized Labor in the Twentieth-Century South*, ed. Zieger (Knoxville: Univ. of Tennessee Press, 1991), 35–59.

4. F. Ray Marshall, *Labor in the South* (Cambridge: Harvard Univ. Press, 1967), 169–71; Bernstein, *Turbulent Years*, 617–20; Galenson, *CIO Challenge to the AFL*, 329–30, 332–33; Kennedy, "History of the TWUA," 64, 72; Richards, "TWUA, 1937–45," 37–41, 47–48, 91–92; Sitkoff, *New Deal for Blacks*, 179–81; Levinson, *Labor on the March*, 239–41; Salmond, *Miss Lucy of the CIO*, 74–86; Adams, *James A. Dombrowski*, 117–19; Frank T. de Vyver, "The Present Status of Labor Unions in the South," *Southern Economic Journal* 5 (Apr. 1939): 485–98; Herman Wolf, "Cotton and the Unions," *Survey Graphic* 27 (Mar. 1938): 147–48; Margaret Lee Neustadt, "Miss Lucy of the CIO: Lucy Randolph Mason, 1882–1959" (M.A. thesis, Univ. of North Carolina at Chapel Hill, 1969), 20–23; Michael Goldfield, "Race and the CIO: The Possibilities for Racial Egalitarianism During the 1930s and 1940s," *International Labor and Working Class History*, no. 44 (Fall 1993): 5–7.

5. "The CIO Campaign in the South," 1937, HC Papers, Box 1. See also Dombrowski, "Outstanding Achievements in 1937"; Dombrowski, confidential memorandum for the staff, May 8, 1937, Box 2; Horton to Sidney Hillman, May 12, 1937, Box 14; "Field Report of Myles Horton to HFS," Sept. 1937, Box 73, all HC Papers; Hawes, report for the year 1937, Box 9; Horton, "Recommendations," ca. Apr. 1937, Box 14, both HFS Coll.; Horton, Finger interview; Horton, Frederickson interview; Rogin, Finger interview; Levinson, *Labor on the March*, 241.

6. Horton, Finger interview.

7. Dombrowski to Anna Bogue, May 8, 1937, Box 51; Horton, untitled report on Lumberton (possibly transcription of wire recording, ca. 1950), 53–57, Box 63; clippings from Charlotte *News*, May 9, 1937, and other unidentified newspapers, May 9, 17, 1937, Box 64, all HC Papers; "Field Report of Horton"; Richards, "TWUA, 1937–45," 59; Lucy Randolph Mason, *To Win These Rights: A Personal Story of the CIO in the South* (New York: Harper and Brothers, 1952), 40–42; Horton, Finger interview.

8. Worker quoted in Mason, *To Win These Rights,* 49–50.

9. Horton, "Comments on the Lumberton Case," ca. Sept. 1937, HC Papers, Box 63.

10. Horton to Robert Wohlforth, La Follette Civil Liberties Committee, May 20, 1937, Box 63, HC Papers; Horton, untitled report on Lumberton, 1–3; "Field Report of Horton"; John Patton [Pate?], "The Struggle at Lumberton," *We The Students,* Winter Term 1939, 64–65, HFS Coll., Box 13; Mason, *To Win These Rights,* 42–43, 50; Horton, Finger interview.

11. Horton, untitled report on Lumberton, 2–3; *Robesonian,* May 26, 1937, HC Papers, Box 64; "Field Report of Horton"; Mason, *To Win These Rights,* 43; Marlowe, "Participation of the Poor," 35–36; Horton, Finger interview.

12. Horton, untitled report on Lumberton, 3–6; Horton, "Comments on the Lumberton Case"; Horton, "Lumberton Case," ca. Jan. 1938, Box 63; *Robesonian,* June 9, 1937; Charlotte *Observer,* June 11, 1937; Fayetteville *Observer,* June 11, 1937, all Box 64, all HC Papers; "Field Report of Horton"; Mason, *To Win These Rights,* 43–45.

13. *Industrial Leader,* Sept. 2, 1937, HC Papers, Box 64.

14. Horton, "Comments on the Lumberton Case."

15. Horton, untitled report on Lumberton, 6–11; Horton, "Comments on the Lumberton Case"; Horton, "Comments on the Lumberton Case: Personal Experiences," ca. Sept. 1937, Box 63; Charlotte *Observer,* June 11, 1937; Raleigh *News and Observer,* June 12, 1937, both Box 64, all HC Papers; Marlowe, "Participation of the Poor," 37–40; Mason, *To Win These Rights,* 44–46; Horton, Finger interview; "Adventures of a Radical Hillbilly," 11–14.

16. Horton, "Comments on the Lumberton Case"; Horton, "Lumberton Case"; telegram, Horton to Robert Wohlforth, June 23, 1937; answer of Lt. A. T. Moore, July 1, 1937, answer of Mansfield Mills, July 2, 1937, and affidavit signed by 196 union members, July 3, 1937; Horton, statement on court appeal, Aug. 19, 1937; numerous newspaper clippings, June, July, Sept. 1937, all Box 64, all HC Papers; "Field Report of Horton"; Mason, *To Win These Rights,* 46–47.

17. Horton, "Comments on the Lumberton Case." See also Horton, "Lumberton Case"; *Industrial Leader,* Sept. 22, 1937, HC Papers, Box 64; Mason, *To Win These Rights,* 47; Horton, Finger interview.

18. "Workers Education Rally, La Follette, Tennessee, May 29–July 5, 1937," in *Field Classes for Labor Unions: An Experiment in Workers' Education* (Monteagle, Tenn.: Highlander Folk School, 1937), 6, HFS Coll., Box 9. See also "The CIO Campaign in the South"; Dombrowski, "Outstanding Achievements in 1937"; Dombrowski to Berthe Daniel, Apr. 25, 1937, Box 10; Charles Handy to Dombrowski, Feb. 1, 1937, Box 14; "Subjects for La Follette Labor Forum (for ACWU)"; "Tentative Plans for Six Weeks of Labor Forums Beginning About Middle of May, 1937," ca. Apr. 1, 1937; Zilphia Horton to Dombrowski, Apr. 28, 1937; tentative outline, "Workers Education Rally, La Follette, Tenn., and Vicinity," n.d., all Box 58; Chattanooga *Times,* June 8, 1937, Microfilm 795, all HC Papers; Zilphia Horton to Myles Horton, May 12, 1937, ZHP, Box 15; *Advance,* Mar. 1937; Marshall, *Labor in the South,* 177.

19. "Workers Education Rally, La Follette," 2–3, 6; news release, May 21, 1937; Dombrowski to Franz Daniel, May 22, 1937; report on first three weeks of rally, May 29–June 15, 1937; "Lecture #2: How the Union Works," Workers Education Rally,

May 29–July 5, 1937; *Shirt-Tale,* no. 1 (June 14, 1937), all Box 58; "Lesson One: Why Workers Need the Union (A Primer of Trade Unionism)," Workers Education Rally, May 29–July 5, 1937, Box 59; Chattanooga *Times,* June 8, 1937; *Advance,* Aug. 1937, both Microfilm 795, all HC Papers.

20. "Workers Education Rally, La Follette," 3–5. See also *Shirt-Tale,* nos. 2, 3 (June 21, 28, 1937), HC Papers, Box 58; A. I. Horton, "Highlander, 1932–61," 134–36; H. G. Thomas, "Highlander, 1932–41," 93–95.

21. "Workers Education Rally, La Follette," 5–6; *Shirt-Tale,* no. 3 (June 28, 1937), HC Papers, Box 58; A. I. Horton, "Highlander, 1932–61," 136–37.

22. Richards, "TWUA, 1937–45," 63–70, 83–84, 95–96, 145, quotation 81–82; Marshall, *Labor in the South,* 171–73; Galenson, *CIO Challenge to the AFL,* 336, 338–41, 347–48; Bernstein, *Turbulent Years,* 621–23; Kennedy, "History of the TWUA," 83–84, 92–93; Garrison, "Paul Revere Christopher," 77–78, 104–9; Mason, *To Win These Rights,* 42.

23. Horton, "The Highlander Folk School Extension Program," Aug. 10, 1942, HC Papers, Box 58. See also Horton, untitled report on Lumberton, 65–66; "Field Report of Horton"; Horton to Dombrowski, Sept. 21, 1937; *Industrial Leader,* Sept. 2, 1937, both Box 64; *Industrial Leader,* May 12, 1938, Microfilm 795, all HC Papers; Horton, weekly reports—TWOC-CIO, Sept. 4, 11, 25, 1937, Horton Papers, Box 4; *Highlander Fling* 2 (Jan. 1939); Horton, Finger interview; A. I. Horton, "Highlander, 1932–61," 137.

24. Mary Lawrance, *Education Unlimited: A Handbook on Union Education in the South* (Monteagle, Tenn.: Highlander Folk School, 1945), 6–9, 11, HFS Coll., Box 12. See also summaries of fieldwork programs, 1933–1942, Box 58; Aimee Horton, notes on interview with Mary Lawrance Elkuss, Nov. 7, 1963, Box 64; Atlanta *Constitution,* ca. Nov. 1942; *Tennessee CIO News,* Mar. 19, 1945, both Microfilm 795, all HC Papers; A. I. Horton, "Highlander, 1932–61," 164–65. On the impact of the YWCA in awakening and fostering union activism in women like Lawrance, see Mary Frederickson, "'I know which side I'm on': Southern Women in the Labor Movement in the Twentieth Century," in *Women, Work and Protest: A Century of U.S. Women's Labor History,* ed. Ruth Milkman (London: Routledge and Kegan Paul, 1985), 156–80; Salmond, *Miss Lucy of the CIO,* 16 and elsewhere.

25. Bill Elkuss to Lawrance, May 27, 1940; Lawrance to Louise Dichman and Rosanne Walker, June 8, 1940; Lawrance, "Educational Programs with Aluminum Workers, Local 9, Maryville, Tenn. (Summer 1940)," Dec. 1, 1940, all Box 58; highlights of the year 1940, Box 62, all HC Papers.

26. Summaries of fieldwork programs, 1933–42; "Outstanding Achievements in 1940," Box 1; Lawrance to Louise Dichman and Rosanne Walker, June 8, 1940; *AWA News,* nos. 1, 2 (June 15, 22, 1940); Lawrance to Horton, June 16, July 10, 1940; Lawrance to Dichman, ca. June 1940; Lawrance, "Educational Programs with Aluminum Workers," all Box 58, all HC Papers; Lawrance, *Education Unlimited,* 11, 33, 34–35, 37; *Highlander Fling* 2 (Aug. 1940).

27. Horton to Lawrance, July 2, Aug. 16, 1940; Lawrance to Horton, July 28, 1940; Lawrance, "Educational Programs with Aluminum Workers," all HC Papers, Box 58.

28. *CIO News,* Nov. 17, 1941, 14–15. See also Marshall, *Labor in the South,* 225–27.

29. Lawrance, *Education Unlimited,* 17.

30. HFS executive council meeting minutes, Aug. 29, 1942, CIO Org. Comm. Papers, Box 146. See also Horton, "The HFS Extension Program"; Lawrance, *Education Unlimited,* 17–19; Lawrance, "Labor Education in the South," *Ammunition* (Apr. 1945): 14; Joel Seidman, *American Labor from Defense to Reconversion* (Chicago: Univ. of Chicago Press, 1953), 3–4, 42, 89–90, 280–82.

31. Lawrance, *Education Unlimited,* 10–11; Ninth Annual Report, 1941, 16; Horton to Fred C. Pieper, Jan. 14, 1941; Pieper to Horton, Jan. 27, Mar. 19, 1941; New Orleans Extension Program, report on first month Apr. 10–May 10, 1941; Lawrance to Horton and staff, ca. Apr. 26, 1941; Horton, news releases, ca. June 2, 1941, all Box 58, all HC Papers; Lawrance, *Understanding Unionism: An Educational Program in New Orleans* (Monteagle, Tenn.: Highlander Folk School, 1942), 1–2, HFS Coll., Box 9.

32. Ninth Annual Report, 1941, 16–17; New Orleans Extension Program, report on first month; Lawrance, *Understanding Unionism,* 2–5; Lawrance, *Education Unlimited,* 11–12, 38–39; *Highlander Fling* 3 (July 1941).

33. Pieper to Mason, Sept. 5, 1941, Mason Papers. See also Ninth Annual Report, 1941, 16–17; Lawrance to staff, June 2, 1941; Lawrance to Horton, July 8, 1941; Lawrance, "Report on 2nd Session of Educational Program, CIO Industrial Union Council, New Orleans, La.," Aug. 15, 1941, all Box 58; *How To Build Your Union: An Officers, Committeemen, and Stewards' Handbook* (New Orleans: CIO Industrial Union Council, 1942), Box 59, all HC Papers; Lawrance, extension report, 2d session Union Training School, New Orleans Industrial Union Council, July through Sept. 1941, HFS Coll., Box 9; Lawrance, *Understanding Unionism,* 5–6, 10, 17; Lawrance, *Education Unlimited,* 11–13, 15–16, 27, 34; *Highlander Fling* 3 (July, Nov. 1941).

34. Report to the executive council, Oct. 19, 1942, HC Papers, Box 58. See also summaries of fieldwork programs, 1933–42; "John Citizen Listens and Learns," radio script prepared by HFS and broadcast Oct. 2, 1942, Box 57; Lawrance, "Message to Stewards, Officers and Committeemen," Nov. 7, 1941; Lawrance, "4th Session—New Orleans Extension Program," ca. Mar. 1942, both Box 58, all HC Papers; Lawrance to Robert Cruden, Sept. 8, 1942; Pieper to local union officers, Sept. 30, 1942; Lawrance, report on New Orleans "Labor and War" Conference for CIO Unions, Oct. 2, 3, 4, 1942, all CIO Org. Comm. Papers, Box 146; *Highlander Fling* 5 (Feb. 1943); Lawrance, *Education Unlimited,* 14–15.

35. Report on activities, July–Sept. 1941, Box 1; Lawrance, "Extension Program," ca. 1942; report on Oil Workers Institute, Goose Creek, Texas, Oct. 10–11, 1942; Lawrance, "Evaluation of New Orleans Extension Program," ca. Apr. 1942; Lawrance, "The New Orleans Extension Program," ca. Apr. 1942; report to executive council, Oct. 19, 1942, all Box 58, all HC Papers; Lawrance, *Understanding Unionism,* 18; *Highlander Fling* 5 (Feb. 1943).

36. Lawrance, "Atlanta Educational Program, Nov. 1, 1942–May 1, 1943," HFS Coll., Box 9; report to executive council, Dec. 17, 1942, Box 1; Lawrance to staff members, ca. Dec. 24, and ca. Dec. 1942, both Box 58; Atlanta *Constitution,* ca. Nov. 1942, Microfilm 795, all HC Papers; Lawrance, *Education Unlimited,* 12, 38; Lawrance, "Labor Education in the South," 15–16; *Highlander Fling* 5 (Feb. 1943).

37. Lawrance, "Atlanta Educational Program"; executive council meeting minutes, Mar. 28, 1943, Box 1; Lawrance to staff members, ca. Dec. 24, and ca. Dec. 1942;

Lawrance to Horton, Mar. 20, 1943, all Box 58; Atlanta *Constitution,* ca. Nov. 1942, Microfilm 795, all HC Papers; Lawrance to Paul Christopher, Feb. 16, 1943, CIO Org. Comm. Papers, Box 147; Mason to Allan S. Haywood, Mar. 6, 1943, Mason Papers; Lawrance, *Education Unlimited,* 19–21, 25–26, 28–29; Lawrance, "Labor Education in the South," 15–16; *Highlander Fling* 5 (Feb., June 1943).

38. See Lawrance's reports in HC Papers, Box 58; "Highlights of the Year's Activities, 1943," HFS Coll., Box 14; Lawrance, *Education Unlimited,* 12–13, 26–27, 29–30.

39. Paul Christopher to Horton, Sept. 16, 1943, Mar. 4, 1944, both Box 9; "Knoxville Educational Program (cont.), September thru November," ca. Nov. 1943; outline of Rohm-Haas institute classes, Nov. 1943, both Box 58; *CIO News,* Jan. 31, 1944, Microfilm 795, all HC Papers; Lawrance, *Education Unlimited,* 40–41; "Highlights of the Year's Activities, 1943"; *Highlander Fling* 5 (Mar. 1944).

40. Ninth Annual Report, 1941, 17–19; summaries of fieldwork programs, 1933–42; Harry Lasker, "Weekly Report to Myles Horton, Memphis Extension, Oct. 25–Nov. 1, 1941"; Lasker, "Weekly Report—Memphis Extension," Nov. 9–16, Dec. 7–12, 1941, all Box 58; Memphis *Press-Scimitar,* Nov. 5, 1941; Memphis *Commercial Appeal,* Nov. 5, 1941, both Microfilm 795, all HC Papers; *Highlander Fling* 3, 5 (Nov. 1941, Mar. 1944); Horton to Paul Christopher, Jan. 14, 21, 1942; Christopher to Horton, Jan. 28, 1942, all CIO Org. Comm. Papers, Box 146. See also Roger Biles, "Ed Crump versus the Unions: The Labor Movement in Memphis during the 1930s," *Labor History* 25 (Fall 1984): 533–52; Michael K. Honey, *Southern Labor and Black Civil Rights: Organizing Memphis Workers* (Urbana: Univ. of Illinois Press, 1993), 117–35, 177–83; Honey, "Industrial Unionism and Racial Justice in Memphis," in *Organized Labor in the Twentieth-Century South,* 136–42.

41. Lawrance, "Education Department, Tennessee State Industrial Union Council," Dec. 10, 1944, HFS Coll., Box 9; Annual Report, 1944, 6, Box 1; Lawrance to local officers, Memphis IUC, Oct. 25, 1944; "Report for Month of November," 1944, Extension Dept.; report on attendance at educational programs, Memphis, 1944, all Box 58; *CIO News,* Jan. 31, 1944, Microfilm 795, all HC Papers; Lawrance to Paul Christopher, Sept. 16, Nov. 2, 1944, CIO Industrial Union Councils, Tennessee, Papers, Box 31, Manuscript Dept., Perkins Library, Duke Univ. (hereinafter cited as CIO-IUC Papers); *Highlander Fling* 5 (Mar., Nov. 1944, Feb. 1945); Lawrance, *Education Unlimited,* 11–12, 15, 21–24, 30, 39, 40; Honey, *Southern Labor and Black Civil Rights,* 183–97; Honey, "Industrial Unionism and Racial Justice," 142–47.

42. Annual and extension project reports, 1945–47, HC Papers, Boxes 1, 58, 59; HFS, 1946 Program Report, 1–2, CIO Org. Comm. Papers, Box 147; Lawrance, "Report on Chattanooga Educational Program," Aug. 8–Dec. 15, 1945, Horton Papers, Box 3; *Highlander Fling* 5, 6 (Feb. 1945, Feb. 1946, Jan. 1947).

43. List and map of extension classes, 1932–1943, HC Papers, Box 58; table, "Number of Students Attending" residence terms, residence institutes, and extension classes, 1932–1945, HFS Coll., Box 11; *Highlander Fling* 6 (Jan. 1947); Lawrance, *Education Unlimited,* 42–45; Frank T. de Vyver, "The Present Status of Labor Unions in the South—1948," *Southern Economic Journal* 16 (July 1949): 1–22; Marshall, *Labor in the South,* 226–27.

44. Executive council meeting minutes, Jan. 8–9, 1944, HC Papers, Box 1.

5. The CIO Years, 1942–1947

1. David Brody, *Workers in Industrial America: Essays on the Twentieth Century Struggle* (New York: Oxford Univ. Press, 1980), 173–214, quotation 207; Seidman, *American Labor,* 89–90, 195, 209–10, 248–49, 274; de Vyver, "Present Status of Unions in the South— 1948," 4–7, 16–17; Bureau of the Census, *Historical Statistics of the United States, Colonial Times to 1970,* Bicentennial ed. (Washington: Government Printing Office, 1975), pt. 1, 177.

2. Horton, "Highlander's Position in the Southern Labor Movement," ca. 1942, HC Papers, Box 1. See also Ninth Annual Report, 1941, 1; Horton to Lawrance, Feb. 12, 1942, HC Papers, Box 58.

3. Statement of Purpose, Program, and Policy, HFS, Jan. 11, 1942, CIO Org. Comm. Papers, Box 146; executive council meeting minutes, Jan. 11, 1942, HC Papers, Box 1; *Highlander Fling* 4 (Mar. 1942).

4. Annual Reports, 1941, 1944; report to executive council, Dec. 17, 1942; executive council meeting minutes, Jan. 11, 1942, both Box 1; proposal to OCD for Southern Training Center, Jan. 11, 1942; excerpts of letters from various labor union officials supporting HFS proposal to OCD, ca. Feb. 12, 1942, both Box 39; announcement, "Research Department, Highlander Folk School," ca. Nov. 1942; Bill Elkuss to prospective subscribers of research service, Dec. 11, 1942; *Labor News,* nos. 1–17 (Nov. 18, 1942–Feb. 24, 1943), all Box 59; *INFO,* nos. 1–24 (Sept. 1944–Sept. 27, 1945), Box 85, all HC Papers; Horton to Paul Christopher, May 21, 1942; HFS executive council meeting minutes, Aug. 29, 1942, both CIO Org. Comm. Papers, Box 146; *Highlander Fling* 4, 5 (Mar. 1942, Feb. 1943).

5. Executive council meeting minutes, Jan. 11, 1942, HC Papers, Box 1.

6. "Highlander's Position in the Southern Labor Movement"; executive council meeting minutes, Jan. 11, 1942, Box 1; staff meeting minutes, May 3, Sept. 17, 1942, Box 2; financial report, 1941, Box 3; memorandum to HFS supporters regarding Paul Robeson concert, ca. May 11, 1942, Box 45; Leon Wilson, news release, Sept. 29, 1942, Box 66; Chattanooga *Times,* Oct. 24, 26, 1942; Chattanooga *News-Free Press,* Oct. 21, 24, 28, 1942, all Microfilm 795, all HC Papers; fundraising appeal, "The People of the South Will Meet the Challenge," ca. 1942, Box 6; invitation to Highlander National Sponsoring Committee's 10th Anniversary Celebration, ca. Oct. 25, 1942, Box 11, both HFS Coll.; Paul Christopher, "Highlander Money Letter," ca. Jan. 31, 1942; Durward McDaniel, report to the HFS executive council, July 20, 1942, both CIO Org. Comm. Papers, Box 147; *Highlander Fling* 4, 5 (June 1942, Feb. 1943).

7. Report to executive council, Dec. 17, 1942, Box 1; staff meeting minutes, Oct. 26, 1942, Box 2; financial statement, 1945, Box 3, all HC Papers; financial statement, 1943, HFS Coll., Box 13; *Highlander Fling* 5 (Feb. 1943, Feb. 1945).

8. Ninth Annual Report, 1941, 22.

9. The most extensive examination of the circumstances surrounding Dombrowski's departure has been done by Frank Adams in *James A. Dombrowski,* 94– 100, 125–33, 136–37. See also staff meeting minutes, Jan. 20, 1941 [1942?], Jan. 22, 1942, Box 2; Wilson to Durward McDaniel, Jan. 20, 1942, Box 20; Horton to Lawrance, Feb. 12, 1942, Box 58, all HC Papers; *Highlander Fling* 4 (June 1942); Krueger, *And Promises to Keep,* 88–89, 95, 105–6; Horton, interview with author, June 3, 1980.

10. Wilson to staff, Sept. 15, 1942, HC Papers, Box 29.

11. Report to executive council, Dec. 17, 1942, Box 1; staff meeting minutes, Oct. 26, 1942, Box 2; Zilphia Horton to Anita Berenbach, July 15, 1943, Box 5; Zilphia Horton to Ruth Catlin, May 12, 1943, Box 8; Horton to Paul Christopher, Apr. 29, 1943, Box 9; Horton to Gen. Lewis Hershey, Oct. 25, 1942; Wilson "to whom it may concern," Feb. 22, 1943; unidentified newspaper clippings, ca. Mar. 18, Mar. 19, 1943, all Box 29; *Summerfield News* 3 (Mar. 5, 1943), Box 85, all HC Papers; *Highlander Fling* 4 (June 1942).

12. Zilphia Horton to Anita Berenbach, July 15, 1943, HC Papers, Box 5.

13. Executive council meeting minutes, Mar. 28, 1943, Box 1; staff meeting minutes, May 24, 1943, Box 2; Horton to Paul Christopher, Apr. 27, 1943, Box 9; Zilphia Horton to Virginia Durr, May 15, 1943, Box 11; Eva Zhitlowsky to Barney Morel, Mar. 24, 1943, Box 21; Malcolm Ross to Horton, Mar. 15, 1943; Horton to Ross, Apr. 2, 1943, both Box 24; *Summerfield News* 3 (July 1943), Box 85, all HC Papers; *Highlander Fling* 5 (June, Sept. 1943).

14. Annual Report, 1942, Box 1; Wilson to Ruth Reynolds, Nov. 12, 1942, Box 24; announcement, "Six Weeks Summer Term for Southern Workers," ca. Aug. 3, 1942; Horton, "Union Problems," summer term 1942; Lawrance, "Economics," ca. Aug. 3, 1942; Lawrance, "Summer Term 1942: Parliamentary Law," Aug. 4, 1942; Wilson, "Current Events," Aug. 4, 10, 1942; Wilson, "Public Speaking," Aug. 1942; Lawrance, "Union Publicity," Sept. 1, 1942; Wilson, "Notes on dramatics class, taught by Zilphia Horton," Sept. 13, 1942; "Evaluation of the Term—1942," ca. Sept. 14–16, 1942, all Box 62; Horton, news releases, June 14, Sept. 15, 1942, Box 66; *CIO News,* July 20, 1942, Microfilm 795, all HC Papers; leaflet, "Highlander Folk School: A Union School. Summer Term, Six Weeks, Aug. 3–Sept. 13, 1942," HFS Coll., Box 11; *Highlander Fling* 5 (Feb. 1943).

15. Borah to Horton, July 27, 1942, HC Papers, Box 7. See also staff meeting minutes, Apr. 23, 1942, Box 2; Horton to Borah, July 15, 1942, Box 7, both HC Papers; Horton to Paul Christopher, July 15, 1942; Christopher to Horton, Aug. 8, 1942; Christopher to Durward McDaniel, Aug. 13, 1942; HFS executive council meeting minutes, Aug. 29, 1942, all CIO Org. Comm. Papers, Box 146; Zilphia Horton to Myles Horton, Mar. 6, 1942, ZHP, Box 15.

16. Executive council meeting minutes, Mar. 28, 1943, Box 1; staff meeting minutes, Sept. 13, 1943, Box 2; Zilphia Horton to *Nation* editor, May 7, 1943; Horton, news release, Apr. 27, 1943, both Box 66; Pennsylvania *Labor News,* Aug. 13, 1943, Microfilm 795, all HC Papers; "Highlights of the Year's Activities, 1943," HFS Coll., Box 14; report to HFS executive council, July 24, 1943, CIO Org. Comm. Papers, Box 147; *Highlander Fling* 5 (Feb., June, Sept. 1943).

17. Staff meeting minutes, May 24, 1943, HC Papers, Box 2.

18. Horton to Morris Lasker, May 30, 1944, HC Papers, Box 53; Horton, memorandum to HFS executive council members, Mar. 18, 1943, CIO Org. Comm. Papers, Box 147; Garrison, "Paul Revere Christopher," 152–53; Seidman, *American Labor,* 200–202; Brody, *Workers in Industrial America,* 217–19; James Caldwell Foster, *The Union Politic: The CIO Political Action Committee* (Columbia: Univ. of Missouri Press, 1975), 3–15, 39–40, 45–48; Bert Cochran, *Labor and Communism: The Conflict that*

Shaped American Unions (Princeton: Princeton Univ. Press, 1977), 231–32; Daniel A. Powell, "PAC to COPE: Thirty-Two Years of Southern Labor in Politics," in *Essays in Southern Labor History: Selected Papers, Southern Labor History Conference, 1976,* ed. Gary M. Fink and Merl E. Reed (Westport, Conn.: Greenwood Press, 1977), 244.

19. Nashville *Banner,* ca. Aug. 1944; Knoxville *News-Sentinel,* Sept. 2, 1944, both HC Papers, Microfilm 795.

20. Annual Report, 1944, 4; staff meeting minutes, Apr. 16, 1945, Box 2; "Nashville Banner Attacks PAC Meeting at Highlander," ca. Feb. 14, 1945; Dorothy McDade, news release, Feb. 11, 1945, both Box 66; Paul R. Christopher, memorandum re TCPAC, Aug. 30, 1944, Box 73; Nashville *Banner,* Feb. 16, Mar. 12, 1945, Microfilm 795, all HC Papers; *Highlander Fling* 5 (Nov. 1944, Feb. 1945); Garrison, "Paul Revere Christopher," 153–54; Foster, *Union Politic,* 17–29, 44, 49, 64; Seidman, *American Labor,* 202–5; Brody, *Workers in Industrial America,* 217–19; Cochran, *Labor and Communism,* 237–43; Powell, "PAC to COPE," 246–47; J. David Greenstone, *Labor in American Politics* (New York: Alfred A. Knopf, 1969), 50–51; Joseph Gaer, *The First Round: The Story of the CIO Political Action Committee* (New York: Duell, Sloan and Pearce, 1944), 104–11, 149–51, 178–217, 266–67, 287.

21. "Plan for 1944," HC Papers, Box 1. See also staff meeting minutes, Dec. 3, 1943, Mar. 24, 1944, Box 2; Horton, news release, Jan. 13, 1944; Christopher, memorandum re special one-month CIO educational program for southern CIO members, May 1944, at HFS, ca. May 1944, both Box 59, all HC Papers; announcement, *The Southern CIO Regional Directors Proudly Announce: A Southern CIO School, May 1–28, 1944, Highlander Folk School, Monteagle, Tennessee,* HFS Coll., Box 11; HFS staff and executive council, minutes of meeting with southern regional directors, Nov. 3, 1943; Christopher to Allan S. Haywood, Nov. 15, 1943, both CIO Org. Comm. Papers, Box 147; *Highlander Fling* 5 (Mar. 1944).

22. Annual Report, 1944, 1–2, 8, 9; Horton to Lawrance, June 2, 1944, Box 11; [Catherine Winston?] to Tefferteller, May 31, 1944, Box 27; Horton, news release, May 1, 1944; Virginia Hart, report on community relations class of CIO term, May 1944; outline of things CIO unions can do on racial discrimination, May 1944; outline of things that local unions can do for the service men, May 1944; E. A. Larsen, Training Within Industry, news release, May 1944; list of speakers and visiting organizers during May CIO session, May 1–28, 1944, all Box 59; Horton, news releases, ca. May 15, May 21, 28, 1944, Box 66, all HC Papers; *Highlander Fling* 5 (July 1944, Feb. 1945); A. I. Horton, "Highlander, 1932–61," 181–83.

23. Students and Mason quoted in Annual Report, 1944, 1. See also Nolan Trent to C. W. Dickinson, Dallas-Tarrant County Joint Industrial Union Council, July 3, 1944, HC Papers, Box 28.

24. Annual Report, 1944, 1–2; C. W. Danenburg to Horton, June 13, 1944, Box 12; Horton to Dan Ross, Dec. 19, 1944, Box 24; Nolan Trent, news release, May 1944, Box 28, all HC Papers; Horton to Paul Christopher, May 30, 1944, CIO Org. Comm. Papers, Box 147; *Highlander Fling* 5 (Feb. 1945).

25. Sumner M. Rosen, "The CIO Era, 1935–1955," in *The Negro and the American Labor Movement,* ed. Julius Jacobson (Garden City, N.Y.: Doubleday, 1968), 188–208; Seidman, *American Labor,* 165–71; Sitkoff, *New Deal for Blacks,* 169–70; William H. Harris,

The Harder We Run: Black Workers Since the Civil War (New York: Oxford Univ. Press, 1982), 114–15. See also James S. Olson, "Organized Black Leadership and Industrial Unionism: The Racial Response, 1936–1945," *Labor History* 10 (Summer 1969): 475–86.

26. "Highlights of the Year's Activities," 1943. See also executive council meeting minutes, Jan. 11, 1942, Box 1; staff meeting minutes, July 12, 1943, Box 2; Horton to Malcolm Ross, July 31, 1943, Box 24; "Highlander Offers to Help with Race Problems," 1943; Zilphia Horton, "Community Reaction to Negroes at Highlander," 1946, both Box 39; Horton to Lawrance, Jan. 26, 1944, Box 58; Horton to Alton Lawrence, Apr. 27, 1943; "Dr. Max Yergan and the Highlander Inter-Racial Conference," ca. May 4, 1943, both Box 76, all HC Papers; HFS executive council meeting minutes, Aug. 29, 1942, CIO Org. Comm. Papers, Box 146; Mark Starr, "The Current Panorama," in *Workers' Education in the United States*, ed. Theodore Brameld (New York: Harper and Brothers, 1941), 99–100; "An Interracial School for Southerners," *Events and Trends in Race Relations: A Monthly Survey* 4 (Mar. 1947): 240.

27. Annual Report, 1944, 2–3; Horton to Thyra Edwards, June 28, 1944, Box 11; Horton to Lilian W. Johnson, June 12, 1944, Box 16; Lawrance to Horton, Jan. 22, 1944; Horton to Lawrance, Jan. 26, 1944, both Box 58; daily schedule, UAW School, June 5–11, 1944; *United Automobile Worker,* July 15, 1944, both Box 61, all HC Papers; list of participants, UAW Session, June 5–10, [1944]; Sylvia MacMillan, HFS news release, June 11, 1944, both Christopher Papers, Box 24; *Highlander Fling* 5 (July 1944); Rosen, "The CIO Era," 204–5; Goldfield, "Race and the CIO," 11–13.

28. Horton to Morris Lasker, June 12, 1944, HC Papers, Box 53.

29. Annual Report, 1944, 3; Horton to Lawrance, June 13, 1944, Box 11; staff member to Carolyn Finkelstein, June 13, 1944, Box 12; Horton to Kathleen Trager, July 1, 1944, Box 28; William H. Levitt, "Reporting on Education," Box 61; report of Resolutions Committee, 1944 convention, Tennessee State IUC, Box 73, all HC Papers; Lawrance to Paul Christopher, July 31, 1944, CIO-IUC Papers, Box 31; *Highlander Fling* 5 (July 1944).

30. Annual Report, 1944, 3–4, 6–7; Horton to Wilson, July 24, Aug. 22, 1944, Box 29; Horton to Eva Zhitlowsky, July 24, 1944, Box 30; Horton to Lawrance, Aug. 7, 1944, Box 58; Catherine Winston to Charles H. Gillman, July 28, 1944; recommendations of Political Action Class, August Workers' Term, 1944; student-staff list, Aug. 1944, all Box 62; Ann Drucker, news release, July 31, 1944; Horton, news release, Aug. 11, 1944; Winston, news release, Aug. 27, 1944, all Box 66, all HC Papers; *Highlander Fling* 5 (Nov. 1944).

31. W. A. Copeland to Larry Rogin, Aug. 7, 1944, Textile Workers Union of America Papers (Mss 129A), 8A-1, Box 7, State Historical Society of Wisconsin.

32. Annual Report, 1944, 1; summary of Annual Report, 1944; executive council meeting minutes, Jan. 20–21, 1945, both Box 1; Horton to Dombrowski, Dec. 20, 1944, Box 10; list of 1944 contributors, Box 59; Horton, news release, Jan. 22, 1945, Box 66; Chattanooga *Times,* Jan. 22, 1945, Microfilm 795, all HC Papers; George S. Mitchell to Ann Drucker, Aug. 29, 1944, Christopher Papers, Box 24; *Highlander Fling* 5 (Mar. 1944, Feb. 1945).

33. Executive council meeting minutes, Jan. 20–21, 1945, Box 1; staff meeting minutes, Apr. 6, 1945, Box 2; staff meeting minutes, May 1, 1945, Box 2; Horton to

Frank Bender, Maryland regional director, Mar. 19, 1945; Horton to sponsors of the CIO school and executive council members, May 12, 1945; "Evaluation of CIO Term, May 1945," June 4, 1945, all Box 60, all HC Papers; Paul Christopher to Emil Rieve, Mar. 10, 1945, TWUA Papers (Mss 396), Carton 54; Horton to southern CIO regional directors, Apr. 13, 1945, HFS Coll., Box 11; William Smith to Christopher, Mar. 14, 1945; Christopher to Horton, Apr. 5, 1945; announcement, *Second Southern CIO School, May 7–June 3, 1945,* all Christopher Papers, Box 33.

34. Joseph D. Cannon to Christopher, Mar. 9, 1945, Christopher Papers, Box 33. See also Zilphia Horton, "Community Reaction to Negroes"; staff meeting minutes, Feb. 12, 1945, Box 2; Christopher to E. L. Sandefur, Carolinas regional director, Mar. 4, 1945, Box 60, both HC Papers; letters from CIO directors to Christopher, Mar. 6–13, 1945, Christopher Papers, Box 33; Honey, "Industrial Unionism and Racial Justice," 144–46; Honey, *Southern Labor and Black Civil Rights,* 212; Goldfield, "Race and the CIO," 17.

35. Horton to Durward McDaniel, Apr. 4, 1945, HC Papers, Box 20.

36. Staff meeting minutes, Apr. 6, 1945, Box 2; Horton to Aubrey Williams, National Farmers' Union, May 4, 29, 1945; Williams to Horton, May 10, 1945, all Box 42; Horton to Lawrance and Catherine Winston, Apr. 20, 1945, Box 58; Horton to Dombrowski, Mar. 29, 1945; Lawrance to Horton, Apr. 8, 1945; W. A. Copeland to Dorothy McDade, Apr. 9, 1945; Carey Haigler to Paul Christopher, Apr. 23, 1945; Christopher to Haigler, Apr. 28, 1945, all Box 60, all HC Papers; Christopher to Haigler and Charles Gillman, Mar. 28, 1945, Christopher Papers, Box 33.

37. Report of 1945 Activities, 1, Box 1; local officer's news letter, United Transport Service Employees of America, June 16, Aug. 25, 1945, Box 29; list of CIO School staff and visiting speakers, May 7–June 3, 1945; weekly reports on CIO School; *Southern CIO School Monitor,* May 12, June 2, 1945, all Box 60; Catherine Winston, news releases, ca. May 7, June 3, 1945, Box 66; *Tennessee CIO News,* June 18, 1945, Microfilm 795, all HC Papers; *Highlander Fling* 5 (June 1945); Honey, *Southern Labor and Black Civil Rights,* 212.

38. "Evaluation of CIO Term, May 1945."

39. Report of 1945 Activities, 2; staff meeting minutes, May 26, 1945, Box 2; minutes of executive board meeting, Arkansas-Oklahoma IUCs, June 24, 1945, Box 21; George D. Stein to Paul Christopher, June 9, 1945, Box 26; Dorothy Bobo to staff members, June 19, 1945, Box 60; *International Oil Worker,* July 1945; *Tennessee CIO News,* Dec. 24, 1945, both Microfilm 795, all HC Papers; "Evaluation of CIO Term, May 1945"; Horton to Christopher, June 27, 1945, Christopher Papers, Box 33; *Highlander Fling* 5 (June 1945).

40. Report of 1945 Activities, 2–3; staff meeting minutes, June 17, July 7, 1945, Box 2; announcement, "Two Weeks School for Southern URWA," ca. Feb. 1945, Box 61; Federated Press news releases, July 13, Aug. 10, 1945; Catherine Winston, news release, ca. June 17, 1945, all Box 66; *CIO News,* July 16, 1945; St. Louis *Post-Dispatch,* Sept. 26, 1945, both Microfilm 795, all HC Papers; Dorothy McDade to Paul Christopher, June 21, 1945, Christopher Papers, Box 33; *Highlander Fling* 5, 6 (Nov. 1945, Feb. 1946).

41. Seidman, *American Labor,* 213–69; Brody, *Workers in Industrial America,* 175–92, 222; Nelson Lichtenstein, *Labor's War at Home: The CIO in World War II* (Cambridge: Cambridge Univ. Press, 1982), 203–32.

42. Executive council meeting minutes, Apr. 12, 1946, Box 1; staff meeting minutes, Nov. 19, 1945, Apr. 1, 1946, Box 2; Charles H. Gillman to Catherine Winston, Nov. 16, 1945; Paul Christopher to E. L. Sandefur, Jan. 4, 1946; Horton to Christopher, Mar. 20, 1946; Christopher to George Addes, Apr. 4, 1946, all Box 60; Winston, news releases, ca. May 6, May 13, ca. June 2, 1946, Box 66; Chattanooga *Times*, May 26, 1946, Microfilm 795, all HC Papers; announcement, *CIO Unions: The Southern CIO Regional Directors Urge You to Attend Southern CIO School, May 6–June 2, 1946, at the Highlander Folk School, Monteagle, Tennessee*, Box 11; *Tomorrow Is Ours*, written and published by students at the 3d annual Southern C.I.O. School—1946, Box 13, both HFS Coll.; *Highlander Fling* 6 (July 1946, Jan. 1947).

43. Joseph Stephens, response to HFS questionnaire, 1946, Box 32; *Union Leader* 1 (May 18, 1946); student evaluation, ca. June 2, 1946; evaluation of CIO term, staff meeting minutes, June 3, 1946; list of union contributions to 1946 CIO term, ca. May 1946, all Box 60; Catherine Winston, news release, ca. June 2, 1946, Box 66, all HC Papers; *Tomorrow Is Ours*, 13–14; *Highlander Fling* 6 (July 1946).

44. Lawrance, "A Study of the Methods and Results of Workers Education in the South," 1948, 58–60, HC Papers, Box 32; evaluation of CIO term, staff meeting minutes, June 3, 1946.

45. Bittner quoted in *New York Times*, Apr. 19, 1946. See also Marshall, *Labor in the South*, 246–69; Krueger, *And Promises to Keep*, 139–40; J. B. S. Hardman, "The Southern Union Campaign Is in the National Interest," *Labor and Nation* 1 (Apr.–May 1946): 32–34; "Southern Drive Is Launched," *American Federationist* 53 (June 1946): 6–7; Honey, *Southern Labor and Black Civil Rights*, 216–17, 229–30, 236; Salmond, *Miss Lucy of the CIO*, 124–28; Barbara S. Griffith, *The Crisis of American Labor: Operation Dixie and the Defeat of the CIO* (Philadelphia: Temple Univ. Press, 1988); Michael Honey, "Operation Dixie: Labor and Civil Rights in the Postwar South," *Mississippi Quarterly* 45 (Fall 1992): 439–52.

46. Staff meeting minutes, July 29, 1946, HC Papers, Box 2.

47. Executive council meeting minutes, Apr. 12, 1946, HC Papers, Box 1; Krueger, *And Promises to Keep*, 140–43; Brody, *Workers in Industrial America*, 225–26; A. G. Mezerik, "The C.I.O. Southern Drive," *Nation* 164 (Jan. 11, 1947): 38–40; *CIO News*, Jan. 13, 1947; Garrison, "Paul Revere Christopher," 160–62; Honey, "Industrial Unionism and Racial Justice," 146–48.

48. Staff meeting minutes, July 10, 1946, HC Papers, Box 2.

49. Annual Report, 1947, 8; executive council meeting minutes, Apr. 12, 1946, Jan. 31, 1947, Jan. 14–15, 1948, all Box 1; staff meeting minutes, Mar. 31, June 4, Oct. 28, 1946, Jan. 30, June 5, Aug. 22, 1947, Box 2; budget, 1946; financial reports, 1946, 1947, all Box 3; Catherine Winston to Carey E. Haigler, July 9, 1946, Box 14; Horton, report on Highlander committees, Nov. 1946, Box 45; Marc Siegel to Horton, Dec. 16, 1946, Box 46; fundraising flier, "The Drive Is On!" ca. July 1946, Box 66, all HC Papers; executive board meeting minutes, Tennessee State CIO Council, Dec. 14, 1946, CIO-IUC Papers, Box 29; Haigler to W. H. Crawford, July 17, 1946, MHP, Box 10; announcement publicizing Frank Sinatra donation, ca. July 9, 1946, United Packinghouse Workers of America Papers, Box 344, State Historical Society of Wisconsin; *Highlander Fling* 6 (Feb. 1946, Jan. 1947); Alden Stevens, "Small-Town America,"

Nation 162 (June 29, 1946): 784; Catherine Winston, "Choose Up for the Highlander Fling!" *Motive* 6 (Dec. 1945): 19; A. Gilbert Belles, "The Julius Rosenwald Fund: Efforts in Race Relations, 1928–1948" (Ph.D. diss., Vanderbilt Univ., 1972), 91–93.

50. Executive council meeting minutes, Apr. 12, 1946; program for 1946, 2–3, 6–7, both Box 1; staff meeting minutes, Mar. 31, July 29, 1946, Box 2; lists of students, AFHW institutes, Apr. 13–14, Oct. 26–27, 1946, Box 59; Catherine Winston to Cornelia Anderson, Mar. 20, Apr. 2, 1946; list of students and faculty at FTA term, Apr. 21–27, 1946, all Box 60; Winston, news releases, ca. Apr. 14, 27, July 6, Oct. 27, 1946, Box 66, all HC Papers; *Highlander Fling* 6 (July 1946).

51. Program for 1946, 7; Lawrance to James E. Jackson, Jr., Southern Negro Youth Congress, Sept. 15, 1946; *Highlander Highlights,* Sept. 1946; list of students, union leadership training course, Sept. 15–29, 1946; staff evaluation, fall term, Sept. 15–29, 1946; Lawrance, "Highlander Folk School, Fall Term 1946," 20–26, all Box 62; news release, Oct. 1, 1946, Box 66, all HC Papers.

52. Christopher to Horton, June 11, 1947, Christopher Papers, Box 52A; Horton to Christopher, June 13, 1947, CIO Org. Comm. Papers, Box 147.

53. Annual Report, 1947, 1–3; staff meeting minutes, Jan. 30, May 9, July 12, 1947, Box 2; list of students, Hosiery Workers Institute, Feb. 22–23, 1947; list of students, AFHW-CIO regional term, July 20–26, 1947, both Box 59; Catherine Winston to George Guernsey, Mar. 20, 1947; announcement of CIO term, CIO Department of Research and Education, Apr. 21, 1947; *Great Day. FTA-CIO leadership training session, May 11–24, 1947, Highlander Folk School*; report on labor journalism workshop, CIO term, June 15–July 12, 1947, all Box 60; [Bill Elkuss?], "Institute in Educational Techniques, Mine, Mill and Smelter Workers," Dec. 6–8, 1947, Box 61; Winston, news release, June 2, 1947, Box 66; *CIO News,* July 21, 1947; *Hosiery Worker,* Nov. 11, 1947; unidentified MMSW newspaper, Dec. 1947, all Microfilm 795, all HC Papers; *Rubber Workers School News* 1 (Aug. 14, 1947), Box 12; *We're on the Freedom Trail,* CIO leadership training session, June 15–July 12, 1947, Box 13; Elaine Van Brink, "Having Been at Highlander," Oct. 1947, 3–5, 7–9, Box 16, all HFS Coll.; A. I. Horton, "Highlander, 1932–61," 192–96.

54. Staff meeting minutes, Jan. 30, 1947, Box 2; Horton to Lilian Johnson, May 10, 1947, Box 16, both HC Papers.

55. Staff evaluation, Rubber Workers term, Aug. 3–17, 1947, HC Papers, Box 61. See also Mary Lawrance Elkuss to Joseph Vaught, Jan. 21, 1948, HC Papers, Box 61; Alonzo L. Hamby, *Beyond the New Deal: Harry S. Truman and American Liberalism* (New York: Columbia Univ. Press, 1973), 147–68.

56. Lawrance, "Follow-up of Highlander Students" (from Rosenwald Study of Adult Education), 1946; Mary Lawrance Elkuss, "From Workers' Education," 1946, both Box 48; memorandum, Fred G. Wale to Edwin R. Embree, Rosenwald Fund, Oct. 28, 1946, Box 50; "Highlander Folk School: A Brief History," MS, June 1946, 4–5, Box 82, all HC Papers; *Highlander Fling* 6 (Jan. 1947). See also Charles H. Martin, "Southern Labor Relations in Transition: Gadsden, Alabama, 1930–1943," *Journal of Southern History* 47 (Nov. 1981): 545–68.

57. Brody, *Workers in Industrial America,* 198–229; Seidman, *American Labor,* 248–49, 254–69, 280–82; Marshall, *Labor in the South,* 225–27; Greenstone, *Labor in American Politics,* 65–66.

58. Christopher to Horton, Dec. 30, 1946, CIO Org. Comm. Papers, Box 147.

59. Minutes of joint meeting, HFS executive committee and committee from Tennessee State CIO Council, ca. Jan. 30, 1947, Horton Papers, Box 3. See also Christopher to James B. Carey, Dec. 30, 1946, HC Papers, Box 9; Horton to Christopher, Aug. 8, Dec. 20, 1946; Christopher to Horton, Dec. 22, 1946; Carey to Christopher, Jan. 13, 1947, all CIO Org. Comm. Papers, Box 147; Horton to Larry Rogin, Apr. 10, 1947; Rogin to Horton, Apr. 17, 1947, both (Mss 129A), 8A-1, Box 7; interoffice memorandum, Rogin to William Pollock, Aug. 29, 1947, (Mss 396), Carton 54, all TWUA Papers; Honey, "Industrial Unionism and Racial Justice," 148.

60. Executive council meeting minutes, Jan. 14–15, 1948, HC Papers, Box 1. See also Annual Report, 1947, 8; Fred G. Wale to Edwin R. Embree, Oct. 28, 1946, HC Papers, Box 50; Horton to Paul Christopher, Dec. 12, 1946, CIO Org. Comm. Papers, Box 147.

61. Horton, Frederickson interview. See also Horton, "The Spark That Ignites," *Southern Exposure* 4 (Spring–Summer 1976): 153–56; Robert Korstad and Nelson Lichtenstein, "Opportunities Found and Lost: Labor, Radicals, and the Early Civil Rights Movement," *Journal of American History* 75 (Dec. 1988): 786–811; Lichtenstein, "Auto Worker Militancy and the Structure of Factory Life, 1937–1955," *Journal of American History* 67 (Sept. 1980): 335–53.

6. Transition Years, 1944–1953

1. Horton, "Farm-Labor Unity," *Prophetic Religion* 8 (Fall 1947): 79–82, 93, quotations 79, 93. See also executive council meeting minutes, Jan. 14–15, 1948, Box 1; Horton, untitled essay on Highlander's work with the Farmers' Union, ca. 1948; "Educating toward Democratic Unity through Small-Farm Organizations," ca. Oct. 1946, both Box 43, all HC Papers; Horton, interview with author, Aug. 9, 1978; Horton, interview with Bill Olson, *Working Papers for Ryegrass School* 1 (Jan. 1979).

2. Robert L. Tontz, "Membership in General Farmers' Organizations, United States, 1874–1960," *Agricultural History* 38 (July 1964): 143–56; William P. Tucker, "Populism Up-to-Date: The Story of the Farmers' Union," *Agricultural History* 21 (Oct. 1947): 198–207; Gladys Talbott Edwards, *The Farmers Union Triangle* (Jamestown, N.D.: Farmers Union Education Service, 1941), 34–35, 56–59; Theodore Saloutos, *Farmer Movements in the South, 1865–1933* (Berkeley: Univ. of California Press, 1960), 184–212; *Tennessee Union Farmer* 1 (Aug. 1946).

3. John A. Crampton, *The National Farmers Union: Ideology of a Pressure Group* (Lincoln: Univ. of Nebraska Press, 1965), 7–40, 47–60, 163–71, 231–33; Tucker, "Populism Up-to-Date," 205–8; Edwards, *Farmers Union Triangle,* 57, 102–6, 155–60; William P. Tucker, "The Farmers Union: The Social Thought of a Current Agrarian Movement," *Southwestern Social Science Quarterly* 27 (June 1946): 45–53; Gladys Talbott Edwards, *United We Stand* (Denver: National Farmers Union, 1945), 10–12, 20–21, 52–53, 55–56; Tucker, "The Farmers Union Cooperatives," *Sociology and Social Research* 31 (July–Aug. 1947): 436–44; Ladd Haystead and Gilbert C. Fite, *The Agricultural Regions of the United States* (Norman: Univ. of Oklahoma Press, 1955), 82–96;

Tennessee Union Farmer 1 (Aug. 1946). See also Michael W. Flamm, "The National Farmers Union and the Evolution of Agrarian Liberalism, 1937–1946," *Agricultural History* 68 (Summer 1994): 54–80.

4. Horton to Gardiner Jackson, Mar. 4, 1943, Box 16; Horton to Milton C. Rose, William C. Whitney Foundation, Feb. 24, 1944, Box 51, both HC Papers.

5. Executive council meeting minutes, Mar. 28, 1943, Jan. 8–9, 1944, HC Papers, Box 1.

6. Annual Report, 1944, 5; "Plan for 1944"; Horton to Aubrey Williams, Feb. 2, Mar. 7, May 30, 1944; Williams to Horton, Apr. 28, 1944, all HC Papers, Box 42; Horton, untitled essay on work with the Farmers' Union; *Highlander Fling* 5 (Mar., July 1944); *National Union Farmer* 24 (Sept. 15, 1945).

7. Annual Report, 1944, 7; "Educating toward Democratic Unity"; Report of 1945 Activities, 4–5; announcement, "Political Action Meeting Sunday," ca. Mar. 1944, Box 44; "Farmers Union Education in Tennessee," Nov. 1, 1945, Box 51; *Summerfield News* 4 (Apr. 8, May 6, 1944), Box 85, all HC Papers; 1946 Program Report, 4; *Highlander Fling* 5 (July 1944, Feb. 1945); *Tennessee Union Farmer* 1 (Aug., Sept. 1946); *National Union Farmer* 25 (Feb. 1, 1946).

8. News releases, "From the Shoulder" and "From the Shoulder-Up," ca. Apr. 1945, HC Papers, Box 42. See also Nov. [1944] report, Box 1; staff report for Mar. [1945], Box 2; Horton to Aubrey Williams, Mar. 2, Apr. 9, 1945; Crabtree to Horton, Apr. 2, 1945, all Box 42; Nashville *Banner,* Dec. 17, 1945, Microfilm 795, all HC Papers; *Tennessee Union Farmer* 1 (Aug. 1946).

9. Leaflet quoted in *Highlander Fling* 5 (Nov. 1945): 1. See also Report of 1945 Activities, 4; Horton to Aubrey Williams, June 7, 1945; Crabtree to Horton, May 28, 1945; Horton to Paul Christopher, S. A. Para, Hollis Reid, and T. O. Denham, Sept. 5, 1945, all Box 42; Horton, "The Farmers Union in Tennessee," ca. Oct. 10, 1945, Box 43; "Farmers Union Education in Tennessee," Nov. 1, 1945, Box 51; Federated Press release, Aug. 10, 1945, Box 66, all HC Papers; 1946 Program Report, 4; *National Union Farmer* 23 (Sept. 1, 1945).

10. *Tennessee Union Farmer* 1 (Aug. 1946): 1.

11. Staff meeting minutes, Oct. 11, 1945, Box 2; Horton to Aubrey Williams, July 30, Aug. 18, Sept. 7, 1945; Williams to Horton, Aug. 23, Sept. 4, 1945; Horton to Paul Christopher, July 17, 1945; Horton to Christopher, T. O. Denham, Steve Para, and Hollis Reid, Aug. 16, Sept. 5, 1945; Para to A. F. Whitney, Brotherhood of Railroad Trainmen, Sept. 12, Oct. 15, 1945, all Box 42; notes on meetings of Tennessee Joint Labor Legislative Committee, Apr. 16, June 19, 1945, Box 43; minutes of meeting of the Tennessee Farmers' Union, State Committee, May 24, 1946, Box 44; Nashville *Tennessean,* May 25, 1946, Microfilm 795, all HC Papers; *Tennessee Union Farmer* 1 (Aug. 1946); *Highlander Fling* 5, 6 (Nov. 1945, Feb., July 1946); Horton, interview with author, Aug. 9, 1978.

12. Tom Ludwig, interview with author, New Market, Tenn., Aug. 10, 1978; Ludwig, interview with Alice Cobb, Jan. 30, 1979, copy in possession of author; Lawrance to Horton, Dec. 5, 1945, HC Papers, Box 11.

13. Horton quoted in *Highlander Fling* 5 (Nov. 1945): 1.

14. Report of 1945 Activities, 4–5; Horton to Paul Christopher, Steve Para, Hollis Reid, and T. O. Denham, Aug. 16, 1945; Horton to Para, Oct. 6, Dec. 6, 1945, all Box 42; *Tennessee Labor Bulletin* 1 (Aug. 1945); Horton to Glenn Talbott, North Dakota Farmers' Union, Aug. 28, 1945; J. J. King, Jr., to Horton, ca. Dec. 1945; Horton to King, ca. Dec. 1945, all Box 43; Horton, "Summary of Organizational Activities, Tennessee Farmers Union, Oct. 29 to Nov. 25—4 Weeks," 1945, Box 44, all HC Papers; *Tennessee Union Farmer* 1 (Aug. 1946); Armand Peter Ruderman, "Rural Awakening in the Near South," *Nation* 167 (Aug. 28, 1948): 234–35.

15. Executive council meeting minutes, Apr. 12, 1946; Annual Report, 1947, 4–5, both HC Papers, Box 1; 1946 Program Report, 3; HFS executive council meeting minutes, June 21–22, 1947, CIO Org. Comm. Papers, Box 147; *Tennessee Union Farmer* 1, 2 (Aug., Nov., Dec. 1946, Feb., June, Nov. 1947); Ludwig, Cobb interview; Ruderman, "Rural Awakening in the Near South," 235.

16. News release, Nov. 8, 1948, HC Papers, Box 66; *Tennessee Union Farmer* 2, 3 (July, Dec. 1947, Jan. 1948); *Union Farmer* 3 (Feb., June 1948); *National Union Farmer* 25, 26 (Nov. 1947, Dec. 1948).

17. Annual Reports, 1948, 1950, both Box 1; Horton to Russell Smith, June 16, 1949, Box 42; E. B. Reed to Krainock, Jan. 31, 1949; J. Lynch Jones to Greene County farmers, Mar. 28, 1949; Horton to Sen. Estes Kefauver, Apr. 12, 1949; Horton to Jones, June 16, 1949; Greene County Farmers' Union news release, Aug. 10, 1949; Lee Fryer, National Farmers' Union, "Report on the South," ca. May 1949, all Box 43, all HC Papers; *Union Farmer* 3, 4 (Sept., Nov., Dec. 1948, May 1949).

18. Report of 1945 Activities, 4; Annual Report, 1947, 4; executive council meeting minutes, Apr. 12, 1946; "Report from the Mountains: The 1948 Spring and Summer Program of the Highlander Folk School," 3, both Box 1; staff meeting minutes, July 29, 1946, Box 2; Ludwig to James Lee Taylor, Dec. 27, 1945; Lange to Crabtree, Feb. 9, 1946; Lange to Horton, Feb. 19, 1946; Lange to Ludwig, Mar. 30, 1946; James Patton to Lange, June 27, 1946; Chet Kinsey, Progressive Party of Montana, to Krainock, June 6, 1949, all Box 42, all HC Papers; "Educating toward Democratic Unity"; 1946 Program Report, 3; *Tennessee Union Farmer* 1, 2 (Aug., Oct. 1946, Apr., May, Dec. 1947); *Union Farmer* 3 (Feb. 1948); *National Union Farmer* 25 (Mar. 1, 1947); Zilphia Horton, "People Like to Sing," *Food for Thought* 8 (Mar. 1948): 18–19.

19. Patton to Will Alexander, Rosenwald Fund, Nov. 10, 1946, HC Papers, Box 50.

20. Executive council meeting minutes, Jan. 14–15, 1948, HC Papers, Box 1.

21. Report of 1945 Activities, 4–5; Annual Report, 1947, 3–4; executive council meeting minutes, Apr. 12, 1946, Jan. 14–15, 1948, Box 1; Horton to Steve Para, Jan. 1, 1946; Patton to Horton, Dec. 19, 1947; Horton to Patton, Jan. 7, 27, 1948, all Box 42; memorandum, Fred G. Wale to Edwin R. Embree, Oct. 28, 1946, Box 50; Tennessee Farmers' Union press release, Nov. 2, 1946, Box 66, all HC Papers; "Educating toward Democratic Unity"; Horton, "The Farmers Union in Tennessee"; 1946 Program Report, 3–4; HFS executive council meeting minutes, June 21–22, 1947, CIO Org. Comm. Papers, Box 147; *Highlander Fling* 6 (Jan., Mar. 1947); *Tennessee Union Farmer* 1, 2 (Aug., Oct., Nov., Dec. 1946, Jan., Feb., Mar., July 1947, Jan. 1948); *National Union Farmer* 25 (Feb. 1, Aug. 15, Sept. 15, 1946).

22. Horton to Patton, Feb. 25, 1947, HC Papers, Box 43.

23. *Tennessee Union Farmer* 2 (Sept. 1947), quoted in A. I. Horton, "Highlander, 1932–61," 225.

24. Annual Reports, 1947–49, Box 1; staff meeting minutes, Nov. 1, 1948, Box 2; Marc Siegel to Margaret Lamont, Feb. 26, 1947, Box 18; Horton to Gladys Edwards, Feb. 25, 1947; *Farmers Union Workshop News* 1 (July 31, 1947), both Box 43; "Report on the Farmers Union School, October 17–October 22, 1948"; Horton to Ludwig, Oct. 26, 1948, both Box 44; Catherine Winston to "Muriel and Lav," Feb. 25, 1947, Box 45; Chattanooga *Times,* Aug. 4, 1947, Microfilm 795, all HC Papers; *Highlander Fling* 6 (Mar. 1947); *Tennessee Union Farmer* 2 (Feb., Mar., Aug., Sept. 1947); *Union Farmer* 3, 4 (Nov., Dec. 1948, Jan. 1949); *National Union Farmer* 25, 26 (Sept. 1, 1947, Nov. 1948).

25. HFS executive council meeting minutes, June 21–22, 1947, CIO Org. Comm. Papers, Box 147.

26. Annual Report, 1947, 1–2; staff meeting minutes, Aug. 19, 1947, Box 2; Horton to Steve Para, Aug. 6, 1947; list of students, staff, and visitors attending the Farmer-Labor term, Sept. 14–27, 1947; HFS Farmer-Labor Cooperative Association minutes, Sept. 15, 18, 1947, all Box 43; Catherine Winston, news release, Sept. 27, 1947, Box 66, all HC Papers; Horton to Paul Christopher, Aug. 19, 1947, CIO Org. Comm. Papers, Box 147; *Tennessee Union Farmer* 2 (Nov. 1947).

27. Lee Fryer, "Notes on Southern F.U. Meeting, Nashville, Tennessee," Dec. 1–3, 1947, 24–25, HFS Coll., Box 10.

28. Annual Reports, 1948–50, Box 1; Horton to William and Mary Elkuss, Feb. 16, 1950, Box 11; confidential proposal submitted to Brotherhood of Railway Trainmen by National Farmers' Union, Farmers Educational Foundation, and HFS, 1948; Lee Fryer, "Report on the South," ca. May 1949, both Box 43, all HC Papers; *Union Farmer* 3 (Feb., June 1948); *National Union Farmer* 26 (June 1948).

29. Annual Report, 1948, 1; executive council meeting minutes, Jan. 22–23, 1949, Box 1; Lee Fryer, "Operating Guide for the Southern Area," Mar. 1, 1949, Box 42; Ludwig, minutes, "A Meeting of Organizations Interested in Establishing a Cooperative Fertilizer Manufacturing Plant," May 4, 1947, Box 43, all HC Papers; Fryer, "Report on the South"; *Tennessee Union Farmer* 2 (June, Aug., Sept., Nov. 1947); *Union Farmer* 3, 4 (Aug. 1948, Feb. 1949); *National Union Farmer* 26, 27, 28 (Apr. 1948, Feb., Dec. 1949, Jan. 1950).

30. Fryer, "Operating Guide for the Southern Area."

31. Annual Reports, 1950, 1951, Box 1; Catherine Winston, "Report on Altoona Project," Feb. 24, 1950; Horton to Robert and Kay Levin, Mar. 14, 1950, both Box 44, all HC Papers; Fryer, "Report on the South"; *Union Farmer* 4 (Apr., May 1949); *National Union Farmer* 27, 28 (May, Nov. 1949, Jan., Feb., June, July, Dec. 1950).

32. Horton to E. B. Reed, June 16, 1949, HC Papers, Box 43. See also executive council meeting minutes, Jan. 22–23, 1949, Box 1; Horton to Lange, Sept. 20, 1948, Box 42; Patton to Horton, Feb. 28, 1947, Box 43, all HC Papers; *National Union Farmer* 28 (Jan., Mar. 1950).

33. Horton to Ludwig, Jan. 11, 1949; Horton to Fryer, Mar. 17, 1949, both HC Papers, Box 42; Theodore Saloutos, "Agricultural Organizations and Farm Policy in the South after World War II," *Agricultural History* 53 (Jan. 1979): 377–404; Tontz, "Membership in General Farmers' Organizations," 155–56; Crampton, *National Farmers Union,* 193, 209.

34. Horton to Russell Smith, June 16, 1949, HC Papers, Box 42; "Farmers Union Left-Wing Program Put on Display at Clanton," *Alabama: The News Magazine of the Deep South* 14 (Dec. 9, 1949): 5, 10–11.

35. Ludwig to C. E. Huff, Mar. 30, 1952, Horton Papers, Box 4. See also Horton to James E. Payne, June 14, 1948, HC Papers, Box 43; *National Union Farmer* 28 (Sept. 1950); Crampton, *National Farmers Union,* 50, 160.

36. Ludwig, interview with author; Ludwig, Cobb interview; A. I. Horton, "Highlander, 1932–61," 207–8, 233–36.

37. "Report from the Mountains," 1–2; Annual Reports, 1948, 1949; executive council meeting minutes, Nov. 29–30, 1949, Box 1; staff meeting minutes, July 28, Aug. 27, 29, 1948, Box 2; Mary L. Elkuss to William Rafsky, Jan. 22, 1948, Box 59; flier advertising Southern States CIO Leadership Training Term, Sept. 19–Oct. 2, 1948; Elkuss, report on CIO term, ca. Oct. 2, 1948; George Guernsey to Horton, Oct. 12, 1948, all Box 60, all HC Papers; Horton to HFS interim committee, ca. Apr. 29, 1949, CIO Org. Comm. Papers, Box 147; *CIO United,* Fifth Annual CIO Southern School, 1948, HFS Coll., Box 12.

38. "Report from the Mountains," 5; Annual Reports, 1948–53; executive council meeting minutes, Dec. 8–9, 1952, all Box 1; Jean Krainock to Ludwig, Aug. 16, 1948; yearly progress report, Film Center, Oct. 1949–Sept. 1950; Horton, "Proposal for Film Center Unit and Highlander Permanent Staff Agreement," ca. Apr. 1951; activities report, Film Center, Oct. 1, 1953–Apr. 30, 1954, all Box 44, all HC Papers; yearly progress report, Film Center, Jan. 24–Sept. 30, 1949, HFS Coll., Box 5; *Union Farmer* 4 (May 1949).

39. Report of 1945 Activities, 5–6; Annual Reports, 1947–53; executive council meeting minutes, Jan. 22–23, 1951, Dec. 8, 1952, Box 1; staff meeting minutes, July 28, 1948, Box 2; Creighton, report on HFS community participation, ca. Jan. 1949; report of the HFS Community Program, Jan.–July 1949; Nursery and Community Report, Sept. 30, 1950–Mar. 31, 1951; Aimee Horton, notes on interview with Joey (Creighton) Willimetz, July 11, 1963, all Box 65, all HC Papers; 1946 Program Report, 5; Horton to interim committee, HFS executive council, Sept. 27, 1948, CIO Org. Comm. Papers, Box 147; Joanna Creighton Willimetz, "How Come Me To Be Here?" *Wellesley Alumnae Magazine* (Oct. 1949).

40. Mary Elkuss to Charles Wilson and Alton Lawrence, Feb. 11, 1948, HC Papers, Box 59.

41. Horton and Danenburg quoted in executive council meeting minutes, Jan. 22–23, 1949, HC Papers, Box 1. See also financial reports, 1946–51, Box 3; Horton to prospective donors, ca. 1949; Horton to Elizabeth Wisner (form letter), Oct. 1950, both Box 44; St. Louis *Post-Dispatch,* June 20, 1949; *Christian Science Monitor,* Mar. 8, 1951; Minneapolis *Star,* Apr. 11, 1951, all Microfilm 795, all HC Papers; "Highlander Folk School," *New World Commentator* (Dec. 1949): 12–16, HFS Coll., Box 16; *Highlander Fling* 6 (June 1948).

42. The most extensive analyses of the CIO's expulsion of Communist-dominated unions are Harvey A. Levenstein, *Communism, Anticommunism, and the CIO* (Westport, Conn.: Greenwood Press, 1981), 208–329; Cochran, *Labor and Communism,* 248–315; Max M. Kampelman, *The Communist Party vs. the C.I.O.: A Study in Power*

Politics (New York: Frederick A. Praeger, 1957); and Steve Rosswurm, ed., *The CIO's Left-Led Unions* (New Brunswick, N.J.: Rutgers Univ. Press, 1992). See also David M. Oshinsky, "Labor's Cold War: The CIO and the Communists," in *The Specter: Original Essays on the Cold War and the Origins of McCarthyism,* ed. Robert Griffith and Athan Theoharis (New York: New Viewpoints, 1974), 116–51; John A. Fitch, "The CIO and Its Communists," *Survey* 85 (Dec. 1949): 642–47; Brody, *Workers in Industrial America,* 223–29; Lichtenstein, *Labor's War at Home,* 233–45; Honey, "Industrial Unionism and Racial Justice," 148–51; Lawrence Rogin, interview with James A. Cavanaugh, May 2, 1978, Textile Workers Union of America Oral History Project, State Historical Society of Wisconsin.

43. Brownie Lee Jones, Southern School for Workers, to Horton, Nov. 7, 1950; Horton to Jones, Nov. 13, 1950, both HC Papers, Box 4; Jones to Mason, Nov. 2, 1948, Mason Papers; Mason to Horton, June 10, 1950, Horton Papers, Box 3; Norman Markowitz, "A View from the Left: From the Popular Front to Cold War Liberalism," in *The Specter,* 103–15; Rogin, Cavanaugh interview; Levenstein, *Communism, Anticommunism, and the CIO,* 330–40; Cochran, *Labor and Communism,* 312–22; Krueger, *And Promises to Keep,* 179–87, 191; Robert Bendiner, "Surgery in the C.I.O.," *Nation* 169 (Nov. 12, 1949): 458–59; Atlanta *Constitution,* Feb. 26, 1950.

44. Horton to George Mitchell, Dec. 16, 1948, HC Papers, Box 21.

45. Horton to Paul Christopher, Apr. 13, 1948, CIO Org. Comm. Papers, Box 147.

46. Horton to George Mitchell, Dec. 16, 1948, HC Papers, Box 21. See also staff meeting minutes, July 29, 1948, Box 2; Horton, interview on *Cross Section USA,* Columbia Broadcasting System, Feb. 14, 1948, Box 66, both HC Papers; Horton to Christopher, Oct. 31, 1947; Christopher to Horton, Nov. 3, 1947; Horton to HFS executive council members, Apr. 13, 1948; Horton to interim committee, HFS executive council, Nov. 6, 1948, all CIO Org. Comm. Papers, Box 147; A. I. Horton, "Highlander, 1932–61," 201; Goldfield, "Race and the CIO," 13–18; Honey, *Southern Labor and Black Civil Rights,* 214–36; Griffith, *Crisis of American Labor,* xiv–xv, 152–54, and elsewhere.

47. Executive council meeting minutes, Jan. 22–23, 1949, HC Papers, Box 1.

48. Horton to George Mitchell, Mar. 17, 1949, HC Papers, Box 21.

49. Ruttenberg to Horton, July 5, 1949, Horton Papers, Box 3.

50. Ruttenberg to Horton, Aug. 19, 1949, Horton Papers, Box 3. See also memorandum, Horton to executive council members, Sept. 1949, HC Papers, Box 41; Horton to Guernsey, May 31, 1949; Guernsey to Horton, June 14, 1949; A. L. Lewis to Horton, July 7, 14, 1949; Lewis to Guernsey, July 7, 1949; Horton to Ruttenberg, Aug. 1, 1949; Horton to George Mitchell, Aug. 29, 1949, all Horton Papers, Box 3.

51. Horton to Ruttenberg, Aug. 26, 1949, Horton Papers, Box 3.

52. Memorandum, Horton to executive council members, Sept. 1949, HC Papers, Box 41. See also Horton to Gladys Dickason, Sept. 5, 1949; Horton to Roger Baldwin, Sept. 5, 13, 1949; Horton to Christopher, Sept. 5, 1949; Horton to Aubrey Williams, Sept. 10, 1949; Horton, "Notes on Conversation with Anthony Smith," ca. Nov. 1949, all Horton Papers, Box 3.

53. Christopher to Ruttenberg, Aug. 30, 1949, CIO Org. Comm. Papers, Box 147.

54. Baldwin to Horton, Sept. 9, 1949, Horton Papers, Box 3. See also George S. Mitchell to Horton, Aug. 3, 1949, Box 21; Tom White to Horton, Sept. 18, 1949, Box 28; Charles C. Webber to Ruttenberg, Sept. 3, 1949, Box 29, all HC Papers; Horton to Baldwin, Sept. 13, 23, 1949; Kermit Eby to Horton, Sept. 14, 1949; Baldwin to Horton, Sept. 16, 1949; Fleming James to Horton, Nov. 18, 1949, all Horton Papers, Box 3.

55. Executive council meeting minutes, Nov. 29–30, 1949, HC Papers, Box 1. See also Statement of Purpose, Program and Policy, Nov. 29, 1949, Box 1; Horton, comments on CIO controversy, ca. 1949, Box 41, both HC Papers; draft statement enclosed in Horton to Paul Christopher, Nov. 24, 1949, CIO Org. Comm. Papers, Box 147; Salmond, *Miss Lucy of the CIO*, 151–52.

56. Executive council meeting minutes, Nov. 29–30, 1949 (revised version, incorrectly dated 1950), HFS Coll., Box 5.

57. Executive council meeting minutes, Apr. 3, 1950, HC Papers, Box 1; Horton to Mason, Dec. 24, 1949; Mason to Horton, Jan. 4, 1950 (incorrectly dated 1949); Horton to Guernsey, Jan. 7, 1950; Horton to Baldwin, Jan. 16, 1950; Horton to Williams, Feb. 13, 1950; Horton to J. Lewis Henderson, Feb. 13, 25, 1950; Henderson to Horton, Feb. 19, Mar. 5, 1950; Henderson to Mason, Feb. 26, 1950; Mason to Williams, Mar. 17, 1950; staff meeting minutes, Mar. 29, 1950; Horton to Hilda W. Smith, Mar. 30, 1950; Mason to Ruttenberg and Guernsey, Apr. 7, 1950, all Horton Papers, Box 3; Statement of Purpose, Program and Policy, Apr. 3, 1950, HFS Coll., Box 5; Horton, Frederickson interview; Rogin, Finger interview; Rogin, Cavanaugh interview.

58. Staff meeting minutes, Mar. 29, 1950; Horton to E. K. Bowers, Apr. 6, 1950, both Horton Papers, Box 3.

59. Horton to Mason, June 21, 1950, Horton Papers, Box 3. See also Annual Report, 1950, 2; Horton to Fleming James, Apr. 6, 1950; Horton to Hilda W. Smith, Apr. 6, 1950; Ruttenberg to Baldanzi, May 10, 1950, all Horton Papers, Box 3; *CIO News*, May 22, 1950.

60. Horton to Hugh H. Clegg, Dec. 10, 1950, HC Papers, Box 33.

61. Horton to HFS supporters, Feb. 1951, HC Papers, Box 33.

62. Quotations from Hoover's marginal comments on memorandum, D. M. Ladd to The Director, Feb. 23, 1951, *FBI File on HFS*. Other declassified documents reveal that the FBI's subsequent standard response to inquiries about Highlander was to report that while it once had Communist party members on its staff and welcomed Communists as students, "the school has never offered courses of instruction in communist matters nor has the communist element ever completely controlled the institution." FBI, confidential report on Highlander Folk School, Mrs. Miles [*sic*] Horton, and Mr. Miles [*sic*] Horton, Apr. 27, 1956; confidential note to SAC [Special Agent in Charge], Knoxville bureau, Feb. 4, 1958; confidential memorandum to U.S. Legal Attache, Bonn [Germany], June 29, 1961; memorandum, F. J. Baumgardner to W. C. Sullivan, July 26, 1963, *FBI File on HFS*.

63. Executive council meeting minutes, Jan. 22–23, Nov. 19–20, 1951, Box 1; Horton to Guernsey, Oct. 9, 1950; Horton to Sen. Estes Kefauver, Oct. 11, 1950; Hugh H. Clegg to Horton, Jan. 3, 1951; Horton to J. Howard McGrath, Jan. 31, 1951; J. Edgar Hoover to Baldwin, Feb. 26, 1951; St. Louis *Post-Dispatch*, Mar. 5, 21,

1951; notes on community meeting, Mar. 7, 1951; Horton's talk to community residents, Mar. 7, 1951; Peyton Ford to Rep. Adam Clayton Powell, Jr., Mar. 20, 1951; Horton to Herbert Monte Levy, Mar. 24, Apr. 14, June 5, 1951; Levy to Horton, Mar. 29, 1951; Levy to Hoover, Apr. 18, 1951; Hoover to Levy, Apr. 20, 1951; memorandum, Horton to interim committee, HFS executive council, June 7, 1951, all Box 33; Raymond B. Bragg to Morley Wolfe, June 7, 1951, Box 77; New York *Daily Compass,* Mar. 18, 1951; St. Louis *Post-Dispatch,* Mar. 19, 1951, both Microfilm 795, all HC Papers.

64. Annual Reports, 1950–53; announcements and lists of staff and students, CIO Schools for the South, 1950, 1951; *News: From the CIO Upper South Summer School,* nos. 1, 3, 4 (June 22–28, 1952); Bulletin 5, Tennessee Area CIO School, June 26, 1953, all Box 60; report on Religion and Labor workshop, Sept. 25, 1950, Box 61; Horton, report to council members and participants, International Problems Conference, Apr. 2, 1950; announcement, conference on U.S. Labor and World Affairs, ca. Dec. 8, 1951, Box 78; *Advance,* Nov. 15, 1951, Microfilm 795, all HC Papers; Joanna Willimetz, program highlights, Oct. 1951–Mar. 1952, HFS Coll., Box 6; "How-To-Do-It," *Highlights: A Newsletter for Organizations,* no. 6 (July–Aug. 1950): 5–6; *CIO News,* July 13, 1953; Horton, interview with author, Aug. 9, 1978.

65. Annual Report, 1951, 1; Christopher to Horton, July 3, 1951; Horton to Christopher, Aug. 9, 1951, both Box 9; "Highlander's Relation to UPWA Educational Department," ca. Dec. 10, 1951, Box 74; *Packinghouse Worker* 10 (Oct. 1951), Microfilm 795, all HC Papers; Horton to Ralph Helstein, Dec. 10, 1951; Helstein to Horton, Dec. 31, 1951, both UPWA Papers, Box 75; John Hope II, *Equality of Opportunity: A Union Approach to Fair Employment* (Washington, D.C.: Public Affairs Press, 1956), 1–2, 5–7, 16–19, 85–86, 100–102, 105; Theodore V. Purcell, *The Worker Speaks His Mind: On Company and Union* (Cambridge: Harvard Univ. Press, 1953), 64–73; Catherine Winston, "Workers' Education: New Style," *Nation* 173 (Nov. 17, 1951): inside front cover; Hope, "The Self-Survey of the Packinghouse Union: A Technique for Effecting Change," *Journal of Social Issues* 9 (1953): 28–36; Goldfield, "Race and the CIO," 18–20; Horton, interview with author, Aug. 9, 1978. See also Jeff Zacharakis-Jutz, "Straight to the Heart of a Union, Straight to the Heart of a Movement: Workers' Education in the United Packinghouse Workers of America, 1951–1953" (Ph.D. diss., Northern Illinois University, 1991); Rick Halpern, "Interracial Unionism in the Southwest: Fort Worth's Packinghouse Workers, 1937–1954," in *Organized Labor in the Twentieth-Century South,* 158–82.

66. Winston, "Workers' Education."

67. "Highlander's Relation to UPWA Educational Department"; Horton, HFS proposal to United Packinghouse Workers, ca. 1952, UPWA Papers, Box 347. See also Annual Reports, 1951, 1952; memorandum, Horton to UPWA district directors, Jan. 8, 1952; "Copy of Approved Agreement" between HFS and UPWA, ca. Mar. 1952, both Box 74; Federated Press release in San Francisco newspaper, Nov. 16, 1951, Microfilm 795, all HC Papers; memorandum, Horton to executive council, committee members, and sponsors, Oct. 29, 1951, CIO Org. Comm. Papers, Box 147; memorandum, Horton to UPWA educational representatives, ca. Apr. 1952, UPWA Papers, Box 347; Kermit Eby, "The 'Drip' Theory in Labor Unions," *Antioch Review* 13 (Spring 1953): 95–102.

68. *Proceedings, Eighth Constitutional Convention of the United Packinghouse Workers of America, CIO,* Denver, Colo., May 12–16, 1952, 123–28, quotation 124, HFS Coll., Box 10. See also Annual Report, 1952, 1–3; *Eighth Constitutional Convention, UPWA-CIO: Officers Report,* Denver, Colo., May 12–16, 1952, 45–51; memorandum, Horton to UPWA educational representatives, Mar. 6, 1952; UPWA Education Dept., *Instructor's Manual No. 1 for Steward Training,* ca. 1952; *Instructor's Manual No. 2 for Steward Training,* ca. 1952, all Box 74; *Packinghouse Worker,* Feb., ca. May 1952, Microfilm 795, all HC Papers; Horton, 1952 Progress Report, UPWA-CIO Education Dept., 1–4, HFS Coll., Box 10.

69. Annual Report, 1952, 2–3. See also Horton, reports to Ralph Helstein, Sept., Nov. 1952; Hy Kornbluh, resume of procedures and methods in instructor program, Oct. 30, 1952; "Instructor Training Program, UPWA-CIO: Developing the Instructor Program in a Local," Dec. 12, 1952, all HC Papers, Box 74; Horton, "Educational Dept. Report to Helstein: Analysis of Methods Used in UPWA Schools and Examples of Results," ca. Aug. 1952; Horton, 1952 Progress Report, UPWA-CIO Education Dept., 2–5, both HFS Coll., Box 10.

70. *Labor Stuff* 1 (Apr. 1952): 1, 11, HC Papers, Box 5.

71. Horton to Jordan Stokes III, July 2, 1952; Patrick E. Gorman to Horton, July 10, 1952; Horton to Gorman, Dec. 19, 1952, all Box 5; Ernest C. Smith to Russell Lasley, Aug. 7, 1952, Box 74; Gorman to Horton, Mar. 28, 1951; Horton to Russell Bull, June 28, 1952; Horton to Gorman, July 2, 1952; "The Proof!" [UPWA response to Amalgamated charges], ca. summer 1952; Max Semenick, UPWA local president, Indianapolis, response to questionnaire on UPWA education program, ca. Dec. 27, 1952, all Box 75, all HC Papers; Lasley to Horton, Feb. 18, June 6, 1952; Horton to Lasley, Feb. 26, June 30, 1952, all UPWA Papers, Box 347; Hope, *Equality of Opportunity,* 122.

72. Stephens to Horton, Oct. 21, 1952, UPWA Papers, Box 347.

73. Horton to Ralph Helstein, Sept. 29, 1952; Adrian O. McKinney to Horton, Oct. 2, 1952; Horton to McKinney, Oct. 8, 1952; Horton to Hy Kornbluh, Mar. 27, July 9, Sept. 16, Dec. 18, 1952, all HC Papers, Box 74; Horton to A. T. Stephens, Oct. 14, Nov. 19, 1952; Stephens to Horton, Aug. 19, 1952, all UPWA Papers, Box 347; Eby, "The 'Drip' Theory," 97.

74. Executive council meeting minutes, Dec. 8–9, 1952, HC Papers, Box 1; Grover R. Hathaway, UPWA, notes taken at HFS executive council meeting, Dec. 9, 1952, UPWA Papers, Box 303.

75. Horton to Goodwin Watson, May 2, 1953, HFS Coll., Box 10.

76. Annual Report, 1953, 4, 9–10; Horton, special report to executive council members, Nov. 11, 1953, 1–5, Box 1; Horton to Christopher, Oct. 27, 1953, Box 41; Horton to Ralph Helstein, Jan. 26, Mar. 14, 1953; memoranda, Horton to UPWA educational staff, Jan. 29, ca. Mar. 1953; Horton to Hy Kornbluh, Mar. 23, 1953, all Box 74; schedule of International Staff School, Feb. 28–Mar. 6, 1953, Box 75; *Packinghouse Worker,* Mar. 1953, Microfilm 795, all HC Papers; Hope, *Equality of Opportunity,* 110–12.

77. Horton to Christopher, Oct. 27, 1953, HC Papers, Box 41.

78. Horton to Barbara Wertheimer, Dec. 15, 1953, HC Papers, Box 41; Horton to William Stix, Nov. 23, 1953, HC Papers, Box 48; Christopher to Horton, Aug. 22, 1953; Horton to Christopher, Sept. 14, Dec. 3, 1953, all Christopher Papers, Box 2.

79. Annual Report, 1952, 4, 8; financial report, Oct. 1, 1951–Sept. 30, 1952, Box 3; Zilphia Horton to [?], ca. Feb. 1952, Box 15; Joanna Willimetz to Mrs. Louis S. Weiss (form letter), Mar. 10, 1952, Box 44; Willimetz, "Reports and Suggestions: To Committees and Areas Where New Committees Are Being Established," Apr. 1952, Box 45; news release, ca. Feb. 13, 1952, Box 66, all HC Papers; Willimetz, program highlights, Oct. 1951–Mar. 1952, HFS Coll., Box 6; Nashville *Tennessean,* Feb. 14, 15, 1952.

80. Horton to "Bill" (form letter), Apr. 2, 1953, HC Papers, Box 46.

81. Zilphia Horton quoted in G. Thomas, "Hear the Music Ringing," 41.

82. Executive council meeting minutes, Dec. 9, 1952, HC Papers, Box 1. See also Annual Report, 1953, 3; Horton to Maxwell Hahn, Jan. 7, 1953, HC Papers, Box 49; Horton to J. L. Maloney (form letter), Mar. 27, 1953, Christopher Papers, Box 2; Horton, interview with author, Aug. 9, 1978; "Adventures of a Radical Hillbilly," 21; Egerton, *Speak Now Against the Day,* 567–68.

7. From School Desegregation to Student Sit-Ins, 1953–1961

1. Report of special executive council meeting, Apr. 27–28, 1953, HC Papers, Box 1.

2. Carl T. Rowan, *South of Freedom* (New York: Alfred A. Knopf, 1952), 205–6. See also Horton, interview with author, Aug. 9, 1978; Aimee Horton, "The Highlander Folk School: Pioneer of Integration in the South," *Teachers College Record* 68 (Dec. 1966): 242–43.

3. Report of special executive council meeting, Apr. 27–28, 1953. See also news release, May 1, 1953, HC Papers, Box 66; Grover R. Hathaway, notes on special session of HFS executive council, Apr. 27, 1953, UPWA Papers, Box 303; "Adventures of a Radical Hillbilly," 21; Horton, interview with author, Aug. 9, 1978.

4. "A Summary of Workshop on the Supreme Court Decision and the Public Schools with Selected Resource Materials, July 12–18, 1953," HC Papers, Box 78. See also Annual Report, 1953, 4, 7; *Report from Highlander,* Dec. 1953, 2–3, Box 1; Horton to Brandeis Workers Education Fund (form letter), June 22, 1953, Box 49; news release, July 20, 1953, Box 66; "Notes on How One Community Started," July 12–Aug. 8, 1953, Box 67; pamphlet, *Highlander Announces Summer Workshops on Supreme Court Decisions and the Public Schools, July 12–Aug. 8, 1953, Aug. 9–15, 1953*; lists of participants, workshops on the Supreme Court Decisions and the Public Schools, July 12–Aug. 8, Aug. 9–15, 1953, all Box 78, all HC Papers; Horton to Christopher, May 20, 27, 1953, Christopher Papers, Box 2; Horton and Septima Clark, "The Human Frontiers in the Southern Mountains," *Journal of Human Relations* 6 (Summer 1958): 86–87.

5. *Report from Highlander,* 1–3. See also Annual Report, 1953, 4; list of films previewed by students, 1953, Box 44; "Working Toward Integrated Public Schools in Your Own Community: A Guide to Action," July 12–Aug. 8, 1953; "On Use of Filmstrip: *The High Cost of Segregation,*" ca. 1953; report on "Teachers and Integration of the Public Schools," Aug. 9–15, 1953, all Box 78, all HC Papers; "Summary of Workshop on the Supreme Court Decision"; summary of workshop sessions, July 20–25, 1953,

Labadie Collection, Subject VF, ff. Highlander Folk School, Dept. of Rare Books and Special Collections, Univ. of Michigan Library, Ann Arbor.

6. Horton, special report to executive council members, Nov. 11, 1953, 7, HC Papers, Box 1.

7. Annual Reports, 1953, 1954; memorandum, Horton to executive council members, Dec. 16, 1953; executive council meeting minutes, Feb. 15–16, 1954, both Box 1; Horton to Henry Shipherd, Apr. 12, 1954; Elizabeth K. Shipherd to John B. Thompson, Aug. 17, 1954, both Box 26; Horton to George and Bee Wolfe, Apr. 1, 1954, Box 34; Horton to Ralph Tefferteller, Oct. 13, 1954, Box 47; "News from Highlander," Sept. 30, 1954, Box 66, all HC Papers.

8. Horton to Tefferteller, June 10, 1954, HC Papers, Box 47. See also Horton to John Wesley Dobbs, June 3, 1954, HC Papers, Box 10; Richard Kluger, *Simple Justice: The History of Brown v. Board of Education and Black America's Struggle for Equality* (New York: Alfred A. Knopf, 1976), 700–714; Harvard Sitkoff, *The Struggle for Black Equality, 1954–1992*, rev. ed. (New York: Hill and Wang, 1993), 21–23; Robert H. Brisbane, Black *Activism: Racial Revolution in the United States, 1954–1970* (Valley Forge, Pa.: Judson Press, 1974), 23–24.

9. Annual Report, 1954, 1.

10. "A South Carolina Public School Teacher Tells Her People about Highlander," Sept. 1, 1954, HC Papers, Box 78. See also Annual Report, 1954, 2; Tuskegee *Herald,* July 13, 1954, Box 16; Henry Shipherd to Nicholas Roosevelt, Aug. 27, 1954, Box 48; pamphlet, *Highlander Workshop: The Supreme Court Decision on Segregation in the Public Schools, June 27–July 4, 1954;* "Summary of Discussions on Goals and Procedures for Community Action on the Supreme Court Decision on Segregation in the Public Schools Workshop, June 27–July 4, 1954"; list of participants, workshop on segregation, June 27–July 4, 1954; news release, July 7, 1954; "Suggested Community Workshop Procedures Discussed at the Supreme Court Decision on Segregation in the Public Schools Workshop," July 12, 1954; excerpts of letters from Nancy Gough to Horton, July 12, 1954; James Carey, report on HFS, ca. July 1954, all Box 78, all HC Papers; audio recording, workshop on the Supreme Court Decision on Segregation in the Public Schools, June 29, 1954, Highlander Research and Education Center Tape Collection, 515A/144, State Historical Society of Wisconsin (hereinafter cited as HC Tape Coll.).

11. Clark to "Biddie" [Julie Mabee], May 17, 1955, HC Papers, Box 9. See also data sheet and list of civic, educational, and religious activities of Septima P. Clark, ca. Sept. 1957, Box 3; Clark to Horton, July 22, 1954, Box 9, both HC Papers; Clark, *Echo in My Soul,* 12–121; Clark, interview with author, Charleston, S.C., Nov. 24–25, 1980. See also Grace Jordan McFadden, "Septima Clark and the Struggle for Human Rights," in *Women in the Civil Rights Movement: Trailblazers and Torchbearers, 1941–1965,* ed. Vicki L. Crawford, Jacqueline Anne Rouse, and Barbara Woods (Bloomington: Indiana Univ. Press, 1993), 85–97; Cynthia Stokes Brown, ed., *Ready from Within: Septima Clark and the Civil Rights Movement* (Trenton, N.J.: Africa World Press, 1990), 85–102, 114–18.

12. "Summary of Discussions and Projects Which Developed out of Workshop on World Problems, the United Nations and You," Aug. 1–8, 1954, HC Papers, Box 78.

13. "Excerpts from Tape Recordings of Discussions during 1954 Workshop on the United Nations," HFS Coll., Box 15. See also Annual Report, 1954, 2; Clark, notes on workshop on United Nations problems, Aug. 1–5, 1954; list of participants, Workshop on World Problems, the United Nations and You, Aug. 1–8, 1954; news release, Aug. 9, 1954, all Box 78, all HC Papers; "Summary of Discussions and Projects"; audio recordings, Workshop on World Problems, the United Nations and You, Aug. 1–8, 1954, HC Tape Coll., 515A/151, 152, 155; pamphlet, *Highlander Workshop on World Problems, the United Nations and You*, Aug. 1–8, 1954, HFS Coll., Box 15; Clark, interview with author; Avrahm G. Mezerik, "Experiment in the South," *Nation* 179 (Nov. 27, 1954): 465; Clark, *Echo in My Soul*, 121; Guy and Candie Carawan, eds., *Ain't You Got a Right to the Tree of Life? The People of Johns Island, South Carolina—Their Faces, Their Words and Their Songs* (New York: Simon and Schuster, 1966; rev. ed., Univ. of Georgia Press, 1989), 168 (page numbers from first edition).

14. Horton, notes on speech to teachers conference, Wilmette (Ill.) public schools, Sept. 1954, HC Papers, Box 39.

15. Annual Reports, 1953–55; executive council meeting minutes, Mar. 26–27, 1955, Box 1; financial reports, 1952, 1954; analysis of cash balance for the year ended Sept. 30, 1955, all Box 3; Horton to George and Bee Wolfe, Apr. 1, 1954, Box 34; Henry Shipherd to Morris Lasker, Dec. 6, 1954, Box 47; Shipherd to Howard Wolf, Mar. 10, 1955; Horton and Shipherd, fundraising form letter, Mar. 10, 1955, both Box 48; Horton and Shipherd to Maxwell Hahn, Jan. 26, 1955, Box 49, all HC Papers.

16. Executive council meeting minutes, Mar. 26–27, 1955, HC Papers, Box 1. See also Henry F. Shipherd, fundraising form letter, Oct. 13, 1954, HC Papers, Box 26.

17. Horton to Harvey O'Connor, Oct. 31, 1955, HC Papers, Box 22.

18. Annual Report, 1955, 4; Horton to Chester Bowles, July 12, 1955, Box 7; transcript of leadership discussion, United Furniture Workers School, June 1955, Box 61; Bernice White [Robinson] to Myles and Zilphia Horton, July 19, 1955, Box 67; announcement and list of participants, the United Nations and You workshop, July 3–9, 1955, Box 78; *Furniture Workers Press*, June 1955, Microfilm 795, all HC Papers; transcript, "1955 United Nations Workshop—Discussion on Setting up a Credit Union on Johns Island," July 3–9, 1955, HFS Coll., Box 15; Bernice Robinson, interview with Eliot Wigginton and Sue Thrasher, Nov. 9, 1980, transcript in Highlander Center library; Clark, *Echo in My Soul*, 121–22.

19. Annual Report, 1955, 1; Florence Singleton, speech to Johns Island Civic Club on desegregation workshop at HFS, July 24–Aug. 3, 1955, Box 67; synopsis of program and list of participants, workshop on desegregation, July 24–Aug. 6, 1955, Box 78, all HC Papers; transcript of general discussion, desegregation workshop, July 25, 1955, Box 3; pamphlet, *Highlander: The South Prepares to Carry out the Supreme Court Decision Outlawing Segregation in Public Schools, July 24–Aug. 6, 1955*, Box 7, both HFS Coll.; Rosa Parks, report on the Montgomery, Ala., passive resistance protest, Mar. 3–4, 1956, Horton Papers, Box 5; Robinson, Wigginton and Thrasher interview; Clark, interview with author; A. Horton, "Pioneer of Integration," 246; Kluger, *Simple Justice*, 716–46.

20. Annual Report, 1955, 1–2; Singleton, speech to Johns Island Civic Club; synopsis of program, workshop on desegregation; "Basic Policies for Presentation to Local School Boards," July 24–Aug. 6, 1955; "Outline of Recommendations for School

Integration," ca. July 1955; "Necessary Education Accompanying Integration," ca. July 1955; news release, Aug. 8, 1955, all Box 78, all HC Papers; *A Guide to Community Action for Public School Integration* (Monteagle, Tenn.: Highlander Folk School, 1955), HFS Coll., Box 7; A. Horton, "Pioneer of Integration," 247–49.

21. Minutes of the joint meeting of the executive council and advisory committee for integration, Oct. 15–16, 1955, HC Papers, Box 1. See also Henry Shipherd to Allan K. Chalmers, Sept. 22, 1955, Box 45; Horton to Tefferteller, Jan. 3, 1956, Box 47; Shipherd to Maxwell Hahn, Oct. 4, 1955; Horton and Shipherd to Hahn, Jan. 26, 1956, both Box 49, all HC Papers; Horton to editor, *New Republic,* Oct. 18, 1955, HFS Coll., Box 5.

22. Martin Luther King, Jr., *Stride toward Freedom: The Montgomery Story* (New York: Harper and Brothers, 1958), 44.

23. Parks quoted in Howell Raines, *My Soul Is Rested: Movement Days in the Deep South Remembered* (New York: Bantam Books, 1978), 35; Virginia Durr to Myles and Zilphia Horton, Jan. 30, 1956, HC Papers, Box 11.

24. Parks to Elizabeth Shipherd, July 6, 1955; Parks to Horton, Feb. 25, 1956; excerpted quotation of Parks at Loop College community workshop, Chicago, May 13, 1970, all HC Papers, Box 22; audio recording, public school integration workshop, Aug. 25, 1956, HC Tape Coll., 515A/176; Parks, report on the Montgomery passive resistance protest; Clark, interview with author; "Adventures of a Radical Hillbilly," 18–19; J. Mills Thornton III, "Challenge and Response in the Montgomery Bus Boycott of 1955–1956," *Alabama Review* 33 (July 1980): 194–96; Sitkoff, *Struggle for Black Equality,* 37–38; Raines, *My Soul Is Rested,* 31–35; King, *Stride toward Freedom,* 43–44; Eugene Pierce Walker, "A History of the Southern Christian Leadership Conference, 1955–1965: The Evolution of a Southern Strategy for Social Change" (Ph.D. diss., Duke Univ., 1978), 8–9; Aldon D. Morris, *The Origins of the Civil Rights Movement: Black Communities Organizing for Change* (New York: Free Press, 1984), 51–52, 148–49.

25. Parks, report on the Montgomery passive resistance protest; Horton, interview with author, New Market, Tenn., Aug. 6, 1982; Sitkoff, *Struggle for Black Equality,* 38–55; Thornton, "Challenge and Response," 196–235; Brisbane, *Black Activism,* 33–41; Walker, "History of SCLC," 8–30; King, *Stride toward Freedom,* 44–174; Raines, *My Soul Is Rested,* 33–44; Morris, *Origins of the Civil Rights Movement,* 17–25, 52–55; David Levering Lewis, *King: A Biography,* 2d ed. (Urbana: Univ. of Illinois Press, 1978), 47–84; Adam Fairclough, *To Redeem the Soul of America: The Southern Christian Leadership Conference and Martin Luther King, Jr.* (Athens: Univ. of Georgia Press, 1987), 15–18. See also Jo Ann Gibson Robinson, *The Montgomery Bus Boycott and the Women Who Started It* (Knoxville: Univ. of Tennessee Press, 1987); Mary Fair Burks, "Trailblazers: Women in the Montgomery Bus Boycott," in *Women in the Civil Rights Movement,* 71–83; Fairclough, "The Preachers and the People: The Origins and Early Years of the Southern Christian Leadership Conference, 1955–1959," *Journal of Southern History* 52 (Aug. 1986): 403–40; David J. Garrow, *Bearing the Cross: Martin Luther King, Jr., and the Southern Christian Leadership Conference* (New York: W. Morrow, 1986), 11–82; Taylor Branch, *Parting the Waters: America in the King Years, 1954–63* (New York: Simon and Schuster, 1988), 128–205.

26. Clark to Horton, Mar. 15, 1957, Box 9; Virginia Durr to Horton, Feb. 18, 1956; Durr to Myles and Zilphia Horton, Feb. 24, 1956; Horton to Durr, Feb. 29,

Nov. 7, 1956, all Box 11; Parks to Horton, Feb. 25, 1956; Progressive Civic League, Detroit, to "Fellow Citizens," ca. June 12, 1960, both Box 22; Stewart Meacham to Horton, May 19, 1956; Horton to Charlotte Meacham, Feb. 16, 1957, both Box 47, all HC Papers; Clark, interview with author; Clark, interview with Jacquelyn Hall, July 25, 1976, Southern Oral History Program, SHC.

27. Minutes of planning conference on public school integration workshops, Mar. 3–4, 1956; notes on advisory committee meeting, Mar. 4, 1956, both HC Papers, Box 79.

28. Horton to "Mike and Camille" [Ross], June 25, 1956, HC Papers, Box 54; Attending Physician's Statement, Mrs. Myles Horton, Apr. 9, 1956; Certificate of Death, Zilphia Horton, Apr. 11, 1956, both ZHP, Box 15; Myles Horton, notes on Zilphia, ca. 1986–87, MHP, Box 4.

29. Horton, interview with Bill Olson, *Working Papers for Ryegrass School* 1 (May 1979). See also *Highlander Reports,* July 1956, 2, HC Papers, Box 1; Horton to Connie Burden, Aug. 4, 1957, Horton Papers, Box 2.

30. Clark, interview with author; Tom Ludwig to author, Nov. 18, 1986, Mar. 27, 1987; Aleine Austin to author, May 8, 1987; May Justus to author, May 16, 1987; Mary L. Elkuss to author, May 20, 1987; Myles and Charis Horton, telephone conversation with author, May 25, 1987; Joanna and Emil Willimetz to author, June 5, 1987; Catherine W. Male to author, June 10, 1987; Eve Z. Milton to author, June 24, 1987.

31. Henry Shipherd to Geoffrey S. Smith, Jan. 24, 1955, HC Papers, Box 48.

32. Statement read by Horton at staff meeting, Apr. 16, 1956, HC Papers, Box 47. See also Henry Shipherd to Geoffrey S. Smith, Dec. 8, 1954; Shipherd to William Fulton Kurtz, Jan. 12, 1955, both HC Papers, Box 48; Clark, interview with author.

33. "Official Statement Mutually Agreed upon Regarding the Shipherds' Resignation, Apr. 30, 1956," HC Papers, Box 2.

34. Betty Shipherd to Tefferteller, May 9, 1956, Box 47; Horton to Bea Schneiderman, May 3, 1956, Box 45, both HC Papers. See also minutes of emergency meeting of the executive council, Apr. 21, 1956; "Settlement and Release," Apr. 30, 1956; memorandum, Horton to executive council, May 4, 1956, all Box 2; memorandum, Henry and Betty Shipherd to Horton, Apr. 18, 1956, Box 47, all HC Papers.

35. *Highlander Reports,* July 1956, 4; Annual Report, 1956, 3, Box 1; memorandum, Horton to executive council, May 7, 1956, Box 2; news release, June 7, 1956, Box 66; Clark, list of services rendered, May–July 1956, Box 67, all HC Papers; announcement, *Highlander Workshops on Public School Integration, July 15–21, Aug. 5–11, Aug. 19–25, 1956,* HFS Coll., Box 7; Clark, *Echo in My Soul,* 111–18, 168–69; Clark, Hall interview; Clark, interview with author; McFadden, "Septima P. Clark," 89; Brown, *Septima Clark,* 23–42; Branch, *Parting the Waters,* 263–64.

36. Annual Report, 1956, 1, 2.

37. Report of program activities since Oct. 1, 1955, Box 1; reports on integration workshops, July 15–21, Aug. 5–11, Aug. 19–25, 1956, Box 79, all HC Papers; report on passive resistance, Aug. 19–25, 1956, Box 7; Clark, *Champions of Democracy* (Monteagle: Highlander Folk School, 1956), Box 12, both HFS Coll.; reports on integration workshops, 1956, Labadie Coll.

38. Annual Reports, 1956, 1957, Box 1; report on joint executive council and consultants meeting, Jan. 5–6, 1957; Clark, extension report to executive council, Jan.

5–6, 1957, both Box 2; staff report on visit of Clinton students, Dec. 14, 15, 16, 1956, Box 39, all HC Papers; Ludwig, interview with author; Benjamin Muse, *Ten Years of Prelude: The Story of Integration since the Supreme Court's 1954 Decision* (New York: Viking Press, 1964), 92–103; Hugh Davis Graham, *Crisis in Print: Desegregation and the Press in Tennessee* (Nashville: Vanderbilt Univ. Press, 1967), 92–108, 114; Lester C. Lamon, *Blacks in Tennessee, 1791–1970* (Knoxville: Univ. of Tennessee Press, 1981), 100–101.

39. Horton to Theodore and Ona Brameld, Jan. 28, 1957, HC Papers, Box 7. See also executive council meeting minutes, Sept. 25, 1956, Box 2; analysis of fund balance for year ended Sept. 30, 1956, Box 3; Horton to Charlotte Meacham, Feb. 16, 1957, Box 47; Horton to Frederick D. Patterson, Oct. 18, 1956, Box 50; "Summary of September [1956] Meetings at Highlander to Plan for Anniversary Year," Box 79, all HC Papers; evaluation of public school integration workshop, Aug. 25, 1956, HC Tape Coll., 515A/176; budget for the calendar year 1957, Box 6; *Highlander Announces 12 Workshops in 1957 on Public School Integration,* Box 7, both HFS Coll.

40. Report on joint executive council and consultants meeting, Jan. 5–6, 1957. See also Annual Report, 1957, 3–4; Clark, extension report to executive council, Jan. 5–6, 1957; executive council meeting minutes, Jan. 5–6, Apr. 13–14, 1957, Box 2; operating fund income and expenses, fiscal year ended Sept. 30, 1957, Box 3, both HC Papers; memorandum, Horton to executive council members, Feb. 14, 1957, HFS Coll., Box 5; Clark, Hall interview; Sitkoff, *Struggle for Black Equality,* 57–60; Numan V. Bartley, *The Rise of Massive Resistance: Race and Politics in the South During the 1950's* (Baton Rouge: Louisiana State Univ. Press, 1969), 83–85, 143–44.

41. Annual Report, 1957, 2–3; "Summary of Residential and Extension Activities of 1957 and Proposed Program for 1958," Jan. 15, 1958, Box 1; Horton to Aubrey Williams, June 19, 1957, Box 29; notes, workshop on integration, July 1957 (incorrectly dated), Box 78; workshop reports, Jan. 19–25, Feb. 9–15, 1957; Clark, "Southern Negroes' Attitude Is Encouraging," Dec. 5, 1957, all Box 79, all HC Papers; Cortez Puryear, summary of NAACP chapter's accomplishments during 1956 and plans for 1957, ca. Jan. 19–25, 1957, HC Tape Coll., 515A/176; attendance figures for workshops, 1956–59, HFS Coll., Box 6.

42. Program, "The South Thinking Ahead: The Human Aspects of the Integration Struggle," Aug. 30–Sept. 2, 1957, HC Papers, Box 79.

43. Annual Report, 1957, 2; news releases, June 20, Aug. 2, 1957, Box 66; workshop report, "The Implications of Integration for Education," ca. Aug. 30–Sept. 2, 1957, Box 78; "The South Thinking Ahead" seminar schedule; attendance list, twenty-fifth anniversary seminar, Aug. 30–Sept. 2, 1957; workshop reports, Aug. 31–Sept. 2, 1957; news release, Sept. 6, 1957, all Box 79; *New York Times,* July 7, 1957; Nashville *Tennessean,* Sept. 1, 1957, both Microfilm 795, all HC Papers; *The South Looks Ahead: Report on the 25th Anniversary, Highlander Folk School* (Monteagle: Highlander Folk School, [1957 or 1958]), HFS Coll., Box 7.

44. *The South Looks Ahead,* 11.

45. Aubrey Williams, "The South Is Playing with Fire," address delivered at the twenty-fifth anniversary, Sept. 2, 1957, HC Papers, Box 79.

46. Martin Luther King, Jr., "The Look to the Future," address delivered at the twenty-fifth anniversary, Sept. 2, 1957, HC Papers, Box 79.

47. Nashville *Banner,* Aug. 31, Sept. 3, 1957, HC Papers, Microfilm 795.

48. *Highlander Folk School: Communist Training School, Monteagle, Tenn.* (Atlanta: Georgia Commission on Education, 1957), HFS Coll., Box 8. See also *The South Looks Ahead,* 1; John Salmond, "Vanguard of the Civil Rights Movement: The Post New Deal Career of Aubrey Willis Williams," *Historian* 44 (Nov. 1981): 64.

49. Executive council meeting minutes, Jan. 18–19, 1958, HC Papers, Box 2. See also Annual Report, 1958, 4, Box 1; operating fund income and expenses, fiscal years ended Sept. 30, 1958, Sept. 30, 1959, Box 3; Horton to George Mitchell, May 29, 1958, Box 21, all HC Papers.

50. Annual Report, 1959, 1–3, Box 1; executive council meeting minutes, Oct. 2–3, 1959, Box 2; Cobb, vita, ca. 1959, Box 3; Carawan to Friends of Highlander, ca. July–Aug. 1959; Carawan to Horton and Conrad Browne, six-year summary of work in the South, 1965, both Box 37; news release, Sept. 18, 1959, Box 66; Carawan, vita, ca. 1961, Box 92; Carawan, biographical material, Jan. 25, 1967, Box 104, all HC Papers; Guy Carawan, interview with Ron Cohen, Jan. 24, 1991, copy in possession of author; Carawan, interview with author, June 25, 1994.

51. Annual Report, 1959, 2; report on last six months' activities, Aug. 3, 1959, Box 1; Justine Wise Polier to Maxwell Hahn, June 1, 1959, Box 49; Horton to Prynce Hopkins, July 10, 1958, Box 50; news releases, Apr. 12, 1958, Feb. 16, June 12, 1959, Box 66; workshop reports, May 1958, May 1959, Box 79, all HC Papers; Velma Deloris Richberg, "The Highlander Folk School Involvement in the Civil Rights Movement from 1957 to 1961" (M.A. thesis, Fisk Univ., 1973), 15–17.

52. Chattanooga *News-Free Press,* June 19, 1958, HC Papers, Microfilm 795.

53. Annual Reports, 1958, 1959; report on last six months' activities, Aug. 3, 1959; Clark, report on 1958 workshops on Citizenship and Integration, ca. Sept. 1958, Box 1; report on workshop on Registration and Voting, June 21–26, 1959; fundraising report on Eleanor Roosevelt visit, ca. July 1958, both Box 79; Chattanooga *Times,* June 18, 1958; Chattanooga *News-Free Press,* June 18, 1958, both Microfilm 795, all HC Papers.

54. Annual Report, 1959, 2. See also Annual Report, 1958, 3; Clark, report on 1958 workshops; Horton to Carl Tjerandsen, Aug. 2, 1958, Box 51; *M.I.A.* (Montgomery Improvement Association newsletter) 2 (Oct. 7, 1959): 1–2, Box 64; workshop notes and summaries, July 1958, July 1959, all Box 79, all HC Papers.

55. Annual Reports, 1958–60; quarterly report, winter 1960, all Box 1; Horton to new [noncontributing] foundations (form letter), Jan. 27, 1958, Box 49; news releases, Sept. 8, Oct. 12, 1959, Box 66; Horton, notes on problems of migrants, ca. Mar. 1958; notes from audio recording, "Conference on the Problems of Migrants, Sept. 5–7, 1958"; report, "The Citizenship School—an Idea and a Reality," Sept. 1959, all Box 79; reports, Social Needs and Social Resources workshops, Oct. 11–12, Nov. 27–28, 1959, Box 80; *Afro-American,* Sept. 19, 1958, Microfilm 795, all HC Papers.

56. Horton to John B. Thompson, Apr. 7, 1960, HC Papers, Box 28.

57. William H. Chafe, *Civilities and Civil Rights: Greensboro, North Carolina, and the Black Struggle for Freedom* (New York: Oxford Univ. Press, 1980), 71–101; Clayborne Carson, *In Struggle: SNCC and the Black Awakening of the 1960s* (Cambridge: Harvard Univ. Press, 1981), 9–18; Howard Zinn, *SNCC: The New Abolitionists* (Boston: Beacon Press, 1964), 16–32; Raines, *My Soul Is Rested,* 73–104; Sitkoff, *Struggle for Black*

Equality, 61–82; Morris, *Origins of the Civil Rights Movement,* 188–215; Eugene Pfaff, Jr., "Greensboro Sit-ins: Interviews with William Thomas, Elizabeth Laizner, Clarence Malone and Willa Player," *Southern Exposure* 9 (Spring 1981): 23–28; "Nashville Sit-ins—Nonviolence Emerges: Interviews with Marion Barry and John Lewis," *Southern Exposure* 9 (Spring 1981): 30–32.

58. Horton, remarks during class on Nashville sit-ins, Social Needs and Social Resources workshop, Mar. 18–20, 1960, HC Papers, Box 80.

59. Annual Report, 1959, 2; Horton to Lewis W. Jones, Mar. 15, 1960, Box 17; Horton to A. A. Liveright, Mar. 15, 1960, Box 19; Clark to John B. Thompson, Apr. 7, 1959, Box 28; Horton, "Social Adjustments," ca. 1960, Box 40; college workshop reports, 1954, 1958, 1959, Box 78, all HC Papers; Horton, remarks during class on Nashville sit-ins; Morris, *Origins of the Civil Rights Movement,* 147–48.

60. Annual Report, 1960, 2; Nashville *Tennessean,* Apr. 4, 1960; Chattanooga *Times,* Apr. 4, 1960, both HC Papers, Microfilm 795; "The New Generation Fights for Equality," report of the seventh annual college workshop, Apr. 1–3, 1960, 1, 8, HFS Coll., Box 5; Nashville *Tennessean,* Apr. 3, 1960, Horton Papers, Box 7.

61. "New Generation Fights for Equality," 2–4. See also excerpt from audio recording, college workshop, Apr. 1, 1960; transcription of audio recording, college workshop, Apr. 3, 1960, both HC Papers, Box 78; Richberg, "HFS Involvement," 36–39; *Southern Patriot* 18 (June 1960): 3.

62. Transcribed excerpts of college workshop audio recording, general session, Apr. 1–2, 1960, HC Papers, Box 78.

63. "New Generation Fights for Equality," 4–7. See also transcription of audio recording, college workshop, Apr. 3, 1960, Box 78; Nashville *Tennessean,* Apr. 4, 1960, Microfilm 795, both HC Papers; Nashville *Tennessean,* Apr. 3, 1960, Horton Papers, Box 7; Richberg, "HFS Involvement," 35, 37–39; Branch, *Parting the Waters,* 263.

64. Annual Report, 1961, 4, Box 1; "Random Notes by Myles Horton on Singing and Music at Highlander," ca. 1961, Box 13; Carawan, six-year summary of work in the South, 1965, Box 37, all HC Papers; G. Thomas, "Hear the Music Ringing," 41–44; Maggie Lewis, "Guy and Candie Carawan: Song Leaders for Social Change," *Christian Science Monitor,* Sept. 2, 1982, 3–4; Carawan, interview with author, June 25, 1994.

65. Annual Report, 1960, 3; Carawan, six-year summary of work in the South; "We Will Overcome," *People's Songs* 5 (Sept. 1948): 8; Bob Smith, "The Making of a Folk Song: 1963," unidentified newspaper, Aug. 31, 1963; Knoxville *News-Sentinel,* Aug. 30, 1968, all Box 69, all HC Papers; Robert E. Smith, "We Shall Overcome: Where the Civil Rights Anthem Came From," *Southern Courier,* Jan. 22, 1966, Highlander Papers, Ser. 2, Box 4; pamphlet, Candie and Guy Carawan, *Highlander Center: An Approach to Culture and Social Change,* n.d., Highlander Center library; "Moment of History," *New Yorker* 41 (Mar. 27, 1965): 37–38; G. Thomas, "Hear the Music Ringing," 44–45; David King Dunaway, *How Can I Keep from Singing: Pete Seeger* (New York: McGraw-Hill, 1981), 222–23; Bradley Rentzel, "The Highlander Idea: A History of Its Development, 1932–1972" (M.D. thesis, Union Theological Seminary, 1973), 48–50. See also Guy and Candie Carawan, "Protest Music," *Southern Exposure* 22 (Fall 1994): 64; Carawan, "'Freedom in the Air': An Overview of the Songs of the Civil Rights Movement," *Black Music Research Bulletin* 12 (Spring 1990): 1–4; Bernice Johnson Reagon, "The Lined Hymn as a Song of Freedom," ibid., 4–7.

66. Carawan, six-year summary of work in the South; Smith, "We Shall Overcome"; "Moment of History," 37–38; Carson, *In Struggle,* 19–25, 28–29, 157, 186; Zinn, *SNCC,* 32–35; Sitkoff, *Struggle for Black Equality,* 82–87; Raines, *My Soul Is Rested,* 104–6; Morris, *Origins of the Civil Rights Movement,* 215–21; Branch, *Parting the Waters,* 290–93; Kenneth B. Clark, "The Civil Rights Movement: Momentum and Organization," *Daedalus* 95 (Winter 1966): 258–60; Archie E. Allen, "John Lewis: Keeper of the Dream," *New South* 26 (Spring 1971): 15–16, 20, 23; Adam Fairclough, "The Southern Christian Leadership Conference and the Second Reconstruction, 1957–1973," *South Atlantic Quarterly* 80 (Spring 1981): 180–81; Charles Payne, "Ella Baker and Models of Social Change," *Signs* 14 (Summer 1989): 885–99.

67. Executive council meeting minutes, July 21–22, 1960, HC Papers, Box 2.

68. Horton to Willard Uphaus, Apr. 30, 1960, HC Papers, Box 28.

69. Horton quoted in news release, Aug. 20, 1960, HC Papers, Box 66. See also memorandum, Horton to executive council members, May 1, 1960, Box 2; staff meeting minutes, July 21, 24, 1960; Horton, personal notes, Jan. 1961, all Box 3; Horton to John B. Thompson, Apr. 7, 1960, Box 28, all HC Papers; unedited draft of executive council meeting minutes, July 21–22, 1960, HFS Coll., Box 5; Horton, interview with author, Aug. 9, 1978.

70. *Southern Patriot* 18 (Sept. 1960): 4. See also Annual Report, 1960, 2; news release, June 1, 1960, Box 66; excerpt from audio recording, "The Place of the White Southerner" workshop, May 25, 1960, Box 80; Chattanooga *Times,* May 27, 1960, Microfilm 795, all HC Papers; audio recordings, "The Place of the White Southerner" workshop, May 25–28, 1961, HC Tape Coll., 515A/194, 199; reports on "The Place of the White Southerner" workshop, May 25–28, 1960, HFS Coll., Box 4; *New Agenda for the White Southerner*; Richberg, "HFS Involvement," 40–46.

71. Annual Report, 1961, 2; news release, Nov. 17, 1960, Box 66; "Highlander Workshop," New South Writer's Service, ca. Nov. 15, 1960; Judith P. Gregory to "Pat," Nov. 15, 1960; Gregory, notes on "The Place of Non-violent Direct Action (Including Civil Disobedience) in the Current Struggle in the South," ca. Nov. 15, 1960, all Box 78; *Sewanee Purple,* Nov. 16, 1960; *Catholic Worker,* Dec. 1960, both Microfilm 795, all HC Papers; *Considerations by Southern White Students of Their Roles in the Struggle for Democracy in the South* (Monteagle, Tenn.: Highlander Folk School, 1961), HFS Coll., Box 12; Richberg, "HFS Involvement," 46–49; *Southern Patriot* 19 (Jan. 1961): 4.

72. Annual Report, 1961, 2; Ernestine Brown to Clark, Apr. 14, 1961, Box 5; Clark to S. S. Seay, June 2, 1960, Box 25; Jane Stembridge to Anne Lockwood, Nov. 20, 1960, Box 26; report and list of participants, "New Frontiers" workshop, Apr. 7–9, 1961; "Freedom Riders Who Have Been at Highlander, 1960–1961," all Box 78; Clark to Ella Baker, June 14, 1960, Box 79, all HC Papers; notes on audio recording from college workshop, Apr. 8, 1961 (incorrectly dated), Highlander Papers; Richberg, "HFS Involvement," 61–63.

73. Annual Report, 1960, 2–3; tabulation of enrollment, fiscal year ending Sept. 30, 1960, Box 1; news release, July 29, 1960, Box 66; workshop announcements, June, July, Aug. 1960, Boxes 79, 80; Nashville *Banner,* July 1, 1960; Chattanooga *Times,* July 1, 30, 1960, all Microfilm 795, all HC Papers.

74. Annual Report, 1960, 3; Horton to Jane Lee Eddy, July 1, 1960, Box 51; prospectus, Summer Youth Project, July 6–Aug. 16, 1960; Lewis W. Jones and Herbert Haberland, "The 1960 Highlander Folk School Youth Project: Observations and Appraisal," 1–3, both Box 84, all HC Papers.

75. Annual Reports, 1960, 1961; Jones and Haberland, "The 1960 HFS Youth Project," 19, 82, 93, 95; Horton, report to executive council members, ca. June 21, 1961, Box 2; Youth Project Budget, July 6–Aug. 16, 1960, Box 3; Horton to Harry Belafonte, July 21, 1961, Box 6; Horton to Adolph Hirsch, Sept. 17, 1960, Box 51; Belafonte, fundraising letter, June 1, 1960; Anne Lockwood to Bess Barrows, July 19, Aug. 22, 1960, all Box 52; news releases, July 13, 22, 1960, Box 66; student evaluations, 1960 Youth Project; list of participants, Youth Project, July 1–Aug. 12, 1961, all Box 84; Chattanooga *Times,* Aug. 19, 1960, July 23, 1961; Knoxville *Journal,* July 23, 1960; Nashville *Banner,* Aug. 17, 1960, all Microfilm 795, all HC Papers; Nashville *Tennessean,* Aug. 18, 1960; *Afro-American,* Sept. 24, 1960; Chattanooga *Times,* Nov. 16, 1960, all HFS Coll., Box 14; "Most Hated School in the South," *Sepia* (Oct. 1962): 20–23.

76. Shuttlesworth quoted in news release, Feb. 27, 1961, HC Papers, Box 66. See also Annual Report, 1961, 2; staff meeting minutes, Oct. 3, 27, Dec. 5, 1960, Box 3; news release, Jan. 17, 1961, Box 66; Horton to Lewis Killion, Feb. 8, 1960; workshop announcements and notes, Jan., Feb. 1961, all Box 80, all HC Papers; notes of audio recording, beauticians' workshop, Jan. 15–17, 1961, Highlander Papers; A. I. Horton, "Highlander, 1932–61," 310–13; Richberg, "HFS Involvement," 51–60.

77. Annual Report, 1961, 3; Horton to "friend of Highlander," Mar. 1, 1961; announcement and list of participants, New Agenda workshop, May 5–7, 1961, all HC Papers, Box 80; Richberg, "HFS Involvement," 63–65.

78. Carawan, six-year summary of work in the South; "Freedom Riders Who Have Been at Highlander"; Carson, *In Struggle,* 33–37; Zinn, *SNCC,* 40–57; Sitkoff, *Struggle for Black Equality,* 88–103; Raines, *My Soul Is Rested,* 114–38; Brisbane, *Black Activism,* 52–57.

79. Annual Report, 1961, 1, 3; memorandum, Anne Lockwood to staff, July 20, 1961; proposed agenda, SNCC executive committee meeting, Aug. 11–13, 1961, both Box 71; Chattanooga *Times,* Oct. 10, 1961, Microfilm 795, all HC Papers; Ella Baker, interview with Eugene Walker, Sept. 4, 1974, Southern Oral History Program, SHC; Carson, *In Struggle,* 37–42; Zinn, *SNCC,* 57–59; Sitkoff, *Struggle for Black Equality,* 103–6; Lewis, *King,* 136–37; Branch, *Parting the Waters,* 485–87.

80. Morris, *Origins of the Civil Rights Movement,* 139–57.

8. The Citizenship Schools, 1953–1961

1. Horton, interview with author, Aug. 6, 1982; Carl Tjerandsen, *Education for Citizenship: A Foundation's Experience* (Santa Cruz, Calif.: Emil Schwarzhaupt Foundation, 1980), 139–40, 149–50; "Reading, Writing, and Voting," *Southern Exposure* 10 (Sept./Oct. 1982): 28.

2. Proposed report for Project for Leadership Training for Local Communities in the South, ca. Mar. 1953, HC Papers, Box 39. See also "Need for Participation in Dealing with Community Problems," ca. 1953; "The Reasons and Needs for Developing Democratic Community Leaders," ca. 1953, both Box 39; summary and application to the Schwarzhaupt Foundation, ca. Mar. 1953; Leo Gerngross to Horton, June 4, 1953, both Box 51, all HC Papers; Tjerandsen, *Education for Citizenship,* 141–44; Horton, interview with author, Aug. 6, 1982.

3. Leadership Training Program staff meeting minutes, Sept. 31–Oct. 1, 1953, HC Papers, Box 39.

4. Ibid., Dec. 11–12, 1953.

5. Summary report, Community Leadership Training Program, Dec. 1953; Leadership Training Program staff meeting minutes, Sept. 28, Sept. 31–Oct. 1, Oct. 8, 15, Nov. 20, 21, Dec. 11–12, 1953, all Box 39; Mabee, report on Community Leadership Training Program in Monteagle, Tenn., begun in Aug. 1953, Box 40; Horton to Carl Tjerandsen, Oct. 6, 1953, Feb. 4, 1955, Box 51, all HC Papers; Horton, interview with author, Aug. 6, 1982; Tjerandsen, *Education for Citizenship,* 144–46.

6. Notes on Community Leadership Training Program, ca. 1954, HC Papers, Box 39. See also Horton to Carl Tjerandsen, Dec. 9, 1954; Horton to Leo Gerngross, Apr. 30, 1956, both HC Papers, Box 51.

7. Horton to Robert J. Blakely, Mar. 26, 1955; Horton, report on meeting with Tom Ludwig regarding Greeneville and Kodak, Dec. 25–26, 1954; Julie Mabee, report on conference with Ludwig, Apr. 17, 1955; Index of Developments in Kodak, July 23, 1955; Ludwig, "Why Kodak Built a Community Organization," Dec. 31, 1955, all Box 39; Horton to Leo Gerngross, Apr. 30, 1956, Box 51, all HC Papers; Horton, interview with author, Aug. 6, 1982; Tjerandsen, *Education for Citizenship,* 146–47.

8. Horton to Leo Gerngross, Apr. 30, 1956, HC Papers, Box 51. See also Annual Report, 1956, 3; Index of Developments in Kodak; Ludwig, "Why Kodak Built a Community Organization"; Mabee, report on conference with Ludwig, Apr. 17, 1955; Ludwig, notes on Kodak project, ca. Apr. 24, 1955, Box 39; notes on conversations with Horton on Sevier County projects, Apr. 23, 1959, Box 40; conversation between Horton and Ludwig, Dec. 25, 1955, Box 43; Horton to Tjerandsen, Oct. 5, 1955, Nov. 1, 1956, Feb. 16, 1957, all Box 51, all HC Papers; "Highlights from letters and reports by Myles Horton, Tom Ludwig and Harry Greene" on Kodak project, May 31, 1955; Horton, report on Knoxville, Washington College, and Kodak, Tenn., trip, Oct. 6–9, 1955; evaluation of Kodak project, ca. 1955, all HFS Coll., Box 2; Horton, interview with author, Aug. 6, 1982.

9. Horton to Leo Gerngross, Apr. 30, 1956, HC Papers, Box 51.

10. Annual Report, 1955, 2–3; Index of Developments in Kodak; notes on conversations with Horton on Sevier County projects; Horton to Tjerandsen, July 23, Oct. 5, Nov. 5, 1955, all Box 51; report on Community Leadership workshop, Aug. 28–Sept. 3, 1955, Box 78, all HC Papers; tentative outline for an analysis of a Rural Community Leadership Training Program, Feb. 1955; comments on tentative outline, 1955, both HFS Coll., Box 2; Horton, interview with author, Aug. 6, 1982; Tjerandsen, *Education for Citizenship,* 148–49.

11. Horton to Leo Gerngross, Apr. 30, 1956, Box 51; Clark, notes on Johns Island, South Carolina, ca. 1956; "Island Lore," enclosed in Clark to Horton, Mar. 29, 1955, both Box 67, all HC Papers; Horton, field trip report, Charleston and Johns Island, S.C., Dec. 11, 12, 13, 1954, Box 3; excerpts from tape recordings of discussions during 1954 workshop on United Nations, Box 15, both HFS Coll.; program, "Esau Jenkins: A Retrospective View of the Man and His Times. An Exhibit and Seminar, Feb. 5–29, 1984," sponsored by the Avery Institute of Afro-American History and Culture, the College of Charleston, and the South Carolina State Museum, MHP, Box 10; Clark, *Echo in My Soul,* 51, 137–38; Mary A. Twining and Keith E. Baird, "Introduction to Sea Island Folklife," *Journal of Black Studies* 10 (June 1980): 387–416; Cynthia Stokes Brown, "Literacy as Power," *Radical Teacher,* no. 8 (May 1978): 10; Brown, *Septima Clark,* 104–10; Richard A. Couto, *Ain't Gonna Let Nobody Turn Me Round: The Pursuit of Racial Justice in the Rural South* (Philadelphia: Temple Univ. Press, 1991), 120–22.

12. Notes on Esau Jenkins, ca. 1966, Box 55; summary of Community Leadership Training activities involving Esau Jenkins, Johns Island, S.C., through Mar. 1955, Box 67; Charleston *News and Courier,* July 28, 1968, Microfilm 795, all HC Papers; excerpts from tape recordings during 1954 workshop on United Nations; Horton, interview with author, Aug. 6, 1982; Carawan, *Ain't You Got a Right,* 158–59, 163–64, 172–73; Tjerandsen, *Education for Citizenship,* 150–51; Septima Poinsett[e] Clark and Mary A. Twining, "Voting Does Count: A Brief Excerpt from *A Fabulous Decade,*" *Journal of Black Studies* 10 (June 1980): 445–46; Brown, *Septima Clark,* 42–47; Couto, *Ain't Gonna,* 122–27.

13. Transcript of audio recording, "Highlander Folk School—Background," ca. Dec. 1959, Box 34; Clark, untitled MS on Citizenship Schools, Jan. 7, 1960, Box 67; Charleston *News and Courier,* July 28, 1968, Microfilm 795, all HC Papers; Carawan, *Ain't You Got a Right,* 160–63, 167; Tjerandsen, *Education for Citizenship,* 151–52; Clark, *Echo in My Soul,* 135–37; Brown, "Literacy as Power," 10–11; interview transcript, Esau Jenkins on organizing Progressive Club, 1962 SNCC workshop, MHP, Box 13; Robinson, Wigginton and Thrasher interview. Excerpts of this interview have been published in "Reading, Writing, and Voting," 28–29.

14. "Highlander Folk School—Background"; summary of activities involving Jenkins; Jenkins to Horton, Sept. 20, 1954, HC Papers, Box 67; Horton, field trip report, Charleston and Johns Island, Dec. 11–13, 1954, HFS Coll., Box 3; Clark, *Champions of Democracy*; Robinson, Wigginton and Thrasher interview; Clark, interview with author; Carawan, *Ain't You Got a Right,* 168, 170; Tjerandsen, *Education for Citizenship,* 152–53; Morris, *Origins of the Civil Rights Movement,* 150; Couto, *Ain't Gonna,* 127–28.

15. Horton, field trip report, Charleston and Johns Island, Dec. 11–13, 1954, HFS Coll., Box 3.

16. List of staff activities since Oct. 1, 1954, Box 1; Horton to Tjerandsen, June 1, 4, 1955; Horton to Leo Gerngross, Apr. 30, 1956, all Box 51; reports and correspondence regarding trips to Johns Island, Nov. 1954–Dec. 1955, Box 67, all HC Papers; evaluation sheet for Johns Island, Dec. 1954; "Report of Myles' Trip to the Sea Islands," Jan. 30, 1958, both Box 3; Clark, report on meetings on Wadmalaw and Johns Island, May 28, 29, 1955, Box 5, all HFS Coll.; Jerome D. Franson, "Citizenship Education in the South Carolina Sea Islands, 1954–1966" (Ph.D. diss., George

Peabody College for Teachers, 1977), 48–50; Clark, interview with author; Horton, interview with author, Aug. 6, 1982; Tjerandsen, *Education for Citizenship*, 152–55.

17. Jenkins to Horton, Apr. 28, 1955, HC Papers, Box 67. See also Horton to Tjerandsen, Mar. 28, 1955, Box 51; Horton, report on the Feb. 28–Mar. 4 [1955] trip to Charleston and Johns Island; Horton, conference with Clark, Mar. 18, 1955; Horton, conference on Leadership Training, Charleston, Mar. 19, 1955; notes on trip to Charleston and Johns Island, May 24–26, 1955; Index of Developments on Johns Island, July 22, 1955; transcript of conversation between Justine Wise Polier, Clark and Horton, May 1959, 10–13, all Box 67, all HC Papers; Tjerandsen, *Education for Citizenship*, 153–57; Clark, interview with author; Horton, interview with author, Aug. 6, 1982.

18. Horton to Tjerandsen, June 1, July 11, 1955, Mar. 1, 1956; report from Clark, July 14, 1955, all Box 51; report on planning meeting for series of workshops in Charleston County, Oct. 19, 1955; Clark to Horton, Jan. 8, 1956; notes on Johns Island workshop, Feb. 5, 1956, all Box 67; mimeographed booklet, "Materials on a Highlander Workshop," 1958, 9–10, Box 78, all HC Papers; Index of Developments on Johns Island, July 22, 1955; meeting to plan workshop, Dec. 3, 1955, HFS Coll., Box 3; Tjerandsen, *Education for Citizenship*, 157–59; Franson, "Citizenship Education," 51–52; Clark, interview with author.

19. Clark to Horton, Sept. 14, 1955, HC Papers, Box 67. See also executive council meeting minutes, Mar. 26–27, 1955, Box 1; Horton, notes on crisis situations, Feb. 5, 1955, Box 39; Clark, report on special meeting at the Methodist Center, May 29, 1955; Clark to Horton, Jan. 8, 1956; "Johns Island Civic Club—Leadership Training Program: Bench-mark Facts and Observations," ca. 1955; Clark, comments on Esau Jenkins's Civic Club meeting, Jan. 2, 1956, all Box 67, all HC Papers; Jenkins to Horton, Aug. 19, 1956, HFS Coll., Box 5; Tjerandsen, *Education for Citizenship*, 153–55, 158; Franson, "Citizenship Education," 55–56; Clark, interview with author; Horton, interview with author, Aug. 6, 1982.

20. Horton to Leo Gerngross, Apr. 30, 1956, Box 51; Horton, notes on Johns Island residence school, ca. 1955–56, Box 67, both HC Papers; Tjerandsen, *Education for Citizenship*, 159–60; Franson, "Citizenship Education," 64–68.

21. Clark, "Summary of Residential and Extension Activities of 1957"; Leo Gerngross to Horton, July 18, 1956; Horton to Tjerandsen, Feb. 16, 1957, both Box 51; transcript of meeting concerning the beginning of the Johns Island School, ca. June 30, 1957, Box 67, all HC Papers; Clark, untitled MS on Citizenship Schools; Clark, interview with author; Franson, "Citizenship Education," 68–70; Clark, *Echo in My Soul*, 138–39; Tjerandsen, *Education for Citizenship*, 160–61.

22. Conversation between Polier, Clark, and Horton, 20–21; Clark, *Echo in My Soul*, 139–42; Horton and Dorothy Cotton, "Citizenship Schools," in *Roots of Open Education in America: Reminiscences and Reflections,* ed. Ruth Dropkin and Arthur Tobier (New York: City College Workshop Center for Open Education, 1976), 111–12; Robinson, Wigginton and Thrasher interview; Brown, *Septima Clark*, 48–49.

23. Horton to Tjerandsen, Feb. 16, 1957, HC Papers, Box 51; Robinson, Wigginton and Thrasher interview; Clark, interview with author; Clark, *Echo in My Soul*, 147–51; Tjerandsen, *Education for Citizenship*, 161, 163; Franson, "Citizenship Education," 70–71; Brown, *Septima Clark*, 50–51.

24. Conversation between Polier, Clark, and Horton, 6–8; Clark, untitled MS on Citizenship Schools; Franson, "Citizenship Education," 71–73; Clark, *Echo in My Soul*, 147–50, 152–53, 155; Tjerandsen, *Education for Citizenship*, 161–63; Robinson, Wigginton and Thrasher interview.

25. Quotations from Horton to Tjerandsen, Feb. 16, 1957, HC Papers, Box 51.

26. Accounts of the first adult school on Johns Island have become more dramatic and occasionally less clear with the passage of time. At some point, either Horton or the students decided that it was more appropriate to call the literacy education program the Citizenship School program. Accounts also differ on the number of students who registered to vote in February 1958. Annual Report, 1957, 3; Clark, "Summary of Residential and Extension Activities of 1957"; transcript of meeting concerning the beginning of the Johns Island school; Clark, untitled MS on Citizenship Schools; Clark, *Echo in My Soul*, 153–54; Franson, "Citizenship Education," 74; Tjerandsen, *Education for Citizenship*, 162–63; Morris, *Origins of the Civil Rights Movement*, 151–53; Brown, "Literacy as Power," 12; Robinson, Wigginton and Thrasher interview; Clark, interview with author.

27. Charleston *News and Courier*, Mar. 11, 12, 1959, HC Papers, Microfilm 795.

28. Justine Wise Polier to Maxwell Hahn, June 1, 1959, Box 49; Horton to Tjerandsen, Aug. 2, 1958, May 18, 1959, Box 51; report on Sea Island Programs, Jan.–July 1959, Box 67, all HC Papers; conversation between Polier, Clark, and Horton, 1–3; Tjerandsen, *Education for Citizenship*, 163–64; Franson, "Citizenship Education," 84–85; Robinson, Wigginton and Thrasher interview.

29. Horton to Maxwell Hahn, Oct. 29, 1958, HC Papers, Box 49.

30. "The Sea Island Citizenship Project," ca. June 1958, HC Papers, Box 38; conversation between Polier, Clark, and Horton, 11–12; Clark, untitled MS on Citizenship Schools; "Report of Myles' Trip to the Sea Islands"; Tjerandsen, *Education for Citizenship*, 164–68; Clark, *Echo in My Soul*, 156–59, 161–66; Horton and Cotton, "Citizenship Schools," 113–14; Franson, "Citizenship Education," 86–88.

31. "Sea Island Citizenship Project"; Horton to Tjerandsen, May 7, Aug. 2, 1958, Box 51; Alice Cobb, report on Sea Island Citizenship Project, ca. June 1960, Box 67, all HC Papers; Clark, untitled MS on Citizenship Schools; audio recording, Clark reporting on Sea Island activities, ca. Mar. 1959, HC Tape Coll., 807A/12; Robinson, Wigginton and Thrasher interview; Tjerandsen, *Education for Citizenship*, 163, 167–70; Franson, "Citizenship Education," 75–78; Clark, *Echo in My Soul*, 157–59, 162–63, 166.

32. Recorded figures on enrollment in these Citizenship Schools vary. Annual Reports, 1959, 1960; tabulation of enrollment, Citizenship Classes, Oct. 1960–June 1961, Box 34; Alleen S. Brewer, factual report of adult school, Edisto Island, S.C., Mar. 27, 1961, Box 38; news release, Mar. 10, 1960, Box 66; reports on Citizenship Schools, 1958–60; Mrs. H. L. Leonard to Horton, Nov. 16, 1960, all Box 67, all HC Papers; Clark, *Echo in My Soul*, 150, 160–61; Tjerandsen, *Education for Citizenship*, 167–68.

33. Annual Reports, 1959, 1960; "Highlander Folk School—Background"; Carawan, report of work with adult school program, S.C. Sea Islands, 1960–61, Box 8; Cobb, Consumer Education Project proposal, ca. Jan. 1960, and report, Apr. 21, 1960, both Box 41; news release, Jan. 12, 1960, Box 66; report on Sea Island Programs, Jan. 1–July 1959; Carawan, "Spiritual Singing in the South Carolina Sea Islands," ca. Feb.

1960, both Box 67, all HC Papers; Clark, *Echo in My Soul,* 196–205; Franson, "Citizenship Education," 79–80; Carawan, *Ain't You Got a Right,* 10; Tjerandsen, *Education for Citizenship,* 162, 168; Cobb, "Residential Workshops: The Case for Them," *Adult Leadership* 9 (Mar. 1961): 281; Carawan, interview with author, June 25, 1994.

34. Annual Reports, 1959, 1961; special report on Charleston, S.C., and Sea Island activities, ca. 1961, Box 1; edited transcript of audio recording of Highlander Center board of directors meeting, 1965, Box 2, all HC Papers; Robinson, Wigginton and Thrasher interview; Carawan, *Ain't You Got a Right,* 169; Franson, "Citizenship Education," 80–81, 83–84; Clark, *Echo in My Soul,* 160; Tjerandsen, *Education for Citizenship,* 167–69.

35. Jenkins quoted in Carawan, *Ain't You Got a Right,* 168. See also edited transcript, Highlander Center board meeting, 1965; summary of programs and enrollments, 1953–61, Box 1; information about Esau Jenkins, ca. 1966, Box 55; J. Palmer Gaillard, Jr., to Jenkins, Apr. 25, 1961, Box 67; Charleston *News and Courier,* June 18, 1960, Microfilm 795, all HC Papers; Horton, memorandum on Citizenship School Training Program, Dec. 1960, HFS Coll., Box 2; Franson, "Citizenship Education," 82, 84.

36. Conversation between Polier, Clark, and Horton, 22.

37. Annual Report, 1959, 3; executive council meeting minutes, July 21–22, 1960, Box 2; progress report on the Citizenship School Program, Jan. 27, 1961, Box 67, both HC Papers; audio recording, Polier, Clark, and Horton, conversation on Sea Islands projects, May 19, 1959, HC Tape Coll., 515A/46.2; Franson, "Citizenship Education," 89–91; "Literacy—Louisiana Style," *New Republic* 140 (Mar. 9, 1959): 9; Henry Lee Moon, "The Negro Voter," *Nation* 191 (Sept. 17, 1960): 155–57.

38. Annual Report, 1960, 3; tabulation of enrollment, Citizenship Classes, Oct. 1960–June 1961, Box 34; Clark to Horton, ca. Oct. 6, 1960; Horton to Clark, Oct. 6, 1960; Clark to Hosea L. Williams, Dec. 6, 1960, all Box 38, all HC Papers; Clark, "Recent Developments in 'The Citizenship School Idea,'" Sept. 25, 1960; memorandum on Citizenship Program, June 26, 1961, both HFS Coll., Box 2; Tjerandsen, *Education for Citizenship,* 173–74; Franson, "Citizenship Education," 91–92; Clark, interview with author.

39. Progress report on the Citizenship School Program; Horton, memorandum on Citizenship School Training Program, Dec. 1960, HFS Coll., Box 2; memorandum, Anne Lockwood to B. R. Brazeal, Aug. 30, 1961, Horton Papers, Box 1; Robinson, Wigginton and Thrasher interview.

40. Annual Report, 1961, 2; staff meeting minutes, Apr. 24, 1961, Box 3; progress report on the Citizenship School Program; progress report, HFS, Mar. 15, 1961; selection of teachers for Citizenship Schools, ca. 1961; Clark to Dorothy Cotton, Mar. 19, Apr. 20, 1961, all Box 38; James L. Macanic to Clark, report of Feb. 13–18 workshop, Mar. 4, 1961; Clark, report on training workshop, Mar. 13–18, 1961, both Box 67; partial transcript of experimental workshop, Jan. 19–21, 1961; Clark and Bernice V. Robinson, report on training leaders for Citizenship Schools, Apr. 10–15, 1961, both Box 80, all HC Papers; audio recording, experimental workshop on adult education, Jan. 21, 1961, HC Tape Coll., 515A/207.1; mimeographed booklet, "Highlander Folk School Citizenship School Training Program," Nov. 1960; tabulation of enrollment, citizenship training and refresher workshops, Nov. 1960–June 1961, both Box 2;

report on workshop on training leaders for Citizenship Schools, Jan. 19–21, 1961, Box 4, all HFS Coll.; Franson, "Citizenship Education," 93–96; Tjerandsen, *Education for Citizenship,* 176–78; A. I. Horton, "Highlander, 1932–1961," 286–91.

41. Annual Report, 1961, 2; news release, May 4, 1961, HC Papers, Box 66; tabulation of enrollment, citizenship training and refresher workshops; Bernice Robinson, reports on training leaders for Citizenship Schools workshop, June 16–18, July 17–23, 1961; memorandum on Citizenship Program, June 26, 1961, all HFS Coll., Box 2; Clark, *Echo in My Soul,* 212–13.

42. Staff meeting minutes, May 8, 1961, Box 3; Horton to Maurice McCrackin, ca. June 1961, Box 20; Horton to Justine Wise Polier, Nov. 8, 1960, Box 23; tabulation of enrollment, Citizenship Classes, Oct. 1960–June 1961, Box 34; John Reilly to Horton, Sept. 13, 1960; Horton to Charlie Fisher, May 12, 1961, both Box 38; excerpt from newsletter, Montgomery Improvement Association, Mar. 15, 1961, Box 64; Operation Freedom fundraising letter, Jan. 1961, Box 65, all HC Papers; memorandum on Citizenship Program, June 26, 1961; pamphlet, *Tent City: "Home of the Brave"* (Washington: Industrial Union Department, AFL-CIO, [1961]), Highlander Papers, Ser. 3, Box 2; Clark, interview with author; *Southern Patriot* 18, 25 (Dec. 1960, Nov. 1967); Lamon, *Blacks in Tennessee,* 85–87, 102–4; Graham, *Crisis in Print,* 20, 190–91; Richard A. Couto, *Lifting the Veil: A Political History of the Struggles for Emancipation* (Knoxville: Univ. of Tennessee Press, 1993), 185–206 and elsewhere; Couto, *Ain't Gonna,* 247–48.

43. Tabulation of enrollment, Citizenship Classes; Horton, report on Savannah, Ga., trip, Jan. 7, 1961; Hosea Williams to Clark, Feb. 9, 1961; memorandum, Horton to Jane Lee Eddy, ca. Apr. 1961, all Box 38; Horton to Eddy, May 15, 1961, Box 51; lists of workshop participants and training leaders for Citizenship Schools, Feb. 13–18, Mar. 13–18, Apr. 10–15, 1961, Box 80, all HC Papers; memorandum on Citizenship Program, June 26, 1961; Tjerandsen, *Education for Citizenship,* 178–80.

44. Tjerandsen, *Education for Citizenship,* 180–81; Clark, "Literacy and Liberation," *Freedomways* 4 (Winter 1964): 118–19.

45. Executive council meeting minutes, July 28–29, 1961, Box 2; memorandum on SCLC-HFS financial agreements, Dec. 1, 1960; Anne Lockwood and Clark, report on discussions with Jim Wood and Dorothy Cotton re Citizenship School, Jan. 30, 1961; Clark to Cotton, Apr. 20, 1961, all Box 38; news release, May 4, 1961, Box 66, all HC Papers; pamphlet, *Southern Christian Leadership Conference Launches Leadership Training Program,* ca. Oct. 1960, HFS Coll., Box 2; memorandum, Lockwood to B. R. Brazeal, Aug. 30, 1961, Horton Papers, Box 1; Cotton, interview with Eliot Wigginton and Sue Thrasher, June 20, 1981, copy in Highlander Center library, published in part in "To Make the World We Want," *Southern Exposure* 10 (Sept./Oct. 1982): 25–31; Horton, interview with author, Aug. 6, 1982; Tjerandsen, *Education for Citizenship,* 181–82; Walker, "History of SCLC," 89–90.

46. *New York Times,* Feb. 23, 1961, Box 17; Pittsburgh *Courier,* Mar. 11, 1961, Box 38; Nashville *Banner,* Feb. 23, 1961; Chattanooga *Times,* Feb. 23, 1961; Chattanooga *News-Free Press,* Feb. 23, 1961, all Microfilm 795, all HC Papers.

47. Horton, report to executive council members, ca. June 21, 1961; "Items for Consideration at the July 28–29 Executive Council Meeting," July 24, 1961; execu-

tive council meeting minutes, July 28–29, 1961, all Box 2; Herman Long to Horton, May 25, 1961; Wood to Hotchkiss, June 6, 1961; Citizenship School Committee meeting minutes, June 8, 1961; Horton to Hotchkiss, June 26, 1961; Hahn to Hotchkiss, July 13, 1961, all Box 38, all HC Papers; memorandum, Anne Lockwood to B. R. Brazeal, Aug. 30, 1961, Horton Papers, Box 1; Horton, interview with author, Aug. 6, 1982; Couto, *Ain't Gonna*, 245–46.

48. Young to Robert Spike, Apr. 25, 1961, HC Papers, Box 30.

49. Annual Report, 1961, 2; Horton, report to executive council members, ca. June 21, 1961, Box 2; staff meeting minutes, May 8, 1961, Box 3; Young to Horton, June 20, 1961; Citizenship School Committee meeting minutes, June 8, July 12, 1961; Horton to Clark, June 12, 1961, all Box 38; Horton to Charles Jones, May 23, 1961, Box 67, all HC Papers; Clark, interview with Eugene Walker, July 30, 1976, Southern Oral History Program, SHC; Robinson, Wigginton and Thrasher interview; Cotton, Wigginton and Thrasher interview; Young, interview with Eliot Wigginton, July 8, 1981, copy in Highlander Center library; Horton, interview with author, Aug. 6, 1982; Clark, *Echo in My Soul*, 213, 215; David J. Garrow, *The FBI and Martin Luther King, Jr.: From "Solo" to Memphis* (New York: W. W. Norton, 1981), 28–29; Branch, *Parting the Waters*, 575–76; Andrew Young, *A Way Out of No Way: The Spiritual Memoirs of Andrew Young* (Nashville: Thomas Nelson, 1994), 49–53.

50. Memorandum, Clark to Anne Lockwood, Horton, and Alice Cobb, ca. Nov. 18–20, 1960, HC Papers, Box 80.

51. Clark and Robinson to Horton, June 19, 1961, Horton Papers, Box 1.

52. Horton to B. R. Brazeal, May 30, 1961, Box 34; Horton to Clark, June 12, 1961; Horton to Maxwell Hahn, June 19, 1961, both Box 38; news release, May 29, 1961, Box 66; Chattanooga *News-Free Press*, May 29, 1961, Microfilm 795, all HC Papers; Clark to Horton, May 4, June 29, July 3, 1961; memorandum, Horton to staff, June 21, 1961; Horton to Clark, June 21, 1961; Horton to Robinson, June 21, 28, 1961; Robinson to Horton, June 25, 1961; memorandum, Lockwood to Brazeal, Aug. 30, 1961, all Horton Papers, Box 1; Clark, interview with author; Horton, interview with author, Aug. 6, 1982.

53. Annual Report, 1961, 4; executive council meeting minutes, July 28–29, 1961, Box 2; Robinson to Dorothy Cotton, Aug. 1, 1961, Box 38, all HC Papers; Horton to Clark, July 3, 1961; memorandum, Lockwood to Brazeal, Aug. 30, 1961, both Horton Papers, Box 1; Clark, Walker interview; Horton, interview with author, Aug. 6, 1982; Morris, *Origins of the Civil Rights Movement*, 236–38; Fairclough, *To Redeem the Soul of America*, 68–70, 169; McFadden, "Septima P. Clark," 90–94; Garrow, *Bearing the Cross*, 149–64; Branch, *Parting the Waters*, 576–77, 588. See also Couto, *Ain't Gonna*, 128, 243–47.

54. Quotation from Young, Wigginton interview. See also tabulation of enrollment, Extension Program in Citizenship and Community Leadership Development, 1953–1961, Box 1; R. Elizabeth Johns, *Refinement by Fire* (Atlanta: SCLC Citizenship Education Program, 1965), Box 9; Horton to Esau Jenkins, Aug. 1, 1961, Box 67, all HC Papers; Clark, Hall interview; Clark, Walker interview; Clark, interview with author; Cotton, Wigginton and Thrasher interview; Horton and Cotton, "Citizenship Schools," 104–7; Franson, "Citizenship Education," 97.

55. Summary of programs and enrollments, 1953–61, HC Papers, Box 1. See also Sandra B. Oldendorf, "Highlander Folk School and the South Carolina Sea Island Citizenship Schools: Implications for the Social Sciences" (Ph.D. diss., Univ. of Kentucky, 1987); Oldendorf, "The South Carolina Sea Island Citizenship Schools, 1957–1961," in *Women in the Civil Rights Movement*, 169–82.

56. "An Interview with Myles Horton," *Concern* 15 (Oct. 23, 1959): 5.

9. Highlander under Attack, 1953–1962

1. Further general observations can be found in interview of John Thompson, Feb. 21, 1964, HC Tape Coll., 515A/125; "Adventures of a Radical Hillbilly," 1–2, 10; Anne Braden, "A View from the Fringes," *Southern Exposure* 9 (Spring 1981): 72. Another account of the struggle between HFS and its opponents is Joan Hobbs, "Politics of Repression: The Prosecution of the Highlander Folk School, 1957–1959" (M.A. thesis, Vanderbilt Univ., 1973).

2. Chattanooga *Times*, Sept. 22, 1953, HC Papers, Microfilm 795. On the "Great Fear," see, among many other studies of post–World War II anticommunism, David E. Caute, *The Great Fear: The Anti-Communist Purge under Truman and Eisenhower* (New York: Simon and Schuster, 1978). Caute describes Crouch as "one of the most brazen and colorful liars" in the government informant "business" (126). See also Willard Shelton, "Paul Crouch, Informer," *New Republic* 132 (July 19, 1954): 7–9; *New York Times*, Nov. 19, 1955, HC Papers, Box 38.

3. Horton to Gerhard Van Arkel, Oct. 27, 1953, HC Papers, Box 33. See also Michael Law, "Adult Education, McCarthyism and the Cold War," paper presented to the Adult Education Research Conference, Calgary, Alberta, Canada, May 1988, MHP, Box 9; Egerton, *Speak Now Against the Day*, 446–48.

4. Horton to Sutton, Nov. 23, Dec. 4, 1953; Sutton to Horton, Dec. 1, 1953, all Box 33; Horton to Kefauver, Dec. 15, 1953; Chattanooga *Times*, ca. Apr. 9, 1954, both Box 17; Chattanooga *News-Free Press*, Dec. 3, 1953, Microfilm 795, all HC Papers; Graham, *Crisis in Print*, 64–65, 273–74.

5. Nashville *Tennessean*, Mar. 10, 1954, HC Papers, Microfilm 795; Bartley, *Rise of Massive Resistance*, 53–54, 117–19; Caute, *The Great Fear*, 104–5, 166–67. The following account of the Eastland hearings is based in part on Jennings Perry, "The Congressional Inquisition Moves South," *I. F. Stone's Weekly* (Mar. 29, 1954): 2–3; Alfred Maund, "Battle of New Orleans: Eastland Meets His Match," *Nation* 178 (Apr. 3, 1954): 282–83; Irwin Klibaner, "The Southern Conference Educational Fund: A History" (Ph.D. diss., Univ. of Wisconsin, 1971), 35–36, 62–156; Klibaner, "The Travail of Southern Radicals: The Southern Conference Educational Fund, 1946–1976," *Journal of Southern History* 49 (May 1983): 179–88; John Salmond, *A Southern Rebel: The Life and Times of Aubrey Willis Williams, 1890–1965* (Chapel Hill: Univ. of North Carolina Press, 1983), 219–42. See also Egerton, *Speak Now Against the Day*, 569–72; Adams, *James A. Dombrowski*, 222–32; Klibaner, *Conscience of a Troubled South: The*

Southern Conference Educational Fund, 1946–1966 (Brooklyn, N.Y.: Carlson, 1989), 73–84; John A. Salmond, *The Conscience of a Lawyer: Clifford J. Durr and American Civil Liberties, 1899–1975* (Tuscaloosa: Univ. of Alabama Press, 1990), 158–65.

6. Eastland was to have been joined in New Orleans by his Democratic colleagues on the Internal Security Subcommittee, Senators Patrick McCarran of Nevada and John L. McClellan of Arkansas. But after Virginia Durr, Horton, and Williams appealed to their friends in the Senate to call off the inquiry, Senate minority leader Lyndon B. Johnson of Texas persuaded McCarran and McClellan to stay in Washington and let Eastland handle the investigation himself. Horton to Kefauver, Feb. 9, 1954, HC Papers, Box 17; Clifford Durr, interview with Allen Tullos and Candance Waid, Dec. 29, 1974, Southern Oral History Program, SHC; Hollinger F. Barnard, ed., *Outside the Magic Circle: The Autobiography of Virginia Foster Durr* (University: Univ. of Alabama Press, 1985), 256; Salmond, *Clifford J. Durr*, 160–61.

7. *Southern Conference Educational Fund, Inc.: Hearings before the Subcommittee to Investigate the Administration of the Internal Security Act and Other Internal Security Laws of the Committee on the Judiciary*, U.S. Senate, 83d Cong., 2d sess., Mar. 18–20, 1954 (Washington: Government Printing Office, 1955), 1–83, quotations 52 (hereinafter cited as *SCEF Hearings*); Dombrowski to J. Waties Waring, Apr. 9, 1954, HC Papers, Box 34.

8. Maund, "Battle of New Orleans," 282.

9. *SCEF Hearings*, 84–122, quotation 117; New Orleans *States*, Mar. 20, 1954; New Orleans *Times-Picayune*, Mar. 20, 21, 1954, both HC Papers, Microfilm 795; Clifford Durr, Tullos and Waid interview; Barnard, *Virginia Foster Durr*, 254–63, 266–73.

10. *SCEF Hearings*, 122–48, quotations 124, 125, 126, 136; New Orleans *States*, Mar. 20, 1954; Chattanooga *Times*, Mar. 23, 1954, both HC Papers, Microfilm 795; Clifford Durr, Tullos and Waid interview.

11. "Statement of Myles Horton," Mar. 18, 1954, HC Papers, Box 33. See also Horton, handwritten notes on back of prepared statement for SCEF hearings, ca. Mar. 20, 1954; Horton, "Comments on the New Orleans Hearing from Memory," ca. June 1954, both Box 33; New Orleans *Item*, Mar. 19, 1954; Chattanooga *News-Free Press*, Mar. 25, 1954, both Microfilm 795, all HC Papers.

12. *SCEF Hearings*, 151. In his copy of the hearings, Horton wrote that Eastland edited the transcript to make it seem that Horton had said, "you listened to Communists . . ." Horton denied saying this, and some newspaper accounts seem to substantiate his charge.

13. New Orleans *States*, Mar. 20, 1954; *New York Times*, Mar. 21, 1954, HC Papers, Microfilm 795.

14. *SCEF Hearings*, 150–51; Horton, handwritten notes on back of prepared statement for SCEF hearings; "Statement by Myles Horton in connection with hearings before subcommittee on Internal Security, New Orleans, Louisiana, March 18–20, 1954"; Horton to Gerhard Van Arkel, Mar. 22, 1954; Horton to Arthur Carstens, Mar. 22, 1954, all Box 33; Horton to Ellis McGhee, June 7, 1954, Box 34; New Orleans *Times-Picayune*, Mar. 21, 1954; Nashville *Tennessean*, Mar. 21, 1954; Murfreesboro *Daily News Journal*, Mar. 21, 1954, all Microfilm 795, all HC Papers. Horton later checked Highlander's files and found no record of a student named Mildred White. He recalled that she had once been a secretary for regional CIO director Paul Christopher, but Christopher

assured Horton that White had never been an HFS student. Horton to Christopher, Apr. 16, 1954; Christopher to Horton, Apr. 26, 1954, Christopher Papers, Box 2.

15. *SCEF Hearings,* 154.

16. New Orleans *States,* Mar. 20, 1954; *New York Times,* Mar. 21, 1954; Montgomery *Journal,* Mar. 25, 1954, all HC Papers, Microfilm 795; Clifford Durr, Tullos and Waid interview.

17. *SCEF Hearings,* 152–54; Chattanooga *Times,* Mar. 21, 23, 1954; New Orleans *Times-Picayune,* Mar. 21, 1954; Nashville *Tennessean,* Mar. 21, 24, 1954; Murfreesboro *Daily News Journal,* Mar. 21, 1954; Montgomery *Journal,* Mar. 25, 1954, all HC Papers, Microfilm 795; Clifford Durr, Tullos and Waid interview; Barnard, *Virginia Foster Durr,* 263–65.

18. Chattanooga *Times,* Mar. 23, 1954, HC Papers, Microfilm 795.

19. Montgomery *Journal,* Mar. 25, 1954, HC Papers, Microfilm 795.

20. Chattanooga *News-Free Press,* Mar. 22, 1954; Grundy County *Herald,* Mar. 25, 1954, both HC Papers, Microfilm 795. See also "Statements from Responsible Citizens about Eastland Hearings," ca. Apr. 3, 1954, Box 33; Eleanor Roosevelt, et al., to Sen. William Langer, ca. Mar. 20, 1954; Horton to Elaine Wright Handy, Apr. 1, 1954; Horton to Arthur Schlesinger, Jr., Apr. 16, 1954, all Box 34; Littleton (Colo.) *Independent,* Mar. 26, 1954; Chicago *Sun-Times,* Mar. 30, 1954; *Afro-American,* Apr. 3, 1954; San Francisco *Sun-Reporter,* Apr. 17, 1954, all Microfilm 795, all HC Papers; Horton to Christopher, Apr. 16, 1954, Christopher Papers, Box 2.

21. Nashville *Banner,* Mar. 26, 1954, HC Papers, Microfilm 795.

22. Horton to "Friend of Highlander," Apr. 3, 1954; *New York Times,* Nov. 19, 1955, both Box 33; Joanna Willimetz, notes on community-press meeting on Eastland hearings, Mar. 25, 1954; Horton to Callie Thomas, Apr. 13, 1954, both Box 34; Mabee, report on meeting at Highlander re Eastland Hearings, Apr. 2, 1954, Box 40; Chattanooga *Times,* Mar. 26, 28, 1954; Nashville *Tennessean,* Mar. 25, 26, 1954; Chattanooga *News-Free Press,* Mar. 26, 1954, all Microfilm 795, all HC Papers; Horton, reports to staff and community meeting on Eastland hearings, Mar. 1954, HC Tape Coll., 807A/2; *SCEF Hearings,* Report of Senate Internal Security Subcommittee, v–viii; Salmond, *A Southern Rebel,* 242–46; Klibaner, "Travail of Southern Radicals," 188–95, 201–2; Klibaner, "SCEF," 156–60, 170–72, 176–77; Klibaner, *SCEF,* 84–86, 92–93, 95–99; Salmond, *Clifford J. Durr,* 166–69.

23. Eastland and Griffin quoted in Bartley, *Rise of Massive Resistance,* 67–68. See also Neil R. McMillen, *The Citizens' Council: Organized Resistance to the Second Reconstruction, 1954–64* (Urbana: Univ. of Illinois Press, 1971), 9–10.

24. Bartley, *Rise of Massive Resistance,* 67–107, 115–16, 121–25, 143, and elsewhere; McMillen, *Citizens' Council,* 9–11, 15–40, and elsewhere; Sitkoff, *Struggle for Black Equality,* 25–28; Harold C. Fleming, "Resistance Movements and Racial Desegregation," *Annals of the American Academy of Political and Social Science* 304 (Mar. 1956): 44–52.

25. Swartz to HFS, Feb. 20, 1957, HC Papers, Box 34. See also Annual Report, 1957, 4; "Brief of Protestant, before the Commissioner of Internal Revenue, Department of the Treasury, re Highlander Folk School: Protest against Revocation of Tax Exempt Status," May 8, 1957, 1–2, 16–24, HFS Coll., Box 8 (hereinafter cited as "Highlander Protest").

26. Unidentified, unsigned copy of petition, ca. Sept. 1957, HC Papers, Box 34. See also Annual Report, 1957, 2–4; memorandum, Horton to executive council, Sept. 23, 1957, Box 2; Horton to Kefauver, Oct. 22, 1957, Box 17; memorandum, Horton to contributors, ca. Mar. 1957; letters to the Commissioner of Internal Revenue from adult educators, May 6–June 22, 1957, all Box 34; Horton, fundraising letters, May 17, Aug. 13, 1957, Box 44; Horton to Dombrowski, May 23, 1957, Box 71; Chattanooga *News-Free Press,* Sept. 7, 1957, Microfilm 795, all HC Papers; "Highlander Protest"; Horton to Morris Mitchell, May 1, Sept. 25, 1957, Morris R. Mitchell Papers, Box 5, SHC.

27. "Amendment to Charter of Incorporation," Sept. 1957, Box 1; memorandum, Horton to executive council, Sept. 23, 1957, Box 2; memorandum, Horton and Clark to Highlander personnel, Apr. 24, 1958; operating fund income and expenses, fiscal years ended Sept. 30, 1957, 1958, all Box 3; H. T. Swartz to HFS, Dec. 18, 1957; Horton, notice to contributors, Dec. 22, 1957, both Box 34, all HC Papers.

28. Annual Reports, 1956–58; "Summary of Residential and Extension Activities of 1957"; Ernest Morgan to Martin Luther King, Jr., Aug. 15, 1956, Box 56; Horton, news releases, July 2, 1956, Oct. 5, 1957, Box 66; *New York Times,* Oct. 5, 1957, Microfilm 795, all HC Papers; Horton, "The Status of Our Civil Rights," undelivered speech to Emergency Civil Liberties Committee, Dec. 15, 1959, HFS Coll., Box 1; "Georgia: Wrong Target," *Time* 72 (Aug. 4, 1958): 17; Bartley, *Rise of Massive Resistance,* 54, 182, 223; Raines, *My Soul Is Rested,* 435–37; Robert W. Dubay to author, Dec. 10, 1981. This account of the GBI investigation of Koinonia and Highlander relies upon Dubay's thorough examination of the Samuel Marvin Griffin Papers deposited at Bainbridge Junior College.

29. Horton to Maxwell Hahn, Oct. 10, 1957; Horton to Fred Routh, Oct. 10, 1957; Lois E. Gratz to Horton, Oct. 16, 1957; Horton to Gratz, Dec. 29, 1957, all Box 34; Horton, news release, Oct. 5, 1957, Box 66; Nashville *Tennessean,* Feb. 21, 1959, Microfilm 795, all HC Papers; Horton, interview with author, June 3, 1980; Clark, interview with author; Raines, *My Soul Is Rested,* 437–39.

30. *New York Times,* Oct. 5, 1957; Chattanooga *Times,* Oct. 5, 1957, both HC Papers, Microfilm 795.

31. Horton to Tefferteller, Oct. 10, 1957, HC Papers, Box 47. See also Berry to Horton, Oct. 18, 1957, Box 34; Horton to Prynce Hopkins, Oct. 10, 1957, Box 50; Horton, news release, Oct. 5, 1957, Box 66, all HC Papers; Horton, interview with author, June 3, 1980; *Daily Worker,* Sept. 10, 1957; *Southern School News* 4 (Nov. 1957): 9.

32. HFS: *Communist Training School.* See also Bartley, *Rise of Massive Resistance,* 188–89; Salmond, *A Southern Rebel,* 258.

33. Maryville-Alcoa *Times,* Dec. 16, 1957; Atlanta *Constitution,* Dec. 15–21, 1957, both HC Papers, Microfilm 795. See also Horton to Leon Wilson, Jan. 9, 1958, Box 29; Clark to Ralph McGill, Jan. 7, 1958, Box 34; Chattanooga *News-Free Press,* Sept. 3, Dec. 23, 1957, Microfilm 795, all HC Papers; Horton, "Status of Our Civil Rights"; Raines, *My Soul Is Rested,* 435–36, 440; "Georgia: Wrong Target," 17; Bartley, *Rise of Massive Resistance,* 183, 188–89.

34. Postcard, "A Training School for Communists," (Belmont, Mass.: *American Opinion,* n.d.), Box 34; Nashville *Tennessean,* July 25, 1965, Box 37, both HC Papers; *Communism and the NAACP* (Atlanta: Georgia Commission on Education, 1958), HFS

Coll., Box 16; *New York Times,* July 13, 1963; Salmond, *A Southern Rebel,* 259; Garrow, *The FBI and King,* 63; Branch, *Parting the Waters,* 853–54.

35. Arapahoe *Herald,* Oct. 16, 1957, quoted in news releases, Oct. 1957, HC Papers, Box 34.

36. "National Leaders Answer Griffin's Attack on Highlander," Dec. 18, 1957, Box 34; *New York Times,* Dec. 22, 1957, Microfilm 795, both HC Papers.

37. *Southern School News* 4 (Nov. 1957): 9; memorandum, Horton to executive council, Jan. 18–19, 1958, HC Papers, Box 2.

38. Executive council meeting minutes, Jan. 18–19, 1958, HC Papers, Box 2. See also memorandum, Clark to executive council members, ca. Dec. 11, 1957; memorandum, Horton to executive council members, Dec. 19, 1957, both Box 2; Horton to Maxwell Hahn, Oct. 10, 1957; reprint of "Georgia Invades Ohio," *Christian Century,* Oct. 30, 1957; news releases, Oct. 1957, all Box 34; Horton, "Education for Integration: The Full Highlander Story," speech given in Cincinnati, Ohio, Jan. 16, 1958, Box 40; Horton to Robert Levin, Oct. 21, 1957; Levin to Horton, Nov. 13, 1957, both Box 46; Tefferteller to John Thompson, Nov. 21, 1957, Box 47; news release, Dec. 20, 1957, Box 66; Chattanooga *Times,* Oct. 7, 1957; *Packinghouse Worker,* Nov. 1957, both Microfilm 795, all HC Papers; *Southern Newsletter* 2 (Dec. 1957): 10–11, HFS Coll., Box 16.

39. Horton to George S. Mitchell, May 29, 1958, Box 21; Chattanooga *Times,* July 28, 1958; Memphis *Press-Scimitar,* Jan. 6, 1959, both Microfilm 795, all HC Papers; *New York Times,* July 13, 1963; Horton, interview with author, June 3, 1980; Garrow, *The FBI and King,* 24–25; Bartley, *Rise of Massive Resistance,* 183; Raines, *My Soul Is Rested,* 439.

40. Horton to George Mitchell, May 29, 1958, HC Papers, Box 21.

41. Executive council meeting minutes, Nov. 1–2, 1958, Box 2; Max V. Cate to Horton, May 5, 1958, Box 33; copy of Horton telegram to contributors, Apr. 30, 1958; Horton, memorandum re cancellation of fire insurance, May 8, 1958, both Box 45; Horton to Luther Tucker, Sept. 16, 1958, Box 46; Horton, memorandum on fire insurance, June 30, 1958, Box 47, all HC Papers; *Common Sense,* Sept. 15, 1958; *White Sentinel* (official publication of National Citizens Protective Association) 8 (Nov. 1958): 3–5, both 81st General Assembly, State of Tennessee, Highlander Folk School Special Investigating Committee Papers, Box 11, Tennessee State Library and Archives (hereinafter cited as HFS Inv. Comm. Papers); Justus, Cobb interview; Bartley, *Rise of Massive Resistance,* 251–78; Graham, *Crisis in Print,* 140–44, 162–63.

42. Report of hearing before the special education committee of the Arkansas Legislative Council, Dec. 16, 17, 18, 1958, HFS Inv. Comm. Papers, Box 11. See also Bartley, *Rise of Massive Resistance,* 187–88, 222, 224; Wilma Dykeman and James Stokely, "McCarthyism under the Magnolias," *Progressive* 23 (July 1959): 6–10; Walter Goodman, *The Committee: The Extraordinary Career of the House Committee on Un-American Activities* (New York: Farrar, Straus and Giroux, 1968), 335–37, 419–20.

43. Nashville *Banner,* Jan. 20, 1959; Chattanooga *News-Free Press,* Jan. 20, 1959, both HC Papers, Microfilm 795. See also Horton to Harris Wofford, Jr., Feb. 17, 1959, Box 30; Horton and B. R. Brazeal, "Arkansas' Attorney General Proposes Closing Highlander," Feb. 2, 1959, Box 34; Chattanooga *News-Free Press,* Jan. 23, 1959; Nashville *Banner,* Jan. 27, 1959; Nashville *Tennessean,* Jan. 29, 1959, all Microfilm 795, all HC Papers; Bartley, *Rise of Massive Resistance,* 212–21.

44. Copy of House Joint Resolution Number 26: A Resolution to Appoint an Investigating Committee to Investigate the Subversive Activities of Highlander Folk School, Grundy County, Tennessee, and Other Organizations Affiliated Therewith, Jan. 1959, HC Papers, Box 35; *Tenn. House Journal,* Jan. 26, 1959, 203.

45. Nashville *Banner,* Jan. 28, 1959; Chattanooga *Times,* Jan. 29, 1959; Knoxville *News-Sentinel,* Jan. 29, 1959, all HC Papers, Microfilm 795. See also Horton and Brazeal, "Arkansas' Attorney General Proposes Closing Highlander"; Nashville *Banner,* Jan. 27, 1959; Nashville *Tennessean,* Jan. 29, 30, Feb. 17, 1959, all HC Papers, Microfilm 795; *Tenn. House Journal,* Jan. 28, 1959, 233–34; *Tenn. Senate Journal,* Jan. 28, 1959, 205–6.

46. Senter quoted in Chattanooga *News-Free Press,* Feb. 5, 1959; Knoxville *News-Sentinel,* Feb. 5, 1959, both HC Papers, Microfilm 795. See also Horton and Brazeal, "Arkansas' Attorney General Proposes Closing Highlander"; Horton to Rhinehart and Senter, Jan. 31, 1959, Box 35; various newspaper clippings, Jan. 29–Feb. 4, 1959, all Microfilm 795, all HC Papers; *Tenn. Senate Journal,* Jan. 29, Feb. 3, 1959, 221, 237; *Tenn. House Journal,* Jan. 29, Feb. 3, 4, 1959, 244, 288, 291–92, 313–14; *Tenn. Public Acts,* 1959, 1091–94; *Southern School News* 5 (Mar. 1959): 12.

47. Recorded proceedings, 81st General Assembly, Tenn. State Senate, Feb. 10, 1959, Tennessee State Library and Archives, Nashville. See also Nashville *Tennessean,* Feb. 3, 11, 1959; Chattanooga *News-Free Press,* Feb. 11, 1959; Knoxville *News-Sentinel,* Feb. 12, 1959, all HC Papers, Microfilm 795; *Tenn. Senate Journal,* Feb. 10, 1959, 309–10; *Tenn. House Journal,* Feb. 10, 12, 1959, 379, 422.

48. Nashville *Tennessean,* Jan. 29, Feb. 1, 8, 11, 1959; Chattanooga *Times,* Feb. 1, 2, 1959; Knoxville *News-Sentinel,* Feb. 11, 1959; St. Louis *Post-Dispatch,* Feb. 9, 1959; Arapahoe *Herald,* Feb. 10, 1959; Chattanooga *News-Free Press,* Jan. 27, 1959; Charleston *News and Courier,* Feb. 24, 28, Mar. 3, 1959, all HC Papers, Microfilm 795; Hamilton County *Herald,* Feb. 13, 1959, HFS Inv. Comm. Papers, Box 11.

49. Niebuhr to Horton, Feb. 16, 1959, Box 35; Nashville *Tennessean,* Feb. 25, 1959, Microfilm 795, both HC Papers. See also Annual Report, 1959, 2, 4; Henry S. Randolph to Gov. Buford Ellington, Feb. 10, 1959, Box 35; Nashville *Banner,* Feb. 11, 23, 1959; Memphis *Commercial Appeal,* Feb. 2, 1959; Chattanooga *News-Free Press,* Feb. 3, 5, 21, 1959; Chattanooga *Times,* Feb. 5, 1959; Knoxville *News-Sentinel,* Feb. 5, 1959, all Microfilm 795, all HC Papers; numerous letters to Ellington regarding HFS investigation, Jan. 28–Mar. 22, 1959; Oakley Melton, Jr., to Ellington, Feb. 17, 1959, all Buford Ellington Papers, Box 72, Tennessee State Library and Archives.

50. Bennett quoted in Nashville *Tennessean,* Feb. 21, 1959, HC Papers, Microfilm 795. See also Horton to Maxwell Hahn, Feb. 6, 1959, Box 49; Nashville *Tennessean,* Feb. 17, 1959; Nashville *Banner,* Feb. 18, 19, 23, 1959, all Microfilm 795, all HC Papers; minutes of Joint Legislative Committee for Investigation of Highlander Folk School, Feb. 20, 1959; Chattanooga *News-Free Press,* Feb. 21, 1959, both HFS Inv. Comm. Papers, Box 11.

51. *Before the Legislative Committee of the Tennessee Legislature in the Matter of: Investigation of Highlander Folk School, Grundy County, Tennessee. Closed Hearing,* Tracy City, Feb. 21, 1959 (Nashville: Hix Brothers, 1959), 3–51, 128–44, quotation 9 (hereinafter cited as *Closed Hearing,* Tracy City). For newspaper reports on the Tracy City hearings, see Knoxville *News-Sentinel,* Feb. [21?], 27, 1959; Nashville *Tennessean,* Feb. 22, 27, 1959;

Chattanooga *Times,* Feb. 22, 27, 1959; Nashville *Banner,* Feb. 23, 27, 1959; Memphis *Press-Scimitar,* Feb. 27, 1959, all HC Papers, Microfilm 795; Chattanooga *News-Free Press,* Feb. 21, 1959; Nashville *Banner,* Feb. 21, 1959, HFS Inv. Comm. Papers, Box 11.

52. A Pentagon official later informed Horton that Scruggs had never been "affiliated in any manner with Army Intelligence." "False Witness Number One: Carrington Scruggs, Specialist 5th Class," HC Papers, Box 35.

53. *Closed Hearing,* Tracy City, 51–128, quotations 62, 76, 100, 101, 107, 121.

54. *Before the Joint Legislative Investigating Committee, State of Tennessee, in the Matter of: Investigation of the Highlander Folk School, Grundy County, Tennessee. Public Hearing,* Tracy City, Feb. 26, 1959 (Nashville: Hix Brothers, 1959), 4–69, 76–85, 88–108, 111–27, 197–236, quotations 11, 89, 120, 199–200, 219 (hereinafter cited as *Public Hearing,* Tracy City).

55. Ibid., 69–75; executive council meeting minutes, Sept. 25, 1956, Apr. 13–14, 1957, Box 2; George Mitchell to Horton, Nov. 17, 1959, Box 21; Clark, "To Whom It May Concern," June 1, 1957; board of directors meeting minutes, Aug. 7, 1957, both Box 54, all HC Papers; J. H. McCartt to Viola [*sic*] Burnett [Crutchfield], Feb. 23, 1959, HFS Inv. Comm. Papers, Box 11.

56. *Public Hearing,* Tracy City, 133–97, quotations 143, 148, 162, 189.

57. *Before the Joint Legislative Investigating Committee, State of Tennessee, in the Matter of: Investigation of Highlander Folk School, Grundy County, Tennessee. Public Hearing,* Nashville, Mar. 4, 5, 1959 (Nashville: Hix Brothers, 1959), 246–58, quotations 257 (hereinafter cited as *Public Hearing,* Nashville). Press accounts of the Nashville hearings include Knoxville *News-Sentinel,* Mar. 4, 5, 6, 1959; Nashville *Banner,* Mar. 4, 5, 6, 1959; Nashville *Tennessean,* Mar. 5, 6, 1959; Chattanooga *News-Free Press,* Mar. 5, 9, 1959; Memphis *Press-Scimitar,* Mar. 5, 1959; Memphis *Commercial Appeal,* Mar. 5, 1959; Charleston *News and Courier,* Mar. 5, 6, 1959; Chattanooga *Times,* Mar. 6, 1959, all HC Papers, Microfilm 795.

58. *Public Hearing,* Nashville, 258–73, 283–307, 313–19, 361–422, quotations 294, 319, 377, 378, 401, 403.

59. Hanover's comment in Memphis *Press-Scimitar* and Memphis *Commercial Appeal,* Mar. 5, 1959, both HC Papers, Microfilm 795. See also *Public Hearing,* Nashville, 277–83, 319–57, 422–26, quotation 321.

60. Bennett's remark in Nashville *Tennessean,* Mar. 5, 1959, HC Papers, Microfilm 795. See also *Public Hearing,* Nashville, 427–96, quotations 447, 486, 493; U.S. House of Representatives, Information from the Files of the Committee on Un-American Activities, Feb. 26, 27, 1959; list of HUAC citations on Pete Seeger, n.d., both HFS Inv. Comm. Papers, Box 11.

61. Nashville *Tennessean,* Mar. 6, 1959; Knoxville *News-Sentinel,* Mar. 6, 1959, both HC Papers, Microfilm 795.

62. *Public Hearing,* Nashville, 496–605, quotations 555, 562, 589, 598.

63. Committee Report: To the Members of the 81st Session of the General Assembly of the State of Tennessee at Nashville, Tennessee, Mar. 6, 1959, reprinted in *Tenn. House Journal,* Mar. 10, 1959, 1043–56, and *Tenn. Senate Journal,* Mar. 10, 1959, 787–800. See also *Tenn. Public Acts,* 1959, 1235; Nashville *Tennessean,* Mar. 9, 11, 13, 1959; Nashville *Banner,* Mar. 11, 1959; Chattanooga *Times,* Mar. 11, 1959; Knoxville *News-Sentinel,* Mar. 11, 1959; Knoxville *Journal,* Mar. 11, 1959, all HC Papers, Microfilm 795.

64. Roger L. Shinn, "The Rumpus About Highlander," *Christianity and Crisis* 19 (Nov. 30, 1959): 171.

65. Knoxville *News-Sentinel,* Mar. 19, 1959; Nashville *Tennessean,* Mar. 20, 1959, both HC Papers, Microfilm 795.

66. Horton to Rep. Wayne L. Hays, Mar. 30, 1959, HC Papers, Box 13.

67. Horton to Robert A. Childers, June 1, 1959, HC Papers, Box 8. See also Horton to Harry Golden, Mar. 12, 1959, Box 13; Horton to A. A. Liveright, Apr. 2, 1959, Box 19; memorandum, Horton to May Justus and Eugene Kayden, ca. Mar. 1959, Box 34; Horton, memoranda on legislative investigation and Ed Friend, ca. Mar. 1959, Box 36; Nashville *Tennessean,* Mar. 4, 6, 7, 8, 10, 11, 13, 22, 1959; Chattanooga *Times,* Mar. 6, 11, 12, 23, 27, 1959; Knoxville *Independent Call,* Mar. 7, 1959; Nash-' ville *Banner,* Mar. 11, 1959; Knoxville *News-Sentinel,* Mar. 11, 12, 15, 19, 1959; Chattanooga *News-Free Press,* Mar. 12, 14, 1959; Charleston *News and Courier,* Mar. 12, 28, 1959; Knoxville *Journal,* Mar. 14, 1959; Kingsport *Times-News,* Mar. 15, 1959; *Afro-American,* Mar. 21, 1959, all Microfilm 795, all HC Papers; E. H. Alexander, "The Highlander School Unmasked," *American Mercury* (July 1959): 149–50, Horton Papers, Box 1; *Southern School News* 5 (Apr. 1959): 9; *Southern Patriot* 17 (Apr. 1959): 4; "Unfortunate Hearings," *Concern* 14 (Mar. 27, 1959): 2.

68. All quotations in this account of the raid are from "Report on July 31 Raid," Aug. 4, 1959, HC Papers, Box 34, and Clark, *Echo in My Soul,* 3–9. See also Annual Report, 1959, 2, 4; "Points to be Covered in Executive Council Session," Aug. 3, 1959, Box 2; statements regarding raid transcribed from audio recording, Aug. 1, 1959; Linda Bastian and Sally Freedman, "Report on July 31 Raid," Aug. 5, 1959; Clark to Horton, Aug. 7, 1959; statements to "Friends of Highlander," Aug. 13, 27, 1959, all Box 34; *M I A,* 2 (Oct. 7, 1959): 2, Box 64; Chattanooga *Times,* Aug. 2, 3, 1959; Nashville *Tennessean,* Aug. 2, 1959; Grundy County *Herald,* Aug. 6, 1959; *Antioch College Record,* Nov. 6, 1959, all Microfilm 795, all HC Papers; Justus, Cobb interview; Robinson, Wigginton and Thrasher interview; Clark, interview with author, "Moment of History," 38; Maggie Lewis, "Guy and Candie Carawan," 21; John Egerton, "The Trial of the Highlander Folk School," *Southern Exposure* 6 (Spring 1978): 83; Brown, *Septima Clark,* 55–59.

69. Nashville *Tennessean,* Aug. 2, 1959, HC Papers, Microfilm 795. See also Annual Report, 1959, 4; statements regarding raid transcribed from audio recording; statement to "Friends of Highlander," Aug. 13, 1959; *M.I.A.* 2 (Oct. 7, 1959): 2–3; Chattanooga *Times,* Aug. 2, 3, 1959; Knoxville *Journal,* Aug. 4, 1959; Nashville *Banner,* ca. Aug. 1959, all Microfilm 795, all HC Papers; audio recording, discussion of raid on Highlander, Aug. 1, 1959, HC Tape Coll., 515A/19.

70. Both closing arguments in Chattanooga *Times,* Aug. 7, 1959, HC Papers, Microfilm 795.

71. *Before the Honorable John P. Wright and the Honorable J. L. Locke, Justices of the Peace for Grundy County, Tennessee, in the Matter of: State of Tennessee vs. Mrs. Septima P. Clark,* Altamont, Aug. 6, 1959 (Nashville: Wells and Hamlin, 1959), quotations 90, 98; Chattanooga *News-Free Press,* Aug. 7, 1959; Nashville *Banner,* Aug. 7, 1959, both HC Papers, Microfilm 795; Cecil Branstetter, interview with John Egerton, Aug. 9, 1981, copy in Highlander Center library.

72. "A Brief History of the Present Litigation Involving Highlander Folk School," ca. 1960, 3, HFS Coll., Box 8. See also *Before the Honorable John P. Wright and the Honorable J. L. Locke, Justices of the Peace for Grundy County, Tennessee, at Altamont, in the Matter of: State of Tennessee vs. Guy Hughes Carawan, Jr., Perry MacKay Sturges, Brent Eugene Barksdale,* Aug. 12, 1959 (Nashville: Wells and Hamlin, 1959); Chattanooga *Times,* Aug. 13, 1959; Chattanooga *News-Free Press,* Aug. 13, 1959; Nashville *Tennessean,* Aug. 13, 1959, all HC Papers, Microfilm 795; Clark, *Echo in My Soul,* 10.

73. "Original Bill and Notice, to the Honorable Chester C. Chattin, Circuit Judge, Holding the Circuit Court for Grundy County, Tennessee," Aug. 12, 1959, HC Papers, Box 36. See also Chattanooga *Times,* Aug. 13, 1959; Chattanooga *News-Free Press,* Aug. 13, 1959; Nashville *Tennessean,* Aug. 13, 1959; *New York Times,* Aug. 13, 1959, all HC Papers, Microfilm 795; "Brief History of the Present Litigation," 3.

74. Nashville *Tennessean,* Aug. 21, 1959; *Carolina Times,* Sept. 19, 1959, both HC Papers, Microfilm 795.

75. Chattanooga *Times,* Aug. 16, 1959; Nashville *Tennessean,* Aug. 16, 1959, both HC Papers, Microfilm 795.

76. Clark to newspaper editors, Aug. 27, 1959, and Horton to "Fellow Tennesseans," Sept. 8, 1959, both HC Papers, Box 34. See also Annual Report, 1959, 4; "Testimonials from Friends of Highlander," Aug., Sept. 1959, Box 34; news releases, Aug. 14, Sept. 8, 1959, Box 66; Chattanooga *Times,* Aug. 9, 11, 13, 14, 1959; Nashville *Tennessean,* Aug. 13, 20, 1959; Nashville *Banner,* Aug. 17, 1959; Charleston *News and Courier,* ca. Aug. 22, 1959; *Afro-American,* Aug. 22, Sept. 12, 19, 1959; Milwaukee *Journal,* Aug. 30, 1959; St. Louis *Post-Dispatch,* Aug. 31, 1959; Chattanooga *News-Free Press,* Aug. 31, Sept. 9, 1959; New York *Post,* Sept. 14, 1959, all Microfilm 795, all HC Papers; Clark, *Echo in My Soul,* 10–11, 206–10.

77. Chattanooga *Times,* Sept. 15, 1959, HC Papers, Microfilm 795.

78. *In the Circuit Court of Grundy County, Tennessee, at Altamont, in the Matter of: State of Tennessee, ex rel., A. F. Sloan, Attorney General of the 18th Judicial Circuit, vs. Highlander Folk School, a Corp.; Myles Horton; May Justus; and Septima Clark,* Docket No. 37358, Sept. 14, 15, 16, 1959 (Nashville: Wells and Hamlin, 1959), 62 (hereinafter cited as *Tennessee vs. HFS,* Sept.). Newspaper accounts include Chattanooga *Times,* Sept. 15, 16, 17, 1959; Chattanooga *News-Free Press,* Sept. 15, 16, 1959; Nashville *Tennessean,* Sept. 15, 16, 17, 1959; Nashville *Banner,* Sept. 15, 16, 1959; Milwaukee *Journal,* Sept. 15, 16, 17, 1959; *New York Times,* Sept. 15, 17, 1959; New York *Post,* Sept. 16, 1959; *National Guardian,* Sept. 28, 1959, all HC Papers, Microfilm 795. See also Anne Braden, "Mountain Witch Hunt," 1959, HFS Coll., Box 8; Braden, notes on hearing, Sept. 15, 16, 1959, Braden Papers, Box 50; Alice Cobb, "The Trial and Charges Against Highlander," *Concern* 15 (Oct. 23, 1959): 4, 8; *Southern Patriot* 17 (Oct. 1959): 4; Dan Wakefield, "The Siege at Highlander," *Nation* 189 (Nov. 7, 1959): 323–25; Branstetter, Egerton interview; Egerton, "Trial of HFS," 85–86.

79. *Tennessee vs. HFS,* Sept., 20–39, 77–112, 131–60, 232–92, quotations 87, 92, 238.

80. Ibid., 40–76, 112–30, 161–231, 293–94, 382–422, quotations 56, 75.

81. Ibid., 295–320, 324–81, quotations 295, 319, 325, 326, 335, 347, 359.

82. Chattanooga *Times,* Sept. 16, 1959, HC Papers, Microfilm 795.

83. *Tennessee vs. HFS,* Sept., 423–52, 519–32, 546–94, 611–15, quotations 549.

84. Ibid., 503–18, 595–610, 616–50, quotations 610, 629, 643.

85. Ibid., 454–502, 533–45, quotations 461, 491; Clark, interview with author; "Adventures of a Radical Hillbilly," 22.

86. *Tennessee vs. HFS,* Sept., 667–85, quotations 683; Anne Braden, notes on hearing, Sept. 16, 1959; "Brief History of the Present Litigation," 4.

87. News release, Oct. 12, 1959, Box 66; Nashville *Tennessean,* Sept. 27, 1959; Chattanooga *Times,* Sept. 27, 1959; Chattanooga *News-Free Press,* Sept. 28, 1959; Nashville *Banner,* Sept. 28, 1959; *Afro-American,* Oct. 24, 1959, all Microfilm 795, all HC Papers.

88. Annual Report, 1959, 4; executive council meeting minutes, Oct. 2–3, 1959, Box 2; Horton to Martin Luther King, Jr., Oct. 8, 1959; Pittsburgh *Courier,* Oct. 10, 1959; statement of support signed by prominent citizens, Dec. 1959, all Box 34; news releases, Sept. 18, 28, Oct. 2, 8, ca. Oct. 12, Nov. 1, 5, Dec. 2, 1959, Box 66; Nashville *Tennessean,* Sept. 14, 17, 21, Nov. 1, 1959; Chattanooga *News-Free Press,* Sept. 15, 29, 1959; St. Louis *Post-Dispatch,* Oct. 9, 1959; Chattanooga *Times,* Oct. 10, 29, 1959; Knoxville *News-Sentinel,* Oct. 24, 1959; Nashville *Banner,* Feb. 23, 1960, all Microfilm 795, all HC Papers; "Small Beer," *Nation* 189 (Oct. 3, 1959): 183; "In Defense of Highlander," *Concern* 15 (Oct. 23, 1959): 2; Wakefield, "The Siege at Highlander," 323–25; *Southern Patriot* 17 (Oct. 1959): 4; (Nov. 1959): 4.

89. "Order Allowing Amendment to Original Bill," *State of Tennessee, ex rel. A. F. Sloan, & etc., vs. Highlander Folk School, et al.,* Oct. 29, 1959, Grundy County Circuit Court Clerk office, Altamont, Tenn. See also Chattanooga *Times,* Oct. 29, 1959; Nashville *Tennessean,* Oct. 29, 30, Nov. 1, 3, 1959, all HC Papers, Microfilm 795; "Brief History of the Present Litigation," 4–5; Shinn, "The Rumpus About Highlander," 171.

90. Nashville *Tennessean,* Oct. 29, 1959; Nashville *Banner,* Oct. 29, 1959, both HC Papers, Microfilm 795.

91. Demurrer to the original Bill as amended, *State of Tennessee ex rel. A. F. Sloan vs. Highlander Folk School, etc.,* ca. Oct. 29, 1959, 6, HC Papers, Box 36.

92. Sloan quoted in Nashville *Tennessean,* Oct. 29, 1959, Microfilm 795; Horton, news release, Oct. 30, 1959, Box 66, both HC Papers. See also Nashville *Tennessean,* Nov. 1, 3, 1959; Nashville *Banner,* Nov. 2, 1959, both HC Papers, Microfilm 795.

93. *In the Circuit Court of Grundy County, Tennessee, at Altamont, in the Matter of: State of Tennessee, ex rel., A. F. Sloan, v. Highlander Folk School, a Corp., Nov. 3, 4, 5, and 6, 1959* (Nashville: Wells and Hamlin, 1959), 1–291, quotation 18 (hereinafter cited as *Tennessee v. HFS,* Nov.). Like the September hearing, the November trial received extensive press coverage. See the more than two dozen clippings, HC Papers, Microfilm 795. See also John Thompson, notes on court case, Nov. 9, 1959; transcript of audio recording of November trial played on KPFA-FM radio program, *The Highlander Folk School,* Berkeley, Calif., May 31, 1960, both Box 34; memorandum brief, *State of Tennessee ex rel. A. F. Sloan vs. Highlander Folk School etc.,* Dec. 21, 1959, Box 36, all HC Papers; "Brief History of the Present Litigation," 5–6; *Southern Patriot* 17 (Dec. 1959): 3; Egerton, "Trial of HFS," 86–87; Branstetter, Egerton interview; Horton, interview with author, Aug. 6, 1982.

94. *Tennessee v. HFS,* Nov., 331–42, 443–56, 469–519, 523–66, 569–76.

95. Ibid., 292–330, 361–414, 457–65.

96. Ibid., 578–97, quotations 593.

97. Ibid., 598–697, 765–73, quotations 649, 665, 666, 684, 685, 772.

98. Ibid., 698–765, quotations 702.

99. Ibid., 774–824, quotations 788, 792, 799, 812, 817, 823.

100. Ibid., 783–84, 825–37; unsigned article, "Why They Don't Like Highlander," ca. Nov. 6, 1959; John Thompson, notes on court case, Nov. 9, 1959; "Memo from Highlander," Nov. 10, 1959, all Box 34, all HC Papers; memorandum brief, *Tennessee vs. HFS*; jury decision, Nov. 6, 1959, and orders of Judge Chester C. Chattin, Dec. 2, 1959, Jan. 12, 1960, *Tennessee* vs. *HFS,* Grundy County Circuit Court Clerk office.

101. Opinion of Judge Chester C. Chattin, *Tennessee vs. HFS,* Circuit Court, Grundy County, Tenn., No. 90, Feb. 16, 1960, HC Papers, Box 36. See also memorandum, Horton to supporters, Mar. 8, 1960, Box 34; Chattanooga *News-Free Press,* Feb. 16, 1960; Chattanooga *Times,* Feb. 17, 26, Mar. 8, 1960; *New York Times,* Feb. 17, 1960, all Microfilm 795, all HC Papers; Chattin, Final Order, *Tennessee vs. HFS,* Mar. 7, 1960, Grundy County Circuit Court Clerk office; *Southern School News* 6 (Mar. 1960): 2.

102. Chattanooga *News-Free Press,* Feb. 17, 1960; Chattanooga *Times,* Feb. 17, 1960, both HC Papers, Microfilm 795, and see many other clippings, ibid. See also "The Highlander Controversy," *Mountain Life and Work* 35 (Winter 1959): 23–25; Shinn, "The Rumpus About Highlander," 171; Graham, *Crisis in Print,* 205–6.

103. Horton to Malcolm Ross, Apr. 26, 1960, HC Papers, Box 24. See also notes on executive council meeting, Feb. 23–24, 1960; memorandum, Horton to executive council members, May 19, 1960, both Box 2; Horton to John B. Thompson, Mar. 24, Apr. 7, 1960, Box 28; Thompson, notes on court case, Nov. 9, 1959; memoranda to "Friends of Highlander from the Executive Council," Nov. 23, 1959, Mar. 10, 1960; "Memo from Myles Horton," Mar. 8, 1960, all Box 34; news releases, Dec. 23, 1959, Feb. 24, Mar. 10, May 14, 1960, Box 66; Nashville *Tennessean,* Nov. 12, 1959, Feb. 17, 25, 1960; Chattanooga *Times,* Feb. 24, 25, 1960; Nashville *Banner,* Feb. 17, 24, 26, 1960; *New York Times,* Feb. 17, 24, 1960, all Microfilm 795, all HC Papers; transcript of KPFA-FM program, *The Highlander Folk School*; *Southern School News* 6 (Mar. 1960): 2; Horton, interview with author, June 3, 1980.

104. Notes on executive council meeting, Feb. 23–24, 1960; memoranda, Horton to executive council members, May 1, 19, June 19, 1960; proposed Highlander Research and Training Center Trust Agreement, n.d., all Box 2; Horton to George D. Pratt, Jr., July 9, 1960, Box 23; Horton to John Thompson, Apr. 7, 1960, Box 28; Thompson, notes on court case, Nov. 9, 1959, Box 34; Horton to Prynce Hopkins, June 19, 1960, Box 50; Nashville *Banner,* Feb. 26, 1960, Microfilm 795, all HC Papers.

105. Executive council meeting minutes, July 21–22, 1960, Box 2; Motion for a New Trial and/or Rehearing, *Tennessee vs. HFS,* Apr. 1960, Box 36; news releases, June 24, July 22, 1960, Box 66; Chattanooga *Times,* June 19, 25, July 23, 1960; Nashville *Tennessean,* June 19, 25, July 23, 1960, Feb. 15, 1961; Nashville *Banner,* June 24, 1960, Apr. 4, 1961; Chattanooga *News-Free Press,* June 25, July 23, 1960; Knoxville *Journal,* July 23, 1960, Microfilm 795, all HC Papers; Order Overruling Motions for New Trial and Granting Appeal, *State on Relation of A. F. Sloan vs. Highlander Folk School and etc.,* July 1, 1960, Grundy County Circuit Court Clerk office.

106. Opinion of the Supreme Court of Tennessee, *State of Tennessee ex rel., A. F. Sloan, District Attorney General v. Highlander Folk School,* Apr. 5, 1961, HFS Coll., Box 8. See also "Memo from Highlander," Apr. 10, May 9, 1961; Branstetter to Horton,

May 26, 1961, Box 34; *Excerpted from Assignments of Error, Brief and Argument of Plaintiffs-in-Error, in the Supreme Court of Tennessee, Highlander Folk School . . . vs. The State of Tennessee . . .* , ca. Apr. 5, 1961; Petition to Rehear, *Highlander Folk School, etc., et al., vs. The State of Tennessee ex rel. A. F. Sloan, etc., et al.,* ca. Apr. 10, 1961; Opinion and Judgment of the Supreme Court of Tennessee on Petitions for Rehearing, *State of Tennessee . . . v. Highlander Folk School,* May 5, 1961, all Box 36, all HC Papers; Horton, interview with author, June 3, 1980; Branstetter, Egerton interview.

107. Horton to Wesley Hotchkiss, July 28, 1961, HC Papers, Box 34.

108. Eastland quoted in "Memo from Highlander," Apr. 10, 1961, Box 34; St. Louis *Post-Dispatch,* Apr. 10, 1961, Microfilm 795, both HC Papers.

109. Annual Report, 1961, 4; memorandum, Horton to executive council members, July 12, 1961; executive council meeting minutes, July 28–29, 1961, both Box 2; operating fund income and expenses, fiscal years ended Sept. 30, 1959, 1960, 1961, Box 3; program, "Benefit Program of Folk Music, Carnegie Hall, Feb. 10, 1961," Box 27; Horton to John Thompson, June 20, 1961, Box 28; Marge Frantz to Berkeley (Calif.) Friends of Highlander, Feb. 4, 17, 1961; announcement, Pete Seeger benefit concert for HFS, Boston, Apr. 18, 1961; memorandum, Horton to Friends of Highlander, May 4, 1961, all Box 45, all HC Papers.

110. Cecil D. Branstetter and George E. Barrett, Petition for a Writ of Certiorari to the Supreme Court of Tennessee, *In the Supreme Court of the United States, October Term 1961. Highlander Folk School, et al. v. State of Tennessee ex rel. A. F. Sloan, District Attorney General, 18th Judicial Circuit,* Aug. 1961, HC Papers, Box 36. See also Branstetter to Morris Lasker, July 27, 1961, Box 34; Chattanooga *Times,* Aug. 4, 1961; Nashville *Banner,* Sept. [28?], 1961, both Microfilm 795, all HC Papers.

111. Cox to Gerhard Van Arkel, July 24, 1961, HC Papers, Box 34.

112. Horton, report to executive council members, July 1, 1961, Box 2; staff meeting minutes, Aug. 14, 1961, Box 3; Cox to Charles O. Gregory, July 19, 1961, Box 13; Branstetter to Horton, Apr. 14, Aug. 9, 1961; Horton to Niebuhr, July 6, 1961; Niebuhr to Horton, July 11, 29, 1961; Branstetter to Patrick M. Malin, July 11, 1961; Marshall to Walter Johnson (same letter to other HFS supporters), July 19, 1961; Marshall to Branstetter, Aug. 7, 1961; Marshall to Sen. Alexander Wiley, Aug. 29, 1961; "Individuals Who Have Responded to Highlander's Request for Assistance in Bringing Our Case to the Attention of the Department of Justice," ca. Aug. 1961, all Box 34, all HC Papers; "Some Responses to Highlander's Request for Assistance in Bringing Our Case to the Attention of the Department of Justice," July 1961, HFS Coll., Box 8; Horton, interviews with author, June 3, 1980, Aug. 6, 1982; Branstetter, Egerton interview.

113. Ludwig subsequently lost his job with the UMWA Welfare and Retirement Fund for renting the Riverside Drive property to Highlander. Annual Report, 1961, 1; Charter of Incorporation, Highlander Research and Education Center, Aug. 21, 1961, Box 1; memoranda, Horton to executive council, July 28–29, Sept. 12, 1961; Highlander Center incorporators meeting minutes, Aug. 30, 1961; executive council meeting minutes, Sept. 30, 1961, all Box 2; Horton to George and Bee Wolfe, Nov. 25, 1961, Box 30; Knoxville *News-Sentinel,* Oct. 8, 11, 31, Nov. 2, 7, 1961; Nashville *Tennessean,* Oct. 8, 10, 1961, all Microfilm 795, all HC Papers; *Southern School News* 7 (Nov. 1961): 6; Branstetter, Egerton interview.

114. Horton to Mrs. Joseph Barnes, Oct. 3, 1961, HC Papers, Box 6. See also Roger N. Baldwin to Horton, Oct. 12, Nov. 28, 1961; Horton to Baldwin, Nov. 24, 1961, Jan. 8, 1962, all Box 6; Samuel L. Kuhn to Horton, Nov. 13, 1961, Box 17; Jay Lavenson to Horton, Nov. 15, 1961, Box 18; Horton to A. A. Liveright, Oct. 3, 1961, Box 19; Branstetter to Lavenson, Jan. 3, 1962, Box 34; Horton, "Confidential Memorandum to 300 Friends of Highlander," Oct. 6, 1961, Box 44; Chattanooga *News-Free Press,* Oct. 9, 13, 1961; Nashville *Banner,* Oct. 10, 1961; Nashville *Tennessean,* Oct. 11, 1961, all Microfilm 795, all HC Papers; H. E. Baggenstoss to Buford Ellington, Oct. 9, 1961; Ellington to Baggenstoss, Oct. 10, 1961 (similar letter to others), both Ellington Papers, Box 72; Horton, interview with author, June 3, 1980.

115. Chattanooga *Times,* Oct. 10, 1961, HC Papers, Microfilm 795.

116. Memorandum, Horton to executive council members, Dec. 12, 1961, Box 2; final financial statements, HFS, Oct. 1, 1961–Nov. 14, 1961, Box 3; Horton to Dombrowski, Jan. 6, 1962, Box 10; F. Nat Brown to Director of Internal Revenue, Nov. 25, 1961, Box 34; Horton to "Friend of Highlander," Nov. 8, 1961, Box 44; Nashville *Banner,* Oct. 9, 1961; Nashville *Tennessean,* Oct. 10, 17, 1961, all Microfilm 795, all HC Papers; *Southern School News* 7 (Nov. 1961): 6; *Southern Patriot* 19 (Nov. 1961): 1–2; Egerton, "Trial of HFS," 87–88.

117. Bates quoted in Egerton, "Trial of HFS," 88. See also Horton to Richard Griffin, Mar. 19, 1963, Box 12; Horton to George and Bee Wolfe, Nov. 25, 1961, Box 30; Chattanooga *Times,* Dec. 17, 19, 1961, Microfilm 795, all HC Papers; Branstetter, Egerton interview.

118. Memoranda, Horton to Highlander Center board of directors, June 2, 14, 1962; confidential memorandum, B. R. Brazeal to board of directors, June 22, 1962, all Box 2; Horton to Ethel Clyde, June 18, July 2, 1962, Box 9; Horton to Dorothy W. Douglas, July 20, 1962, Box 10; Howard Frazier, draft of personal and confidential letter to "Friend of Highlander Folk School," June 7, 1962; Frazier to Horton, June 12, 1962; Horton to Frazier, July 13, 1962, all Box 12; Horton to James H. Slater, Jan. 11, 1962, Box 26; George and Bee Wolfe to Horton, June 6, 1962; Horton to the Wolfes, June 12, 1962, both Box 30; Branstetter to Howard D. Willits, May 4, 1962, Box 34; memorandum, Horton to contributors, July 2, 1962, Box 44; Nashville *Tennessean,* June 22, July 9, 1962; Knoxville *News-Sentinel,* July 8, 1962; Chattanooga *Times,* July 8, 1962; Chattanooga *News-Free Press,* July 9, 1962, all Microfilm 795, all HC Papers.

119. Summerfield residents, interviews with Mikii Marlowe regarding HFS, 1963, HC Papers, Box 52; John Thompson, interview, Feb. 21, 1964, HC Tape Coll., 515A/125.

10. Highlander Center:
New Directions, New Struggles

1. First Annual Report, Highlander Center, 1962; summary of activities, Sept. 1, 1962–Aug. 31, 1963, both Box 1; Horton, progress report to the executive council, Dec. 12, 1961; memorandum, Horton to friends in the Knoxville area, Jan. 26, 1962, both Box 2; staff meeting minutes, Feb. 9, 1962, Box 3; Horton to friends of Highlander (form letter), Feb. 9, 1962, Box 44, all HC Papers; Horton, interview with author, Aug. 9, 1978.

2. Pamphlet, *Why Must Knoxville Organize?* Knoxville Citizens' Council Organizational Committee, ca. Sept. 27, 1962, Box 33; Knoxville *Journal,* Oct. 13, 1962, May 20, 1963, Microfilm 795, all HC Papers.

3. Board of directors meeting minutes, Aug. 30, 1961; memorandum, Horton to friends in the Knoxville area, Jan. 26, 1962, both Box 2; Aimee I. Horton to J. R. Kidd, Dec. 13, 1961, Box 17; Horton to Burke Marshall, Jan. 11, 1962, Box 20; J. F. Worley to Highlander Center, Mar. 21, 1962, Feb. 27, 1963; Horton to Commissioner of Internal Revenue, Mar. 13, 1963; Horton to Justine Polier, Mar. 28, 1963, all Box 23; Worley to Highlander Center, Mar. 25, 1963, Box 52; Knoxville *Journal,* Nov. 2, 8, Dec. 1, 1961; Knoxville *News-Sentinel,* Nov. 7, 8, 25, 1961, all Microfilm 795, all HC Papers.

4. *Highlander Reports: Three-Year Report,* Aug. 28, 1961–Dec. 31, 1964, Box 1; financial statement, fiscal years ended Aug. 31, 1962, 1963, Box 3, all HC Papers.

5. Bernice Robinson, Mississippi Voter-Education Report, July 19, 1962, HC Papers, Box 1; Branch, *Parting the Waters,* 717, 719n., 825.

6. On the 1962–63 Mississippi voter registration campaign, see *Three-Year Report*; summary of activities, 1962–63; Robinson, Mississippi Voter-Education Report; proposed area program, ca. May 1963, Box 1; Horton, notes on current programs, ca. June 1963, Box 66; Horton, notes on Highlander's Role in the Development of SNCC's Educational Program, ca. June 1964, Box 71; pamphlet, *The Eventful Past/The Eventful Present,* Fall 1963, Box 85, all HC Papers; Tjerandsen, *Education for Citizenship,* 182–85; Carson, *In Struggle,* 66, 77–82, 96–98; Zinn, *SNCC,* 81–93; Mary Aickin Rothschild, *A Case of Black and White: Northern Volunteers and the Southern Freedom Summers, 1964–1965* (Westport, Conn.: Greenwood Press, 1982), 13–20; Allen J. Matusow, "From Civil Rights to Black Power: The Case of SNCC, 1960–1966," in *Twentieth-Century America: Recent Interpretations,* ed. Barton J. Bernstein and Matusow (New York: Harcourt, Brace and World, 1969), 536–37; Steven F. Lawson, *Running for Freedom: Civil Rights and Black Politics in America Since 1941* (New York: McGraw Hill, 1991), 86–91; John Dittmer, *Local People: The Struggle for Civil Rights in Mississippi* (Urbana: University of Illinois Press, 1994), 148–49, 207. On the desire to develop adult schools independent of Highlander, see Horton, "Highlander-Type Centers," May 28, 1964, MHP, Box 3.

7. *Three-Year Report*; Horton, report on Council of Federated Organizations Workshop, Greenville, Miss., Nov. 11–17, 1963, HC Papers, Box 41; report on White Community Project workshop, Gulfport, Miss., July 27–28, 1964, Highlander Papers, Ser. 2, Box 4; Horton, "Notes on the Civil Rights chapter," re Adams, *Unearthing Seeds of Fire,* ca. 1975, MHP, Box 10. Among the many studies of the Mississippi Freedom Summer, see Carson, *In Struggle,* 96–123; Rothschild, *A Case of Black and White*; Zinn, *SNCC,* 242–50; Dittmer, *Local People*; Doug McAdam, *Freedom Summer* (New York: Oxford Univ. Press, 1988).

8. *Three-Year Report*; prospectus, SNCC's Education Program, ca. 1963, HC Papers, Box 9; Horton, notes on Highlander's Role in the Development of SNCC's Educational Program; Carson, *In Struggle,* 115–29; Lawson, *Running for Freedom,* 95–102; Matusow, "From Civil Rights to Black Power," 539–45; Zinn, *SNCC,* 250–51; Vincent Harding, "Black Radicalism: The Road from Montgomery," in *Dissent: Explorations in the History of American Radicalism,* ed. Alfred F. Young (DeKalb: Northern Illinois Univ. Press, 1968), 338–39.

9. *Three-Year Report*; summary of activities, 1962–63; Proposed Southwide Voter Education Project, ca. May 1963, Box 1; report on Southwide Voter Education Internship Program, July 15–Oct. 26, 1963, Box 67, both HC Papers; Carawan, six-year summary of work in the South; Julius Lester, "Excerpt from Newport Folk Festival," July 1966, HCadd, Box 35; Tjerandsen, *Education for Citizenship,* 188–89.

10. *Three-Year Report*; summary of activities, May 17, 1965–May 15, 1966; summary of programs, May 1, 1966–May 1, 1967, both Box 1; report on Southwide Voter Education Internship Project, ca. Aug. 1, 1964; summary of project, Apr. 15–Aug. 31, 1965, both Box 68; *Highlander Workshop News* 2 (Nov. 1965): 1–3, Box 84, all HC Papers; Carson, *In Struggle,* 73–74; Zinn, *SNCC,* 93–96; Branch, *Parting the Waters,* 819–20; Dittmer, *Local People,* 170–73; Kay Mills, *This Little Light of Mine: The Life of Fannie Lou Hamer* (New York: Dutton, 1993), 54, 75–76.

11. *Highlander Reports: Black Power in Mississippi,* ca. 1968; summary of programs, 1966–67, Apr. 26, 1968–Apr. 25, 1969, all Box 1; announcement, City, County and State Negro Candidates workshop, June 19–24, 1966, Box 81; memorandum, Horton to C. Conrad Browne, Mar. 20, 1968, Box 96; proposal for City, County and State Negro Candidates workshops, Mar. 1968; proposal, post-election workshop for Negro officials, Apr. 1968, both Box 103, all HC Papers; Tjerandsen, *Education for Citizenship,* 190.

12. *Three-Year Report*; Horton to Bill and Diane Meeks, Jan. 13, 1966, Box 19; Mrs. Walter Johnson and A. A. Liveright, summary report to friends of Highlander on work-camp situation, ca. July 9, 1963; Sam Clark, memorandum on North-South Work Camp, July 1963, both Box 36; Knoxville *News-Sentinel,* Mar. 23, June 20, 24, July 5, 1963; Maryville-Alcoa *Daily Times,* June 20, 24, 25, 27, July 8, 1963; Knoxville *Journal,* June 21, 22, 24, 25, 26, July 6, 1963; Edward D. Lynch, "Memorandum Regarding the Facts and Law Regarding the Cases Involving the State of Tennessee vs. Certain Individuals at the Smoky Mountain North-South Work Camp Located on Rich Mountain in Blount County, near Townsend, Tennessee," ca. July 9, 1963; Nashville *Tennessean,* July 25, 1965, all Box 37, all HC Papers; *Southern Patriot* 21 (Sept. 1963): 1–3; Stephen B. Oates, *Let the Trumpet Sound: The Life of Martin Luther King, Jr.* (New York: Harper and Row, 1982), 360–61; Branch, *Parting the Waters,* 825–26.

13. Transcripts of audio recordings sponsored by "The Shame of Knoxville," ca. Sept. 8, 1965, and Valley Products, Nov. 1966, Feb. 1, 1967, HC Papers, Box 100.

14. Copies of Tenn. House Joint Resolutions 13 and 14, Jan. 1967, HC Papers, Box 101.

15. Memoranda, C. Conrad Browne to board of directors and sponsors, ca. May 5, Sept. 2, 1967, Box 2; Horton to Alice Lynch, Aug. 4, 1966, Box 19; Browne to Margrit de Sabloniere, Oct. 22, 1965, Box 25; memorandum, Browne to board of directors, Jan. 15, 1968, Box 92; news release, Oct. 7, 1966, Box 94; Browne to John Doar, Sept. 8, Nov. 30, 1965, Box 100; numerous clippings from Knoxville *Journal,* Knoxville *News-Sentinel,* and Nashville *Tennessean,* July 1966–Jan. 1968, Boxes 100, 101, Microfilm 795, all HC Papers; Knoxville *News-Sentinel,* May 27, 1967; Nashville *Tennessean,* June 22, 1967, both Highlander Papers, Ser. 2, Box 1; *Southern Patriot* 24, 25, 26 (Nov. 1966, Feb. 1967, Feb. 1968).

16. *Three-Year Report*; "Highlander's Statement on Black Power and Charges of Communism," Oct. 15, 1966; Horton, notes on Black Power, ca. 1971, both Box 71;

C. Conrad Browne to David L. Rothkop, Nov. 26, 1968, Box 98; Horton to Patrick J. Whelan, Sept. 25, 1967, Box 105, all HC Papers; transcripts of board of directors meetings, 1964, spring 1968, Horton Papers, Box 2; Stokely Carmichael, "What We Want," *New York Review of Books* 7 (Sept. 22, 1966): 5–8; Matusow, "From Civil Rights to Black Power," 551–56; Carson, *In Struggle,* 215–28. See also William L. Van Deburg, *New Day in Babylon: The Black Power Movement and American Culture, 1965–1975* (Chicago: Univ. of Chicago Press, 1992).

17. Myles Horton, "Civil Rights and Appalachia," comment given during meeting of Highlander Board of Directors—Appalachian Program, ca. 1968, MHP, Box 9; Anne Braden to Bea Schneiderman, Mar. 12, 1964, HC Papers, Box 7; Michael Clark, interview with author, Aug. 10, 1978; Kate Black, "The Roving Picket Movement and the Appalachian Committee for Full Employment, 1959–1965: A Narrative," *Journal of the Appalachian Studies Association* 2 (1990): 110–27.

18. Quotation from report on Appalachia Workshop, Mar. 12–14, 1964, Horton Papers, Box 8. See also *Three-Year Report*; memorandum, Myles Horton to Appalachian Provisional Organizing Committee, ca. Nov. 1964, Box 32; Highlander press releases, Mar. 2, 17, 1964; notes on Appalachia Workshop, ca. Mar. 12–14, 1964, Box 80, all HC Papers; transcript of audio recording of "Hazard Workshop," Mar. 12–13, 1964, HCadd, Current files.

19. *Three-Year Report*; Carol Stevens, "A Proposal for Organizing Appalachia," ca. Nov. 7, 1964; memorandum, Highlander Center Appalachian Conference, Nov. 7 and 8, 1964; Myles Horton to John Chater, Jan. 20, 1965; memorandum, Horton to C. Conrad Browne, ca. Feb. 1965; memorandum, Horton to Appalachian Project Staff, Apr. 22, 1965; Frank Adams, "Highlander Appalachian Project," Summer 1965, Box 32; Guy Carawan, report on East Kentucky Mountain Project, June 1–Dec. 15, 1967, Box 37; "Myles Horton's Report on Field Trip to Development Residential Centers in Appalachia," July 2–7, 1967, Box 100; Horton to Carl and Anne Braden, Mar. 18, 1967, Box 106; report on Appalachian Community Leaders Workshop, Jan. 13–16, 1967; Jerry Knoll to Horton, Mar. 17, 1967; announcement of public programs, "Appalachia: Its Human and Natural Resources," June 2–5, 1967; memorandum, Joe Mulloy to Community Leaders invited to attend the fifth Appalachian Community Leadership Workshop, Nov. 17, 1967; Appalachian Report: Five Highlander Community Leadership Workshops—Two Adult Education Centers in Appalachia Founded by Highlander Workshop Participants, Mar. 1968, Box 108; Karen Mulloy, report on Mountain Organizer Training Workshop, May 8, 1968, Box 109, all HC Papers; Horton, "Civil Rights and Appalachia," ca. 1968, MHP, Box 9; audio recording, Appalachian Project Meeting, June 16, 1965, HC Tape Coll., 515A/16; Guy and Candie Carawan, "Sowing on the Mountain: Nurturing Cultural Roots and Creativity for Community Change," in *Fighting Back in Appalachia: Traditions of Resistance and Change,* ed. Stephen L. Fisher (Philadelphia: Temple Univ. Press, 1993), 247–51.

20. Memorandum, Myles Horton to Appalachian Project Staff, Apr. 22, 1965, HC Papers, Box 32.

21. Memorandum, Myles Horton to Highlander board of directors, Nov. 9, 1965, Box 2; Appalachian Pilot Project meeting minutes, Oct. 31, 1964, Box 32; Horton to Wilfred J. Unruh, Sept. 25, 1967, Box 97; Horton to Anne Braden, May

16, 1967, Box 106; Horton, "Introductory Remarks (Revised), Appalachian Community Leadership Workshop," Oct. 6–9, 1967, Box 108, all HC Papers; Horton, "Rough Notes on organizing in Appalachia," ca. 1967, Highlander Papers, Ser. I, Box 4; Horton, "Civil Rights and Appalachia," ca. 1968; "Myles' rough notes," Sept. 22, 1968, MHP, Box 9; Mike Clark, interview with Colin Greer, Dec. 1990, copy in author's possession. An edited version of this interview appears in *Social Policy* 21 (Winter 1991): 53–57.

22. Quotation from Highlander board of directors meeting minutes, ca. 1967, Horton Papers, Box 2. See also "Myles Talking about Appalachia," May 1967, Box 2; Proposed Highlander Center Project for Appalachian Poor, 1966, Box 32; Horton to Abram Nightingale, Oct. 2, 1966, Box 97, all HC Papers; Highlander board of directors meeting minutes, Spring 1968, Horton Papers, Box 2; Horton, "Civil Rights and Appalachia," ca. 1968, MHP, Box 9; "Excerpts from an interview with Myles Horton, Director of Highlander Center, by James Coleman, a graduate student," Feb. 1968, Highlander Papers, Ser. I, Box 4.

23. Fairclough, *To Redeem the Soul of America*, 358–83, quotation 369.

24. *Highlander Reports,* Fall 1968, Box 1; C. Conrad Browne to David and Toby Brooks, Feb. 23, 1968, Box 95; Browne to Lucy Montgomery, Aug. 9, 1968, Box 97; Myles Horton, notes on southern mountain coalition, Sept. 30, 1968, Box 100; Horton, report on Poor People's Cultural Workshop, Resurrection City, Washington, D.C., May 20–June 29, 1968, Box 109, all HC Papers; resume, Michael S. Clark, Fall 1977, HCadd, Box 32; transcript of meeting on Resurrection City and the Poor People's Campaign, June 6, 1968; Horton, notes on the Poor People's Campaign, June 23, 1968; Horton, report on Poor People's Coalition Convention, Washington, D.C., June 24–27, 1968; Horton, report on Highlander Center Poor People's Workshop, Hawthorne School, Washington, D.C., June 29–30, 1968; Joe and Karen Mulloy, Special Report on the Poor People's Campaign: The Appalachian Contingent, ca. June 1968, all Highlander Papers, Ser. III, Box 7; Horton, Appalachian Education Program, ca. 1968, Horton Papers, Box 1; Clark, critique of Charles Fager MS on Poor People's Campaign, Dec. 13, 1968; [Clark], "The Third Phase of Highlander's Program: The Coalition Idea," ca. 1969, Mike Clark Papers, Box 1, Highlander Research and Education Center (hereinafter cited as Clark Papers); Clark, personal notes on Resurrection City, ca. June 1968, Clark Papers, Box 2; Elizabeth Sutherland, "Resurrection City: Eyewitness," *Guardian,* June 8, 1968; Calvin Trillin, "Resurrection City: Metaphors," *New Yorker* 44 (June 15, 1968): 71–80; New York *Post,* June 20, 1968; *New York Times Magazine,* July 7, 1968; Charles Fager, *Uncertain Resurrection: The Poor People's Washington Campaign* (Grand Rapids, Mich.: Williams B. Eerdmans, 1969); Fairclough, *To Redeem the Soul of America,* 385–89; Fairclough, "SCLC and the Second Reconstruction," 189–91; Horton, interview with author, Aug. 9, 1978; Clark, interview with author, Aug. 10, 1978.

25. C. Conrad Browne to Norman Clement Stone, Mar. 21, 1968, HC Papers, Box 99; David Whisnant, *Modernizing the Mountaineer: People, Power, and Planning in Appalachia,* rev. ed. (Knoxville: Univ. of Tennessee Press, 1994): 101–19, 191–208; John M. Glen, "The War on Poverty in Appalachia—A Preliminary Report," *Register of the Kentucky Historical Society* 87 (Winter 1989): 48–55.

26. *Highlander Reports,* Winter 1969, Spring, Summer, Dec. 1970, Box 1; Horton, report on Southwest and Chicago programs, ca. Feb. 11, 1970, Box 101; The Highlander Center Program 1971, Box 105; memorandum, Horton to staff on Western Committee, July 7, 1970, Box 108; Horton, field report on Chicago project, ca. Sept. 28, 1969, Box 109, all HC Papers; "A Proposal for Multi-Racial Poor Peoples Workshops at Highlander Center," ca. 1972, Box 14; Horton, Report to the Highlander Center Board of Directors on the Multi-racial Poor People's Program, July 1, 1972, Box 33, both HCadd; staff meeting minutes, Dec. 15, 1971, Box 2; notes on staff meeting, July 3, 1970, Box 2A, both Highlander Papers, Ser. I; *Highlander Reports,* Summer 1969, Braden Papers, Box 77; *Highlander Reports,* Mar., Sept. 1971, author's possession; Rodolfo Acuña, *Occupied America: A History of Chicanos,* 2d ed. (New York: Harper and Row, 1981), 362–64.

27. Myles Horton to Cathy Male, Sept. 3, 1969, HC Papers, Box 97; "Transcript of Appalachian Staff Meeting," Apr. 18, 1969, Horton Papers, Box 1.

28. C. Conrad Browne to Gerald Kreider, Aug. 27, 1968, Box 96; Browne to David L. Rothkop, Nov. 26, 1968, Box 98, both HC Papers; Appalachian Program Staff Report, Apr. 26, 1969, Highlander Papers, Ser. II, Box 1; Myles Horton, "Civil Rights and Appalachia," ca. 1968, MHP, Box 9.

29. *Highlander Reports,* Winter 1969, Spring, Summer, Dec. 1970, Box 1; Appalachian Program Staff Report, Apr. 26, 1969, Box 92; proposal, Appalachian Self-Education Program, ca. 1968; Myles Horton, "Suggestions for Appalachian Program," Mar. 15–16, 1969, both Box 100; The Highlander Center Program 1971, Box 105; Horton to Dorothy Cotton, Apr. 21, 1969, Box 106, all HC Papers; prospectus, Appalachian Education Program, ca. 1968; program proposal, Highlander Center, ca. Apr. 1970, both HCadd, Box 14; *Today's Highlander Program: A Logical Succession of 37 Years of Tumultuous History* (Knoxville: Highlander Research and Education Center, ca. 1969), Highlander Papers, Ser. II, Box 4; *Highlander Reports,* Summer 1969, Braden Papers, Box 77; John Egerton, "Appalachia: The View from the Hills," *Progressive* 39 (Feb. 1975): 26–30; "Adventures of a Radical Hillbilly," 23–25; Mike Clark, interview with author, Aug. 10, 1978; Clark to author, Mar. 22, 1991.

30. Quotation from Almetor King, Mike Clark, and Michael Kline, Report on the Appalachian Self-Education Program, Apr. 1970, Highlander Papers, Ser. I, Box 1. See also Clark to "Herme," Sept. 19, 1969, Ser. I, Box 1; "Text of a talk to VISTA workers by Mike Clark of the Highlander Center staff," Oct. 1969, Ser. IV, Box 1, both Highlander Papers; Clark, "Cult of the organizers" and other notes, ca. 1969, Clark Papers, Box 2.

31. Appalachian Program Staff Report, Apr. 26, 1969; King, Clark, and Kline, Report on the Appalachian Self-Education Program, Apr. 1970, Ser. I, Box 1; Clark, "Poor People Develop Poor People's Power," Mar. 20, 1969; Clark and King, "The Appalachian Self-Education Staff Report to the Highlander Board, 1970–71"; Highlander Center: The Appalachian Self-Education Program—A Two Year Report, Oct. 1971, all Ser. II, Box 1, all Highlander Papers; Horton, notes on the Council of the Southern Mountains, ca. 1971, Horton Papers, Box 1; Sue Easterling, "Greetings from the Youth Commission of the Council of the Southern Mountains," ca. Jan. 1969, Appalachian Volunteers Papers, Box 46, Southern Appalachian Archives, Berea College,

Berea, Ky.; *Highlander Reports,* Sept. 1971, author's possession; *Mountain Life and Work* 45 (May 1969): 4–26; (June 1969): 3, 23; 46 (June 1970): 9–13, 22–23; Whisnant, *Modernizing the Mountaineer,* 26–33; John Glen, "The Council [of the Southern Mountains] and the War [on Poverty]," *Now and Then* 5 (Fall 1988): 4–12; Sue Ella Kobak to author, Mar. 23, 1991.

32. King, Clark, and Kline, Report on the Appalachian Self-Education Program, Apr. 1970; Herman and Betty Liveright, report on Highlander activities, ca. 1970, Box 1; Sam W. Howie, field report, July 8–12, 1969; Clark, field report, Mar. 13, 1970; Clark, field trip report to Pickett Co. [Tenn.], Mar. 12–13, 1971, Box 2; Charles Maggard, field reports, May 1971, Oct. 4, 1971, Box 2A, all Highlander Papers, Ser. I; Clark and King, "The Appalachian Self-Education Staff Report to the Highlander Board, 1970–71"; Highlander Center: The Appalachian Self-Education Program—A Two Year Report, Oct. 1971, both Highlander Papers, Ser. II, Box 1; Howie, field report, July 18–24, 1969; Clark, field report, Nov. 21, 1969, Box 100; The Highlander Center Program 1971, Box 105, all HC Papers.

33. Quotation from *Highlander Reports,* Mar. 1971 (copies of this and all subsequent *Highlander Reports* in author's possession). See also Highlander staff meeting minutes, Dec. 15, 1971, Ser. I, Box 2; Clark and King, "The Appalachian Self-Education Staff Report to the Highlander Board, 1970–71"; Highlander Center: The Appalachian Self-Education Program—A Two Year Report, Oct. 1971, Ser. II, Box 1, all Highlander Papers; King and Clark, Appalachian Staff Report, Apr. 1971, HCadd, Box 14; *Highlander Reports,* June 1974; *New York Times,* Apr. 23, 1972; Clark, interview with author, Aug. 10, 1978; Clark to author, Mar. 22, 1991.

34. Mike Clark, Report to the Highlander Center Board of Directors: The Appalachian Program—A General Statement, July 1972, HCadd, Box 33.

35. Quotation from Highlander staff meeting minutes, Nov. 7, 1972, Highlander Papers, Ser. I, Box 2. See also "Myles Horton's Field Trips," Oct. 31–Nov. 19, 1972; Mike Clark, report on Area Development District Meetings, Whitesburg, Ky., Nov. 10–13, 1972, both Highlander Papers, Ser. I, Box 2; Leslie Callaway, "Appalachian Development Districts: A Guide," May 1977, HCadd, Box 32; *Highlander Reports,* June 1973, June 1974; Clark to author, Mar. 22, 1991.

36. James Branscome, "Appalachia's People Begin to Unite," *South Today,* Dec. 1972; Branscome, Report to the [Highlander] Board, Mar. 1, 1974, HCadd; Box 36.

37. "Jim Branscome's Staff Report," Feb. 28–Mar. 3, 1973, Highlander Papers, Ser. I, Box 2; Charles Maggard, Report to the Highlander Board of Directors on the Appalachian Program, ca. Mar. 1973, Box 17; Highlander staff meeting minutes, Feb. 15–16, 1973; Mike Clark and Mike Smathers to Ralph Bohrson, Ford Foundation, memorandum re Notes on Development Strategy for Appalachia, Feb. 14, 1975, both Box 32; Maggard, Report to the Highlander Center Board of Directors on the Appalachian Program, July 1972, Box 33; Maggard, Report to the Highlander Center Board of Directors on the Appalachian Program, Mar. 1974, Box 36, all HCadd; Clark, interview with author, Aug. 10, 1978; Maggard, interview with author, Apr. 1, 1991.

38. *Highlander Reports,* Winter 1969, Dec. 1970, Jan. 1972, Jan. 1973, all Box 1; memorandum, Browne to board of directors, Mar. 25, 1970, Box 92, all HC Papers; Clark, President's Report to the Highlander Center Board of Directors, Apr. 14–15,

1973, Box 33; David Whisnant to Clark, May 8, 1975; Clark to Whisnant, May 13, 1975, Box 35, all HCadd; memorandum, Horton to Browne and Herman Liveright, July 10, 1969; executive committee meeting minutes, Nov. 1, 1969, Aug. 19, 1972; board of directors meeting minutes, Apr. 18, 1970, Aug. 19, 1972; Herman and Betty Liveright, report to the board of directors on the capital campaign, July 1972, all Box 1; "The Need for a New Highlander Center," ca. 1969; memorandum, Horton to the Liverights and other staff members, Dec. 21, 1970; staff meeting minutes, June 3, Dec. 15, 1971, Nov. 7, 1972, all Box 2; staff meeting minutes, June 2, 1971, Feb. 15–16, 1973, Apr. 10, May 10, Aug. 9, Nov. 12, 1974, Apr. 11, 1975, Box 2A, all Highlander Papers, Ser. I; memorandum, Horton to Browne, Oct. 6, 1969, MHP, Box 6; *Highlander Reports*, June 1973; pamphlet, *Highlander's New Home: A Progress Report*, ca. Jan. 1974; Clark, interview with author, Aug. 10, 1978; Clark to author, Mar. 22, 1991.

39. Quotations from Highlander staff meeting minutes, Dec. 13–14, 1974, Apr. 11, 1975, Highlander Papers, Ser. I, Box 2A. See also memorandum, Mike Clark to Members of the Highlander Board of Directors and the Land Trust, Nov. 30, 1973, Box 17; Clark, Report to the Highlander Board of Directors, June 1980, Box 22; Myles Horton, "In Staff Memorandum," Feb. 10, 1976; Highlander executive committee meeting minutes, Jan. 22, 1977; Highlander staff meeting minutes, Oct. 18, 1976, Apr. 14, 1977; memorandum, Beth Spence to Appalachian Alliance Members, June 12, 1977, all Box 32; report, "Who Highlander Worked With," 1976, Box 33; Clark, President's Report to the Highlander Center Board of Directors, Apr. 6–7, 1974, Box 35; Clark, President's Report to the Highlander Center Board of Directors, Mar. 1974, Administrative files, all HCadd; staff meeting minutes, Feb. 15–16, 1973, Nov. 26, Dec. 13–14, 1974, Apr. 11, 1975, all Highlander Papers, Ser. I, Box 2A; *Highlander Reports*, Sept. 1978; Clark, "Appalachia: The Changing Times," *W.I.N.* 12 (Aug. 19, 1976): 5–8; Guy and Candie Caravan, *Voices from the Mountains* (Urbana. Univ. of Illinois Press, 1975), ix–xiii.

40. Proposal, Appalachian Health Exchange Project, ca. 1977; Helen M. Lewis to David Ramage, Jr., New World Foundation, Sept. 8, 1978, both Box 6; Highlander Center in a Changing Appalachia: 1977–78 Program Report and Proposal for Further Activities; Highlander Center in a New Decade—1979 Program Report and Proposal for Future Activities, Jan. 1980; Helen M. Lewis, Health Program: Report 1977; Lewis and Robin Gregg, Highlander Health Program Annual Report, Apr. 1979; Lewis and Gregg, 1979–80 Annual Report—Highlander Health Program; Mike Clark, Report to the Highlander Board of Directors, June 1980; Gregg, Health Program Report to the Highlander Board of Directors, June 1981, all Box 22; Highlander executive committee meeting minutes, Jan. 22, 1977; "Minutes from Community Health Clinic Workshop," Mar. 25–27, 1977, both Box 32; "Myles Horton's Health Program ideas," ca. 1975; Delivering Health Care in Rural Appalachia: A Proposal for Support of the Appalachian Health Education Leadership Program, Mar. 14, 1979; Lewis and Gregg to Ramage, Oct. 9, 1979; Appalachian Health Education Program—Update of Program Activities, Oct. 1979, all Box 35; Proposal for Leadership Development Workshops for Emerging Leaders, July 1980; newsletter, *Appalachian Health Providers* 1 (Oct. 1980); Highlander Center General Proposal, Winter/Spring 1982; Highlander's 1976

Program Report; Ron Short, Report to the Highlander Board: Appalachian Health Project, May 7, 1977, all Box 43, all HCadd; Lewis, *The Highlander Health Program* (New Market, Tenn.: Highlander Research and Education Center, n.d.); *Mountain Eagle,* May 11, 1978, Jan. 4, 1979; *Highlander Reports,* Sept. 1978, July 1980; Roger M. Williams, "TVA and the Strippers," *World,* June 19, 1973; Steve Fisher, "Teaching Pride and Power," *In These Times,* Apr. 25–May 1, 1979; Patricia Beaver, "You've Got to Be Converted: An Interview with Helen Matthews Lewis," *Appalachian Journal* 15 (Spring 1988): 255–56.

41. Highlander Center in a Changing Appalachia, 1977–78; Highlander Center in a New Decade, Jan. 1980; June Rostan, Labor Education Program—Board Report, June 1980, Box 20; Bingham Graves, Report to the Board—High School Equivalency Program, Spring 1978; Mike Clark, Report to the Highlander Board of Directors, June 1980, both Box 22; Highlander executive committee meeting minutes, Jan. 22, 1977, Box 32; Highlander's 1976 Program Report; Graves, Report to the Board: Labor Program, May 7–8, 1977; Proposal for Leadership Development Workshops for Emerging Leaders, July 1980; Highlander Center General Proposal, Winter/Spring 1982, all Box 43; report to board, GED Program, Spring 1978; memorandum, Helen Lewis to Highlander Board of Directors, Mar. 7, 1979, Current files, all HCadd; *Highlander Reports,* Sept. 1978; Clark, interview with author, Aug. 10, 1978.

42. Highlander Center in a Changing Appalachia, 1977–78; Highlander Center in a New Decade, Jan. 1980; WKPT radio editorial, Jan. 21, 1981, Box 20; Resource Center Report to the Board, May 1978, May 1980, May 1981; Mike Clark, Report to the Highlander Board of Directors, June 1980, all Box 22; Helen M. Lewis, Preparing Appalachian Communities for Changing Environmental and Occupational Health Needs: A Final Report, July 15, 1980, Box 36; Highlander's 1976 Program Report; Gaventa, Staff Report on Resource Center, Apr. 19, 1977; Highlander Center General Proposal, Winter/Spring 1982, all Box 43; Clark to Janet and Doug Gamble, Jan. 19, 1979, Administrative file; John Gaventa, Notes on Participatory Research at Highlander, ca. 1981; Final Report to the Ford Foundation from the Appalachian Public Policy Resources Program for Period of Four Years to Apr. 19, 1982, Current files, all HCadd; *Highlander Reports,* Sept. 1978, Feb. 1980; Kingsport *Times-News,* Apr. 5, 1979, Jan. 16, 1981; Appalachian Alliance, *Appalachia 1978: A Protest from the Colony* (n.p.: Appalachian Alliance, 1978); "Helen Matthews Lewis," 256; *Highlander Special Report: Who Owns the Land and Minerals?* Sept. 1981; John Egerton, "Appalachia's Absentee Landlords," *Progressive* 45 (June 1981): 42–45; "Who Owns Appalachia?" *Southern Exposure* 10 (Jan./Feb. 1982): 33–48; Patricia D. Beaver, "Participatory Research on Land Ownership in Rural Appalachia," in *Appalachia and America: Autonomy and Regional Dependence,* ed. Allen Batteau (Lexington: Univ. Press of Kentucky, 1983), 252–66; Margaret Ripley Wolfe, *Kingsport, Tennessee: A Planned American City* (Lexington: Univ. Press of Kentucky, 1987), 198–204; Clark to author, Mar. 22, 1991; Lewis, interview with author, Mar. 23, 1991; Joe Szakos, Kentuckians For The Commonwealth, interview with author, Apr. 10, 1991. Appalachian Land Ownership Task Force, *Who Owns Appalachia? Landownership and Its Impact* (Lexington: Univ. Press of Kentucky, 1983), summarizes the findings of the land study project.

43. Highlander Center in a Changing Appalachia, 1977–78; Highlander Center in a New Decade, Jan. 1980; Southern Appalachian Leadership Training Fellowship Program, ca. Oct. 1979, Box 6; Guy and Candie Carawan, Report to the Board, 1982 Cultural Program, Box 20; Carawans, Report to the Board: Music and Culture Program, Spring 1978; Carawans, Cultural Program: Report to the Board, May 1980, Box 22; Bingham Graves, Staff Report (June 1975 to Mar. 1976), Box 32; Southern Appalachian Leadership Training Fellowship Program, Education Project, ca. 1977–78; Sharon Branscome to Pat Edwards, Jan. 2, 1980; Tom Gjelten, "SALT: Training grass-roots leaders in Appalachia," manuscript for *Community Jobs,* June 25, 1980; Southern Appalachian Leadership Training Program Narrative, ca. 1980, all Box 36; Carawans, Report to the Board: Music and Culture Program, May 7–8, 1977; Carawans, Summary of Cultural Activities—1977; Highlander Center General Proposal, Winter/Spring 1982, all Box 43; Southern Appalachian Leadership Training Program, Final Narrative Report, Oct. 1978; workshop announcement, "They'll Never Keep Us Down": The Role of the Cultural Worker in Our Changing South, May 28–31, 1982, both Current files; Proposal for Funding of the Southern Appalachian Leadership Training Program (SALT), ca. 1978–79, Administrative files; newsletter, *Alliance Advocate* 1 (Feb. 1982), Research files, all HCadd; Carawans, overview of Highlander cultural program, ca. 1978, Clark Papers, general files; Carawans, "Sowing on the Mountain," 252–58; *Appalachia in the Eighties: A Time for Action* (New Market, Tenn.: Appalachian Alliance, 1982).

44. Bingham Graves, Staff Report (June 1975 to Mar. 1976); Highlander staff meeting minutes, Aug. 17, 1977; Peter Wood, chairperson, Highlander board of directors, to Mike Clark, Dec. 14, 1977; Helen Lewis, June Rostan, and Candie Carawan, A Proposal for an In-House Workshop on Women's Issues at Highlander, Apr. 23–24, 1978, all Box 32; Highlander board of directors meeting minutes, May 5–6, 1978, Box 33; Highlander Center General Proposal, Winter/Spring 1982, Box 43; Leslie Lilly, Southeast Women's Employment Coalition, to Mary Jane Harlan, National Organization for Women, July 25, 1979, Research files, all HCadd; Leah Langworthy, "Struggles within Struggles: Women's Experience at the Highlander Folk School," undergraduate thesis, Department of History, Carleton College, 1990; Kingsport *Times-News,* Jan. 16, 1981; *Highlander Reports,* Dec. 1984, Spring 1986; Helen Lewis, interview with author, Mar. 23, 1991; Sue Ella Kobak to author, Mar. 23, 1991; Joyce Dukes to author, Apr. 16, 1991; Guy and Candie Carawan, interview with author, June 25, 1994.

45. Mike Clark, "Sowing on the Mountain: Highlander in the Seventies," ca. May 5, 1990, copy in author's possession; John Gaventa, interview with author, June 26, 1994.

46. Quotations from Notes from the Highlander Board and Staff Workshop, Jan. 7–9, 1983, HCadd, Box 45. See also memorandum, Mike Clark to Highlander staff, Nov. 30, 1979, Box 17; Clark to Peter Wood, Nov. 10, 1981; Clark to Highlander board of directors, Dec. 4, 1981; Highlander staff meeting minutes, Dec. 28, 1981, all Box 20; David Whisnant to Clark, May 25, 1978; Highlander board of directors meeting minutes, May 5, 1979; Clark, Report to the Highlander Board of Directors, June 1980, all Box 22; memorandum, "Pam" to staff members, May 24, 1977;

Bingham Graves, "Thoughts about Educational Evaluation of Highlander Work (a working paper presented with accompanying ideas by John Gaventa)," Mar. 12, 1978, both Box 32; memorandum, Doug Gamble to Highlander staff, Jan. 2, 1980; Robin Gregg, "Setting the Context for Evaluation," Jan. 27, 1981, both Box 33; Bruce Raynor, ACTWU, to Wood, Jan. 5, 1979; Wood to Raynor, Jan. 15, 1979; Clark to Wood, Jan. 20, 1979, all Box 35; memorandum, Juliet Merrifield to Highlander staff, Jan. 10, 1983, Current files; memorandum, June Rostan to Highlander staff, Jan. 10, 1980, Director's files; Highlander board of directors meeting minutes, May 20–22, 1983; Transition Discussion, Mar. 16, 1983; notes on Staff Meeting Retreat, May 7, 1983, all General Correspondence files, all HCadd; Clark to Myles Horton, Aug. 20, 1979; Clark to Mark Harris, Jan. 9, 1988, both MHP, Box 6; *Highlander Reports,* Mar. 1982; announcement, "Highlander Board Appoints New Director," ca. June 19, 1982; Clark to author, Mar. 22, 1991; Charles Maggard, interview with author, Apr. 1, 1991.

47. Quotation from U.S. Senate, debate on H.R. 3706, 98th Cong., 1st sess., Oct. 3, 1983, *Congressional Record* 129: 13458. See also Ronald V. Dellums and Andrew Young to The Norwegian Nobel Committee, Oct. 14, 1982; Alice Walker to The Norwegian Nobel Committee, Jan. 31, 1983, both MHP, Box 14; memorandum and attachments, Tom Schlesinger to Board Members and Friends of Highlander, Apr. 26, 1984, HCadd, Box 45.

48. Highlander staff meeting minutes, Nov. 4, 1981; John Gaventa, Acting Director, 1982 Program Report to the Highlander Board; memorandum, Robin Gregg to staff, June 29, 1982, all Box 20; memorandum, Helen Lewis, Acting Director, to Highlander Board, Apr. 1979; Mike Clark, President's Report to the Board of Directors, June 1981, both Box 22, all HCadd.

49. Quotation from John Gaventa, interview with author, June 26, 1994. See also Highlander executive committee meeting minutes, Jan. 14–15, 1984; Highlander board of directors meeting minutes, May 11–13, 1984; Highlander staff meeting minutes, Nov. 20, 1984, all Box 14; Highlander Center general proposal, Winter/Spring 1982, Box 43; Highlander executive committee meeting minutes, Aug. 15, Nov. 6, 1983; memorandum, Sue Thrasher to Members of the Highlander Board, Apr. 15, 1984; Hubert Sapp, Report to the Board, Apr. 26, 1984; Guy and Candie Carawan and Jane W. Sapp, Report to the Board, 1984 Cultural Program; Annual Report to Highlander's Board of Directors, Apr. 9, 1985, all Box 45; Sapp, Director's Report to the Highlander Board of Directors, Apr. 22, 1983; Highlander board of directors meeting minutes, May 20–22, 1983, both General Correspondence files, all HCadd; Annual Report to the Board of Directors, Apr. 25–27, 1986; Annual Report, Highlander Research and Education Center, Sept. 1, 1986–Aug. 31, 1987, both author's possession; *Highlander Reports,* Apr., July 1983, Nov. 1984, Spring 1985, Summer 1986, Winter 1988; *Highlander Review—1987* (New Market, Tenn.: Highlander Research and Education Center, ca. 1988); *Culture—The Roots of Community Spirit and Power: The Highlander Culture Program* (New Market, Tenn.: Highlander Research and Education Center, ca. 1988); "Helen Matthews Lewis," 259; Maxine Waller, "Local Organizing: Ivanhoe, Virginia," *Social Policy* 21 (Winter 1991): 62–67; Guy and Candie Carawan, interview with author, June 25, 1994.

50. Highlander executive committee meeting minutes, Jan. 14–15, 1984; Highlander board of directors meeting minutes, May 11–13, 1984, both Box 14; memorandum, Mike Clark re Yellow Creek Concerned Citizens in Middlesboro, Ky., Feb. 19, 1981, Box 18; Robin Gregg, Report to the Board, 1982 Health Program/Human Needs Project, Box 20; memorandum, Clark re Toxic Wastes Project, Aug. 14, 1981, Box 33; Ben Drake, Report to the Board, 1983–84, Toxics Program; Annual Report to Highlander's Board of Directors, Apr. 9, 1985, both Box 45; Juliet Merrifield, Report to the Board, 1982–83; Highlander board of directors meeting minutes, May 20–22, 1983, both General Correspondence files, all HCadd; Annual Report to the Board of Directors, Apr. 25–27, 1986, author's possession; *Highlander Reports*, Apr., July 1983, Apr. 1984, Winter 1987, Winter 1988, Spring, Fall 1989; *Highlander Review—1987.*

51. Highlander staff meeting minutes, Mar. 15, 1984, Box 14; June Rostan, Report on Labor Education, Mar. 17, 1982; Rostan, Report to the Board, 1982 Labor Education Program, both Box 20; Rostan, Staff Report: Labor Education, June 1980–June 1981, Box 22; Highlander Center general proposal, Winter/Spring 1982, Box 43; Highlander executive committee meeting minutes, Aug. 15, Nov. 6, 1983; Hubert E. Sapp, Report to the Board, Apr. 26, 1984; Annual Report to Highlander's Board of Directors, Apr. 9, 1985, all Box 45, all HCadd; "Analysis of Labor Education Program," ca. 1982, MHP, Box 13; Annual Report to the Board of Directors, Apr. 25–27, 1986, author's possession; *Highlander Reports,* Dec. 1984, Winter, Spring, Summer 1986, Spring, Summer, Fall 1989; *Highlander Review—1987;* "Helen Matthews Lewis," 259, 263; Carawans, "Sowing on the Mountain," 259. See also John Gaventa, "The Poverty of Abundance Revisited," *Appalachian Journal* 15 (Fall 1987): 24–33; Gaventa, Barbara Ellen Smith, and Alex Willingham, ed., *Communities in Economic Crisis: Appalachia and the South* (Philadelphia: Temple Univ. Press, 1990); Jim Sessions and Fran Ansley, "Singing Across Dark Spaces: The Union/Community Takeover of Pittston's Moss 3 Plant," in *Fighting Back in Appalachia,* 195–223.

52. Highlander board of directors meeting minutes, May 11–13, 1984, Box 14; board of directors meeting minutes, Nov. 8–9, 1986, Box 43; Hubert E. Sapp, Report to the Board, Apr. 26, 1984; Annual Report to Highlander's Board of Directors, Apr. 9, 1985, both Box 45; summary of Southern and Appalachian Leadership Training Fellowship Program, ca. 1988, Current files; John Gaventa, Report to the Board, Apr. 20, 1983, General Correspondence files, all HCadd; Annual Report to the Highlander Board of Directors, Apr. 25–27,1986; Annual Report, Highlander Research and Education Center, Sept. 1, 1986–Aug. 31, 1987, both author's possession; *Highlander Review—1987; Highlander Reports,* Sept. 1984, Summer, Fall 1986, Summer 1987, Winter 1988, Spring, Summer, Fall, Winter 1989, Fall 1990, Winter 1992, July–Sept., Oct.–Dec. 1993; excerpt from *Southern Growth,* Sept. 1987.

53. Highlander Center in a New Decade, Jan. 1980; Highlander board of directors meeting minutes, May 11–13, 1984; Highlander staff meeting minutes, Nov. 20, 1984, all Box 14; memorandum, Sue Thrasher to Members of the Highlander Board, Apr. 15, 1984; John Gaventa and Juliet Merrifield, Report of a Participatory Research Adventure in India, May 1984; Annual Report to Highlander's Board of Directors, Apr. 9, 1985, all Box 45; Highlander's Programmatic Work—1983, Administrative

files; memorandum, Mike Clark to staff, Aug. 22, 1980, Current files; John Gaventa, Report to the Board, Apr. 20, 1983; Highlander board of directors meeting minutes, May 20–22, 1983, both General Correspondence files, all HCadd; Annual Report to the Board of Directors, Apr. 25–27, 1986, author's possession; *Highlander Reports,* Apr., Oct. 1983, Apr. 1984, Spring, Fall 1985, Winter 1986, Summer 1987, Spring 1988, Summer, Fall 1989; *Highlander Review—1987;* "Helen Matthews Lewis," 259–63. See also Helen Lewis and Myles Horton, "Transnational Corporations and the Migration of Industries in Latin America and Appalachia," in *Appalachia/America: Proceedings of the 1980 Appalachian Studies Conference,* ed. Wilson Somerville (Boone, N.C.: Appalachian Consortium Press, 1981), 22–33.

54. Highlander executive committee meeting minutes, Jan. 14–15, 1984; Highlander board of directors meeting minutes, May 11–13, 1984, both Box 14; memorandum, John Gaventa and Juliet Merrifield to staff, Jan. 26, 1981, Box 18; Gaventa and Merrifield, Research Program: Report to the Highlander Board, May 1982, Box 20; Highlander Center general proposal, Winter/Spring 1982; Summary of program activities, FY 86, both Box 43; Tom Schlesinger, Defense Industry Project Activity in 1983; Helen M. Lewis and Rob Currie, Highlander Research Program: Field Staff Report, Apr. 1984; Annual Report to Highlander's Board of Directors, Apr. 9, 1985, all Box 45; Highlander Programmatic Work—1983, Administrative files; Highlander board of directors meeting minutes, May 20–22, 1983, General Correspondence files, all HCadd; Annual Report to the Highlander Board of Directors, Apr. 25–27, 1986; Annual Report, Highlander Research and Education Center, Sept. 1, 1986–Aug. 31, 1987, author's possession; *Highlander Reports,* Mar. 1981, Apr., Oct. 1983, Sept. 1984, Winter 1987, Fall, Winter 1988, Winter 1989; *Highlander Review—1987;* Tom Schlesinger, *Our Own Worst Enemy: The Impact of Military Production on the Upper South* and *How To Research Your Local Military Contractor* (New Market, Tenn.: Highlander Research and Education Center, 1983); *Picking Up The Pieces: Women In and Out of Work In the Rural South* (New Market, Tenn.: Highlander Research and Education Center, 1986); *Communities in Economic Crisis;* Jane Harris Woodside, "Creating the Path as You Go: John Gaventa and Highlander," *Now and Then* 7 (Fall 1990): 17–19; Gaventa, interview with author, June 26, 1994.

55. Highlander staff meeting minutes, Oct. 5, 1983; Highlander board of directors meeting minutes, May 11–13, 1984, both Box 14; John Gaventa, 1982 Program Report to the Highlander Board, Box 20; Statement of Support, Revenue and Expenses and Changes in Fund Balances, Year Ended Aug. 31, 1986; Highlander board of directors meeting minutes, Nov. 8–9, 1986; memorandum, Juliet Merrifield to Highlander board members, Apr. 24, 1987, all Box 43; Notes from the Highlander Board and Staff Workshop, Jan. 7–9, 1983; notes on executive committee meeting, Apr. 7–8, 1984, both Box 45; Karl Mathiasen III, Management Assistance Group, to Peter Wood and Hubert Sapp, Oct. 20, 1986, Administrative files; memorandum, Jane Sapp to Program Staff, Oct. 29, 1987; Highlander Program Staff meeting minutes, July 11, 1988, both Current files; notes from Highlander Fall Retreat, Sept. 17–18, 1984, Director's files; Highlander board of directors meeting minutes, May 20–22, 1983, General Correspondence files, all HCadd; Erica Kohl, journal of visits to Highlander and Ivanhoe, Va., Oct.–Nov. 1988, Box 4; Mike Clark to Mark Harris, Jan. 9,

1988, Box 6, both MHP; Audited Financial Statements, Highlander Research and Education Center, Aug. 31, 1980–Aug. 31, 1985; memorandum, Mathiasen to Highlander board of directors, executive committee, and staff, Mar. 6, 1986; Annual Report to the Board of Directors, Apr. 25–27, 1986; Annual Report, Highlander Research and Education Center, Sept. 1, 1986–Aug. 31, 1987, all author's possession; *Highlander Reports,* Winter, Spring 1985, Summer 1986; Joe Szakos, interview with author, Apr. 10, 1991; Guy and Candie Carawan, interview with author, June 25, 1994; John Gaventa, interview with author, June 26, 1994; Statement of Highlander's Mission, Nov. 1987.

56. "Press Release: Myles Horton of Highlander Dies," ca. Jan. 19, 1990; wire service obituary, "Rights Activist Succumbs," Jan. 21, 1990; Peter Applebome, "Nurturing New Seeds In a Garden Of Hopes," *New York Times,* Jan. 29, 1990; Knoxville *News-Sentinel,* May 6, 1990; *Highlander Reports,* Summer 1989–Winter 1995; John Gaventa, "Carrying On . . . ," *Social Policy* 21 (Winter 1991): 68–70; Jane Harris Woodside, "Myles Horton: Pushing the Boundaries," *Now and Then* 7 (Fall 1990): 22–23; Woodside, "Creating the Path," 20–21; panel presentation, Tom Heaney, Judy Austermiller, Lee Williams, and Gaventa, "Learning from the Highlander Experience: Contributions of the Post–Civil Rights Period," 35th Annual Adult Education Research Conference, May 20–22, 1994; Gaventa, interview with author, June 26, 1994.

Bibliographical Essay

Studying the history of the Highlander Folk School and its role in twentieth-century southern dissent and reform has presented both challenges and problems. There is a wealth of primary material concerning Highlander and the major figures and organizations associated with it in archives, university libraries, and other institutions throughout the South and in other parts of the country. Until recently, however, there has been little scholarly literature on the history of the organized labor and civil rights movements in the South since 1932 or on the social and economic history of Appalachia. Only a handful of studies have examined modern southern farm groups. Fortunately, a growing number of scholars have started to look more closely into these topics and the changes and conflicts that have characterized much of the region's history from 1930 to the present. Blending fresh perspectives with traditional as well as new research approaches, including oral history, they have begun to develop a fuller understanding of the social, economic, and political forces that have shaped the modern South, their impact on the lives of ordinary black and white southerners, and the efforts of a diverse group of southern radicals to help these people challenge oppression and injustice.

The intent of this essay is to indicate the primary and secondary sources that have been instrumental in chronicling Highlander's history and in placing it in a regional and national context, as well as to suggest potential areas for further exploration. This is not meant to be an exhaustive list of works consulted during the writing of this book; for a more complete account, and for more precise citations, see my "On the Cutting Edge: A History of the Highlander Folk School, 1932–1962" (Ph.D. diss., Vanderbilt University, 1985). Here, I want only to identify and evaluate the kinds of materials that have helped to clarify and explain Highlander's fascinating, complex, and often controversial story.

Manuscripts

Nothing aided my research more than the Highlander staff's practice of retaining the vast majority of its records. Through these papers and audio recordings, staff members monitored the progress of their programs, promoted a historical awareness among their students, and assessed their achievements in light of past performances. The bulk of the folk school's files traveled from Monteagle to Myles Horton's home in Knoxville and from there to New Market before being placed in the Social Action Collection at the State Historical Society of Wisconsin in Madison in 1971. The Highlander Research and Education Center collection currently includes well over one hundred boxes of correspondence, administrative and financial records, workshop and extension project reports, class materials, song sheets and books, play scripts, newspaper clippings, speeches and articles about Highlander, legal documents, scattered personal papers, and hundreds of audio recordings and photographs covering the activities of both the folk school and the center. Fifty-two boxes of material dating from the period 1965–1987, added to the collection in 1990, are only partially processed. The Highlander Folk School manuscript collection in the Tennessee State Library and Archives in Nashville and the Highlander Folk School papers in the Labadie Collection at the University of Michigan in Ann Arbor contain portions of the folk school's records, but both are far less comprehensive than the collection in Madison. Another major source for Highlander's more recent work is the center's own archive in New Market, which is divided into administrative, program, subject, and publications files.

The personal papers of Highlander staff members provide valuable insights into the internal operations of the school, its relations with labor, farm, civil rights, Appalachian, and other reform organizations, and the emotions of the staff and its allies. Located in the Highlander Center archive are the papers of Myles Horton, Michael Clark, Emil and Joanna Creighton Willimetz, and Guy and Candie Carawan. The archive also contains audio recordings from Johns Island, the 1963 Birmingham civil rights demonstrations, and the Mississippi voter education projects of the mid-1960s, as well as hundreds of video recordings documenting the center's residential and extension programs. The State Historical Society of Wisconsin also holds the Myles Horton Papers, which largely date from his career before and after his direct association with Highlander, and the Zilphia Horton Papers, consisting mostly of correspondence and material on music and theater. Their love letters as newlyweds reveal their passion for their work and for each other. The personal and organizational papers of Septima Clark, Bernice Robinson, and Esau Jenkins are located at the Avery Research Center for African American History and Culture, Charleston, South Carolina.

Nearly equal in importance are the manuscript collections of individuals and organizations who campaigned with Highlander for economic and social reform. Useful perspectives on the school can be found in the papers of several southern activists, including the papers of Carl and Anne Braden, co-directors of the Southern Conference Educational Fund (State Historical Society of Wisconsin); Lucy Randolph Mason, southern public relations director of the Congress of Industrial Organizations (Duke University); AFL-CIO Region VIII director Paul Revere Christopher (Georgia State University); religious radical Howard Anderson Kester and educational reformer Morris Randolph Mitchell (University of North Carolina). The interaction between labor union officials and Highlander is partially disclosed in the papers of the Textile Workers Union of America and the United Packinghouse Workers of America (State Historical Society of Wisconsin), the Tennessee CIO Industrial Union Councils, Organizing Committee, and Political Action Committee papers (Duke University), and the Southern Tenant Farmers' Union papers (University of North Carolina), as well as in the Paul Christopher papers. The Socialist Party of America Papers (Duke University) and the Fellowship of Southern Churchmen Papers (University of North Carolina) give a few suggestions about the extent of Highlander's radicalism during the 1930s. The papers of the 81st General Assembly of Tennessee, Highlander Folk School Special Investigating Committee, and those of Tennessee Governor Buford Ellington (Tennessee State Library and Archives) indicate the approach state officials intended to take in their prosecution of the folk school in the late 1950s. The microfilmed *FBI File on the Highlander Folk School* (Wilmington, Del.: Scholarly Resources, 1990), though censored, discloses that the FBI closed its investigation of the school in 1943 and of Myles Horton in 1944 after it concluded that no reliable information existed that Horton was either "interested or active in Communist Party affairs" and that "much of the subversive, derogatory information" about HFS had been "repudiated." Nevertheless, the bureau continued to receive allegations of individual Communists "connected" with the school into the 1960s.

Oral Interviews

Supplementing the richness of the manuscript collections are oral interviews with Highlander teachers, students, and supporters. These personal recollections and interpretations not only reveal the connections between Highlander's private concerns and its well-publicized programs, but also illuminate various periods and themes in the school's past.

Interviews with Myles Horton are most rewarding when the examiner goes beyond the popular and superficial images of Highlander. Having been questioned for years about the school and his career, Horton tended to give facile, somewhat superficial answers to my initial inquiries in 1978. But as my questions became more knowledgeable and pointed during interviews in 1980, 1982, and 1983, Horton readily responded with information and insights that untangled several complicated episodes and gave greater coherence to the manuscript material. Other substantive interviews of Horton have been conducted by Dana Ford Thomas in 1959 (quoted at length in Thomas Bledsoe, *Or We'll All Hang Separately: The Highlander Idea* [Boston: Beacon Press, 1969]); by William R. Finger in 1974 and by Mary Frederickson in 1975 for the Southern Oral History Program at the University of North Carolina, the latter interview appearing in *Southern Exposure* 4 (Spring/Summer 1976): 153–56; by Bill Olson in 1977, serialized in *Working Papers for Ryegrass School* (1979); by Bill Moyers in 1981 for his Public Broadcasting System series *Bill Moyers' Journal*; and by Gary J. Conti and Robert A. Fellenz for "Myles Horton: Ideas that have Withstood the Test of Time," *Adult Literacy and Basic Education* 10, no. 1 (1986): 1–18.

Former staff members and friends of the folk school have also contributed to the oral record. Septima Poinsette Clark was interviewed twice in 1976 for the Southern Oral History Program by Jacquelyn Hall and Eugene Walker, and she patiently answered my questions in her Charleston home in 1980. Tom Ludwig recounted his long association with HFS in interviews with me in 1978 and with Alice Cobb in 1979. The Southern Oral History Program collection contains useful interviews with Howard Kester (1974), Clifford Durr (1974), and Lawrence Rogin (1975). Former TWUA

of the Adult Learner: Using Nonformal Education for Social Action," *Convergence* 11 (1978): 44–52, are more recent recapitulations of the form, function, and objectives of the residence and extension programs. See also the published oral interviews listed above and the autobiography of Myles Horton cited below.

Zilphia Horton wrote very little about the integral role of music at Highlander, but Guy and Candie Carawan have carefully collected the words and music of the black southerners and rural Appalachians who have inspired the staff's work. In addition to numerous recordings, the Carawans' publications include *We Shall Overcome* (New York: Oak Publications, 1963), *Ain't You Got a Right to the Tree of Life?* (New York: Simon and Schuster, 1966; revised and expanded ed., Univ. of Georgia Press, 1989), *Freedom is a Constant Struggle: Songs of the Freedom Movement* (New York: Oak Publications, 1968), *Voices from the Mountains* (Urbana: Univ. of Illinois Press, 1975), "'Freedom in the Air': An Overview of the Songs of the Civil Rights Movement," *Black Music Research Bulletin* 12 (Spring 1990): 1–4, and "Protest Music," *Southern Exposure* 22 (Fall 1994): 64.

Opposition to Highlander is well documented. "A Good School Under Fire," *New Republic* 103 (Dec. 9, 1940): 776, notes the Grundy County Crusaders' assault on the school. Jennings Perry, "The Congressional Inquisition Moves South," *I. F. Stone's Weekly,* Mar. 29, 1954, and Alfred E. Maund, "The Battle of New Orleans: Eastland Meets His Match," *Nation* 178 (Apr. 3, 1954): 281–82, critically report on Mississippi Senator James O. Eastland's attempt to discredit Myles Horton and other SCEF officers in 1954. The Tennessee state legislature's investigation of Highlander and the subsequent courtroom battle over the school's charter is sympathetically described in a number of sources, including Alice Cobb, "'Subversion' in Tennessee," *Concern* 14 (Mar. 27, 1959): 3; "The Trouble at Highlander," a special issue of *Concern* 15 (Oct. 23, 1959); Dan Wakefield, "The Siege at Highlander," *Nation* 189 (Nov. 7, 1959): 323–25; and Roger L. Shinn, "The Rumpus About Highlander," *Christianity and Crisis* 19 (Nov. 30, 1959): 170–71.

Throughout its history Highlander has attracted the attention of local, state, regional, and national newspapers. Since it would have been impossible to conduct a systematic search of these papers for this study, I relied mainly on the many clippings contained in the manuscript collections cited above. These news stories mirrored and in some cases generated the controversies about the folk school throughout its history; indeed, few newspapers remained neutral toward Highlander. Leading the charge against the institution were the Chattanooga *News* and the Chattanooga *Free Press,* whose merger in the late 1930s did nothing to alter their attitude, and the staunchly conservative Nashville *Banner.* Other newspapers critical of the school have included the Knoxville *Journal,* the Charleston *News and Courier,* and the Grundy County *Herald.* On the other hand, the Chattanooga *Times* did not always approve of Highlander's activities, but it consistently defended its right to exist, a position eventually shared by the Nashville *Tennessean* and the Knoxville *News-Sentinel.* The distance between East Tennessee and Memphis evidently explains the limited attention given to Highlander by that city's *Press-Scimitar* and *Commercial Appeal.* National newspapers such as the *New York Times* and the St. Louis *Post-Dispatch* carried brief and generally positive reports of events at Highlander. The *CIO News, National Union Farmer, Tennessee Union Farmer,* and various papers and bulletins of individual labor unions contained spirited stories of the school's workshops and extension programs. The *Southern School News* sought to offer a balanced picture of Highlander's troubles with the state of Tennessee in the late 1950s, while the *Southern Patriot* stridently supported the civil rights activities of the school and denounced its enemies.

A number of contemporary accounts provide the intellectual background for the establishment of Highlander. Reinhold Niebuhr strongly influenced the political and economic content of Myles Horton's ideas on education, as is suggested by his *Moral Man and Immoral Society: A Study in Ethics and Politics* (New York: Charles Scribner's Sons, 1932). Other formative influences include Harry F. Ward, *Our Economic Morality and the Ethic of Jesus* (New York: Macmillan, 1929); Joseph K. Hart, *Light from the North: the Danish Folk Highschools: Their Meanings for America* (New York: Henry Holt, 1927); and Holger Begtrup, Hans Lund, and Peter Manniche, *The Folk High Schools of Denmark and the Development of a Farming Community* (London: Oxford Univ. Press, 1926). Donald West, "Knott County, Kentucky: A Study" (B.D. thesis, Vanderbilt Univ., 1932), expresses the social gospel impulse in the thinking of Highlander's co-founder and foreshadows his subsequent radicalization during the 1930s.

The CIO southern organizing drives of the 1930s and 1940s are described in Lucy Randolph Mason, *To Win These Rights: A Personal Story of the CIO in the South* (New York: Harper and Brothers, 1952). Frank T. de Vyver furnishes a statistical picture of the significant yet ultimately limited gains made by the CIO in the region in "The Present Status of Labor Unions in the South," *Southern Economic Journal* 5 (Apr. 1939): 485–98, and "The Present Status of Labor Unions in the South—1948," *Southern Economic Journal* 16 (July 1949): 1–22. Robert Bendiner, "Surgery in the C.I.O.," *Nation* 169 (Nov. 12, 1949): 458–59, and John A. Fitch, "The CIO and Its Communists," *Survey* 85 (Dec. 1949): 642–47, report on the

CIO purge of Communist-oriented unions after World War II, recorded in detail in the *1949 Proceedings of the Eleventh Constitutional Convention of the Congress of Industrial Organizations* (Washington, D.C., 1949). John Hope II, *Equality of Opportunity: A Union Approach to Fair Employment* (Washington, D.C.: Public Affairs Press, 1956), and "The Self-Survey of the Packinghouse Union: A Technique for Effecting Change," *Journal of Social Issues* 9 (1953): 28–36, set forth the policies and practices of the United Packinghouse Workers that persuaded Horton to make one more attempt to work with organized labor in the early 1950s.

National Farmers' Union education director Gladys Talbott Edwards furnishes an insider's perspective on that organization's history and programs in *The Farmers Union Triangle* (Jamestown, N.D.: Farmers' Union Education Service, 1941), *United We Stand* (Denver: National Farmers' Union, 1945), and *This Is the Farmers Union* (Denver: National Farmers' Union, 1951). Another contemporary view comes from three articles by William P. Tucker: "The Farmers' Union: The Social Thought of a Current Agrarian Movement," *Southwestern Social Science Quarterly* 27 (June 1946): 45–53; "The Farmers' Union Cooperatives," *Sociology and Social Research* 31 (July–Aug. 1947): 435–45; and "Populism Up-to-Date: The Story of the Farmers' Union," *Agricultural History* 21 (Oct. 1947): 198–208. Tucker blames the union's inability to grow in the South in part on the poverty, illiteracy, and shiftlessness of its members.

The massive outpouring of books and articles on the civil rights movement during the 1950s and 1960s produced a few publications of lasting value. Martin Luther King, Jr., *Stride Toward Freedom: The Montgomery Story* (New York: Harper and Brothers, 1958), remains an essential account of the Montgomery bus boycott and the evolution of King's nonviolent philosophy. Harold C. Fleming, "Resistance Movements and Racial Desegregation," *Annals of the American Academy of Political and Social Science* 304 (Mar. 1956): 44–52, is an early overview of organized white opposition to racial change in the South. Howard Zinn, *SNCC: The New Abolitionists* (Boston: Beacon Press, 1964), is a mostly sanguine history of the student sit-ins and freedom rides of the early 1960s, while Kenneth B. Clark, "The Civil Rights Movement: Momentum and Organization," *Daedalus* 95 (Winter 1966): 239–67, is a more cautious appraisal of the problems and potential facing civil rights groups in the mid-1960s. "Moment of History," *New Yorker* 41 (Mar. 27, 1965): 37–38, is one of several articles tracing the evolution of the civil rights anthem, "We Shall Overcome."

The legal documents generated by the assault on Highlander during the 1950s not only detail the battle between Highlander and public officials seeking to close the school, but also shed light on the strategies of segregationists who made southern white civil rights activists their special target for attack. Senator James Eastland's investigation into alleged subversion in the South is captured in *Southern Conference Educational Fund, Inc.: Hearings before the Subcommittee to Investigate the Administration of the Internal Security Act and Other Internal Security Laws of the Committee on the Judiciary,* U.S. Senate, 83d Cong., 2d sess., Mar. 18–20, 1954 (Washington, D.C.: Government Printing Office, 1955). The process by which Tennessee state officials managed to revoke Highlander's charter and confiscate its property can be followed in a number of government documents: the *Senate Journal* and *House Journal* of the 81st General Assembly of the State of Tennessee (Nashville, 1959); *Before the Legislative Committee of the Tennessee Legislature in the Matter of: Investigation of Highlander Folk School, Grundy County, Tennessee,* vols. 1–4 (Nashville: Hix Brothers, 1959); *In the Circuit Court of Grundy County, Tennessee, at Altamont, in the Matter of: State of Tennessee, ex rel. A. F. Sloan . . . vs. Highlander Folk School, a Corp.; Myles Horton; May Justus; and Septima Clark,* Docket No. 37358, Sept. 14–16, 1959 (Nashville: Wells and Hamlin, 1959); *In the Circuit Court of Grundy County, Tennessee, at Altamont, in the Matter of State of Tennessee, ex rel. A. F. Sloan, v. Highlander Folk School, a Corp.; Nov. 3, 4, 5, 6, 1959* (Nashville: Wells and Hamlin, 1959); and various legal briefs, petitions, and orders filed in the Grundy Circuit Court Clerk's office, Altamont, Tennessee.

Secondary Sources

Much of the literature on dissent and reform in the South derives its inspiration from the civil rights movement of the 1950s and 1960s. In its wake, scholars have uncovered increasing evidence that the "Other South" historian Carl Degler found in the nineteenth century persisted into the twentieth century and reached significant proportions after World War II. They have shed new light on the contributions of southern men and women willing to challenge the prevailing views and values of the region, to assert the equal importance of race and class in southern society, and to unite blacks and whites in the pursuit of common interests. Their research has re-emphasized the point that the South has always contained ideas and movements that run counter to its traditional image.

The starting point for an overview of modern southern dissent is George Brown Tindall, *The Emergence of the New South, 1913–1945* (Baton Rouge: Louisiana State Univ. Press, 1967), which describes the impact of the Great Depression and New Deal on the growth of organized labor in the South and on a "scattered tribe" of southern liberals and radicals advocating economic and racial reforms. Morton Sosna, *In Search of the Silent South: Southern Liberals and the Race Issue* (New York: Columbia Univ. Press, 1977), attempts to trace the development of southern white liberalism from the late nineteenth century to the end of the 1940s. Sosna's insistence that "the ultimate test of the white Southern liberal was his willingness or unwillingness to criticize racial mores," his apparent desire that this test be met dramatically and unequivocally, and his focus on the intellectual elite of southern liberalism limit the effectiveness of his book. Anthony P. Dunbar stresses the Christian basis of southern radicalism in *Against the Grain: Southern Radicals and Prophets, 1929–1959* (Charlottesville: Univ. Press of Virginia, 1981). *Southern Exposure* is a valuable source of articles on the history of protest movements in the South. The journal's issues "No More Moanin': Voices of Southern Struggle" 3 (Winter 1974), "Here Come a Wind: Labor on the Move" 4 (Spring/Summer 1976), "Stayed on Freedom" 9 (Spring 1981), and "Who Owns Appalachia?" 10 (Jan./Feb. 1982) are particularly useful. Though the task would be formidable, there is still a need for a comprehensive, analytical synthesis of southern dissent since the beginning of the Depression; fortunately, John Egerton has gone a long way toward meeting this challenge in his encyclopedic *Speak Now Against the Day: The Generation Before the Civil Rights Movement in the South* (New York: Alfred A. Knopf, 1994). Numan V. Bartley, *The New South, 1945–1980* (Baton Rouge: Louisiana State Univ. Press, 1995), appeared too late to be used in this study but should offer a comprehensive synthesis of far-reaching regional changes that both advanced and challenged southern activism.

Previous histories of Highlander have been limited in scope, uneven in quality, and generous in their sympathy toward the institution. With few exceptions, their stories end with the closing of the folk school in 1961. Frank Adams, with Myles Horton, *Unearthing Seeds of Fire: The Idea of Highlander* (Winston-Salem, N.C.: John F. Blair, 1975), is a glib and dramatic version of Highlander's history. As some staff members admit, its primary intention is to win support and contributions for the school. It is certainly more balanced than Thomas Bledsoe, *Or We'll All Hang Separately,* previously cited, which makes no pretense to objectivity. Aimee I. Horton, "The Highlander Folk School: A History of the Development of Its Major Programs Related to Social Movements in the South, 1932–1961" (Ph.D. diss., Univ. of Chicago, 1971), is more restrained, but it too stresses the positive results of HFS programs; it has been published as *The Highlander Folk School: A History of Its Major Programs, 1932–1961* (Brooklyn, N.Y.:

Carlson, 1989). See also her "The Highlander Folk School: Pioneer of Integration in the South," *Teachers College Record* 68 (Dec. 1966): 242–50.

Shortly before his death Myles Horton sought to explain once more his life's work and the educational process pursued at Highlander. In *The Long Haul: An Autobiography* (New York: Doubleday, 1990), written with Judith Kohl and Herbert Kohl, Horton not only describes his personal development and the more dramatic episodes of the school's history, but also reflects upon such subjects as charisma, democracy, self-knowledge, organizing, and adult education around the world. He also collaborated with noted Brazilian adult educator Paulo Freire to "speak a book" entitled *We Make the Road by Walking: Conversations on Education and Social Change,* ed. Brenda Bell, John Gaventa, and John Peters (Philadelphia: Temple Univ. Press, 1990), a sweeping discussion that reveals mutual respect, friendship, and common ground in the two men's personal and professional experiences. See also Jane Harris Woodside, "Myles Horton: Pushing the Boundaries," *Now and Then* 7 (Fall 1990): 22–23.

The past three decades have witnessed a steadily growing body of scholarship on specific phases of Highlander's history. The first to give serious academic attention to the school was Hulan Glyn Thomas, who explores the development of its labor education programs in "A History of the Highlander Folk School, 1932–1941" (M.A. thesis, Vanderbilt Univ., 1964), and summarizes his findings in "The Highlander Folk School: The Depression Years," *Tennessee Historical Quarterly* 23 (Dec. 1964): 358–71. Joan Hobbs, "Politics of Repression: The Prosecution of the Highlander Folk School, 1957–1959" (M.A. thesis, Vanderbilt Univ., 1973), recounts the long-running campaign against Highlander with barely concealed hostility toward the school's enemies. Other, more specialized studies are Neil J. O'Connell, "The Religious Origins and Support of the Highlander Folk School," paper presented at the 1978 Southern Labor History Conference, Atlanta; Michael E. Price, "The New Deal in Tennessee: The Highlander Folk School and Worker Response in Grundy County," *Tennessee Historical Quarterly* 43 (Summer 1984): 99–120; Michele Fowlkes Marlowe, "Participation of the Poor: The Southern White in Social Movements" (M.S. thesis, Univ. of Tennessee, 1967); Anne W. Petty, "Dramatic Activities and Workers' Education at Highlander Folk School, 1932–1942" (Ph.D. diss., Bowling Green State Univ., 1979); Velma Deloris Richberg, "The Highlander Folk School Involvement in the Civil Rights Movement from 1957 to 1961" (M.A. thesis, Fisk Univ., 1973); and Bradley Rentzel, "The Highlander Idea: A History of Its Development, 1932–1972" (M.D. thesis, Union Theological Seminary, 1973). Glyn Thomas, "Hear the Music Ringing," *New South* 23 (Summer 1968): 37–46, and Maggie Lewis, "Guy and Candie Carawan: Song Leaders for Social Change," *Christian Science Monitor*, Sept. 2, 1982, are helpful surveys of the role of music at Highlander. John Egerton offers an interesting look at Highlander's battle with Tennessee officials in "The Trial of the Highlander Folk School," *Southern Exposure* 6 (Spring 1978): 82–89.

Recent studies of Highlander include Jane Harris Woodside, "Creating the Path as You Go: John Gaventa and Highlander," *Now and Then* 7 (Fall 1990): 15–21; Leah Langworthy, "Struggles within Struggles: Women's Experience at the Highlander Folk School" (undergraduate thesis, Department of History, Carleton College, 1990); "Building Movements, Educating Citizens: Myles Horton and the Highlander Folk School," special issue of *Social Policy* 21 (Winter 1991); John P. Beck, "Highlander Folk School's Junior Union Camps, 1940–1944," *Labor's Heritage* 5 (Spring 1993): 28–41; and John Egerton, "Highlander in the Thirties: An Appalachian Seedbed for Social Change," *Appalachian Heritage* 22 (Winter 1994): 5–9.

The Citizenship School project of the 1950s has been analyzed more thoroughly than any other Highlander program. The best and most complete treatment is Carl Tjerandsen, *Education for Citizenship: A Foundation's Experience* (Santa Cruz, Calif.: Emil Schwarzhaupt Foundation, 1980), 139–231. Other informative accounts are Jerome D. Franson, "Citizenship Education in the South Carolina Sea Islands, 1954–1966" (Ph.D. diss., George Peabody College for Teachers, 1977); Guy and Candie Carawan, *Ain't You Got a Right to the Tree of Life?*; Mary A. Twining and Keith A. Baird, ed., special issue on "Sea Island Culture," *Journal of Black Studies* 10 (June 1980); and Cynthia Stokes Brown, "Literacy as Power," *Radical Teacher*, no. 8 (May 1978): 10–14. In *A Way Out Of No Way: The Spiritual Memoirs of Andrew Young* (Nashville: Thomas Nelson, 1994), Young gives a brief account of his brush with Highlander and work for SCLC's Citizenship School Program. Richard A. Couto, *Ain't Gonna Let Nobody Turn Me Round: The Pursuit of Racial Justice in the Rural South* (Philadelphia: Temple Univ. Press, 1991), suggests how black struggles for change on the Sea Islands, in Haywood County, Tennessee, and elsewhere extended beyond civil rights to encompass health, land, education, and political reform. Couto places the civil rights movement in the context of the lives of Haywood County's black residents in *Lifting the Veil: A Political History of Struggles for Emancipation* (Knoxville: Univ. of Tennessee Press, 1993).

An increasing number of works concerning individuals, organizations, and institutions allied with Highlander have appeared in recent years. Richard Wightman Fox, *Reinhold Niebuhr: A Biography* (New York: Pantheon,

1985), is an admirable portrait that offers several insights into the long relationship between the theologian and Highlander. Based on extensive interviews, Frank T. Adams's *James A. Dombrowski: An American Heretic, 1897–1983* (Knoxville: Univ. of Tennessee Press, 1992) tells the life story of a self-effacing man who was pivotal in keeping alive the vision of economic and racial justice between the 1930s and 1960s. John A. Salmond, *A Southern Rebel: The Life and Times of Aubrey Willis Williams, 1890–1965* (Chapel Hill: Univ. of North Carolina Press, 1982), is a solid biography of the most prominent southern reform figure between the 1930s and 1950s. Equally useful are Salmond's *Miss Lucy of the CIO: The Life and Times of Lucy Randolph Mason, 1882–1959* (Athens: Univ. of Georgia Press, 1988), and *The Conscience of a Lawyer: Clifford J. Durr and American Civil Liberties, 1899–1975* (Tuscaloosa: Univ. of Alabama Press, 1990). Hollinger F. Bernard, ed., *Outside the Magic Circle: The Autobiography of Virginia Foster Durr* (University, Ala.: Univ. of Alabama Press, 1985), draws upon a collection of interviews in which Durr traces "The Emancipation of Pure White Southern Womanhood." Other pertinent biographies include Stanley Lincoln Harbison, "The Social Gospel Career of Alva Wilmot Taylor" (Ph.D. diss., Vanderbilt Univ., 1975); Robert F. Martin, "A Prophet's Pilgrimage: The Religious Radicalism of Howard Anderson Kester, 1921–1941," *Journal of Southern History* 48 (Nov. 1982): 511–30; Martin's excellent *Howard Kester and the Struggle for Social Justice in the South, 1904–77* (Charlottesville: Univ. Press of Virginia, 1991); and David King Dunaway, *How Can I Keep From Singing? Pete Seeger* (New York: McGraw-Hill, 1981).

The turbulent history of a major southern interracial reform organization and its more radical offspring can be followed in Thomas A. Krueger, *And Promises to Keep: The Southern Conference for Human Welfare, 1938–1948* (Nashville: Vanderbilt Univ. Press, 1967); Irwin Klibaner, *Conscience of a Troubled South: The Southern Conference Educational Fund, 1946–1966* (Brooklyn, N.Y.: Carlson, 1989); and Klibaner, "The Travail of Southern Radicals: The Southern Conference Educational Fund, 1946–1976," *Journal of Southern History* 49 (May 1983): 179–202. Unlike Krueger and Klibaner, Linda Reed, in *Simple Decency & Common Sense: The Southern Conference Movement, 1938–1963* (Bloomington: Indiana Univ. Press, 1991), finds greater continuity in the efforts of both SCHW and SCEF to achieve racial equality for African Americans in the South. Philanthropic support of southern racial reform is described in A. Gilbert Belles, "The Julius Rosenwald Fund: Efforts in Race Relations, 1928–1948" (Ph.D. diss., Vanderbilt Univ., 1972), and Carl Tjerandsen's report of the activities sponsored by the Emil Schwarzhaupt Fund in *Education for Citizenship.*

Several accounts provide some insight into the relationship between Highlander and other intellectual and educational trends in the South and the nation. Richard J. Altenbaugh, *Education for Struggle: The American Labor Colleges of the 1920s and 1930s* (Philadelphia: Temple Univ. Press, 1990), a comparative analysis of Brookwood Labor College, Commonwealth College, and Work People's College in Minnesota, offers a good perspective on Highlander's early labor education programs. Charles F. Howlett takes a more thematic approach in *Brookwood Labor College and the Struggle for Peace and Social Justice in America* (New York: Edwin Mellen Press, 1993), and "Brookwood Labor College and Worker Commitment to Social Reform," *Mid-America* 61 (Jan. 1979): 47–66. See also Sue Thrasher, "Radical Education in the Thirties," *Southern Exposure* 1 (Winter 1974): 204–9; Raymond and Charlotte Koch, *Educational Commune: The Story of Commonwealth College* (New York: Schocken Books, 1972); Mary Frederickson, "A Place to Speak Our Minds: The Southern School for Women Workers" (Ph.D. diss., Univ. of North Carolina, 1981); and Joyce L. Kornbluh and Mary Frederickson, ed., *Sisterhood and Solidarity: Workers' Education for Women, 1914–1984* (Philadelphia: Temple Univ. Press, 1984). Donald B. Meyer, *The Protestant Search for Political Realism, 1919–1941* (Berkeley: Univ. of California Press, 1961); Richard H. Pells, *Radical Visions and American Dreams: Culture and Social Thought in the Depression Years* (New York: Harper and Row, 1973); Alonzo L. Hamby, *Beyond the New Deal: Harry S. Truman and American Liberalism* (New York: Columbia Univ. Press, 1973); Morton Sosna, *In Search of the Silent South*; and John Egerton, *Speak Now Against the Day,* establish a general context for the efforts of HFS staff members and other southern activists between the 1930s and 1950s.

Although much of the story of organized labor in the South remains unwritten, there have been recent signs of progress. Michael K. Honey, in *Southern Labor and Black Civil Rights: Organizing Memphis Workers* (Urbana: Univ. of Illinois Press, 1993), ably demonstrates how southern labor history can illuminate the relationship between race and class in the region; his study also provides a valuable context for Highlander's extension work in the city during late 1930s and early 1940s. Other important contributions to the field are collected in a fine anthology edited by Robert H. Zieger, *Organized Labor in the Twentieth-Century South* (Knoxville: Univ. of Tennessee Press, 1991). F. Ray Marshall's *Labor in the South* (Cambridge: Harvard Univ. Press, 1967), a more traditional narrative of the growth of unions in the region, emphasizes the activities of union leadership rather than the rank and file and only partially reveals the economic, social, and political factors influencing the unionization of southern industrial workers after 1930.

David Brody constructs a more useful interpretive framework in *Workers in Industrial America: Essays on the Twentieth Century Struggle* (New York: Oxford Univ. Press, 1980), 82–166, and "The Expansion of the American Labor Movement: Institutional Sources of Stimulus and Restraint," in *The American Labor Movement,* ed. Brody (New York: Harper and Row, 1971), 119–37. While acknowledging the importance of New Deal policies in the labor upsurge of the 1930s, Brody also stresses the rise of a new militancy among factory and mill workers and the ability of the CIO to rally them around the idea of industrial unionism. J. Wayne Flynt, "The New Deal and Southern Labor," *The New Deal and the South,* ed. James C. Cobb and Michael V. Namorato (Jackson, Miss.: Univ. Press of Mississippi, 1984), 63–95, briefly but effectively applies this analysis to southern industrial workers.

Other major treatments of organized labor during the Great Depression include Irving Bernstein, *Turbulent Years: A History of the American Worker, 1933–1941* (Boston: Houghton Mifflin, 1971); Walter Galenson, *The CIO Challenge to the AFL: A History of the American Labor Movement, 1935–1941* (Cambridge: Harvard Univ. Press, 1960); Milton Derber and Edwin Young, ed., *Labor and the New Deal* (Madison: Univ. of Wisconsin Press, 1957); James A. Hodges, *New Deal Labor Policy and the Southern Cotton Textile Industry, 1933–1941* (Knoxville: Univ. of Tennessee Press, 1986); Michael Goldfield, "Race and the CIO: The Possibilities for Racial Egalitarianism During the 1930s and 1940s," *International Labor and Working-Class History,* no. 44 (Fall 1993): 1–32; and Robert H. Zieger, *The CIO, 1935–1955* (Chapel Hill: Univ. of North Carolina Press, 1995). John W. Hevener, *Which Side Are You On? The Harlan County Coal Miners, 1931–1939* (Urbana: Univ. of Illinois Press, 1978); and Philip Taft, "Violence in American Labor Disputes," *Annals of the American Academy of Political and Social Science* 364 (Mar. 1966): 127–40, focus on the bloody side of labor-management conflict during the 1930s. Mary Frederickson highlights the tradition of activism among southern women workers in "'I Know Which Side I'm On': Southern Women in the Labor Movement in the Twentieth Century," in *Women, Work and Protest: A Century of U.S. Women's Labor History,* ed. Ruth Milkman (London: Routledge & Kegan Paul, 1985), 156–80, a theme also examined by Jacquelyn Dowd Hall in "Disorderly Women: Gender and Labor Militancy in the Appalachian South," *Journal of American History* 73 (Sept. 1986): 354–82.

A number of unpublished monographs begin to explore the interrelationship between the unrest among southern industrial workers, the organizing strategies of the CIO in the South, and the New Deal. They include Vernon F. Perry, "The Labor Struggle at Wilder, Tennessee" (B.D. thesis,

Vanderbilt Univ., 1934); Fount F. Crabtree, "The Wilder Coal Strike of 1932–33" (M.A. thesis, George Peabody College for Teachers, 1937); John Wesley Kennedy, "A History of the Textile Workers Union of America, C.I.O." (Ph.D. diss., Univ. of North Carolina, 1950); Margaret Lee Neustadt, "Miss Lucy of the CIO: Lucy Randolph Mason, 1882–1959" (M.A. thesis, Univ. of North Carolina at Chapel Hill, 1969); Joseph Yates Garrison, "Paul Revere Christopher: Southern Labor Leader, 1910–1974" (Ph.D. diss., Georgia State Univ., 1976); and Paul David Richards, "The History of the Textile Workers Union of America, CIO, in the South, 1937 to 1945" (Ph.D. diss., Univ. of Wisconsin, 1978).

World War II marked a second important phase of union expansion in the South, but as yet little attention has been devoted to the subject. Brody, *Workers in Industrial America,* 173–257, and Joel Seidman, *American Labor from Defense to Reconversion* (Chicago: Univ. of Chicago Press, 1953), provide a general understanding of the period. In *Labor's War at Home: The CIO in World War II* (Cambridge: Cambridge Univ. Press, 1982), Nelson Lichtenstein critically examines the suppression of rank-and-file militancy by national CIO leaders as they moved to create "an increasingly bureaucratic and politically timid industrial union federation." Other wartime and postwar developments are discussed in Sumner M. Rosen, "The CIO Era, 1935–1955," in *The Negro and the American Labor Movement,* ed. Julius Jacobson (Garden City, N.Y.: Doubleday, 1968); James Caldwell Foster, *The Union Politic: The CIO Political Action Committee* (Columbia: Univ. of Missouri Press, 1975); Nelson Lichtenstein, "Auto Worker Militancy and the Structure of Factory Life, 1937–1955," *Journal of American History* 67 (Sept. 1980): 335–53; Barbara S. Griffith, *The Crisis of American Labor: Operation Dixie and the Defeat of the CIO* (Philadelphia: Temple Univ. Press, 1988); and Michael Honey, "Operation Dixie: Labor and Civil Rights in the Postwar South," *Mississippi Quarterly* 45 (Fall 1992): 439–52.

Scholarly investigations of the declining relationship between organized labor and the political left after World War II shed light on the estrangement of Highlander from the CIO in 1949–50. Harvey A. Levenstein, in *Communism, Anticommunism, and the CIO* (Westport, Conn.: Greenwood Press, 1981), persuasively argues that disputes over the level of class consciousness among industrial workers and controversies over union ideology had less to do with the fate of radicals in the labor movement than the struggle for control of the CIO and an overriding concern with "job-related issues." Max Kampelman, *The Communist Party vs. the C.I.O.: A Study in Power Politics* (New York: Frederick A. Praeger, 1957), defends the CIO expulsion of Communist unionists in 1949, while James R. Prickett, "Communists and the Communist Issue in the American Labor Movement, 1920–1950" (Ph.D. diss., Univ. of California at Los Angeles, 1975), and the essays in Steve Rosswurn, ed., *The CIO's Left-Led Unions* (New Brunswick, N.J.: Rutgers Univ. Press, 1992), are critical of the CIO hierarchy and sympathetic to the position of left-wing unions. Bert Cochran, *Labor and Communism: The Conflict That Shaped American Unions* (Princeton, N.J.: Princeton Univ. Press, 1977); and David M. Oshinsky, "Labor's Cold War: The CIO and the Communists," in *The Specter: Original Essays on the Cold War and the Origins of McCarthyism,* ed. Robert Griffith and Athan Theoharis (New York: New Viewpoints, 1974), 118–51, attempt to steer a middle course between the traditional and revisionist interpretations of the CIO purge.

The story of southern agriculture and farm organizations in the twentieth century and in particular the checkered history of the Farmers' Union in the region are ripe areas for research and analysis. In *Farmer Movements in the South, 1865–1933* (Berkeley: Univ. of California Press, 1960) and "Agricultural Organizations and Farm Policy in the South After World War II," *Agricultural History* 53 (Jan. 1979): 377–404, Theodore Saloutos begins to define the dimensions of the field. Gilbert C. Fite, *Cotton Fields No More: Southern Agriculture, 1865–1980* (Lexington: Univ. Press of Kentucky, 1984), and Jack Temple Kirby, *Rural Worlds Lost: The American South, 1920–1960* (Baton Rouge: Louisiana State Univ. Press, 1987), offer a more comprehensive framework. John A. Crampton, *The National Farmers Union: Ideology of a Pressure Group* (Lincoln: Univ. of Nebraska Press, 1965), remains the most thorough treatment of the union, but it deals primarily with the policies, operations, and leadership of the national organization. Louis B. Schmidt, "The Role and Techniques of Agrarian Pressure Groups," *Agricultural History* 30 (Apr. 1956): 49–58; Robert L. Tontz, "Membership in General Farmers' Organizations, United States, 1874–1960," *Agricultural History* 38 (July 1964): 143–56; and the articles by William C. Tucker previously cited provide further information on the Farmers' Union and its postwar decline in the South.

Recent years have seen major advances in the scholarly treatment of the civil rights movement as historians and other writers have gained the perspective and the willingness to reexamine the drive to transform race relations in the South. Leading the way are two Pulitzer Prize–winning volumes: David J. Garrow, *Bearing the Cross: Martin Luther King, Jr., and the Southern Christian Leadership Conference* (New York: William Morrow, 1986), and Taylor Branch, *Parting the Waters: America in the King Years, 1954–63* (New York: Simon and Schuster, 1988). Two anthologies on the history of the movement—Charles W. Eagles, ed., *The Civil Rights Move-*

ment in America (Jackson: Univ. Press of Mississippi, 1986), and Armstead L. Robinson and Patricia Sullivan, ed., *New Directions in Civil Rights Studies* (Charlottesville: Univ. Press of Virginia, 1991)—reflect the field's interpretive growth. Among the better shorter overviews are Fred Powledge, *Free At Last? The Civil Rights Movement and the People Who Made It* (New York: Little, Brown and Company, 1991); Robert Weisbrot, *Freedom Bound: A History of America's Civil Rights Movement* (New York: W. W. Norton, 1991); Harvard Sitkoff, *The Struggle for Black Equality, 1954–1992*, rev. ed. (New York: Hill and Wang, 1993); and Steven F. Lawson, *Running for Freedom: Civil Rights and Black Politics in America Since 1941* (New York: McGraw-Hill, 1991), a study distinguished not only by its emphasis on politics but also by its chronological and geographical breadth. Howell Raines, *My Soul Is Rested: Movement Days in the Deep South Remembered* (New York: Bantam Books, 1978), is a fine collection of interviews with those who participated in and fought against the movement, and John Hope Franklin and Isidore Starr, ed., *The Negro in Twentieth Century America: A Reader on the Struggle for Civil Rights* (New York: Vintage Books, 1967), is a representative compilation of contemporary observations, articles, and speeches.

Intensive studies of major protests and the organizations and individuals involved in them have produced a more complex and useful framework for understanding the dynamics of the civil rights movement than that offered by earlier accounts. Aldon D. Morris, *The Origins of the Civil Rights Movement: Black Communities Organizing for Change* (New York: Free Press, 1984), is a worthwhile reminder that the drive for racial equality during the 1950s and early 1960s arose from within southern black communities themselves, aided by "Movement Half-way Houses" like Highlander. No other analysis of the Supreme Court's historic 1954 school desegregation decision approaches the breadth and quality of Richard Kluger, *Simple Justice: The History of Brown v. Board of Education and Black America's Struggle for Equality* (New York: Alfred A. Knopf, 1976). Benjamin Muse, *Ten Years of Prelude: The Story of Integration Since the Supreme Court's 1954 Decision* (New York: Viking Press, 1964), details the impact of the ruling on public school desegregation before 1960. J. Mills Thornton III, "Challenge and Response in the Montgomery Bus Boycott of 1955–1956," *Alabama Review* 33 (July 1980): 163–235, is a well-researched investigation of the political and legal battle over segregation that ushered in a new era of black protest. Hugh Davis Graham traces the implementation of a federal "policy revolution" that responded to the black civil rights and feminist movements in *The Civil Rights Era: Origins and Development of National Policy, 1960–1972* (New York: Oxford Univ. Press, 1990).

In addition to David Garrow's *Bearing the Cross* and Taylor Branch's *Parting the Waters,* the life and times of Martin Luther King, Jr., continue to fascinate students of the era. David Levering Lewis, *King: A Biography,* 2d ed. (Urbana: Univ. of Illinois Press, 1978), remains a highly influential assessment of King's role in the southern struggle. Despite its lack of documentation, Lewis's work is more instructive than Stephen B. Oates, *Let the Trumpet Sound: The Life of Martin Luther King, Jr.* (New York: Harper and Row, 1982). Adam Fairclough, in *To Redeem the Soul of America: The Southern Christian Leadership Conference and Martin Luther King, Jr.* (Athens: Univ. of Georgia Press, 1987), confirms the idea that the organization was more than an extension of a single personality. See also Fairclough's "The Southern Christian Leadership Conference and the Second Reconstruction, 1957–1973," *South Atlantic Quarterly* 80 (Spring 1981): 177–94; his "The Preachers and the People: The Origins and Early Years of the Southern Christian Leadership Conference, 1955–1959," *Journal of Southern History* 52 (Aug. 1986): 403–40; and Eugene Pierce Walker's "A History of the Southern Christian Leadership Conference, 1955–1965: The Evolution of a Southern Strategy for Social Change" (Ph.D. diss., Duke Univ., 1978).

The story of the student sit-ins of 1960–61 has not yet been completed. Case studies of the demonstrations in Nashville, Atlanta, and other southern cities would help reveal both the changes and the continuities in the struggle between black communities and white civic leaders over the desegregation of public facilities. William H. Chafe establishes a solid foundation for this approach in *Civilities and Civil Rights: Greensboro, North Carolina, and the Black Struggle for Freedom* (New York: Oxford Univ. Press, 1980); see also Lester C. Lamon, *Blacks in Tennessee, 1791–1970* (Knoxville: Univ. of Tennessee Press, 1981), 99–109; and Aldon Morris, "Black Southern Sit-In Movement: An Analysis of Internal Organization," *American Sociological Review* 46 (Dec. 1981): 744–67.

The evolution of black radicalism after the sit-ins, exemplified by the history of the Student Nonviolent Coordinating Committee, is described in Clayborne Carson's outstanding *In Struggle: SNCC and the Black Awakening of the 1960s* (Cambridge: Harvard Univ. Press, 1981); Allen J. Matusow's perceptive "From Civil Rights to Black Power: The Case of SNCC, 1960–1966," in *Twentieth-Century America: Recent Interpretations,* ed. Barton J. Bernstein and Matusow (New York: Harcourt, 1969), 531–57; and Archie E. Allen, "John Lewis: Keeper of the Dream," *New South* 26 (Spring 1971): 15–25. Robert H. Brisbane, *Black Activism: Racial Revolution in the United States, 1954–1970* (Valley Forge, Pa.: Judson Press, 1974); August Meier and Elliott Rudwick, ed., *Black Protest in the Sixties* (Chicago: Quadrangle

Books, 1970); Vincent Harding, "Black Radicalism: The Road from Montgomery," in *Dissent: Explorations in the History of American Radicalism,* ed. Alfred F. Young (DeKalb: Northern Illinois Univ. Press, 1968), 320–54; and William L. Van Deburg, *New Day in Babylon: The Black Power Movement and American Culture, 1965–1975* (Chicago: Univ. of Chicago Press, 1992), trace the origins, ascendancy, and decline of black militancy in the 1960s. The story of Mississippi Freedom Summer has generated two outstanding studies: Doug McAdam, *Freedom Summer* (New York: Oxford Univ. Press, 1988), and John Dittmer, *Local People: The Struggle for Civil Rights in Mississippi* (Urbana: Univ. of Illinois Press, 1994).

The impact of the civil rights movement on black and white women, and their significant participation in it, has yet to receive the full scholarly attention it deserves. The memoirs of Jo Ann Gibson Robinson, *The Montgomery Bus Boycott and the Women Who Started It* (Knoxville: Univ. of Tennessee Press, 1987), calls attention to the leadership role played by the Women's Political Council during that momentous protest. Mary Aickin Rothschild, *A Case of Black and White: Northern Volunteers and the Southern Freedom Summers, 1964–1965* (Westport, Conn.: Greenwood Press, 1982), depicts the voter registration project involving SNCC and other young black and white activists as an especially radicalizing experience and the beginning of the women's liberation movement, a theme examined more broadly by Sara Evans in *Personal Politics: The Roots of Women's Liberation in the Civil Rights Movement and the New Left* (New York: Alfred A. Knopf, 1979). Kay Mills, in *This Little Light of Mine: The Life of Fannie Lou Hamer* (New York: Dutton, 1993), offers a flattering portrait of a charismatic woman. Similar profiles can be found in Vicki L. Crawford, Jacqueline Anne Rouse, and Barbara Woods, ed., *Women in the Civil Rights Movement: Trailblazers and Torchbearers, 1943–1965* (Bloomington: Indiana Univ. Press, 1993); Charles Payne, "Ella Baker and Models of Social Change," *Signs: Journal of Women in Culture and Society* 14 (Summer 1989): 885–99, and Cynthia Griggs Fleming, "Black Women Activists and the Student Nonviolent Coordinating Committee: The Case of Ruby Doris Smith Robinson," *Journal of Women's History* 4 (Winter 1993): 64–82.

Southern white opposition to school desegregation and to groups like the Highlander staff often combined anti-Communist investigations and propaganda with well-organized, well-publicized defenses of white supremacy. Numan V. Bartley ably describes this strategy of reaction in *The Rise of Massive Resistance: Race and Politics in the South during the 1950's* (Baton Rouge: Louisiana State Univ. Press, 1969). Neil R. McMillen, *The Citizens' Council: Organized Resistance to the Second Reconstruction, 1954–64*

(Urbana: Univ. of Illinois Press, 1971), focuses on the most "respectable" wing of the resistance movement, while Hugh Davis Graham, *Crisis in Print: Desegregation and the Press in Tennessee* (Nashville: Vanderbilt Univ. Press, 1967), points out the diversity of editorial responses among Tennessee newspapers to the prospect of a fundamental change in southern race relations. The attempts of congressional committees and the Federal Bureau of Investigation to repress what they perceived as threats to the status quo are examined thoroughly in David E. Caute, *The Great Fear: The Anti-Communist Purge under Truman and Eisenhower* (New York: Simon and Schuster, 1978); Walter Goodman, *The Committee: The Extraordinary Career of the House Committee on Un-American Activities* (New York: Farrar, Straus and Giroux, 1968); and David J. Garrow, *The FBI and Martin Luther King, Jr.: From "Solo" to Memphis* (New York: W. W. Norton, 1981).

Several monographs reflect Highlander's long-standing approach to the problems of the Appalachian region. For many years, observers and would-be reformers stereotyped Appalachia as a subculture with unique customs, values, and ways of life that were obsolete and tied to the poverty, isolation, and powerlessness of the area. In the 1960s, however, critics of the subcultural model, drawing on Harry M. Caudill, *Night Comes to the Cumberlands: A Biography of a Depressed Area* (Boston: Little, Brown, 1963); and C. Vann Woodward, *Origins of the New South, 1877–1913* (Baton Rouge: Louisiana State Univ. Press, 1951), began to assert that Appalachia was an "internal colony" suffering persistent social and economic ills because of the continued exploitation and domination of outside corporate and cultural interests. It is an argument expressed by Highlander staff members as early as the 1930s, and during the 1970s and much of the 1980s Appalachian scholarship drew upon this colonialism argument, including Helen Matthews Lewis, Linda Johnson, and Donald Askins, ed., *Colonialism in Modern America: The Appalachian Case* (Boone, N.C.: Appalachian Consortium Press, 1978); Henry D. Shapiro, *Appalachia On Our Mind: The Southern Mountains and Mountaineers in the American Consciousness, 1870–1920* (Chapel Hill: Univ. of North Carolina Press, 1978); David E. Whisnant, *Modernizing the Mountaineer: People, Power, and Planning in Appalachia* (Boone, N.C.: Appalachian Consortium Press, 1980, revised ed., Univ. of Tennessee Press, 1994); Whisnant, *All That Is Native and Fine: The Politics of Culture in an American Region* (Chapel Hill: Univ. of North Carolina Press, 1983); Ronald D. Eller, *Miners, Millhands, and Mountaineers: Industrialization of the Appalachian South, 1880–1930* (Knoxville: Univ. of Tennessee Press, 1982); and Allen W. Batteau, *The Invention of Appalachia* (Tucson: Univ. of Arizona Press, 1990).

Highlander's contribution to the development of Appalachian studies can be found in John Egerton, "Appalachia: The View from the Hills," *Progressive* 39 (Feb. 1975): 26–30; Lewis, Johnson, and Askins, ed., *Colonialism in Modern America,* 9–31, 113–57, 199–227; John Gaventa, *Power and Powerlessness: Quiescence and Rebellion in an Appalachian Valley* (Urbana: Univ. of Illinois Press, 1980); Helen Lewis and Myles Horton, "Transnational Corporations and the Migration of Industries in Latin America and Appalachia," in *Appalachia/America: Proceedings of the 1980 Appalachian Studies Conference,* ed. Wilson Somerville (Boone, N.C.: Appalachian Consortium Press, 1981), 22–33; Patricia D. Beaver, "Participatory Research on Land Ownership in Rural Appalachia," in *Appalachia and America: Autonomy and Regional Dependence,* ed. Allen Batteau (Lexington: Univ. Press of Kentucky, 1983), 252–66; the Appalachian Land Ownership Task Force, *Who Owns Appalachia? Landownership and Its Impact* (Lexington: Univ. Press of Kentucky, 1983); and John Gaventa, "The Poverty of Abundance Revisited," *Appalachian Journal* 15 (Fall 1987): 24–33. Two recent important anthologies bring together organizers and scholars to document the extent and variety of citizen activism in Appalachia since the mid-1960s: John Gaventa, Barbara Ellen Smith, and Alex Willingham, ed., *Communities in Economic Crisis: Appalachia and the South* (Philadelphia: Temple Univ. Press, 1990); and Stephen L. Fisher, ed., *Fighting Back in Appalachia: Traditions of Resistance and Change* (Philadelphia: Temple Univ. Press, 1993), which includes my "Like a Flower Slowly Blooming. Highlander and the Nurturing of an Appalachian Movement"; Guy and Candie Carawan, "Sowing on the Mountain: Nurturing Cultural Roots and Creativity for Community Change"; and Jim Sessions and Fran Ansley, "Singing Across Dark Spaces: The Union/Community Takeover of Pittson's Moss 3 Plant."

The largest task facing students of the history of progressive reform in Appalachia and the South since 1930 remains the same as when the first edition of this book appeared in 1988: to examine and analyze rigorously the social movements that have helped to reshape these regions. The broad outlines of the struggle for economic and racial justice have been established, and recent scholarship has begun to fill in the framework. The need now is for a better, more nuanced understanding of the course of the southern and Appalachian labor, farm, and civil rights movements; the individuals and institutions involved in them over the past six decades; and the ways in which current activists have sought to fulfill that legacy and extend it into new fields of citizen resistance and struggle.

Index

United Nations, 158–59, 160, 183, 189, 194, 205, 214, 220, 247
United Packinghouse Workers of America (UPWA), 119, 147–51, 155
United Rubber Workers of America (URWA), 83, 110, 119, 123, 124
United States Department of Justice, 146, 181, 202, 247–48
United States Employment Service, 97
United States Supreme Court, 155, 156, 157, 159, 160–61, 163, 206, 215, 239, 240; and HFS, 157, 182, 183, 207, 239, 244–48; *see also Brown v. Board of Education*
United Steel Workers, 115
United Sugar Workers, 97
United Textile Workers of America (UTWA), 37, 39, 44, 56, 85, 92

Vastine, Annie, 195
Vaughn, Dolph, 60–61, 63
Vincent, Craig, 262
Vivian, C. T., 179

Walker, Cas, 257
Walker, Rosanne, 62
Walker, Wyatt Tee, 179
Wallace, Henry A., 125, 126, 139, 142, 143
Waller, Maxine, 273
Walsh, J. Raymond, 112
War Labor Board, 100, 104, 119
War Manpower Commission, 112
War on Poverty, 258, 259, 260, 261, 264, 267
War Production Board, 97
Ward, Harry F., 12–13
Waring, J. Waties, 167
Water: You Have to Drink It with a Fork, 276
"We Shall Overcome," 172, 176–77, 232
Weaver, George, 118
West, Constance, 33, 293n45
West, Don, 21–25, 27–28, 30–33, 44–45, 51, 128, 292–93n45
Whisnant, David, 5, 17

White, Henry, 118
White, Mildred, 212–13, 353–54n14
White Community Project, 255
Wilder, Tenn., coal miners' strike, 29–32
Wilder Emergency Relief Committee, 30
Williams, Aubrey, 70, 130, 136–38, 143, 145, 170, 210–11, 217–18, 229, 353n6
Williams, Claude, 43
Williams, Hosea L., 200, 202
Williams, Truman V., Jr., 216, 217, 220
Willimetz, Emil, 140, 156, 186–87
Willimetz, Joanna Creighton, 141, 156
Wilson, Harry Leon, Jr., 68, 75, 78, 108–9
Wilson, Larry, 274
Wine, Alice, 190, 195
Winston, Catherine, 101, 122
Witt, Shirley, 262
Women's Political Council, 163
Wood, James, 179, 181, 204
work camps, 68–69, 141
Work Camps for America, 69
Workers Alliance, 59, 60, 64, 72
Workers' Defense League, 80
Workers' Folk School, 19
Works Progress Administration (WPA), 48–50, 59–64, 188
Wright, Marion, 239
writers' workshops, 68

Yellow Creek (Ky.) Concerned Citizens, 274
Yergan, Max, 113
York, Alvin, 132, 135
Young, Andrew, 179, 204, 205–6, 260, 272, 278
Young Communist League, 226
Youth Project (later Summer Youth Workshops), 180–81, 275

Zellner, Robert, 179
Zhitlowsky, Eva, 64
Zwerg, James, 182

NORTHERN COLLEGE LIBRARY
76504 BARNSLEY S75 3ET

JR204